The

CHAPLIN

ENCYCLOPEDIA

The

CHAPLIN

ENCYCLOPEDIA

Glenn Mitchell

B.T BATSFORD LTD LONDON

Printed in China

for the publishers
B.T. Batsford Ltd
583 Fulham Road
London SW6 5BY

ISBN 0 7134 79388

Designed by DWN Ltd London.

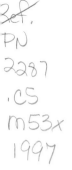

In memory of my father, James Mitchell
(1924–1997), who made everything
possible.

ACKNOWLEDGEMENTS

The illustrations in this book consist
mostly of stills issued for publicity
purposes by the following organizations:
Keystone, Essanay, Mutual, First
National, United Artists, Archway and
Universal. Others, where known, are
identified in the captions.
All Chaplin films made post 1918,
Property and Copyright © ROY
EXPORT COMPANY
ESTABLISHMENT.
Chaplin image Property and Copyright ©
BUBBLES INCORPORATED S.A.
All rights reserved.

Although effort has been made to trace
all other present copyright owners,
apologies are offered in advance for any
unintentional omission or neglect; we
will be happy to insert appropriate
acknowledgement to companies or
individuals in subsequent editions of the
book. Details of stage and screen plays
are quoted in the text as a matter of
historical record and for the purposes of
study and constructive criticism.

INTRODUCTION

It has become near-compulsory to preface a Chaplin study with the question, 'Why another Chaplin book?' One might just as well ask why there are so many volumes dedicated to Shakespeare or, indeed, any pre-eminent figure in a given field. One answer is that, despite the large number of accounts (some of them seemingly exhaustive), there is always something new to be said about Chaplin (or, for that matter, Shakespeare). Alistair Cooke summed up Chaplin's vast reputation with a quote from humorist Will Rogers: 'The Zulus know Chaplin better than Arkansas knows Garbo.' Chaplin's story has, admittedly, been documented, scrutinized and variously juggled with sufficient frequency to deter a would-be chronicler, but the main purpose of the present work is, as in my earlier encyclopedia surveys of Laurel & Hardy and the Marx Brothers, to assemble useful or amusing data in a format instantly accessible to the reader. Inevitably, this book must overlap with much that has gone before, although it is hoped that much 'new' information may be gleaned from these pages.

Unlike my previous books, the present volume is intended as a concentration upon the films themselves. Although the basics of Chaplin's life are covered – also, at times, more than the basics – it is my opinion that most admirers are interested primarily in Chaplin's artistic achievements rather than in any political or sexual intrigues. Another difficulty is that of scale. When I mentioned this project to an interested friend, the response was a daunting 'but Chaplin was *everywhere*', thus reinforcing the decision for selectivity. An absolutely complete Chaplin encyclopedia, detailing everything said or written about the man, would probably dwarf most public buildings. All one can hope for is to be representative.

A key difference between the *Laurel & Hardy Encyclopedia* and the *Marx Brothers Encyclopedia* was the first book's rôle as 'consumer guide'. Available copies of the Marx Brothers films, in any case fewer in number, tend to vary far less in condition. By contrast, Chaplin's much-revived early comedies have been subject to considerable mangling, rendering the consumer guide aspect even more important than in the *Laurel & Hardy Encyclopedia*. Where possible, alternative prints of the Chaplin films have been examined, in an attempt to document the action fully while at the same time permitting comparisons (this becomes even more complex when examining the variations that derive from alternative camera negatives, a subject hitherto neglected in Chaplin histories). Numerous prints of the early comedies continue to circulate among collectors, even in this video-dominated age.

There was once a time when Chaplin was the last person to need defending in print, at least artistically. There have been many instances where the political and moral vilification inflicted upon him by post-war America has paled alongside the near-compulsory denigration of his art over the last three decades. Strangely, comedy enthusiasts have come to favour a certain partisanship – or in other words, if you like Keaton, you aren't supposed to like Chaplin, or if you enjoy Laurel & Hardy, you aren't supposed to approve of the Marx Brothers, and so on. This strikes the author as unnecessary and inappropriate. There is no reason for a single viewer's taste to be confined to one specific style, nor did any of these comedians have exclusive claim on the public's attention; they were indeed sometimes quoted as praising their contemporaries. The 'Chaplin-bashers' might take note that virtually all of comedy's big names of the period cited Chaplin as the greatest in their profession, and it is significant that he remains the common denominator whenever comparisons are made.

Much of this has to do with the extensive period in which Chaplin was praised virtually to the exclusion of his contemporaries. A consequent desire to give other comedians their due was both correct and ultimately beneficial to the common heritage, but Chaplin – as again with Shakespeare and, to an extent, Walt Disney – has suffered unfairly from a backlash based upon the maxim that 'He's had it too good for too long.'

It is no real compliment when praise for one artist has to be to the detriment of another. The battle for Chaplin's contemporaries has been won, to the point where it is Chaplin himself who today seems in need of defence.

In his essay on *City Lights* – for many, Chaplin's masterpiece – the journalist Alexander Woollcott described how, over a period of fifteen years, he had periodically been informed of various comedians who were considered 'funnier than Chaplin'. Woollcott expressed surprise at the frequent comparison, because 'I never think of the dauntless Charlie as a figure of fun. Or at least not as primarily a figure of fun. Primarily Charlie is innocent courage, gallantry – the unquenchable in mankind – taking on flesh and walking this earth to give us heart.'

In conclusion, I would like to offer my heartfelt thanks to: Kate Guyonvarch, of the Roy Export Company Establishment, for the loan of several rare stills; Michael Pointon, for numerous discoveries and his customary guidance; Mark Newell, for digging into his extensive files once more; Robert G. Dickson, who finds all manner of goodies; Bonnie McCourt and David Totheroh, of the Charlie Chaplin Film Co.; Hooman Mehran, who supplied much valued material and information; Annette M. D'Agostino, for assistance with the supporting players; Adrian Rigelsford, for considerable help in picture research; Tony Barker and Barry Anthony, for assistance concerning Fred Karno, Chaplin's parents, Leo Dryden and the music-hall scene in general; Roy Hudd, for information and photographs concerning Chaplin's connection with the Grand Order of Water Rats; Graeme Foot; Claudia Sassen; Frank Hill, for details of Billie Ritchie; Wesley Butters; Carolyn Whitaker, literary agent and finder of cuttings; David Wyatt, for filling several gaps in the film collection and other valued advice; Frank Scheide, who with Tony Fletcher and Tony Merrick has done much valued research into Chaplin's early life; Robert S. Lewis; Annie Shead; the British Film Institute; the Study Room at the Theatre Museum, Covent Garden; the British Library; Westminster Public Libraries; Huw Jones; Batsford editors Richard Reynolds and Janina Godowska; and, of course, Nora Nettlerash.

Glenn Mitchell
London, 1997

ABANDONED PROJECTS

It is inevitable that, in a career as productive as Chaplin's, there should have been many instances where projects did not come to fruition. When at Essanay (*qv*), Chaplin commenced work on *Life*, a feature-length tragi-comedy set amid urban poverty. A reference to this in the studio's own publication, *Essanay News*, claimed that the feature 'will not interfere at all with the other releases', but it was evidently concern over deadlines for the short comedies that led Essanay to persuade Chaplin to abandon the idea. Extracts from *Life* were later incorporated into *Police* and *Triple Trouble* (both *qv*).

According to Mary Pickford's biographer, Scott Eyman, Chaplin wanted to co-star with the actress as early in 1917, in a film to be called *Bread*. He despatched Syd Chaplin (*qv*) with an offer of $10,000 per week – to match the salary then being paid her by Adolph Zukor – but Mary declined. From around the same time, during Chaplin's contract with Mutual (*qv*), the documentary series *Unknown Chaplin* (*qv*) revealed two aborted storylines that proved to be embryonic versions of *The Immigrant* (*qv*) – one a Svengali tale set in an artists' café, the other a disembodied restaurant sketch utilizing the same set. The same source reveals an unfinished, final Mutual comedy called *The Golf Links* or simply *Golf* (itself the title of a much later Larry Semon film), the footage being put aside instead for *How To Make Movies* (*qv*), itself an abandoned project. The golfing routine was later reworked into *The Idle Class* (*qv*); following its completion, Chaplin commenced work on *Come Seven*, depicting himself and Mack Swain (*qv*) as

wealthy plumbers who drive to work in a limousine. This was abandoned in favour of a different 'workman' story, *Pay Day*. (Stills from the abortive *Come Seven* were included, presumably in error, within a *Pay Day* montage in Chaplin's book, *My Life in Pictures*.) Another First National, *A Dog's Life*, was briefly interrupted by an abortive tale named *Wiggle and Son*.

Again from *Unknown Chaplin* is a segment called *The Professor*, one of Chaplin's periodic attempts to break away from his usual character. As 'Professor Bosco' (subsequently the name of an illusionist in *The Circus* [*qv*]), Chaplin sports a top hat and frock coat. He is disguised under bushy moustache and eyebrows, the whole complemented by a corncob pipe. The Professor owns a flea circus, with which he checks into a back-alley flophouse (not unlike that in the *Life* extracts). He settles, but one of the fleas must be retrieved from his clothing, hopping into the box after a leap through the 'hoop' formed by Bosco's thumb and forefinger. A bearded Henry Bergman (*qv*) starts to scratch; Bosco finds a flea in the man's beard, but returns it as an outsider. Bosco's fleas escape *en masse* and, though he seems to have recaptured them, the Professor soon realises they have taken up residence on a dog. He is last seen pursuing the infested animal through an alleyway.

Chaplin's attempts to launch Edna Purviance (*qv*) on an independent career, culminating in *A Woman of Paris* (*qv*) and a never-released project known as *Sea Gulls*, *The Sea Gull* or *A Woman of the Sea* (described in the entry on Edna Purviance), also included plans to star her in an adaptation of *The Trojan Women* and, later, as the Empress Josephine, opposite Chaplin as Napoleon. Chaplin later recalled how Napoleon increasingly 'got in the way' of any concentration upon Josephine and, although several stills were taken of him costumed as the French Emperor, he decided in the end to restrict his impersonation to costume parties, at least, as noted below, until the early 1930s.

Another, more controversial idea was for Chaplin to play Christ (see **Religion**), though one imagines this to have been the type of notion both coined and forgotten within the space of one social gathering. There is evidence elsewhere of Chaplin being discouraged from a growing desire for seriousness. On 21 November 1925, *Picture Show* announced that Chaplin would soon embark on *The Clown*, a film eventually

released as *The Circus*. Chaplin had decided on this project instead of two potential dramatic subjects, Robert Louis Stevenson's story *The Suicide Club* (or *The Club of Suicides*) and *The Dandy*, after the success of *The Gold Rush* (*qv*) proved how 'the public like Charlie in humorous films that lend themselves to pathos'. Jack Spears' profile of Robert Florey (*qv*), in *Hollywood: The Golden Era*, describes Florey's wish to film John Kendrick Bangs' novel, *A Houseboat on the Styx*, in which various personages from history and literature meet in hell; amid a truly all-star cast, Chaplin was recommended to play Hamlet. The idea had been drawn up at Christmas 1927, during a party at Pickfair, but was quietly dropped from UA's schedule as celebration made way for practicality.

When talking pictures became standard during production of *City Lights* (*qv*), there were rumours of both a sound-film revamp of the project plus an unexpected leap into Chaplin's past with the production of *Mumming Birds* as a talking picture. As Fred Karno (*qv*) was then both seeking work in the USA and feeding ambitious tales to the press, one may perhaps pinpoint the origin of the story; irrespective of its genesis, the report soon gained sufficient currency for a 1929 edition of *Film Weekly* to speculate that Syd Chaplin had gone to America in order to assist Charlie in its production. It was never made. Nor was a film suggested to Chaplin by the British government during his visit of 1931; according to Paul Holt, in the *Daily Sketch* of 28 May that year, the comedian had been invited 'to devise and direct a British talkie of national significance', seemingly about 'the London he loves so well'.

In the summer of 1933, the young Alistair Cooke, filling in for six weeks for the *Observer's* film critic, C.A. Lejeune, embarked on a series of articles about Hollywood; he approached Chaplin via Alf Reeves (*qv*) and became a welcome guest. During his stay, Cooke made a home movie of Chaplin's pet impersonation of Napoleon, and was later invited to return the next summer, to work with Chaplin on a screenplay based on Napoleon's experiences in St. Helena. Most of summer 1934 was spent on the script, until Chaplin suddenly announced that it would be 'a beautiful idea – for someone else'. For unrelated reasons, Cooke reluctantly declined Chaplin's offer to remain as an assistant on *Modern Times*, and was all the more surprised when Chaplin wanted to launch him as a light comedian. At this time, Chaplin also told Cooke of an idea which was left unmade, a revue-format film with religious overtones. The Napoleon idea resurfaced after Chaplin's Far Eastern jaunt of 1936–7, during which he worked on three stories, the others being *Stowaway* (eventually made as *A Countess From Hong Kong*) and *Regency*.

As noted in the main entry, *Monsieur Verdoux* was based upon an original idea by Orson Welles. When interviewed by Peter Bogdanovich (in *This is Orson Welles*), he recalled having conceived a second idea for Chaplin, pairing him with Greta Garbo in a film 'based on the love affair between D'Annunzio and Eleonora Duse'. Welles' rationale was that Garbo, having played comedy in *Ninotchka* (1939), might be willing to try farce. Both stars claimed it was too beautiful a story to be played for laughs.

During 1941–2, Chaplin intended to produce another serious film called *Shadow and Substance*, based on the play by Paul Vincent Carroll. A potential leading lady, Joan Barry, proved less than stable and was responsible for Chaplin being taken to court (unjustly, as it turns out) on paternity and other charges. More positively, another choice for leading lady was Oona O'Neill (*qv*), who, instead of making *Shadow and Substance*, became Chaplin's wife.

The 1940s saw Chaplin's abandonment of the tramp character, but there were occasional suggestions that it might be revived. One suspects Chaplin to have been too old for the part by 1952, but on 11 October of that year, the *Daily Mail* quoted him to the effect that it might happen, albeit without dialogue. The concept had become even less plausible when Chaplin made a similar statement, again to the *Mail*, in February 1964.

In 1962, Chaplin announced his intention to make two more films, one of them a 'real slapstick burlesque' starring his son, Sydney, the other a parody of the then-popular historical spectacles; these came to nothing, as did rumours that he planned to make a film in the USSR or (according to *Le Figaro* of 27 November 1962) appear in a movie written by Paddy Chayevsky. According to contemporary publicity, Chaplin was approached to play a part in Otto Preminger's ultimately disastrous *Skidoo* (1968); both he and, oddly, Senator Dirksen declined the offer, which was accepted instead by Groucho

Marx (*qv*). Chaplin had himself considered a similar concept, in which he played a stuffy old judge whose son eventually converts him into a hippie. There was also talk of Chaplin, in a dual rôle, portraying both a crazed Roman emperor and his slave.

The idea of Chaplin's supposed Jewish heritage (see **Religion**) produced an interesting tale at a late stage in his life. One doubts if he genuinely knew anything of a film project detailed in the *Daily Sketch* of 30 January 1968, intended to première in Jerusalem as part of Israel's 21st birthday celebrations. Entitled *Two Thousand Years, My Love*, it was to tell the story of the Jewish people and would be financed by 'Jews all over the world'. According to this report, Chaplin had agreed to star in the £4 million film for a fee of precisely 8 shillings, then the equivalent of one US dollar.

An even more intriguing non-starter of this period was *The Freak*, about a winged, flying girl, discovered in Chile, whom the natives adore as an angel descended from heaven. Two criminals from Britain abduct the girl, taking her to London, where she is exploited by an evangelist. The girl escapes, flying across London until she reaches the Opera House in Covent Garden, where *Swan Lake* is being performed; inside the theatre, she takes refuge disguised as one of the swans. The imposture ends when the girl takes flight above the startled audience. A rabies scare is put around, and the girl is pursued through the countryside by the army. She disappears within a costume party at a country mansion, but is ultimately captured, whereupon a court has to decide if the caged girl is human or an animal. Jerry Epstein (*qv*), upon whose account this description is based, saw it as a combination of *E.T.* and *The Elephant Man*, with the potential to have been Chaplin's greatest work since *City Lights*. Chaplin's daughter, Victoria, was to play the lead, with her sister, Josephine, in a co-starring rôle; their father intended to contribute a cameo appearance as a drunk who is baffled by the flying apparition. Tests were filmed at Shepperton during 1969 or 1970, but nothing more. Epstein's version is that Oona, concerned for her husband's health, was convinced he would not survive such an elaborate project and cancelled it. Chaplin's 1974 memoir, *My Life in Pictures*, refers to him having rehearsed a few scenes with Victoria until she decided to forsake the idea in favour

of matrimony. Her marriage took place in 1971, yet, as late as May 1974, another daughter, Geraldine, mentioned the project (by name) to reporters in London. She claimed that her father would soon be in London to discuss finances, that he was very excited about the film, and that he had recently been 'very busy in other directions, writing music and so on'. This statement may have been prompted by a recent family gathering, where Victoria had been photographed wearing the wings, thus reawakening Chaplin's interest in the film. Chaplin's subsequent comments make it clear that he fully intended to make *The Freak*, at least until shortly before his death. Those who have seen the script have not necessarily shared Epstein's enthusiasm, but Victoria's subsequent stage work suggests she would have been very effective.

(See also: Aircraft; Awards, honours; *The Chaplin Revue*; Children; Dual rôles; Home movies; Karno Company, the; Marriages; Music; Pathos; Pickford, Mary; Public appearances; Religion; Suicide; Women)

ADDAMS, DAWN
(1930–85)

English-born actress, RADA-trained, who adopted an American accent for her rôle as 'Ann Kay', television hustler, in *A King in New York* (*qv*). Originally on the British stage, by the early 1950s she had established herself in American films, sometimes those with an English locale (as in 1952's *The Hour of Thirteen*). She auditioned as 'Terry' in *Limelight* (*qv*) and, though not accepted, formed a friendship with Chaplin and his wife, Oona; they were present at her wedding (to an Italian aristocrat) in 1954. Her other films, from both sides of the Atlantic, include *The Robe* (1953), *Young Bess* (1953), *Riders to the Stars* (1954), *The Silent Enemy* (1958), *The Two Faces of Dr. Jekyll* (1960), *Come Fly With Me* (1962), *Ballad in Blue* (1964) and *The Vampire Lovers* (1970). Also many British TV appearances, as in a November 1959 ITV 'Play of the Week' called *Sweet Poison*, the action series *The Saint, Danger Man* and *Department S*, also the early 1960s hospital soap, *Emergency Ward 10*.

(See also: Bloom, Claire; O'Neill, Oona)

Dawn Addams plays the TV advertising girl in *A King in New York*

THE ADDING MACHINE 🎩

See: Epstein, Jerry

THE ADVENTURER 🎩

Released by Mutual, 23 October 1917. Written and directed by Charles Chaplin. Photographed by Rollie Totheroh. Two reels. 1,845 feet.

With Charlie Chaplin (himself, as 'The Eel', an escaped convict), Edna Purviance (the heiress), Eric Campbell (her suitor), Frank J. Coleman (prison guard), (?) Marta Golden (Edna's mother), Henry Bergman (pierside spectator/Edna's father, Judge Brown), Albert Austin (butler), Kono (chauffeur).

At the beach, prison guards are seeking an escaped convict. One of the guards is taking a rest when the convict, Charlie, digs his way out from beneath the sand. Charlie, face to face with a rifle barrel, attempts to re-submerge, but tries instead to sneak away while the guard snoozes. He almost succeeds, but the guard is awakened when he tumbles into the hole left by Charlie. The guard fires after Charlie, who scurries up a cliff face. Charlie throws down a rock at his pursuer, believing himself safe until another guard steps on his hand. Charlie eludes the guard, kicking him over the edge to join his colleague. Charlie rushes down to the beach, runs straight into the guards, and runs back up the hill again. When a guard has Charlie cornered on a

ledge, he fires a seemingly fatal shot. He examines the convict, who, returning to life, kicks the guard off the ledge. Charlie escapes down to the beach, ducking through caves until he catches one of the guards by surprise. Armed with his rifle, Charlie backs away to the sea. He loses the rifle when he trips over a rock, but has gained a lead. The officers try to follow in a rowing boat, but are defeated by a mighty wave. Charlie swims to another boat, whose occupant is trying to pull a sweater over his head. Charlie, unnoticed, borrows the man's swimming costume. At a seaside café, bearded giant Eric is trying to impress Edna with his mighty biceps. Edna's attention is diverted to the screams of her mother, who has fallen from the pier. Eric takes his time in playing hero, so Edna leaps into the sea, the result being two drowning ladies. Eric offers half-hearted cries for help as a dispassionate passerby looks on. When both men lean over the rail, it breaks and there are suddenly *four* people in distress. Nearby, Charlie swims to shore. Hearing cries for help, he swims to the scene, passing over Edna's mother to save the younger woman first. This done, he brings in Edna's mother and suitor (the passerby having presumably been left to float contentedly). Charlie gives Edna's mother a drink; Eric expects one, but Charlie drinks it himself, using Eric's beard as napkin. The family chauffeur carries mother to her car by stretcher. Charlie explains that he heard their cries

from his 'yacht', then returns to fetch Eric. He is unharmed but quite prepared to be carried; Charlie picks up one end of the stretcher, and Eric slides back into the sea. Charlie dives back to retrieve him; as they climb the ladder to the pier, Eric kicks Charlie into the water. The chauffeur is sent to find Charlie. He finds the unconscious rescuer drifting to shore and takes him back to the car. They drive away. Charlie awakens to find himself wearing striped pyjamas. These, and the iron-barred bedstead, give him the momentary impression of being back in jail. The illusion is dispelled by the arrival of a butler bringing him a set of dinner clothes. Downstairs, a party is in progress. Eric continues to force his attentions on Edna. Charlie joins the gathering by accepting a drink from the butler, not from a glass but by spraying soda into the bottle. He is greeted by Edna, who introduces him to some other guests. Eric snubs him, but Charlie lands a kick when Eric bows to a society lady. Edna plays piano as Charlie leans against the instrument. Eric returns Charlie's kick, but receives a jet of soda in return. Outside, Eric looks at a newspaper, which carries an account of Charlie's escape, complete with photograph. Eric compares the likeness. In the house, Edna introduces Charlie to her father, Judge Brown; they recognize each other, but only Charlie realizes why. Eric walks in, scrutinizing the stranger; outside, Charlie finds the incriminating paper and, taking a pen, makes alterations. Eric brings the Judge in order to confront Charlie with the evidence, but Charlie has added a beard to the picture, making it look like Eric. The Judge cannot understand Eric's protests. Charlie returns to the party, emptying one glass then switching it for someone else's drink. In the kitchen downstairs, the maid is entertaining one of the prison guards. As his fellow-guests retire upstairs, Charlie collects all their wine dregs into one glass. Edna escorts Charlie down to the kitchen. The maid conceals her boyfriend in a cupboard, fooling neither Edna nor Charlie. He acknowledges the situation roguishly, takes a peek inside the cupboard and, recognizing its occupant, takes to his heels. The guard fails to recognize him and makes his own escape through the window. Charlie approaches the verandah, but withdraws on seeing the guard sneaking past. Inside, Charlie involuntarily puts up his hands when the butler pops a champagne cork. Edna

takes him upstairs to the ballroom. An elderly dancing couple obscure their path; once inside, Charlie considers stabbing the matron's behind with a pin but, out of deference to Edna, changes his mind. Eric telephones the prison; thus alerted, officers rush to the scene. Charlie and Edna retire from the dance floor to the balcony, where they are served ice cream. Charlie spills his into the front of his ill-fitting trousers; he permits it to slide out through his trouser leg, pushing it through the floor grating. The frozen delicacy lands down the back of a matron's dress, whose panic is not alleviated by Eric's attempts to retrieve it. An onlooker gets the blame. The prison guards arrive, and Eric offers them directions. Charlie is pursued upstairs through the ballroom, back down to the foyer – where he pauses to kiss Edna – thence to the verandah, where a guard descends from the balcony above. The chase resumes back upstairs, Charlie leaping from the balcony to escape one guard, only to meet another below. In the foyer, Charlie dons a lampshade to adopt the rôle of standard lamp as the guard rushes past. Eric arrives, making a grab at Edna, until Charlie drops his pose and overpowers the big man. Back to the verandah, where Charlie removes the shade to see a guard; he is chased back to the ballroom, where he dodges the guard using a sliding door. He catches the guard's head between door and frame, doing the same to Eric when his head pops through. Charlie kicks the guard away, leaving Eric's head secured

between the sliding doors, using the guard's handcuffs. Charlie leaps to the verandah, hoping to explain himself to Edna. As she is unwilling to listen, Charlie walks dejectedly away. The guard descends from the balcony, and Charlie's liberty seems at an end. The gentlemanly convict pauses to introduce the guard to Edna and, as the guard pauses to shake her hand, Charlie makes his getaway.

The last of Chaplin's comedies for Mutual (*qv*), *The Adventurer* is also one of the most famous because, as Isobel Quigley has pointed out, virtually everyone seems to have seen it on 8mm over the years (a situation doubtless reversed of late by the predominance of home video). It was, sadly, also the final appearance of Eric Campbell (*qv*), who was killed in a road accident soon after.

As the final entry in the series, *The Adventurer*'s forthcoming UK release brought a moment's reflection from the British magazine *Pictures and the Picturegoer*. In the issue of 17 November 1917, Chaplin's publicist Elsie Codd noted delays in production, first from Chaplin's decision to visit the East, then from 'an indisposition that kept him housebound for a fortnight'. Anxious to dispel notions of a purely fun-filled occupation, the article insisted that 'no mugwump in his audience thinks the job unfunnier than Mr. Chaplin does himself'. It is well known that Chaplin did not work from a script until *Modern Times* (*qv*); in describing Chaplin's

improvisational methods, Codd speaks of 'the machinery of the Lone Star Studio' being 'at once set in motion as soon as Mr. Chaplin has announced the tremendous advent of the Main Idea'. Examples cited of such 'main ideas' are props, as in an alarm clock (*The Pawnshop* [*qv*]), or sets, such as a Turkish Bath (*The Cure* [*qv*]). It is revealed that 'when work has started ... Mr. Chaplin most probably has not the remotest idea how his story is going to begin, to end, or, in fact, [what it is] to be about'. The story's direction would be determined by ways in which the 'Main Idea' relates to the comedian's character and its 'possibilities of distress and inconvenience to the persons of the other folk'. At times the 'Main Idea' would be shelved on the development of a greater inspiration (as clearly occurred during *The Immigrant* [*qv*]). Also noted are the irregularities of Chaplin's filming schedules, by which 'on a lucky day' perhaps over 1,000 feet of film might be exposed, while another day might see no filming at all. Supporting players would be paid for remaining idle; this became almost the rule for the later features, when actors would happily accept Chaplin's lower pay rates because it would guarantee an income during his protracted absences. The studio would be inactive while Chaplin developed ideas; Codd's account describes the comedian's preference for solitude, seeming absent-mindedness, 'mental sluggishness' and a look of harassment – this and occasional

House-guest Charlie is served ice cream in **The Adventurer***; it soon slides down a matron's back*

temperament (preserved in a few out-takes) induced by sleeplessness. Chaplin's insomniac hours would be used in the making of audio notes – unusual for the time – by means of a dictaphone. When the ideas flowed again, Chaplin seemed to lose twenty years in appearance and would energetically arrange his stock company as required. The article notes Chaplin's directorial method, to which he adhered even up to *A Countess From Hong Kong* (*qv*): although he might watch, patiently if pained, his actors' first attempts at interpretation, Chaplin would customarily instruct each individual player in how the rôles should be played; the impression one obtains is of Chaplin preferring to play every rôle in the film but resorting to a supporting cast only as a physical necessity. Selection of the film's title, it seems, was postponed until the end of production, Chaplin's preference being for concise simplicity (though some Chaplin titles, notably *The Idle Class*, contain a measure of irony). Once shooting was completed, the supporting cast could disappear, but Chaplin was left with the considerable burden of editing. Codd's text, substantiated by other sources, cites the length of an uncut Chaplin Mutual as anywhere between 20,000 and 90,000 feet (*The Immigrant* went to the latter extreme), from which a comedy running approximately 2,000 feet would need to be assembled. It was usual for Chaplin to work until dawn before finally returning home to bed.

Of the Mutuals, *The Adventurer* has the highest slapstick content and fastest pace (accentuated by an uncharacteristic use of undercranking when Charlie scales a cliff face) but is rescued from potentially Keystone-like chaos by construction, characterization and Chaplin's high-speed grace. His pursuit by the guards, both at the beginning and during the climactic scenes, differs from the received idea of silent-comedy 'chase' through ingenuity (e.g. Charlie's impromptu pose as a lamp) and the much-discussed balletic quality that Chaplin, under the influence of several well-meaning commentators, would later take rather too seriously. The only structural fault in *The Adventurer* becomes apparent when viewing the documentary series *Unknown Chaplin* (*qv*): in the ballroom sequence, it is evident that Charlie has sat down on a radiator, but nothing comes of it in the finished film; instead, out-takes preserve the development of a deleted gag in which Charlie's behind is singed when the radiator is accidentally turned on.

A footnote: Charlie's lifeguard act in this film found a real-life parallel during rehearsals, near Topango Canyon, Santa Monica. Another *Pictures and Picturegoer* item describes Chaplin's rescue of seven-year-old Mildred Morrison, the daughter of a New Rochelle stockbroker, who had fallen into the sea while excitedly watching the comedian at work.

[See also: Alcohol; Austin, Albert; Ballet; Bergman, Henry; Boats, ships; Cars; 'Chaplin Craze', The; Coleman, Frank J.; Costume; Dual rôles; Food; *His New Profession*; Home movies; Keystone; Kono, Toraichi; Policemen; Prisons; Purviance, Edna; Rand, John; Television; Trick photography; Video releases]

AGEE, JAMES

See: *Monsieur Verdoux* and *Work*

AIRCRAFT

'(Chaplin films *qv*)
The bulk of Chaplin's film work pre-dates an age in which air travel has become commonplace, though he takes potshots at First World War aeroplanes in *Shoulder Arms* and, from a retrospective point of view, *The Great Dictator*. In the immediate period before his departure from the USA, Chaplin shied away from air travel – perhaps through fear of an attempt on his life – though his fictional exiled monarch in *A King in New York* shares none of these qualms.

This may be the point to dwell upon Chaplin's first experiences of flying, amid the aviation craze that followed the First World War. *Picture Show* of 27 March 1921 carried a story from Chaplin's publicist, Elsie Codd, recalling an incident 'some time ago' when the comedian took his first flight in an aircraft. His main worry, according to the piece, surrounded the padded clothes required for the journey, which he considered indicative of a likelihood to crash. He survived a 'loop-the-loop' but did not wish to repeat the experience. Despite this unnerving introduction, the piece was accompanied by photos of Chaplin embarking on a more recent flight, this time to San Diego. It may have been this experience that prompted a report in *Pictures and Picturegoer* of 25 October 1919, announcing that 'Charlie Chaplin's next comedy will ...

make sport of aviation, most of its scenes being taken in and around airplanes and up in the air.' If Chaplin did contemplate such a film, it must have been in a passing moment of enthusiasm, for it was never made (though David Robinson's *Chaplin: His Life and Art* lists the shooting of a publicity film of Chaplin in an aeroplane at this location on 8 August 1919). Another *Picture Show* story, from 20 December 1920, reported Chaplin, his wife Mildred Harris (*qv*), Mary Pickford (*qv*), Douglas Fairbanks (*qv*) and Marjorie Daw having 'motored to the Chaplin Aerodrome' (presumably a strip of land purchased for such use), where they were taken up in pairs, 'Douglas and Charlie going first, followed by Mary and Mildred, and then by Marjorie Daw. All the film celebrities were given a thrilling time in the air,' Chaplin and Fairbanks being 'treated' to twelve loops, three nose dives, one 'side slip' and a tailspin. A photo recording the event says in its caption: 'This adventure caused thrills for the actors, and shivers for their managers and insurance companies.'

[See also: Abandoned projects; Bloom, Claire; Coogan, Jackie; Royalty; Wartime]

ALCOHOL

(Chaplin films *qv*)
Scenes of comic drunkenness have been part of theatrical tradition since classical times. It is a general rule that the best comic drunks are in real life moderate drinkers, if not teetotallers; there are exceptions, but Chaplin, despite many superbly alcoholic scenes, was not fond of drink (though he had a brief flirtation with it in his late teens, during a stint of unemployment following *Sherlock Holmes*). This is hardly surprising, for it was alcoholism that brought about the death of Charles Chaplin Senior (*qv*) at the early age of 37. What is more remarkable is that, despite this tragedy, Chaplin should be so adept at humorous intoxication when in character. (It might be noted in passing that his uncle, Spencer Chaplin, was a publican who in 1890 built the Queen's Head, on Black Prince Road.) His stage role in *Mumming Birds* (*qv*), later transferred to film as *A Night in the Show*, is perhaps the best-known example; the Keystones, in which he mostly portrays a less sympathetic figure than later on, see him imbibing very freely, as when creating a nuisance

Alcohol: Essanay supplied a cut-out Charlie to promote the Bass brewery; his friends look too young to be drinking

in the early *Mabel's Strange Predicament* and *Caught in the Rain*, propping up a bar in *His Favorite Pastime*, helping himself to the landlady's booze in *The Star Boarder*, deserting his duties in *His New Profession*, out on the razzle with Fatty Arbuckle (*qv*) in *The Rounders*, acquiring belated Dutch courage in *Mabel's Married Life* or depicting a broken man in *The Face on the Bar Room Floor*. Of the Essanays, *A Night Out* recalls both *The Rounders* and *Mabel's Strange Predicament* by pairing him with Ben Turpin (*qv*) as a pair of pugnacious revellers; in *The Champion*, Charlie's fight training is punctuated by frequent pulls at a jug of beer (he is similarly fortified in his work as *The Property Man*), while in *By the Sea* it is the turn of Billy Armstrong (*qv*) to be under the influence. Charlie meets other drunks in *Police* and its offshoot, *Triple Trouble*.

The more polished Mutual comedies provide less space for out-and-out rowdyism, and Chaplin's drunk performance in *One A.M.* concentrates primarily on his attempts to cope with his own house while rendered incapable of doing so. A contemporary review of the film in *Pictures and the Picturegoer* makes an interesting point in regarding the consequences of Charlie's intoxication in this film, itself 'muzzy' rather than aggressive, as more a recommendation of temperance than glorification of drunkenness. He plays an

equally dapper tippler in *The Cure*, organized to the point of having a trunk fully equipped as a travelling bar (the contents of which are dumped into a health spring). From the First National films, it is a wallet stolen from a well-heeled drunk that eventually provides financial security for Charlie and Edna in *A Dog's Life*. Charlie's wealthy alter ego in *The Idle Class* endangers his marriage with a fondness for the bottle. Detailed elsewhere is the celebrated gag where he seems reduced to tears by his wife's threatened departure, but is seen instead to be mixing yet another drink (an even more elaborate mixing of a cocktail may be seen in *The Rink*). The film's immediate successor, *Pay Day*, concludes with a drunken Charlie ejected from the house by his wife. Chaplin's next film, *The Pilgrim*, suggests hypocrisy in the ostensibly clean-living deacon, from whose back pocket protrudes a bottle of whisky. A saloon sequence later in the film is explained by a title card that sets the story before Prohibition.

Among the best drinking scenes in the Chaplin canon are those in the much later *City Lights*, when Charlie hits the town with a drunken millionaire who fails to recognize his companion once sober. In *Modern Times*, Charlie, as a night-watchman, gets drunk with a group of burglars, one of whom is a former colleague. The darker side of alcohol is only really explored in his troubled music-hall comedian from *Limelight*, who even then conveys the grace and wit expected from Chaplin's earlier portrayals.

It might be expected that several Chaplin films depict specific settings for drinking; some are detailed above, but one might mention the bar-room setting that opens *The Vagabond*, the café setting of *Caught in a Cabaret*, the dance halls in *A Dog's Life* and *The Gold Rush* and the nightclub from *A King in New York*. That the on-screen Charlie is the most habitual of bar patrons is suggested by a drunken moment in *A Night Out*, when his foot reaches for an absent rail beneath a hotel desk; this gag acquires greater incongruity in *The Bond*, when a sober Charlie does the same when standing before a church altar.

Since the 1960s there has been a pub named after Chaplin near his childhood haunts in the Elephant and Castle; another pub, The Roebuck, was a few doors from his commemorative plaque in the Kennington Road and spent the early 1990s bearing the name 'Charlie

Chaplins" (sic) but has since undergone a further rechristening. The association of alcohol with Chaplin's screen character was noticed very early on: Essanay (*qv*), always astute in terms of publicity, once arranged a publicity tie-in with Bass, a UK brewery. Ironically, the much later *A King in New York* incorporates not merely the deposed monarch's refusal to endorse a 'King's Lager Beer', but also a supposed TV commercial in which a seductive woman's sales pitch turns out to be for a similar brew. Although films have traditionally used fictional products in such instances, on this occasion a genuine, British brewery is named – doubly strange given that it is a brand probably unknown in the United States.

(See also: Allen, Phyllis; Early stage appearances; Karno Company, the; Home movies; Keystone; Mutual; Myers, Harry; Sandford, Stanley J. 'Tiny')

ALDRICH, ROBERT (1918–83)

American producer-director, whose work ranged from the robust spectacle of *Vera Cruz* (1954), via the high-pitched histrionics of *Whatever Happened to Baby Jane?* (1962) to some ambitious latter-day failures .
Credited as associate director on *Limelight* (*qv*).

(See also: Bennett, Marjorie)

ALLEN, PHYLLIS (1861–1938)

(Chaplin films *qv*)
New York-born character actress, of imposing frame and demeanour. Formerly in vaudeville and musical comedy, she entered films in 1910, initially for Selig and Keystone (*qv*); her work for the latter includes *Riot*, *Murphy's IOU* (both 1913) and *A Fatal Sweet Tooth* (1914). She appeared frequently with Roscoe 'Fatty' Arbuckle (*qv*); among many other Sennett films are *Hogan's Wild Oats* (1915) with Charlie Murray (*qv*), plus a number of comedies with Syd Chaplin (*qv*), such as *Giddy, Gay and Ticklish* (detailed under the **Keystone** entry) and his best-known Sennett film, *A Submarine Pirate*. She left Keystone for Fox in March 1916. In Charlie Chaplin's Keystones, she is present in *Caught in a Cabaret, The Property Man, Dough and Dynamite,*

Gentlemen of Nerve and *Tillie's Punctured Romance* (also, reportedly, *A Busy Day*), in addition to serving as intimidating spouse for Mack Swain (*qv*) in both *His Trysting Place* and *Getting Acquainted*, ditto for Charlie in *The Rounders*. She repeated the task much later in *Pay Day*, a First National film in which fellow old-Keystonian Swain also appears.

(See also: First National; Wilson, Jack; Women)

ALTERNATIVE VERSIONS

See: *Count, The; Dog's Life, A; Easy Street; Floorwalker, The; Gold Rush, The; Kid, The; Pay Day,* and *Shoulder Arms*

ANDERSON, G.M.
(1880 or 1882–1971)

Born Max Aronson, Gilbert M. Anderson played at least two parts in Edison's pioneering 1903 western (made in the east), *The Great Train Robbery*, and thus set his screen career for nearly two decades. As 'Broncho Billy', Anderson became the early cinema's archetypal cowboy star, in films produced by the Essanay company (*qv*) which Anderson had formed with George K. Spoor (also *qv*) in 1907. Chaplin's memoirs make it clear that his relationship with Anderson was extremely cordial, at least in his initial months with Essanay. On 17 April 1915, *Pictures and Picturegoer* announced that Anderson's sister, Leona, would be Chaplin's leading lady, even though Edna Purviance (*qv*) had already been assigned to that rôle. Miss Anderson did not get the job, but her brother made a guest appearance in Chaplin's *The Champion*, a favour reciprocated when Chaplin contributed comic business to Anderson's *His Regeneration* (*qv*). Anderson sold out his interest in Essanay to Spoor, venturing instead into independent production, almost as soon as Chaplin had left the company's employ. Anderson had always acted as intermediary between Spoor and Chaplin, and there are those who see this gesture as a show of loyalty to the comedian over the *Carmen* lawsuit. In the 1920s, Anderson produced a series of comedies starring Chaplin's old colleague, Stan Laurel (*qv*), the pilot for which, *A Lucky Dog*, brought about a chance appearance with future team-mate Oliver Hardy.

Although successful, the Laurel-Anderson films came to an end when the producer reneged on contractual matters (a situation reminiscent of some of Chaplin's problems at Essanay). Anderson lived to enjoy a lengthy retirement (popping up for a cameo in a 1954 Randolph Scott film, *The Bounty Hunter*), and in 1957 was honoured with a special Academy Award for his part in the industry's fledgling days.

(See also: Arbuckle, Roscoe 'Fatty'; *Carmen; Film Johnnie, A;* Swanson, Gloria)

ANIMALS

(Chaplin films *qv*)
Chaplin was the kind of talent able to ignore the showbusiness maxim of never working with children or animals. When touring in *Sherlock Holmes* as a teenager, he surreptitiously kept a pet rabbit in his lodgings. In his autobiography, Chaplin recalled the animal was not housetrained but nonetheless briefed to rush into its makeshift hutch when there was a knock at the door. In the films, as early as *Caught in a Cabaret*, Charlie was accompanied by a sausage dog on a lead; the resultant entanglements anticipate similar business in *A Dog's Life* and *The Gold Rush*. Another dog proves to be Charlie's rescuer in *The Champion*, while still another insists on chewing his foot in an extant sequence deleted from *The Circus*. Again in *The Gold Rush*, Charlie adopts canine methods when burying a gun in the snow; the same film introduces us to a grizzly bear (ultimately eaten!) and Big Jim's hallucination of Charlie as a chicken. *The Circus*, again, has Charlie seemingly ready to make a meal of a passing chicken, only to fool his audience by contenting himself with an egg. *The Circus*, not surprisingly, brings him into frequent contact with the animal world, not least a caged lion (fortunately, less hungry than the smaller cats in *Pay Day*!), an ailing horse (whose pill enters Charlie's stomach) and the monkeys who plague him while on the high wire. Another nemesis in this film is an intermittently angry mule, an infinitely less co-operative specimen than that towing the cart in *His Musical Career*. In *City Lights*, Charlie, as a roadsweeper, avoids a group of mules only to see a circus elephant trotting through. Another of the childhood experiences in Chaplin's autobiography concerns his story at Methley Street, and the abattoir that stood nearby. His laughter at the antics of a runaway sheep turned to horror at the thought of its imminent slaughter on recapture. Recalling the incident, Chaplin suspected it may have influenced the blending of comedy and tragedy in his later work.

(See also: Animation; Early stage appearances; Impersonators; Risqué humour; *Unknown Chaplin*)

Animals: 'Scraps' – whose real name was 'Mut' – proved an ideal parallel to Charlie and Edna in A Dog's Life

ANIMATION

As noted elsewhere, the 'Chaplin Craze' (*qv*) produced replicas of various kinds. Chaplin's army of impersonators (*qv*) did not meet with his approval, but he chose at least to tolerate an in-house imitation in the field of animated cartoons and, subsequently, to encourage at least one series of such films based on his character and exploits. The earlier example dates from Chaplin's tenure with Essanay (*qv*) during 1915. Essanay had a series of cartoon films in which 'Dreamy Dud Draws ...' whoever happened to be the subject. One of these, *Dreamy Dud Draws Charlie Chaplin*, typifies Essanay's keenness to exploit its biggest signing.

In the earlier weeks of 1916, a San Francisco-based firm, the Movca Film Studios, announced a weekly series of 'Star Comedy Cartoons' starring 'Charlie – Fatty – Maybelle [*sic*]', evidently designed to reflect Chaplin's Keystone work with Arbuckle and Normand. The cartoons were released on a State's Rights basis through the Herald Film Corporation, New York.

The series actively encouraged by Chaplin was produced by the Pat Sullivan studio, starting in 1916. For the task, Sullivan hired as animator Otto Messmer, who went on to create the studio's main attraction, Felix the Cat. In John Canemaker's 1977 documentary *Otto Messmer and Felix the Cat*, Messmer recalled how Chaplin would supply autographed stills of his various poses. The comedian evidently regarded the cartoons as being more an advertisement for him than the outright competition presented by flesh-and-blood imitators (he may not have been aware of 'Charlie' appearing in *Romeo and Juliet*, a British cartoon made for Hepworth by Anson Dyer in 1920). One of these cartoons, *How Charlie Captured the Kaiser*, was announced in August 1918 and seems to have anticipated – perhaps through access to stills – Chaplin's forthcoming *Shoulder Arms* (*qv*).

Messmer used the experience by incorporating many facets of the Chaplin character into Felix, who, as Leonard Maltin has noted, was often described as the 'Charlie Chaplin of cartoon characters'; the debt was acknowledged in a 1923 Felix adventure, *Felix in Hollywood*, in which Felix does a Chaplin act only for the Tramp to admonish him with a severe, 'Stealing my stuff, eh?' The following year brought an *avant-garde* animated

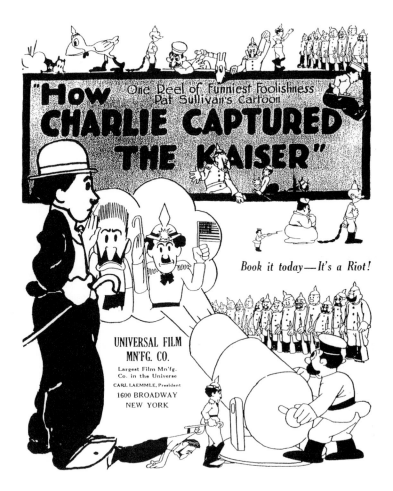

Animation: one of Otto Messmer's Chaplin cartoons for Pat Sullivan parallels Shoulder Arms
By courtesy of Claudia Sassen

film from France, *Charlot présente le Ballet Mécanique*, presenting the Tramp as a collection of angular, disjointed components. The design was very similar to a drawing made of Chaplin two years later by the Russian director Sergei Yutkevitch. The French film was used by Britain's Channel 4 in a 1989 documentary tribute, *Our Charlie* (the station also employed a sequence based upon it as the motif for its entire Chaplin centenary celebrations).

Post-dating these more or less 'official' Chaplin cartoons are examples typical of the movie-star caricatures employed by animation studios in the 1930s and 40s. Most of these take place in films where several stars are caricatured, though there are

exceptions. Ub Iwerks produced a series of cartoons starring 'Flip the Frog', who, in a 1931 entry called *Movie Mad*, consults a book called *How to be a movie actor*. The first illustration is of Chaplin, whom Flip impersonates while the music switches to the opening chords of *City Lights* (*qv*). Another Iwerks cartoon, 1935's *Balloonland* (a.k.a. *Pincushion Man*), takes place in a land populated by folk composed of balloons; the first three to pass the camera are Oliver Hardy, Stan Laurel (*qv*) and Charlie Chaplin! (Chaplin and Hardy are also among the numerous dancing figures to be glimpsed in a 1988 animated film from the Netherlands, *Pas à Deux*.) Iwerks was an early associate of Walt Disney, from whom he spent a decade away before returning as a special-effects expert. Disney himself was fond of the movie-star motif, hence Charlie Chaplin featuring in a trade ad celebrating Mickey Mouse's seventh birthday in 1935 or, in a film released the following year, joining *Mickey's Polo Team* (in which Charlie rides a horse which has a similar walk to his own!). In a prior Disney entry, Charlie attends *Mickey's Gala Première* (1933) without an invitation, crawling in on all fours. The Warner Brothers cartoons were fond of incorporating caricatured film stars but seldom featured Chaplin, possibly owing to his limited output in latter days. One of the few examples is a black-and-white 'Looney Tune' of 1937, *Porky's Road Race*, in which a cartoon Charlie performs his 'skidding turn'. An odd footnote is that this is one of the monochrome Warner cartoons retraced into colour for TV, with the result that Charlie has been given blond curls in the evident belief that he is Harpo Marx!

More peripherally, the *Motion Picture News* of 10 August 1918 contains a review of a Chaplin burlesque using animated dolls, entitled *The Burglar Man*. This, the first of an intended series of 'Doll Comedies', was made by the Emerald Manufacturing Company and distributed by General Film (Essanay's one-time outlet). Chaplin was represented as an inept porter, as in *The Bank* (*qv*); although the film was considered to be essentially for children, the reviewer conceded there were 'several mildly funny incidents' leading to 'a real Mack Sennett riot at the end'.

Returning to two-dimensional animation, there are those who detect the shades of Charlie and Eric Campbell (*qv*) in the 'Foo Foo' and 'Gogo' characters created by animators Halas & Batchelor for a 1950s British TV series. Subsequent Chaplin animations have been sparse, even counting the brief title sections of the 'Charlie Chaplin Comedy Theatre' package distributed to TV in the 1960s or the credits for *Unknown Chaplin* (*qv*). A notable exception may be found in Richard Williams' animated credits for *The Return of the Pink Panther* (1974), showing the titular character imitating Chaplin, among other stars. As if to prove how time can stand still in cartoons, the Panther uses his tail to simulate Chaplin's cane, just as Felix did in 1923.

(See also: Ballet; Caricatures; Documentaries, compilations; Marx, Groucho; *Nice and Friendly*; Television)

ARBUCKLE, ROSCOE 🎩 'FATTY' (1887–1933)

(Chaplin films *qv*)
Rotund comedian, whose first films were made for Selig in 1909. He joined Keystone (*qv*) in 1913, and was an established name when Chaplin arrived at the end of the year. According to legend, Arbuckle loaned Chaplin the oversized trousers and undersized hat when the 'tramp' costume was first assembled; he was also among those to support Chaplin when Mack Sennett (*qv*) considered firing him. In his biography of Arbuckle, *The Day the Laughter Stopped*, David Yallop quotes Arbuckle's first wife, Minta Durfee (*qv*), to the effect that Sennett had found Chaplin's methods too slow, mostly in terms of meeting deadlines. 'Listen,' Arbuckle told him, 'he's doing beautiful things. Don't worry about the shipping dates. We'll make them.' Sennett had sufficient confidence in Arbuckle to allow Chaplin to continue. Arbuckle appears in Chaplin's *A Film Johnnie*, *Tango Tangles*, *His Favorite Pastime*, *The Masquerader*, *His New Profession* (almost unrecognizably, as the barman) and, perhaps best of all, *The Rounders*. Chaplin also contributes to Arbuckle's *The Knockout* as a crooked fight referee. The comedians' friendship survived after Chaplin had left Keystone for Essanay (*qv*): on 26 June 1915, *Pictures and the Picturegoer* reported Chaplin, Arbuckle and G.M. Anderson (*qv*) having been spotted sharing a box at a Los Angeles theatre, whereupon they were obliged to forsake their seats and perform a 40-minute turn for the audience. Among other occasions, Yallop reports Chaplin's presence at a banquet given in Arbuckle's honour prior to his departure on a 'personal appearance' tour during 1917. Just as Chaplin left Sennett for greater opportunities, so did Arbuckle depart in 1916. He signed with Joseph M. Schenck for a series of comedies in which Arbuckle was to have total autonomy: one of Arbuckle's first acts was to lure away an ex-vaudevillian from a promising Broadway career; Buster Keaton (*qv*). They appeared together regularly until Arbuckle, having been promoted to full-length comedies for Paramount, abdicated the short subjects to Keaton. In 1921, Arbuckle was in his prime when a party held in his hotel suite went disastrously wrong; one of the guests, a young actress, was taken ill and subsequently died. Those in certain quarters found it in their interests to fabricate a story of Arbuckle

having attacked the girl, and the case went to trial. Arbuckle was condemned by the newspapers and hounded by virtually every pressure group in existence. Loyal friends, who knew Arbuckle to be anything but the monster portrayed in the media, found their comments ignored: for example, Chaplin, in London at the time of Arbuckle's arrest, considered the accusations 'preposterous', but the press did not quote him. Arbuckle was, at length, acquitted – with an unprecedented apology from the jury – but his acting career was ruined. He was permitted to direct, using the pseudonym 'William Goodrich', but had been officially barred from appearing on screen. There was support for Arbuckle – Chaplin attended Arbuckle's second marriage in 1925, with Buster Keaton as best man, and both were among the many stars to attend Arbuckle's reopening of the Plantation Club, as did Mabel Normand, Douglas Fairbanks and Mary Pickford (all *qv*) – but his name had been permanently and unjustly tarnished. Eventually, during 1932–3, Arbuckle was permitted to star in a series of sound shorts for Vitaphone. They were a success, and he was signed to appear in features for Warner Brothers. That night, Arbuckle suffered a heart attack and died, aged 46. Even now, Arbuckle myth continues to be perpetuated, and this more than two decades after Yallop's work established the comedian's innocence beyond question.

(See also: Allen, Phyllis; Arnold, Cecile; Ballet; Conklin, Chester; Coogan, Jackie; Costume; Edwards, Vivian; Fighting; Grey, Lita; Guest appearances; Lehrman, Henry 'Pathé'; Pearce, Peggy; Risqué humour; St. John, Al; Sterling, Ford)

ARMSTRONG, BILLY 🎩 (1891–?1924)

(Chaplin films *qv*)
One of the several British players in Chaplin's stock company over the years, Bristol-born Billy Armstrong had been a music-hall comedian in his native country and, like Chaplin, spent time with Fred Karno (*qv*) before travelling to the USA, where he obtained rôles at various comedy studios. Armstrong worked with Chaplin at Essanay (*qv*), appearing in *The Tramp*, *By the Sea*, *Work*, *A Woman*, *The Bank* and *Shanghaied*; he is also present in *Police* and *Triple Trouble*, in scenes evidently shot for the abandoned feature film, *Life*

Billy Armstrong *provides ample support for Charlie's flirtation; a posed shot from* The Bank

(see **Abandoned projects**). After Essanay, Armstrong worked in David Horsley's Cub Comedies; post-Chaplin film credits include *The Twin Trunk Mystery*, *A Lover's Might*, *Double Double Cross*, *M.T. Dome's Awful Night* (all 1916), *A Royal Rogue*, *A Shanghaied Jonah*, *Hula Hula Land*, *Mr. Shoestring in a Hole* (all 1917), *Love, Honor and Behave*, *Down On the Farm* (both 1920) and *Skirts* (1921). A quoted date of death, 1 March 1924, is probably accurate, but an obituary section in *The Performer Who's Who in Variety* for 1950 mentions a William Armstrong having died on 3 May 1940.

(See also: Florey, Robert)

ARNOLD, CECILE
(c.1895–1931)

(Chaplin films *qv*)
Blonde actress at Keystone (*qv*), often sharing second female lead with Vivian Edwards (*qv*). In Chaplin's *The Masquerader* she is one of the two distracting starlets who cause Charlie to miss his cue; in *Those Love Pangs* and *Getting Acquainted* she is a similar, parkside enticement; she is embroiled in further parkside intrigues in *His New Profession*; she is a seductive waitress in *Dough and Dynamite*, Charlie's faithless lover in *The Face on the Bar Room Floor* and one of the Stone Age women of *His Prehistoric Past*. She is, in the author's opinion, among the racetrack spectators in *Gentlemen of Nerve*. Miss Arnold appeared in at least two Keystone comedies with Syd Chaplin (*qv*) during 1915 and was later known professionally as 'Cecile Arley'. Biographical details have tended to be

sparse; there have been claims that she was born Cecile Arnole in Kentucky, and it was believed that she died in Hong Kong during 1931, a victim of influenza. This last was confirmed by her half-sister, a Mrs Zedrick Moore, in a letter to the Dallas Public Library in 1961. According to this source, Cecile was born 'about 66 years ago' in New York, her real name being Cecile Laval Arnoux. Her father was a Frenchman – reputedly a count – named Anthony Arnoux, who married an American, Susan Campbell. The marriage ended in divorce, following which Arnoux returned to France. Cecile's mother remarried and settled with her second husband, Albert Evans, in St. Louis. Mrs Moore was Evans' daughter. The family subsequently moved to Forth Worth, Texas. Cecile returned to New York and spent time in the *Ziegfeld Follies* prior to joining Keystone in California. It was thought that she worked with Roscoe 'Fatty' Arbuckle (*qv*), whom she knew well, and was said to have been offered the female lead in a 1917 film starring Jack Pickford. Mrs Moore further recalled Cecile having been directed by Roy and Hampton Del Ruth. At some time around the First World War, Cecile visited Honolulu, where she had a brother (or presumably half-brother) working on a newspaper. From Honolulu, she and a friend travelled to China, where Cecile met and married a prosperous, English-born banker. She did not resume her career. Although based in China, Cecile travelled to San Francisco to ensure that her son was born in the United States. He was Robert Arnoux Evans (a surname – coincidentally? – matching that of her stepfather), who later became a petroleum engineer with an oil company in West Texas. Again

according to Mrs Moore, Cecile died from a particularly virulent flu virus – seemingly the only illness she had ever suffered – during the 1931 Hong Kong trip mentioned above. She was buried there, in accordance with her request for interment in whichever place she died.

(See also: *His Musical Career*; Parks; Risqué humour)

ARTISTS

(Chaplin films *qv*)
Artists, of the oil-and-canvas type, are occasionally depicted in the Chaplin films. Charlie is a painter whose life is ruined by a faithless lover in *The Face on the Bar Room Floor*; another romance is endangered by an artistic rival in *The Vagabond*; an artist engages Charlie and Edna as models in *The Immigrant*; still another is the natural father of *The Kid*; *A Woman of Paris* centres around a society girl's broken romance with an artist; while *The Great Dictator* is captured by artists during momentary pauses amid his busy schedule. In real life, Chaplin occasionally dabbled in painting, but otherwise left formal portraits to more trained hands. As noted under **Auctions**, Chaplin sometimes acquired works of art. In June 1975 he paid £100 for a carving of a woman at prayer, by a Mrs Barbara Kent of Lincoln. The piece was sold to benefit the Lincoln Cathedral fabric fund. In the March 1978 *McCall's* magazine, Chaplin's daughter, Geraldine, spoke of the way global success had merely left her father insecure, citing as an example a family visit to a Paris art exhibition a few years before. 'It was an incredible show,' she recalled, 'but daddy got more disgruntled as we moved along. When we left the gallery he said very quietly, "You see, no one knows me anymore." Yet all through the exhibition people had been clapping as they recognized him.' Geraldine attributed his failure to hear to a preoccupation with his youth and early acclamation.

(See also: Animation; Bergman, Henry; Caricatures; Children; Left-handedness; Purviance, Edna; Religion; Statues; Suicide)

AUCTIONS

The collectability of Chaplin artifacts is evidenced by the prices they tend to fetch at auction. For example, as recently as

November 1996, an original poster for *The Kid* (*qv*) fetched £13,800 at Christie's in London. Twelve months before, a silver shoe, thought to have been presented by Chaplin in 1933, was priced at £6,000 when offered at the Olympia Fine Art and Antiques Fair. In Monaco during May 1995, Chaplin's 1931 Rolls-Royce Phantom II convertible was sold to a Scandinavian collector for £101,165. In December 1989, Christie's auctioned three pieces of promotional art, one of them a French colour litho poster (*c*.1920) by August Leymarie, advertising Everest Films' Chaplin releases. The second poster showed a broad-grinned caricature of Chaplin bearing the name 'Charlot' in large letters. The third, again a colour litho of French origin, advertised *A Woman* (*qv*) under the title 'Mademoiselle Charlot', naming the Himalaya Film Co. as distributor. There were also two self-caricatures, dated 1942 and 1944, plus a cartoon signed 'Swamy 1940' and inscribed 'Sincere Wishes Charlie Chaplin'. More commonplace but not without interest was a souvenir menu, signed by Chaplin, for the Critics' Circle Film Section Luncheon given in his honour at London's Empress Club on 10 October 1952. Chaplin himself sometimes acquired items at auction. It was presumably in remembrance of his upbringing that he purchased four engravings of scenes from the capital at a London auction in February 1957. At an earlier Christie's auction, in December 1987, a set of Chaplin's hat, cane and boots fetched £82,500; the boots went to a museum for £38,500. There was much interest when the effects of John R. Freuler, the one-time president of Mutual (*qv*), were auctioned at two Illinois venues in October and November 1984; almost a decade later, in July 1994, a total of 31 Chaplin lots surfaced in a 'Cinema Posters and Collectibles' auction at Burbank, California. These included many rare photographs, paperwork, sheet music, comics and toys. Perhaps the most interesting items were an original copy of *Charlie Chaplin's Own Story*, a signed copy of *My Trip Abroad* and an original Keystone-Mutual poster for *Laughing Gas* (*qv*).

(See also: Artists; Books; Caricatures; Childhood; Public appearances)

AUDLEY, MAXINE
(b. 1923)

British actress, from the stage, who plays the estranged, exiled 'Queen Irene' in *A King in New York* (*qv*). Her many other films include *The Barretts of Wimpole Street* (1957), *Our Man in Havana* (1959) and *The Trials of Oscar Wilde* (1960).

AUSTIN, ALBERT 🎩
(1882–1953)

(Chaplin films *qv*)
Gangling British comedian, born in Birmingham, with whom Chaplin had worked for Fred Karno (*qv*) when touring the USA. Like Stan Laurel (*qv*) and others, Austin was among those to remain behind, trying his luck on the American stage, when the troupe disbanded following Chaplin's departure for Keystone (*qv*). Austin re-entered Chaplin's story early in 1916 when he was hired to appear in the new series for Mutual (*qv*). He quickly became a valued member of the team, both as an actor (he is the only supporting player in *One A.M.*) and as one of Chaplin's advisers. On screen, he frequently adopted a bushy moustache, typical both of silent comedies of the day and of young bloods of an only slightly earlier generation. He appears thus in his baffled clerk rôle of *The Floorwalker* or, most memorably, the owner of an ultimately dismembered alarm clock in *The Pawnshop*. The moustache would sometimes be omitted, especially on the many occasions when he was required to play more than one part (e.g. *Easy Street*, in which he is both a clean-shaven preacher and a moustachioed policeman). He is both a chef and a skater in *The Rink*, while *The Immigrant* sees him as a Russian émigré in the first reel and a disgusted diner in the second. Austin was given at least five rôles in *Shoulder Arms*, variously two soldiers on each side of the war, plus an army physician in a deleted opening sequence. Another doctor, that in *Sunnyside*, is sometimes identified as Austin, but this is probably an error (his contribution was in another deleted scene, as the victim of Charlie's barbershop technique). Elsewhere in the Chaplin films, he is one of the brigade in *The Fireman*; a member of the German band in *The Vagabond*; a monocled party guest in *The Count*; the stagehand whose lunch Charlie 'shares' in *Behind the Screen*; an attendant in *The Cure*; a butler in *The Adventurer*; a sneaky-looking thief in both *A Dog's Life* and *The Kid*, and is Charlie's scrounging friend in *The Bond*. His latter-day contributions to the Chaplin films were essentially behind the camera; he is credited as one of three assistant directors on *City Lights*, in which he also takes a small part as Charlie's roadsweeping colleague. He is in the cast of Mary Pickford's *Suds* (1920); he also directed Jackie Coogan (*qv*) in *Trouble*, *Keep Smiling* (credited after Gil Pratt), *My Boy* (credited after Victor Heerman) and *A Prince of a King*. An obituary in *Variety* reports Austin to have spent his last eleven years as a guard at the Warner Brothers studio.

(See also: Bergman, Henry; Crocker, Harry; Dual rôles; Karno Company, The; Riesner, Dean; *Unknown Chaplin*)

AVERY, CHARLES
See: Costume and *Knockout, The*

AWARDS, HONOURS 🎩

(Chaplin films *qv*)
In the initial 'Chaplin Craze' (*qv*), the comedian had a habit of topping popularity polls, e.g. that in *Pictures and the Picturegoer* which named him the 'Cleverest British Player' for 1915, even though he was not working in his native land.

The first year of the Academy Awards brought Chaplin a special Oscar for *The Circus*, probably more in recognition of his contribution to the industry as a whole. *The Great Dictator*, released twelve years later, brought Chaplin the New York Critics' Best Actor Award (which, for reasons suggested elsewhere, Chaplin declined). Jack Oakie (*qv*) was nominated by the Academy as Best Supporting Actor.

Overseas, in 1921, Chaplin was decorated by the French – who made him Officier de l'Instruction Publique – after attending the Paris opening of *The Kid*; he was awarded the Légion d'Honneur when revisiting Paris ten years later.

May 1956 brought an honour from both his native country and chosen profession when he was made an Honorary Life Member of the film technicians' union, ACT (later ACTT and now BECTU). According to Roy Fowler in the May 1989 *Film and*

Television Technician, it had been noticed that Chaplin had been working in a British studio without possessing a ticket, and the award seemed the best solution. In his speech, the union's president, film director Anthony Asquith, jokingly chided Chaplin for having commenced *A King in New York* without joining the union. 'As a newcomer to British studios there is some excuse for you,' said Asquith. Chaplin, in his turn, promised to go on strike with everyone else.

Returning to the international field, Chaplin became a Grand Officer of the Italian Order of Merit in December 1952, when visiting Rome for the Italian première of *Limelight*. In 1954, Chaplin was awarded the World Peace Prize, the proceeds of which were distributed to the needy of Paris and Lambeth. In 1962, he received honorary doctorates from both Oxford and Durham universities – appropriate recognition for a self-educated man (thoroughly so) whose formal schooling had been barely extant. June 1965 saw Chaplin in Amsterdam, to receive the Erasmus Prize, alongside Swedish filmmaker Ingmar Bergman; the presentation was made by Prince Bernhard, in the presence of Queen Juliana and Princess Beatrix. Chaplin was photographed at the event with Peter Ustinov.

In 1971, the Grande Medaille de Vermeil was awarded to Chaplin by the City of Paris; a year later, his name was belatedly added to Hollywood's 'Walk of Fame', presumably in anticipation of his visit to accept a special Oscar; after arriving in New York, he was presented with the city's most prestigious cultural prize, the Handel Medallion, where he told photographers, 'I'm smiling. I'm afraid my teeth will fall out.' On 16 April – his birthday – he received the Oscar in Hollywood. Later, in 1972, the Venice Film Festival honoured Chaplin with the Golden Lion.

The British New Year's Honours List for 1975 announced what had seemed inevitable but strangely postponed: a knighthood. It was rumoured at the time that Chaplin had privately declined this honour in the early 1930s, something hinted at in a 1931 *Daily Sketch* item. This describes the British government's invitation to Chaplin to make a film on their behalf (see also **Abandoned projects**), adding: 'It is possible that a signal mark of honour will be the outcome for the world's greatest comedian.' When

Awards, honours: *Chaplin receives his second Oscar in 1972*

questioned about the absent knighthood at the 1974 launch of *My Life in Pictures*, he said: 'I started my life as plain Mr. Chaplin and it's a handle that hasn't done me any harm in life. I'm content.' He was nonetheless delighted to become 'Sir Charles', and was thus dubbed by Queen Elizabeth II on 4 March 1975. Afterwards, reporters asked Chaplin what had been said by the Queen; 'She thanked me for all that I had done,' said the comedian. 'She said the films had helped her a great deal.' Chaplin, smiling, admitted having been too 'dumbfounded' to respond to the remark. It has been said that Labour Prime Minister Harold Wilson wanted to arrange the honour in 1970, but had been prevented; by the end of 1974, Wilson was again in 10 Downing Street and this time encountered less opposition to the proposal.

The Queen was present once more to congratulate Sir Charles when, in the spring of 1976, he was made a Fellow of the British Academy of Film and Television Arts; he had been presented with Honorary Membership of the then British Film Academy twenty years earlier. June 1976 brought recognition once more, with Honorary Membership of the American Academy of Arts and Letters and the National Institute of Arts and Letters.

(See also: Books; Childhood; Coogan, Jackie; Hale, Georgia; Newsreels; Public appearances; Raye, Martha; Royalty; Statues)

AYRES, AGNES
(1898–1940)

Leading lady of the 1920s whose early experience included a stint at Essanay (*qv*), where, like Gloria Swanson (*qv*), she appeared as an extra in Chaplin's *His New Job* (*qv*). It seems reasonable to suggest that various young actresses were being considered as Chaplin's permanent leading lady until Edna Purviance (*qv*) was hired. In feature films, she is perhaps best recalled for Valentino's *The Sheik* (1921) and DeMille's *The Ten Commandments* (1923); by the later 1920s her career was in decline and she became one of several faltering stars to appear in Hal Roach comedy shorts, such as *Eve's Love Letters* (1927) with Stan Laurel (*qv*).

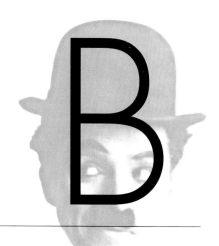

BACON, LLOYD 🎩
(1890–1955)

(Chaplin films *qv*)
Born in San Jose, California, Lloyd F. Bacon was the son of Frank Bacon, a famous stage actor. The younger Bacon initially studied law, but instead took up an acting career; after stage work (including a production of Wilde's *Salome*), Bacon made his first film in 1914, and by the following year was a member of Chaplin's stock company at Essanay (*qv*). He appears in *The Champion* as a fight trainer; *In the Park* sees him as a pickpocket (not the hot dog vendor, as is sometimes claimed); he is a butler in *A Jitney Elopement*; Charlie loses Edna Purviance (*qv*) to him in *The Tramp*, and he is one of the thieves in *The Bank*. Lloyd Bacon was one of several players to continue with Chaplin in his new series for Mutual (*qv*). Bacon actually has the title rôle in *The Floorwalker*, a corrupt individual whose place is taken by Charlie; he plays another crook, this time an insurance fraudster, in *The Fireman*; *The Vagabond* parallels *The Tramp*, with Bacon as Charlie's handsome rival for the girl; he is the comedy director in *Behind the Screen*, and one of Edna's party guests in *The Rink*. His final Chaplin film, *Easy Street*, provides his grittiest character, that of a basement-dwelling drug addict who has Edna at his mercy. War service interrupted Bacon's career, but he returned to film comedy at Triangle in 1919. By 1921, Bacon had moved into directing, initially for comedian Lloyd Hamilton (with whom he had worked as an actor), then for Sennett (*qv*), Universal and Warner Brothers. Among his best-known films as director are Jolson's *The Singing Fool* (1928) and *Wonder Bar* (1934), *Moby Dick* (1930), Joan Blondell's *Miss*

Pinkerton (1932), James Cagney's *The Picture Snatcher* (1933), the Busby Berkeley musicals *42nd Street* (1933), *Footlight Parade* (1933) and *Gold Diggers of 1937*; *Devil Dogs of the Air* (1935), *San Quentin* (1937), *Marked Woman* (1937) with Bette Davis and Humphrey Bogart, *A Slight Case of Murder* (1938), the Cagney-Bogart *The Oklahoma Kid* (1939), *Invisible Stripes* (1940) with Bogart and George Raft, *Brother Orchid* (1940) with Edward G. Robinson, *Give My Regards to Broadway* (1948) and a censor's nightmare of 1954 (thanks to Jane Russell's costume), *The French Line*.

(See also: Trick photography)

BAKER, NELLIE BLY 🎩
(1894–?)

(Chaplin films *qv*)
Long employed by Chaplin in a secretarial capacity – she may be seen thus in *How to Make Movies* (*qv*) – Nellie Bly Baker portrays the housewife with whom Charlie flirts in *The Kid*, and is also the scene-stealing, contemptuous masseuse in *A Woman of Paris*. Other screen work includes *Broadway Hostess* and *Love and the Devil*, both films for First National (*qv*); also M-G-M's *The Bishop Murder Case*. She is also in Von Sternberg's *The Salvation Hunters*, a frankly peculiar film for which Chaplin had great enthusiasm (see **Edna Purviance**). On 30 November 1929, *Picture Show*, noting her long-term status as Chaplin's secretary, mentioned also her new function as elocution teacher (a task evidently made redundant by Chaplin's decision not to incorporate dialogue into *City Lights*).

BALLET 🎩

(Chaplin films *qv*)
Of the many quotes popularly attributed to W.C. Fields, one of the best-known is that in which a pays a seemingly reluctant and certainly backhanded compliment to Chaplin by describing him as a ballet dancer, albeit the greatest that ever lived. It's easy to see why such a comment should be made: *The Floorwalker* has Charlie pirouetting quite extensively before being clobbered by Eric Campbell (*qv*); he reacts similarly when struck by Cupid's arrow in *The Bond*. As explained in his introduction to *The Chaplin Revue* (*qv*), Chaplin saw his blend of silent action with music as 'a sort of a comic

ballet'. The association of Chaplin's tramp with the dance formed the basis for a short film of the 1920s, detailed under **Animation**, in which an abstract 'Charlie' performs a fragmented ballet. A keen *balletomane* in real life, Chaplin met Nijinsky shortly before the dancer's mental collapse, and was embarrassed when the master delayed a performance to engage him in trivial chat. Chaplin's renowned dance with the nymphs in *Sunnyside*, dating from a brief period when 'serious' critics had turned his head somewhat, is a slightly more serious foray than earlier examples; despite its slapstick overtones, a more accurate reflection of Chaplin's alternately serious and satirical view of ballet comes from David Yallop's biography of Roscoe Arbuckle (*qv*), describing Arbuckle and Chaplin staging a humorous 'benefit ballet' for Mack Sennett (*qv*) at the Sunset Inn. Wearing tablecloths to approximate Isadora Duncan's costumes, they performed 'The Rustle of Spring' in the company of Buster Keaton, Ben Turpin, Mack Swain, Charlie Murray, Al St. John, Ford Sterling and Chester Conklin (all *qv*). In the same vein is a home-movie fragment used in the series *Unknown Chaplin* (*qv*), in which the comedian, clad in a type of classical tunic, performs an embryonic version of Hynkel's dance with the globe in *The Great Dictator*. For *Limelight*, his most concentrated exploration of the art, Chaplin created a ballet of his own, 'The Death of Columbine'.

(See also: *Adventurer, The*; Home movies)

THE BANK 🎩

(Chaplin film)
Released by General Film Company, 9 August 1915. Produced by Essanay. Written and directed by Charles Chaplin. Photographed by Harry Ensign. British title: *Charlie at the Bank*. Sometimes known in reissue as *In the Bank*. Two reels. 1,985 feet.

With Charlie Chaplin (himself, as bank janitor), Edna Purviance (Edna, the typist), Billy Armstrong (Charlie's colleague), Carl Stockdale (Charles, a cashier), Charles Insley (bank president), Lawrence A. Bowes (a bond salesman), Leo White (bank executive), Bud Jamison, Paddy McGuire (members of the gang), Carrie Clark Ward.

Charlie interrupts his journey to work. He

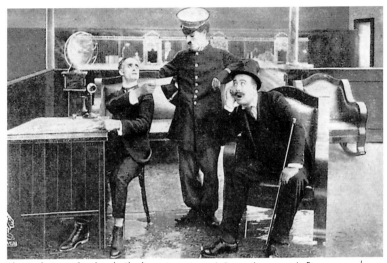

The Bank: Leo White hands Charlie an important missive, as Lawrence A. Bowes eavesdrops

has somehow managed to trip on a pin, which he attaches to his trousers. He enters the bank premises, after more than the usual turn within a revolving door. Charlie walks past a busy janitor, carefully moving his derrière out of the way. Exuding dignity, Charlie goes through the elaborate business of remembering the combination to the strongroom. This open, he exchanges hat, coat and cane for a mop and bucket. The door is sealed, and from within the bucket are pulled Charlie's tunic and cap. He sets to work as janitor. His fellow-janitor enters the bank president's office, stopping for a bite to eat and a drink from a can of water. Charlie disrupts business on the main floor. Charlie joins his colleague in the office, allowing his mop to drip into the water can as the man delivers a lecture. The other janitor takes a drink from the can and reacts accordingly. In the adjoining office, he protests but Charlie drops the can into his bucket. On the main floor, a bank executive is dealing with a customer. The bank's president arrives, and the customer tries to sell him some bonds. The president, ignoring the man's pleas, pushes him aside. The two janitors are sweeping up paperwork in the adjoining offices. Charlie brushes the contents of his room into the next; his colleague sweeps it all back. Charlie makes to leave with his mop and bucket, but the other janitor refuses to sweep up. Their subsequent fight is broken up by the bank executive, who sends the other janitor into the business area. The exiled janitor brandishes his broom at Charlie, striking the bond salesman; Charlie returns the flourish, splashing the executive with his

mop. Charlie begins to pick up the paper but, warm from the effort, switches on an electric fan, sending down another stream of litter. Elsewhere, another Charles, one of the cashiers, is celebrating his birthday. Edna, the typist, walks past the tills into the office, where she is saluted by an adoring Charlie. Edna is carrying a present. Charlie the janitor watches her in devotion before going about his business. Charlie heads downstairs, catching his mop on the executive and his customer while en route. His colleague is scrubbing the floor. Charlie's foot is jammed in his bucket; once freed, the bucket is jammed under Charlie's own and is carried off. A fight begins when the other janitor reclaims them both. Charlie knocks him senseless, separates the pails and leaves

him with both. In the office, Edna examines the tie she has bought for the cashier. She types an accompanying note that reads 'To Charles with love from Edna', leaving the gift on a desk. In her absence, Charlie the janitor sees the present, assuming it to be for him. Edna takes the cashier's present to his window, discreetly leaving it for him to find. On her return, Charlie is tongue-tied. He composes a letter to Edna, which is left for her along with a small bouquet. Charlie returns to the customer area, where he sees the president and the would-be bond salesman. The president tears up the worthless documents and orders the desperate man from the premises. He departs, uttering threats. The president gives Charlie a letter to post. He meets the desperate customer and, suspecting all is not well, carries out an impromptu medical examination. In the end, all he wants is for the man to put out his tongue in order to lick the stamp. Charlie reaches the post box but has to tear up the outsized letter to fit the slot. On the return journey, he thoughtfully replaces the man's tongue. Edna and the cashier find their respective presents. Charles the cashier visits the office to thank Edna for the tie. When she offers return thanks for the note and flowers, she is told they must be from Charlie the janitor. Returning to the office, Charlie's face drops as Edna consigns his flowers and the letter to a waste bin. Her reaction turns from contempt to scornful amusement. Charlie retrieves the flowers and meets the cashier, sporting his new tie. Charlie examines the tie with disdain. Downstairs, he finds the other

Charlie rests on a bustle in this posed shot from **The Bank**

A rare behind-the-scenes pose from **The Bank**, *with Leo White and Billy Armstrong*

janitor preening himself in similar fashion and administers a swift kick. Charlie sits in the corner, debating whether or not to place the flowers in a dustbin. Charlie closes his eyes and the scene fades. The bank president takes inventory of some bags of cash, aided by Edna and the cashier. In the business area, the man who was ordered out has returned, accompanied by henchmen. The other janitor is overpowered by the gang; in the office, the president is attacked just after Edna and the cashier have departed with the money. On opening the strongroom they are ambushed; Edna cries for help but the cashier, pushing her to the floor, flees in terror. The president is fighting off an attacker; the cashier is intercepted by one of the gang. Edna is being carried into the strongroom when Charlie, hearing her screams, dashes to the rescue. He forces three of the gang into the strongroom, seals it and carries the unconscious Edna on his shoulder. Using a pistol taken from the gang, he corners the robber who has been holding the cashier at gunpoint. The cashier makes a run for it. Charlie, still carrying Edna, forces the criminal into the office. When he places Edna into a chair, the tables are turned and the villain has Charlie by the throat. Edna, now recovered, takes the gun and holds the criminal at bay. Next door, the president has finally been overpowered but Charlie knocks out the attacker with a sack of coins. Charlie, ringing for the police, discovers the cashier hiding beneath the desk. The

thieves are arrested and the president congratulates Charlie and Edna. The cashier, suitably shamed, is dismissed. Charlie still has the flowers, which are this time accepted. Edna is in his arms as the scene fades. Fade up and Charlie is sitting in the corner, hugging and kissing his mop. He awakens, splutters and, carrying the flowers, walks away. He passes Edna and the cashier, who, seeing Charlie, depart to do their canoodling elsewhere. Charlie throws away the flowers, giving them a back-kick as he goes about his mundane duties. He manages a jaunty shrug.

Four films after his first acknowledged 'classic', *The Tramp* (*qv*), Chaplin took his character's emotional development several stages further. The first glimmerings of a sympathetic Charlie had appeared in 1914's *The New Janitor* (*qv*), of which *The Bank* is a more sophisticated reworking; Chaplin's later film has the expected quota of simple, knockabout humour (Chaplin barely exploits a prop revolving door, in stark comparison to later business in *The Cure* [*qv*]), but its central figure combines inelegance with panache – as per his dignified entrance – underlined by the hopelessness of a would-be gentleman who is doomed never to rise above his humble station. In earlier films, Charlie is quite content to maintain the role of outlaw and is only interested in higher things for what he can get. The optimistic dreamer of Chaplin's mature work is more obvious here than in any other of the Essanay comedies, a facet complemented by the genuine drama and suspense in the robbery sequence. According to MacDonald, Conway and Ricci's Chaplin study, a week's delay in *The Bank*'s release prompted contemporary speculation as to whether Chaplin had produced either a poor comedy or else one too vulgar for the censor to pass; Sime Silverman, of *Variety*, had been highly critical of Chaplin's recent Essanays in terms of both inadequate storyline and alleged vulgarity. That Chaplin was aware of such complaints is evidenced by a contemporary letter from Fred Goodwins (*qv*) to Britain's *Pictures and the Picturegoer*, details from which were published in September 1915. Goodwins describes *The Bank* as representing 'Charlie's new line of work, the dramatic-comedy ... so much adverse criticism has cropped up among the public of USA (which is inclined to be very Puritanical) about some of the "naughty" little incidents in certain of Charlie's comedies, that he has decided to turn his

attention to a much more legitimate line of work – viz., dramatic stories in which he, in comedy vein, pulls off all the rescues, traps the thieves, and so on.' According to Goodwins, Essanay's Chicago office saw the result of this policy and responded instantly with a wire stating, 'Congratulations to Charles Chaplin and Company on *The Bank*. It is a bear!' 'This is the first time he has received one of these,' continued Goodwins. 'He was so pleased with himself and us that nothing could be wrong that day.' *Variety*, at least, was similarly pleased: when *The Bank* was eventually released, the recently-hostile Sime noted fewer loud laughs from 'upstairs' but a better reception overall from those less enamoured of Chaplin's earlier vulgarity. Sime evaluated it as 'the most legitimate comedy film Chaplin has played in in many a long day, perhaps since he's been in pictures'. He also thought Chaplin had employed a 'book' (i.e. pre-written scenario), but the comedian's improvisational methods are known to have continued throughout his silent work.

Some prints, including a UK video release, fade out on Charlie's awakening after the dream. In certain copies, the sequence of events varies slightly, in that Edna discovers the true sender of the flowers prior to the scene of Charlie mailing a letter. This applies to the BBC version (itself missing several shots), which may or may not be correct; the sequence quoted above is from a full-frame, silent-era reissue. Sub-titles in this print are a mixture of those probably based on the original text, interspersed with others (of a different design) commenting unnecessarily on the action. As noted elsewhere, it was common practice to pad out reissues by the addition of superfluous titling. This version bears out Theodore Huff's description of the dubious customer as being a bond salesman; this seems more in keeping than the rôle implied in titling for the BBC version, in which he is supposedly in need of a loan. Filmographies have tended to identify the character as being played by John Rand (*qv*), but this does not seem to be the case; Goodwins' report from the set identifies him instead as Lawrence A. Bowes (*qv*), who also plays the ship's captain in *Shanghaied* (*qv*).

(See also: *Carmen*; Dreams; Essanay; Home movies; Jamison, William 'Bud'; McGuire, Paddy; Reissues; Ruggles, Wesley; Television; Titling; Video releases; Ward, Carrie Clark)

BARRY, JOAN

See: Women

BARRY, VIOLA

See: Pearce, Peggy

BEHIND THE SCREEN

(Chaplin film)
Released by Mutual, 13 November 1916.
Written and directed by Charles
Chaplin. Photographed by Rollie
Totheroh. Two reels. 1,796 feet.

With Charlie Chaplin (himself, as
assistant stagehand), Eric Campbell
('Goliath'), Edna Purviance (aspiring
actress), Frank J. Coleman (supervisor),
Henry Bergman (director), James T.
Kelly (cameraman), Charlotte Mineau
(actress), Albert Austin, John Rand
(stagehands).

Charlie discovers a sleeping Edna in a posed shot from **Behind the Screen**
BFI Stills, Posters and Designs

Day begins at the Gigantic picture
studios, where Edna, an aspiring actress,
finds there is no call for her services. A
title introduces 'Goliath, the stage-hand'
and 'David, his assistant'. 'David' is
Charlie, doing all the work for the large,
slothful stagehand. Charlie's efforts
extend to separating scantily-clad statues,
supplying cushions for Goliath, knocking
over the camera and causing havoc when
moving a pillar in the drama set. After
Charlie has expended great effort, the
boss arrives and, seeing Charlie sitting
dazed on the floor, accuses him of
laziness. Elsewhere, Charlie tries to sit for
a moment (having first moved a spiked
German helmet) but is again accused of
slacking. Carrying a huge burden of
chairs plus an upright piano, Charlie
resembles a porcupine which has
stumbled into the removal business.
Goliath finally stirs, and Charlie, taking
a moment's rest, is once more accused of
loafing. Later, when the scene has been
prepared, Charlie dresses a prop bearskin
rug with the panache of a hairdresser.
Again, Goliath briefly emerges from
slumber, and Charlie, taking a well-
earned break, is thought to be slacking.
At lunch, Charlie measures Goliath's
huge array of pies in relation to his
stomach, then is nearly asphyxiated by
the spring onions eaten by a neighbour.
Charlie's own repast, consisting of slices
of bread, is eked out when placed over
his neighbour's hambone. Goliath has
consumed a large collection of pies, their
tin trays providing Charlie with a set of

makeshift kettle drums. Charlie returns
to work as Goliath takes another nap.
Also dozing are the other stagehands,
who, taking umbrage at being awakened,
go on strike. Charlie and Goliath refuse
to take part, and are thanked by a
grateful boss; Edna, who has been
observing from the sidelines, borrows a
set of the strikers' overalls and,
masquerading as a boy, volunteers as a
stagehand. On the set of a melodrama,
Charlie is asked to open a trapdoor on
the firing of a revolver. The gun fails to
shoot, and Goliath is called over to help.
He is standing on the trap and, on firing
the gun, plummets through the floor.
Charlie, attempting to close the trap,
unwittingly jams Goliath's head between
the doors. Charlie oils both the lever and
his arm before realizing the problem.
Helping ineptly to lift Goliath, Charlie
receives a kick in the rear and drops the
unfortunate propman. Goliath is freed,
and in his subsequent fight with Charlie,
the lever is pushed back and forth so that
the actors and their director all disappear
through the trap. Another, portly,
director tries to help but is next to go
through the trap, splitting the seat of his
trousers. Charlie takes his leave, to find
the male-attired Edna singing and
playing the guitar. Edna pauses and,
forgetting her disguise, powders her nose.
Charlie makes fun of the 'boy' and his
supposed effeminacy until the portly
director asks Edna to sew his torn

trousers. Edna faints, and Charlie
removes her cap. Seeing her female
hairstyle, Charlie realizes Edna's true
gender and starts to kiss her. Her cap is
back in place, and Goliath, stunned by
what he sees, mocks them with a series of
outrageously camp gestures. On
neighbouring sets, the company is
preparing a costume drama and
rehearsing a 'new idea' for the comedy
department, a pie fight. An actor in
police costume fails to throw with any
accuracy; he is replaced by Goliath, who
lands his pies unerringly on a second
actor, playing a cook. The actor quits in
disgust at 'this highbrow stuff'.
Elsewhere, the strikers plan revenge by
planting dynamite, but are overheard by
Edna. On set, Charlie is recruited to take
the cook's place, but ignores a brief to
take a pie from Goliath. Instead, the
giant is splattered, and stray pies make
their way into the drama set. Battle
escalates as Charlie, still unscathed,
shelters behind a table. Edna knocks out
one of the strikers; as the pie fight
continues on set, the ringleader lights the
fuse to a keg of dynamite, planting it in
the prop trapdoor. He discovers Edna,
and there is a struggle; Charlie, pursued
by Goliath, is caught above the trapdoor
and is knocked against the switch,
opening the doors beneath Goliath.
Charlie rescues Edna, kicking the strike
leader down into the trap. Goliath is
climbing out when there is a terrific

explosion. There is a close-up of Charlie kissing Edna, giving the audience a wink as the scene fades.

Behind the Screen incorporates elements of the Keystone comedies *Dough and Dynamite, A Film Johnnie, The Property Man* (all *qv*) and, to a lesser degree, *The Masquerader* (*qv*). It is also the culmination of them, sharing with the Essanay film *His New Job* (*qv*) a conscious lampooning of Sennett's early methods. The television series *Unknown Chaplin* (*qv*) uncovered several out-takes from this film, one of them an unusual (for Chaplin) trick effect in which, using reverse photography, an axe-wielding player narrowly misses Charlie's feet as he walks past. Another juxtaposes a graceful dance troupe with Charlie leading a group of cleaning ladies in a similar routine. Also of interest is an alternative shot of Edna Purviance (*qv*), disguised as a boy, playing a small harp instead of the guitar used in the finished film. The narration suggests the conscious substitution of a traditionally more masculine instrument.

(See also: Bergman, Henry; Camera-looks; Essanay; Food; Hair; Kelly, James T.; Keystone; Politics; Risqué humour; Sennett, Mack; Slapstick; Television; Trick photography)

BELL, MONTA
(1891–1958)

Producer and director, born in Washington; after experience as journalist and stage actor, he joined Chaplin as an assistant, initially to replace publicist Carlyle Robinson. He appears on-screen in *How To Make Movies* (*qv*). Bell is believed either to have ghostwritten or at least transcribed Chaplin's account of his 1921 tour into book form (known variously as *My Trip Abroad* and *My Wonderful Visit*), and is credited with 'editorial direction' for *A Woman of Paris* (*qv*). It was reportedly the film's co-star, Adolphe Menjou (*qv*), who recommended Bell to Warner Brothers as writer and director; his directorial credits away from Chaplin include Garbo's *The Torrent* (1926). Bell was subsequently in charge of Paramount's Long Island studio, and thus became the Marx Brothers' first movie producer. Later productions include *Men in White* (1934), *The Birth of the Blues* (1941) and *Beyond the Blue Horizon* (1942).

(See also: Books; De Limur, Jean; Florey, Robert; Marx, Groucho; Public appearances)

BENNETT, BILLIE
(1874–1951)

Indiana-born supporting actress, real name Emily B. Mulhausen, who appears in two Chaplin Keystones, *Mabel's Busy Day* and *Tillie's Punctured Romance* (both *qv*). Her other films include *The Amateur Gentleman* (1927) and frequent rôles in westerns.

(See also: Keystone)

BENNETT, CHARLES
(?1889–?1943)

(Chaplin films *qv*)
Actor in two Chaplin Keystones, *Tillie's Punctured Romance* (as Tillie's uncle) and *The Property Man*. Among his other films are: *Her Husband's Friend* (1913), *Salvation Sal* (1913), *Master of the Mine* (1914), *Tony, the Greaser* (1914), *The Adventures of Ruth* (1919), Griffith's *America* (1924) and M-G-M's 1934 version of *Treasure Island*.

(See also: Griffith, D.W.)

BENNETT, MARJORIE
(?1895–1982)

Australian-born character actress, sister of Enid Bennett (1895–1969); like many Australians, frequently called upon to play Londoners in American films. She is maid to Mme Grosnay in *Monsieur Verdoux* (*qv*) and landlady Mrs Alsop in *Limelight* (also *qv*). Other films include *The Man Who Cheated Himself* (1950), *Two Flags West* (1950), *Sail a Crooked Ship* (1961), Robert Aldrich's *Autumn Leaves* (1956), *Whatever Happened to Baby Jane?* (1962) and *Four For Texas* (1963), Walt Disney's *Mary Poppins* (1964), *My Fair Lady* (1964), Don Siegel's *Coogan's Bluff* (1968) and *Charley Varrick* (1973), also *Better Late Than Never* (1979). She contributed voice work to Disney's *101 Dalmatians* in 1961.

(See also: Aldrich, Robert; Elsom, Isobel)

BERGMAN, HENRY
(1868–1946)

(Chaplin films *qv*)
Stoutly-built actor, from the legitimate

Henry Bergman was arguably the most supportive – at times literally – of Chaplin's colleagues
Photos by courtesy and copyright of the Roy Export Company Establishment

stage, who first joined Chaplin's company as the proprietor of *The Pawnshop* (*qv*) and remained in the comedian's exclusive employ for the rest of his life. Bergman became one of Chaplin's trusted advisers, functioning also as an assistant director (for which he is credited on *City Lights*). On-screen, it is Bergman who tries to direct a costume drama in *Behind the Screen*, dons a Russian hat amid the rowdies of *Easy Street*, provides heavy-handed massage in *The Cure* and is one of the builders in *Pay Day*. He plays the sheriff on the train in *The Pilgrim*, offers Charlie accommodation in *The Gold Rush* and attempts to instruct him in clowning in *The Circus*. Bergman was also the type of player who, suitably disguised, could take more than one rôle per film. In *The Rink*, he doubles up as both 'Mrs Stout' and an outraged restaurant patron (who is served soap and a scrubbing brush!); similarly, *The Immigrant* casts him as a large lady (with a small husband) and, later, an artist. *The Adventurer* sees him as an expectorating spectator on the pierside and, by contrast, a judge who just happens to be Edna's father. Bergman contributes three characters to *A Dog's Life*, variously the hot dog vendor, a man at the employment office and a tearful fat lady in the café scene. He performs a comparable feat in *Shoulder Arms*, this time as a bewhiskered German soldier, the Kaiser's general and a bartender within Charlie's dream of home comforts. He forms still another trio in *A Day's Pleasure*, as the boat's captain, a fat cop and, once more, an amply-proportioned lady. He returned to dual rôles for *The Kid* (an impresario and the flophouse owner), *The Idle Class* (a sleeping tramp and a party guest), and *City Lights* (the mayor and the blind girl's downstairs neighbour). He also plays the maître d' in *A Woman of Paris* and has been credited as Edna's father in *Sunnyside*. In *Modern Times* he plays the owner of a café, a rôle not dissimilar to his real-life, extracurricular activities. Bergman operated a restaurant, 'Henry's', on the northern side of Hollywood Boulevard, an establishment semi-specializing in German cuisine and in which Chaplin, its initial financier, retained an interest. A description of 'Henry's' in the *Picture Show* annual for 1929 refers to an unimposing exterior but a loyal clientele of actors and writers filling the booths around the walls. As the restaurant was open both day and night, most of these types would congregate there at around two in the morning. Favoured delicacies were turkey sandwiches, coffee cake and coffee itself. Bergman's origins are difficult to determine, due mainly to his Münchausen-like treatment of facts when giving interviews. Some sources give his place of birth as Germany, others claim he was American-born of German parentage. Alistair Cooke, who worked briefly with Chaplin in the 1930s, described Bergman as 'a gentle old German'. Publicity material for *The Chaplin Revue* (*qv*) describes him as of 'Swedish extraction', noting also his

presence at Lehrman's L-KO studio and Joker Comedies prior to joining Chaplin's company.

(See also: Abandoned projects; *Bond, The*; Dual rôles; Food; Lehrman, Henry 'Pathé'; Policemen; Purviance, Edna; Underwood, Loyal)

BERLE, MILTON

See: Impersonators; Raye, Martha, and *Tillie's Punctured Romance*

BETWEEN SHOWERS

(Chaplin film)
Keystone Comedy released by Mutual, 28 February 1914. Produced by Mack Sennett. Directed by Henry Lehrman and, reportedly, Mack Sennett. Photography attributed to Frank D. Williams. Reissued as *The Flirts* and under the original title. One reel. 1,020 feet (UK length cited in *Bioscope*). With Ford Sterling (a masher), Charlie Chaplin (another masher), Emma Clifton (girl), Chester Conklin (first cop), Sadie Lampe (housemaid).

Ford Sterling has a broken umbrella. He swaps it for an unbroken one belonging to a cop and his girlfriend, a housemaid. Ford disappears before the substitution is noticed. There being no sign of the culprit, the cop is chastised by the housemaid and instructed to solve the crime himself. 'After the shower' (according to a sub-title), Ford sees a girl trying to cross a deep puddle in the kerb. He gauges the water's depth with the umbrella, which he hands to the girl before disappearing to fetch some wood to use as a bridge. In Ford's absence, Charlie arrives, offering help. He too tests the water's depth, earning a bootful of water in the process. Ford is busy removing a wooden post; Charlie in turn steals a plank of wood from a nearby building site. In the mean time, a second cop has carried the girl safely across the puddle. Ford and Charlie return to discover what has happened. The girl has crossed the road to a park, where she is pursued by Ford. He wants the umbrella back, but she construes it as having been a gift. Charlie, who has been engaging the policeman in backchat, is amused to see Ford's struggle to regain the umbrella, the more so after Ford is pushed to the ground and struck with the umbrella. His amusement is tempered when the girl pushes Ford back across the street, into Charlie. Ford kicks Charlie before returning to the girl; Charlie intercedes on her behalf, but Ford throttles Charlie

A Chaplin–Sterling confrontation as Emma Clifton seeks refuge with officer Chester Conklin: a posed shot from **Between Showers**

and throws him aside. Landing beside a lake, Charlie throws bricks at Ford's face; returning fire, Ford knocks a bystander into the lake. The rivals continue to push bricks into each other's faces as the girl runs off. Ford catches up with her, grabs the umbrella and, despite Charlie's efforts, makes off with it; Charlie gives pursuit, stuns Ford with a brick over the head (before jabbing the umbrella in Ford's rear!), then returns the umbrella to the girl. Charlie is making progress with her as Ford summons a policeman – unaware that he is the very officer who is trying to reconstruct the theft of his umbrella. By the time they reach Charlie, the girl has taken umbrage and departed, leaving the umbrella. The policeman recognizes it, and when challenged, Charlie concedes ownership of the umbrella to his rival. Ford claims the item, but, belatedly realizing the truth, is arrested for its theft. Charlie is amused until the second cop reappears and, with a blow of his truncheon, sends Charlie on his way.

Available prints of *Between Showers* tend to omit this brief postscript to the tale, finishing instead on Sterling's arrest; the above account is based on material from two silent theatrical reissues and a subsequent 9.5mm home movie edition, from which the 'missing' finale is drawn. One of the two theatrical reissues is lacking various shots from early in the film, such as the policeman lifting the girl across the puddle and some of the kerbside byplay between Chaplin and Sterling. The W.H. Productions reissue lacks only the final moment quoted above.

Bo Berglund's 1989 *Sight and Sound* article (see **Kid Auto Races at Venice, CA**) points out that *Between Showers* was the immediate legacy of genuine torrential rain that had hindered production considerably in the early part of 1914, hence the huge puddle present at the roadside. Considering it is only Chaplin's fourth comedy, *Between Showers* has much of the familiar 'Charlie' character, not least the 90-degree skidding turn; he is without the cane, but at one point twirls the umbrella in like fashion. One might add that the cane's absence was probably deliberate, facilitating use of the umbrella as plot point just as the cane makes way for a pet's lead in *A Dog's Life* (*qv*). Less typical is Chaplin's use of exaggerated facial expression when struck by Sterling, of the type associated with less subtle

visual comics. Chaplin was to abandon such things very quickly. Although Sterling serves as plot mover, Chaplin gets most of the comic footage, and this is at least as much a Chaplin film as a vehicle for Sterling. As with many Keystones, a degree of scrutiny is necessary to determine the characters' motivation: Sterling's initial attempt to assist the stranded girl (Emma Clifton) may have been brought about by gallantry and/or sexual interest, but thereafter he is concerned solely with retrieving the umbrella; Charlie, however, is attracted to the girl throughout but seems just as content to win the umbrella. That the two comedians are usually misconstrued as rivals for the girl's attention is suggested by several descriptions from over the years, some of them dating back to contemporary reviews. One of these, in the *Bioscope* of 25 June 1914, describes Chaplin and Sterling as the girl's 'two fatuous adorers', true in Chaplin's case but certainly not Sterling's. (A synopsis published on 7 March 1914 in the *Motion Picture News* gives a correct account; Chaplin's name does not appear, but there is reference to 'the new English comedian of the Keystone Company'.) The action in these early, improvised 'park' comedies was often somewhat confusing, even after Chaplin had wrested directorial control from other hands. *Between Showers* was the last Chaplin film for which Henry Lehrman (*qv*) performed any directing duties, prior to his departure from Keystone.

(See also: Clifton, Emma; Conklin, Chester; Keystone; Mutual; Parks; Policemen; Sterling, Ford; Streetcars; Walk, the; Williams, Frank D.)

BIRTH

Charles Spencer Chaplin was born at 8 p.m. on 16 April 1889 in East Street, Walworth, in South London. Then and now, East Street was known to locals (and not-so-locals) as 'East Lane', the venue for a popular Sunday-morning market. There is no available birth certificate for Chaplin, who seems to have relied on his family for details. (It should be noted that David Robinson's *Chaplin: His Life and Art* reprints a contemporary announcement of the birth, placing the date as *15* April.) Although registration of births was compulsory, many such events went

unrecorded at that time. By way of contrast, Chaplin's friend and contemporary, Groucho Marx (*qv*), was the only child in his family whose birth *was* officially registered. There is also doubt as to the exact house in which he was born, which has been cited variously as number 87, 91, 191, 256, 258 and 260 (it is believed that the house, whichever one it was, succumbed to bombing during the Second World War). This uncertainty over the location has prohibited the commemoration of Chaplin's birth by means of an official blue plaque (there is instead one at his father's old home, 287 Kennington Road, where Charlie and Syd once stayed). Instead, Southwark Council installed one of its own on 16 April 1993, at the corner of East Street and the Walworth Road. It was placed above what had by then become a shoe shop, perhaps in keeping with the belief that Chaplin had been born upstairs in his grandfather's bootmaking shop. According to a local paper, the *Southwark Sparrow*, the campaign had been led by the council's deputy leader, Jeremy Fraser. Another report, from the *South London Press*, describes the efforts of a retired film technician, Reginald Cane, to have Chaplin and the area's other notables commemorated in this way. Zoe Brooks, manager of the Vauxhall Heritage Centre, pointed out to the *South London Press* that much of Chaplin's film work was based on his early experiences in Kennington. At that

Birth: *a 1921 photograph claims this as an authentic view of Chaplin's birthplace, at the rear of East Lane*

time, the Kennington Lane centre was drawing up plans for a Charlie Chaplin heritage walk, in the hope of attracting sponsors for a series of plaques marking out the route.

Amid the uncertainty, various myths have gained currency regarding Chaplin's entry into the world. A few earlier sources quote the year as 1890, but the most absurd claim originates in an unreliable biography of 1916, called *Charlie Chaplin's Own Story*. This account has Chaplin born of a wealthy French family in Fontainebleu: novelist Thomas Burke repeated it in an essay on the comedian, but had learned the truth by the time of a later work; and yet despite massive documentary evidence to the contrary, there are *still* people who believe one of the most famous Britons to have been born in France.

Chaplin's centenary in 1989 drew considerable attention, not least in his native country. The event was commemorated in a season of TV screenings on Channel 4 and an exhibition, *The Worlds of Charlie Chaplin*, at London's Museum of the Moving Image.

(See also: Books; Chaplin, Charles Sr; Chaplin, Hannah; Chaplin, Syd; Childhood; Parks; Statues)

BLOOM, CLAIRE
(b. 1931)

British actress who plays 'Terry' in *Limelight* (*qv*). She was appearing in *Ring Around the Moon* in London when playwright Arthur Laurents recommended her to her Chaplin. She was asked to send some photographs to Hollywood but failed to do so, being scarcely able to believe that Chaplin would be interested. Two weeks later, a wire arrived from Chaplin, asking, 'Where are the photographs?' They were duly sent, following which Chaplin, via publicist Harry Crocker (*qv*), invited the actress and her mother to a meeting in New York. After his prior difficulties, Chaplin wanted to ensure a chaperone when meeting a young lady. New York had been chosen as a compromise, Miss Bloom's stage commitments allowing only a comparatively brief trip; at this time Chaplin was averse to flying, and had crossed the USA by train. Chaplin and Jerry Epstein (*qv*) took the trouble to meet their visitors at the airport; this, and the comedian's concern for the

Claire Bloom with Sydney Chaplin in Limelight

actress's safety, eliminated any nervousness she had in his presence. The meeting was successful, and a test was shot, with Chaplin employing his customary method of demonstrating every action he required. Miss Bloom returned to *Ring Around the Moon* after a week's absence; the show had continued with an understudy and, of the cast, only Margaret Rutherford (*qv*) was interested in hearing about Bloom's association with Chaplin.

Three months later, a telegram arrived from Crocker, confirming she had been hired for the rôle. During filming, the actress came to think of Chaplin as a 'supportive and brilliant partner', while forming a close friendship with Chaplin and his wife, Oona. They were reunited when the Chaplins travelled to England for *Limelight*'s UK première – during which Chaplin was barred from returning to America – and took a trip around Covent Garden. The actress recalled no fuss or requests for autographs, simply a murmured 'God bless, Charlie' from the stallholders as he passed by –a touching acknowledgement to a returning Londoner. Miss Bloom, currently appearing as Shakespeare's Juliet at the Old Vic, could not attend the première but sat beside Chaplin at the press screening a few days before. Silence greeted the film's conclusion, but a lengthy ovation awaited Chaplin when he arrived in the foyer. The audience had delayed any reaction until Chaplin was there to hear it. His leading lady, overcome, threw her arms around

Chaplin's neck and kissed him. Claire Bloom, whose relationship with the Chaplins continued long after their professional association, has chronicled her experiences in two memoirs, *Limelight and After: The Education of an Actress* (1982) and *Leaving a Doll's House* (1996).

(See also: Aircraft; Keaton, Buster; O'Neill, Oona; Politics; Women)

BOATS, SHIPS

(Chaplin films *qv*)
There are occasional maritime forays in the Chaplin films. *A Busy Day* was shot at the opening of San Pedro harbour; *The Rounders* take to a rowing boat, only to disappear into the lake; the climactic scenes of *Tillie's Punctured Romance* offer Keystone's idea of seaborne cops; *By the Sea*, though short on boats, offers comic business with a lifebelt; *Shanghaied* is self-explanatory; *The Immigrant* is ferried to the USA by sea; *The Adventurer* steals a swimming costume from a man in a rowing boat; *A Day's Pleasure* is anything but, when Charlie and family take to the waves; *The Gold Rush* finishes with a wealthy Charlie finding his lost love on an ocean liner; while politician Ogden discovers an intriguing stowaway in *A Countess From Hong Kong*.

Syd Chaplin (*qv*) pursued a real-life merchant career prior to becoming a comedian. Charlie's first trip to the USA, with the Karno Company (*qv*) in 1910, was on the *Cairnrona*. Their second visit, after which Chaplin remained in America, was made on the *Oceanic*. His next visit home, in 1921, was on board the *Olympic*, by which he returned to America. The *Mauretania* took him back to England a decade later; Chaplin's extensive wanderings in this period encompassed the Far East, concluding in June 1932, when he, Syd and valet Kono left Japan for the USA on the *Hikawa Maru*. A year later, Chaplin acquired a yacht, the *Panacea*; an intended Hawaiian trip of 1936, aboard the *Coolidge*, became another Far East tour. Chaplin's permanent departure from the USA – though he did not know it until en route – was in 1952, when he and his family sailed for England on the *Queen Elizabeth*.

(See also: Abandoned projects; Aircraft; Murder; Politics; Public appearances)

Boats, ships: *Charlie feigns seasickness when travelling to the USA for the first time in 1910*

'BOGUS CHAPLINS'

Along with the rash of impersonators (*qv*), 'bogus Chaplins' – or, in other words, unauthorized films in which the comedian was claimed to appear – were an inevitable by-product of the 'Chaplin Craze' (*qv*). Several of these were assembled using extracts from the Keystone films (*qv*), many of which were not copyrighted, mixed with newly-shot material that would often employ a double. Theodore Huff noted an entire serial derived from Chaplin-Keystone footage, entitled *The Perils of Patrick* (a deliberate nod towards Pathé and its famous Pearl White serial, *The Perils of Pauline*). On 20 November 1915, Essanay (*qv*) placed a full-page advertisement in the *Moving Picture World* headed 'an appeal for fair play'. The appeal was ostensibly on behalf of Chaplin himself, in response to 'letters of protest received from numerous exhibitors who secured from so-called film exchanges the conglomerations entitled Charles Chaplin in "The Mix-Up," "Ambition" and "The Review"'. Both Chaplin and Essanay denied responsibility for these 'patched-up

films', which they dismissed as a rehash of scenes from his earlier work, assembled 'without regard to sequence or story'. Ironically, it was Essanay itself that went on to produce no less than five 'strays' from the Chaplin canon, namely the feature-length version of *Carmen* (*qv*), an abridged version of *Police* (*qv*), two feature-length anthologies, *Chase Me, Charlie* (*qv*) and *The Essanay-Chaplin-Revue of 1916*, plus a supposedly withheld two-reeler, *Triple Trouble* (*qv*). (It is evident that the Essanay subjects had also been cut around by other hands. A contemporary advertisement for the *Revue* warns all would-be pirates that each Essanay-Chaplin subject had been copyrighted with the Library of Congress.) As stated elsewhere, Chaplin tried in vain to prohibit the release of the extended *Carmen*, which may perhaps explain his failure to combat Essanay's subsequent mutilations. He was more successful when acting against five other films during the autumn of 1917, soon after signing with First National (*qv*). The *Moving Picture World* of 27 October that year reports an alliance between 'Chaplin, his attorneys, and the members of the First National Exhibitors' Circuit', taking the form of a 'national vigilance committee', aiming to stem the large number of imitators (or at least those claiming to be the genuine article) plus the various unauthorized films bearing the comedian's name. The *World* reprints a letter from Nathan Burkan, First National's legal representative, describing the temporary restraining order granted in New York against a feature-length subject, *The Fall of the Rummy-Nuffs*, featuring *Charles Chaplin*, the two-reel films *The Dishonor System* and *One Law For Both* (produced by the Motion Picture Film Company), in addition to a further brace of faked Chaplins, *Charlie in a Harem* and *Charlie Chaplin in 'A Son of the Gods'* (from the New Apollo Feature Film Company). As with the cobbled-together serial described above, these films set out to guy specific dramatic films of the period (such as Annette Kellerman's *A Daughter of the Gods*), and had been compiled from old Chaplin material, using a double to provide necessary linking footage. Chaplin prevented their further distribution, seeking also financial redress from the producers, the laboratory where the material was duped, the firm manufacturing the display posters and even, in the case of *Fall of the Rummy-Nuffs*, the theatre where the picture was

shown. 'Several suits will be started against each and every exhibitor in this and other cities for exhibiting spurious Charlie Chaplin pictures,' added Burkan. It was to combat such fraudulent releases that Chaplin decided to authenticate the main title of each First National film by signing it as the camera turned (see **Titling**).

(See also: Reissues)

THE BOND 🎩

(Chaplin film)
Made for and distributed free of charge by the Liberty Loan Committee in 1918 (see below). Produced, written and directed by Charles Chaplin. Photographed by Rollie Totheroh. Copyrighted as *Charlie Chaplin in a Liberty Loan Appeal*. Half reel.
With Charlie Chaplin, Edna Purviance, Albert Austin, Sydney Chaplin.

This episodic reel was part of Chaplin's work in promoting the sale of war bonds during the Fourth Liberty Loan Drive. It consists of brief vignettes demonstrating the various types of 'bonds'. One is the bond of friendship, when Albert Austin (*qv*), standing by a lamp-post, greets Charlie, keeping him from an appointment; despite Charlie's frequent attempts to excuse himself, Austin brings him up to date on recent happenings, tells him an obviously tedious joke and, ultimately, taps him for money. This done, Austin suggests a visit to a bar, which Charlie declines before finally being allowed on his way. Another is the bond of love, as an unusually flirty Edna Purviance (*qv*) lures Charlie by a wicked lift of her skirt. Charlie hangs his cane on the moon and, while resting against a park bench, is easy prey for Cupid's arrow, which lands in his behind. Charlie responds with a delirious ballet before he and Edna are 'bonded' by a ribbon hurled by Cupid. Still another is the bond of matrimony, Edna having got Charlie to the altar. Charlie produces a well-wrapped ring and has to pay off first the clergyman then the usher, in order to retrieve his top hat. Albert Austin throws large quantities of rice, knocking the bridegroom senseless when also hurling a shoe. Finally, and, most importantly, there is the Liberty Bond, symbolized by Edna as the Statue of Liberty. Miss Liberty is endangered when the Kaiser appears from the shadows; fortunately, a doughboy is on hand to bring the Kaiser to submission. Charlie buys a Liberty Bond from Uncle Sam. The proceeds are given to a blacksmith, representing 'industry', who in turn hands a rifle to a doughboy. Charlie is sufficiently impressed to turn over an additional sum, concealed in his trouser leg. The blacksmith is thus able to present a second rifle, this time to the US Navy. Uncle Sam, Charlie and the blacksmith shake hands. The Kaiser makes a speech, unaware of Charlie's surreptitious approach, bearing a large mallet marked 'Liberty Bonds'. After several devastating blows, Charlie knocks out the Kaiser before delivering a rousing (if inaudible) curtain speech.

It was probably *The Bond*'s extracurricular nature – interrupting his series for First National (*qv*) – that encouraged Chaplin to use a setting composed of abstract, white-on-black cut-outs and props. This approach, unique in Chaplin's work, was considerably ahead of its time and may have influenced some of the 1920s' *avant-garde* talents. There is, however, a slight continuity error; when Charlie hangs his cane on the crescent moon, it momentarily disappears when Cupid peeps over the moon in close-up! This same sequence employs a moment of trick photography (*qv*), when Cupid's arrow lands in Charlie's rump. This was evidently filmed with the camera turning backwards, enabling the arrow simply to be yanked out of a concealed pad; the device is given away by Chaplin reacting to the arrow just a fraction too soon. The white-on-black technique is particularly effective in the Statue of Liberty scene, where a spotlight fades up first on the Kaiser, then on the soldier who defends Miss Liberty. As in *Shoulder Arms* (*qv*), the Kaiser is portrayed by Syd Chaplin (also *qv*).

The Bond was one of several propaganda films in which movie stars donated their services to the war effort. Others to have made them include Douglas Fairbanks, Mary Pickford and Roscoe 'Fatty' Arbuckle (all *qv*). Of these, Fairbanks' film at least is known to have used similar abstract sets to *The Bond*. According to a report in the New York Times, *The Bond* was among a selection of these films screened at New York's Strand Theater late in September 1918, which is slightly at odds with the film's usually accepted release date of 4 October. At around the same time, Chaplin appeared with Scottish music-hall star Harry Lauder in a film to

Charlie conks the Kaiser – alias Syd Chaplin – in **The Bond**

benefit the British war loan. This item is believed to have remained unreleased, but Chaplin's *My Life in Pictures* prints several stills from both productions, including two showing Henry Bergman (*qv*) costumed as 'John Bull'. Bergman does not appear in *The Bond*, but was presumably in its British equivalent, as one still suggests the use of the same set but with John Bull in lieu of Uncle Sam. The 'Liberty Bonds' sign above the sales kiosk reads instead 'War Bonds', and the British flag replaces that of the United States. Another still depicts Chaplin and Lauder impersonating each other: they have exchanged hats and walking sticks; Chaplin is smoking a pipe, while Lauder has a cigarette, and each is imitating the other's stance. Film of this mutual impersonation may be found among the out-takes used in the series *Unknown Chaplin* (*qv*). Also included are Chaplin greeting Lauder at the studio, a sequence with them revising William Tell's most famous shot, and a scene in which Lauder draws Chaplin's likeness in chalk.

(See also: Alcohol; Ballet; Children; Early stage appearances; *Funniest Man in the World, The*; Parks; Race; Religion; Smoking; Trick photography; Wartime; Women)

BOOKS

This volume is only one of a very large number of Chaplin studies – in several languages – to have been published over the years; a bibliography compiled for

Classic Images had to be split into sections for consecutive issues. For this reason, the present account must concern itself with those works either directly linked to Chaplin and his immediate family, books indicative of the times, or English-language studies that have been regarded as standard reference.

The 'Chaplin Craze' (*qv*) brought such things as *The Charlie Chaplin Book*, consisting essentially of portraits and verse. Essanay's London representative, Langford Reed, put together *The Chronicles of Charlie Chaplin*. Fleetway, also in London, published *The Charlie Chaplin Scream Book* and *The Charlie Chaplin Laugh Book* in 1915. The rarest is *Charlie Chaplin's Own Story*, published in 1916 by Bobbs-Merrill; ostensibly by Chaplin, it was instead ghostwritten, and its departures from fact caused sufficient embarrassment for Chaplin to have it withdrawn.

It was reportedly Monta Bell (*qv*) who wrote down Chaplin's account of his 1921 tour, published a year later in America as *My Trip Abroad* (Harper) and in Britain as *My Wonderful Visit* (Hurst & Blackett). In 1937, Chaplin wrote a preface to a book by Gilbert Seldes, *Movies for the Millions*. Chaplin kept the world waiting for his authentic memoirs, titled simply *My Autobiography* (Bodley Head). He had worked on it for a few years when, in June 1962, he told *The Times* that he was 'polishing it – one week putting in a comma, the next week taking it out again'. The publishers were then hoping to have it in print before the new year, but in the end it did not appear until 1964. The general opinion of the book is of some curious omissions and occasional pomposity, compensated by frankness and periodic self-effacement. Contemporary reaction favoured the chapters detailing Chaplin's childhood and young adult years, which were later published separately as *My Early Life*. Several of the autobiography's omissions were compensated for in a follow-up, *My Life in Pictures* (Bodley Head), assembled in 1974 with the help of Francis Wyndham.

A few Chaplin family members have written books. Charles Chaplin Jr, with N. and M. Rau, produced *My Father, Charlie Chaplin* (Random House, 1960); his mother, Lita Grey (*qv*), entered the field with *My Life with Chaplin* (Bernard Geis Associates, 1966); in the same year, another son, Michael, had his experiences published as *I Couldn't Smoke the Grass on My Father's Lawn* (UK: Leslie Frewin/US:

Putnam); while Michael's former wife has recently written a biography of Oona Chaplin. Not quite family but certainly very close was Jerry Epstein (*qv*), whose book, *Remembering Charlie*, is detailed elsewhere.

For many years, the definitive reference work was considered to be Theodore Huff's *Charlie Chaplin*, first published in 1951 and based on his 1940s researches. It is still one of the key volumes, one which many believe Chaplin used as a guide when chronicling his own history. Others from the 1950s include Peter Cotes' and Thelma Niklaus' *The Little Fellow* (1951); R.J. Minney's 1954 study, *The Immortal Tramp*, to which Syd Chaplin (*qv*) is believed to have contributed, and Robert Payne's analytical *The Great Charlie* (a.k.a. *The Great God Pan*), from 1957. The Citadel Press 'Films of' series brought forward one of the most useful and widely-circulated guides, *The Films of Charlie Chaplin* (1965) by Gerald McDonald, Michael Conway and Mark Ricci. Donald W. McCaffrey's *Focus On Chaplin* (1971) proved a useful collection of Chaplin essays. John McCabe's *Charlie Chaplin* (1978) remains one of the better histories, aided in part by the author's interviews with Stan Laurel (*qv*). David Robinson's *Chaplin: The Mirror of Opinion* (1983) was closely followed by the exhaustive *Chaplin: His Life and Art* (1985), which is regarded as a classic. A further Robinson study, *Charlie Chaplin: The Art of Comedy*, was published a decade later. Mention might also be made of the first volume of Harry Geduld's *Chapliniana*, a detailed study of the Keystone films.

(See also: Bibliography; Censorship; Children; Florey, Robert; Keystone; O'Neill, Oona; Public appearances)

BORDEAUX, JOE (OR BORDEAU)
(?1894–1950)

(all films *qv*)
Supporting actor in Chaplin Keystones: in *The Property Man* he is an old-school thespian; *His Musical Career* casts him as the pauper who unexpectedly receives a new piano; while he is reported as one of the many disreputable types in *Mabel at the Wheel* and among the Keystone Cops in *The Knockout* and *Tillie's Punctured Romance*.
(See also: Keystone)

BOWES, LAWRENCE A. (ALFRED)

(Chaplin films *qv*)
Born in Newark, California, Lawrence A. Bowes (not Bowles) worked with Chaplin at Essanay (*qv*) and is believed also to have appeared in films for Selig and Universal. He appears in *Shanghaied* as the captain and in *The Bank* as the top-hatted leader of the robbery. Both rôles have sometimes been misattributed to John Rand (*qv*). Bowes is reported also in Chaplin's *Carmen*.

BOXING

See: *Champion, The*; *City Lights*, and Fighting

BRADBURY, KITTY

(Chaplin films *qv*)
When Chaplin wrote *My Life in Pictures* in 1974, he could neither recall the name of the beautiful, elderly lady who played the mother of Edna Purviance (*qv*) in *The Immigrant* nor recount what became of her later on. She has been identified as character actress Kitty Bradbury, and one can only assume a (forgivable) lapse in memory on Chaplin's part, for she is credited on-screen in his own reissue of *The Pilgrim*, in which she again plays Edna's mother. She may also be seen as the bride's mother in the wedding sequence of *The Kid*, though this is deleted in Chaplin's own reissue. Among Miss Bradbury's other films are *The Brand of Lopez* (1920) and *Code of the Wilderness* (1924).

(See also: *Chaplin Revue, The*; Reissues)

BRANDO, MARLON
(b. 1924)

Leading man of *A Countess From Hong Kong* (*qv*), Marlon Brando's distinguished career, like that of co-star Sophia Loren (*qv*), need not be detailed in these pages. It is believed that Chaplin selected Brando for the film after first considering Sean Connery, who was at that time associated primarily with the 'James Bond' films. Brando's admiration for Chaplin's talent was known: a 1962 biography by Charles Hamblett, titled simply *Brando*, quotes his description of Chaplin as 'the greatest artist that movies have ever produced. No, I don't know him personally, nor am I interested in what people say about him – either his morals or his politics. I still think he's a great actor ... the greatest.' When Brando finally made Chaplin's acquaintance, relations quickly became strained. The essential difficulty seems to have been in

***Marlon Brando**'s relationship with Chaplin deteriorated while making* A Countess From Hong Kong*; a truce is clearly in evidence*

the profound difference between their methods: Chaplin, as director, was accustomed to showing his actors exactly how he wanted a scene performed, and would act it through; Brando, as actor, was accustomed to providing his own interpretation. Sophia Loren later recalled her embarrassment when Brando slept through Chaplin's enactment of the script at his home in Vevey; the actor later explained that he was suffering from jet-lag. It is believed that Brando further disapproved of the essentially offhand manner in which Chaplin dealt with his son, Sydney, who played the second male lead. There are times in any walk of life when an employer, anxious to ward off accusations of nepotism, will deliberately be strict with a blood relation; the reasons for Chaplin's attitude on this and some other reputed occasions are suggested in the main entry for *Countess*. Both Chaplin and Brando seem otherwise to have established good working relations with their *Countess* colleagues, and one may regret the essential incompatibility between the two. Brando's memoirs, published nearly thirty years after the event, suggest ego and tyranny on Chaplin's part, but concede his status as the film medium's greatest talent; 'he makes everybody else look Lilliputian,' wrote the actor.

(See also: Children; Rutherford, Margaret)

BRUCE, NIGEL
(1895–1953)

Although possessed of fairly illustrious British parents (Sir William Waller Bruce and Lady Angelica Mary Bruce, *née* Selby), Nigel Bruce was actually born overseas, quoted variously as the USA or Mexico. He was educated in England, served as a private in the First World War during 1914–15, but was wounded in France and subsequently invalided out. His theatrical debut was in *Why Marry?* at the Comedy Theatre, London, in May 1920; later that year saw him in Canada, from which he returned to the British stage. Aside from New York engagements in November 1926 and October–December 1931, Bruce remained in Britain until 1937. He had commenced film work in 1930 and, after a number of such rôles (among them 1933's *Channel Crossing*, with Max Miller), Bruce moved to America, where he became an English archetype (as when playing W.S. Gilbert in *Knights of Song*

Charlie as a distraught lady having **A Busy Day**
BFI Stills, Posters and Designs

on Broadway in 1938). He was ultimately identified as 'Dr Watson' to Basil Rathbone's 'Sherlock Holmes' in a long-running series of adventures. In *Limelight* (*qv*), he is 'Postant', an impresario whose name bears uncanny similarity to that of the stage manager in a *Holmes* production in which Chaplin appeared during 1905.

(See also: Daniell, Henry; Early stage appearances)

BRYAN, VINCENT
See: Essanay

A BUSY DAY

(Chaplin film)
Keystone Comedy released by Mutual, 7 May 1914. Produced by Mack Sennett. Written and directed by Charles Chaplin. Photography attributed to Frank D. Williams. Split reel, accompanied by a factual subject, *The Morning Papers*. Also known as *Militant Suffragette*. 441 feet (UK length cited in *Bioscope*).

With Charlie Chaplin (wife), Mack Swain (her husband), Phyllis Allen (see below).

A turbulent couple sit in a crowd of spectators, awaiting a parade and military band. The wife's character may be gauged from a garrulous manner and willingness to blow her nose on her skirt; the husband in turn displays his preoccupations by sloping off after a

pretty girl. Setting out in pursuit, the wife is distracted by a newsreel cameraman, pauses before the lens and must be removed, the while doing battle with a cop. The comic action pauses for a view of the 'torpedo boat flotilla'. Catching up with her husband, she dismisses the girl and proceeds to beat up her spouse. He retaliates, shoving his wife into the policeman. She is booted back to her husband, on whom she renews attack. The policeman intervenes, but both he and the wife are disposed of by the husband, who goes off into the crowd. The husband sees speedboats being launched before being distracted by the return of his girlfriend. Elsewhere, his wife performs an eccentric dance to the music of the band. Once finished, she seeks out her husband, attacking both the girl and her errant man. They are on the jetty, and the struggle sends the wife into the sea. She struggles for a while before disappearing beneath the waves.

Once thought lost, *A Busy Day* exists in often excellent prints bearing the original Keystone titling and, in some copies, an alias (presumably coined for a British reissue), *Militant Suffragette*. The most commonplace edition, from Blackhawk Films, could be taken as a pristine original, but in fact is not. The title card and tracking shot representing the 'torpedo boat flotilla' are missing, as is a brief moment in which the cop slaps the 'wife' before kicking her back into the newsreel camera's range. These additional segments are from an alternate Keystone print, bearing titles of slightly different typography and, in the case of the first sub-title, a variant in text. The film was shot at the opening of San Pedro harbour, Greater Los Angeles (identified in a banner visible in the parade): the alternate print's first sub-title sets the scene as 'Opening day at Los Angeles Harbor'; that in Blackhawk's copy states merely 'Gathered to see the parade and hear the band play', suggesting an early reissue with the topical aspect eliminated. The seemingly earlier version is mutilated in a quite different way, omitting Chaplin's descent into the sea and final close-up in the water. In their stead is a long-shot of someone else falling from a quite different jetty!

Chaplin's first on-screen female impersonation follows the knockabout tradition of British pantomime dame, in which respect it differs from later examples in *The Masquerader* and *A Woman* (both *qv*). Chaplin is said to have borrowed the dress from veteran actress Alice Davenport (*qv*). Another Keystone stalwart, Mack Swain (*qv*), appears without his usual 'Ambrose' make-up on this occasion. Swain's extramarital partner is sometimes credited as played by Phyllis Allen (*qv*), but the actress in that rôle is very obviously younger and smaller of build.

In common with *Kid Auto Races at Venice* (*qv*) and the later *Recreation* (also *qv*), *A Busy Day* was originally released on the same reel as a quite unrelated item. Further parallels with *Auto Races* are Chaplin's posing before a newsreel camera and, especially, the Keystone practice of shooting at a genuine public event. The author once examined a bizarre hybrid of the two films, intercut into a full 35mm reel as though the events were taking place simultaneously. This may explain why *Militant Suffragette* has also been cited as a reissue title for *Kid Auto Races*. Intriguingly, a May 1920 trade advertisement brackets both films in relation to *Militant Suffragette*, suggesting a date for this strange combination. Blackhawk Films paired the films once more – not intercut! – for their 8 and 16mm releases.

In a trade advertisement placed in *Bioscope* of 8 October 1914, Sennett's UK distributors, the Western Import Co., seemed almost as interested in promoting it as a travelogue: 'Chas. Chaplin as the lady who had a day off, got into trouble with the police and finished in the harbour. Includes interesting views of Los Angeles harbour,

the American navy, etc.' When reviewed in that journal on 22 October, there was acknowledgement of Chaplin's female impersonation and 'an amazing exhibition of acrobatic humour'.

(See also: Boats, ships; Female impersonation; Home movies; Keystone; Leno, Dan; Newsreels; *Recreation*; Reissues; Williams, Frank D.)

BY THE SEA 🎩

(Chaplin film)
Released by General Film Company, 29 April 1915. Produced by Essanay. Written and directed by Charles Chaplin. Photographed by Harry Ensign. British title: *Charlie by the Sea*. One reel. 997 feet (UK length cited in *Bioscope*). With Charlie Chaplin (himself), Bud Jamison (burly man), Edna Purviance (his wife), Billy Armstrong (Charlie's opponent), Margie Reiger (Billy's wife), Snub Pollard (ice cream salesman).

Billy and his wife are at the sea front. It is a breezy day, so Billy's hat is attached with string. Billy's wife goes off alone, ordering him to stay put. Billy struggles against the elements. Charlie ambles along the boardwalk, munching a banana. His hat is similarly tethered – all the more useful when he takes a dive over the banana's discarded peel, the result of having used the wrong leg to kick it away. He passes Billy, and their hats, blown into the air, become

swapped, entangling the two men in string. Tempers are aroused, and during the scuffle the string becomes detached from Billy's clothing. Charlie runs away, taking both hats with him. Billy catches up, taking Charlie by the throat; he is eventually given back his hat, though Charlie has extricated it at the cost of half its brim. Billy strikes Charlie, squaring up for a fight; Charlie makes his escape after administering some well-aimed kicks. Looking back, Charlie laughs and leans back, knocking a life belt over his head. Still covered in string, Charlie becomes entangled once more. He calls over a dazed Billy. Charlie soon tricks him into a position of helplessness, Billy's neck being encircled by Charlie's left arm as his right hand delivers blows. Charlie notices some passengers on Billy's head, who seem acrobatic. A lady passes by, with whom Charlie flirts when not punching Billy's head. Charlie arranges his unconscious opponent into a perch while making time with the attractive stranger. Unimpressed, she continues on her way. Charlie, having hooked Billy to the stand intended for the life belt, follows on. The lady's frostiness is thawed into laughter when the string on Charlie's hat becomes caught across his face. Billy, now semi-conscious, staggers over in fighting mode. When the lady looks away, Charlie pushes his adversary out of view. On landing, Billy's rump becomes wedged in the life belt. Freed, Billy hurls the life belt, which passes around Charlie. When it has reached ankle level,

By the Sea: *Charlie has an ice cream with Billy Armstrong, as vendor Snub Pollard looks on...*

(See also: Abandoned projects; Boats, ships; Essanay; Jamison, William 'Bud'; Leno, Dan; Parks; Pollard, Harry 'Snub'; Purviance, Edna; Stockdale, Carl; Television)

... but his immediate past soon catches up with him

Billy pulls the rope and Charlie topples over. For the lady's benefit, Charlie pretends it is a game; the illusion is over when Billy throws the belt around Charlie a second time, and he is dragged over for a renewed scrap. The lady departs for the bench where her burly husband is waiting. Charlie and Billy are still squabbling when a rather stooped policeman takes an interest. When Billy accidentally flattens the officer, he and Charlie agree to become friends. They have departed when Billy's wife returns; she calls for Billy and becomes increasingly irritated by his absence. Charlie offers to buy ice cream for himself and Billy. They are enjoying their ices while the burly gentleman buys a cigar from a neighbouring kiosk. Their argument is renewed when Charlie insists Billy should pay for their cones. The ice cream becomes a weapon, splattering both ice cream salesman and the man buying a cigar. When the burly man joins the fight, Charlie leaves him to throttle Billy and takes a seat beside his wife. The cop reappears to arrest Billy. The ice cream salesman still wants his money but is pushed over by the large man. He returns to the bench, where Charlie is attempting to flirt with his wife. The threat of violence is enough to dispose of Charlie, who avoids a second cop only to meet the ice cream salesman. Money is demanded, so Charlie produces a coin from his waistcoat pocket. Placing it straight back there, he departs. The burly man wants to go after Charlie, but is dissuaded by his wife. Charlie meets Billy's wife and, joining her on a bench, starts to flirt once more. Billy escapes from the cop; the other couple make their way over

and Charlie is surrounded. Coyly, Charlie has placed his hat over his face and is at first unaware of the situation. Believing the woman is still beside him, Charlie strokes Billy's face, and the truth dawns. Charlie reacts with a start, toppling over the bench and its occupants.

By the Sea is a 'park' comedy without the trees, unremarkable in itself, though possessing, as Theodore Huff observed, 'a certain impromptu charm'. In common with Chaplin's other one-reeler for Essanay, *In the Park* (*qv*), the impression is of an interim effort designed to maintain public attention between the more elaborate two-reel subjects. Not that *By the Sea* is a poor effort; there is a reasonable proportion of imaginative byplay, not least when Charlie observes the to-and-fro cavortings of the fleas supposedly residing in an adversary's hair. Chaplin, who would never forget a worthwhile gag, elaborated upon this momentary bit of business many years later, in the 'animal trainer' routine from *Limelight* (*qv*). Available prints of *By the Sea* are very grainy but watchable. The BBC's *Chaplin SuperClown* edition is of fair quality but lacks sub-titles; the author's print, from a UK reissue by Equity-British, lacks a small section (where Charlie blunders into the life belt) but includes sub-titles that probably match the original text. These serve to clarify the action somewhat: two cards establish the respective couples as being married, a situation otherwise unspecified; another makes it plain that Charlie has offered to treat Billy Armstrong (*qv*) to ice cream, hence the man's subsequent protest at being asked to pay.

CAMERA SPEEDS
See: Trick photography

CAMERA-LOOKS 🎩

(Chaplin films *qv*)
As noted in the main entry, most prints of *The Fireman* are missing a shot in which Charlie and Leo White (*qv*) sit before the camera, visibly repeating the words 'Help! Fire!' When discussing *Tillie's Punctured Romance*, Theodore Huff noted the frequent straight-to-camera looks and even full soliloquys offered by the players. This was ascribed to the film's stage origins and an overall theatrical legacy that came to be supplanted during 1914, as cinema developed its own techniques (Stan Laurel [*qv*] recalled Chaplin fixing stage audiences with a look suggesting him to be *genuinely* crazy!). Just the same, Leo

White favours the device rather heavily in *The Champion*, as does Fred Goodwins (*qv*) during *A Jitney Elopement*. At the conclusion of both films, Charlie and Edna Purviance (*qv*) acknowledge the camera prior to their final embrace. A similar glance is given the audience at the end of *Behind the Screen*. Generally, Charlie uses such moments as an opportunity to take the audience into his confidence, as when tipping us the wink after using a hard-luck story to ingratiate himself with the maid in *Work*. In this respect Chaplin's camera-looks are in keeping with those used later by Oliver Hardy, since both comedians wordlessly invite an audience's opinion and thus remain in character, as opposed to the detached, verbal comments made by comedians such as Groucho Marx (*qv*). Chaplin employed the motif sparingly, but it can still be seen in later pictures, as when Charlie consumes a pepped-up prison meal in *Modern Times*.

(See also: Karno Company, The; Mental illness)

CAMERAMEN
See: Totheroh, Rollie; Struss, Karl; Williams, Frank D., and Wilson, Jack

CAMPBELL, ERIC 🎩
(1878–1917)

(Chaplin films *qv*)
Large-framed actor, widely reported to have been born in Dunoon, Scotland (as

Eric Stuart Campbell or Alfred Eric Campbell – see below). Campbell joined Chaplin's stock company as regular villain for the Mutual series. His distinctive appearance – generally either bullet-headed thug or, more commonly, lavishly-whiskered-and-eyebrowed giant – identifies him for many as the definitive Chaplin adversary. In *The Floorwalker*, Campbell plays the corrupt store manager; *The Fireman* casts him as a fire chief willing to help an arsonist; *The Vagabond* presents him as a bullying gypsy, taking a whip to Edna Purviance (*qv*); *The Count* sees Campbell as an opportunistic tailor, vying with Charlie for the attentions of Miss Moneybags; in *The Pawnshop* he is a gun-toting jewel thief; in *Behind the Screen* he is Charlie's indolent foreman; in *The Rink* he is a lecherous nuisance; he terrorizes an entire neighbourhood, including the police, in *Easy Street*; he portrays another lecher, this time gout-ridden, in *The Cure*; he is the intimidating head waiter in *The Immigrant*, a rôle originally intended for Henry Bergman (*qv*), and is Charlie's lecherous, cowardly and underhanded rival in *The Adventurer*. In short, Eric Campbell was called upon to represent the world's less desirable characters – an image reportedly quite at odds with his gentle, real-life demeanour. John McCabe, a biographer of both Chaplin and Stan Laurel (*qv*), quoted the latter's recollection of Campbell as 'such a wonderful guy. People used to say he had a heart as big as himself.' Laurel believed that Campbell's excellent singing voice would have brought him great success in talking pictures, despite being, like Chaplin, somewhat shy. Laurel agreed, in a sense, with Campbell's description of himself as an 'elephant', in the sense of being 'big, gentle, lovable'. Eric Campbell was killed in a road accident after completing the Mutual series. Had he lived, Campbell would most certainly have continued with Chaplin, as noted below; equally likely is that, in common with Henry Bergman and Albert Austin (both *qv*), he would have contributed on both sides of the camera. The last footage taken of Campbell was for an intended Mutual comedy with a golfing theme, a routine used eventually for *The Idle Class* (*qv*), with Mack Swain (*qv*) in lieu of Campbell. Stills supposedly depicting Campbell in *The Idle Class* baffled historians until the discarded footage was recovered and edited into *How to Make Movies* (*qv*).

At the 1995 Edinburgh Film Festival,

Camera-looks: the sly fade-out from *Behind the Screen* it was decided that Campbell may well have been Scotland's first film star – a dubious claim, but undeniably an efficient means of drawing attention. The festival's director, Mark Cousins, made an appeal for information, the result being that the following year's festival was able to screen a new tribute to the man. In the *Daily Telegraph* of 10 August 1996, Chris Peachment reported how film historian Kevin MacDonald (a grandson of filmmaker Emeric Pressburger) had directed a 50-minute documentary, *Chaplin's Goliath: In Search of Scotland's Forgotten Star* (named in the article as *The Search For Eric Campbell*), which had been selected as the 1996 festival's closing item on 24 August. The film, produced by Fran Robertson, was made by Figment Films and the Scottish Arts Council Lottery Fund, in association with the Scottish Film Production Fund for Scottish Television. Among the interviewees were Chaplin biographer David Robinson, film historian Sam Gill, Rollie Totheroh's grandson David, Bonnie McCourt of the Charlie Chaplin Film Co. society and, most intriguingly, Eric Campbell's granddaughter, Brenda Bull, who was discovered to be living in Devon.

Chaplin's Goliath shows the unveiling of a commemorative plaque in Dunoon. The film clears up several mysteries, not least that of Campbell's true birthdate. His age at death was reported as 39, yet the year of birth has sometimes been quoted as 1870 instead of 1878. This was the result of Campbell's first marriage, at the age of 20, to a Gertrude Rowbotham. They seem to have eloped, and Campbell, at that time a minor, needed to falsify his age. There remains no confirmation of his claim to have worked in the D'Oyly Carte Company; traced instead were details of Campbell's stage debut (as a Chinaman in *Five O'Clock Tea*) when aged eight; photos of him in barnstorming melodramas touring Scotland and Wales; a report of him in Glasgow during 1908; details of his singing career in music-hall and in a production of *Dick Whittington* at the Theatre Royal, Birmingham; confirmation of his employment in the Karno Company (*qv*), playing 'Big Ben' in *The Yap-Yaps*; and details of his arrival in New York in July 1914, having been engaged by Klaw and Erlanger for their show, *Tipping the Winner*. Despite its closure after only twelve performances, Campbell remained in New York, where he found greater success in *The Irish Dragoon*. He was joined by his wife and daughter in 1915, and a year later was recognized by

Eric Campbell was the archetype of Chaplin's villains, as in this pained predicament from The Cure

his former colleagues, Charlie and Syd Chaplin, when they saw him on stage in *Pom Pom*. They were in New York to sign with Mutual, and it was this chance encounter that resulted in Campbell's engagement for the new series.

Chaplin's Goliath suggests Campbell to have participated in Chaplin's gag sessions, implying further that his sudden loss may explain the alleged self-obsession, and softened edge, characterizing Chaplin's First Nationals. Illustrating their collaboration are stills, extracts from the films themselves and, best of all, selected Mutual out-takes. Many of these overlap with *Unknown Chaplin* (*qv*), but not all; gems include Chaplin, Edna and Eric breaking into laughter during *The Immigrant* and Chaplin directing Campbell (in *The Floorwalker*) while being held up by the

neck. The circumstances leading up to Campbell's death, on 20 December 1917, are at last clarified: after the sudden death of his first wife, Campbell hastily remarried. The new bride was Pearl Gilman, vaudevillian and reputed gold-digger, from whom he was separated after two months. Campbell moved into rooms adjoining Chaplin's at the Los Angeles Athletic Club while his wife prepared for divorce, citing doubtless trumped-up charges of cruelty and insobriety. Chaplin, meanwhile, had successfully re-engaged his friend and colleague for the First National series (despite lucrative offers from elsewhere) and, while building his new studio, loaned him to Mary Pickford (*qv*) for a dramatic rôle in *Amarilly of Clothes-Line Alley*. Three days into shooting, Campbell attempted to drive home from a party while under the influence of drink, probably the result of his ongoing divorce. Campbell was driving at 60 m.p.h. on the wrong side of the road, becoming involved in a collision in which he was killed outright. It was known that Chaplin had considerable difficulty in replacing Campbell (in a sense, he never did); *Chaplin's Goliath* illustrates the problem, using hitherto-unseen footage of those who auditioned for the job.

Campbell's remains were cremated and, in the absence of any contact from relatives, returned to the undertaker. After 21 years, his ashes were sent to the Rosedale Cemetery, Los Angeles, where another 13 years elapsed prior to interment. The exact burial site is unknown, but a new memorial plaque has been placed in the cemetery. The plaque cites his year of birth as 1880 and his real name as Alfred Eric Campbell, both of which might be argued by historians. None would dispute his epitaph, which reads: 'A Big Man – A Big Star'.

(See also: Abandoned projects; Animation; Chaplin, Syd; Documentaries, compilations; Impersonators; First National; Mutual; Risqué humour; Sickness; Sport; Stamps, coins; *Unknown Chaplin*; Villains; Wartime)

CARGILL, PATRICK
(1918–96)

British actor who plays Hudson, the valet, in *A Countess From Hong Kong* (*qv*). Cargill's background was in the Indian Army; he became one of British theatre's most highly-regarded *farceurs*, a skill he brought to BBC Television for a series of Feydeau comedies, *Oo-La-La!* Cargill's best-remembered TV work is the Thames sitcom *Father, Dear Father*.

CARICATURES

(Chaplin films *qv*)
Caricatures of Chaplin have proliferated since his initial fame as a stage comedian. An early example was mentioned in the *Performer* of 31 May 1951, courtesy of a letter received from a Mrs Nellie Cooke of Blackpool. Her late husband, George, had been a professional caricaturist; they met Chaplin in Hanley, Staffordshire, when he was touring in *Sherlock Holmes* (see **Early stage appearances**) during

Caricatures: Charlie was, and remains, a favourite of cartoonists, as in this 1915 UK specimen; the central portrait dates from Karno days

1905. Charlie was quite delighted with George's caricature of him, a coloured drawing for which he paid 7s 6d (all he could afford at the time!).

Publicity and newspaper reviews from the Karno period often depict Chaplin in his celebrated rôle of comic drunk. When his early film successes initiated the 'Chaplin Craze' (*qv*), such caricatures became numerous. Rick de Croix's 'Fighting For Reappraisal' series (*Classic Images*, October 1983) reproduces a cartoon panel from the June 1915 *Motion Picture* magazine, in which the world, personified as one being, gratefully shakes Charlie by the hand. Chaplin's own personal favourite, representing the tramp as a sealion, is reproduced in the book *My Wonderful Visit* (a.k.a. *My Trip Abroad*).

Charlie's distinctive image made him a natural hero of the cartoon strips. Britain's comic papers had for some years depicted music-hall comedians in this fashion – Dan Leno (*qv*) had his own paper in 1898 – and it was Charlie's turn when *The Funny Wonder* began to publish his adventures (drawn by Bertie Brown) in February 1915. The strip initially credited Essanay (*qv*) at the top, but continued for nearly thirty years after Chaplin's tenure with the company. Syd Chaplin (*qv*) became a strip-cartoon hero in *Firefly*. Rival comics sometimes offered 'bootleg' Charlies under other names, such as 'Dicky Doenut'. Later in the decade, Charlie's antics were drawn for American papers by E.C. Segar,

known later as the creator of *Popeye*. In 1975, F.C. MacKnight (in *Classic Film Collector*) estimated that Chaplin appeared in perhaps six syndicated newspaper strips during the 1910s. A children's book of the 1920s, published in London by T. Werner Laurie Ltd, provided cut-out 'negative' portraits of film stars which, when held before a lamp, threw a positive image. Chaplin's portrait was that chosen as the cover illustration.

Chaplin's personal difficulties of the 1920s drew considerable press attention, most of it unwelcome; he had his defenders, however, one of them an artist sympathizing with his gigantic payout to Lita Grey (*qv*). Perhaps the best was drawn in 1927 by Rollin Kirby of the *New York World*, showing the tramp unsullied despite the liberal hurling of rotting fruit and worse. The figure is labelled 'Chaplin the Artist'; the caption reads 'What Remains Untouched'.

Chaplin's private nightmares had subsided for a while when, on 23 December 1929, *Film Weekly* published a cartoon, 'The Filmgoer's Xmas Nightmare', in which various stars were shown impersonating others. Chaplin was drawn in Jolson mode, disguised in blackface, his white-gloved hands spread wide and pools of tears accumulating by his feet.

There are occasional caricatures within the films themselves: a drawing of Charlie is chalked on a wall in *The Property Man*; in *The Adventurer* he turns a newspaper photo of himself into a caricature of Eric Campbell (*qv*); while his attempted portrait of Edna Purviance (*qv*) in *The Vagabond* is more caricature than anything else. Chaplin would sometimes add a brief self-caricature when signing autographs, a semi-abstract representation of the hat, cane, moustache and boots. In January 1978, the *Daily Mail* reported the discovery of a self-portrait by Chaplin, dating from a 1946 visit to the California studio of dancer and painter Tilly Losch (later Countess of Carnarvon). Chaplin picked up a brush, producing a simple figure of the tramp with the message, 'It's Me – Charlie.' Tilly Losch, who died two years before the story appeared, gave the picture to her biographer, Billy Hamilton.

The 1970s also brought a series of comic-books, using artwork of European origin and licensed by Chaplin's own company, Bubbles, Inc., formed to sanction toys, novelties, and so on. There is a book translating *The Gold Rush* into strip form, drawn by Philippe Magniaux; Drake Publishing produced an edition in New York during 1975.

Promo artwork for Chaplin's films sometimes appears for sale (see **Auctions**). One of the top showbiz caricaturists, Al Hirshfeld, first drew Chaplin in the 1920s. The première issue of *Limelight*, the Chaplin magazine, describes Chaplin's visit to Hirschfeld's home in Bali, where none of the artist's houseboys had ever seen a film, much less heard of Chaplin. He earned himself a new reputation as comedian with the old trick of making his hat spring into the air. Chaplin bought several of Hirschfeld's pictures, thus financing the artist's return to the USA. Hirschfeld later paid a return visit to the Chaplin home and, in 1994, drew the Chaplin caricature issued on a stamp by the United States Postal Service.

One of the more ingenious Chaplin caricatures was that forming the logo for the 25th London Film Festival in 1981. A full-length portrait of Charlie was formed by a collage of famous movie faces, ranging from Felix the Cat to Anthony Perkins in *Psycho*.

One might note in passing the influence of Chaplin's image on later cartoon creations. One character to emerge during the Second World War, George Baker's downtrodden soldier, 'Sad Sack', was described in the *Daily Express* William Hickey column (9 March 1944) as 'surely born of Chaplin. He has, this rissole-nosed, doughnut-eared little soldier, the pathos of "The Gold Rush" and some of the blind ebullience of "Shoulder Arms".'

(See also: Alcohol; Animation; Artists; Auctions; Costume; *Gold Rush, The;* Karno Company, The; Public appearances; *Shoulder Arms;* Skating; Stamps, coins)

CARMEN

(Chaplin film)
Scheduled for released by General Film Company, 18 December 1915, in a two-reel version; released by V-L-S-E, 10 or 22 April 1916 (see below), as *Charlie Chaplin's Burlesque on Carmen*, expanded to four reels. Produced by Essanay. Original version written and directed by Charles Chaplin. Photographed by Harry Ensign.

With Charlie Chaplin (Darn Hosiery, or 'Don José' in later prints), Edna Purviance (Carmen), Leo White (Morales, Captain of the Guard), Jack Henderson (Lillas Pastia, gypsy chief), John Rand (Escamillo, the matador), Wesley Ruggles (tramp), May White (Frasquita) and (in the four-reel version) Ben Turpin (Le Remendado), Wesley Ruggles.

In old Seville, the king's troops are commanded by his bravest soldier, Darn Hosiery. In his fine uniform and plumed helmet, Darn Hosiery cuts a dash, even when drawing a minuscule sword or tripping over a rock, the latter of which he orders to be shot. The chief of a band of gypsy smugglers offers Darn Hosiery a bribe; when he proves incorruptible, the chief assigns his sultry daughter, Carmen, to the task of seducing the soldier. Darn Hosiery resists briefly, then takes what he believes to be her arm. The limb belongs instead to the heavyweight Frasquita, who is duly pushed away. Carmen, a rose in her teeth, flirts with the Captain of the

Top: **Carmen:** *Charlie as the heroic 'Darn Hosiery'*
BFI Stills, Posters and Designs

The World's Famous Comedian
In the Funniest Scream He Ever Made
A Mirth Quake of Roaring Laughs!

CHARLIE CHAPLIN

In His Comedy Super-Play

BURLESQUE ON CARMEN

Supported by a Cast of Celebrated Comedians, Including

Ben Turpin
EDNA PURVIANCE
LEO WHITE
and a Host of Others

The Comedy the Whole World Proclaimed as the Funniest Ever Shown on the Screen

YOU'L LAUGH FOR WEEKS AFTER!

Above: Reissue publicity for Chaplin's mutilated **Carmen**

Guard before pushing the flower into Darn Hosiery's mouth. He follows Carmen as she skips away. When she vamps him, Darn Hosiery acquires a large spider under his tin hat. Once Carmen has gone, a fellow-soldier eliminates the spider by hitting Darn Hosiery with a bottle. At a café, Carmen divides her attentions among several men. Darn Hosiery arrives, to watch a matador clean his plate to the point where it can be used as a mirror. The two men quarrel, but all attention is diverted when Carmen appears in the gallery. They compete for Carmen's attention, the matador losing a fierce game of pat-a-cake. Carmen leads Darn Hosiery to the centre of the floor, where he blunders into the table. He sips a beer before returning to her side. The Captain of the Guard turns his attentions to Carmen, but is dismissed by Darn Hosiery. The matador offers to lift Carmen up to the table, which Darn Hosiery claims as his own prerogative. She is too heavy, and the matador is allowed to perform the task. Carmen dances a flamenco, embracing the matador but allowing Darn Hosiery a kiss; the soldier climbs the table himself, performing a similar dance while kicking the matador out of the way. A bugle sounds for the troops; despite protests from the Captain, Darn Hosiery prefers to carry Carmen away for some fun. As Darn Hosiery deals with the bugler, Carmen colludes with her father. Carmen returns to the soldier and, signalling to her comrades, vamps Darn Hosiery while the gypsies bring in their contraband. Later, a fight breaks out between Carmen and Frasquita, when Carmen tries to steal her boyfriend. Frasquita is vanquished, and Darn Hosiery declares Carmen the winner. The Captain wants to arrest Carmen, but Darn Hosiery forbids it. The soldiers escort her to the café, where the Captain confronts Carmen and her father. Darn Hosiery boots the Captain across the room, and they cross swords; Darn Hosiery treats the battle casually as the other soldiers attempt to break down the door. The Captain lies exhausted while Darn Hosiery plays 'pool', using sword and onions in place of the usual implements. The Captain rallies, and battle resumes. Forced onto a table, Darn Hosiery is nearly throttled; he has regained the advantage when Carmen, aiming for the Captain, strikes Darn Hosiery with a gourd. The fight continues, Darn Hosiery stealing his opponent's wallet while wrestling. The Captain is strangled; Darn Hosiery attempts a *coup de grace* with his sword, which merely curls into a loop. Suddenly aware of his horrific crime, Darn Hosiery examines the Captain's lifeless body. Carmen makes her escape, and Darn Hosiery is advised to do the same. By the time the gates are broken down, Darn Hosiery is with Carmen. He draws a knife, suggesting suicide, when the matador arrives. Carmen embraces the matador, who literally treads on the

soldier's toes. Carmen deserts Darn Hosiery to wed the matador. Darn Hosiery, now an outlaw in peasant's costume (and bowler), sees the couple travel past; the matador leaves his fiancée outside the town gates. Darn Hosiery confronts Carmen, but is treated with scorn. He draws his knife, plunging it into Carmen's heart. Tenderly, he kisses his fallen love then stabs himself, falling across Carmen's inert form. The matador arrives, surveying the tragedy. Darn Hosiery gives him a back-kick, forcing him through the gates. The couple revive, Darn Hosiery showing Carmen how he has used a collapsible stage knife. The scene irises out as they are about to kiss.

The above is designed to approximate the two-reel version intended by Chaplin in 1915. His own edit was shown to reviewers in December of that year, only to be withdrawn after his departure from Essanay (*qv*) and issued as a four-reel subject the following April. Essanay achieved the expansion partly through means of reinstated out-takes, causing some repetition of action: for example, a gag with Darn Hosiery pretending to be a masseur is used both when fighting the Captain and following his seeming demise, a duplication Chaplin would not have included (the second instance follows an obvious join in the negative, suggesting the reinstatement of an out-take). In addition, Essanay intercut a new (and unfunny) sub-plot with Ben Turpin (*qv*), which explains why Turpin and Chaplin appear only in separate shots. Turpin, playing a gypsy, is seen among the smugglers in the expanded version's opening sequence, and is among those seeking favour with May White as the tubby Frasquita; he reappears at the town gates and is intercut with Chaplin's scenes in the café. At the time, George K. Spoor (*qv*) defended the film's expansion, via the studio's own journal, *Essanay News*. Spoor claimed that *Carmen* was Chaplin's 'first attempt at cutting' (it was no such thing), and that his version 'was not acceptable to us, for the reason that Chaplin left out more good stuff than he put in'.

In Chaplin's version, *Carmen* would be among the best of his Essanay comedies, and might well be better known today. Before the final comic twist, the death scenes are played with surprising conviction, comparing favourably with much that was then being done in dramatic films.

Contemporary reviewers thought the film would have been fine in two reels, but expressed dissatisfaction with the four-reeler; Chaplin, enraged by this mutilation of his work, sought redress in the courts, but was unsuccessful. The course of this action can be traced through the pages of the *Moving Picture World*: on 15 April 1916, it was announced that *Carmen*, Chaplin's second feature (the first having been *Tillie's Punctured Romance* [*qv*]), would be released on an open basis to exhibitors by V-L-S-E, the recently-formed distributing organization based on the former Patents Trust; one week later it had become *Charlie Chaplin's Burlesque on 'Carmen'*, with a release date cited of 10 April (earlier than that generally accepted) and the general view that, despite much publicity, 'a goodly portion of the legions of Chaplin's admirers will be disappointed'. The inclusion of repeated gags did not go unnoticed, 'the inference being that the stunt was done twice that the better of the two might be chosen'. Edna Purviance was lauded as Carmen, while the finale was compared to *The Bank* (*qv*) in suggesting how Chaplin was 'not limited to the comedy division of portrayal'. On 6 May it was reported that Chaplin, represented by his attorney, Nathan Burkan, had brought suit against Essanay and V-L-S-E, on the grounds that their expansion of the two-reel film would damage his reputation. In the New York Supreme Court, Justice Nathan Bijur signed an 'order to show cause' against the defendants. Accompanying the injunction was an affidavit signed by Syd Chaplin (*qv*), detailing the conditions under which the film had been made and the adverse publicity it had since attracted. (This account suggests, incidentally, Syd's presence on the Essanay lot immediately after his tenure at Keystone [*qv*].) In effect, Chaplin was making the then unprecedented claim for what has since become known (in Europe, at least) as 'moral rights' for a creative artist. On 24 April, the Essanay company, represented by William Seabury, moved for the case to be dismissed, but the decision was temporarily withheld; there was simultaneously a countersuit issued against Chaplin, alleging breach of contract and demanding damages of $500,000. The company's grounds were that Chaplin had completed four pictures less than the number for which he had been paid a $10,000 bonus during the summer of 1915. The latter case eventually went in Chaplin's favour but, on 8 July, the *Motion Picture World* reported that Judge Hotchkiss, of the Supreme Court, had decided the *Carmen* suit in favour of Essanay. Doubtless in memory of this debacle, Chaplin ensured that subsequent deals would specifically prohibit such studio tampering, though little could be done over amendments to reissues (*qv*).

The edition of *Carmen* presently in circulation is from the Quality Amusement Corporation, titled *Burlesque on Carmen*. This is a three-reel hybrid (with seemingly interminable introductory titles) that is neither Chaplin's nor Essanay's cut. It has been speculated that Chaplin might easily have re-acquired *Carmen* in order to restore his intended release, but examination of the film suggests that no such editing could be undertaken without causing enormous jumps in continuity. Not surprisingly, there have been reissues with scores based on Bizet's original opera; less expected is a UK print current during the 1950s, with narration by a young Peter Sellers.

As a footnote to *Carmen*, it should be remembered that silent film adaptations of opera 'books' were not uncommon; in 1930, there was even a talking but non-musical version of *Carmen* produced in Britain, retitled *Gypsy Blood*. Chaplin's inspiration had been the competing film portrayals of Carmen by Geraldine Farrar and Theda Bara. Soon after completing his film, Chaplin *nearly* saw Miss Farrar portray the character opposite Enrico Caruso at New York's Metropolitan Opera House; however, the star's illness forced a last-minute cancellation and Caruso appeared, minus Miss Farrar, in *Rigoletto*. The parody element did not end with Chaplin: McDonald, Conway and Ricci's *The Films of Charlie Chaplin* refers to a children's burlesque of the Chaplin film entitled *Chip's Carmen*; in turn, Eldon K. Everett, in the Winter 1974–5 edition of *Classic Film Collector*, details a 1916 release called *A Great Imitation of Charlie Chaplin's Burlesque on Carmen*, an unwieldy title that might have been a sub-heading to that quoted by McDonald et al. According to Everett, this was one of several child comedies made by the Juvenile Film Corporation. A youngster named Joseph Monahan took the Chaplin rôle, while Janethel Monahan (a sister?) replaced Edna Purviance (*qv*). The film was directed by James Fitzpatrick.

(See also: 'Bogus Chaplins'; Costume; Henderson, Jack; Home movies; Jamison, William 'Bud'; Murder; Rand, John; Ruggles, Wesley; Suicide; Video releases; White, Leo; White, May)

CARS

(Chaplin films *qv*)
Although Chaplin's comedy tended not to favour mechanical contrivances, there was often a place for that most commonplace of machines, the motor car. The car's position as a then-recent intrusion on the landscape is suggested when, in *The Tramp*, Charlie narrowly escapes being run over by two passing cars (he also has to dodge traffic in *Work*). In *A Film Johnnie*, there is a mass exodus of cars as the Keystone troupe goes off to the scene of a fire, while in *His Favorite Pastime*, Charlie tries to catch up with a woman's cab but falls into the road. Cars provide the means for a climactic chase in both *Tillie's Punctured Romance* and *A Jitney Elopement*, and are involved in formalized competition for *Mabel at the Wheel*, *Mabel's Busy Day* and *Gentlemen of Nerve* (the vehicles in *Kid Auto Races at Venice* are of the push-along variety). Charlie arrives home by taxi in *One A.M.*, makes his escape towed by a car at the end of *The Rink* and, in *The Idle Class*, hitches a lift on a the back of a limousine. Charlie is taken away in a

different limousine for the finale of *The Vagabond*, while yet another limousine ride, in *The Adventurer*, is in Chaplin's own real-life car, a Locomobile (driven by Kono, Chaplin's chauffeur and valet for many years). *The Kid* is initially abandoned in a Pierce-Arrow, a limousine favoured by America's well-to-do at that time. *Monsieur Verdoux* accepts a lift in another luxurious vehicle, but *The Great Dictator* has his own staff car. Charlie is made a gift – at least temporarily – of a Rolls-Royce in *City Lights*. Details of the comedian's own such vehicle may be found under **Auctions**; how extensively it was used remains open to question, for Chaplin disliked big cars and, at least during his latter days in America, favoured a small Ford.

(See also: Kono, Toraichi)

CAUGHT IN A CABARET

(Chaplin film)
Keystone Comedy released by Mutual, 27 April 1914. Produced by Mack Sennett, but credited to Mabel Normand (see below). Written by Charles Chaplin. Directed by Charles Chaplin and Mabel Normand. Photography attributed to Frank D. Williams. Reissue titles include *The Waiter*, *The Jazz Waiter* and *Faking With Society*. Two reels. 2,052 feet (UK length cited in *Bioscope*).

Mabel extracts her vengeance at the end of **Caught in a Cabaret**
BFI Stills, Posters and Designs

*The nominal Chaplin-Normand collaboration on **Caught in a Cabaret** is commemorated in this UK advertisement*

With Charlie Chaplin (the waiter), Mabel Normand (society girl), Harry McCoy (Mabel's erstwhile fiancé), Alice Davenport (Mabel's mother), Hank Mann (Mabel's father), Edgar Kennedy (café owner), Chester Conklin (second waiter), Mack Swain (burly restaurant patron), Minta Durfee (hootchy-kootchy dancer), Gordon Griffith (boy), Phyllis Allen, Alice Howell, Joseph Swickard, Wallace McDonald (in the café).

Charlie waits at table in a rough café-cum-dance hall. He departs for lunch with both his pet sausage dog and strict orders to return on time. Charlie and his dog create a nuisance in the park, but Charlie becomes a hero when saving a society girl from an attempted robbery. Her would-be suitor is unamused, but the girl is much impressed by her rescuer and invites him home. Charlie introduces himself with a bogus visiting card, implying he is a VIP. Charlie is introduced to the girl's parents, and accepts an invitation to their party. The girl's other admirer follows Charlie as he hurries back to work. Peering into the café, he learns Charlie's true status.

Charlie receives a kick in the pants for being late, then gets into a scuffle with another waiter. He has an even bigger fight on his hands when the second waiter cannot budge a burly patron. Charlie is given the job, and orders the man to leave. The customer pulls a gun, and Charlie pretends to take his order. Charlie brings him a drink before administering cranial massage with a large mallet. The unconscious man is dragged away and the dancing continues, Charlie giving the second waiter a thump on the head for good measure. The society girl's party is in full swing as Charlie, in top hat and frock coat, sets off. He is greeted royally, except by his rival for the girl. Inspired by the party's musicians, Charlie serenades the girl, who is charmed if a little unnerved by her guest's increasing drunkenness. When Charlie exits, staggering, his rival suggests a 'slumming' visit to the café. Back at work, Charlie, aghast to see the society crowd, pretends to be slumming there himself. The owner gives the game away, and a fight breaks out, culminating in Charlie being pursued by a furious, gun-toting employer. Charlie knocks him cold and returns to the society girl, who rejects his pleas.

Caught in a Cabaret represents a successful reconciliation between Chaplin and Mabel Normand (*qv*), with whom Chaplin had conflicted during the making of *Mabel at the Wheel* (*qv*). They shared responsibility for directing this film, albeit, significantly, from a screenplay by Chaplin. Contemporary advertising describes *Caught in a Cabaret* as having been produced by Mabel Normand. Chaplin's greater control over its content is reflected in a *Bioscope* review of 22 October 1914, stating that 'Mr. Chaplin has a humour all his own ... [which] he has the opportunity of indulging to the utmost.' Well-

constructed, and with the comparative luxury of two reels, this is one of the more durable Keystones, despite mutilation in various reissues. A version with added music indulges in a trick effect for the finale, when by reverse printing Charlie seems repeatedly to get up after Mabel has knocked him down. This is followed by an 'end' title declaring it 'A Keystone Comedy', albeit superimposed over the final shot of an Essanay film, *The Tramp* (*qv*)! This edition has further been 'improved' with rewritten sub-titling, incorporating old and unnecessary verbal jokes on the lines of, 'You scoundrel, I wish I was that boy's father,' to which the answer is, 'Well, why don't you talk it over with his mother?' Though unattributed in the copy viewed by the author, such titling was added to several reissued Keystones by Syd Chaplin (*qv*). It is this version that is excerpted in *The Funniest Man in the World* (*qv*); one title, in which Chaplin tries to eject Mack Swain (*qv*) with a simple 'OUT!' has been clumsily spliced in, losing the moment where Swain knocks him to the ground. This moment is intact in the Blackhawk Films print and a copy supplied to European TV and video. There is some uncertainty as to the precise identity Charlie adopts for his society friends: the retitled copy shows a card reading 'O.T. Axle, Ambassador for Greece', a punning name doubtless added later; in other material it reads 'Baron Dogbugle, Prime Minister of Greenland'.

(See also: Animals; Conklin, Chester; Dance; Davenport, Alice; Durfee, Minta; Essanay; *Face on the Bar Room Floor, The*; *Her Friend the Bandit*; Kennedy, Edgar; Keystone; *Knockout, The*; MacDonald, Wallace; Mann, Hank; McCoy, Harry; Parks; Politics; Reissues; Video releases; Williams, Frank D.)

CAUGHT IN THE RAIN 🎩

(Chaplin film)

Keystone Comedy released by Mutual, 4 May 1914. Produced by Mack Sennett. Written and directed by Charles Chaplin. Photography attributed to Frank D. Williams. Reissued as *Who Got Stung* and *In the Park* (see below). One reel, 1,015 feet (UK length cited in *Bioscope*).

With Charlie Chaplin (himself), Mack Swain (Ambrose), Alice Davenport (Mrs Ambrose).

Ambrose and his wife are sitting in the park. When Ambrose is visiting a sales kiosk, Charlie, at the drinking fountain, notices Mrs Ambrose. He is flirting and generally being a nuisance when Ambrose returns. Convinced of her infidelity, the furious man takes his wife back to their hotel. Charlie, evidently somewhat drunk, narrowly misses being hit by a streetcar. He stops outside the same hotel and, seeing a pretty girl, follows her inside. In the foyer, Charlie treads on a guest's gouty foot. Checking in, he attempts a fast run upstairs but slides to the floor. After collisions with his fellow-guests, Charlie eventually makes his way upstairs. He enters the wrong room, which just happens to be that occupied by Mr and Mrs Ambrose. The wife is again accused of faithlessness, and Charlie is ejected. In his own room, Charlie prepares for bed, revealing pyjamas beneath his street clothes. Ambrose goes out. His wife begins to sleepwalk; outside, Ambrose is caught in a rainstorm and returns to the hotel just as his somnambulist spouse enters Charlie's room. Charlie watches as she goes through his trouser pockets, carefully removing the garments from her grasp. Ambrose, returning to his bedroom, calls out for his absent wife. A nervous Charlie ventures into the corridor, where Ambrose asks if he has seen his wife. Satisfied with Charlie's denial, Ambrose departs. Back in his room, Charlie is horrified to see Mrs. Ambrose asleep in his bed. She is awakened and hastily escorted back to her own room. Charlie is still with her when Ambrose walks back to his room, and he has to be concealed outside the window, in the pouring rain. A policeman, seeing Charlie, fires a shot, forcing him back inside. Blundering into Ambrose, Charlie rushes into the corridor, but a group of approaching policemen force a retreat into his room. Ambrose at first attacks the police, then directs them to Charlie's room; Charlie sends them running with a thump from his bedroom door, then kicks Ambrose in the stomach. Ambrose collapses on Charlie's bed, while Charlie and Mrs Ambrose follow suit in the corridor.

Chaplin acknowledged *Caught in the Rain* as his first solo effort as writer and director, although a similar case has recently been put for an earlier effort, *Twenty Minutes of Love* (*qv*). The film's basic idea owes a little to that of *Mabel's Strange Predicament* (*qv*), while elements of both were to resurface in the following year's *A Night Out* (*qv*). Confusingly, *Caught in the Rain* has been reissued under the same title as another, later film, *In the Park* (*qv*), although most of the action does not take place there.

(See also: Alcohol; Davenport, Alice; Essanay; Keystone; *Mabel at the Wheel*; Parks; Reissues; Risqué humour; Streetcars; Swain, Mack; Williams, Frank D.)

CENSORSHIP 🎩

(Chaplin films *qv*)
Although public – and private – organizations sought to temper the content of moving pictures from the very beginning, formal censorship only really began to take shape via local authorities and, during 1910–30, on a more centralized basis. Although often deemed risqué, Chaplin's earlier comedies always passed censorship in the USA and Britain (detailed elsewhere is a case of suspected censorship in a reissue of *The Fireman*).

Uno Asplund's Chaplin study is of particular interest for its chronicle of censorship in the author's native Sweden. Though noted later for liberalism, Sweden was, in Chaplin's heyday, extremely strict. *Mabel's Strange Predicament* was considered 'brutalizing' and not shown. The same word was used when banning *Behind the Screen* in 1918, but Asplund believes the censor's true objection was to the homosexual gag with Eric Campbell (*qv*). According to Asplund, the film was granted an 'X' certificate in 1919 and deemed fit for universal exhibition seven years later. 'Brutalizing', clearly the stock expression, was also the rationale for a temporary banning of *Easy Street*. *Caught in the Rain* was banned on initial submission, owing to its bedroom scenes. *The Rounders* arrived in Sweden in 1915, and was not only banned but accused of not being a genuine Chaplin film at all (see **Impersonators**). *A Woman* was submitted for the Swedish censor's approval in 1917, and banned completely. An abridgment was tried in 1920, but the film remained unseen in that country until 1931. *Tillie's Punctured Romance* reached Sweden in 1919, and was totally banned. (In passing, Asplund details a latter-day copy of *Shoulder Arms* imported into Sweden from Germany, from which some of the German officer's greater humiliations had been excised.)

The Kid reached UK audiences only after the British Board of Film Censors removed a gag about checking the baby's sex in order to determine his future name. *A Woman of Paris* seems to have been mostly untroubled by censorship, despite its (for the day) sometimes controversial nature. The party scene – albeit with the implicit presence of a lesbian – is carefully photographed, and there seem to have been no censorship difficulties in the United States. Nor were there any problems surrounding its initial six-week London run, which commenced at the Tivoli on 25 February 1924, or at its appearances in more than 600 provincial theatres around Great Britain; the only exception dates from a year later, when, on 5 March 1925, the *Bioscope* reported a ban in the City of Coventry. In December, the distributors had received a letter from Coventry's Chief Constable stating the film's rejection by the local Watch Committee; there followed six weeks of appeals until a final statement upheld the ban. *Bioscope* pointed out its approval by the British Board of Film Censors, whose judgement was accepted by most local authorities, in addition to noting a critical verdict that *A Woman of Paris* was 'a work of genius'. Given that it was 'in no way subversive of public morals', concluded *Bioscope*, 'the general public may be left to the enjoyment of a new form of puzzle which, for fascination, surely beats the much-vaunted "cross-word" pastime'.

It is believed that the Hays Office disapproved of Chaplin's original intention to lampoon Hitler in *The Great Dictator*, though the comedian's decision was, of course, vindicated. By the time of *Monsieur Verdoux*, that office's strict Production Code has been in effect for over a decade, bringing with it an astonishing set of anomalies. Chaplin was required to guard against exposure 'above the garter' when including a chorus line and, by a fantastic double standard, was permitted to suggest Verdoux's murder of a 'wife', although the office objected to a hint (probably more in the censor's mind than Chaplin's) that they might have engaged in sexual intercourse.

When Gilbert Seldes asked Chaplin to write a preface for his book, *Movies For the Millions*, in 1937, Chaplin took it as an opportunity to lambast the notorious Code, introduced three years earlier. Pointing out the freedoms of the press, novels and the theatre, Chaplin spoke of the difficulties in matching the dramatic events pictured in newsreels when conditions enforced the screenwriter's restriction to 'such subject-matter as a child would read in a rhyming book'. The press, noted Chaplin, had lobbied for strict self-censorship in the film industry on the pretext of shielding young, impressionable minds, yet 'the daily Press features in glaring headlines that any child might read, crimes of violence, strikes and revolutions'. Chaplin's view was that aesthetic criticism might provide a more positive yardstick, in addition to rendering unsuitable the many films passed by the censors despite 'their lack of good taste, their false standards of life and their vulgar treatment'. By contrast, Chaplin believed that 'many forbidden subjects, if judged by aesthetic standards, might be beneficial and constructive, if excelling in artistry, and treated with dignity and intelligence'.

(See also: *Bank, The*; Risqué humour; Swain, Mack)

THE CHAMPION 🎩

(Chaplin film)
Released by General Film Company, 11 March 1915. Produced by Essanay. Written and directed by Charles Chaplin. Photographed by Harry Ensign. British title: *Champion Charlie*. Two reels. 1,939 feet (UK length cited in *Bioscope*).
With Charlie Chaplin (himself), Bud Jamison (Young Hippo), Leo White (crooked gambler), Edna Purviance (girl), Ben Turpin (ringside vendor), G.M. Anderson (spectator), Spike (dog).

A title introduces 'Charlie, a would-be pugilist'. He stops for lunch, consisting of a hot dog withdrawn from an inside pocket, contained in a roll retrieved from within his hat. Charlie's bulldog is offered some of the meat, but seems interested only after his master has taken a bite. Nearby, an aspiring boxing champion named Spike arrives at his training camp. Lunch over, Charlie continues on his way and sees the fighter's advertisement for sparring partners. Charlie dismisses the idea until he finds a horseshoe and, thus fortified with luck, steps in. The boxer tries Charlie with a few practice blows before

eliminating several existing sparring partners. As they are carried out, Charlie, growing increasingly nervous, inserts the horseshoe into his glove. When it is his turn, he knocks the fighter unconscious with the loaded glove. Spike's trainer is much impressed, the more so when Charlie fends off the fighter a second time. Charlie pursues the terrified scrapper into the street, but is interrupted by a policeman. The fighter continues to run. Charlie has to elude a second policeman to re-enter the training camp, where he is carried around like a hero. The fighter is seen hopping aboard a freight train. Forgetting his weighted glove, Charlie slaps his new friends on the back, and the entire party collapses. 'Young Hippo', the champion, is in training. Hippo's trainer shows him a newspaper, announcing the forthcoming bout between Young Hippo and Charlie, the challenger. Charlie is also in training, using Indian clubs, a punch ball that fights back and barbells. Charlie's diet consists of frequent draughts from a jug of beer. As the fight nears, Charlie divides his attention between the barbells and an equally shapely female assistant, Edna. Charlie's trainer has him run round around the camp, having first been careless with the starting pistol. Charlie tries the skipping rope, as Edna looks on; he is then approached by a crooked gambler, who offers Charlie a wad of money if he will throw the fight. Charlie rejects the offer, knocks the man flat and takes the money anyway. The crook follows Charlie into the gym and offers even more money; Charlie, pondering the scheme, scratches the villain's head in mistake for his own. Despite being pummelled by barbells

and punch ball, the crook continues with his scheme. They discuss the deal in the seclusion of the shower; Charlie refuses to co-operate, and when the villain draws a pistol, Charlie gives him a soaking. He is driven from the gym, then finished off with a well-aimed medicine ball. The evening of the fight arrives. Both Charlie and Hippo are limbering up, Charlie shaking his bulldog firmly by the paw as he departs for the ring. The crooked gambler takes his place amid the spectators, just in time to be clambered over by a ringside vendor. Charlie makes an impressive entrance, tripping over the ropes. Charlie's ringcraft consists primarily of evasive action, but Hippo manages, at length, to knock him down. The bout continues, the participants in and out of clinches, each managing the occasional knock-down. One of these catches the referee. There have been several rounds but Charlie notices a ringside card that still reads '1'. He changes it to '20' and the bout continues. The fight is going Hippo's way until Charlie's bulldog, which has joined the spectators, rushes into the fray. The dog clamps his jaws around Hippo's behind as Charlie, taking advantage of his opponent's new handicap, delivers a series of knockout blows. 'To the victor ...' says a sub-title, preceding a shot of Charlie and Edna; '... belong the spoils,' continues the next, as they kiss, their heads concealed by Charlie's jug of beer.

A semi-remake of Arbuckle's *The Knockout* (qv), *The Champion* differs by placing Chaplin in the rôle of pugilistic newcomer and through fewer diversions from the immediate setting. The dog,

The Champion *begins with a hungry Charlie and his choosy pooch*

The Champion: *Leo White tries to influence the result ... but is sent on his way*

named Spike, is sometimes referred to as such in descriptions of the film, though available prints do not name him in the titling. This reduces the evident irony of two characters ('boxers'?) bearing that name, the other being the heavyweight whom Charlie dismisses with a loaded glove. Oddly, the title cards in available prints describe him as 'Spike Hennessy', despite a sign that reads 'Spike Dugan's Training Quarters'.

'There can be few comedians,' said a *Bioscope* review of 6 May 1915, 'who obtain their effects with the apparent ease and simplicity which characterises the art of Charles Chaplin,' though allowing that his skill with elaborate business was far from accidental, being instead 'the result of many years' study and hard work', this combined with 'exceptional natural gifts'. 'He is, in short,' it was decided, 'a man with a great talent who has developed that talent to the uttermost.' *The Champion* (or *Champion Charlie*, as it was called in Britain) was deemed 'as funny a Chaplin film as one has seen', blending 'Chaplin and pugilism – two of England's most popular institutions' in a manner guaranteed to 'bring down almost any house'. The reference to Chaplin as an English institution is an interesting one, reflecting perhaps his existing stage reputation in the UK as much as popular acceptance of his film work in America.

Many current prints of *The Champion* – including an otherwise good copy from Blackhawk Films – are missing

a large section beginning after the recovery of 'Spike' the prizefighter from Charlie's initial blows up to the point where a title card introduces 'Young Hippo'. Thus are lost all scenes of Spike's attempt to fight back, his flight from the training camp, Charlie's encounters with police, his subsequent reception, and Spike's departure by train. One UK video release follows Blackhawk's version; another omits the opening 'lunch' scene, but includes the complete section described above. The BBC *Chaplin SuperClown* copy is complete but for the brief shot of Spike boarding the freight train (though part of the climactic boxing match is transferred at an accelerated speed, presumably for reasons of time). There is little excuse for such an oversight, this shot being available even in a one-reel 8mm abridgment.

(See also: Alcohol; Camera-looks; Fighting; Home movies; Jamison, William 'Bud'; Karno Company, The; Reissues; Risqué humour; Stockdale, Carl; Television; Vagrancy; Video releases; Villains; Women)

CHAMPION CHARLIE

See: *Champion, The*

CHAPLIN
(1992)

(Chaplin Films *qv*)
Richard Attenborough's Chaplin biopic

(produced by Attenborough and Mario Kassar, and directed by Attenborough), known as *Charlie* in its earlier production stage, was an ambitious and, on the face of it, worthwhile project. Attenborough's track record, including as it did the 1982 epic, *Gandhi*, suggested a talent equal to the task of chronicling Chaplin's long, unusually eventful life. (A prior dramatization, TV's *Young Charlie Chaplin* (*qv*), had drawn six 25-minute episodes from the early years alone.) An immediate problem was in finding an actor capable of playing Chaplin. A few hearts sank when an American was announced for the part, but in the end Robert Downey Jr proved remarkably effective. The Americans and the British are notoriously bad at impersonating each other's accents, but Downey's London tones were creditable in the extreme, even during the gradual process of polishing up Chaplin's diction (though, as noted elsewhere, there is some doubt as to whether Chaplin ever spoke with a noticeably downmarket accent). For the benefit of a visiting TV news team, Downey was able to demonstrate several bits of Chaplin 'business' – among them the ear-twisting/smoke-blowing gag – of a type less often in evidence in *Chaplin*'s final cut. Though reassured by the casting, several eyebrows were genially raised – as in the *South London Press* – when it was made known that Chaplin's childhood exploits were to be filmed north of the Thames. The explanation was that too many of the original locations had been demolished, though, as the author pointed out in a contemporary magazine article, much of Victorian South London has survived intact.

The account of Chaplin's early life is striking, made all the more poignant by the casting of Geraldine Chaplin as her own grandmother, Hannah. An interesting point is made by having the same actress, Moira Kelly, portray both Hetty Kelly, Chaplin's first love, and Oona, his last. Most of the story is framed by a conversation during the preparation of Chaplin's autobiography, between Chaplin and a (fictitious) publisher's representative, played by Anthony Hopkins (the film cites Chaplin's *My Autobiography* and David Robinson's *Chaplin: His Life and Art* as source material). This serves both to speed the narrative and suggest the reasons for certain omissions from Chaplin's memoirs. A certain degree of licence, not uncommon in biographical films, seems to have been taken concerning points of detail, along with a compression of time. Charles Chaplin Sr (*qv*) is barely referred to, let alone depicted; Chaplin's stage work of 1898–1907 makes way instead for a very young-looking Charlie auditioning for Fred Karno (*qv*), played by a perhaps surprisingly northern-accented John Thaw; the presence of Rollie Totheroh (*qv*) is hinted at during Keystone days, establishing him in the story far too soon; the Essanay and Mutual films – which, for many people, are the films evoked by Chaplin's name – are concertinaed with disconcerting brevity; while also overlooked are the making of *The Circus* and Chaplin's concurrent, traumatic divorce from Lita Grey (*qv*) (portrayed by Deborah Maria Moore, one of the film's better lookalikes). The same applies to *Monsieur Verdoux*, which was a key factor in America's condemnation of Chaplin in the 1940s. One might also conclude that Chaplin did very little in the twenty years following his exile from the USA, given the absence of any reference to *A King in New York*, *A Countess From Hong Kong* or indeed any of his activities apart from the autobiography.

It is, of course, difficult to convey Chaplin's lengthy, complex history within a comparatively short space (as the author knows only too well!). Prior to the film's release, Richard Attenborough told *Film and Television Technician* of the problems in telling such a story in a movie that needed to play twice in one evening, and that the film had been overlength (there is, at the time of writing, word of a laserdisc containing additional footage). This implies the swift narrative to have been the consequence of heavy cutting; the author's impression on first seeing the film was, 'If it's Tuesday, it must be Essanay.' There are several instances wherein key characters and events may have been painted rather more broadly than one might have preferred. Mabel Normand (*qv*) – strangely, represented as a high-cheekboned blonde, rather than as a round-faced brunette – might also have been portrayed more sympathetically, or at least her talent more fully acknowledged. (Further, one of a few highly debatable points amid the film's concluding résumés is that Mabel did not act on screen after 1922.)

The film really comes to life when Downey imitates Chaplin's comic set-pieces, notably when playing the drunk

in *Mumming Birds* – a magnificent scene, apparently filmed at the Hackney Empire – or when proving his capabilities to a sceptical Mack Sennett (played by Dan Aykroyd). There are occasions when the narrative slips into pastiche silent-movie style, the best of them being that in which *The Kid* has to be edited while in hiding.

There are a number of extracts from Chaplin's own films, understandably avoiding close facial recognition until the final collage, as a tearful, octogenarian Chaplin watches a montage of his work at the 1972 Oscar ceremonies. Here one appreciates a conscious departure from narrative in favour of a tribute to Chaplin's legacy, a body of films immune to any of the disasters befalling the man who made them. Chaplin's last few years – including his knighthood – are covered in the series of résumés mentioned above.

The film received extensive media coverage, both during production and at the time of release; one of the larger spreads was, appropriately, in a Swedish film magazine called *Chaplin*. Critical reaction seemed, at times, unduly harsh, there being instances where, in the author's opinion, reviewers took the opportunity to attack Chaplin himself rather than evaluate this account of his life.

(See also: Awards, honours; Chaplin, Hannah; Childhood; Children; Documentaries, compilations; Early stage appearances; Essanay; Impersonators; Karno Company, the; Keystone; Music; Mutual; O'Neill, Oona; Smoking; Video releases; Women)

CHAPLIN, CHARLES JR
See: Children

CHAPLIN, CHARLES SR
(1863–1901)

The name 'Charles Chaplin' first became known to paying audiences before the more familiar 'Charlie' was born. An obituary in the *Era* of 11 May 1901 suggests that Chaplin's father took to the stage around 1886, a year following his marriage to Hannah Hill (see **Chaplin, Hannah**). In *Chaplin: His Life and Art*, David Robinson notes that Chaplin Sr gave his occupation as 'professional singer' at the time of marriage, but doubts that either he or Hannah had yet begun such a career. As noted in the entry for Hannah Chaplin, historian

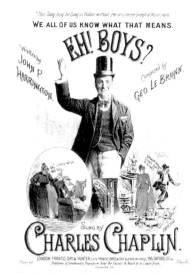

Charles Chaplin Sr *was the named artist on several published songs*
By courtesy of Tony Barker

Barry Anthony has located engagements for Hannah dating back to May 1884, and also suggests that the elder Chaplin may have appeared in minor establishments of the type unreported in the theatrical press. It should be noted that many of the profession's newcomers and lesser lights in general were obliged to perform at informal venues ranging between clubs and, at the lower extreme, impromptu platforms arranged for the occasion. At first specializing in 'mimicry', Chaplin Sr was soon recognized as a comic singer in his own right. Some indication of his comparatively swift rise to popularity may be gleaned from a reference in the *Entr'acte* of 1890, describing him as 'The Already Eminent and Popular Comedian'. His itinerary for the first five months of that year alone was a busy one, taking him to the People's Palace in Newcastle, the Palace in Nottingham, London's Oxford and Standard music-halls, the Brighton Alhambra, London again, the City Varieties in Leeds, then back to London for engagements at the Canterbury and Paragon music-halls. Reviewing his Paragon appearance on 17 May, the *Entr'acte* considered Chaplin's songs 'good in subject and their virtues well revealed by the excellent treatment awarded them by their sponsor, who knows how to get effect'. Chaplin's likeness, as captured by artist H.G. Banks, appears on several published songs for which he is the named artist. Among these are *Oui! Tray Bong! Or My Pal Jones* (written and composed by Norton Atkins); *The Girl Was Young and Pretty* (written and composed by Chaplin Sr); *As the Church Bells Chime* (written by Norton Atkins, composed by Felix McGlennon); and *Eh! Boys?* (written by John P. Harrington, composed by George Le Brunn). Barry Anthony notes another title, *Everyday Life*, which the elder Chaplin is believed to have shared, ironically, with Leo Dryden (see **Dryden, Wheeler**). The nature of these songs is essentially that of the 'masher', or man-about-town, out on the razzle with a group of like-minded revellers. This 'lion-comique' style had been in vogue since at least the days of George Leybourne and Alfred Vance, and would survive into a slightly later generation through such artists as George Lashwood. On 4 October 1931, the *New York Herald-Tribune* covered a reunion between Charlie Chaplin and his former colleague in 'The Eight Lancashire Lads' (see **Early stage appearances**), George Carney, who was then appearing in *The Good Companions*. The article dwelt somewhat on Chaplin Sr, mentioning the debut of *Oui! Tray Bong!* at the Old Gaiety, Birmingham, and of his audience's insistence on six encores of the song at Seabright's in London. It was noted also that Chaplin Sr introduced Carney to his wife, Jenny Pine, on a music-hall itinerary that allegedly featured Hannah – billed under her stage name of Lily Harley – elsewhere on the programme.

The marriage to Hannah did not endure. Once they had parted, Charles took up residence with his mistress, Louise. According to Chaplin's memoirs, they had a son, who went by his mother's surname and of whom no further details seem to have surfaced. Opinions vary as to whether this child was genuinely Chaplin Sr's or that of Louise from an earlier relationship. Young Charlie saw his father onstage – he mentioned seeing him at the Canterbury music-hall, in London – but the estranged parent was not meeting his maintenance payments, causing Hannah the added stress of taking legal action. When Hannah broke down and entered a mental hospital, Syd and Charlie were sent to live with Charles Sr and Louise, an arrangement that lasted until Hannah's release.

One of the occupational hazards of the music-hall profession was its precariousness, as noted of Chaplin Sr in the *Era* obituary: 'Of late years Chaplin was not fortunate, and good engagements, we are afraid, did not often come his way.' He was therefore easy prey for another risk of the profession, a social aspect centring around drink. Like many of his contemporaries, Chaplin Sr developed a chronic and ultimately fatal alcohol problem (the *Era* used the term 'dropsy'), probably not assisted by having a brother, Spencer Chaplin, who owned several pubs in the Lambeth area. When Charles Sr died in St. Thomas's Hospital, London, he was only 37. He was recalled by his son and namesake with a mixture of pride and disappointment, in consideration both of his achievements and of the circumstances surrounding his early death. Charles Chaplin Sr was portrayed by Ian MacShane in the 1989 TV serial *Young Charlie Chaplin* (*qv*).

(See also: Alcohol; Birth; *Chaplin* (1992); Childhood; Documentaries, compilations; Early stage appearances; Food)

THE 'CHAPLIN CRAZE'

'There is no one more talked about than the inimitable Charlie Chaplin,' claimed *Pictures and the Picturegoer* on 18 September 1915. 'In fact, the world is Chaplin-mad,' it continued, describing his name as being 'on everybody's lips, from the smallest street arab to the biggest City "pot"', going on to cite various insane press rumours to the effect that Chaplin might be in an asylum or prison, or 'blind, deaf, dumb, dead, or even a nervous wreck'. (The magazine ran a potted biography at the time, simply to dispel the more outlandish claims.) Similar speculation would later mar the comedian's existence, but in the middle of the second decade of the century it was all part of a more positive obsession dubbed the 'Chaplin Craze'. Virtually everything about Chaplin was a talking point, even his famously white teeth, often bared in a grin that could range from the coy to the downright mischievous.

The flood of Chaplin publicity could often be indirect. One example dates from October 1916, when Marie Doro, then with Famous Players-Lasky, was photographed by the press, herself supposedly taking a close-up picture of studio colleague Blanche Sweet; she was supposedly using a miniature camera presented to her by Chaplin, with whom she had appeared in *Sherlock Holmes* eleven years before. This level of silliness manifested itself further in the various other names given to the 'Chaplin Craze',

among them 'Chaplinoia' and, more commonly, 'Chaplinitis'. Another *Pictures and Picturegoer* report describes an outbreak in Forres, a small town in Scotland: 'No one is exempt from its ravages, and doctors cannot find an antidote for it. It affects the laughter part of the system, causing pains in the side and a running of water from the eyes.' In Scotland, as elsewhere, the demand for film prints was such that, in June 1915, a Glasgow distributor, Green's Film Service, ran a trade ad declaring in large type their practice of buying four copies of each Chaplin subject.

There were innumerable publications cashing in on the trend, among them a publication devoted to Chaplin jokes, called *Moviegrins*. There were several comic strips (see **Caricatures**) and, at the opposite end of the market, serious attention in such august journals as the *Tatler*, which published a large cover portrait of Chaplin out of costume on 15 March 1916 (describing him as 'possibly the widest-known personage in the world'). Despite occasional jokes at Chaplin's expense, *Punch* devoted almost a full page in praise of his talents in the issue of 1 September 1915. One of the most influential essays was that by written in 1916 for *Harpers Weekly* by distinguished actress Minnie Maddern Fiske.

Musical shows would often include dance numbers based on Chaplin, sometimes dressing chorus girls in the appropriate costume. One item, 'That Charlie Chaplin Walk' (words and music by Nat D. Ayer) appeared in the musical *Watch Your Step*; other songs of the period include 'The Moon Shines Bright On Charlie Chaplin' (much recorded at the time), 'Charlie Chaplin, the Funniest of Them All', 'Funny Charlie Chaplin', 'Those Charlie Chaplin Feet' and, in a vague tie-in to *A Jitney Elopement* (*qv*), 'The Jitney Bus'.

W.C. Fields, whom legend insists either decried or ignored Chaplin, was sufficiently aware of him to include a

reference in contemporary sketch material. Wes D. Gehring's *W.C. Fields: A Bio-Bibliography* details a 1919 stage skit by Fields, 'The Mountain Sweep Stakes', sending up various film personages of the day; the hero of the tale, 'Lew "Left-foot" Chaplin', repeats the gag in *The Adventurer* (*qv*), wherein ice cream slides down Charlie's leg, slides through a grating and, ultimately, lands on a dowager's back. The same source quotes Sara Redway's interview with Fields for the September 1925 *Motion Picture Classic* in which Fields, with surprising generosity, names Chaplin as 'the

greatest of all comedians', nominating the ice cream gag as perhaps the funniest he had seen.

The 'Chaplin Craze' brought with it the inevitable impersonators (*qv*), toys, dolls, statuettes, costumes, cut-outs and even animated cartoons. Although the frenzy for Chaplin goods had abated somewhat by the 1920s, there were still novelties to be had, something which remains true even today.

(See also: Animation; 'Bogus Chaplins'; Children; Early stage appearances; Mental illness; Music; Stamps, coins; Walk, The)

CHAPLIN, HANNAH
(1865 or 1866–1928)

Chaplin's mother, *née* Hannah Hill, was, on her mother's side, part-gypsy. Her father, Charles Hill, was an Irish émigré who owned a bootmaker's in East Lane, Walworth (the street where her son, Charlie, was to be born). Hannah was a soubrette on the music-hall stage (as was her younger sister, Kate), working under the name of Lily (sometimes Lilly or Lillie) Harley. Historian Barry Anthony has traced engagements for Hannah (listed in the *Entr'acte*, a theatrical paper) from at least as early as 24 and 31 May 1884, at the Bijou Music Hall, Blackfriars Road. Another historian, Frank Scheide, has found 'Lily Harley' billing at the Castle music hall, Camberwell Road, for 25 November of that year.

A seeming absence thereafter may be explained by her subsequent claim to have gone to South Africa with a wealthy Jewish man named Sydney Hawkes, by whom she bore an illegitimate son in March 1885. Some commentators believe Hawkes to have been no more than a deceiver, his reputed wealth a mere fabrication; also in doubt is the child's birthplace, reported usually as being in South Africa, but said by others to have been in London, after the hasty return of a disillusioned Hannah (at least source quotes Syd's birthplace as 57 Brandon Street, Walworth, the family home at the time).

Three months after giving birth, Hannah married Charles Chaplin Sr (*qv*), whom she had known previously. The child was given his stepfather's surname, and thus became Sydney (or Sidney) Chaplin (*qv*). In July 1885, 'Lily Harley' was listed among the attractions at the Castle Music Hall, Camberwell,

and is believed to have appeared in Dublin, Belfast and Glasgow from December 1885 to January 1886. In the short term, Hannah's career on the halls thrived rather more than is popularly supposed; again, the *Entr'acte* furnishes details, her Scottish engagements occupying at least the first two months of 1886, then a return to London at the Peckham Varieties; from the summer until the end of the year, she could be seen in Bristol, Glasgow, Belfast, Edinburgh, Aberdeen and Dundee. These mostly provincial dates – and a comparatively minor London booking – might, to the uninitiated, suggest a comparatively unsuccessful artist, but it should be remembered that a large number of performers based their careers on such engagements and were quite capable of sustaining themselves with few, if any, bookings at the top-echelon London halls. Her cards in the *Entr'acte* included the following announcement:

Something like success, girls eh? Lily Harley has made a most brilliant hit at the Gaiety and Star, Glasgow, four or five turns every night and heaps of flowers …

As Barry Anthony has observed, such things as Hannah's swift re-engagement at the Folly, Glasgow, suggest an escalating popularity, despite the tendency of such announcements towards exaggeration. David Robinson's *Chaplin: His Life and Art* notes the disappearance of Hannah's engagements from another theatrical paper, the *Era*, in the autumn of 1886. The reason for this is suggested in the *Entr'acte* of 29 January 1887, which published this message: 'To Charles Chaplin — send address to "L.H.", 56 Darwin Street, Old Kent Road, Very ill.' The implication is that Hannah's health problems, and Charles' casual attitude towards his wife, may have commenced at an earlier date than is often assumed. It is probable that, following a period of convalescence, she resumed her career playing minor venues – of the sort overlooked by the trade press – in the weeks immediately preceding her next appearance in the *Entr'acte*, after a gap of almost two years, on 17 November 1888. There is a hint of desperation in her advertisement, which reads: 'The original and refined Lily Harley – terrific success nightly after her indisposition. Bedford, special concerts. Open for pantomime.'

The younger Charles Chaplin was born in April 1889, though it is evident

that his father had left the family home within about a year of the birth. Hannah attributed the failure of their marriage to her husband's drinking. Charlie was aware of his father only on stage, save for one chance meeting on the street. Charlie and Syd idolized their mother. Charlie recalled her violet-blue eyes and long, brown hair and made it plain that her skills as performer and storyteller, albeit at home, influenced most of his later work. As a family unit, albeit fatherless, they were initially quite prosperous. Hannah did not need to rely on her husband's income (an estimated £40 per week, most of which was spent on alcohol) until her own career began to falter, the result of escalating problems with her throat (the probable cause of her 'indisposition' towards the end of 1886). During 1891, she was both working on stage and involved with music-hall singer Leo Dryden who, in November of that year mentioned 'Lillie Harley' in an *Era* announcement to the effect that she was among the few artists permitted to use his song 'Opportunity'. In a later reminiscence for *Bioscope*, Syd recalled a double-act formed by Hannah and his 'father at the time', whose description closely matches that of Dryden. Hannah gave birth to Dryden's illegitimate son, Wheeler Dryden (*qv*), on 31 August 1892, but the child was taken from her during the following spring. It may have been this birth that led Charles Sr to default on his agreed maintenance payments. Hannah took unsuccessful legal action against him.

Detailed under **Early stage appearances** is young Charlie's debut, in 1894, as a surprise deputy when his mother's voice failed. Although her career

was never to recover, there is evidence of occasional bookings. Chaplin's *My Life in Pictures* reprints a programme for Hannah's appearance – as 'Lily Chaplin' – at the Hatcham Liberal Club, New Cross, as late as 8 February 1896. Although a comparatively small, private venue, this was a far from ignominious engagement. The club (which exists today, though it moved to a different building in the area *c*.1910) often employed headliners, and continued to do so for decades thereafter.

As Hannah's circumstances declined, so she took increasingly to religion, moving more in church circles than those of the music-hall. Her meagre living was made primarily as a seamstress, but this income fell away as her health declined. Hannah's breakdowns and the consequences for her children are detailed under **Childhood**. When *Pictures and the Picturegoer* ran a Chaplin biography in 1915, she was referred to discreetly as 'now unfortunately an invalid at Hove'. She was actually in private care at Peckham, but a problem arose at this time, reportedly owing to a mistake rather than through neglect, concerning Charlie and Syd not paying the necessary fees. Charlie and Syd later arranged for Hannah to be taken to the USA, where she arrived in March 1921. Hannah was provided with a house by the sea and suitable care for the last seven years of her life. She was portrayed by Twiggy in the 1989 TV serial *Young Charlie Chaplin* (*qv*), and by her own granddaughter, Geraldine, in the 1992 biopic *Chaplin* (*qv*). Hannah's year of birth is given as 1865, but the date cited on her grave marker is a year later, probably in error.

(See also: Birth; Childhood; Children; Documentaries, compilations; Early stage appearances; Impersonators; Mental illness; Religion; Women)

THE CHAPLIN REVUE
(1959)

Seven years – and one feature film – after leaving the United States, Chaplin assembled three of his First National productions into a new compilation. *The Chaplin Revue* comprises *A Dog's Life*, *Shoulder Arms* and *The Pilgrim* (all *qv*), sub-titled 'Three Comedies without words'.

Chaplin aide Jerry Epstein (*qv*), who

receives on-screen credit for assisting in the project, states in his book, *Remembering Charlie*, that Chaplin had originally conceived the idea during work on *A King in New York* (*qv*) in 1957. According to Epstein, Chaplin considered filming an introduction parodying the framing devices employed in Somerset Maugham's filmed collections of short stories (*Trio*, *Quartet* and *Encore*); Chaplin would be seen in bed, from behind, seemingly in the company of a young woman. Apologizing for being caught at an 'inopportune moment', he would make his introduction as the audience discovered his bedmate to be a collie dog.

In lieu of this amusing segment, the *Revue* opens with scenes intended for the comedian's abortive semi-documentary, *How To Make Movies* (*qv*). We are shown Hollywood 'before it was visited by the Three Horsemen of the Apocalypse – oil, movies and aeronautics' (Chaplin admits to being 'one of the offenders'). The scene alters rapidly as we are shown stop-motion views of the studio in construction. Once the building is complete, Chaplin is seen arriving for work. Next is a comic rehearsal with Edna Purviance (*qv*), Henry Bergman (*qv*) and diminutive Loyal Underwood (*qv*). Chaplin demonstrates what he wants by shaking the little man vigorously, until, suggests Chaplin jokingly, his arms became tired. Chaplin sits at the make-up mirror, applying his moustache, as the narration proclaims his retreat behind a 'curtain of silence' as *A Dog's Life* begins. This copy is mostly converted to sound speed by a process known as 'stretch-printing'. Every other frame is printed twice, slowing the action to normal speed; this often produces an unsatisfactory, jerky result, but here the effect is quite smooth. One scene is left unstretched, that in which Edna makes a heavy-handed attempt at 'flirting'. Prior to commencing *Shoulder Arms*, Chaplin addresses his audience over First World War footage supplied by the Imperial War Museum. The film itself retains the original opening title card, in which Chaplin signs the credits. This time the stretch-printing is used only at intervals, generally where a hastening of movement would be especially obvious. The same applies to *The Pilgrim*, which Chaplin introduces as the closing credits for *Shoulder Arms* are on screen. Having no wish to give too much away, he describes it, guardedly, as 'the story of an escaped convict who steals some clothes – I won't say what kind. By a coincidence he is mistaken for someone else.' *The Pilgrim* is decorated at its beginning and end by a song, *Bound For Texas*, performed by a then little-known British vocalist named Matt Monro (so little-known, in fact, that his surname is misspelled 'Monroe' on the credits). Monro's reputation started to build soon after, when it was revealed that he had supplied the impeccable Sinatra impression for a Peter Sellers album called *Songs For Swingin' Sellers*.

Chaplin made some slight cuts when preparing his films for the *Revue*. Some of these are detailed elsewhere, but it is worth noting a tightening of the action throughout. In *Shoulder Arms*, Charlie, posing as a German officer, is believed to have been up to no good with the captive French girl; absent from the *Revue* is a section in which Charlie tries to respond by repeating an easily lip-read '*Ja Ja*' several times. Detailed under **Smoking** and in the film's main entry is a cut routine based on the superstition concerning three cigarettes on a single match.

Master material is of excellent quality except for one momentary piece of damage, again in *Shoulder Arms*, when Charlie is relieved from sentry duty: a splice in the original is surrounded by a few frames bleached from decomposition, though this is passed off as one of several explosions by a suitable effect from the orchestra.

The comedian composed a new score for the occasion, arranged by Eric James and Eric Spear. Although prepared in London, the soundtrack album was also issued in the USA. The film itself does not seem to have been released in the USA at that time; F.C. MacKnight, in *Classic Film Collector*, recalled having first seen the *Revue* in Canada. This may account for the *Revue* stills that circulate bearing the United Artists logo. Its first screening seems to have been in Paris (as *La Revue de Charlot*) during September 1959, with Chaplin in attendance.

Originally 125 minutes, *The Chaplin Revue* has often been revived in dismembered form. Invariably, *A Dog's Life* has been shown independently, with an opening title of a design similar to that of the *Revue*'s credits but differing from that used in the compilation itself. *Shoulder Arms* and *The Pilgrim* were reissued as a pair (incorporating Chaplin's introduction), omitting the *Revue* titling, and billing what was left as 'two comedies without words'. A small sound edit removed reference to Chaplin having composed

two hours of new music, while a similar cut did the same for Chaplin's 'curtain of silence' remark, which, as noted above, was designed originally to herald *A Dog's Life*. BBC Television, which also screened *A Dog's Life* as a separate entity, advertised this abridgment as 'The Chaplin Revue'. Later screenings on Channel 4 have separated the three films entirely, omitting Chaplin's links and with his spoken comments deleted from *Shoulder Arms*' closing credits. Publicity for a Prague equivalent, entitled *Charlie X2*, suggests a version comprising only *A Dog's Life* and *Shoulder Arms*. The original American video release omitted Chaplin's introduction, but this has been remedied in more recent tapes. Laserdisc collectors can now obtain the films, at the correct speed and 'unstretched', with Chaplin's cuts reinstated. There has yet to be a video edition in Britain.

(See also: Ballet; Costume; Documentaries; compilations; Music; Politics; Reissues; Television; Titling; Trick photography; United Artists; Wartime)

THE CHAPLIN STUDIO

See: First National and *How To Make Movies*

CHAPLIN, SYD
(1885–1965)

The origins of Sydney (or Sidney) Chaplin, Charlie's half-brother, are detailed elsewhere (see **Chaplin, Hannah**). His early professional training, from the age of eleven, was for the sea; as an older boy, he was more often out on his own than Charlie, being little in evidence when Charlie was living with Charles Chaplin Sr (*qv*). Syd later went off alone hop-picking and, for a while, took a job as telegraph boy. He returned to the sea with the Donovan & Castle Line as a bugler, which eased the family finances for a while. On his second trip, he was put ashore in Cape Town, suffering from rheumatism. There was no word from him for weeks, a period during which his mother went insane and was ultimately admitted to a mental hospital. Although both Charlie and Syd intended to pursue acting careers, it was the younger brother who was given his first real opportunity, in *Sherlock Holmes* (see **Early stage appearances**). Syd, who

for a while worked as a barman at a music-hall haunt, the Coal Hole pub in the Strand, later joined him in a provincial tour of the play. Syd's break came in 1906, when Fred Karno (*qv*) signed him up – and sent him briefly to America – after spotting him in a touring comedy troupe run by Charlie Manon. Syd introduced Charlie to Karno in 1908. From here, Charlie began to make his own reputation, particularly after travelling to America. When Charlie left Keystone (*qv*) late in 1914, he recommended Syd as his replacement. Syd spent a year at the studio, usually playing a character called 'Gussle'; his best-known Keystone is *A Submarine Pirate* (1915).

Syd afterwards spent much of his time handling Charlie's interests, and very well – he negotiated the contracts with Mutual and First National (both *qv*), and the first, informal meeting of United Artists (*qv*) was held at his home. The general opinion is that Syd's business skills were the main foundation of his brother's considerable wealth.

Syd did not abandon performing. He appears with Charlie in five films: *A Dog's Life*, *Shoulder Arms*, *Pay Day*, *The Pilgrim* and an item made for the war effort, *The Bond* (all *qv*). In the summer of 1919, Famous Players-Lasky signed Syd to a million-dollar contract, sending him to France to shoot location scenes for the first picture (Syd returned after two months, bearing 30,000 feet of film and the unsurprising opinion that post-war Europe was 'unsettled'). He also worked in the films of others, as in Colleen Moore's *The Perfect Flapper* (1924); his best-known starring vehicles are probably *Charley's Aunt* (1925) and *The Better 'Ole*, a 1927 film directed by Chuck Riesner (*qv*). Charlie named his third son, born in 1926, after Syd. R.J. Minney, a friend of Syd's, drew upon the latter's recollections for a 1954 Chaplin study, *Chaplin: The Immortal Tramp*. Syd spent his last years in France.

(See also: Boats, ships; Books; Campbell, Eric; Childhood; Dual rôles; Karno Company, The; Schade, Fritz; Summerville, George J. 'Slim'; *Young Charlie Chaplin*)

CHAPLIN, SYDNEY EARL
See: Chaplin, Syd; Children; *Countess From Hong Kong, A* and *Limelight*

Syd Chaplin as a young music-hall comic...

... and in 'Archibald' character for a Karno sketch ...

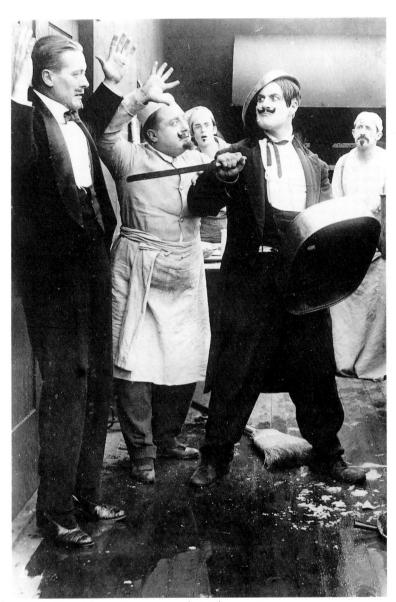

... and in his most famous Keystone comedy, A Submarine Pirate
Portraits by courtesy of Tony Barker

CHAPLIN'S GOLIATH
See: Campbell, Eric

CHARLIE AT/IN THE BANK
See: Bank, The

CHARLIE AT THE SHOW
See: Night in the Show, A

CHARLIE AT WORK
See: Work

CHARLIE BY THE SEA:
See: By the Sea

CHARLIE CHAPLIN'S BURLESQUE ON CARMEN
See: Carmen

CHARLIE IN THE PARK
See: In the Park

CHARLIE IN THE POLICE
See: Police

CHARLIE SHANGHAIED
See: Shanghaied

CHARLIE, THE PERFECT

LADY
See: Woman, A

CHARLIE, THE TRAMP
See: The Tramp

CHARLIE'S ELOPEMENT
See: Jitney Elopement, A

CHARLIE'S NEW JOB
See: His New Job

CHARLIE'S NIGHT OUT
See: Night Out, A

CHASE, CHARLEY
(OR CHARLIE)
(1893–1940)

(Chaplin films *qv*)
Baltimore-born comedian, usually employed in Keystone comedies of the middle of the second decade of the century as little more than a good-looking young man, as in *Love, Loot and Crash* (1915). He may be seen with Chaplin in *The Knockout, The Masquerader, His New Profession, The Rounders, Dough and Dynamite, Gentlemen of Nerve, His Musical Career* and *Tillie's Punctured Romance*; of these, only *His New Profession* gives him any real prominence, although the restored *Gentlemen of Nerve* provides a usually absent moment in which he intimidates Chester Conklin (*qv*). After Chaplin's departure, Chase was allowed to train as a director at Keystone; subsequent acting work included a stint at King Bee, in comedies starring Chaplin imitator Billy West. Chase became director for comedian Lloyd Hamilton *c.*1921 before moving to Hal Roach, where he directed most of the better Snub Pollard films. As a director, Chase was billed as 'Charles Parrott', apparently his real name even though some recent sources claim the reverse (on 11 December 1926, *Picture Show* reported that he had legally changed his name from Parrott to Chase). Confusingly, his brother, James, also directed under the name 'Parrott' but appeared on screen variously as 'Jimmie Parrott' and 'Paul Parrott'. Roach permitted Charley Chase to star in a series of one-reel comedies, commencing in January 1924. Leo McCarey (who later cited Chase as having taught him everything about film-making) took over direction later that year, and the series soon graduated into two-reelers. Chase's best and most inventive work dates from this period, in which his leading-man features and breezy manner contrasted neatly with imaginative visual gags, set within situations designed above all to cause poor Charley the maximum degree of embarrassment. Chase survived more than adequately into the talkie era, remaining almost entirely in short comedies for Hal Roach. When the studio abandoned short subjects (apart from the 'Our Gang' series) in 1936, Chase was tried out in feature work but considered unsatisfactory. He subsequently worked at Columbia, starring in his own two-reelers and

directing those of others, mostly the Three Stooges. His early death, from a heart attack, was the result of an alcohol problem exacerbated by a troubled private life. Charley Chase may perhaps be called the least appreciated of film comedy's authentic geniuses. Although under-used at Keystone and elsewhere, his films for Roach – particularly the silents of 1925–9 – rank among the finest work in the genre, and a great many prominent comedians owed considerable debt to his guidance at various times.

(See also: Goddard, Paulette; Harris, Mildred; Impersonators; Jamison, William 'Bud'; Keystone; Pollard, Harry 'Snub'; Schade, Fritz; Swickard, Joseph)

CHASE ME CHARLIE

(Chaplin films *qv*)
One of the more enigmatic titles in Chaplin filmographies, *Chase Me Charlie* was a feature-length anthology of Essanay comedies assembled in London by the company's representative, Langford Reed, during 1917 (not 1918, as is often stated). A similar collage had been released in America on 23 September the previous year, a five-reeler entitled *The Essanay-Chaplin Revue of 1916*. Contemporary publicity suggests this to have been compiled from *The Tramp, His New Job* and *A Night Out*, starting with Charlie's rescue of a farm girl, his discovery of a rival for her affections, a new career at a film studio and, at the day's end, a drunken spree with Ben Turpin (*qv*). (Rick de Croix, in his 1983 'Fighting For Reappraisal' Chaplin series for *Classic Images*, mentions the hiring of impersonator Graham Douglas to provide linking footage.) According to *Pictures and the Picturegoer* of 1–8 September 1917, Reed's task was to edit 24,000 feet of film into 6,000, 'like a jig-saw puzzle', or in other words to fashion a six-reel feature from various short comedies totalling 24 reels. *Chase Me Charlie* was described as 'the first revue ever filmed' (though allowing that 'he did not actually pose for it'), presumably in ignorance of Essanay's previous compendium and designed as response to a then-current fad for stage revues. Prints of this anthology do not seem to have survived (though a 'Citation Films' release of 1959, bearing the same title, is known to have been compiled from

The Essanay-Chaplin-Revue *was an American precursor of Britain's* **Chase Me Charlie**
By courtesy of Robert G. Dickson

much the same footage), but the published article suggests the film's content to have been similar to its American predecessor.

Reed's story began with Charlie leaving his rural home for London (Reed opted for British place names, despite the films' obviously American setting), in footage derived from *The Tramp*. The girl he rescues, 'Edna Sugar-Plum', is supposed to be the daughter of a rich man, sent to the countryside when proposed to by an unsuitable duke. When another young man seemingly takes precedence in Edna's affections, Charlie continues to London, seeking work (presumably in footage from *His New Job*) but, distracted by his lost love, travels instead to Margate, where he joins a ship's crew (presumably in footage from *By the Sea* and *Shanghaied*). Back on shore, Charlie takes short-lived employment in a bank (*The Bank*) then meets Edna once more, leaning on a gate (again from *Shanghaied*). She explains that the other fellow was her brother; his romance rekindled, Charlie goes out to celebrate (*A Night Out*). Next day he takes a job as sparring partner (*The Champion*) and, aided by a horseshoe, is in line to meet the 'heavyweight champion of Lundy Island'. Charlie emerges as victor and, with the purse, returns to ask Edna's hand (*Shanghaied* again!). Her father arrives and sends him away. They meet again (in footage from *In the Park*), arrange a rendezvous, and go their separate ways. Charlie sees his rival, the 'duke' (Leo White), with another girl; he reports the fact to Edna's father who, refusing to believe such conduct in a duke, once again gives Charlie the boot. Charlie visits an employment office and is sent to a film studio (*His New Job*); he becomes a big star, and is thus sufficiently wealthy for Edna's father to welcome him as son-in-law. Titling for *Chase Me Charlie* (itself a joky, clichéd expression in Britain) was in often excruciating rhyming couplets. An example:

He spent a day at Margate
His misery to lighten,
But his thoughts were in a Blackpool,
His spirits wouldn't Brighton.

Although contemporary British humour had its more advanced practitioners, an essential corniness remained prevalent until after the Second World War. This, in addition to the ruinous effect on the industry of the 1914–18 conflict, may go some way towards explaining why a large number of Britons subsequently preferred to fulfil their ambitions in the United States.

(See also: 'Bogus Chaplins'; Documentaries, compilations; Essanay; Impersonators; Purviance, Edna; Royalty; Wartime; White, Leo)

CHERRILL, VIRGINIA
(1908–96)

Born in Carthage, Illinois, Virginia Cherrill was a society girl, with no background in acting, when Chaplin engaged her as leading lady of *City Lights* (*qv*). Although originally from a moneyed background, the departure of her father, landowner James Cherrill, compelled her mother to obtain work in a private school as a means of financing Virginia's education. Chaplin later recalled their first meeting as having been on a beach, where she approached him with the question, 'When am I going to work for you?' This version has similar currency to a different account, much circulated since the time but known to UK readers of *Picture Show* at least as early as 15 December 1928. In reporting the forthcoming film and its leading lady, *Picture Show* quoted the actress thus: 'I came West to visit Sue Carol, my old school chum ... I really hadn't the slightest idea of going into pictures, though. I had never seen a boxing match, and one night a friend

Virginia Cherrill plays the blind girl in City Lights

invited me to see the Hollywood bouts at the American Legion Stadium. Looking around, I saw a man gazing intently at me. Then I recognized the famous Charlie Chaplin, and was overcome with confusion. I found out afterwards that he was looking so hard at me because he thought I resembled Edna Purviance. The next time I went to the stadium, I found Mr. Chaplin sitting next to me. The man I was with knew him, and introduced me, and the comedian invited me to have a screen test.' Chaplin was pleased to discover her ability to portray a blind girl by looking at him 'inwardly'; she was in this way able to appear sightless while not seeming unattractive. Further, as Miss Cherrill recalled in *Unknown Chaplin* (*qv*), the comedian wanted someone untrained and consequently receptive to his method of directing. In this regard, Virginia was perfect casting but, as noted elsewhere, her fondness for late-night parties nearly caused her to lose the rôle. This was to be their only association, and the actress later admitted a mutual dislike between Chaplin and herself. In the wake of *City Lights*, Virginia Cherrill was signed by the Fox Film Corporation, for whom she appeared in three productions during 1931: an early John Wayne film, *Girls Demand Excitement*, which played New York at the time of *City Lights'* opening; *The Brat* (directed by John Ford); and a Janet Gaynor vehicle, *Delicious*. Her movie career did not progress satisfactorily (she later admitted being 'no great shakes as an actress'), and

concluded after two unmemorable British productions starring James Mason, *Late Extra* (1935) and *Troubled Waters* (1936). By this time she had been married and divorced twice, in addition to her well-publicized engagements to other society men: her first husband was Irving Adler, a Chicago lawyer, whom she wed in 1927 only to divorce a year later (some accounts cite the marriage as being from 1926 to 1927); the second marriage, to actor Cary Grant, began in 1934 but finished in 1935. They met at the première of *Blonde Venus* in 1932 and always remained friendly, to the point where, decades later, Virginia offered to be Grant's 'character witness' in his divorce from actress Dyan Cannon. While in Britain, Virginia met the 9th Earl of Jersey, becoming Lady Jersey on marriage to him in 1937. She spent the Second World War doing charity work, much of it with the American Red Cross, then was divorced from the Earl in 1946. Two years later, she married Florian Martini, a Polish air ace she had met when acting as 'godmother' to 315, the RAF squadron to which he was attached. They moved to Santa Barbara, California, in 1950, remaining there until Virginia's death. The Martinis became a respected couple in the community, Virginia becoming noted for her considerable charity work; her obituary in the Los Angeles *Times* differed from most in being headed 'Virginia Martini' rather than employing her maiden name.

(See also: Purviance, Edna; Sport; Women)

CHILDHOOD

As noted under **Birth**, Chaplin's family told him that he was born in East Street, Walworth, on 16 April 1889. This is the accepted birthplace; a massively discredited work of 1916 (see **Books**) claimed he was born to a well-to-do French family in Fontainebleau, an inaccuracy perpetuated in good faith by his friend, novelist Thomas Burke, in his book *The London Spy* (1922). In *City of Encounters*, published a decade later, Burke mentioned the error while noting a 'certain book of reference' having placed Chaplin's birth in London's East End. The comedian had neither corrected any of these sources nor supplied Burke with the facts. The novelist was unwilling to delve into official records, but thought Chaplin had been born in 'Chester Street, which runs between Kennington Road and Lower Kennington Lane'. Although resolutely a South Londoner, Chaplin is described repeatedly as a 'Cockney' in Burke's text, on the debatable theory that 'true' Cockneys were to be found in what had been London and Westminster's 'earliest suburb', to the immediate south.

Chaplin's early years were spent mostly within a comparatively small radius, encompassing Kennington, Brixton and the area leading up to Westminster. In today's more mobile age, this may seem odd, but at that time people would often spend their entire lives within a single neighbourhood. It should also be recalled that Chaplin was born not only into the music-hall profession but also into its residential suburbs. Kennington, Brixton, Clapham, Balham and Streatham were – and, to some extent, still are – homes to a large number of theatrical types, for whom the attraction at that time was an excellent late-night tramcar service from the West End. Chaplin's account of the area suggests a harsh, downmarket background redolent of Dickens, and although much of the area contained new, somewhat upmarket dwellings, circumstances often forced Hannah and her boys into the less salubrious accommodation that also characterized the neighbourhood. The presence of such varied housing standards within such a small area has led some scholars – mistakenly – to assume Chaplin to have overstated the deprivations of his childhood.

As noted in their respective entries, Chaplin was born to music-hall singers Charles Chaplin Sr and his wife, Hannah, who worked under the name 'Lily Harley'. On their marriage, Charles Sr had accepted and given his surname to Hannah's first child, who became known as Sydney (or Sidney) Chaplin (*qv*). The family's comparative prosperity survived only for a limited period. After settling in Walworth at 68 Camden Street (now Morecambe St.), then at the fairly prestigious West Square, Charles and Hannah parted company around 1890 (a year during which the elder Chaplin appeared in New York). Hannah, her mother and sons moved into comparatively humble lodgings at 94 Barlow Street. Before very long, Charles was failing to pay maintenance. As suggested elsewhere, this may have been the result of Hannah's involvement with another music-hall singer, Leo Dryden, by whom she bore a son, Wheeler Dryden (*qv*) in 1892. Dryden took his son away from Hannah when still an infant. Hannah's career on the music-halls had been troubled even in the late 1880s, and by 1894 her voice had begun to fail to a serious degree; the entry for **Early stage appearances** details the occasion on which the five-year-old Charlie became impromptu deputy for his ailing mother. Hannah's inability to work on the halls, coupled with the absence of support from Chaplin Sr, led to Hannah making something of a living doing odd jobs, primarily as seamstress. Syd went out selling papers, and was once able to supplement their meagre income when he found a laden purse on a bus. As the bills accumulated, Hannah lost her sewing machine, thereby cutting off her income as a seamstress. According to Chaplin's autobiography, in 1895 Hannah was advised to enter Lambeth Workhouse, at Renfrew Road, as a means of forcing her estranged husband to pay maintenance. The account in David Robinson's *Chaplin: His Life and Art*, supported by contemporary documentation, suggests Hannah was instead taken ill in the summer of 1895 and admitted to Lambeth Infirmary; Syd was taken into care by the authorities, variously between Lambeth Workhouse and the West Norwood Schools, while Charlie was for a while in the custody of Hannah's relatives. Hannah's health did not improve sufficiently for the children to be returned; in May 1896, Charlie and Syd were placed in the Newington Workhouse. Chaplin Sr, by this time living with another woman, was prepared to accommodate Charlie but not Syd. To keep them together, in June 1896 the boys were transferred to the Hanwell Schools for Orphan and Destitute Children, located just outside London. Chaplin Sr, deemed able to make a living, was ordered to pay fifteen shillings per week towards the boys' upkeep. The school's regimentation meant they were separated for the first time. Charlie, who had scarcely attended any form of school, received his basic education there, admitting later that Hanwell's treatment was not actually bad except for its strong discipline, administered either with the cane or the birch, and often to boys who had committed no misdemeanour. At the age of seven, Charlie was flogged for a minor deed of which he was in any case innocent. Another traumatic experience was having his head shaved during an outbreak of ringworm. (Chaplin was finally persuaded to revisit Hanwell while in England during 1931. Thomas Burke recorded his reactions, which suggested a certain masochistic pleasure in the experience. Comparing it to 'the dead returning to earth', Chaplin was surprised to see the place extant after a gap of thirty years; 'nothing in America lasts that long,' he claimed.) Syd, when aged eleven, left Hanwell to train for a sea career aboard the *Exmouth*. By the time of Syd's return in 1898, the Hanwell authorities had wearied of Chaplin Sr's irregular payments; his brother, Spencer Chaplin, was the landlord of the nearby Queen's Head pub and settled the arrears (totalling £44 8s). Having decided that Chaplin Sr. should take charge of the boys, the authorities offered a reward of £1 (!) for information concerning his whereabouts. Acting on the word of a Mr Charles Creesey, Chaplin was traced to Kennington Road in December 1897 and arrested. He paid a further sum of £5 6s 3d, but requested that the boys should be discharged into Hannah's care. Hannah, by then living at 10 Farmers Road (presently the site of Kennington Park Gardens), was reunited with her two sons, but continuing money problems enforced frequent 'flits' and a return visit to Lambeth Workhouse, from which the boys were sent back to West Norwood Schools. During their separation, there was a brief reunion when mother and sons contrived a release from their respective institutions, only to return later in the day for re-admission. In September 1898, Hannah went insane and was admitted first to Lambeth Infirmary, then to Cane Hill Asylum. Her boys were sent to live with Chaplin Sr at 289 Kennington Road, where Chaplin resided with his mistress, Louise, and their small son, who was almost four years younger than Charlie. (Chaplin recalled the number as 287, where a plaque has been placed; Robinson has confirmed the address as 289.) Louise, like Chaplin Sr, was a heavy drinker and was not fond of Syd. Hannah was discharged from the asylum in November, and was rejoined by her sons. They were living in comparative comfort at 39 Methley Street, behind Kennington Cross. (A plaque commemorates Chaplin's occupancy of this house.) Charlie was attending Kennington Road School, but was not taught imaginatively, and absorbed very little. He later recalled envy at not being in a school production of *Cinderella*, because the boys who had been chosen for the cast were showing neither effort nor flair, but achieved a measure of fame from his recitation of *Miss Priscilla's Cat*, which Hannah had copied down from a newsagent's window. At the end of 1898, Charlie left to join a touring clog-dancing troupe, 'The Eight Lancashire Lads' (an engagement reportedly obtained through a contact of his father's). His education continued at the various schools in whichever towns they happened to play.

A brief return to Kennington saw Charlie lodging with the show's proprietors, a Mr. and Mrs. Johnson, at 267 Kennington Road, close to Chaplin Sr's lodgings. Charlie remained with the 'Eight Lancashire Lads' until at least the end of 1900. Hannah had written to the troupe's employer, expressing concern for her son's health. The boy was promptly dismissed because of her supposed fussing, but Hannah's fears became justified when Charlie developed asthma. This was in time overcome, despite a reduction in family circumstances that took them to various lodgings before settling at 3 Pownall Terrace (part of an area demolished in the 1960s), virtually opposite Chaplin Sr's residence in the Kennington Road. Hannah was still reliant on sweat-shop sewing and barely able to earn money; there was a brief move away to lodgings with one of Hannah's church friends, but this ended in acrimony and they returned to Pownall Terrace. Chaplin Sr died in May 1901; Charlie last saw him alive in the Three Stags, a pub on the corner of Kennington Road and Lambeth Road, close to the present site of the Imperial

War Museum (the pub survives but, in common with many London hostelries, has recently changed its name as part of an adopted Irish theme). There was talk of Chaplin's funeral being paid for by the Variety Artists' Benevolent Fund, but the amount was met by Albert, his younger brother visiting from Africa. He was buried at Tooting Cemetery.

Charlie tried various means of earning money, variously as flower seller, errand boy, doctor's boy (and subsequently page boy at the physician's home), a job at W.H. Smith's, glassblowing (for one day) and operating a giant printing machine which, from Chaplin's description, seems a direct ancestor of the mechanic-eating monster in *Modern Times* (*qv*). The job finished when Charlie caught influenza and Hannah returned him to school. Syd, utilizing his earlier sea training, obtained a position as a bugler in the Merchant Navy. His advance salary enabled Hannah and Charlie to take better rooms, above a barber's shop in Chester Street. The improved living conditions provided by Syd's money lasted only until the cash was exhausted; Syd returned to sea, while his mother and Charlie moved back to Pownall Terrace. Charlie devised another short-lived enterprise, this time by learning how to make toy boats. His diet was supplemented by eggs appropriated with the assistance of Hannah's father, Charles Hill, who was then being treated in hospital for rheumatism; soon after came the news that Syd, his return overdue, had been put ashore at Cape Town to be treated for the same ailment. Weeks passed before any word arrived from Syd, during which Hannah, whose health was declining owing to malnutrition, lost the little work she received making shirts. Charlie returned home one day to be told by neighbours that she had gone insane. A doctor had been summoned, who on his arrival told Charlie to take Hannah to the infirmary, which he did. Charlie pretended to be staying with an aunt, but returned instead to their empty flat. Hannah was readmitted to Cane Hill, while the landlady kept Charlie in food, despite his reluctance to accept. To avoid being reported to the authorities – and consequently returned to Hanwell – Charlie kept away from home, working among woodcutters. One evening the boss took them to the South London Music Hall to see, prophetically, Fred Karno's *Early Birds*. Once Syd had eventually returned with enough money

to keep them going, the boys visited their mother at Cane Hill.

Both Charlie and Syd were determined to follow theatrical careers, as detailed under **Early stage appearances**. During rehearsals for *Sherlock Holmes*, Charlie and Syd paid a visit to Hannah, who was in a padded room, but rallied a little on seeing her sons. Syd visited her regularly while Charlie was on tour. Syd, less fortunate in his theatrical enquiries, took a job as barman at the Coal Hole, a pub in the Strand that had been one of the embryonic music-halls in the mid-19th century (the 'hole' itself, a downstairs cellar bar, still survives). Charlie arranged for Syd to receive a part in the second *Holmes* tour, and the resultant boost in income enabled them to leave Pownall Terrace for improved lodgings in the Kennington Road. Cane Hill pronounced Hannah recovered, and she joined her sons when they were at Reading. On returning to London, she took the flat they had formerly occupied in Chester Street, with money sent home by Charlie and Syd. During the third tour, she sent news that, ironically, Louise had died in Lambeth Workhouse, and that her son had been sent to the Hanwell school. She visited him on several occasions but, suffering a relapse in her condition, was readmitted to Cane Hill. She remained there for several years until her sons could afford a private nursing home. *Sherlock Holmes* took Charlie into 1906, after which he toured in Wal Pink's sketch, *Repairs*, prior to joining Will Murray's *Casey's Circus* or *The Casey Circus*. Syd, meanwhile, secured himself a place with the Karno Company (*qv*), to which he introduced his younger brother in 1908; at this time, the brothers rented a flat, 15 Glenshaw Mansions, in the Brixton Road near Kennington Oval. From here, Chaplin's adult career may be said to begin, a career which, despite periodic turmoil, would prove to be perhaps the most extraordinary in entertainment history.

This might be the appropriate point to dwell on the subject of Chaplin's original accent. His eventual polished accent is believed by some to be the result of elocution lessons. Chaplin's autobiography states clearly that Hannah ensured Charlie and Syd were taught to speak correctly – logical for a theatrical family. It has been said that Chaplin's polished accent was present even in Karno days, even if his literacy may have needed work (not surprising given his fragmented education). Debatably, the biopic *Chaplin* (*qv*) gives him a somewhat downmarket – if not actually broad – accent, which is gradually refined, with occasional lapses, as time progresses. A September 1915 Chaplin profile in *Pictures and Picturegoer*, describing his on-set manner, refers to his often employing Americanisms but 'in an unmistakable (not Cockney) London dialect'. Thomas Burke, who knew Chaplin from 1921 onwards, remarked on his American way of speech. By contrast, on 20 September 1919, the British magazine *Picture Show* published an account of a visit to Chaplin's studio, in which was mentioned his 'well-bred English voice and clear-cut speech'. In 1982, the author was alternately amused and annoyed when a magazine reviewed a video release of *The Gentleman Tramp* (*qv*), frankly accusing Chaplin of lying about his background (despite overwhelming evidence to the contrary), preferring instead to believe the long-discredited Fontainebleau story. The rationale seems to have been based on the absurd belief that anyone from south London must automatically have been uneducated.

As a footnote to Chaplin's childhood, it may be worth mentioning a film detailed in MacDonald, Conway and Ricci's *The Films of Charlie Chaplin*. Titled *When Charlie Was a Child*, it was not an attempt to chronicle his early days but instead a comedy performed by children in equivalent rôles to those in the contemporary Chaplin films.

(See also: Animals; Birth; Children; Food; Music; Public appearances; Vagrancy; Villains; *Young Charlie Chaplin*)

CHILDREN

(Chaplin films *qv*)
'Children form the majority of my audience,' said Chaplin to *Picture Show* in December 1919, 'and I have to thank them for my position.' A contemporary report in the *Motion Picture News* suggests this not to have been lost on the management of Loew's Theaters in Ohio, who in that same month had secured front-page coverage for *A Day's Pleasure* by arranging a free Christmas première for some 1,500 children from Cleveland's orphanages. On another occasion, Chaplin claimed always to feel more of a child among adults, and there is much of

the disrespectful infant in his screen character. Hal Roach, who worked alongside Chaplin in 1915, often expressed the view that all great comedians, Chaplin included, imitated children, citing as example Chaplin's habit of skidding around corners on one foot. Roach's theory may not apply in every case, but it is a tenable argument with regard to Chaplin.

Perhaps it a sense of rivalry that makes Charlie dismissive or similarly disdainful towards children on screen. They are often depicted as out-and-out brats: the landlady's son in *The Star Boarder*, Dean Riesner (*qv*) in *The Pilgrim* and Robert Parrish (*qv*) (later a respected director) as a newsboy in *City Lights* all come to mind, as does Dee Lampton (*qv*) as the fat boy in *A Night in the Show* and an arrow-happy Cupid in *The Bond*. An *alter ego*, Adenoid Hynkel, is in turn dampened by a baby in *The Great Dictator*. Among the savage residents of *Easy Street*, even a small boy is enough to make policemen flinch.

Charlie does, however, display parental instincts: the prime example is, of course, *The Kid*, but his tenderness towards the baby in *His Trysting Place* is implicit, even when Charlie gives him a revolver as plaything. Charlie is evidently proud of his lookalike sons in *A Day's Pleasure* and one of the deleted sequences from *Shoulder Arms*. The murderous activities of *Monsieur Verdoux*, of course, contrast with a family life that includes a sympathetic young son. Such instincts are

also evident in others; the heroine of *A Woman of Paris* eventually fills her home with adopted orphans, while the orphaned *gamine* of *Modern Times* briefly assumes this rôle with her younger siblings.

Chaplin's first child, a son named Norman Spencer, was the issue of his marriage to Mildred Harris (*qv*). He was born in July 1919 but, being severely handicapped, survived only three days. Chaplin had two sons by his marriage to Lita Grey (*qv*); Charles Spencer Jr, born in 1925, and Sydney Earl (not Earle) in 1926. Chaplin's marriage to Paulette Goddard (*qv*) produced no offspring, but his final spouse, Oona O'Neill (*qv*), presented him with eight more: Geraldine (b. 1944), Michael (b. 1946), Josephine (b. 1949), Victoria (b. 1951), Eugene (b. 1953), Jane (b. 1957), Annette (b. 1959) and Christopher (b. 1962).

Both Charles Jr and Sydney – named after Syd Chaplin (*qv*) but always called 'Tommy' by his mother – served in the Second World War. Charles Jr's career was doubtless not helped by having the hardest act in the world to follow, a problem typified when he was once asked, brusquely, if he was as good as his father. His memoirs, *My Father, Charlie Chaplin*, were first published in 1960, eight years before his early death from a heart attack. Sydney's acting work included rôles in *Limelight* and *A Countess From Hong Kong*; on the stage, he was associated with the Circle Theater (see **Jerry Epstein**), and later drew praise

Children: *Charlie and Oona with six of their children in 1958. From left to right: Jane, Eugene, Victoria, Josephine, Michael and Geraldine*

on Broadway in *Funny Girl*.

Geraldine became an international film star, most notably in *Dr. Zhivago* (1967). In the 1992 film *Chaplin* (qv), she had the unusual experience of portraying her own grandmother, Hannah. Geraldine, Michael and Victoria appear briefly in *Limelight*; Michael plays the child genius in *A King in New York*, and later acting work included a 1966 British comedy, *The Sandwich Man*. Reportedly something of a rebel in the 1960s, Michael wrote a book called *I Couldn't Smoke the Grass on My Father's Lawn*. His former wife, Patrice, has written a biography of Oona. Each of the children has at some time ventured into the entertainment profession. Victoria was intended as lead in her father's last film, *The Freak* (see **Abandoned projects**), but left home to get married. She and her husband, French comedian and illusionist Jean Baptiste Thierrée, have toured the world in their shows *Le Cirque Bonjour* (1971–4), *Le Cirque Imaginaire* (1975–90) and most recently, *Le Cercle Invisible* (1991 to date). Those who attended the latter's season at London's Mermaid Theatre during November 1996 and January 1997 will probably conclude that, of the Chaplin offspring, Victoria's excellent work is the closest in style to her father's.

(See also: *Adventurer, The*; Artists; Books; Chaplin, Hannah; Costume; *Great Dictator, The*; Impersonators; Marriages; Parks; Policemen; Politics; Purviance, Edna; *Unknown Chaplin*; Vagrancy; *Walk, the*; Women)

THE CIRCUS

(Chaplin film)
Released by United Artists, 7 January 1928 (premièred 6 January, Mark Strand Theater, New York). Produced, written and directed by Charles Chaplin. Assistant director: Harry Crocker. Director of photography: Rollie Totheroh. Camera operators: Jack Wilson, Mark Marklatt. An early working title: *The Clown*. Copyrighted 6 January 1928 (LP24830). Seven reels (6,700 or 6,400 feet). Reissued 1969 with music by Charles Chaplin (including a title song, sung by Chaplin), arranged by Lambert Williamson. Musical associate: Eric James. 71 mins.

With Charlie Chaplin (himself), Allan Garcia (circus owner), Merna Kennedy (his stepdaughter, Merna, a circus rider), Harry Crocker (Rex, the tightrope walker), George Davis (Professor Bosco, magician), Henry Bergman (an old clown), Stanley J. 'Tiny' Sandford (head property man), John Rand (his assistant), Betty Morrissey ('vanishing lady'), Steve Murphy (the pickpocket), Doc Stone (prizefighter in deleted section – see below).

A travelling circus visits town. Its star attraction, a young trick rider named Merna, misses a paper hoop and is reprimanded by her stepfather, the show's owner. She is to be denied food that night and, for good measure, is knocked to the ground. The owner also treats his clown troupe with disdain, blaming them for the poor attendance. A tramp, Charlie, wanders among the sideshows. Penniless, money unexpectedly comes his way when a pickpocket, challenged by his victim, dumps a stolen wallet and pocket watch on Charlie. Unaware of the windfall, Charlie filches a snack from a babe in arms. The pickpocket tries to retrieve the loot, but is spotted by a policeman, who assumes the items belong to Charlie. The thief is led away, but breaks free; the pickpocket's true victim sees Charlie with the watch and wallet, and calls a policeman. Both Charlie and the pickpocket are pursued, Charlie taking refuge in a hall of mirrors within the funhouse. The thief follows him. Outside, Charlie poses within a display of mechanical figures; he is joined by the pickpocket who, cosh in hand, demands the loot. Charlie's mechanical rôle sees him hitting the pickpocket with his own cosh, then feigning laughter; the policeman recognizes them when the thief collapses, unconscious. Charlie retreats into the hall of mirrors, enabling him to escape a cop in the confusion. Charlie is pursued into the big top, enlivening a tepid clown act when the audience roars at his evasion of the policeman. Charlie leaves the ring and vanishes. He reappears during the magician's act, when hiding in a prop cabinet. He changes places with the magician's young lady assistant, so that the cop inadvertently strikes her instead of Charlie. Outside, Charlie shakes off the policeman then, seeing the thief apprehended by a different officer, hands over the stolen goods to the law. Off the hook, Charlie stops for a rest. In the ring, the genuine clowns fail to impress, and the owner is intrigued by

calls for 'the funny man', who is asleep in a circus chariot outside the tent. Later, the clowns offer Merna some food, but the girl explains that she is allowed none. The oldest of the clowns insists Merna should take some, but the owner arrives and returns it. Charlie is awakened, offered a job by the owner and told to report to him the following morning. That morning begins with Charlie preparing soup. He takes off after a passing chicken but, contrary to expectations, takes an egg rather than the bird itself. The hungry girl emerges from her caravan and takes Charlie's bread. He tries to stop her, then shares the bread. Merna develops hiccups, passing them on to Charlie. Introductions are made before the owner arrives. Charlie watches disapprovingly as he slaps his stepdaughter around. Charlie is put to work but, returning for his cane, stops to let the girl have the egg he has been cooking. Charlie auditions as a clown, but is hopeless when trying to be funny. He enjoys watching their William Tell and paperhanging acts, but cannot participate in set routines. When Charlie accidentally covers the boss in goo, he is ordered out. His face covered in foam, Charlie is chased by a mule. He meets Merna, who emerges from her caravan in circus costume. She points out

Charlie's moustache began to shrink at the time of **The Circus**

The Circus: *Tiny Sandford and a rookie clown. From a lobby card*

the mess on his face, helps him dry up, then, as the show is to start, asks if he is coming in. Charlie tells her he is leaving, having failed to 'agree terms' with the boss. Merna departs, thanking Charlie for the egg; Charlie watches her until he is chased once more by the mule. In the big top, the propmen quit after a dispute over back pay. Charlie, watching Merna through a hole in the tent, is recruited to take their place. Carrying a stack of plates, he is chased into the ring by the mule; once again he is an inadvertent comic hit, the more so when giving away the magician's tricks. The owner decides to keep Charlie as nominal prop man; he is consequently an unconscious, underpaid star. Neither is Merna's lot improved; while she rehearses the trapeze, Charlie tries to hurl food up to her, but switches to juggling it when the owner appears. He succeeds in delivering some of the food, but a pie falls on the head propman. Charlie blames a passing bird and is put back to work, still unaware that he is the show's star attraction. Charlie must help tend the various animals. One is a horse who needs a pill blown down his throat; the horse blows first. Charlie makes a swift exit, only to be chased again by the mule. He evades the animal, but finds himself sharing a cage with a sleeping lion. The door has locked, and the only exit leads into a tiger's cage. A dog begins to yap at Charlie, who pleads for its silence. Merna arrives but, seeing the danger, passes out. The lion wakes up, but does not attack Charlie. He becomes blasé, and Merna, regaining

consciousness, is impressed. She opens the door, but Charlie is in no hurry to leave. He changes his mind when, over-confident, he approaches the hitherto docile lion and is scared away. The girl catches up with Charlie, who has climbed a tent pole and is pretending to do tricks. He rejoins her for a chat, and is frightened by a passing kitten. The head propman arrives, demanding the horse pill. Instead of summoning a doctor, the pill is brought back up by a kick to Charlie's behind. When Charlie resumes work, he finally learns from Merna that he is the hit of the show. The boss overhears, and hits the girl; Charlie, aware of his position, threatens to quit if it happens again; he also demands a salary increase. He is offered $50 a week, demands 60, and the boss offers to double that figure. 'Nothing less than a hundred,' insists Charlie, thus agreeing to an instant $20 reduction. Life improves for Charlie and Merna. Charlie overhears when the girl's fortune is told: she will marry a 'dark, handsome man who is near you now'. He is delighted, but has not seen a new arrival, Rex the tightrope walker. Rex makes Merna's acquaintance as Charlie buys an appropriate ring from the old clown. Merna returns to the fortune teller, announcing the prediction to have been fulfilled; once more, Charlie overhears, this time as Merna professes love for the tightrope walker. In the ring, Charlie's clowning hardly raises a laugh. After, he

watches girl and tightrope walker in conversation, imagining himself stepping out of his body and knocking his rival down. Charlie is introduced to Rex, and is unimpressed when made to watch his act. Time passes and, in parallel to Merna's blossoming relationship with Rex, so does Charlie develop ambitions as a tightrope walker. His comic expertise is suffering, and he is given only one more chance to improve. Charlie is given a quite different chance when Rex fails to appear; though reluctant to take his place, Charlie does so as an alternative to dismissal. The owner realizes the danger but is unconcerned, having had Charlie insured. In searching for the costume, Charlie opens a trunk filled with monkeys, who seem drawn to Rex's suit. Charlie dons the breakaway costume, beneath which he is supposed to wear tights. Charlie sees Merna before going on, claiming to have a 'charmed life' before bringing a sandbag down on his head. He also bribes the assistant propman to attach a wire to him. Merna asks Charlie not to go through with it. When Charlie sits beside Merna, the wire touches some power cables. Once disconnected, he reassures Merna by demonstrating the wire. He goes on, having been reminded just too late about the missing tights. The act progresses adequately, to the point where Charlie fails to notice the wire's detachment. Once alerted, Charlie starts to wobble, helped not at all when circus monkeys

Charlie braves the high wire in **The Circus**

start to clamber over him. The suit is gradually pulled away, and Charlie is knocked dizzy when a monkey pushes the trapeze swing at his head. Charlie nearly overbalances but, clinging to the rope, makes his way to a tethered bicycle and descends to safety, careering out of the tent and into a general store nearby. There is panic at the circus, and the owner beats his stepdaughter. Charlie attacks his boss, but the head prop man intervenes and pulls him away. Charlie is fired. That night, Merna visits Charlie, who is camping out nearby. Merna tells Charlie she has run away and wants to go with him. Charlie rejects the idea, but has thought of an alternative. He tells Merna to wait. At the circus, the owner asks Rex if he has seen Merna. He has not, and once the owner has gone, Charlie calls to Rex. He explains that he can do nothing for Merna but, handing him the ring he had bought earlier, takes Rex to see her. Next morning, Charlie is best man at their wedding. They return to the circus, where Rex ensures that the owner will treat his new wife with respect. The owner accepts Rex's handshake, but not Charlie's. Rex and his wife will remain with the show on condition that Charlie is reinstated. This is grudgingly agreed to, but Charlie must travel in the rear wagon. Merna and Rex invite him into their wagon, but Charlie declines; suggesting that 'two's company', he closes the door of their wagon. Instead of joining the company, Charlie watches them depart for the next town. He is left alone, sitting on a crate where the sawdust ring had been. Charlie finds a star-decorated remnant of the paper hoop; he compresses it into a ball and, back-kicking it away, resumes his own journey, breaking into a jaunty step.

Chaplin's preceding feature, *The*

Gold Rush (*qv*), had been in release only a matter of months when, on 21 November 1925, *Picture Show* reported his intention not to leave as large a gap between pictures. His new film, provisionally entitled 'The Clown', was to go into immediate production, for completion in approximately six months. In the end, it took some two years, due in no small part to harassment from the US Internal Revenue system and, above all, by the very public and extremely thorough pillorying inflicted by Lita Grey (*qv*) in her divorce case. His tribulations during this period led to a nervous breakdown and the consequent transformation of his partly-greying hair into a disconcerting white. (The scene in which Charlie is harassed by monkeys has often been taken as symbolic of Chaplin's current real-life difficulties, but it is evident that this idea had been devised before his troubles had started.)

Filming began in January 1926. Joining Chaplin were several newcomers, principally leading lady Merna Kennedy (*qv*) and ex-journalist Harry Crocker (also *qv*). In addition to functioning as assistant writer and director, Crocker played the tramp's tightrope-walking rival, Rex. Theodore Huff claimed that Chaplin taught himself wire-walking; David Robinson in turn quotes an interview with Henry Bergman (*qv*) in which, unexpectedly, the rotund actor took credit for having passed on the skill to Chaplin. Bergman is known to have romanticized somewhat in various interviews; a contemporary *Picture Show* report mentions only that Chaplin spent two months mastering the technique.

This was not the only way in which Chaplin had gone to enormous trouble for his new project. Publicity material notes the building of a full-sized circus set and the acquisition of a menagerie of lions, tigers, elephants, horses, monkeys, mules, dogs, pigs and a variety of poultry, housed for more than twelve months at considerable cost. Some scenes, reportedly populated by some 2,000 extras, brought a human feed bill that included over a thousand lollipops, nearly 2,000 pretzels, more than 1,500 sticks of gum, 3,000 gallons of lemonade, 3,622 bottles of soda, 2,602 bags of peanuts and in excess of 5,700 frankfurters plus buns. 'I note,' said Chaplin at the time, 'we didn't use any butter.'

Chaplin embarked on this expensive – if well-catered – production only to discover that the first month's work had

been rendered useless. The negative was scratched, a fault suspected by some to have been caused by sand in the cameras or, more probably, at the laboratory stage. This was remedied and a measure of serenity restored to the proceedings, as when Chaplin was photographed taking tea in a circus tent with Sir Henry and Lady Wood, or else posing in the big top with another distinguished visitor, Lord Astor.

Work was halted again some nine months into shooting, when a fire destroyed the interior stage and props. The circus settings were soaked during attempts to halt the blaze; a further difficulty lay in replacing costumes and other items, which needed to duplicate those seen in the existing footage. (Stills exists of Chaplin wearing an outlandish clown's suit, unseen in the final version. A contemporary photo (illustrated) proves that the coat at least survived the fire, but there is not trace of this outfit in the final film.) According to a later publicity release, Rollie Totheroh (*qv*) shot 250 feet of film showing Chaplin, his usual costume partly covered in a dressing gown, attempted to salvage what

Disaster plagued Chaplin while making **The Circus**. *Here he ponders the film's fire-ravaged set*
Photo by courtesy and copyright of the Roy Export Company Establishment

he could. The film was later used to trail *The Circus* in some theatres.

While the sets were being rebuilt, Chaplin devised a segment that could be shot elsewhere and slotted in afterwards. In this section, Charlie, in his best clothes, takes Merna into town. They meet Rex en route, and Charlie reluctantly accepts that the party has become a threesome. To add to his frustration, Charlie is annoyed by a passing dog, then embarrassed when, anxious to match Rex's gallantry, he attempts to help a lady, only to make a mess of her package of fish. Charlie, Rex and Merna stop at a café. A stranger torments Charlie by throwing sugar cubes at him, but Charlie is persuaded not to retaliate, as the man is a prizefighter. Unknown to Charlie, the fighter has an identical twin who exited earlier. Eventually, something has to be done to save both honour and skin; Charlie quietly approaches the fighter, paying him a small sum to take a dive. The ruse is successful, and the fighter makes his exit. When his twin returns, Charlie assumes it is the same man and, renewing his attack, is soundly beaten. His ego becomes comparably bruised when Rex sees the other man off and is the hero of the day. Charlie retrieves his money from the unconscious man. Chaplin decided not to use this sequence in his final edit, but Rollie Totheroh (*qv*) preserved the rushes in the comedian's archives. An edited version was assembled for the documentary series *Unknown Chaplin* (*qv*); more recently, historian David Shepard has collected the various takes, showing the gradual additions made by Chaplin to improve the scene, for laserdisc issue in the United States. Many filmographies have listed 'Doc' Stone (who plays both prizefighters) in the cast of *The Circus*, despite the excision of his contribution.

Chaplin resumed filming of his main story and, miraculously, had shot most of *The Circus* by November 1926. As with *The Kid* (*qv*), the negative of the new film was in danger of attachment by Lita's attorneys; Chaplin retreated to New York, telling the press that he planned to establish a base there in which to complete *The Circus*, but was instead able to return to his studio by the autumn of 1927. By 24 December, *Picture Show* was able to trail Chaplin's latest production through both a front-cover illustration and a two-page centre spread, in which Paul Thompson quoted the star's definition of *The Circus* as 'A

low-brow comedy for high-brows', or in other words, 'making no attempt at great drama but ... intended purely and simply as a laugh-provoker'. In describing the film's protracted creation, Thompson wrote sympathetically of the comedian's matrimonial traumas and the way in which the pending divorce had inhibited Chaplin's singular, improvisational approach to film-making.

As noted by several reviewers (see below), *The Circus* lived up to its 'low-brow-for-high-brows' brief, both in terms of a higher proportion of straightforward gags than had become Chaplin's custom and in the use of traditional clowning as an overall context (of the sort that Chaplin would choreograph again for *Limelight* and *A King in New York* [both *qv*]). One of its characters, the magician, 'Professor Bosco', takes his name from a flea trainer portrayed by Chaplin in an earlier, abortive film, *The Professor* (see **Abandoned projects**). *The Circus* contrasts its deliberate revival of earlier methods with a remarkable degree of technical sophistication, not least the beautifully-photographed chase in the hall of mirrors and, for Chaplin, some unusual trick work in which Charlie, by means of double-exposure, seems to leave his body in order to strike down his rival. There are one or two loose ends: the title cards do not refer to Merna by name until late in the film, while she in turn refers the circus proprietor as 'Father', despite her billing as his stepdaughter (though such terminology is, admittedly, not uncommon among stepchildren); one might add that the temporary disappearance of Rex is inadequately explained, at least in the final cut.

Any damage inflicted upon Chaplin's personal reputation by the divorce had to some extent subsided when *The Circus* premièred at his favoured New York venue, the Mark Strand, at a late-night screening on Friday, 6 January 1928. Chaplin did not attend in person but instead sent a telegram, read out to the audience, citing the new film as the outstanding achievement of his career. Mordaunt Hall of the *New York Times*, calling Chaplin 'the Grimaldi of modern days', thought *The Circus* 'likely to please intensely those who found something slightly wanting in *The Gold Rush*, but at the same time it will prove a little disappointing to those who revelled in the poetry, the pathos and fine humor of his previous adventure'. There is, in fact, quite the expected quota of pathos, but Hall chose to dwell upon the film's

slapstick, which in his view resembled the Chaplin comedies pre-dating *Gold Rush* or even *The Kid* (*qv*), albeit qualifying that opinion by noting Chaplin's ability to 'set forth old ideas with a toothsome sauce'. His review dwells enthusiastically upon the principal comedy sequences, among them a scene in which the tramp is being instructed in the art of being funny while proving, by instinct, to be more amusing than the clowns. 'Here,' said Hall, 'this born comedian portrays his genius.'

Playwright Robert E. Sherwood had been one of *Gold Rush*'s earliest champions, but his *Life* review welcomed the return to strong, extensive comedy routines in *The Circus*. Alexander Bakshy (in *The Nation*) liked Chaplin's scenes but thought it 'a solo performance', with the supporting cast 'not more than competent', and thought the direction compared unfavourably to that in his dramatic feature, *A Woman of Paris* (*qv*). *Variety* considered it Chaplin's best – a 'corker', no less – but suggested its own preferences when reporting a predominance of broad comedy, a supposed (and highly debatable) absence of subtlety and, above all, tight editing. As a theatrical paper, *Variety* thought some of the gags might be more appreciated among show people than the general public, as when Charlie takes a bow after his high-wire act concludes in a neighbouring store, or when he attempts to join the clowns in such traditional set-pieces as 'The William Tell bit'. Due acknowledgement was made of the pathos overlooked by Hall, and appreciation expressed that a man in his forties (though Chaplin was actually 38), possessed of 'position and wealth', should take the trouble to learn wire-walking simply for one picture. It might be said in passing that genius is often defined as 'an infinite capacity for taking pains'; accurate or not, this definition may certainly be applied to Chaplin.

The Times suggested a comparable opinion when the film opened at the New Gallery, London, in February 1928. Much space was allocated to quoting the opening comic business, after which it was decided: 'That is the trouble with Mr. Chaplin's work – it is so rich in detail that the mind lingers over fragments, neglecting the narrative.' The general opinion, as in most *Circus* reviews, was that any seeming lack in melancholy was balanced by comic ingenuity, and that 'it is at least the equal of anything that Mr. Chaplin has done'. St. John Ervine of the *Observer*, similarly impressed by Chaplin's 'extraordinary' invention, remarked on the way in which the comedian's props, though sparse, were there 'for a purpose'. Ervine chose as example a scene in which Charlie glances at the poster advertising a lady sword swallower, placed not merely to dress the scene but to allow Charlie to compare it with the starving circus girl as she hungrily devours her food. (As further evidence, Ervine marvelled at the way in which the hall-of-mirrors scene had been photographed without reflecting the camera crew.) Ervine's main point, touched upon by other reviews, was in applauding Chaplin's skill in the use of consciously old material when working among the circus clowns. Noting that there is really no such thing as a new joke, but that any joke is new to *somebody*, Ervine reminded his readers that 'stale stuff stalely performed remains stale, even to those to whom it is new'. Chaplin, by contrast, performed 'stale acts in a fresh way, [showing] us how a man of original mind and genius will alter traditional methods under the very eyes of the traditionalists, and make it seem rousingly comic'. Ervine was reluctant to place *The Circus* below *The Gold Rush*, conceding that others held a different opinion; among them was the *Daily Express* reviewer, who, though reporting some 'masterpieces of comic invention', deemed *The Circus* 'a good but not a great "Chaplin"'. Opinion here was that there were perhaps forty minutes of 'good laughter', but with the remaining footage 'too thin to be called funny' and in need of 'judicious pruning'. There was again praise for the mirror business and the belief that, despite Chaplin's intention to make 'a film for the multitude', some effort had been made to cater to 'high-brow' audiences in search of 'the "Pagliacci theme"'. One of the less enthusiastic reviews, from the *Star*, remarked again on a seeming reversion to earlier methods, with the implication that Chaplin might have been playing down to his public. This, it was felt, was 'Chaplin without the "Mr."', or in other words a return to the populist approach after the supposedly more aesthetic pleasures of *The Gold Rush* had instigated a vogue for calling him 'Mr. Chaplin'. The film was considered 'not, looked at all round, a patch on its predecessor', albeit with an admission that any quibbling was the result of Chaplin's own high standards. Whether 'Mr. Chaplin' or 'Charlie', the *Morning Post* implied a superiority to *The*

Gold Rush and welcomed his return to the 'old days' of slapstick, complemented by just enough sentiment 'to give the undercurrent of reality' to his screen character.

The Circus brought Chaplin a special Oscar in the first year of the Academy Awards, but was thereafter consigned to his vaults for a period of forty years. In reviewing the new edition of *The Gold Rush* for *Time* in 1942, James Agee wrote that Chaplin was 'ready to pretty-up *The Circus* for reissue if *The Gold Rush* box office warrants it'. Chaplin's profit on the revival was considerable, but his intended revamp of *The Circus* did not follow until 1969 (though reissue prints carry a copyright date from the previous year). This was not through any shortcomings in the film itself, but more probably the result of Chaplin's extreme trauma in making it; consequently, *The Circus* has never been given its true place in the Chaplin canon as a work comparable to the films released before and after. On 23 May 1969, London's *Evening News* reported how Eric James, Chaplin's musical associate, had persuaded the comedian to sing a 'sentimental ballad' on the new soundtrack. The item in question, 'Swing Little Girl', appears under a new credit sequence, intercut with shots of Merna Kennedy practising on the trapeze (duplicated from elsewhere in the film). In other respects, the reissue is identical in content to the original release. (There are a few old copies around – which are slightly cut – bearing 'part titles', announcing the beginnings and ends of reels, crediting Williams and Ivey as distributors. This is surprising, as they seem otherwise only to have reissued the Mutuals in 16mm prints.) When the revived edition reached the USA in January 1970, *Time* saw it as opportunity to appreciate Chaplin's tramp within a properly constructed vehicle instead of via the customary extracts. Moreover, the point was made of how much was owed Chaplin by other comedians, not just his contemporaries but those from overseas and of subsequent generations, not least Jerry Lewis, Fernandel and Danny Kaye. The following October, Chaplin was invited to the Roundhouse in London – where Harold Lloyd had recently visited – but declined on the grounds of illness, sending instead his revived copy of *The Circus*. It opened officially at London's Curzon cinema in December 1970.

Chaplin's preserved edition of *The Circus*, barring a couple of momentary signs of decomposition, is a joy to watch.

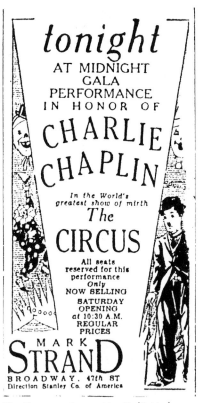

The Circus premieres at New York's Mark Strand Theatre on 6 January 1928 By courtesy of Robert G. Dickson

With so much negative, 'revisionist' writing on Chaplin during recent years, it is a pleasure to note that some of it has been devoted to restoring *The Circus* to prominence within the body of his work.

(See also: Abandoned projects; Animals; Awards; Bergman, Henry; Costume; Crocker, Harry; Dual rôles; Food; Garcia, Allan; Hair; Mental illness; Music; Policemen; Rand, John; Reissues; Sandford, Stanley J. 'Tiny'; Slapstick; Suicide; Television; Trick photography; Twists and transformations; United Artists; Video releases)

CITY LIGHTS ♟

(Chaplin film)
Released by United Artists, 6 February 1931 (Los Angeles première 30 January). Produced, written and directed by Charles Chaplin. Assistant directors: Harry Crocker, Henry Bergman and Albert Austin. Music composed by Charles Chaplin, arranged by Arthur Johnston and directed by Alfred Newman. Settings

(art direction) Charles D. Hall. Photographed by Rollie Totheroh, Gordon Pollock and (uncredited) Mark Marklatt. 9 reels, 86 mins.

With Charlie Chaplin (himself), Virginia Cherrill (blind girl), Harry Myers (millionaire), Henry Bergman (Mayor/blind girl's downstairs neighbour), Hank Mann (prizefighter), Florence Lee (blind girl's grandmother), Allan Garcia (millionaire's butler), Eddie Baker (fight referee), Albert Austin (roadsweeper/crook), James Donnelly (foreman), Robert Parrish (newsboy), John Rand (tramp), Stanley J. 'Tiny' Sandford (pavement lift operator), Stanhope Wheatcroft (wealthy-looking man in restaurant), Blanche Payson and Edith Wilson (ladies in deleted scene – see below), Harry Crocker, Charles Lederer (also in deleted scene), Jean Harlow (reported extra – see below).

City Lights: *Charlie discreetly watches the blind girl going about her work*

Local dignitaries preside over the unveiling of a new statue display, 'Peace and Prosperity'. Peace vanishes when the covers are lifted to reveal the far from prosperous Charlie, asleep on one of the statues. Obligingly, he attempts to leave but becomes caught on a statue's sword. He departs, leaving the occasion in chaos. Later, Charlie is teased by some newsboys, who pull the cane from under his arm and steal a finger from his crumbling glove. Charlie pauses by a shop window to admire a nude statue. Each time he steps back, a pavement lift

rises to fill the void behind him. Eventually, there is a minor spill and Charlie protests to its operator – until he discovers him to be huge. On a street corner, a blind girl sells flowers. There is a traffic jam and, anxious also to avoid a motorcycle cop, Charlie crosses the road by climbing through a stationary limousine. Hearing the car door close, the girl asks Charlie to buy a flower. Charlie does so, but accidentally knocks it from her hand. When she asks if he has picked it up, Charlie realizes she is blind. Charlie pays her, but before he has time to collect his change, a rich man enters the car and drives off. She believes Charlie has gone, allowing her to keep the change. Charlie tiptoes away, then silently takes a seat beside a drinking fountain, to observe the girl. Unaware of his presence, the girl washes out a bucket then unwittingly hurls the water into Charlie's face. Dampened, Charlie tiptoes away once more. That evening, the blind girl returns home to her grandmother. The girl bids good-bye to a sighted girl friend, off for an evening with a beau. Night, and on an embankment, Charlie sees a wealthy-looking drunk tie a noose around his neck, a boulder attached to the other end. Charlie tries to persuade him not to jump in the river. The drunk proceeds in his attempt, but in his stupor accidentally puts the noose around Charlie, who is dumped in the river. The millionaire, extending a hand, is also pulled in, but they both scramble to safety. The process is repeated when the millionaire inadvertently knocks Charlie back in. On the embankment, the millionaire pronounces himself cured and Charlie is his 'friend for life'. Charlie is taken back to his new friend's mansion. The butler announces that the millionaire's wife has 'sent for her baggage' – news that explains his employer's melancholia, despite his reply of 'Good.' The millionaire tries to pour drinks, but empties most of a bottle down Charlie's trousers. The butler's disapproval of Charlie escalates as the guest becomes tipsy. The millionaire's mood changes, and Charlie has to stop him turning a revolver on himself. Having been persuaded to live, the millionaire orders out the Rolls-Royce, in which he takes Charlie to a nightclub. Charlie, in a borrowed tuxedo, drunkenly lights the millionaire's cigar in mistake for his own, then, when his own is finally lit, has to toss it aside to avoid confusion with a sausage on his plate. Charlie's cigar lands on a chair, burning a

society matron's *derrière*. Charlie extinguishes the blaze with a soda syphon. The disturbance over, Charlie is served spaghetti, but eats a paper streamer instead. He is distracted from the meal by a floor show, an *apache* dance in which, taking it seriously, Charlie intervenes. Couples occupy the floor in frenzied dancing; Charlie borrows a partner, whirling her around until she is reclaimed by her husband. Charlie then whirls around with a waiter. Next morning, Charlie has to take the wheel when the millionaire tries drunkenly to drive them home. At the house, Charlie says he likes the Rolls; he is told he can have it. Charlie helps the man inside, but is barred admission by the butler. The blind girl passes with her flowers. The millionaire demands Charlie should be admitted; once inside, Charlie suggests they buy some flowers, and is given enough to buy the whole basket plus a generous tip. Charlie tells the butler to put the flowers in water while he drives the girl home in the Rolls-Royce. He delivers her outside, asking if he can see her home again. 'Whenever you wish, sir,' is the reply. She enters the upstairs flat. Charlie's rapture is interrupted when a flower pot, dislodged by a cat, lands on his head. He perches on a rain barrel to watch the girl through the window, to discover his rapture is shared. When a downstairs neighbour arrives, Charlie overbalances, tipping the rain barrel over the neighbour. Charlie drives away, hurriedly. The sober, hungover millionaire is 'out' to everyone, so Charlie is again refused admission. Needing a smoke, Charlie uses the car to follow a man likely to discard a cigar butt. This is accomplished, though another tramp is astonished to be beaten to a cigar butt by a tuxedo-clad gentleman driving a Rolls. The car is returned to the house. The sober millionaire emerges, just as Charlie pulls up outside. The millionaire, failing to recognize his new pal when sober, gets into the car and drives off. The blind girl is telling her grandmother of the gentleman she has met. Grandmother concludes he must be wealthy; 'Yes,' replies the girl, 'but he's more than that.' That afternoon, Charlie, still in the borrowed tuxedo, bumps into the millionaire, drunk again. Now recognizing Charlie, he takes him home for a party. Amid the wild goings-on, Charlie nearly tucks into someone's bald head instead of a dessert, and succeeds in swallowing a whistle. This, combined

Catering to the flower girl in **City Lights**, *while picking up an unusual buttonhole*

with hiccups, interrupts a singer and unnecessarily summons a cab and a dog when Charlie steps outside. The *soirée* is disrupted further when Charlie returns with a pack of dogs. Next morning, the sober millionaire awakens to find Charlie sharing his bed. Charlie is given his own clothes and thrown out, while the millionaire prepares for a noon departure to Europe. Charlie heads for the blind girl's pitch but, finding her absent, visits the flat instead. Through the window, he sees the doctor in attendance. The girl has a fever and needs careful attention. In order to help, Charlie takes a job as a roadsweeper, attending to his duties, but turning back on seeing mules herded along. Retracing his steps, he is further discouraged when a circus elephant trots through. The girl's grandmother receives a letter concerning their $22 back rent; if this is not settled, she and the girl will be evicted. Grandmother keeps this from the girl as she goes off to deputize as flower-seller. Charlie is due to visit, but grandmother is never there to see him. Charlie washes up for lunch, leaving the soap so that a colleague eats it in mistake for cheese. He departs with a warning to return on time. Despite the millionaire's absence, Charlie keeps up the pretence of affluence. To the flat he brings groceries and a newspaper telling of a Viennese doctor with an operation to cure blindness, offered free to the poor. Charlie is momentarily unnerved at the

thought of her being able to see him. She asks him to hold the wool she is winding; Charlie, unwilling to mention that she has instead caught the wrong strand, sits patiently as his underwear is unravelled. Charlie finds a letter addressed to the girl; she asks him to read it, and thus learns of the rent arrears. Charlie promises to pay it the next morning and departs. Late back to work, Charlie is dismissed but offered some 'easy money' in a prizefight. That evening, he sits in the dressing room, confirming a shady deal by which he splits the $50 purse and will not be hurt. The rules change when his erstwhile opponent disappears after being told the police are after him. A different bruiser is engaged to fight Charlie, one with no interest in splitting the purse. A black boxer, despite a lucky rabbit's foot, is hammered; Charlie's nerves escalate when his opponent flattens a larger man in the dressing room. Charlie spends much of the bout hiding behind the referee, but lands several blows, some of them when flying from the corner. His dartings confuse the other fighter and, when there is a seeming double knockout, it is anybody's guess who will beat the count. Further confusion reigns when Charlie's neck is caught in the bell rope; once freed, the dazed Charlie is knocked out. He regains consciousness in the dressing room, only to be knocked out again by a falling glove. That night,

still hoping to raise the money, Charlie roams the streets; he meets the millionaire, back from Europe and fantastically drunk. At his mansion, the millionaire promises to help the girl and gives Charlie $1,000. Thieves have concealed themselves in the room. After Charlie continues to get in their way, they knock the millionaire cold. Charlie calls the police and chases the thieves away. An officer arrives, and the butler accuses Charlie of the theft. The millionaire regains consciousness and does not remember giving Charlie the $1,000 sum found in his pocket. Charlie grabs the money, douses the lights and rushes to the flat. The money will settle the rent and finance the girl's trip to Vienna. As he leaves, Charlie explains he will be going away for a while. On the street, the newsboys watch as detectives arrest Charlie. Months pass, and the girl, her sight restored, now runs a florist's of her own. Charlie, shabbier than ever but out of prison, revisits her former pitch. A wealthy young gentleman customer arrives in the shop, but the girl is disappointed to realize it is not her benefactor. She watches with amusement as the newsboys tease Charlie when he picks a flower from the gutter. Seeing her through the window, he smiles. 'I've made a conquest,' she says, jokingly, before stepping outside to give Charlie a flower. When she touches his hand, the girl recognizes the truth about him. 'You can see now?' asks Charlie. 'Yes,' replies the girl, 'I can see now,' squeezing his hand and starting a smile. Charlie, full of hope, returns the smile.

Chaplin had intended the opening scene to be that in which Charlie's attention is taken by a piece of wood, jammed into the ventilator grille outside a department store. Charlie makes several attempts to dislodge it with his cane before realizing he has drawn a crowd. Once it has dispersed, he is is observed instead by a dim-looking messenger boy (Charles Lederer), who spits and eats an orange. Charlie disposes of him by disappearing around a corner and, on returning, pauses to examine his cane. A large lady (Blanche Payson) stands over the grille; while she is there, Charlie extends a leg to push down the wood. The lady turns, giving Charlie a terrible look before exiting with her friend (Edith Wilson, wife of cameraman Jack Wilson [*qv*]). A window-dresser (Harry Crocker [*qv*]) walks into the shop display, sees Charlie's efforts and tries,

A desperate means of raising money in **City Lights***; Hank Mann won't throw the fight*

inaudibly, to advise. Thus distracted, he pins a tag to the rear end of a lady assistant. He departs, embarrassed. Charlie is amused, but shares the embarrassment on realizing the presence of another crowd. As he renews his efforts, a policeman arrives to investigate. Fortunately, Charlie is now able to dispose of the wood with a single shove and goes on his way, leaving the officer to disperse the unwelcome onlookers. This leisurely routine seems to have been omitted from the final version of *City Lights* only for reasons of pace. It had never been shown publicly until retrieved from the vaults for the series *Unknown Chaplin* (*qv*), but has since been acknowledged as a Chaplin classic, albeit a disembodied one.

Sub-titled 'a comedy romance in pantomime', *City Lights* was begun in March 1928. Chaplin constructed an elaborate city set, shaped like a 'T' (thus permitting a lengthy street view without noticeable boundaries), filled with cars and, above all, hundreds of extras (most of them, as Theodore Huff remarked, young women under the age of 25!). An immediate task was to select an actress capable of portraying a convincing but attractive blind girl, a part which, as detailed elsewhere, was given to Virginia Cherrill (*qv*). Chaplin expended numerous takes in order to perfect the tramp's first scene with her. *Unknown Chaplin* (*qv*) revealed how he tried various means to convince the girl of

Charlie's apparent wealth, but did not devise the solution – that of Charlie eluding a cop by walking through a limousine, which, after a slam of the door, drives off without him – until September 1930, close to the end of shooting. In *Six Men*, Alistair Cooke records how Chaplin spent three weeks pondering the means by which the blind girl would believe the tramp to be rich, until the solution virtually presented itself. 'I came down one morning,' said Chaplin, 'very glum, a bear, and I looked at the automobile and it hit me: *a slamming door!*'

Other delays were to plague *City Lights*. A six-month hiatus resulted from the simple act of firing actor Henry Clive, who had been cast as the millionaire. Pleading a cold, he had asked for the studio pool to be heated prior to filming the scene of his attempted suicide. Chaplin ordered him to go ahead, and when he continued to refuse, the rôle given instead to Harry Myers (*qv*), with whom all of Clive's earlier scenes were reshot. (Some of the stills from the restaurant scene suggest the presence of Jean Harlow, who was an extra at the time of *City Lights'* commencement, but who had reached stardom prior to its release. She is not readily visible in the film itself, and it seems likely that the scene was retaken without her.) Home-movie film taken on the set – again used in *Unknown Chaplin* – shows Chaplin growing irritable with

assistant Harry Crocker, who was also fired during production (though he was to work for Chaplin as a publicist into the 1950s). A similar fate nearly befell Virginia Cherrill; though an untrained actress, she proved ideal as the blind girl, but her fondness for late-night partying did not fit in with the type of dedication Chaplin required, especially when the effects needed to be carefully concealed using make-up. Virginia was eventually fired for lateness, and her rôle was given to Georgia Hale (*qv*), but she was not right for the part, and Chaplin had in any case expended far too much on existing footage. Reluctantly, Chaplin reinstated Virginia, but not without cost; Marion Davies, a friend of both Chaplin and Virginia, had advised the latter on the advantageousness of her position, and she was thus able to negotiate a significant rise in salary. Chaplin's objections were negated when Virginia pointed out that her initial contract was negotiated before she had reached the age of 21 and was consequently invalid. Not surprisingly, *City Lights* was to be her only film with Chaplin.

Talking pictures had become the norm by the time of *City Lights'* completion. There was for a while speculation as to whether *City Lights* would become at least a part-talkie. On 9 September 1929, *Film Weekly*, asking 'Will Charlie Talk?', offered the opinions of Nathan Burkan, Chaplin's lawyer and business adviser, who was then holidaying in England. 'It is still undecided whether or not this film will be a talkie,' said Burkan. 'Charlie's attitude to talkies at the present time is that they are interesting, but he does not consider that speech is in any way essential to screen art. I, personally, consider that if he were to make a talking picture it would be a great success. He would be marvellous. He has a fine singing and speaking voice, he dances well, and has the advantage of an early stage training. The script of *City Lights* contains dialogue, and it is almost certain that the film will contain some speech; but whether Charlie will break his silence is an open question. If he speaks it will be as a concession to popular taste, and not from personal inclination.' Burkan had reminded Chaplin of his enormous following among children, and of the talkies' popularity with youngsters, but Chaplin, aware of a guaranteed market for his films, whether silent or sound, was not to be swayed; 'he likes to please himself,' explained Burkan, noting how the comedian had rejected several lucrative contracts in order to remain his own master. 'It is this disregard for purely monetary considerations,' Burkan continued, 'that makes him an artist idealised by his friends.' One might query Burkan's reference to scripted dialogue, since those involved in the project remembered there being no script whatever. This, however, is academic, for Chaplin, dismissing sound film as being like 'painting marble statues', employed no spoken dialogue in *City Lights*, preferring instead to supply a soundtrack comprised of music and effects. Again *Film Weekly* supplies details, via an interview conducted by Charles Lapworth and published in the issue of 6 December 1930. When asked why he did not speak in *City Lights*, Chaplin remarked on the absence of any reason why he *should*, going on to cite the many people whose desire for the co-existence of silent and sound films had been ignored. Chaplin had allied himself with those who believed that 'talking pictures could never wholly satisfy', but found himself almost the last representative of that group. The decision to remain silent had been taken after re-running several key scenes from his earlier work and speculating on their effectiveness if punctuated by dialogue. Thus satisfied, he considered further the eloquence of mime – 'the oldest art' – over the spoken word, which 'can defeat the imagination'. 'In an appeal to the emotions,' claimed Chaplin, 'the silent clown with his pantomime can beat every time the throaty tragedian.' He was also conscious of the many fine silent-film players who, through inadequacy or misfortune, had vanished with the advent of talking pictures. There was, in addition, the problem of the international market, at that time frequently catered to by re-shot foreign-language editions instead of dubbing or sub-titling; 'The Chinese children, the Japanese children, the Hindu, the Hottentot, all understand me,' said Chaplin. 'I doubt whether they would understand my Chinese or my Hindustani.'

The musical track consists almost entirely of Chaplin's own compositions, although, as noted in the **Music** entry, wry smiles greeted the unattributed use of Padilla's 'La Violetera' ('Who'll Buy My Violets') as motif for the blind girl. In common with the many silents issued with pre-recorded music-and-effects tracks during 1928–9, *City Lights*

interacts with its accompaniment in a way that a strictly silent picture would not (something all the more true of Chaplin's next film, *Modern Times* [*qv*]). The cutting allows for the use of recurrent themes underlining pivotal moments in the plot, while several gags are dependent upon strategically-placed sound effects. One of these occurs at the beginning, where the fledgling talkies are guyed considerably by the buzzing kazoo noise emanating from the mouths of civic dignitaries. Another is when Charlie, at a party, swallows a whistle and thus produces involuntary, piercing blasts on the instrument.

City Lights premièred at the Los Angeles Theater on 30 January 1931, an occasion marred when, according to Chaplin's memoirs, the manager interrupted the performance after three reels in order to lecture the audience on

Contemporary British artwork for **City Lights**

the delights of the new building; a contemporary report from journalist Donovan Pedelty makes no reference to such an intrusion, claiming instead a delay of an hour and three-quarters

Arriving in Britain for the opening of **City Lights** *...*

owing to Chaplin's car having been caught in the very heavy traffic caused by the occasion. At the evening's end, Chaplin delivered a speech of thanks, in which he felt he might have done better with 'more time' (and this after three years in production). Those he introduced to the audience stood and bowed: Virginia Cherrill, Harry Myers and, unexpectedly, Albert Einstein, whose direct connection with *City Lights* remains obscure. A less disruptive New York opening took place at the George M. Cohan Theater on 6 February. According to Mordaunt Hall of the *New York Times*, Chaplin arrived with a police guard, stopping to greet his friends prior to taking an aisle seat beside veteran actress Constance Collier. The film was received enthusiastically and, at its conclusion, Chaplin walked to the stage to thank his audience. In Hall's opinion, Chaplin 'proved so far as he is concerned the eloquence of silence' with 'an admirable artistry' and plot twists that made him 'the O. Henry of the screen'. One suspects that *Variety* couldn't quite make up its mind, for among its 'miniature reviews', *City Lights* was

deemed a 'Strong Chaplin picture and silent', whereas the main review decided it 'isn't so strong that there isn't some doubt concerning its holdover power' following the initial rush of business. *Variety* decided it was not Chaplin's best, 'because the comedian has sacrificed speed to pathos, and plenty of it ... But the British comic is still the consummate pantomimist, unquestionably one of the greatest the stage or screen has ever known.' An important point is made when stating that there would always be room for Chaplin, even as a silent performer in a world of talking pictures, for he had the 'talent, time and means' to ensure he made good films. The only thing a concession to sound could do for Chaplin would be perhaps to 'make him slightly less important in the general public eye as time goes on'. Alexander Woollcott (*qv*), whose essay on the film was reprinted three years later in his anthology, *While Rome Burns*, was no lover of talkies (except perhaps those of the Marx Brothers) and saw this latter-day silent comedy as 'a gauntlet thrown down to all of Hollywood', though allowing there was 'no proof that any other player would be thus accepted at his face value'. Evaluating Chaplin's comic skills as being at 'high tide', Woollcott compared Charlie's reappearance to that of a comet, returning 'after four years of loitering on the other side of the moon', further likening the art of Chaplin to that of Lewis Carroll and Charles Dickens. Unlike Dickens' gallery of characters, Chaplin had by that time created only one of consequence, 'but that one,' continued Woollcott, 'in his matchless courtesy, in his unfailing gallantry – his preposterous innocent gallantry, in a world of gross Goliaths – that character is – I think, the finest gentleman of our time'. The ragged gentility of Charlie is certainly at its most pronounced in *City Lights*, that misplaced courtliness which ensured that he would tip his hat even to some inanimate abomination he had just tripped over in the street. It was never more evident than when Charlie, a *boulevardier* in rags, was obliged to retrieve the finger stolen from his disintegrating glove by an impudent newsboy. Woollcott claims that the picture was intended to finish with the Tramp tipping his hat and leaving without revealing his identity to the girl, but this seems unlikely, given the survival of an alternate take of the finale, in which Georgia Hale substitutes as the flower

girl. Woollcott's essay concludes with one of the most quoted (or slightly misquoted) summations of Chaplin: 'At all events, his like has not passed this way before. And we shall not see his like again.'

Chaplin was again present when *City Lights* opened at London's Dominion Theatre on 27 February 1931. He had spent the day evading attention while revisiting familiar parts of London, managing a walk through the Strand prior to embarking by taxi for Clerkenwell and Tower Bridge. Journalist S.R. Littlewood told how Chaplin had 'hoaxed half London' by arriving at the theatre an hour early, using a side entrance and changing into evening clothes behind a screen; the expected crowds were left to face an army of police amid pouring rain (Chaplin eventually pacified the crowds in Tottenham Court Road by appearing at an upstairs window, picked out by searchlights as he waved his greetings). A further hoax was perpetrated when a man clad in Chaplin's screen costume appeared from a taxi outside the theatre. He was duly fêted until a small boy cried out, 'That's not him!', whereupon the police escorted the impostor to the road. Seated between Bernard Shaw and Lady Astor, Chaplin recalled due laughter at the pairing of himself and the Irish playwright, magnified when the two were required to stand up together. Reaction, as before, was of hearty laughter and no few tears. As the show concluded, Chaplin again took the stage to deliver a speech, 'so pleasantly spoken,' according to one correspondent, 'that if ever he does fall to the talkies we may still have hope'. Chaplin drew laughter by comparing himself to 'the young chap making his maiden speech, who said: "Ladies and gentlemen, I should like to express my heartmost felt."' 'This is, indeed, a great triumph for me,' he continued. 'It would be silly to try and tell you what I am feeling. One day, when I get a little grey-haired [an ironic reference to his already whitened hair], I may set it down in a book.'

After the performance, Shaw was asked if Chaplin could play Hamlet; Shaw replied in the affirmative, claiming to have been struck by the comedian's 'haunting, tragic expression', even in the days when he dealt entirely in slapstick. On leaving the theatre, Chaplin entertained his party of friends at the Carlton Hotel, then spent much of the following day in bed, suffering from exhaustion. At teatime he received one visitor, a reporter whom Kono (*qv*), his valet, had admitted more than three hours previously. Asked how he felt when seeing his own work, Chaplin believed he could generally take a detached view, enabling him to contemplate improvements to technique and 'the mechanics', while noting audience reaction to the comedy and pathos. In this respect, Chaplin unwittingly anticipated the perils of showing cinema comedy on television for, as he claimed: 'The whole thing is like a symphony in which the audience is as important as the screen.'

... and on stage at the Dominion Theatre

British reviews were at least as appreciative as those in the United States. S.R. Littlewood feared that *City Lights* might be the last appearance of 'Charlie' before his creator moved away from silence to explore other topics; even so, Littlewood saw 'little that is new in it' to point to any 'creative future' in Chaplin's tramp. Nonetheless, the film was deemed 'a masterpiece within its own confessed limits', containing all the best elements of Chaplin's work. The opinion of Ivor Brown in the *Observer* was that 'Charlie, silent as ever, has said everything. To see this film is not only to see a city's lights; it is to hear the whole beat and rhythm of its life, its laughter and its cruelty.' His *Observer* colleague, C.A. Lejeune, compared the 'curious emotional envelope – a sense of associative experience' with the best of European cinema, offering *City Lights* alongside Rene Clair's *Sous les Toits de Paris* as the best example of 'going back to essentials' since the arrival of sound. 'These two directors,' said Lejeune, 'are almost alone in their power of pure film-thinking, without translation through literary or sociological or dramatic idea; they are quite alone in their comic psychology, their sense of the right

movement, gesture or pause to reveal the whole mockable nature of a man's soul. But Chaplin is the surer artist, giving what Clair has never quite succeeded in suggesting, the sense of frustration behind the laughter; there is always at the back of Chaplin's work that emotion without logic which first carried him beyond Sennett and the Keystone comedies to be the world's first clown.' Far from a test case for the survival of silent film, Lejeune considered *City Lights* 'first Chaplin and then a wordless film', just as any talkie he might make would be 'first Chaplin and then a film with words'.

Theodore Huff attributed the 'grayness' and 'flatness' in prints of *City Lights* to the as-yet unperfected incandescent studio lighting and panchromatic film stock that had recently been adopted by the industry. It is true that the usual copies tend to disappoint slightly in this regard, but one should not forget the excellent material used for the 1989 'live cinema' revival (see **Reissues**) and the subsequent TV screening of this presentation. It is probable that the added soundtrack forced Chaplin to make his release prints from a single, duplicate negative instead of those from the multiple cameras customary in silent work (home movies in *Unknown Chaplin* confirm the use of twin cameras). At this time, duplicate negative stock was in its infancy, and one suspects it was this, rather than the camera original, that served to reduce the contrast and clarity of *City Lights'* usual version. Further, the bland-looking, basic design of the main title cards may also be attributed to the addition of a soundtrack, in order to permit a musical preamble to that in which the title is spelled out in light bulbs superimposed over the city scene.

Despite considerable difficulties in its creation, *City Lights* remained Chaplin's own favourite of his films, a view shared by many *aficionados*. Some argue for *The Gold Rush*, but despite evident reworkings from earlier comedies (notably *The Champion* and *The Rounders*, both *qv*), *City Lights* is a less episodic, fully-rounded tale with a profundity of emotion surpassing even that of its closest rival in the Chaplin canon.

(See also: Introduction; Animals; Animation; Awards; Baker, Nellie Bly; Bergman, Henry; Cars; Children; Costume; Fighting; Garcia, Allan; Grand Order of Water Rats, The; Hair; Impersonators; Music; Parrish,

Robert; Policemen; Politics; Prisons; Public appearances; Race; Rand, John; Reissues; Risqué humour; Sandford, Stanley J. 'Tiny'; Smoking; Suicide; Television; Trick photography; United Artists; Vagrancy; Video releases; Women)

CLIFTON, EMMA
(1874–1922)

Actress, born in Philadelphia; in appearance, a slightly chubbier alternative to Mabel Normand (*qv*). Emma Clifton was leading lady of Chaplin's fourth film, *Between Showers* (*qv*); she left Keystone (*qv*) soon after, following its director, Henry 'Pathé' Lehrman (*qv*), to make a rival series of comedies with Ford Sterling (*qv*) (in which her resemblance to Normand was doubtless considered valuable).

COLEMAN, FRANK J.

(Chaplin films *qv*)
Balding, rotund actor visible in the Chaplin Mutuals; he has been credited in several Essanays, but is hard to spot. He is difficult to identify in *The Floorwalker*, but seems to be the pipe-smoking store cleaner. In *The Fireman*, Coleman is one of Charlie's brave fire-fighting colleagues; *The Vagabond* places him among both the German band and the gypsies; *The Count* sees him dressed as a clown at the costume party and, suitably disguised, as a policeman; he is a policeman again in *The Pawnshop* and *Easy Street*, also a prison guard in *The Adventurer*. Coleman plays the film producer in *Behind the Screen* and, continuing in an administrative capacity, is the manager of a restaurant in *The Rink* and of a health spa in *The Cure*. *The Immigrant* presents a slight puzzle in that Coleman is, once again, the restaurant manager; the author's opinion is that Coleman is also the whiskered gambler whom Charlie outwits, a rôle long attributed to Stanley J. 'Tiny' Sandford (*qv*), who worked in Chaplin's later films. Another puzzle is the absence of Coleman's biographical details from most reference works. Details are sparse but, perhaps surprisingly, Coleman was allocated an entry in a multi-volume Italian work of 1957, *Enciclopedia Dello Spettacolo*. According to this source, Coleman was born in Newburg, New York, gaining early theatrical experience in the Garden City Quartette, Bennett-Morton Stock Company and others prior to entering films. Aside from his work with Chaplin,

the text notes a prolific career in silent comedies, citing as other examples *The Tenderfoot* (1917), *A Fresh Start*, *Nonsense* (both 1920), *The Cave Girl*, *The Punch of the Irish* and *A Game Lady* (all 1921). Other known appearances: *Fools in the Desert* (1925) and *Napoleon, Jr.* (1926).

(See also: Dual rôles; Mutual)

COLOUR

(Chaplin films *qv*)
Chaplin had blue eyes and, in youth, black hair (some accounts claim dark brown). As noted elsewhere, Chaplin's hair had started to grey by or before his thirties, and within a decade had gone completely white. Most of his cinema work was, of course, made before colour film had become commonplace, and *A Countess From Hong Kong* was his only project not in monochrome. Tinting was standard procedure in the silent era and, though Chaplin is said to have avoided it in his independently-produced films, there is evidence of it having been employed for some of his earlier comedies (the author once saw an original – or at least first-generation reissue – fragment of *His New Job* on amber stock). One of the first experiments in computer-added colour used an extract from *The Tramp*, but no other Chaplin items seem to have followed, at least in Britain.

(See also: Hair; One A.M.; Race)

COME SEVEN

See: Abandoned projects and *Pay Day*

CONKLIN, CHARLES 'HEINIE'
(1880–1959)

Although a Sennett stalwart, Heinie Conklin – also known as Charlie Lynn – seems to have joined a year after Chaplin's departure (thus disqualifying him from status as an 'original Keystone Cop'), and consequently does not appear in any of his Keystones. He may be seen instead as a workman in *Modern Times* (*qv*), one of the many small rôles he played as a veteran. In his heyday, 'Charlie Lynn' (whose trademark was a long, Chinese-looking moustache curling at the ends) received joint billing with Ben Turpin (*qv*) in the British comic

paper *Film Fun*. Not to be confused with, and seemingly not related to, Chester Conklin (*qv*).

(See also: Keystone; Sennett, Mack)

CONKLIN, CHESTER
(1888–1971)

(Chaplin films *qv*)
Iowa-born comedian (real name Jules Cowles) with experience in stock, vaudeville (as a 'Dutch' comic) and the circus; reportedly studied law for a while, in between various odd jobs. Some accounts claim he entered films in 1913 at the Majestic studio (where some of Chaplin's Essanays would later be made); others say he left either the Al G. Barnes or Barnum Circus for Keystone (*qv*) when the show was wintering in California, then gained additional experience during a brief time away at Majestic. Whatever the exact sequence, Conklin first began to achieve eminence that year amid the Keystone Cops, and especially as the studio's hugely-moustached 'Walrus', a comic villain usually cast opposite Mack Swain (*qv*) as 'Ambrose'. He appears thus in most of Chaplin's Keystones, although he may be seen, barely recognizable, without make-up in *Twenty Minutes of Love* and *The Face On the Bar Room Floor*. On joining the studio, Chaplin was somewhat overawed by his new colleagues, Conklin in particular; yet it was Conklin who persuaded Chaplin not to quit when he had clashed with Mabel Normand (*qv*). The two comedians worked well together and, as noted elsewhere, jointly devised the plot of *Dough and Dynamite*. Conklin has been identified playing two rôles (a tramp and a cop) in Chaplin's first Keystone, *Making a Living*; he is the elderly man occupying the hotel room opposite Mabel Normand in *Mabel's Strange Predicament*; a cop in *Between Showers* and *Mabel's Busy Day*; a costumed dancer in *Tango Tangles*, again rendering him difficult to spot; *Mabel at the Wheel* casts him as father of the titular heroine; he is Charlie's fellow-waiter in *Caught in a Cabaret* and his erstwhile replacement in *The Masquerader*; he is Charlie's romantic rival in *Those Love Pangs* and an unwelcomed guest in *Tillie's Punctured Romance*; while he takes a further pasting from Charlie in *Gentlemen of Nerve*. He has been cited as the butler in *Cruel, Cruel Love* but this is debatable. Conklin remained with Sennett for some time after Chaplin's departure. One of the best-known 'Walrus-Ambrose' films of this

Chester Conklin worked with Chaplin at Keystone, and reappeared much later, as in this scene from Modern Times

period is *Love, Speed and Thrills* (1915); Conklin also appeared as a different character, 'Droppington', as in *Droppington's Family Tree* (1915). Conklin's later silent work – characterized by the addition of thick glasses – included time with Fox's Sunshine Comedies, brief partnerships with Charlie Murray (*qv*) and a trio of Paramount comedy features with W.C. Fields, *Two Flaming Youths* (1927), the 1928 remake of *Tillie's Punctured Romance* (*qv*) and, also from 1928, *Fools For Luck*. Lahue and Gill's *Clown Princes and Court Jesters* reports Conklin working for Joe Rock-Standard Cinema in 1925–6 and with Hank Mann (*qv*) during 1926–7. Among many silent features are *We're in the Navy Now* (1926) and *Gentlemen Prefer Blondes* (1928), which included also Conklin's old Keystone tutor, Ford Sterling (*qv*). Perhaps the most profound picture in Conklin's career is Von Stroheim's *Greed* (1924). Conklin's early talkies include Warners' revue film, *Show of Shows* (1930), and a further film with W.C. Fields, *Her Majesty, Love* (1931, in which Sterling also appears). He was reunited with Chaplin in the later factory scenes of *Modern Times*, and subsequently took a minor rôle in *The Great Dictator* as the barbershop customer who is shaved to music. Conklin also turned up in a number of Three Stooges shorts, as well as being on the usual list when slapstick veterans were sought, as in Fox's *Hollywood*

Cavalcade (1939) and the 1947 fictionalized biopic of Pearl White, *The Perils of Pauline*. By 1954, Conklin's career had wound down, to the point where a syndicated newspaper story revealed he was working as a department store Father Christmas. He took it all from a sanguine viewpoint, explaining how the job combined his love of children with that of acting. A small film rôle, in *Li'l Abner*, followed in 1959, but two years later saw him retiring, for health reasons, to a hospital for veterans of the film industry (he had recently contributed to *Paradise Alley*, released in 1962). This seemed the end of the line, but Chester shocked the nation once more by announcing, in 1965, that he was to marry and set up private residence again. That same year also brought a postscript to his film career in *A Big Hand for the Little Lady* (released in 1966).

(See also: Chase, Charley; Essanay; Lehrman, Henry 'Pathé'; Policemen; Sennett, Mack)

COOGAN, JACKIE
(1914–84)

Child actor, born to parents in vaudeville. Anthony Slide's *Early American Cinema* cites as his first film a 1915 Essanay production, *Skinner's Baby*, when interviewed by Jay Rubin for *Classic Film Collector* in 1976, Coogan could recall nothing of the experience, having been perhaps eighteen months old at the time, but he knew that his mother had been approached by the studio when the family was in Chicago. His father, Jack Coogan Sr, brought the boy on stage when appearing at the Orpheum Theater in Los Angeles; Chaplin was in the audience, watching a by then seven-year-old Jackie doing various bits such as imitations, jokes and a song-and-dance, and decided to seek him out. As Coogan later admitted, there was an element of design in this manoeuvre, for Coogan Sr was well aware of the film industry's habit of recruiting from vaudeville. Chaplin was with theatre owner Sid Grauman, who knew the Coogans and promised an introduction. It was arranged for Jackie to be tested – unpaid! – as one of the children in *A Day's Pleasure* (qv). Coogan told Rubin that Chaplin lost interest in that film, finishing it up quickly because he had developed the basic idea of *The*

Jackie Coogan *met Chaplin again in 1972, reportedly to the comedian's disquiet*

Kid (qv).

In the intervening period, Coogan Sr decided to forsake vaudeville for the movies, and signed with Roscoe 'Fatty' Arbuckle (qv). The younger Coogan told Arbuckle's biographer, David Yallop, of Arbuckle's visits to the Coogan household, where the gentle comedian would play with the youngster. Chaplin heard of 'Jack Coogan' having signed with Arbuckle, and thought the boy's acting talents had been secured; relieved to discover the truth, he signed young Jackie immediately, and *The Kid* entered production.

It has been suggested that Chaplin was prompted to make *The Kid* after the death of his own son, Norman Spencer Chaplin, during production of *A Day's Pleasure*; certainly the presence of a gifted child actor at this time would explain the story's genesis. *The Kid*'s protracted creation worried Chaplin's distributors, First National (qv) who, having had no indication of what had been occupying his time, needed to be reassured. They were invited to the Chaplin studio to see Jackie perform; film of this event may be seen in *The Gentleman Tramp* and *Unknown Chaplin* (both qv), to which Coogan also contributed interviews. Chaplin's lengthy, undisclosed film project, coupled with the presence of the child and the recent loss of his own son,

swiftly combined into unfounded speculation on both his professional and domestic lives. *Picture Show* of 14 February 1920 quoted him as denying three American press rumours: that (a) he was making an aviation picture, (b) he had bought a Chinese house and (c), most importantly, that he had adopted a baby. Chaplin had no intention of adopting Jackie, but a paternal attitude certainly characterized their relationship. One important aspect was Chaplin's ability to communicate exactly what he wanted Jackie to convey. In later interviews, Coogan denied a much-repeated tale to the effect that, in the scene where he is to be taken away by the authorities, he was reduced to tears by a threat to make his abandonment genuine. All Chaplin had needed to do was explain the scene in the fashion of 'you-want-to-go-with-this-man-and-you-don't-want-to-go-with-this-man', after which Jackie understood his supposed dilemma perfectly. Coogan's version is substantiated by an extant photo, from between takes, showing the beaming youngster aboard the orphanage truck. Coogan also recalled having been on a straight salary with Chaplin, and that his father had made more money from *The Kid* than he; despite an existing obligation to Arbuckle, Coogan Sr was taken on as an assistant, checking such things as camera angles, in addition to playing seven minor acting rôles.

Although it would have been easy to assume that Jackie Coogan's success had been entirely due to Chaplin, at least one source, the *New York Times*, suspected otherwise. 'Come on, Jack Coogan,' it declared after *The Kid*'s charity première, 'there must be more of you.' Indeed there was, for, after leaving Chaplin, the youngster starred in a lengthy series of silent features, each extremely successful. (One of the more unexpected sidelights of Coogan's eminence – and its reflection upon his father – is a 1920s 78 r.p.m. record, entitled *Master Jackie Coogan – Introducing His Dad*. Father and son engage in barbed banter, during which it becomes clear who the real 'Mr Coogan' is.) Most of Coogan's starring features have since been lost; one survivor, his 1922 version of *Oliver Twist*, was rediscovered during the early 1970s. Although it was an East European copy, Coogan was able to assist in a re-translation.

Coogan's career started to decline with the onset of adolescence; he made talkie versions of *Tom Sawyer* and *Huckleberry Finn*, but was by then outgrowing his familiar persona. His career reached a hiatus; on 22 October 1932 *Picturegoer* reported that Jackie Coogan was studying at Santa Clara University and was 'in training to be a cheer leader at the football games'. His education completed, Coogan decided to resume his career, touring variety theatres on both sides of the Atlantic prior to making his next movie. On 29 December 1934, *Picture Show* said: 'It is a far different Jackie Coogan who has just returned to films. The director of "Code of the West" discovered that he didn't have a winsome child to deal with when scenes called for Jackie to stage a fight with Allan Wood. Jackie is now six feet tall, weighs just over ten stone, and learned quite a bit about boxing at his university.'

The 1930s brought their most severe shock with the discovery that the money earned by his silent films had disappeared. The young star had never seen any of the millions earned by Jackie Coogan Productions, which had been formed by his father; Coogan Sr was by then deceased, and when his son approached his mother and stepfather for the money, she invoked a California law that made parents entitled to all monies earned by their children. The court case led to new regulations being introduced

to protect the earnings of child artists, this legislation becoming known popularly as the 'Coogan Law'.

Coogan served in the Second World Wa, and eventually returned to acting. In 1951, Chaplin biographer Theodore Huff claimed that Coogan had been reported as 'part-owner of a kitchen-ventilator company'; this may well have been true, but Coogan was certainly also active in show business. In the Rubin interview, he mentions having been in 'surface aircraft' following discharge from the service, but returned to the entertainment profession via nightclub work in 1946 and television two years later; in January 1952 *Picturegoer* noted Coogan playing a gunslinger in a forthcoming western, *Outlaw Woman*. He became better known to the TV generation as 'Uncle Fester' in *The Addams Family* during the mid-1960s.

Coogan had always remained friendly with Chaplin, with whom he was reunited on the comedian's return to America in 1972 (although Carol Matthau relates an amusing story of Chaplin initially trying to ignore him, through an alleged fear that his former colleague might want residuals!). In *My Life in Pictures*, published two years later, Chaplin wrote of the 'touching' experience of seeing Coogan as 'a bald man with a fat tummy!' As noted above, Jackie Coogan was frequently on hand in latter days to supply recollections of Chaplin. One such interview was conducted on BBC Radio 2, during a UK visit of the early 1970s.

(See also: Aircraft; Austin, Albert; Awards; Children; Documentaries, compilations; Essanay; Grey, Lita; *Nice and Friendly*; Politics)

COOKE, ALISTAIR

See: Abandoned projects, *City Lights*, *Height*, *Limelight* and *Unknown Chaplin*

COSTUME 🎩

(Chaplin films *qv*)
The screen image adopted by Charlie Chaplin is the most recognizable in the history of film. As stated elsewhere, it took a few weeks to develop, and his first film, *Making a Living*, presents him in an uncharacteristic top hat, frock coat and drooping moustache (versions of this costume would recur in *Cruel, Cruel Love* and *Mabel at the Wheel*). Minta Durfee

(*qv*) told historian David Yallop that one of Chaplin's early experiments was as a comic fat man, an idea turned down by Mack Sennett (*qv*) on the grounds that Arbuckle was already doing well in that rôle.

Detailed under *Kid Auto Races at Venice* and *Mabel's Strange Predicament* are the conflicting opinions as to when Chaplin introduced his 'tramp' persona. The famous story – repeated here only in the interests of completeness – is that Chaplin was required to assemble a 'funny costume', and did so from the following borrowed elements: Arbuckle's oversized trousers; a small bowler owned by Minta Durfee's father; a tight, cutaway jacket – often fastened with a safety pin – reportedly borrowed from actor/director Charles Avery; large shoes owned by Ford Sterling (*qv*), placed on the wrong feet so they would stay on; a moustache trimmed down from Mack Swain's, and a bamboo cane. The shoes, which brought ungainliness to Chaplin's normally small and graceful feet, added a substantial base to the image. Without them he seems poorly anchored and just a little too nimble in relation to the shuffling walk. They are also the subject of a much-cited gag in *Mabel's Married Life*, when he hangs his hat over a shoe in order to mask a gap worn into the sole. The bowler, a staple of music-hall comics, lent a middle-class aspect (at least to British audiences) and permitted him to use the old trick of rolling it along the length of his arm, prior to catching it (as in *Mabel's Busy Day* and *Police*). The bowler is dented to form a trilby when he is anxious to impress, as in *Twenty Minutes of Love* or *His New Profession*, the latter also betraying a detached brim. (This gag was borrowed, though in a different context, by Stan Laurel [*qv*] in the famous Laurel & Hardy short, *The Music Box*.) Chaplin often received bowler hats as gifts. His publicist, Elsie Codd, issued a story (published in *Picture Show* of 3 April 1920) concerning two such hats sent by an 'unknown admirer in the East', which reached the studio minus packing, in a terrible state and covered in labels bearing affectionate messages, poetry, prose and the like. It was evident that staff at each railroad stop on the journey had decided to add their own message to the long-distance hats, endowing them with 'a striking family resemblance to the "fretful porcupine"'.

Charlie was also in the habit of wearing a collar and tie, again in keeping with a man anxious to preserve

Costume: Chaplin's tramp outfit was composed from various elements

appearances. The cane ties into this strong self-image, inappropriate to a tramp; it would see additional service as a weapon (*The Rink*) or as an extended arm (when appropriating a bag during *In the Park*).

The costume was designed to introduce a series of contradictions, using the contrasting sizes. It should be noted, however, that his very first appearances do not include the large shoes; nor is this necessarily the definitive story. Charles Chaplin Jr (in his book, *My Father, Charlie Chaplin*) told a different version, as related by his father. In this account, Chaplin had once filled in as a caretaker in a music-hall, where he was required to deputize for the star comic. The other comedian's clothes were a poor fit, and Chaplin worked out a routine in which he would fall into a tub of water, causing the huge trousers to inflate with air and thus allow him to float on the surface. (One might note in passing that R.J. Minney's *Chaplin, the Immortal Tramp* – a work which, privately, Chaplin is said to have deemed inaccurate – cites the comedian's rag-and-bone-man rôle in a Karno sketch, *London Suburbia*, as the costume's debut.)

Chaplin adopted a moustache, he claimed, because Sennett had expected someone older; it might be added, though, that at least one photograph of Chaplin with the Karno Company (*qv*) shows him with the toothbrush

moustache as early as 1911. It has sometimes been said that the moustache was painted on, but this is untrue. It is clearly three-dimensional, and film exists of Chaplin applying and trimming the item (see **The Chaplin Revue** and **How To Make Movies**). By the time of *The Circus*, Chaplin, presumably to allow for greater visibility of expression, had reduced the size of his moustache. This remained the case through *City Lights* and *Modern Times*, but the larger version, coincidentally an approximation of Hitler's, made an appropriate reappearance in *The Great Dictator*. According to contemporary publicity, the neat moustache sported by *Monsieur Verdoux* was genuine.

Make-up usually took the standard comedian's technique of whitening out the face. Better-quality prints and production stills reveal a clear division as the made-up portion meets the natural skin colour. Chaplin's make-up around the eyes and to the eyebrows was heavy, partly in accord with industry practice of the day (probably a legacy of the stage rather than through any inadequacy in the film stock). Chaplin retained the heavy eye make-up long after it had passed from general use, although his especially blackened eyes in *The Gold Rush* are intended to convey extreme hardship and near-starvation.

There is a tendency to assume that Chaplin's tramp costume did not vary through the years. Closer examination will reveal such things as an elaborate waistcoat in some of the Essanay films and later, also the occasional use of a lighter-coloured bowler when wishing to seem sporty (as in *A Night Out*, *The Count* or, especially, *Mabel's Busy Day*, in which he wears the loud garb of a racing tout). In the experimental Keystone days, there would be variants such as that noted above, or the top hat in *Mabel's Married Life* (an image often used by imitator Billy West).

Among the more noticeable variants are the tieless, caneless Charlie of *A Dog's Life* and, especially, his appearance at the end of *City Lights*. To suggest the tramp's sacrifice and consequent hardship, his costume is more ragged than ever, and the tie and cane have once more disappeared (there are several gags in *City Lights* concerning his disintegrating gloves and torn trousers). Similarly, in *The Tramp*, Charlie, in fighting mode, pulls his jacket down past his shoulders but replaces it on realizing that Edna can see he has no shirtsleeves. In turn, his striped

shirtsleeves in *Police* and *Triple Trouble* suggest a recent release from prison.

Charlie appears in various types of prison garb for *The Adventurer*, *The Pilgrim*, *Modern Times* and *The Great Dictator*. Other uniforms include a sailor's rig in *Shanghaied*, military equivalents in *His New Job*, *Carmen*, *Shoulder Arms* and *The Great Dictator*, a policeman's uniform in *Easy Street* and a fascist uniform as *The Great Dictator*. Occupations, too, impose a specific costume, such as the waiter's clothes in *The Rink* or *A Countess From Hong Kong*, or a mechanic's overalls in *Modern Times*.

There were also occasions when Charlie could portray something of a man-about-town, as in *The Rounders* and his *alter ego* in *The Idle Class*. As noted under **Alcohol**, it has been suggested that his natty costume in *The Cure* – straw boater and light summer jacket – was designed to offset the more negative aspects of his character's alcoholism. Earlier, in *One A.M.*, he had portrayed a drunken reveller attired in evening dress, similar to his stage character in *Mumming Birds* and its film equivalent, *A Night in the Show*; the elegant clothes serve this time to contrast the man's attempted dignity with his frequent humiliation by inanimate objects, though one also suspects Chaplin to have varied his appearance in order to prove a point. On 21 April 1917, Elsie Codd (in *Pictures and the Picturegoer*) cited *One A.M.* as evidence of Chaplin's ability to be equally funny in 'a normal suit of clothes'. 'Those of his detractors who still persist in the fond illusion that his rise to fame and fortune is entirely due to an outsize in boots and trousers,' she continued, 'have now an opportunity of seeing him beat all his former records faultlessly groomed and immaculately tailored.'

No Chaplin portrayal was as faultlessly groomed as *Monsieur Verdoux*, his first character to post-date the 'tramp' image. That he did not feel able to discard the image completely is implicit when in *Limelight*, his 'Calvero' performs a comic song in a straw-hatted variant on the old costume. It may be significant that many advertisements for the film used this semi-recognizable figure as a central image.

(See also: Alcohol; Arbuckle, Roscoe 'Fatty'; Children; Dual rôles; Essanay; Impersonators; Keystone; Marx, Groucho; Purviance, Edna; Prison; Swain, Mack; Walk, The)

By courtesy of Robert G. Dickson

THE COUNT

The bogus Count makes merry with the heiress and the supply of refreshment
Museum of Modern Art/Film Stills Archive

(Chaplin film)
Released by Mutual, 4 September 1916.
Written and directed by Charles
Chaplin. Photographed by Rollie
Totheroh. Two reels. 2,017 feet.

With Charlie Chaplin (himself, as tailor's
assistant), Edna Purviance (Miss
Moneybags), Eric Campbell (tailor), Eva
Thatcher (cook), Leo White (Count
Broko), Charlotte Mineau (Mrs
Moneybags), James T. Kelly (butler),
Albert Austin, John Rand, Loyal
Underwood (party guests).

Charlie, a tailor's assistant, shows cloth to
a lady customer. Taking her
measurements, Charlie includes
irrelevant areas such as the ear and mouth.
Her waist measurement is taken with the
tape measure around both the customer
and a dressmaker's form. The boss takes
over, but Charlie hinders by tugging at
the tape measure. The lady takes
umbrage and departs. The boss finds that
Charlie has permitted a hot iron to burn
through several layers of cloth. Charlie is
dismissed. At this time, Miss Moneybags
is holding a plush dinner party. In his
shop, the tailor finds a letter in a coat
belonging to a customer. It is a letter
from one Count Broko to Miss
Moneybags' mother, declining the party
invitation but expressing the belief that
he will love the heiress at first sight. The
tailor gets an idea. In the kitchen of the
Moneybags' residence, the butler orders
the cook to destroy some over-strong

cheese. The cook's gentleman friend,
Charlie, calls and is served the cheese.
The tailor sets off to the party, posing as
the Count. Charlie, holding his nose,
consumes the cheese. When the butler
returns, Charlie and the cheese are
concealed in a basket. Charlie throws out
the cheese and the cook replaces it. The
tailor arrives at the front door. Charlie
throws out the cheese again, this time
hitting the butler. The puzzled butler
departs to answer the door. The cheese is
dumped back in the basket. Charlie and
cheese emerge, only for Charlie to hide
in a dumb waiter as the cook greets
another caller, a cop; when the butler
returns, the cop has to share the basket
with the cheese, thoughtfully thrown in
by Charlie. The tailor is shown in by the
butler. While the bogus count is
announced, Charlie enters the hallway via
the dumb waiter. He confronts his former
employer, who, telling him of the
imposture, suggests that Charlie can pose
as his secretary. Charlie pushes in ahead
and is taken for the Count, with the
tailor as 'secretary'. At dinner, Charlie
takes a seat beside the heiress, whose
conversation he cannot hear above the
tailor's slurping of soup. When spaghetti
is served, Charlie amuses his fellow-diners
by gesturing, conjuror-like, as the food
disappears into the tailor's mouth. Next
on the menu is watermelon, which makes
Charlie's ears wet. He solves the problem
by tying a napkin around his head. On
leaving the table, the tailor pats Charlie's

back, sending down a cascade of
silverware from his waistcoat. Charlie
pretends it has come from the tailor's coat
and escorts Miss Moneybags into the
foyer. The cook, seeing Charlie with the
heiress, swoons as Charlie hastily returns
the young lady upstairs to the ballroom.
The tailor leads Mrs Moneybags to the
dance floor while Charlie excuses himself.
Downstairs, he begins to explain matters
to the cook, only to be lured back
upstairs by a pretty guest in a harem
costume. He follows her through the
ballroom, garden and back to the
corridor while the tailor is dancing with
Miss Moneybags. When the harem girl
disappears behind a curtain, Charlie
assumes it is the kind of place where a
gentleman cannot follow. He renews his
pursuit when a man emerges. The first
dance over, the tailor leads Miss
Moneybags from the floor; Charlie takes
over, engaging the heiress in a rather odd
two-step, hooking his cane on the
chandelier in order to stand up. Next is a
tango, from which Charlie exits with
knees bent. They are joined by the other
dancers for an Elizabethan-style dance;
Charlie lands a kick on the tailor, who in
reply lands a kick on Charlie; he in turn
kicks the tailor, whose attempts to
respond are thwarted when Charlie
repeatedly moves the heiress into his
firing line. Charlie and the heiress retire
to the garden. The butler tells the cook
she is wanted upstairs. As the tailor takes
Charlie aside to warn him away from

Miss Moneybags, another guest escorts her back to the dance floor. The tailor rudely interrupts, but it is Charlie who becomes her dancing partner. Spotting the cook, Charlie exits to the buffet table, allowing the tailor to partner the heiress. Downstairs, the real count arrives. Told there is already a 'Count Broko' present, he departs to fetch the authorities. The harem girl returns, and Charlie, flirting, starts to hit the food with his cane. Some of it strikes the tailor and other guests; one of them issues a challenge by hurling a glass of wine in Charlie's face. He responds by pouring the punch bowl over them and takes to his heels, sliding over the dance floor as the tailor fires a revolver. Downstairs, the Count is waiting with the police; Charlie deals with both, and the chase continues upstairs. Charlie throws a cake over the furious nobleman and eludes a second officer; the tailor is led away as Charlie rushes down the street.

An efficient, very amusing farce, *The Count* is largely overlooked among the Mutuals. This may be due in part to the absence of a strong central focus (though the watermelon gag was and is much appreciated) or the fact that it overlaps with several other films in which Charlie masquerades as some sort of dignitary, most notably *Caught in a Cabaret* (*qv*) and a later Mutual, *The Rink* (also *qv*). Whatever the reason, *The Count* maintains the high standard of the series and deserves more prominence in the public memory. Despite a myth concerning Chaplin's 'static' direction, there is again use of a travelling camera in the dinner and ballroom sequences.

Reissue prints have been subject to various cuts, most frequently the section in which spaghetti is served, the stolen cutlery gag and the final shots of the tailor being led away, followed by Charlie's escape down the street. Both the 'Chaplin Carnival' version shown in Britain on Channel 4 and the BBC *Chaplin SuperClown* copy have these sequences intact, though the 'Carnival' seems slightly cropped around the point where Charlie hurls the cheese in the policeman's direction. The BBC version omits an insert of the measurements Charlie has taken of a lady customer ('Neck 12; Ear 1½; Mouth 2; Waste 5 feet; finger 1'). Other inserts, of the Count's letter and calling card, have been unnecessarily replaced in this edition. Footage from *The Count* appears in the 1967 documentary *The Funniest Man in the World* (*qv*), including, intriguingly, a different shot in which Charlie delivers a mule-like kick to a policeman. In most prints, Charlie's kick seems barely to brush against his victim's chest, whereas on this occasion he strikes the cop in the face. The cop also makes more of an attempt to outmanoeuvre him. As noted under *The Floorwalker*, *Easy Street*, *A Dog's Life*, *Shoulder Arms*, *The Kid* and *Pay Day*, such alternate takes of Chaplin material are quite uncommon, the probable result of reissues (*qv*) deriving from a single version.

(See also: Austin, Albert; Campbell, Eric; Costume; Food; Home movies; Kelly, James T.; Mineau, Charlotte; Mutual; Policemen; Purviance, Edna; Rand, John; Television; Thatcher, Eva; Titling; Underwood, Loyal; Video releases; White, Leo)

A COUNTESS FROM HONG KONG

(Chaplin film)
Released by Universal, 5 January 1967 (UK). Produced by Jerome Epstein. Written and directed by Charles Chaplin. Music composed by Charles Chaplin, arranged and conducted by Lambert Williamson. Music associate: Eric James. Director of photography: Arthur Ibbetson, B.S.C. Production supervisor: Denis Johnson. Assistant director: Jack Causey. Editor: Gordon Hales. Art director: Bob Cartwright. Technicolor. 108 mins.

With Marlon Brando (Ogden Mears), Sophia Loren (Natascha), Sydney Chaplin (Harvey), Tippi Hedren (Martha), Patrick Cargill (Hudson), Michael Medwin (John Felix), Oliver Johnston (Clark), John Paul (Captain), Angela Scoular (Society girl), Margaret Rutherford (Miss Gaulswallow), Peter Bartlett (steward), Bill Nagy (Crawford), Dilys Laye (saleswoman), Angela Pringle (Baroness), Jenny Bridges (Countess), Arthur Gross (Immigration Officer), Balbina (French maid), Anthony Chin, Jose Sukhum Boonlyve (Hawaiians), Geraldine Chaplin (girl at dance), Janine Hill (second girl at dance), Burnell Tucker (hotel receptionist), Leonard Trolley (purser), Len Lowe (electrician), Francis Dux (head waiter), Cecil Cheng (taxi driver), Ronald Rubin, Michael Spice, Ray Marlowe (American sailors), Josephine and Victoria Chaplin (two young girls), Kevin Manser

A Countess From Hong Kong: *as usual, Chaplin acted out each rôle; here he deputizes for Sophia Loren in mid-clinch*

(photographer), Marianne Stone, Lew Luton, Larry Cross, Bill Edwards, Drew Russell, John Sterland, Paul Carson, Paul Tamarin (reporters), Carol Cleveland (nurse), Jerry Epstein (cameo as barman), Charles Chaplin (an old steward).

A dance hall in Hong Kong promises the company of genuine countesses at the rate of 50 cents per dance. An ocean liner docks in Hong Kong for an overnight stay. On board is Ogden, a millionaire politician whose own skills are frequently eclipsed when the press reminds everyone of his father, the world's richest oilman. Accompanying Ogden is an associate, Harvey, a secretary, Crawford, and Ogden's valet, Hudson. Harvey mentions Ogden's imminent divorce and likely appointment as US Secretary of State. Word arrives of the job going to someone else, so Ogden agrees to 'celebrate' on the town with Harvey. Ogden's plans for a wild evening seem endangered by the arrival of Mr Clark, a senior director of his father's, but the old man arranges for them to spend an evening with three beautiful women from the dance hall, comprising two countesses and a baroness. At a restaurant, Clark discreetly explains the titles to be genuine, the result of Russian émigrés who had fled initially to Shanghai. Their descendents have led difficult lives; this applies particularly to Natascha, Ogden's date for the evening, who, aged fourteen and alone in the world, had become mistress to a gangster. The next morning, a hungover Ogden awakens to find he has been given a diplomatic job in Saudi Arabia. Another discovery is Natascha, hiding in his closet while the ship is two hours out at sea. She had joined the previous night's revelry and saw her chance to escape to America, leaving behind a world of dance halls and prostitution. Natascha asks to remain in Ogden's suite only until the purser has made a count of the passengers. Ogden is reluctant, but is persuaded to let her stay until the first port of call. Natascha must be fed, and is given a menu, but her choice of food raises eyebrows through being at odds with Ogden's hangover. That night, separate and uneasy sleeping arrangements are made, Ogden turning over his bedroom to Natascha while taking the couch for himself. Next day, Natascha is to depart. Harvey and Crawford inform Ogden of a party of reporters anxious to obtain an interview. Natascha must be concealed despite visits from Hudson and the steward. Natascha takes a leisurely breakfast. Because she has only an evening dress, Ogden attempts to buy her some day clothes, but they are large and old-fashioned. Among the items is a massively oversized bra. Natascha refuses to go ashore, and a furious Ogden tries to force her into changing out of his pyjamas. She has taken refuge in the bathroom just as the journalists are ushered in. During the press conference, Harvey discovers Natascha's presence. Later, Ogden tells Harvey what has happened. He has offered to pay Natascha's fare back to Hong Kong, but she will not go. As it is too late to disembark and abandon Natascha, Harvey agrees to talk to her. When questioned, Natascha foresees no difficulty in entering the United States without passport or visa. Their interview is suspended when an elderly steward calls to inform them of rough weather and a consequent need to close all portholes. Harvey offers to arrange her passage to America, provided she disembarks at Tokyo and takes another boat. A substantial bribe is also offered, but Natascha does not want money. Discussions slow down as the weather induces seasickness. Despite Natascha's threat to fabricate a tale of abduction and assault, the nauseous Ogden decides to tell all to the Captain. He gets no further than the bathroom, and soon all three are heaving. The elderly steward calls again but, also seasick, makes a swift exit. Natascha grows in Ogden's affections when she nurses him through severe seasickness, even to the point of risking herself by wanting to call the ship's doctor. The pyjama-clad Natascha

Chaplin – wearing his glasses – rehearses his small rôle as steward in **A Countess From Hong Kong ...**

remains in Ogden's suite while her host attends a dance. He meets an attractive but tedious society girl who informs him of a lady passenger who has been confined to her quarters throughout the voyage. Harvey calls on Natascha, assuring her that Ogden will miss her after she has gone. When an electrician walks in using a passkey, Harvey suggests she would be safer for a while in the ballroom. Natascha, in her evening gown, is escorted in by Harvey, who goes in search of Ogden. Natascha dances with several partners, one of whom is the Captain. Natascha is taken to be the woman who has been confined to her cabin. Her next partner is Ogden, who is informed of the reasons for her departure from the cabin; the next is one John Felix, who, recognizing Natascha from Hong Kong, offers a her a job in America. 'I'm not looking for *that* kind of work,' she replies. She is reluctant to divulge her cabin number to Felix, who claims he can ask the purser. The persistent man forces Natascha to stay for a drink; Ogden and Harvey sit nearby. Harvey intercepts Felix so that Natascha can return to the cabin, where Ogden expresses his disappointment in her. He calls her a 'common harlot', suggesting she go to the other man's cabin. Natascha decides to give herself up, but Ogden kisses her. She is persuaded to surrender to Ogden rather than the authorities. Next morning, Felix makes enquiries after Natascha and is referred to the lady who has been confined to her cabin; she is Miss Gaulswallow, an elderly hypochondriac.

Flowers arrive for her, but Miss Gaulswallow has her nurse take them away. The Captain arrives, bearing chocolates for Miss Gaulswallow, but is disconcerted to meet the true owner of that name. Felix walks in, carrying a bouquet, takes one look at Miss Gaulswallow and rushes back outside. In their cabin, Ogden and Natascha play chess. Natascha is asked about her boyfriend, the alleged gangster. He had taken care of Natascha but was too old for her, and has since died. Ogden is worried about Natascha obtaining entry to the United States. She plans to disembark at the next port, Hawaii, where such a move will be easier. They are happy, for the moment. Ogden leaves the cabin to send some urgent cablegrams. Harvey arrives, telling Natascha of Felix's continued efforts to trace her, but she is preoccupied. She has fallen for Ogden, and has only two days left with him. Harvey is horrified to learn of Natascha's intention to dive overboard at Honolulu and sneak a boat to shore. The day arrives, and Harvey is cornered on deck by the boring society girl. She has a portable radio, from which Harvey learns that Martha, Ogden's wife, plans to meet him at Honolulu and accompany him to Washington. He finds Ogden, who is already been informed by telegram. His wife plans to board that evening, and has no plans to divorce. Natascha must be passed off as the wife of Hudson, the valet. Hudson has long since been a naturalized American, and would thus be able to bring a 'wife' into the USA. Hudson agrees to a hasty, platonic wedding and a divorce soon after landing in America. Harvey concocts a story of Natascha's papers having been blown overboard, and the Captain agrees to conduct a discreet wedding ceremony. Hudson faints at the words 'till death do you part'. They are to spend their wedding night in the same room but occupying separate beds. Ogden must be on hand to explain Natascha's presence to his wife. Natascha, worried that Hudson may wish to consummate their union, watches incredulously as the excited man leaps around his bed in an attempt to settle. Ogden calls in, asking Hudson to find him some nightclothes. Harvey informs him that Martha will not arrive until four o'clock the next afternoon. Ogden takes Hudson's place in the bedroom. Next morning, Hudson is hurriedly reinstated when a steward calls. Over breakfast, the Captain states that, despite the supposedly lost papers, Natascha will need to prove her identity. Security has been tightened owing to a report of a female stowaway. Without identification, the marriage will not be legal and Natascha will have to face a board of enquiry. The Captain leaves when informed that the purser wants to see him. Hudson is briefed in his account of meeting Natascha on board, of their falling in love at first sight and, even less plausibly, of her papers being lost overboard. Ogden accompanies him to the interview with the authorities. Natascha, arranging to meet Harvey on Waikiki beach (if she makes it), emulates some Hawaiians who are making spectacular dives from the ship. The authorities ask to see Hudson's wife. Martha and her French maid arrive in Ogden's suite, to be greeted by Harvey. Martha is somewhat surprised to learn of Hudson's marriage. The Captain enters, wishing to see Natascha. Harvey pretends she has just finished a bath, leaving the Captain in the uneasy company of Martha. Natascha swims to shore. Ogden meets his wife and the Captain, who explains that the authorities want to see Natascha. Without papers she cannot land anywhere, being technically non-existent. Martha is clearly suspicious. Natascha hops a lift to Waikiki on a truck. The Captain is puzzled by Natascha's disappearance; using mime, Harvey silently tells Ogden of her diving act. The entire vessel will be searched. Martha questions Hudson over his marriage, and is told it has not been consummated. Ogden is dissuaded from going ashore with Harvey in favour of lunch with Martha. Alone, they discuss marital details. A letter from Washington has requested they should remain together for the sake of appearances. If their arrangements do not work out, Martha is interested only in money. They have no children. Martha also has no enthusiasm to live in Saudi Arabia. Harvey takes a cab to Waikiki. He checks into the hotel, and is surprised to learn Waikiki beach is actually outside. On the beach, he meets Natascha. He has brought her some clothes. He arranges a hotel suite for Natascha, claiming she is his wife. Natascha, in her new and overly-tight clothes, checks in just as Martha walks in with Hudson. The valet recognizes his absent wife, but Harvey claims he has said that of several women since Natascha's disappearance. Natascha is introduced to Martha as Harvey's wife.

At dinner, Martha makes frosty conversation about Harvey's supposed marriage. Harvey takes her to the dance floor. Once alone, Ogden tells Natascha that while in Saudi Arabia, he will continue to liaise with Harvey in obtaining her a passport. He mentions also Washington's preference for Martha to join him in Saudi Arabia, for the sake of appearances. He would prefer to give up the whole thing, but Natascha will not let him. As Martha watches from the dance floor, Ogden tries to look dispassionate when declaring his love for Natascha. Martha has not been fooled; she has evidently been talking to Felix and knows Natascha's history. Natascha cannot face saying goodbye, and retires to her room. Next day, Ogden and his wife prepare to sail. Clearing most of her husband's things to make room for her own clothes, Martha finds the huge bra that had been bought for Natascha. She speaks of Natascha being palmed off variously as the wife of both Harvey and the valet, adding contemptuous reference to her background as mistress and prostitute. Ogden asks how Martha might have fared in similar circumstances. The ship sails without Ogden. He contacts Harvey and learns that the immigration officials have given Natascha the benefit of the doubt. Ogden forsakes politics in favour of happiness and, unannounced, meets Natascha at the hotel.

Chaplin had originally written *A Countess From Hong Kong*, in a version entitled 'Stowaway', as a vehicle for Paulette Goddard (*qv*) back in 1937. It had been inspired by a earlier visit to Shanghai, where he found exiled male Russian aristocrats running rickshaws, and their women reduced to working in ten-cent dance halls. Chaplin later discovered how conditions had worsened for them after the Second World War forced a migration to Hong Kong. When the project was eventually revived, the leading male character was modelled somewhat on John F. Kennedy – reportedly a supporter of Chaplin's cause in the US – but disguised somewhat after Kennedy's unexpected death.

When in Amsterdam to receive the Erasmus Prize in June 1965, Chaplin announced that his new film was to be made in England, as part of 'British Quota'. Shooting was expected to take place in the autumn, concluding by or before 1 January 1966, with editing and scoring to follow. Jerry Epstein (*qv*), who

received producer credit on the film, had the unenviable task of settling arguments over billing and, more importantly, sounding out the big studios in America. It was not until 30 October 1965 that the *Daily Express* announced Chaplin's new film for Universal-International. On 1 November, Chaplin was accompanied by his leading lady, Sophia Loren (*qv*), to a press conference at London's Savoy Hotel. The *Daily Mail* quoted him as saying, 'I am the servant of the Muses and when they say: "Get back to work you lazy bum" I get back.' The press conference drew interest from newspapers and magazines around the world, guaranteeing considerable advance coverage.

… and directs Sophia Loren's large pyjamas

Chaplin did not take a starring part, preferring instead the minor rôle of an elderly steward. The delay in production meant that Noël Coward, the first choice for Hudson, the valet, was unavailable; Peter Sellers was considered, but Chaplin, concerned not to overload the film with movie stars, opted instead for Patrick Cargill (*qv*), whose reputation at the time was primarily in the theatre. By contrast, Chaplin had ambitions for his son, Sydney, to become a film star, and thus recruited him after a recent Broadway stint in *Funny Girl*.

Shooting commenced at Pinewood late in January 1966; according to Epstein, leading man Marlon Brando (*qv*) called in sick, requiring the team to film around him for three days. His presence was then required for the ballroom sequence, as the studio was needed for a different production. Brando arrived late and was bawled out by Chaplin. Surprisingly, he accepted it quietly and was on time for the rest of the filming.

It is often said that the relationship between Chaplin and Brando suffered from an immediate clash of personalities and approach, particularly when Chaplin insisted, as usual, in demonstrating how each part should be played. Epstein's version is that Loren and Brando were entertained by Chaplin's method of acting out each part and there was much laughter on the set. Brando was supposed to have said, at the time, 'This is the easiest picture I've ever made. I don't have to do anything. Charlie's doing it all!' Their rapport is believed to have crumbled after Chaplin became abrupt and impatient when directing Sydney. Sydney, apparently, was slow to absorb his father's direction and understood the need for discipline; Brando, however, saw it differently and was thereafter cool towards Chaplin, even though melting periodically when watching him enact bits of comic business.

In the finished film, Brando's work suggests little of Chaplin's 'do-it-this-way' approach, but the Chaplin influence is apparent elsewhere; even Sophia Loren, at one point, pads across the cabin in precisely the way Chaplin might, if impersonating a young woman. Perhaps the best and most typically Chaplinesque moments are from Patrick Cargill, who, in preparing for a celibate wedding night, makes a tangle of his bedsheets, disappears behind the bed, emerges to

say 'boo' to his reluctant bride, then, after some time beneath the covers, decides which direction he would prefer to face. One can also discern the shade of 'Charlie' when Hudson repeatedly peeps over the covers at Natascha. Among the cast, Cargill was by far the most experienced in this kind of bedroom farce, but it is easy to conclude that Chaplin acted this out for him (there may be those who would have preferred a film in which Chaplin performed the entire script).

Since he was not working in his own studio, Chaplin could not control the large number of visitors to the set, many of them Britons seizing their one and only chance to meet the comedian. Among the more prestigious callers was Gloria Swanson (*qv*), in the company of historian Kevin Brownlow. On 11 March 1966, *Screen* carried a story from UPI to the effect that Chaplin, in order to get the job done, had closed the set even to his own publicists. One suspects a measure of publicity in the story itself, for six days later *The Times* carried a report from the set, describing Chaplin's directorial approach and opinions on the use of colour, mainly that it should be muted in a light comedy. The next day's *Sun*, in an article by David Nathan, speaks of the respect commanded by Chaplin of his technicians and cast. 'My instinct,' Brando told Nathan, 'is to sort of take time and slosh around. That isn't permitted by Chaplin and he's absolutely right. He knows exactly what he wants

and he insists on getting it. It comes as a great relief. I don't really question whether he is right or wrong.' It is difficult to interpret these as words of respect or of resignation, especially when admitting to being one of a pair of 'glorified marionettes', but Brando's comments from later in the piece are essentially in praise of Chaplin: 'I've done comedies before but they've always turned out tragedies, very unfunny, heavy-footed. I don't think I could play this role with any success without Chaplin.'

Chaplin's alleged desire for privacy seems also to have been ignored when a party celebrating his 77th birthday was held on the set. Chaplin attacked the cake – topped with a miniature 'tramp' – in a joky impersonation of a knife-wielding maniac.

Margaret Rutherford (*qv*), who rather steals the show as elderly hypochondriac Miss Gaulswallow, described in her memoirs an example of Chaplin's insistence on detail: Chaplin wanted a precise duplication of Hong Kong's Mandarin Hotel, necessitating the use of a specific type of chandlier. Two such chandeliers were traced to a private address in London and were duly hired, dismantled, reassembled and thereafter mostly overlooked when shooting. 'In the final film,' recalled the actress, 'there was a quick shot of one of the chandeliers and that was all. But it was authentic and it did look like the Mandarin Hotel in Hong Kong, and that was all that mattered to Mr. Chaplin.' (Comedy *aficionados* may spot Carol Cleveland as Miss Gaulswallow's nurse, a few years before her sometimes revealing work in *Monty Python's Flying Circus*.)

The opening scenes were, not unusually, shot last; less expected is that they were filmed at the showrooms of tentmaker John Edgington in the Old Kent Road, close to Chaplin's birthplace. According to Terry Coleman in the *Guardian* of 11 May 1966, the art director (Bob Cartwright) had called in to buy a tent and 'admired the 1830s elegance of its slender cast-iron columns'; thus Edgington's underwent temporary conversion into a Hong Kong nightclub.

Once shooting was completed, Chaplin went to work on post-production; after 11 October he was working with a leg in plaster after sustaining a broken ankle on an uneven section of pavement. The *Evening News* of 28 October quoted Chaplin on a possible return to America for the film's première,

Sydney Chaplin joins his father's birthday celebrations on the **Countess** *set*

but this was not to be. A London press preview, on 2 January 1967, was ruined by faulty projection. Although Loren was unable to attend, the première itself was well received; the reviews, however, were already in. Brando later called Loren, praising her work but saying 'The critics just destroyed all of us.'

The Times, aware of the film's original conception as a vehicle for Paulette Goddard, speculated on how effective it might have been with Chaplin and Goddard as leads; otherwise, an opportunity was taken to revisit a long-held suspicion – unconfirmable in the absence of *A Woman of Paris* (*qv*) – that Chaplin was less a good director than a skilled presenter of his own performances. *Countess*, it was thought, 'is likely to be a saddening experience for all lovers of Chaplin's earlier work'. Patrick Gibbs of the *Daily Telegraph* dwelt more than somewhat on Chaplin's programme notes for the screening, contrasting the director's search for 'realism' with the essentially artificial farce of the plot. Again questioned was the suitability of the leads to such farce material, extended by a belief that they had not been directed in the necessary fashion. Clive Hirschorn of the *Sunday Express* thought the film possessed 'about as much bang and sparkle as a bagful of sawdust', its gags 'old-fashioned' and plot 'predictable'. Ernest Betts of the *People* considered it 'as dated as one of those silent movies we see now and then' and 'always in perfect taste. That's probably what's wrong with it.' Comments on Brando's performance are perhaps typified by Alexander Walker of the London *Evening Standard*, who referred to him being 'directed to act in two styles, one reminiscent of a speak-your-weight machine and the other a sudden manic frenzy peculiar to bedroom farces'. Penelope Gilliatt of the *Observer* took a kindlier view, admitting to genuinely funny business, albeit within a mostly leaden and ponderous film; in *The Sunday Times*, Dilys Powell believed *Countess* bore Chaplin's signature, but compared it to a letter drafted by an old friend 'but rewritten, I would go so far as to say botched, by someone else'. Once more, the leading man's qualifications were queried; Brando was deemed 'magnificent in the portrayal of tragically defeated characters ... But give him a joke and he turns it into a groan.' Virtually its only supporter was Cecil Wilson of the *Daily Mail*, who saw

Countess as 'Not by a long chalk the best of Chaplin, but all the same an agreeable escapist send-off for the New Year.'

Audience reaction was, reportedly, rather better, with Chaplin receiving many personal letters praising the film and contradicting the critics; in Paris on 11 January, shortly before the French première, a furious Chaplin told *The Times* of an incognito visit to a cinema, where he found 'ordinary cinema-goers roaring with laughter'. The Paris opening, after perhaps six minutes of small cuts, drew favourable comment and a degree of wonderment at London's poor reaction; a few more cuts preceded the US opening, which was treated savagely. The New York *Daily News* called the film 'almost pathetic'; *Time*, twisting the knife, evaluated it as 'probably the best movie ever made by a 77-year-old man. Unhappily it is the worst movie ever made by Charlie Chaplin.' Perhaps the most vitriolic was Bosley Crowther of the *New York Times* (who, by the way, roasted *Monsieur Verdoux* in 1947 but reversed his opinion on its revival in 1964). Representative of Crowther's lengthy condemnation is his use of the word 'awful' and comparison, for the benefit of older readers, with the ancient stage farce *Up in Mabel's Room*. Jerry Epstein later suggested Crowther to have been prejudiced by Chaplin's reluctance to grant him a private interview, and the absence of a private screening.

The concensus among most *Countess* reviews is that the film is old-fashioned. David Nathan suggested exactly that possibility when visiting the set, only to be refuted by the two stars. 'The theme isn't particularly modern or particularly antiquated,' said Brando. 'It's a vehicle for the expression of Chaplin's comedic notions and sentiments.' Loren, concurring, declared, 'When you deal with real sentiments it is never out of date.' The use of an opening title card may not have helped, but *A Countess From Hong Kong* did not benefit from being released in the 1960s, a period given to decrying anything not in then-current mode, and frequently obsessed with its own innovations. This is not to say that nothing of value was introduced at that time, for quite the reverse is true, but much of what was favoured in the 1960s has been treated harshly by posterity.

While *A Countess From Hong Kong* is far from the 'awful' film suggested by contemporary critics, it does not rate as

an outstanding work. It lacks the pace necessary to bedroom farce, and much of it is heavy-handed. The more liberated 1960s allowed Chaplin to be comparatively explicit, but aside from being able to identify his heroine as a prostitute, this freedom extends little beyond jokes about oversized bras. The more basic seasickness gags are handled abruptly, resembling more the unsubtle moments in *Shanghaied* or *A Day's Pleasure* than the cleverness of *The Immigrant*. By far the biggest success of the film is its score, especially *This Is My Song* (see also **Music**).

One might still put aside such quibbling and leave the last word instead to Margaret Rutherford. 'It was sad that the film did not get better notices,' she recalled later on, 'but then film critics can sometimes be very tiresome gentlemen.'

(See also: Abandoned projects; Boats, ships; Colour; Costume; Johnston, Oliver; Music; Politics; Religion; Risqué humour; Sickness; Television; *Tillie's Punctured Romance*; Video releases; Villains)

CROCKER, HARRY
(1895–1958)

(Chaplin films *qv*)
Actor and sometime journalist (including publicity work for Chaplin into the early 1950s), born and educated in San Francisco. Crocker was assistant director on *The Circus* in addition to playing Rex, the tightrope walker, and was credited again as assistant director, with Henry Bergman (*qv*), on *City Lights*. His acting rôle in *City Lights*, that of a window dresser, was deleted prior to release but may be seen in *Unknown Chaplin* (*qv*). Crocker appeared in *Tillie the Toiler*, starring Marion Davies (*qv*), who was mistress to Crocker's newspaper employer, William Randolph Hearst. His other films include *Becky*, *Sally in Our Alley* and *South Sea Love*.

(See also: Bloom, Claire)

CRUEL, CRUEL LOVE

(Chaplin film)
Keystone Comedy released by Mutual, 26 March 1914. Produced by Mack Sennett. Directed either by Sennett or George Nichols. Reissue titles include *Lord Helpus*. Photography attributed to Frank D. Williams. One reel. 1,035 feet

(UK length cited in *Bioscope*).
With Charlie Chaplin (a gentleman), Minta Durfee (his fiancée), Hank Mann (gardener), Alice Davenport (? maid), Chester Conklin (? butler).

Charlie, a well-to-do gentleman, proposes to his lady love. Her maid observes from behind a curtain, amused by Charlie's falling to the floor in the absence of a chair and miming the couple's likely progeny. The lady of the house, aware of an onlooker, catches the maid and sends her away. Outside, the maid confides in her boyfriend, the gardener. Charlie takes his leave. In the garden, the maid trips over, and gallant Charlie helps to the maid to her feet, only to become locked in her embrace. His fiancée, witnessing his seeming faithlessness, ends their engagement. Distraught, Charlie drives home. When the lady scolds her maid, the gardener explains what really happened. At home, Charlie takes what he believes is poison; his butler, spying from the next room, laughs, being aware it is only water. Charlie has a vision of being tortured by pitchfork-wielding demons surrounded by flame. Suddenly the idea of suicide pales. The gardener rushes to Charlie's residence with a note from his lady employer. Charlie, meanwhile, is going through the agonies of poisoning, pulling the curtains down over his head. The gardener arrives with the letter and is shown through by the laughing butler. Charlie reads that all is forgiven but claims it is too late. He pushes away the gardener, who stumbles into the butler. The gardener runs from the house. Charlie, panicking, telephones his physicians, who set off immediately.

As an interim measure, Charlie tries drinking milk as an antidote. The gardener, reaching home, informs the lady of Charlie's poisoning, and they rush to his home by taxi. Both the cab and the doctors' horse-drawn buggy race to the scene. The doctors arrive, but meet resistance when trying to pump Charlie's stomach. His fiancée is greeted by the butler, who informs her that Charlie has only taken water. She bursts in on Charlie to reassure him. After brief thanks to the heavens, Charlie boots the butler through the curtain, also knocking over the gardener. The two begin to scrap, and Charlie attacks his doctors. General mayhem breaks out as the ambulancemen arrive, but they join the others in watching the happy couple embrace.

One 1960s source refers to there being no known copy of *Cruel, Cruel Love*. At least one print was rediscovered – seemingly from a Latin-American release – by the mid-1970s, when new home-movie copies were offered for sale. The film has since been issued on video in America. Available material does indeed seem to suggest imminent extinction of the original at the time of copying, the image being covered in the type of spots indicative of fairly advanced decomposition.

Descriptions of the film have frequently identified Chaplin's character by the punning name 'Lord Helpus', probably deriving from a reissue bearing that title. Chaplin's aristocratic status is reflected in the re-use of his costume and make-up from *Making a Living* (*qv*); it would be used again, though with Charlie's customary moustache, in *Mabel at the Wheel* (*qv*).

(See also: Conklin, Chester; Costume; Davenport, Alice; Home movies; *Monsieur Verdoux*; Religion; Suicide; Video releases; Williams, Frank D.)

THE CURE

(Chaplin film)
Released by Mutual, 16 April 1917. Written and directed by Charles Chaplin. Photographed by Rollie Totheroh. Two reels. 1,834 feet.

With Charlie Chaplin (himself), Edna Purviance (girl), Eric Campbell (gouty giant), Frank J. Coleman (spa manager), John Rand, Albert Austin (attendants), James T. Kelly (elderly bellhop), Henry Bergman (masseur), Loyal Underwood (discoverer of the spring), Janet Miller Sully (patient).

Charlie arrives at a spa clinic, based around a spring discovered by a man of incredibly frail constitution. Charlie is to be 'cured of drinking', a condition emphasized by his wandering into the spring instead of towards the clinic. This is compounded by an inability to negotiate a revolving door, giving his attendant the runaround and trapping the foot of a gouty patient. Another handicap is his 'wardrobe', a trunk comprising a

Our hero visualizes the worst when attempting suicide in **Cruel, Cruel Love**

Cruel, Cruel Love was reissued in 1920 as Lord Helpus
By courtesy of Claudia Sassen

Eric Campbell dozes and John Rand attends as Charlie takes **The Cure**

fully-stocked bar. Another attendant takes Charlie down to the spring. Charlie, who is more interested in a pretty nurse than in any spa water, allows his mug to drain into his hat. When finally taking a drink, he rushes back to his room and a rapid slug from his 'wardrobe'. Having booted out the attendant, Charlie discovers the ancient bellboy has been sampling his private stock. Elsewhere in the clinic, Edna (her presence in the spa unexplained) is being pestered by the gouty patient. They are seated in the lounge when Charlie, walking downstairs, drops a cigarette end in the man's coffee. Charlie, sitting between them, mistakes the man's flirtation as being for him; Charlie responds coyly, then, after an exchange of contempt, whirls around the 'love-seat' he is occupying so that he sits nearer to Edna, falls to the floor. The manager orders Charlie to leave, but Edna comes to his defence. The guilty party and Charlie assume, respectively, the melodramatic poses of thwarted villain and hero. Charlie kisses Edna's hand before falling on the gouty man's foot. Charlie is escorted to the baths, where he is examined by a heavyweight masseur. The manager checks Charlie's room, discovering the booze, a drunken bellhop and a somewhat tipsy attendant. The attendant, ordered to throw out the drink, dumps it into the spring. In the baths, the gouty man and a fellow-patient are getting undressed when each is struck by a flying shoe. They blame each other until they discover a swimsuit-clad Charlie behind a set of curtains. At the swimming pool, Charlie barely puts a leg in the water, but dries himself as if immersed for hours. Outside, the clinic's sober ladies partake of the heavily-laced water. Back at the baths, Charlie, observing the pummelling of a weedy patient, raises the masseur's arm as the 'winner'. He is reluctant to take his turn, and dodges furiously, eventually backing into the next room in judo-style defence. Charlie is impressive except when burning his behind on a radiator. The masseur is sent into the pool, taking the gouty man with him; an attendant, trying to combat Charlie, backs into the sizzling radiator and leaps for the pool unassisted. By the time Charlie has dressed, he and Edna are almost the only sober people left in the building. Charlie rescues the girl from some obnoxious drunks, using a gentlemanly pull of the cane to remove one of the unconscious men from her path. At the well, Edna prevails upon Charlie to take the health-giving water. To his surprise, Charlie finds it enjoyable and is soon very drunk. Edna storms off in disgust; Charlie, in trying to follow, is caught again in the revolving door. The gouty man is being pushed past in a wheelchair; Charlie, blundering out, pushes him down some steps into the well. Charlie spins out of the door, staggers upstairs and, still spinning, falls into the swimming pool. The following day, the clinic is filled with hungover patients. Charlie, appearing very slowly

through the revolving door, removes his hat to reveal a block of ice perched beneath. Edna, having discovered the truth about the well, asks Charlie's forgiveness. Charlie, unaware of the booze-laden water, goes for another drink, but Edna persuades him to swear off. Charlie, taking Edna's arm, steps out for a life without alcohol, only to disappear immediately down the contaminated well.

Most available prints of *The Cure* fade out immediately prior to the final gag, so that Charlie's descent into the spring is lost. This was considered the film's usual state until 1973, when the BBC's *Chaplin SuperClown* copy was unveiled, presenting this moment intact. Another edition, later supplied to Channel 4, also includes this section. The latter copy at least seems to have had this conclusion reinstated from an inferior print; both the Channel 4 and BBC material have heavy vertical scratching during this section, which may have been the reason for its deletion in prior revivals. An otherwise impeccably researched documentary once surprised a few collectors with the claim that all surviving prints faded out as described above, even though the true conclusion was known to exist.

Although presenting its star in unfamiliar straw boater and lightweight blazer (a well-to-do image designed to offset the character's alcoholism), *The Cure* is often regarded as highly representative of Chaplin, especially in its well-timed business with the revolving door and Chaplin's oft-repeated motif of transposition, as when treating the masseur as a champion wrestler. Only slightly dated is a scene in which Charlie imitates the 'Tableaux', a risqué burlesque presentation of the day in which young lovelies in body tights would pose momentarily as the curtains opened and closed. Of all the Mutuals, *The Cure* is among the brightest, its mostly sunny backdrop shining through even the greyer prints in circulation.

(See also: Alcohol; Austin, Albert; Bergman, Henry; Campbell, Eric; Costume; Documentaries; Costume; Kelly, James T.; *King in New York, A*; Mutual; Purviance, Edna; Rand, John; Risqué humour; Sickness; Smoking; Television; Twists and Transformations; *Unknown Chaplin*; Vagrancy)

the Sea (1961) and *My Fair Lady* (1964, released after the actor's death).

(See also: Bruce, Nigel)

DAVENPORT, ALICE
(1864–1936)

(Chaplin films *qv*)
Veteran actress, *née* Shepard, on stage from childhood, and who became part of an illustrious American theatrical family by marriage to Harry Bryant Davenport. Born in New York, she studied at Miss Irving's School, and went on to appear in some 800 theatrical productions between 1869 and 1894. Her film debut is believed to have been in a Nestor comedy of 1911, *The Best Man Wins*; present in Keystone comedies from their inception (where Alice was nicknamed 'Mother Davenport'), she is Chaplin's potential mother-in-law in *Making a Living*, a prudish hotel guest in *Mabel's Strange Predicament*, the landlord's lady friend in *The Star Boarder*, a society woman in *Caught in a Cabaret*, Mrs 'Ambrose' in *Caught in the Rain*, a waitress in *Gentlemen of Nerve*, a nosy neighbour in *Mabel's Married Life* and one of the party guests in *Tillie's Punctured Romance*. She has been identified as the maid in *Cruel, Cruel Love* and as one of the 'Goo-Goo Sisters' in *The Property Man*, but in each case the actress in question seems too young. She has also been cited in the cast of *The New Janitor* but, again, does not seem to be present. It is believed that she supplied the dress for Chaplin's female impersonation in *A Busy Day*. Latterly in Fox's Sunshine Comedies.

(See also: Female impersonation; Keystone; Lehrman, Henry 'Pathé'; Swain, Mack)

DAVIES, MARION

See: Guest appearances, Murder and Women

DAVIS, GEORGE
(1889–1965)

Plays 'Professor Bosco', the magician in *The Circus* (*qv*). Appeared with Buster Keaton (*qv*) in his classic *Sherlock, Jr.* (1924) and the somewhat later (and lesser) *Parlor, Bedroom and Bath* (1931). Davis was born in Holland, for which reason he was much in demand for foreign-language films. Among many Hollywood

D'ABBADIE D'ARRAST,  HENRI (OR HARRY)
(1897–1968)

(Chaplin films *qv*)
Chaplin associate, from the French nobility; some sources cite his birthplace as Argentina but his education, at least, took place in Europe. He was in the USA from 1922 and is credited on-screen, with Jean di Limur (*qv*), in *A Woman of Paris* for 'research' and as co-assistant director (with Chuck Riesner [*qv*]) of *The Gold Rush*. Also a director in his own right, as in *A Gentleman of Paris* (1927), *The Magnificent Flirt* (1928), *Raffles* (1930), *Laughter* (1930) and *Topaze* (1933). According to Jack Spears' *Hollywood: The Golden Era*, d'Arrast's friendship with Chaplin paled in later years, especially when Chaplin reportedly declined to help in the financing and distribution of some d'Arrast projects. Chaplin is claimed to have thought at least one of them too similar to his own work, the result not of conscious imitation but of Chaplin's influence upon his former colleague. Spears also mentions d'Arrast attending the reissue of *The Gold Rush* with actress Eleanor Boardman, predicting, accurately, that his name would be absent from the credits.

DANIELL, HENRY
(1894–1963)

British actor who plays 'Garbitsch', the Goebbels figure in Chaplin's *The Great Dictator* (*qv*). Often seen as 'Moriarty' in Basil Rathbone's 'Sherlock Holmes' series; many other films include *Firefly* (1937), *The Philadelphia Story* (1940), *Wake of the Red Witch* (1948), *The Egyptian* (1954), *Voyage to the Bottom of*

appearances are Chaney's *He Who Gets Slapped* (1925), *The Magic Flame* (1928), Garbo's *The Kiss* (1929), *Arsène Lupin* (1932), *Love Me Tonight* (1932), *The Black Cat* (1934), *Topper Takes a Trip* (1939), *Ninotchka* (1939, again with Garbo), Danny Kaye's *The Kid From Brooklyn* (1946), the Betty Grable vehicle *Mother Wore Tights* (1947) and Howard Hawks' *Gentlemen Prefer Blondes* (1953).

A DAY'S PLEASURE

(Chaplin film)
Released by First National, 7 December 1919. Produced, written and directed by Charles Chaplin. Photographed by Rollie Totheroh. Working titles: *Charlie's Picnic* and *Ford Story*. Two reels.

With Charlie Chaplin (himself), Edna Purviance (Charlie's wife), Jackie Coogan, (?) Raymond Lee (their sons), Jean 'Babe' London (seasick girl), Tom Wilson (her boyfriend), Albert Austin, Henry Bergman (captain/whiskered man in limousine/fat cop), Loyal Underwood (swearing pedestrian).

'Off for a rattling good time', Charlie's wife and two small sons take their place in the family Model T. The car refuses to co-operate and Charlie examines the engine with a watchmaker's glass. He is about to tinker with the car when it starts into life. Charlie boards the undulating vehicle with some difficulty and the party sets off. At the quayside, Charlie's wife heads down the gangplank as her husband follows, carrying the boys because 'children in arms go free'. They settle down, but when Charlie disappears for a moment, a fat girl and her large boyfriend take Charlie's seat. He returns, and has to squeeze in. Charlie takes a pin, which he jabs into the man's leg, then disappears ashore. The boat is moving when a latecomer rushes aboard, a large lady with a pram. The pram is pushed aboard, but the lady is caught between jetty and boat, forming a human gangplank; Charlie uses her as such when returning to the boat. The large man tries to pull in the unfortunate woman, now hanging on to the boat's edge. Charlie tries using a boathook, doing more harm than good, but eventually he and the other man bring the latecomer to safety and the journey begins. The captain starts the black jazz band playing. Charlie and his wife are among the couples dancing to the frenzied music; this and the boat's violent rocking start to induce seasickness, especially within

Charlie. After he has blundered into a female passenger, Charlie's wife goes off, huffily. Charlie takes a seat beside the band, whose trombonist's slide continually pops under Charlie's nose. Charlie, the drummer and trombonist become very queasy; the trombonist actually turns pale. Charlie staggers away, trying to ignore someone selling ham sandwiches, buttered popcorn, cigars and cigarettes. In desperation, Charlie kicks over tray and vendor. Elsewhere, the large man and his chubby girlfriend are eating snacks. Charlie, finding his wife and sons asleep in deckchairs, tries to put up a deckchair of his own, but becomes horribly tangled. The large man, becoming seasick, disappears for a while; Charlie, abandoning the deckchair and still decidedly queasy, sits by the man's girlfriend. Their shared nausea sees them wilting into an intertwined heap. An attendant places a blanket over them. The boyfriend returns with a drink for his girl. She declines it, as does Charlie, concealed beneath the blanket. Furious at finding another man with his girl, the boyfriend shoves Charlie away. He lands at his wife's feet. Not content with hurling Charlie away, the man comes along to throttle him. Charlie, seasick, does not have energy to fight back, but respite comes when his attacker suddenly needs to head for the rail. Charlie recovers sufficiently to launch his own assault, but soon has to retire, seasick again. Charlie renews the fight and, despite intervention by the captain, is still punching the big man as the scene irises out. Journey's end, and the passengers disembark. The big man has evidently fared worse than Charlie. In the car, Charlie and family are delayed when a policeman tells them to wait at a crossroads. They are held up further by a group of people standing in front of them. One is an old man, perched on the mudguard, whom Charlie dislodges by backing up. Charlie covers his ears as the old man protests. The family proceeds, but their turn has been missed. The cop tries to send them back, and Charlie, arguing the point, receives a ticket. He backs up, straight into a heavily-laden truck, causing a crate to fall on a neighbouring limousine. In the confusion, a tar wagon is knocked over. Another, fat policeman becomes anchored in its spillage. He strides out of the mess, taking with him a manhole cover directly behind his colleague, who is arguing with Charlie. The officer steps back, disappearing into the hole. The fat officer, unaware of the mishap, replaces the cover. Charlie surveys the differently-shaped officer, remarking,

By courtesy of Claudia Sassen

'How you have changed.' Charlie leaves his vehicle and, standing in the tar, argues with the cop. Stuck fast, Charlie is able to stand at virtually a 45-degree angle. He bobs around like a child's toy, then shoves the policeman's hands into the tar. Trying to release him, Charlie becomes trapped even further. The first policeman emerges from the manhole. Lunging at Charlie, he becomes another of the tar's victims. Charlie, who sacrifices a shoe in order to escape the tar, drives away with his family.

The above account is based upon the sequence of events in present-day copies of *A Day's Pleasure*. A cutting continuity (i.e. written list of shots as they appear in the edited film) is reproduced in Chaplin's *My Life in Pictures*, as is a list of sub-titles; these confirm a long-held belief that the comedian rearranged the film for reissue. (It should be noted, however, that a contemporary review from the *Chicago Herald* – quoted by MacDonald *et al* in *The Films of Charlie Chaplin* – places the order of scenes as per the supposed revision.) In the original version, the scene at the crossroads was placed between the family's departure from home and their arrival at the quayside.

From the point of view of gags, *A Day's Pleasure* is fairly obvious stuff, at least by Chaplin's standards, although it must be allowed that general audiences might find it more amusing than some of his more restrained comedies. The topic of seasickness is not, for example, handled as well as in *The Immigrant* (qv), nor is the effect of a rocking boat, on this occasion evidently achieved simply through a swaying camera rather than in tandem with

an elaborate, tilting stage. In this regard the film more closely resembles *Shanghaied* (qv), a much earlier and less elaborate effort. There is also a racial joke, the type of easy laugh to which Chaplin seldom resorted. When *A Day's Pleasure* opened in New York at the Strand (supporting *Jubilo*, a Goldwyn feature starring Will Rogers), the *New York Times* considered Chaplin 'screamingly funny' when battling with a deckchair and applauded the 'many little bits of pantomime and burlesque, in which he is inimitable'. 'But most of the time,' it continued, 'he depends for comedy upon seasickness, a Ford car, and biff-bang slapstick, with which he is little, if any, funnier than many other screen comedians.' There is an overall sense of effort in the film, which was not an unqualified success in its day. Each of the First Nationals made enough money to satisfy the distributors,

Charlie's disagreement with Tom Wilson in **A Day's Pleasure**
Museum of Modern Art/Film Stills Archive

but Chaplin's own inspiration was, by his later admission, briefly impaired at this point in his career. Marriage to Mildred Harris (*qv*) proved less than idyllic, a situation helped not at all by the death of their child, Norman Spencer Chaplin, during production of this film. Such unfortunate circumstances add to the irony of this being one of Charlie's infrequent appearances as a family man. The grotesquerie might have been even greater but for a decision, noted in David Robinson's *Chaplin: His Life and Art*, to have Edna Purviance (*qv*) play Charlie's wife; Chaplin had initially chosen Tom Wood, the fat boy in *Sunnyside* (*qv*), for the rôle. One of Charlie's sons was played by a recent Chaplin discovery, Jackie Coogan (*qv*).

(See also: Bergman, Henry; Boats, ships; Cars; Children; Dual rôles; First National; Lee, Raymond; London, Jean 'Babe'; Policemen; Race; Reissues; Religion; Sickness; Underwood, Loyal)

DE HAVEN, CARTER

See: *Modern Times*

DE LIMUR, JEAN
(1886 or 1887–1976)

One of the several French expatriates known to Robert Florey (*qv*), Jean de Limur arrived in the USA in 1920. In common with Harry d'Abbadie d'Arrast (*qv*), de Limur had been a French war hero; his initial Hollywood work was as an actor in films starring Douglas Fairbanks, Mary Pickford, Max Linder (all *qv*) and others. Chaplin employed de Limur, d'Arrast and Monta Bell (*qv*) to advise him while making *A Woman of Paris* (*qv*). De Limur was afterwards frequently associated with d'Arrast and Bell in screenplay work. In 1929, Bell produced *The Letter*, directed by de Limur and starring Jeanne Eagels; the rest of de Limur's career was spent largely in Europe.

DEAN, DINKY

See: *Pilgrim, The*; Riesner, Dean, and *Unknown Chaplin*

DEATH

Sir Charles Spencer Chaplin died in the early hours of Christmas Day, 1977. On

12 December, Jean and Dido Renoir had sent the Chaplins a letter (reprinted in Renoir's published correspondence), saying: 'Fortunately you made films and every frame of your films brings us a thousand messages of affection. We are happy to play our part in this symphony of love.' The note concludes with wishes for a merry Christmas and a happy new year. Chaplin did not live to see either, and on the 28th, the day after the funeral, Renoir composed a further letter, addressed to Oona: 'Dido and I forget that Charlie was the genius of the century. We think only of the deep sorrow which is ours. For you the trial must be unbearable. Please, dear Oona, accept our sincerest condolences.'

Chaplin was buried near his home in Vevey. The strangest postscript to his death was the bizarre theft of his body, and ransom demand, in March 1978. It was recovered after sixteen days, buried in a farmer's field. The culprits were subsequently brought to trial, and the farmer, an innocent party in the affair, placed a memorial of his own on the spot where the body once lay; it is a cross with an inscription translating to 'Here slept, in peace, Charlie Chaplin'. The body was re-buried in a secure, concrete tomb. By coincidence, the remains of Chaplin's friend, Groucho Marx (*qv*), were also temporarily moved shortly after interment.

It might be preferable to close this entry with a reference to publicity for an international 1976 reissue of *Modern Times* (*qv*), which reprints the comments of journalist Mike Harris of *The Australian*: 'Seeing his films helps one understand how he has become legendary: they are his immortality.'

(See also: Documentaries, compilations; Public appearances; Purviance, Edna; Sickness)

DESLYS, KAY
(1899–1974)

Chubby, London-born comedy actress, one of the dance hall girls in *The Gold Rush* (*qv*). Originally on stage, Kay Deslys entered films in 1923 and appeared frequently in Hal Roach comedies of the 1920s and 1930s.

DESMONDE, JERRY
(1908–67)

Suave British actor, known as straight man for Sid Field (see also

Impersonators); their sketches together are preserved in *London Town* (1946), directed by Wesley Ruggles (*qv*). He later worked as foil to Norman Wisdom. In Chaplin's *A King in New York* (*qv*) he plays Prime Minister Voudel, the corrupt official who absconds with his monarch's wealth.

(See also: Villains)

DOCUMENTARIES, COMPILATIONS

(Chaplin films *qv*)
The earliest compilations of Chaplin's work were the innumerable bootlegs: Theodore Huff noted the assembly of the Keystones into a serial entitled *The Perils of Patrick*; Griffith and Mayer's *The Movies* mentions the Chaplin shorts having been strung together in the 'Near East' for a feature-length anthology called *Charlie's Life*. By contrast, Essanay's anthologies *The Essanay-Chaplin Revue of 1916* and *Chase Me, Charlie* (*qv*) were legal if still perhaps unethical. A later 'Chase Me Charlie' produced by Edwin G. O'Brien in 1959, incorporates footage from *His New Job*, *A Night Out*, *The Champion*, *The Tramp* and *A Night in the Show*. Huff also noted a British compilation two-reeler with added sound, *Comedy Cocktail*, and a 1948 French anthology, *La Grande Parade de Charlot*.

The AFI's *Catalog of Motion Pictures* details a five-reel compilation, trade-shown in incomplete form on 16 August 1917. Called *The National Association's All-Star Picture*, it was assembled by the National Association of the Motion Picture Industry and distributed on a State's Rights basis. Advertisements promised a total of thirty stars, in thematically-arranged extracts from successful films. One of the known extracts is of Douglas Fairbanks (*qv*) in the fight scene of *Reggie Mixes In* (1916); among the many clips were scenes of Mary Pickford (*qv*) and of Chaplin, though the nature of these extracts remains unknown at present.

The 1950s saw a number of hybrids reviving old, public-domain footage, one of them a 45-minute UK effort called *Laughter Allowed*, comprising extracts from *The Masquerader*, *The Champion*, *The Bank*, *Laughing Gas*, *Gentlemen of Nerve* and *A Night in the Show*. Others from the period include DUK's *Lifetime of Comedy*. Uno Asplund mentioned a compilation shown at least in Sweden, *Merry Go Round* (1962), which

comprises material from *By the Sea, Triple Trouble, The Tramp* and *The Champion*. Chaplin himself entered the market with *The Chaplin Revue* (*qv*); otherwise, the most worthwhile anthologies were those assembled by Robert Youngson, who used Chaplin clips in *When Comedy Was King* (1960), *Days of Thrills and Laughter* (1961) and *Thirty Years of Fun* (1964).

Among more recent documentaries, *The Funniest Man in the World, The Gentleman Tramp* and *Unknown Chaplin* are detailed under separate entries. Particularly worthy of note is Harry Hurwitz's perhaps definitive examination of Chaplin's screen character, *The Eternal Tramp* (1970), narrated by Gloria Swanson (*qv*). Hurwitz presented Chaplin with a 16mm copy of the film when they met in 1972. *Our Charlie*, shown on Britain's Channel 4 at the time of Chaplin's centenary, is of especial interest for its use of an unauthorized biographical film, *The Life Story of Charles Chaplin* (1926), which Chaplin suppressed at the time. In a similar category was the late 1960s TV documentary about Chaplin's childhood, introduced by Tommy Steele. Chaplin did not sanction the project and was going to sue; he changed his mind after being sent a copy of the programme, which he enjoyed to the point of being moved to tears. (An earlier BBC TV tribute, *The Little Fellow*, was hosted by Llewellyn Rees and broadcast on 17 April 1959.) A much later dramatization of Chaplin's early life, Thames TV's *Young Charlie Chaplin* (*qv*), was transmitted in six episodes in 1989; 1992 brought Richard Attenborough's biopic *Chaplin* (*qv*).

Extant at the BFI is a Swedish-made TV documentary of the 1960s, which captured such childhood haunts as Pownall Terrace prior to demolition. Its title translates to 'A Comedian in Lambeth'.

Among the many other documentaries are *The Emerging Chaplin*, introduced by Douglas Fairbanks Jr; *Charlie – the Little Tramp*, hosted by Joel Grey; and *Charlie Chaplin – a Celebration*, released to the UK via sell-through video. A 1996 documentary about Eric Campbell (*qv*), *Chaplin's Goliath*, is detailed within the actor's own entry. Perhaps the oddest of the bunch was shown in 1994, when BBC 2's *Arena* presented a dramatization based on the theft of Chaplin's body, *The Grave Case of Charlie Chaplin.*

Chaplin has been detailed within more general TV film documentaries over the years, notably in Brownlow and Gill's *Hollywood*. During 1965, BBC-1 broadcast an American-made series called *Hollywood and the Stars*, narrated by Joseph Cotten. On 24 April they screened the first of a two-part episode called 'Funny Men', which was advertised in the listings magazine *Radio Times* as including 'a rare sequence of the greatest of them all, Charlie Chaplin, in rehearsal (out of make-up) for *City Lights*'. This was presumably the footage of a civilian-clad Chaplin rehearsing the scene in which he studies a statue in a shop window, a clip used many years later in *Unknown Chaplin*.

(See also: Childhood; Death; Home movies; Kono, Toraichi; Pickford, Mary; Radio; Reissues; Television; Trick photography; Video releases)

A DOG'S LIFE

(Chaplin film)
Released by First National, 14 April 1918. Produced, written and directed by Charles Chaplin. Photographed by Rollie Totheroh. Three reels.

With Charlie Chaplin (himself), Edna Purviance (dance hall girl), Bud Jamison, Albert Austin (thieves), Henry Bergman (hot dog vendor/man at employment office/fat lady), Tom Wilson (policeman), Syd Chaplin (owner of lunch wagon), James T. Kelly (hot dog vendor's customer), Chuck Riesner (employment office clerk/drummer), Park Jones, Janet Miller Sully, Loyal Underwood, Billy White, Scraps (dog).

At dawn, Charlie is sleeping beside a fence in the open air. He awakens to plug a draught in the stonework beneath the fence. Nearby, Scraps, a canine equivalent to Charlie, also struggles for existence. Through a hole in the fence, Charlie steals breakfast from a hot dog vendor. A policeman sees him, but Charlie avoids the officer by rolling to and fro beneath the fence. He disposes of the officer, and a colleague then tries his luck at the employment office, where brewery jobs are being advertised. Charlie is consistently pushed to the end of the queue, and is beaten to the clerk's window each time. On the street and penniless, Charlie searches in vain for food; so does Scraps, who finds some and is promptly set upon by a pack of other, larger dogs. Charlie rescues Scraps, and a chase ensues through the streets, culminating in most of the dogs plundering a butcher's shop. Charlie takes Scraps to safety, despite another tenacious hound gripping the seat of his trousers. Recognizing a kindred spirit, Charlie feeds Scraps from the dregs of a milk bottle, dipping the dog's tail in the milk. Nearby, revelry takes place at the Green Lantern, a bar-cum-dance hall. Outside, Charlie stops by a lunch wagon, where he swipes mouthfuls from the counter each time the proprietor's back is

Charlie's signature authenticated **A Dog's Life** *as the first 'Million Dollar Chaplin'*

Charlie and the Green Lantern's drummer – played by Chuck Riesner – in **A Dog's Life**

A Dog's Life: Charlie returns to the Green Lantern with sufficient funds to propose marriage

turned. The suspicious owner can do nothing without proof; Charlie is eventually spied by the policeman, who investigates but is clobbered when the owner tries to hit Charlie with a German sausage. At the Green Lantern, thieves are at work. Charlie wanders in, but is refused admission because of the dog. Scraps is duly concealed within Charlie's trousers, a tail protruding through a tear in the fabric. Charlie remains unaware of his unusual appendage until, standing

near the band, Scraps' wagging tail starts to beat the bass drum. The drummer queries the spectacle, and Charlie confides to him the dog's presence, while spiriting away part of the musician's snack. The rowdy stage show gives way to Edna, a young innocent, singing a heartrending ballad. All are reduced to tears, although the drummer, confusingly, seems to be smiling. A fat lady produces sufficient tears for Charlie to think that Scraps has left a puddle. Edna forsakes the stage for her official task – namely persuading the customers to buy drink by offering them a smile and a wink. When inexperienced Edna tries to wink seductively at Charlie, he at first thinks she has something in her eye. Having established that she is 'flirting', they take to the dance floor. Their steps are complicated by Charlie having a dog on a lead, and by a sudden stop when Charlie treads on chewing gum discarded by the fat lady. They sit at a table, but Charlie is thrown out for not buying Edna a drink. Charlie considers hurling a brick inside, but is dissuaded by the arrival of a policeman. Around the corner, two of the Green Lantern's resident thieves pounce upon a well-to-do drunk. The local cop is on hand, but the villains escape. One of the thieves buries the drunk's wallet in the spot where Charlie has been sleeping rough. The villain rejoins his accomplice at the Green Lantern. Charlie returns to his open-air 'home' with Scraps. They settle down to sleep, Charlie using the dog as a pillow despite the presence of fleas. At the Green Lantern, the thieves notice Edna. She is approached by the larger man, but the boss sees her repulse him. Edna is fired. Charlie is awakened by Scraps' furious digging. The wallet is unearthed, and Charlie suddenly has sufficient means to start anew. He arrives at the Green Lantern to find a tearful Edna, who has been refused money in lieu of notice. Her tears evaporate when she sees Charlie. Showing her the wallet, Charlie outlines a future for them in the countryside. The dream is over when the villains, recognizing the wallet, knock Charlie on the head and reclaim their haul. Charlie, believed to be drunk, is ejected. Edna joins him outside, but is told to wait as Charlie sneaks back, crawling behind the bar. The two thieves are drinking in an alcove; from behind a curtain, Charlie knocks one of them cold, replacing the unconscious man's arms with his own. He is able to manipulate the thief's inert form,

collecting half the stolen money and, at length, persuading the larger man to lean forward so that he, too, can be knocked out. Charlie takes the wallet and crawls back behind the bar, but is apprehended by the barman. The thieves regain consciousness; at first the larger man blames his comrade for knocking him out, but the truth is soon apparent. The wallet is passed from hand to hand until Charlie grabs it and makes a run. Outside, Charlie takes refuge in the lunch wagon, where he and the proprietor have to dodge the thieves' gunshots. Charlie is cornered in the wagon, and the larger thief starts to throttle him. Charlie passes the wallet down to Scraps, who takes it to Edna. The police arrive to arrest the thieves; Charlie rejoins Edna, Scraps and the wallet as the lunch wagon's dazed owner recovers his senses. We next see Charlie in a ploughed field, planting seeds by hand. Edna calls him to the kitchen. Their domestic bliss is completed by a wicker basket, denoting the presence of young. They sigh happily when contemplating the basket's occupants: Scraps and a litter of puppies.

The first of Chaplin's 'Million Dollar Comedies' for First National (qv), *A Dog's Life* was also Chaplin's debut at his new, purpose-built studio (barring sections of the abortive *How To Make Movies* [qv]). Aside from *Tillie's Punctured Romance* (qv), which Chaplin did not write or direct, and the unofficially expanded *Carmen* (qv), this three-reel comedy was Chaplin's longest subject to date, and was an indication of his ambition to produce features. This increased length permitted Chaplin to develop his central characters; it might be added that *A Dog's Life*, while possessing its share of knockabout, employs a modest shift away from slapstick in favour of situation and bits of 'business'. This may have been in response to some of Chaplin's critics, at least in the USA. Charlie's costume is even more vagrant-like than usual, his tie having disappeared along with that other symbol of gentrification, the cane. The latter omission was probably designed to make it easier for Charlie to hold the dog's lead, though it should be noted that a *New York Times* review of his next film, *Shoulder Arms* (qv), describes a contemporary view that the cane had 'begun to lose its comic character through overuse'. (The *New York Times*' view of *A Dog's Life* was, incidentally, both non-committal and, one suspects, complacent. 'Charlie Chaplin, at the Strand, is Charlie Chaplin,' it was said. 'Thousands know him and like him and will see him this week.')

Supporting casts for the new films remained much as those for Mutual (*qv*); Chaplin had lost an important foil with the untimely death of Eric Campbell (*qv*), but a pleasant addition was his half-brother, Syd Chaplin (*qv*), who may be seen in *A Dog's Life* as the moustached proprietor of a lunch wagon. Other newcomers included Chuck Riesner (*qv*) and Park Jones. Bud Jamison (*qv*), formerly with Chaplin at Essanay (*qv*), briefly rejoined the team.

A Dog's Life was reissued at intervals during the silent era (as in Pathé's UK revival of the mid-1920s), but was long unavailable, at least officially, until its inclusion in *The Chaplin Revue* (*qv*). This version was separated from later incarnations of the *Revue*, as in the BBC and Channel 4 screenings, but included in the US video release. Chaplin's reissue omits the brief opening shot of a sunrise, which has been reinstated in an American laserdisc edition.

As with several titles noted elsewhere, *A Dog's Life* exists in material deriving from more than one camera negative. It is thought that Syd Chaplin tried unsuccessfully to convince Charlie to have *three* cameras turning for each shot, as a means of providing a further, mint negative for future revivals. It is known that the original negative of *A Dog's Life* had deteriorated considerably by the 1940s, for which reason Rollie Totheroh (*qv*), whose photographic duties extended to archival maintenance, was obliged to compile a new master incorporating alternate takes of at least some shots. This is probably the reason why, on this occasion, the variants take the form of slightly different action rather than a noticeable difference in perspective (though Charlie's first tableside chat with the dance hall girl is obviously taken from a different angle, as is the moment where Charlie uses the dog as pillow). This is particularly apparent in the scene where Charlie conceals the dog in his trousers when entering the Green Lantern. In the *Chaplin Revue* copy, the dog is at first concealed apart from a protruding tail; another print, from a silent, British reissue, sees the dog's head pop out from beneath Charlie's coat-tail. The next shot, as Charlie walks the length of the dance hall, is also a different take; in the

Revue print, a woman seated at a table reacts with rather less shock when Charlie seems to have a tail. Soon after, Charlie passes a bar patron who is seen drinking in one version but eating in the other. When Charlie explains the animal's presence to the drummer, the *Revue* copy has Charlie sitting down with Scraps' head peeping over the top of his trousers, whereas the other print shows the drummer lifting the dog out completely. Business during the scene where Charlie dances with Edna Purviance (*qv*) differs quite noticeably; the entanglements between Charlie, Edna and Scraps are quite dissimilar, and the *Revue* print avoids a gag where Charlie, his shoe stuck on chewing gum, falls to the floor when trying to free himself. Also missing is his revenge on the fat lady – played by Henry Bergman (*qv*) – who carelessly dropped the gum. These are not edits in the material but quite separate takes, rather as if Chaplin was consciously toning down the slapstick content for the USA but retaining it for overseas. Equally noticeable is Charlie's subsequent ejection from the café; in the *Revue* version, Charlie holds Scraps' lead using the right hand, whereas in the other copy he uses the left. When he returns to see Edna sitting at a table, Scraps jumps up to greet her in one print but not in the other. The justly famous – and much-imitated – scene where Charlie's hands substitute for those of the unconscious Albert Austin (*qv*) offers similar variations, both in Charlie's mime (each print has business absent from the other) and in terms of editing; the *Revue* copy presents it in an uninterrupted shot, whereas the alternate print includes an insert of Austin's puzzled accomplice. Later, when Charlie and the lunch wagon owner hide from the gun-toting thieves, their heads bob up and down in unison in the *Revue* print, but take turns in the British reissue. The *Revue* uses a close shot of Charlie handing the wallet to Scraps, which remains in long-shot for the other version. Unlike the silent copy, the *Revue* edition does not show the villains actually being taken away. The film's rural postscript, in the *Revue*, opens on a fade-up of Charlie planting seeds; the other print irises up on an otherwise missing shot of Edna carrying a hot kettle from fireplace to table, before fading in a differently-angled view of Charlie in the fields. In the kitchen, the usual print shows Charlie kissing Edna once, on the nose, then receiving

A Dog's Life: *Charlie retrieves the stolen wallet from the thieves, but is intercepted by the café owner; Edna and Scraps remain outside during this scene, but join the other players for a posed still*

Chaplin and two visiting journalists on the set of **A Dog's Life**

an evidently sloppy kiss on the ear in return. In the other copy, Charlie kisses Edna several times around nose, mouth and cheeks, but the kiss on his ear is postponed until they have gone to examine the contents of the basket. As noted elsewhere, such variations are not common in available Chaplin films, which tend to be seen in reissues deriving from a single negative.

(See also: Animals; Costume; *Count, The;*

DORO, MARIE

See: 'Chaplin Craze', The; Early stage appearances, and Women

DOUGH AND DYNAMITE ♟

(Chaplin film)
Keystone Comedy released by Mutual, 26 October 1914. Produced by Mack Sennett. Reportedly written by Charles Chaplin and Mack Sennett, the latter receiving sole credit in the copyright entry. Directed by Charles Chaplin. Photography attributed to Frank D. Williams. Reissued 1923 (under the original title) by 'WAFILMS, Inc.' as amended by Syd Chaplin, re-edited and with new sub-titles; other reissue titles include *The Cook* and *Doughnut Designers*. Two reels. 2,010 feet.

With Charlie Chaplin (himself), Chester Conklin (rival waiter), Fritz Schade (proprietor), Norma Nichols (his wife), Vivian Edwards (seductive customer), Cecile Arnold (waitress), Slim Summerville, Edgar Kennedy (bakers), Phyllis Allen, Jack Dillon, Charley Chase (diners).

Charlie is working as waiter in an eat-in bakery, but is far more interested in the waitresses and prettier customers. In the kitchen, he blunders over his fellow-waiter and, returning through the restaurant, collides with the bakers when descending the steps leading from a pair of trap doors. Downstairs, Charlie gets in the way of the ovens before going back to the restaurant. He stops to make time with a waitress, then returns to the kitchen. The other waiter protests when Charlie, supposedly helping to wash up, drops the dishes. When the bakers decide to strike, the proprietor enlists Charlie to take their place. The head baker points a knife at Charlie, who turns it back on him before giving it a slight push. Charlie sets to work. The strikers depart, swearing vengeance on the proprietor and Charlie. In the kitchen, Charlie speaks to the second waiter, who reports

to the proprietor and is also put to work as baker. Amid great difficulty, Charlie lugs a huge bag of flour from the kitchen to the trap doors, where he drops it on his colleague. Charlie prepares the oven, shovels up the dough, then takes a rest on the sack. His colleague lies beneath, but is soon freed. In their hiding place, the strikers plan revenge using dynamite. At the counter, the proprietor is horrified as Charlie drops loaves of bread to the floor. Charlie's colleague summons him downstairs via the trap; as the other man tugs on Charlie's legs, his head becomes trapped between the doors. Once freed, Charlie battles the other waiter with dough. The head striker returns to the bakery to buy a loaf of bread. The waitresses climb downstairs, and Charlie, putting the other man to work, has their undivided attention; they perch on a worktop, unaware it is covered in flour. The strikers, meanwhile, place a stick of dynamite inside the loaf and set off for the bakery. In the back yard, the second waiter is burning rubbish when, from over the fence, the strikers beat him over the head. He retreats back to the bakery. Charlie goes to the back yard instead. He resumes the task of burning the rubbish when he, too, is clubbed. Dazed, he staggers downstairs to commence another dough fight with his colleague. The waitresses return upstairs; one of them collects an order from the proprietor, turning to reveal a flour-coated behind. Work continues at the oven while the strikers send in a small girl to return the seemingly heavy loaf, actually laden with explosive. The proprietor notices a patch of flour on the other waitress's posterior. His wife takes the loaf down to Charlie to have it baked for longer. She observes Charlie's singular method of making doughnuts, in which he rolls out dough then wraps it around his wrist. The offending loaf is returned to the oven. Charlie has innocently placed floury hand-prints on the wife's lower back, which are noticed by her husband when she returns to take customers' orders. The angry boss rushes downstairs to attack Charlie, but is booted over to the other waiter. The boss pauses to hit the other man before Charlie throws more pastry. Charlie fights off the proprietor, but is chased through the restaurant into the kitchen. Charlie borrows a pie from the cook, aiming it at the boss but hitting a diner instead. The cook takes a swing at Charlie; he ducks and the boss gets it. Charlie sends the cook running with a

hefty kick. The angry customer swings at Charlie, but once again the boss takes the blow. Charlie rushes downstairs, his boss in pursuit; he engages proprietor and colleague in a battle of flour bags and dough until the doctored loaf explodes inside the oven. The explosion sets off the strikers' box of dynamite in their hide-out, sending them flying. In the bakery, proprietor and waiter lie dazed beneath the rubble, while Charlie's head struggles out from beneath a layer of dough.

As noted elsewhere, *Dough and Dynamite* grew out of a sequence intended for *Those Love Pangs* (*qv*). After completion of *Dough and Dynamite*, Chaplin and much of the same cast returned to the original idea, which was completed and released before *Dough and Dynamite* reached the public. There is no truth in the occasional claim that *Dough and Dynamite*'s release was delayed until 1916. On 24 October 1914, Peter Milne of the *Motion Picture News* gave it a rave review, regarding the presence of Chaplin and Chester Conklin (*qv*) as a guarantee of 'slapstick comedy of the highest order'. Milne was particularly impressed by the stars' ability to be 'uproariously funny' without resorting to the vulgarity of many contemporaries, some of whom 'demand a good stretch of the imagination to be termed humorous at all' (Milne had evidently turned a blind eye to a gag in which Charlie compares an undulating female to a sign reading 'Assorted French Tarts'!). The review noted the confinement of the action to comparatively few scenes, despite the two-reel length. Mack Sennett (*qv*) was said to have proven again 'his remarkable ability as producer of this variety of comedy'.

Sennett later regarded *Dough and Dynamite* as the best film Chaplin had made up until that time. It is certainly well-paced and edited, but, like most Chaplin Keystones, has been subject to abuse on its many revivals. Most copies seem to crop the short opening section prior to Charlie's flirtation with Vivian Edwards (*qv*). This applies also to the revived edition edited and retitled by Syd Chaplin (*qv*) (one of whose excessive gag titles reads 'Sorry I'm late – I've been watching a "Sweet Cookie" with a "Bun" on'). Also missing from this edition is the scene of the bakers putting their demands to the owner and a knife to Charlie's stomach, relegating details of the strike to a new title when Conklin is put to work as baker. It does, however, include two sections absent from many prints: one shows the strikers buying a loaf, while the other, more importantly, provides a fuller ending rather than the usual cut-off after the strikers are blown up with their own dynamite. The intended finale, of Charlie emerging from within the dough, anticipates the famous conclusion of Chaplin's later comedy, *Work* (*qv*).

(See also: Documentaries, compilations; Female impersonation; *Funniest Man in the World, The*; Keystone; MacDonald, Wallace; Politics; Reissues; Risqué humour; Summerville, George J. 'Slim'; Williams, Frank D.)

DREAMS

(Chaplin films *qv*)
An oft-used device for fantasy, dreams facilitate the action in *His Prehistoric Past*, *The Bank* and *Shoulder Arms*. *Sunnyside* owes at least part of its surreal nature to no less than *two* dream sequences – one of them Charlie's dance with the wood nymphs, the other his nightmare of a city slicker taking Edna away from him. *The Kid* includes Charlie's dream of heaven, while a dream sequence in *The Gold Rush* gives us his 'Dance of the Rolls'. One might stretch the point further by including, from the same film, Big Jim's hallucinations when desperate for food.

(See also: Food; Mental illness; Trick photography)

DRESSLER, MARIE
(1869–1934)

Heavyweight comedy actress, born Leila Koerber in Coburg, Canada. Her greatest stage success was in the play *Tillie's Nightmare*, filmed at Keystone (*qv*) as *Tillie's Punctured Romance* (*qv*). As noted in the main entry, Mack Sennett (*qv*) required an outside name in order to sell a feature-length comedy; he chose Marie Dressler, mainly on the strength of a meeting years before.

In her dictated memoirs, *My Own Story*, the actress conveys the opinion that Chaplin was then an unknown, and that she had chosen him for the cast; this of course is quite untrue but any grandiose notions she may have entertained at the time are tempered by

Sennett's recollection that she and Chaplin got along well. According to this source, Miss Dressler's only objection to Chaplin concerned his wearing the same collar for sixteen days, something she would have been prepared to overlook but for the piece of squashed banana adorning the collar throughout. Decaying fruit notwithstanding, there is evidence to suggest a continued friendship between the two stars, even though they made only one film together. Miss Dressler visited the set of *Shoulder Arms* (*qv*) and appeared alongside Chaplin, Douglas Fairbanks (*qv*) and Mary Pickford (*qv*) at a Liberty Loan Drive (*illustrated* under **Wartime**).

In the wake of *Tillie's Punctured Romance*, Marie Dressler appeared in two implied sequels for different studios. One of these was *Tillie's Tomato Surprise* (1915) at Lubin, the other *Tillie Wakes Up* (1917) for Peerless-World. The latter film was made available to collectors by Blackhawk Films in 1974.

Her career was always subject to periodic doldrums, and was rescued again by the arrival of talking pictures. During 1929 she found work in sound shorts, among them Al Christie's *Dangerous Females*, which first teamed her with Polly Moran. She received particular acclaim for her rôle in Garbo's talkie debut, *Anna Christie* (1930), and was voted Best Actress for another film of that year, *Min and Bill*, co-starring Wallace Beery. Other films include a number of features with Polly Moran (*Reducing*, *Prosperity* and others), a reunion with Beery in *Tugboat Annie* (1933) and the plush MGM version of the Kaufman-Ferber play *Dinner at Eight* (1933).

(See also: Riesner, Charles F. 'Chuck'; Wartime)

DRYDEN, LEO
See: Chaplin, Charles Sr; Chaplin, Hannah, and Dryden, Wheeler

DRYDEN, WHEELER
(1892–1957)

(Chaplin films *qv*)
Chaplin's somewhat unorthodox family background meant that he had at least two half-brothers. Hannah's elder child, Syd Chaplin (*qv*) was fully acknowledged by Charlie, having been officially

accepted by Charles Chaplin Sr (*qv*) and given his surname; a quite different situation was presented by the offspring of Hannah and music-hall singer Leo Dryden (1863–1939). The boy was given his father's real name, George Dryden Wheeler, but was known also as Leo George Dryden, George Wheeler Dryden and, most frequently, Wheeler Dryden. The elder Dryden was in turn known variously as 'the Kipling of the Halls' and 'the Popular Patriot', on the strength of his songs detailing Britain and its empire. One of these, *The Miner's Dream of Home*, remains familiar today. (Dryden recorded this and other items for Berliner in 1898 and, although file copies are believed to exist at EMI, none have been reissued at the time of writing.) Historian Barry Anthony (in the April 1986 *Music-Hall* magazine) notes an early career parallel between Dryden and Chaplin, in that each had a temporary boyhood occupation as printer's layer-on. Noted also are close parallels to Chaplin Sr, who was born in the same year and had, like Dryden, taken to describing himself as a professional singer by around 1885. As noted elsewhere, they seem to have shared at least one song and, as has become obvious, the favours of Hannah. Chaplin's later recollections are of his mother having been 'seduced' by Dryden, but this is very much open to question; Dryden's later version to his son is that they had lived together for a year or two. The same applies to Dryden's motives in removing his six-month-old son from Hannah's keeping in the spring of 1893. Generally perceived as a selfish act, Dryden's seizing of the child has been construed by some commentators as a reaction to Hannah's increasing difficulty in caring for her family. (There are references to Dryden taking along *two* sons. Details are vague at best, but one suspects the second child, if any, to have had a different mother.) Dryden is said to have taken the boy to America; more specifically, Wheeler Dryden is known to have accompanied his father's variety company to India in 1912. He continued to tour the East until 1915, when, according to David Robinson's *Chaplin: His Life and Art*, he received a letter from his father detailing his origins and connections to the Chaplin family. Again according to Robinson, he tried unsuccessfully to contact Charlie and Syd in California, even to the point of writing to Edna Purviance (*qv*) (Dryden had by 1919

WHEELER DRYDEN
(SON OF THE FAMOUS LEO DRYDEN).

AT PRESENT PORTRAYING THE CHARACTER OF *ASHLEY* IN THE
ORIGINAL NEW YORK PRODUCTION OF "WHITE CARGO" AT THE
COMEDY THEATRE, NEW YORK CITY, N.Y., U.S.A.

A 1920s trade ad for **Wheeler Dryden** ...

... and a 1902 portrait of his father, Leo

arrived in the United States and was
making comedy films in New York for
Gray Seal Productions). They had
become reconciled by the 1920s, when
Hannah was finally reunited with her
son. When Syd returned to England later
in the decade, Wheeler was on hand to
participate in his film projects there (he
directed Syd's 1928 BIP vehicle, *A Little
Bit of Fluff*). He is also known to have
continued his stage career in Britain.
Wheeler later assisted in the directing of
The Great Dictator and *Monsieur
Verdoux*, and may be seen as both the
doctor and a clown in *Limelight*, on
which he is further credited as an
'assistant' to Chaplin. Many
commentators feel that Chaplin's
'Calvero' in *Limelight* is based in part on
Leo Dryden, especially with regard to the
character's much-married history (in
addition to other dalliances, Dryden
married at least three times) and the fact
that Dryden, like Calvero, is known to
have sung in the streets when
engagements had dwindled to nothing.
Contrary to myth, this occurred not

towards the end of Dryden's life but
during periods on either side of the First
World War. Although Dryden's career
was rescued somewhat by the 'Veterans
of Variety' revival, his financial state
remained such that his final two years
were spent at Brinsworth, the variety
artists' retirement home.

(See also: Chaplin, Hannah; Childhood;
Early stage appearances)

DUAL RÔLES 🎩

(Chaplin films *qv*)
The theatrical tradition of an artist
playing more than one rôle was made far
simpler in film by the trickery available.
Chaplin plays dual rôles in *A Night in the
Show*, *The Idle Class*, *The Great Dictator*
and the Mountbatten home movie *Nice
and Friendly* (*qv*). The supporting players
often doubled up, either for the sake of
economy or through ambitions to
display versatility. Henry Bergman (*qv*)
frequently essayed twin rôles, as in *The
Rink*, *The Immigrant*, *The Adventurer* and
A Day's Pleasure. *Shoulder Arms* uses
Bergman in perhaps as many as four. His
contribution to *The Pilgrim*, as a sheriff
whom Charlie meets in the railroad
station and, again, on the train, is not a
dual rôle as is sometimes implied, but
simply a matter of the character
reappearing later in the story. Syd
Chaplin (*qv*) contributes two different
characters to both *Shoulder Arms* –
Charlie's comrade and the Kaiser – and
The Idle Class, in which he plays one of
Charlie's workmates and the proprietor
of a lunch wagon.

Bergman's habitual ubiquity applies
similarly to Albert Austin and Frank J.
Coleman (both *qv*), as again detailed
under *Shoulder Arms*, also *The
Immigrant*, *Easy Street* and others. John
Rand (*qv*) is allocated two rôles in both
Easy Street and *The Immigrant*; in
common with Bergman's rôle in *The
Pilgrim*, Rand's reported doublings in
The Cure and *The Idle Class* seem more a
case of the same character reappearing
later in the story.

Less easy to spot – except in the one
or two good prints – is Edgar Kennedy
(*qv*) playing two parts in *Tillie's
Punctured Romance*. He is usually
credited as a restaurant owner but
seldom spotted also as a butler at the
Banks residence. Relegated to the out-
take department is a dual rôle for Doc
Stone, in a sequence deleted from the

final version of *The Circus*.

(See also: Abandoned projects; Female
impersonation; Trick photography;
Underwood, Loyal)

DURFEE, MINTA 🎩
(?1891–1975)
(all films *qv*)

Comedy actress, on stage in musical
comedy from 1908; she became the first
wife of Roscoe 'Fatty' Arbuckle (*qv*) later
that year. (Minta Durfee's birthdate is
sometimes given as 1897, which is
unlikely unless she was married at the
age of eleven.) After nearly five years of
touring together, Minta and Roscoe were
taken on at Keystone (*qv*). In the films,
Minta would often play Roscoe's wife or
girlfriend, as in, respectively, *The
Rounders* and *The Knockout*. She appears
in Chaplin's debut at Keystone, *Making a
Living*, and in effect plays herself, a
movie actress, in *A Film Johnnie* and *The
Masquerader*. She is a hat-check girl in
Tango Tangles and, in a less salubrious
establishment, a hootchy-kootchy dancer
in *Caught in a Cabaret*. She is the typist
in *The New Janitor*, a maidservant in
Tillie's Punctured Romance and fiancée to
Edgar Kennedy (*qv*) in *Twenty Minutes of
Love*. She is a somewhat more upmarket
fiancée for Charlie in *Cruel, Cruel Love*,
and is his landlady in *The Star Boarder*.
Minta Durfee is sometimes listed in the
cast of *His New Profession* but does not
seem to be present. Her marriage to
Arbuckle did not endure, but they
remained on friendly terms; she was
among those to provide Arbuckle with
support and comfort during his court
ordeal of 1921–2.

(See also: Costume)

EARLY STAGE APPEARANCES

With both parents belonging to the music-hall profession, it was inevitable that young Charlie should be destined for a theatrical career. It was indeed as unplanned deputy for his mother, Hannah, that Charlie made his debut in 1894, at the age of five. Hannah had been engaged at the canteen, Aldershot, when her voice failed. The youngster stepped in with a coster song recently introduced on the halls by Gus Elen (1862–1940), *'E Dunno Where 'E Are* (Wright-Eplett). The delighted audience poured money on the stage, which Charlie announced he would pick up before continuing with his act (!). He followed this with the Irish song that Hannah had intended to perform.

The Gus Elen song is sometimes assumed to have been a very old ditty entitled 'Jack Jones' (actually the first words of the lyric), but in fact had been written only the previous year. Although Elen owned exclusive music-hall rights to the song, he probably would not have enforced the matter under such conditions, even if alerted to its use. Elen (pronounced *Ee*-len, by the way) recorded the song on three occasions, for Berliner in February 1899, Sterno in September 1931 and Decca in May the following year. Gus Elen's repertoire would remain in Chaplin's memory, albeit subconsciously. On 27 September 1919, a *Picture Show* correspondent described having met Chaplin in Levy's, a Los Angeles restaurant. 'You're English, aren't you?' said Chaplin, asking, 'How on earth does Gus Elen's song, *The Golden Dustman*, go? I can't remember all the words.' The reporter duly obliged with the lyric. (Historian Frank Scheide

has unearthed a billing for Hannah – as 'Lily Harley' at the Castle, Camberwell Road, in 1884. Elsewhere on the bill is an 'E. Elen', presumably Gus at a time when he still used his full name of Ernest Augustus Elen.)

Chaplin's formal entry into the music-hall world was as part of 'The Eight Lancashire Lads', whose membership obviously required no strict Lancastrian connections, but depended instead upon some aptitude for clog-dancing. Though essentially a northern pastime, clog-dancing enjoyed considerable vogue throughout Britain in the latter 19th century. Charlie is believed to have joined the troupe, run by a Mr and Mrs John William Jackson, towards the end of 1898, despite his recollection of being eight years old at the time. The act consisted mostly of Jackson's family, one of them a daughter sporting a boyish haircut. The 'Lads' toured the provinces, attending school in whichever town they visited. Jackson, by all accounts a kindly employer, took pride in the fact that his charges, unlike other stage children, used no make-up; instead, Jackson would cheat slightly by having them pinch their faces before going on, to enhance the 'rosy-cheeked' look. The tour brought the young Charlie valuable experience, and served to fuel ambition; prophetically, he spoke of teaming with another member of the troupe, named Bristol, as 'Bristol and Chaplin, the Millionaire Tramps'. Chaplin toured with the 'Lads' until December 1900, when he recalled them taking part in the pantomime *Cinderella* at the London Hippodrome. This is difficult to verify, but examination of a programme from the run suggests any such appearance to have been temporary and unbilled. There was a constantly-changing variety bill supporting the pantomime, suggesting a possible week's engagement in which some of the 'Lads' might also have contributed to *Cinderella*. Chaplin's later recollection was of playing a cat, or in some accounts a dog; even in a cat skin, Charlie's actions were essentially canine, for he described ad-libbing some business in which he sniffed a dog's rear quarters, winking at the audience, before going on to sniff the proscenium arch prior to lifting his leg. The audience loved it, but not the stage manager, who, standing in the wings, gestured for him to stop. There seems no truth to similar claims that Chaplin appeared at the Hippodrome in *Giddy Ostend*, starring

Little Tich, during January 1900, which was also supported by a variety bill (nor is there evidence that Chaplin appeared in the stage run of *Peter Pan*). It was at the Hippodrome that Chaplin claimed to have seen, from the wings, such top stars as Marie Lloyd, Dan Leno (*qv*) (himself formerly a champion clog-dancer) and Bransby Williams. One of Williams' strengths was in the portrayal of characters from Dickens. When Chaplin began to imitate Williams' interpretations, Jackson took note and thrust the boy on stage in a pastiche Williams piece based on *The Old Curiosity Shop*. The audience failed to appreciate the subtlety, and the experiment was not repeated. One particular irony was the troupe's contribution to a benefit for Charles Chaplin Sr (*qv*), then in poor health and close to death. It was, in turn, oncoming asthma that brought about the younger Chaplin's departure from the troupe.

Chaplin obtained his next stage work by registering at Blackmore's Theatrical Agency in London, which obtained for him the part of Billy, the page boy, in Charles Frohman's touring company of William Gillette's play *Sherlock Holmes*. This was preceded by an engagement at Kingston, in a play called *Jim, a Romance of Cockayne* ('Cockayne' being an archaic simile for London). The playwright was H.A. Saintsbury, who was also to play Holmes on the tour. Charlie's fee was £2 10s per week, both for the Kingston production and during the *Holmes* tour. Even then, Charlie abdicated financial dealings to Syd Chaplin (*qv*), who tried (unsuccessfully) to negotiate an increase. After rehearsals at Drury Lane, the play opened at the Royal Court Theatre, Kingston upon Thames, on 6 July 1903. The critics hated it, with the exception of an *Era* reviewer, who, during a second week at Fulham, found praise for young Chaplin's 'most realistic picture of the cheeky, honest, loyal, self-reliant, philosophic street Arab'. The first tour of *Holmes* ran between July 1903 and June 1904; David Robinson's *Chaplin: His Life and Art* reprints an *Era* advertisement of August 1904, for Ernest Stern's production of *Rags to Riches*, starring Chaplin, but suggests it may never have received any engagements. Another *Holmes* tour, with a different lead, ran from the autumn of 1904 into the spring of 1905. It has often been said that Charlie arranged for Syd to receive a part in this second tour, but a

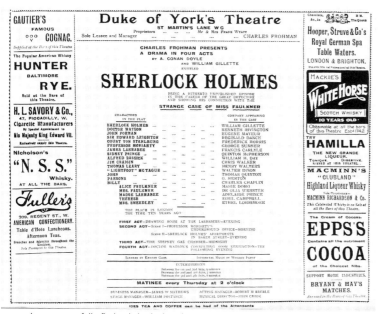

PRECEDED AT 8.30 BY

"THE PAINFUL PREDICAMENT OF SHERLOCK HOLMES"

A FANTASY — IN ABOUT ONE-TENTH OF AN ACT

GWENDOLYN COBB   MISS IRENE VANBRUGH

SHERLOCK HOLMES   MR WILLIAM GILLETTE

BILLY   MASTER CHARLES CHAPLIN

IT ALL TRANSPIRES IN SHERLOCK HOLMES' BAKER STREET APARTMENTS SOMEWHERE
ABOUT THE DATE OF DAY BEFORE YESTERDAY   THE TIME OF DAY IS NOT STATED

BUSINESS MANAGER — JAMES W MATHEWS   ACTING MANAGER — ROBERT M EBERLE
STAGE MANAGER — WILLIAM POSTANCE   MUSICAL DIRECTOR — JOHN CROOK

Early stage appearances: Master Charles Chaplin in an additional prologue for Clarice ...

... and again in a fully-fledged Sherlock Holmes *revival*

Billy, had the distinction of taking a revolver from the pocket of arch-villain Moriarty; he played the part one last time, again under Harry Yorke, in a brief tour occupying the first ten weeks of 1906. The photographs taken of Chaplin in the rôle disappointed him at the time, but they had grown on him by the time of his reminiscences for *My Life in Pictures*, in 1974. When Chaplin directed the Circle Theater more than half a century later, Jerry Epstein (*qv*) marvelled at Chaplin's ability to recall the *Holmes* text verbatim.

In his autobiography, Chaplin recalled having loftily turned down an audition with Mrs Madge Kendal for a provincial tour, the result being ten months of unemployment. It was instead a matter of weeks, for Syd, touring with Charlie Manon's company, obtained Charlie a job in a sketch called *Repairs*, written by Wal Pink. In May 1906, Charlie left to join 'Casey's Court', a group of juvenile comics under the auspices of Will Murray (1877–1955). *Casey's Court* itself is best encapsulated by its bill matter from a later era, calling it 'A Street Urchin's Idea of Producing a Music Hall Show'. Murray played Mrs Casey, presiding over an alley filled with cheeky youngsters; he later took immense pride in the comedians he had trained, using their names – with Chaplin's especially prominent – in publicity material for decades thereafter.

Chaplin is thought to have participated not in the main *Casey's Court*, but in a type of spin-off, known as *Casey's Court Circus*, *The Casey Circus* and variants thereon. The author had hoped to locate a script in the Lord Chamberlain's collection, but found only a fragment of that year's *Casey's Court*. Chaplin's memoirs detail his impersonations in this show, of Beerbohm Tree as Fagin and medical charlatan ,'Dr' Walford Bodie (whom Chaplin had observed first-hand at the funeral of Sir Henry Irving). The latter turned to farce when Chaplin attempted to hang his cane on his arm but had it upside-down. The cane of course hit the stage and, when he tried to retrieve it, Chaplin's top hat fell off. In its absence, the paper wadding fell around his head. The audience, believing the action deliberate, laughed mightily. This suggested to Chaplin the satisfactions of comedy, as did another mishap, recalled by Murray in 1925 for the *Era* (and subsequently reprinted by *Picture Show*):

programme from the Theatre Royal, Bradford, dated 16 May 1904, is from the first production, billing Saintsbury as lead, Charles Chaplin as Billy and Sidney Chaplin in the rôle of Count Von Stalberg. (The programme is reproduced in Sobel and Francis' *Chaplin: Genesis of a Clown*.) *Sherlock Holmes* later transferred to a lesser, provincial company under Harry Yorke, during which Charlie was invited to work at the Duke of York's Theatre with William Gillette (1855–1937), author of the play and the prime Holmes interpreter of his generation. The invitation was from William Postance, the theatre's stage manager, whom Chaplin was to commemorate as impresario Postant in *Limelight* (*qv*). Gillette had travelled from his native America with actress Marie Doro, but their play, a new comedy called *Clarice*, had received bad notices, due in part to his American mode of speech. In response, Gillette wrote a prologue called *The Painful*

Predicament of Sherlock Holmes, in which the famed detective sits, mute, while harangued by a crazed woman (played by Irene Vanburgh). Chaplin, again as Billy, was added to the programme for this segment. *Painful Predicament* seemingly lasted only three nights, from 4 October 1905. The *Illustrated Sporting and Dramatic News* of 21 October mentions in retrospect this addition to the evening's entertainment. Several drawings are reproduced, one of which depicts Holmes' terrible ordeal with his female visitor. Examination of available dates and programmes suggests an overlap between the replacement of *Clarice* with a fully-fledged *Holmes* revival; later programmes bill *Clarice* above a prologue entitled simply *Sherlock Holmes*, with no cast list provided. Whatever the case, *Holmes* soon ousted *Clarice*, and continued until 2 December. The piece was sub-titled 'The Strange Case of Miss Faulkner', the eponymous Alice Faulkner being played by Marie Doro. Chaplin, as

Early stage appearances: Chaplin (centre row, fourth from right) in Will Murray's company, 1906

Early stage appearances: Chaplin never really left music-hall behind. Alice Lloyd visits his studio in 1926 ...

... while Charlie and George Robey exchange impersonations in London, 1931 By courtesy of Tony Barker

Charlie's principal part in the sketch was that of the ring-master; another part he had was that of Dick Turpin in a burlesque of the famous ride to York. Upon the arrival of the Bow Street Runners, Charlie had to dash round and round the ring hotly pursued by the 'coppers', and make a swift exit through the wings. The impetus of his run always used to carry Charlie into some obstacle upon which he barked his shins. From that unfortunate habit arose the famous Chaplin 'stagger'. I instructed him to halt suddenly on one foot when he reached the wings and balance himself. The first time Charlie tried it he nearly broke his nose on the floor. I then explained to him that he must throw out his chest to preserve his balance, otherwise he would swing forward on his face as he done on the first occasion. Charlie succeeded in mastering the 'stunt', and it has served him well ever since.

Chaplin's 'Casey' tenure ended in July 1907 at Sadler's Wells, London. Following this, he tried out as a single at an East End hall, the Forester's. There was a contemporary vogue for Jewish dialect comedians, and the young Chaplin attempted a notably barbed and inept version for a predominantly Jewish audience. He was pelted, and made a swift exit. This ignominious engagement effectively concluded Chaplin's early stage career. His next employment, by the Karno company (qv), was to bring him considerable renown, both on the British variety stage and, soon after, in silent films.

As suggested earlier, Chaplin never really left music-hall behind, and was indeed accepted into the Grand Order of Water Rats (qv) in November 1931. Many of his films offer a retrospective glance towards this period in his life, in terms of material or, sometimes, characters. Harry Lauder was filmed visiting the Chaplin studio in 1918, and is believed to have taken part in an unreleased Chaplin reel intended to aid the British war effort (see The Bond). When Chaplin was in London for the UK première of City Lights (qv), he met up with music-hall legend George Robey (later Sir George) and posed for photographs, each comic impersonating the other. Variety theatres are depicted in The Property Man, A Night in the Show and Limelight (all qv). Among the visitors to the Limelight set was 'Wee' Georgie Wood, the pint-sized and outspoken Scot who is reported to have confronted Chaplin about a supposed lack of authenticity in the film. Wood was one of several music-hall veterans to call at the Chaplin studio when in America. Illustrated is an example from 1926, when Alice Lloyd renewed acquaintance with Chaplin. Alice Lloyd was a sister of Marie Lloyd, a giant of the halls whom Chaplin had seen during his 'Eight Lancashire Lads' stint. Despite Marie's legendary status, Alice, surprisingly, was the bigger name in America. Another variety legend, Fred Emney, met Chaplin in California shortly after the First World War. Emney, recently out of the army, had decided to try his luck in the USA. In relating the incident to Michael Pointon, Emney recalled introducing himself to Chaplin in a restaurant. Chaplin had known Emney's father, who bore the same forename, and greeted him warmly. Emney was invited to visit the Chaplin studio the following day, but, on arrival at the gate, could not get past the guard. Seeing Chaplin once more at the restaurant, he explained what had happened and was assured of admission the next day. Again, Emney was halted by the guard, and this time gave up. The two men were reunited some forty years later, at a function held in London. Emney reminded Chaplin of the appointment they had made four decades earlier. Chaplin, in mock outrage, offered an expletive, followed by 'You're late!'

(See also: Chaplin, Hannah; Childhood; Public appearances; Race; Religion; Vagrancy; Women; Young Charlie Chaplin)

EASY STREET

(Chaplin film)
Released by Mutual, 22 January 1917.
Written and directed by Charles
Chaplin. Photographed by Rollie

Totheroh. Two reels. 1,757 feet.

With Charlie Chaplin (himself), Edna Purviance (mission worker), Eric Campbell (bully), Albert Austin (minister/policeman), James T. Kelly (missionary), John Rand (drunk/policeman), Janet Miller Sully (woman in congregation), Loyal Underwood (father of brood/policeman),

Easy Street: *Officer Charlie meets the local bully ...*

... and, in the film's most famous gag and one of screen comedy's classic moments, anaesthetizes Eric Campbell using a gas lamp

Frank J. Coleman, Henry Bergman, Charlotte Mineau.
Charlie, a derelict, takes shelter in a mission hall and joins the congregation. When handed a hymn book, he misunderstands and places it in his pocket. During the sermon, Charlie is given a baby to hold; its bottle leaks and Charlie momentarily believes the moisture derives from elsewhere. Charlie does not contribute when the collecting box is passed along; another dubious arrival,

obviously drunk, even tries to take a drink from it. Another hymn is sung, and the meeting ends. Charlie is not impressed by the religious message until suitably entranced by the minister's assistant, a beautiful young woman. She and the minister persuade Charlie to mend his ways, so much so that he pauses to hand back the collection on his way out. Nearby is the notorious Easy Street, a lawless neighbourhood presided over by one particularly large bully. Policemen who venture near are lucky to escape merely with torn uniforms. Turnover of officers is so great that a notice is placed outside the station, advertising for new recruits. Charlie, seeing an opportunity to reform, has several thoughts about applying, but eventually makes his way in. Equipped with uniform and truncheon, he is assigned to Easy Street. Outside the station, one of the local hoodlums takes in the spectacle of Charlie in an ill-fitting uniform and a helmet worn back-to-front. He laughs heartily until Charlie, spinning his truncheon, knocks the man cold. In Easy Street, the bully shakes money from a pair of policeman's trousers. He hogs the entire amount, sending his grubby neighbours scurrying. In consequence, only the bully remains when Charlie arrives. The bully follows the new cop as he inspects the scenes of mayhem. Charlie nervously tries to use the police telephone, but is intimidated into pretending it is a flute or to be looking for some sort of blockage in the earpiece. Thinking the bully to be distracted, Charlie lands several blows on his head, to no avail. Putting Charlie to one side, the bully demonstrates his vast strength by bending a lamp-post. Seizing his opportunity, Charlie leaps on the villain's back and jams his head inside the gas lamp, rendering him unconscious with the fumes. Charlie has to lie on the ground in order to call the station. Easy Street's other residents observe the triumphant lawman, scattering whenever he turns suddenly. The other officers cautiously make their way into Easy Street, flinching even at one of the local children. The unconscious bully is carried away, and Charlie, pausing to light a cigarette, causes a gas explosion from the damaged lamp-post. Across the road, the bully's wife steals food from a sleeping greengrocer. Charlie catches her, but, moved by her tears, takes more food for her to conceal in her apron. The mission girl arrives and, on recognizing Charlie in his new calling, assists in helping the pregnant-looking woman into her house. They are chatting outside when

the woman, reverting to type, drops a plant pot from the upstairs window. Across the road, Charlie and the mission girl engage in charity work for a huge family. The father of this immense brood is a frail-looking man, whom Charlie congratulates by temporarily awarding him his badge. In the police station, the bully regains consciousness. Breaking free, he returns home and is immediately battling with his wife. Charlie goes to investigate, and is soon being chased by the burly monster, dodging in and out of doorways, windows, up and down stairs and through a neighbouring street. When they are back in the flat, the bully locks the door and swallows the key. Charlie dodges the bully, at one point hurling a jug that hits a man watching from across the street. Charlie escapes via the drainpipe, but is pursued by the bully's henchmen. He disappears back upstairs, only to meet the bully coming down. Charlie gives him the slip, and returns upstairs while the furious bully is outside. Charlie heaves a stove through the window and flattens him. The mission girl is abducted by the crowd and put into a cellar housing a crazed drug addict. Charlie is also overpowered by the mob and dumped into the cellar. Dazed, Charlie cannot put up much of a fight, and the addict knocks him over; Charlie lands on the addict's needle, giving him the superhuman energy to mop up the Easy Street gang. As a postscript, we see a New Mission at the end of Easy Street, attended by its now-respectable residents. Even the bully attends, a reformed gentleman who deliberately pauses in order to walk at his wife's right hand. Charlie, delighted in any case, brightens even more on seeing the girl, whom he escorts into the mission hall.

Probably Chaplin's most famous short comedy, *Easy Street* is generally believed to replicate the more run-down London streets Chaplin would have known in childhood, some of which still remain; even the name 'Easy Street' is redolent of East Street, his accepted birthplace. As in his earlier *Police* (*qv*), Chaplin presented his comedy within an exaggerated yet authentically horrifying world of poverty and violence, accompanied not merely by the usual accoutrements of alcohol and crime, but also, prophetically, drugs (which in 1917 had yet to be established as a major social problem). A similar gag was to surface years later in *Modern Times* (*qv*). It might also be noted that 'Easy Street' represents something of an immigrants' ghetto; many of the inhabitants seem Russian, given some of the costumes and the portraits of the Tsar and Tsarina on the wall of the cellar.

Despite frequent revival, *Easy Street* tends to survive in reasonable condition, though modern-day prints often lose a few minor shots. One of these is a second close-up of the police chief prior to the exploding lamp-post gag; another shows Eric Campbell (*qv*), in perhaps his finest appearance, being propped up in the police station prior to regaining consciousness. Even the famous sequence of Campbell's gassing is subject to minor trims; usually he seems to become anaesthetized rather too quickly, but complete prints include several additional shots of his head inside the lamp. (One might add in passing that, during shooting, the lamp fell across Chaplin's nose, necessitating stitches.)

The missing sections of the lamp sequence may be seen in both *The Funniest Man in the World* (*qv*) and the restored BBC *Chaplin SuperClown* print. Though by no means the best quality available, the BBC edition appears to be complete, albeit incorporating remade titles employing a probably unreliable text. Some of the author's prints (there are several!) carry primitive-looking sub-titles that are sometimes at odds with the action itself: for example, when Edna Purviance (*qv*) finds a uniformed Chaplin helping the bully's wife, she seems delighted (she can easily be lip-read saying 'Why, Mister Chaplin'!) and, clearly unaware of his aiding the theft of food, helps him assist the woman into the house. The titling, however, has her say, 'A policeman! And you promised to reform,' a seeming condemnation which is neither appropriate nor particularly well-phrased.

Despite this minor quibble, the BBC's *Easy Street* is evidently the product of painstaking assembly, acquiring further interest by the use of some alternative camera material. In silent days, the absence of good duplicate negative stock necessitated the use of twin cameras to produce negatives for domestic and overseas use; in consequence, it is sometimes possible to find separate versions of silent films taken from slightly different angles. In *Easy Street*, the difference becomes obvious in the close-ups of Charlie and Edna, when she persuades him to remain in the mission hall: in most prints they are more or less full-face, whereas the BBC copy presents them in virtual semi-

profile. Similar variants are noted under *The Floorwalker*, *The Count*, *A Dog's Life*, *Shoulder Arms*, *The Kid* and *Pay Day*, but they remain unusual in available Chaplin material.

(See also: Costume; Documentaries; Food; Home movies; Kelly, James T.; Policemen; Rand, John; Reissues; Risqué humour; Television; Titling; Underwood, Loyal; Video releases)

EDWARDS, VIVIAN 🎩
(1897–?)

(Chaplin films *qv*)
Slender, Los Angeles-born brunette, often working in tandem with Cecile Arnold (*qv*) at Keystone (*qv*); she began as an extra during 1914 and was gradually given more to do as the year progressed. Vivian may be seen in Chaplin's *The Face On the Bar Room Floor*, *The Masquerader*, *Those Love Pangs*, *Dough and Dynamite* and, in the author's opinion, as part of the motor-racing audience in *Gentlemen of Nerve*. Other Keystone films include *Hogan, the Porter* with Charlie Murray (*qv*), *A Modern Enoch Arden*, *The Village Blacksmith*, *His Lying Heart* (with Ford Sterling [*qv*]) and the famous Arbuckle-Normand three-reeler *Fatty and Mabel Adrift*, released in early January 1916.

(See also: Arbuckle, Roscoe 'Fatty'; Normand, Mabel; Risqué humour; Women)

ELSOM, ISOBEL
(1893–1981)

English-born actress (real name Isobel Reed) plays Marie Grosnay in Chaplin's *Monsieur Verdoux* (*qv*). Prolific in British films from the middle of the second decade of the century, among them *Dick Turpin's Ride To York* (1922), directed by Maurice Elvey (1887–1967), to whom she was once married. Latterly in America, where her films included *Ladies in Retirement* (1941), *You Were Never Lovelier* (1942), *The Ghost and Mrs. Muir* (1947), *Desirée* (1954) with Marlon Brando (*qv*), Jerry Lewis' *Rock-a-Bye-Baby* (1958) and *Who's Minding the Store* (1963), also *My Fair Lady* (1964), which, coincidentally, also has in its cast Marjorie Bennett (*qv*), who plays Mme Grosnay's maid in *Monsieur Verdoux*.

ENSIGN, HARRY
See: Totheroh, Rollie

EPSTEIN, JEROME (JERRY) 🎩
(1922–91)

(Chaplin films *qv*)
Stage and screen director, also screenwriter, Jerry Epstein's initial contact with the Chaplin family was via the comedian's son, Sydney, an associate of Epstein's in the Circle Theater. Established in 1946, the Circle Theater began on a strictly informal basis, but grew quickly into a thriving entity, not least after Sydney's father began to take an interest. Chaplin and his wife, Oona, drew attention to this early 'in-the-round' group by attending Sydney's performance in *The Adding Machine* and putting out word among their friends. Chaplin began making suggestions for the Circle's productions and became uncredited director. His directing methods remained much as they were in film, demonstrating to each player how the rôle should be interpreted. As ever, Chaplin strove for 'reality', telling his actors to 'Make the audience feel they're looking through a keyhole.' Epstein also recalled a pleasant visit to the Silent Movie House in Los Angeles, when he and Sydney watched some early Chaplin shorts. They enjoyed the films, but not so much as the man behind them, laughing maniacally. On turning to investigate, they discovered the laughter to be from Charlie himself; Chaplin was never one to confuse modesty with a detached view of what was good.

Chaplin's involvement with the Circle Theater spanned the years 1947 to 1951, overlapping with production of *Monsieur Verdoux*. One of their biggest successes, Somerset Maugham's story *Rain*, had been suggested by Chaplin, who also directed – and slightly embellished – a production of *School For Scandal*, with Marie Wilson. Chaplin had wanted Epstein as assistant director for his next film, *Limelight*, but was persuaded otherwise. Instead, Epstein was hired as personal assistant. The Circle personnel were further represented by Sydney as the young composer and Julian Ludwig – making up as older than he really was – as one of the buskers. Chaplin was pleased with Epstein, who among other things rescued the film from a disorganized cutting session; after the Chaplins' departure from the USA, Epstein was invited to stay with them in Switzerland and continued to see them regularly, joining them on trips revisiting the comedian's old stamping grounds in

London. Epstein was involved again, as associate producer, in Chaplin's *A King in New York* and assisted in the preparation of *The Chaplin Revue* (*qv*), incorporating unseen archive material, which, despite Chaplin's orders, Epstein had not destroyed. He was subsequently producer of *A Countess From Hong Kong* (in which he makes a cameo appearances as a barman) and moved permanently to London in 1969. When Epstein directed the film version of *The Adding Machine*, Chaplin contributed a number of gags to the 'Heaven' sequence, in addition to composing – on the spot – a theme used eventually for the title sequence.

Epstein's book, *Remembering Charlie*, was first published in 1988. At the time, the British press took great interest in the theft of Epstein's photos of the Chaplin family, which were subsequently recovered. A 'centenary' edition of *Remembering Charlie* appeared in 1989, a time when, naturally, Chaplin-consciousness was high (Epstein gave several interviews in England at this time, one of them for BBC TV's *Daytime Live*). The American promotion of *Remembering Charlie* brought Epstein into contact with Bonnie McCourt, whose existing enthusiasm for Chaplin was suddenly being more widely comprehended. Epstein encouraged McCourt in her ambitions to launch both a regular magazine and a permanent society. Epstein's comparatively early death – from a heart attack complicated by asthma – meant that he did not see the result, a society called the Charlie Chaplin Film Co. and a journal named after *Limelight*.

(See also: Children; Childhood; Keaton, Buster; O'Neill, Oona; Politics; Reissues; Trick photography)

ESSANAY

(Chaplin films *qv*)
The Essanay Film Manufacturing Company was founded in 1907 by George K. Spoor and G.M. 'Broncho Billy' Anderson (both *qv*), from whose initials derived the name. Their distinctive trademark, the head of a Red Indian chief, was taken from that on a coin. According to Terry Ramsaye's *A Million and One Nights*, it was a contest held by Essanay that first brought about the term 'photoplay'. The studio, based at Chicago, was best-known for its 'Broncho Billy' westerns with Anderson as star. Despite

being based in the east, Essanay's westerns were shot in authentic locations. Also noted from the studio's output were the dramatic films pairing Francis X. Bushman and Beverly Bayne, and those starring J. Warren Kerrigan; comedy was represented by Augustus Carney as 'Alkali Ike', the rustic humour of the 'Snakeville' comedies and an odd little man who had been hired as early as 1909, Ben Turpin (*qv*). Turpin was thus on hand when Chaplin joined Essanay at the beginning of 1915. Terry Ramsaye's account tells of Anderson meeting Chaplin in Los Angeles, when the comedian had decided to leave Keystone (*qv*). Chaplin's financial demands grew increasingly higher, but Anderson cabled Spoor to the effect that they could probably get Chaplin for the admittedly large sum of $1,000 per week. Spoor, seemingly unaware of Chaplin's existence, sought the opinion of studio publicist Frank Suttle. On being assured of Chaplin's status at Keystone as 'the best they've got', Spoor approved the offer. Anderson returned to Chaplin, who, aware of his bargaining power, increased the figure to $1,250. A pet anecdote of Chaplin's concerned Essanay's change of mind over the large fee, claiming Chaplin not to be that popular; he changed their minds when, at their meeting in Chicago's Alexandra Hotel, he had himself paged and thus drew a gigantic crowd!

The deal itself was made in November 1914. Essanay wasted no time in the promotion of their new acquisition, taking out full-page ads on 16 January 1915 in both the *Motion Picture News* and *Moving Picture World*. Each made it plain that the world's 'greatest', 'funniest' comedian was now with Essanay. 'Mr. Chaplin's Latest Comedy Successes', proclaimed the *World* announcement, 'Can Be Booked Through ALL the Branch Offices of the *General Film Co.*' (the distribution arm of the Motion Picture Patents Company, of which Essanay was a member). The British trade saw a similar advertisement twelve days later in the *Bioscope*, bearing the comedian's name in huge letters: 'CHAS. CHAPLIN, (The Greatest Motion Picture Comedian the world has ever seen), is NOW PRODUCING his famous comedies FOR ESSANAY. Watch for First Releases — Coming Soon.' The new films took slightly longer to reach UK audiences, but were much previewed by news snippets from the American press. Another ingredient of the exploitation campaign was a short film item, *Introducing Charlie Chaplin*, which was

designed to accompany screenings of the Essanay comedies.

On arriving at Essanay's Chicago studio, Chaplin felt decidedly let down. He was horrified by the studio's penny-pinching habit of screening rushes in negative form, to save the cost of printing; nor was he impressed by Spoor's frequent absence or the assumption of a subordinate that he would accept a script from the head of the scenario department, Louella Parsons (later a famous gossip columnist). Chaplin insisted on writing his own material and, in his memoirs, compared the company's habit of allocating scripts each Monday morning to the dealing of cards. Above all, he was depressed by the climate of the 'windy city', rather a comedown after the Californian locale of Keystone. Only one Chaplin film, *His New Job*, was made in Chicago. *A Night Out*, *The Champion*, *In the Park*, *A Jitney Elopement* and *The Tramp* were shot after a move to Essanay's California facility at 147 North Hill Street in Niles, a suburb of San Francisco (where Anderson's 'Broncho Billy' westerns were made). Space quickly became a problem, and Chaplin's comedies – along with full studio and laboratory personnel – were relocated to the old Majestic studios in Fairview Avenue, just outside central Los Angeles. The move began on 8 April 1915, with production resuming in mid-May. As an interim measure, *By the Sea* was shot on location at Crystal Pier.

Work, the next release, was promoted as the first in Chaplin's 'newest series'. It was made not at Majestic, but at the former Bradbury mansion, whose peculiar frontage may be seen in the film itself. *A Woman* was about to go into release when, on 10 July 1915, the *Moving Picture World* reported on a visit to the Chaplin unit, noting a deep embankment on three sides of the property and a degree of secrecy unparalleled in the movie industry. This, it seemed, had been forced upon production manager Jesse Robbins by 'the great amount of curiosity to see Chaplin at work', though it became known later that Essanay was anxious to discourage the many potential visitors who sought to lure Chaplin to other studios. Robbins' supervisory capacity extended to that of assistant director to Chaplin (a contemporary piece by Fred Goodwins [*qv*] describes Robbins as 'Director-Chief'). Anderson visited from Niles at least once every fortnight. David Robinson's *Chaplin: His Life and Art* cites screenwriter Vincent Bryan as assisting Chaplin on this series and his subsequent comedies for Mutual (*qv*). Publicity was handled by M.A. Breslauer, who, functioning also as Chaplin's secretary, was obliged to cope with the mountains of fan mail. The leading members of Chaplin's supporting cast are named as Billy Armstrong (*qv*), Leo White (*qv*) and Edna Purviance (*qv*), with additional rôles played by Marta Golden, Paddy McGuire (*qv*), Ernest Van Pelt, Charles Insley (*qv*), Carl Stockdale (*qv*) and Bud Jamison (*qv*). At this time, Hal Roach – whose independent career was in brief hiatus – directed a further Essanay unit alongside Chaplin's. The *World* piece cites among Roach's company Harry 'Snub' Pollard (*qv*) and Margie Reiger (spelt 'Rieger' on this occasion), both of whom are also in Chaplin's *By the Sea* (Margie Reiger appears again in *A Woman*). The next Essanay-Chaplin, *The Bank,* had just been completed when a similar glimpse was provided in the above-mentioned account furnished by Fred Goodwins (*qv*) for the British *Pictures and the Picturegoer* (18 September 1915). As would later become apparent in *Unknown Chaplin* (*qv*), Chaplin's even temperament could snap when on-camera business did not go as intended; mentioned also is a tendency to shoot as many as five or six takes of each scene (which would soon escalate to many more), and this after as many rehearsals. According to this source, Chaplin as director was 'all of a nervous tension, screwing his fingers into his mouth, and bending forward in eager anxiety'. Chaplin believed in the director supplying the on-set atmosphere; 'thus,' continued the piece, 'if it is a mob scene, and he wants anger and excitement, he will stand beside the camera and spur them on (regardless of language in a case like this!) until the crowd is almost in a real rage'. For *The Bank*, he guided his actors through the robbery scene with a series of barely-audible whispers on the lines of, 'Sh! Come on, boys; not a sound,' until they truly felt as though the Bank President might descend at any moment. Noted elsewhere are Goodwins' comments on the maritime hazards faced when commencing *Shanghaied*. The final Essanays were *A Night in the Show, Carmen* and *Police*. The last two films were subjected to mutilation by Essanay following Chaplin's departure for Mutual (*qv*). His intended two-reel cut of *Carmen* was released but hastily withdrawn and, as described in the main entry, expanded into an unsatisfactory four-reel edition.

Chaplin had formed a reasonably close friendship with Anderson,

CHARLES CHAPLIN

MILLIONS ARE LAUGHING WITH

Charles Chaplin

The World's Greatest Comedian is now with

ESSANAY

MR. CHAPLIN IS WORKING ON A NUMBER OF SCREAMINGLY FUNNY NEW COMEDIES THAT WILL BE RELEASED IN THE NEAR FUTURE.

Apply For Your Bookings Now

RELEASES BOOKED THROUGH ALL THE BRANCHES OF THE GENERAL FILM CO.

Essanay Film Mfg. Co.

1333 Argyle Street, Chicago

TRADEMARK
Reg. U. S. Pat. 1907

contributing as a guest to Anderson's *His Regeneration* (*qv*), while Anderson in turn made a cameo appearance in *The Champion*. There is speculation that Chaplin's work under Anderson extended to producing some non-starring Essanay films. Anderson seems to have sold out his interest in Essanay shortly after Chaplin had left, rendering it likely that Spoor alone was responsible for the subsequent abuse of Chaplin's Essanay material, as detailed above, and through the release of three patchwork subjects, *The Essanay-Chaplin-Revue of 1916, Chase Me Charlie* (*qv*) and *Triple Trouble* (*qv*). (It is further tempting to blame Spoor for Chaplin's initial difficulties in collecting his large salary, but it should be noted that Stan Laurel [*qv*] encountered similar problems when working for Anderson during 1922–3.) By the time of

these posthumous Essanay-Chaplins, the studio had become part of V-L-S-E (Vitagraph, Lubin, Selig and Essanay), a vestige of the former Motion Picture Patents Company, which had been massively opposed by the industry's many independents. Both this organization and Essanay itself had vanished by the 1920s. Anthony Slide, in his *Early American Cinema*, is probably correct in stating that Essanay would be completely forgotten but for the Chaplin films.

(See also: Alcohol; Animation; Caricatures; Impersonators; Insley, Charles; Public appearances; Policemen; Prisons)

THE FACE ON THE BAR ROOM FLOOR

(Chaplin film)
Keystone Comedy released by Mutual, 10 August 1914. Produced by Mack Sennett. Written and directed by Charles Chaplin. Photography attributed to Frank D. Williams. Reissued as *The Ham Artist* (see below). One reel. 1,002 feet (UK length cited in *Bioscope*).

With Charlie Chaplin (artist), Cecile Arnold (Madeline/Madeleine), Vivian Edwards (artist's model), Fritz Schade (Charlie's client), Chester Conklin, Hank Mann, Joseph Swickard, Harry McCoy, Wallace MacDonald (bar-room patrons).

In a burlesque of the classic sentimental poem by Hugh Antoine D'Arcy, Charlie becomes the artist who descends into alcoholism over a lost love. ''Twas a balmy summer's evening, and a goodly crowd was there,' we are told, as the scene opens on a busy tavern. A 'vagabond', Charlie, appears, and in repayment for drink tells the assembled customers of a time when, as a painter, 'I was rated pretty good.' In flashback, an opulent-looking Charlie is painting a full-length portrait of the fair Madeline, who poses with another model reclining at her feet. His subject is respectably draped in classical mode, but Charlie's portrait is semi-nude, completed as far as waist level. He continues his painting with what resembles at first a well-rounded rear (and angular thigh); he seems then to add bloomers, but the image becomes instead a large pot, standing on a plinth and obscuring the subject's midriff. When he adds a handle, the pot seems to be of the *boudoir* variety, but the addition of a second

handle plus some suitable plant life renders it more respectable. Charlie shows Madeline the painting and expresses his love, but she seems amused. In the bar-room, Charlie continues his narrative amid collapse and further drinks. He recalls working on a painting of 'a fair-haired boy, a friend of mine, who lived across the way', and in flashback he is seen painting a dark-haired, balding, decidedly middle-aged customer. Madeline, seeing the portrait, 'would like to know the man who had such dreamy eyes'. They are introduced, and soon make a furtive exit together, leaving Charlie a letter attached to the painting's nose. Charlie discovers the note and, having first discarded the note instead of the envelope, reads of his love's departure. Distraught, he reproaches the portrait of his rival, poking it in the eye as a prelude to fuller destruction. A now destitute Charlie takes a seat in the park, where Madeline and Charlie's former friend pass by with several children. Disconsolate, Charlie goes on his way as the scene fades. Back at the bar-room, Charlie is given chalk with which to draw Madeline upon the wooden floor. When not tumbling over, he produces an amateurish sketch consisting of a circle with horizontal lines representing her features. He is booted out into the street, where he continues scribbling on the pavement. A passing cop sends him back to the bar-room, and a fight ensues. Charlie sends the others packing before

returning to his picture. He falls 'across the picture, dead .... drunk', and gives up, finishing flat on his back.

The Face On the Bar Room Floor serves as a lesson in the way prints of early Chaplins, the Keystones in particular, often require a measure of 'shopping around'. The author's material derives from two reissue versions, one of them a W.H. Productions reissue retitled *The Ham Artist*; the other is an Official Films print bearing the correct title but of the distributor's own manufacture. *Ham Artist* is slightly the longer of the two, and seems to present the action in its correct sequence. One title card is misplaced, that concerning the 'fair-haired boy', which is used as an unnecessary, additional card before we first see Charlie in flashback (it should, of course, serve as ironic comment on his ageing client, a joke repeated when *Mad* published its own parody in the 1950s). This version is missing at least two sections, which may be seen instead in the Official Films print: the first segment is a brief establishing shot of the bar-room before Charlie's arrival, which is designed to separate two title cards introducing, respectively, the customers and the destitute artist who wanders in (*Ham Artist* presents these titles uninterrupted); the second concerns Charlie's discovery of the farewell note and consequent destruction of the painting, which in *Ham Artist* cuts off as

Charlie, pre-downfall in **The Face On the Bar Room Floor**
BFI Stills, Posters and Designs

he starts to read; this leads into the park scene, again absent from *Ham Artist*, and linked in Official's version by a title reading 'two months elapsed'. Collectors have long disputed the correct chronological position of the park sequence, some believing it to belong after Charlie's abandonment, others insisting it to be the film's intended conclusion. The latter is less probable, as the scene ends on a slight fade-out, in keeping with the other flashbacks, while the bar-room fight typifies Keystone's motif of a climactic scuffle rounded off by general collapse. The author's interpretation is that Charlie's tale of decline should conclude with this parkside encounter, after which he embarks on the chalk portrait. Official Films' print is from an extensively re-edited version, in which the order of events has been confusingly rearranged. In this copy, his rival's portrait has been painted first; next, the girl is shown her own, completed portrait *before* the scene in which Charlie is busy painting it. There is also a cut within the final bar-room sequence, so that Charlie's brief departure into the street is lost. Official Films' master is sparsely titled (using their own cards), their absence resulting in several jump-cuts. As *The Ham Artist*, the action is described in sub-titles using selected verses from the original poem; Swedish historian Uno P. Asplund reports an edition quoting the complete work, but this is probably from a European reissue rather than the original. *Ham Artist*'s sub-titles are remakes, using italics on a plain background, but are probably faithful to the original text; W.H. Productions' reissues of these comedies seem reasonably conscientious, quoting both Sennett/Keystone origins while supplying the film's original title beneath the new. The poem's 'Madeleine' becomes 'Madeline' in sub-titling, an amendment that may not derive from the Keystone version.

A review in *Bioscope* of 31 December 1914 quotes the name 'Madeleine', and suggests the final scene to have been Charlie's collapse on the floor. Mention is also made of 'a distinctly humorous poem (cleverly distributed among the sub-titles)', suggesting at least a version of the original to have served as narrative. *Bioscope* included it among contemporary releases worthy of greater attention: 'As a medium for the quaint mannerisms of Charles Chaplin, this film so very admirably serves its purpose that special remark is fully deserved ... a series

of evolutions which will evoke screams of laughter ... Extremely broad in its humour, but never offensive.' Perhaps in reaction to this rave review, Sennett's UK distributors placed an ad making reference to this as a 'Chaplin "extra-special"'.

John McCabe's Chaplin study cites this film as the first instance of Charlie as a *bona fide*, rather than implied, tramp, a debatable point; volume one of Harry M. Geduld's *Chapliniana* considers it the first of Chaplin's few explorations of the flashback technique, though an earlier, brief example may be found in *Caught in a Cabaret* (*qv*).

(See also: Alcohol; Arnold, Cecile; Artists; Conklin, Chester; Edwards, Vivian; Home movies; Keystone; Left-handedness; MacDonald, Wallace; Mann, Hank; McCoy, Harry; Mutual; Parks; Reissues; Schade, Fritz; Sennett, Mack; Titling; Vagrancy; Williams, Frank D.)

FAIRBANKS, DOUGLAS (DOUGLAS ULLMAN)
(1883–1939)

Actor, later typed as a 'swashbuckler', but known initially as a comedian from the Broadway theatre. He was engaged by the Triangle Film Corporation in 1915 to film his stage success, *The Lamb* (supervised by D.W. Griffith [*qv*]), and appeared subsequently in bright, breezy rôles scripted by Anita Loos, such as *His Picture in the Papers* (1916), *Reggie Mixes In* (1916) and *The Americano* (1916). It was during this period that he became friends with Chaplin. Ralph Hancock and Letitia Fairbanks (the actor's niece), in their *Douglas Fairbanks: The Fourth Musketeer*, describe the first meeting of Chaplin and Fairbanks as follows: Chaplin was scrutinizing posters of Fairbanks outside a movie theatre; noticing a man standing beside him, Chaplin asked, 'Have you seen this show?' The other man replied in the affirmative, adding, when questioned as to its merits, 'Why, he's the best in the business. He's a scream! Never laughed so much at anyone in all my life.' When asked if he was as good as Chaplin, the man expressed an opinion that Fairbanks was vastly superior. Chaplin drew himself up. 'I'm Chaplin,' he said, indignantly. 'I know you are,' replied the other man, 'I'm Fairbanks!' The moment turned to laughter, following which Chaplin accepted a dinner invitation to the

Fairbanks residence. Their friendship was cemented when Chaplin, for the benefit of his fellow-guests, named Fairbanks as 'the foremost comedian of the stage'; Fairbanks in turn cited Chaplin as 'the foremost comedian of the age'.

On 24 February 1917, the British *Pictures and the Picturegoer* published Bennie Zeidman's lengthy account of Fairbanks visiting Chaplin at the Lone Star studio. Much of it reads like a publicist's fabrication, but the accompanying photos – in which Chaplin mimics a low-key Fairbanks stunt while his friend tries the hat and cane – are perhaps the earliest visual record of their acquaintance.

By the spring of 1917, Fairbanks' films – such as the memorable *Wild and Woolly* – were being made for Paramount, as were those of Mary Pickford (*qv*). They were first introduced at New York's Algonquin Hotel, at a party given by proprietor Frank Case. Each had suffered a failed marriage, but they became Hollywood's ideal couple on their wedding in 1920. It was in the preceding year that Mary proposed the formation of United Artists (*qv*). The history of that studio is detailed elsewhere, but it is worth listing some of the Fairbanks films released under that banner, among them *When the Clouds Roll By* (1919), *The Mark of Zorro* (1920), *The Nut* (1921; see **Guest appearances**), *The Three Musketeers* (1921), *The Thief of Bagdad* (1924), *The Black Pirate* (1926), *The Gaucho* (1927), *The Iron Mask* (1929) and a unique co-starring rôle with Mary Pickford, a 1929 talkie version of Shakespeare's *The Taming of the Shrew*. Sound film work was less prolific, but a more whimsical spirit guided *Mr. Robinson Crusoe* (1932) and *The Private Life of Don Juan* (1934).

Douglas Fairbanks was Chaplin's closest friend; with Mary Pickford, they were arguably Hollywood's most inseparable trio. When the couple's home, Pickfair, was being built, Chaplin bought the land next door and insisted on testing the well that was being dug on their land. Chaplin professed to enjoy the peace and quiet at the bottom of the well shaft, until a sudden earthquake prompted his exit. Another story has Chaplin visiting the set of Fairbanks' 1922 epic, *Robin Hood*, improvising an unannounced scene – sadly not filmed – on the castle drawbridge. The Tramp walked through the portals, pausing to put out the cat and collect his morning milk and newspaper. Still another

*Charlie and **Douglas Fairbanks** clown for the camera early in 1917*

anecdote concerns Chaplin's hoax call to the mayor of Los Angeles, consisting only of a whispered 'beware'. Fairbanks had urged him on, but when the newspapers carried details of the 'threat', there was a worried retreat to Pickfair. Fairbanks completed Chaplin's panic by arranging a bogus raid, carried out by studio police, while Chaplin escaped through the back of the house.

Fairbanks died after suddenly developing heart trouble; his last meeting with Chaplin was on the set of *The Great Dictator* (*qv*). Douglas Fairbanks Jr – the offspring of Fairbanks Sr from his first marriage – introduces *The Funniest Man in the World* (*qv*).

(See also: *Bond, The*; De Limur, Jean; Documentaries, compilations; Florey, Robert; London, Jean 'Babe'; Mutual; *Nice and Friendly*; *Pilgrim, The*; Public appearances; Sport)

THE FATAL MALLET 🎩

(Chaplin film)
Keystone Comedy released by Mutual, 1 June 1914. Produced by Mack Sennett. Screenplay attributed variously to Chaplin or Sennett. Direction attributed as a collaboration between Sennett, Chaplin and Mabel Normand. Photography attributed to Frank D. Williams. One reel. Reissue titles include (from W.H. Productions) *The Pile Driver*. One reel. 1,120 feet (UK length cited in *Bioscope*).

With Charlie Chaplin, Mabel Normand, Mack Sennett, Mack Swain.

Charlie takes an amorous interest in Mabel, but she rejects him for Mack Sennett. Their rivalry starts a brick-throwing fight; Mabel retaliates on Sennett's behalf but, at closer quarters, Charlie knocks his rival senseless. Mabel goes off instead with Mack Swain, and the two men unite against a common adversary, who is sitting beside Mabel on a swing. They find that bricks do no more damage to Swain's head than mild irritation, and are chased away. Hiding in a barn, they hit Swain again; when he hurls a brick in return, he accidentally strikes Mabel. She receives a further bump when Charlie and Sennett open the barn door. Pursued by the brick-throwing Swain, the thwarted pair take refuge in another barn, where they find a mallet. Thus armed, Charlie interrupts Swain's dalliance with Mabel by means of a knockout blow. Swain is carried to the barn, where Charlie renders his other rival unconscious. Charlie locks them both in and returns to Mabel, who is being pestered by a small boy. Charlie disposes of the lad, but the others, having regained consciousness, break out of the barn to confront him. Swain tries to kick Charlie into the lake, but finishes up there himself; Sennett congratulates his friend, boots him into the water with Swain, and walks off with Mabel.

The Fatal Mallet is rough stuff, even by Keystone-Chaplin standards, and is of interest primarily because of the interaction between Chaplin and Mack Sennett (*qv*), who tended not to share scenes even when present in the same film. Despite the critical tendency to divide screenplay credit between Sennett and Chaplin, barnyard antics such as these are more Sennett's forte than Chaplin's. Similarly, the idea of anything like formal direction between the three principals is less likely than an informal free-for-all constructed on a whim. *Fatal Mallet*'s reliance on one-dimensional violence was adequate in 1914 (*Bioscope* of 29 October thought 'the employment of a deadly mallet gives these indescribable comedians the opportunity for another genuinely funny farce'), but posterity takes a different view. This may explain in part its infrequent revival, though sections of the film, presented out of order, may be seen in a 1955 British compilation, *All in Good Fun*. One clip shows Mabel Normand (*qv*) repulsing Charlie by means of a well-aimed slap, another Mabel and Sennett standing beside the swing, hurling bricks at Charlie; these belong to a lengthy opening segment that is missing from many prints of this film. It is understood that extant UK material is longer than that in the United States.

(See also: Documentaries, compilations; Keystone; Parks; Slapstick; Swain, Mack; Williams, Frank D.)

*Charlie and Mack Sennett carry off Mack Swain, a victim of **The Fatal Mallet**; Mabel is rightly distressed*
BFI Stills, Posters and Designs

FEMALE IMPERSONATION

(Chaplin films *qv*)
A comedy staple, particularly in Great Britain, female impersonation can be either ostensibly realistic or purely farcical, as in the pantomime dame. Chaplin essayed both, the latter in *A Busy Day* (with overtones of Leno and, interestingly, Mabel Normand), the former in *The Masquerader* and *A Woman*. These two films share the common motif of a male victim unwittingly making advances to a disguised man, a principle compared by Rick de Croix (in *Classic Images*) to the 1981 Dustin Hoffman film, *Tootsie*. Chaplin is remarkably convincing in female guise – several commentators have spoken of his 'feminine hands' – and it is interesting to note how, in turn, he has often been impersonated by women (see **Impersonators**). Scott Eyman, biographer of Mary Pickford (*qv*), has related an interesting sidelight from the making of Pickford's 1917 film, *A Little Princess*; needing a close-up of Mary bursting into laughter, director Marshall Neilan persuaded Chaplin and Mary's brother, Jack Pickford, to visit the set; dressed in 'outlandish drag', the two men danced to Neilan's whistling of the 'Spring Song'. Mary reacted with appropriate mirth.

Other female impersonations appear in the Chaplin films. A victimized cook in *Dough and Dynamite* is obviously a man in drag, as is Leo White (*qv*) as a gypsy crone in *The Vagabond*. Henry Bergman (*qv*) regularly contributed female rôles, as in *The Rink*, *The Immigrant* and *A Dog's Life*. A reversal of this trend may be found when Edna Purviance poses as a boy in *Behind the Screen*.

(See also: Leno, Dan; Mutual; Normand, Mabel; Risqué humour; Schade, Fritz; Swain, Mack)

FIELD, SID

See: Desmonde, Jerry; Impersonators, and Ruggles, Wesley

FIELDS, W.C.

See: Ballet; 'Chaplin Craze', The, and Raye, Martha

FIGHTING

(Chaplin films *qv*)
An integral part of Chaplin's screen character is his gift for survival, manifesting itself on occasion in the necessary street-fighting skills. Detailed under *Gentlemen of Nerve* is an example of Chaplin's ability to elevate a commonplace scrap by means of elaborate preparation; there are, by contrast, straightforward brawls, as in several Keystones and the hasty exit from a flophouse in *Triple Trouble*. Reviewing *A Jitney Elopement* on 3 June 1915, *Bioscope* noted how Charlie 'fights with the agility of a boxing kangaroo, and with almost as much disregard for the rules of warfare'.

Charlie spends much of *The Pawnshop* scrapping with colleague John Rand (*qv*), displaying an interesting technique when Charlie ducks all of Rand's blows, then catches him each time by pretending to strike, allowing Rand time to flinch, before actually doing so. This incongruous grace is topped by a smooth, well-timed return to duty when the pawnbroker returns unexpectedly.

Chaplin fared less well in a real-life scrap with Louis B. Mayer at the Alexandria Hotel, Los Angeles, in April 1920. Mayer was by then producing films starring Chaplin's estranged wife, Mildred Harris (*qv*), but the comedian was not interested in discussing the matter. A scuffle broke out, Chaplin coming off rather the worse. After describing a youthful fight, in Paris during 1909, Chaplin claimed never to have fought anyone since; clearly, he had preferred to erase the Mayer incident from his memory.

More formally arranged violence, in the form of boxing, also makes its presence known in the Chaplin saga. According to Arbuckle biographer David Yallop, Chaplin and Arbuckle would regularly act as 'seconds' for boxing matches at the athletic club where Chaplin lived. Boxing is at the centre of Arbuckle's *The Knockout* (*qv*) and Chaplin's *The Champion*; Charlie takes to the ring again, versus Hank Mann (*qv*), in the much later *City Lights*.

(See also: Campbell, Eric; Kennedy, Edgar; Sport; Wartime)

Fighting: *Charlie takes a beating in* City Lights

A FILM JOHNNIE

(Chaplin film)
Keystone Comedy released by Mutual, 2 March 1914. Produced by Mack Sennett. Reportedly supervised by Mack Sennett; directed by George Nichols. Photography attributed to Frank D. Williams. Reissued by W.H. Productions as *His Million Dollar Job*. One reel. 1,020 feet (UK length cited in *Bioscope*).

With Charlie Chaplin (himself), Virginia Kirtley ('Keystone girl'), Roscoe 'Fatty' Arbuckle (himself), Ford Sterling (himself), Edgar Kennedy (director), Minta Durfee (actress).

Charlie is outside a cinema, scrutinizing the posters advertising various attractions, including the latest Keystone comedy. Inside, he is moved by a Civil War drama, but taken most of all by the Keystone film and its delightful leading lady. Charlie's strong reactions create a disturbance, and he is thrown out.

Noting the studio's name from the poster, Charlie visits the Keystone lot, hanging around outside as the players arrive for work. He meets such luminaries as Arbuckle and Sterling, praising their abilities and copping a handout from each. Charlie attempts to follow them inside, but the director does not want any 'bums' around. Charlie gets past the doorman and makes a nuisance of himself, tripping over props and getting in the stagehands' way. Charlie finds a genuine revolver among the props. Having spotted the 'Keystone girl' he saw earlier, he intrudes himself into the scene she is filming, dispenses with the villain, kisses the leading lady and fires the revolver around the set. Having made his point, Charlie wanders outside, firing the gun for sport, while attempts are made to resume filming. Away from the studio, a Keystone representative sees a fire in progress. Considering this an ideal conclusion for their present comedy, he phones the information through to the studio. Both the company and Charlie make their way to the conflagration. The Keystone players try to stage their antics before the flames, but Charlie intrudes once more. There is a fight, complicated by the presence of fire hoses. Charlie, already half-throttled by the leading lady, is the final target of the water.

Charlie's interest in the 'Keystone Girl' leads to his becoming **A Film Johnnie**
BFI Stills, Posters and Designs

Publicity for these first Keystones, in Britain at least, made much of Chaplin's recent stardom with Fred Karno (*qv*); Keystone's UK distributor, Western Import, described this in a trade advertisement as 'Another triumph for the old Karno comedian'. The title of this film has been given variously as *A Film Johnnie* and, as an alternative spelling, *A Film Johnny*; the print

examined by the author, the W.H. Productions reissue called *His Million Dollar Job*, cites the original title as '*The* Film Johnnie', a definite rather than indefinite article. Although this series of reissues seems more conscientious than most, such niceties become somewhat doubtful when, as in this instance, the comedian is billed as 'Charley' Chaplin (as in the same company's reissue of *His Favorite Pastime* [*qv*]). *Bioscope* of 2 July 1914 refers to it quite clearly as 'A Film Johnnie', as do contemporary trade ads such as that quoted above.

Definite or indefinite articles aside, *Film Johnnie* is one of a lengthy line of comedies based around the Sennett studio itself, perhaps the best of which is the much later *Hollywood Kid* (1924), which, incidentally, features a Chaplin lookalike as propman. Other such 'in-jokes', as they may perhaps be regarded, include Chaplin's *The Masquerader* (*qv*). Use of the undisguised studio premises – and, in this instance, the also undisguised, civilian-clad Roscoe Arbuckle and Ford Sterling (both *qv*) – is in keeping with Keystone's habit of using absolutely anything as backdrop, such as the real-life public events of *Kid Auto Races at Venice, CA* and *A Busy Day* (both *qv*).

The cinema posters on display at the beginning of the film depict not just a Keystone subject, but others in the then-current release programme of Keystone's parent organization, the New York Motion Picture Company. One visible trademark is for 'Broncho', a name not to be confused with the films starring G.M. Anderson (*qv*) as 'Broncho Billy'.

(See also: *Behind the Screen*; Cars; Essanay; Impersonators; Keystone; Kirtley, Virginia; Smoking; *Tango Tangles*; Williams, Frank D.)

FILM STUDIOS

See: *Behind the Screen*; *Chaplin Revue, The*; Essanay; *Film Johnnie, A*; First National; *His New Job*; *How To Make Movies*; Keystone; *Masquerader, The*; Mutual; United Artists.

THE FIREMAN

(Chaplin film)
Released by Mutual, 12 June 1916.
Written and directed by Charles Chaplin.
Photographed by William C. Foster and Rollie Totheroh. Two reels. 1,921 feet.

With Charlie Chaplin (himself), Eric Campbell (captain), Edna Purviance (captain's sweetheart), Lloyd Bacon (Edna's father), Leo White (frantic householder), Albert Austin, James T. Kelly, John Rand and Frank J. Coleman (firemen).

The captain of the fire brigade assembles his intrepid team for drill; as the bell rings, all are poised around the engine except for its driver, Charlie, who is asleep in bed. Charlie is eventually awakened and, fully clothed, leaps from his bed. His ability with horses is such that he can reverse them into harness. Charlie leads the engine into the street, leaving his comrades behind; called back, he puts the horses again into reverse, knocking over the rest of the brigade. In the station, the captain warns him not to miss another bell, reinforcing the point with a well-aimed kick. Charlie earns a second kick with his left-handed salute. The men are cleaning the engine when Charlie gets into a scrap with his colleagues; he turns his attention to dusting one of the horses, and is booted thoroughly by the captain. In the canteen, Charlie is playing dice with a colleague when the captain walks in. Charlie remains on all fours, scurrying under a table used by the cook. When the captain signals mealtime with a hand-bell, Charlie misinterprets and rushes to his position at the engine. He is retrieved and put to work serving soup. Charlie provides coffee using water from the engine's boiler. When the milkman arrives ringing his bell, Charlie again misinterprets and rushes back to the engine, dumping soup over captain and crew. Charlie, furious, throws away the milkman's bell, and a fight ensues. The captain is caught up, and Charlie flees into the stable. The captain hits him so hard that it seems Charlie will not get up; the captain is concerned, but Charlie, having feigned unconsciousness, springs up, kicking him into the horse trough. Charlie escapes by shinning up the firemen's pole; the captain attempts to follow, but is pushed back down. The captain reaches ground level just as his sweetheart and her father have arrived. His suddenly genteel manner reverts to type when Charlie falls downstairs, but the girl calms his anger. Charlie is dismissed to the canteen while the father talks business with the captain. The father wants to burn his house for the insurance money; if the captain permits it to happen, he can marry the daughter.

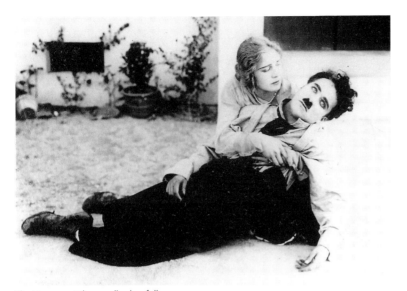

The Fireman: *Edna cradles her fallen rescuer*
BFI Stills, Posters and Designs

The captain, though shocked at first, agrees. Charlie returns to the engine, and finds the daughter receptive to his flirting. She deliberately drops a handkerchief, which Charlie hands to her. They are becoming friendly when Charlie, observed by her father and the captain, makes a discreet exit. The captain has escorted them home when a real fire breaks out elsewhere in town. The distraught householder sets off the alarm, which Charlie silences when it interferes with his game of checkers with a colleague. Charlie loses the game in any case. The householder telephones the station, but Charlie accidentally pulls out the cord. The man rushes to the station, where he runs up and down in a panic. Charlie pacifies him, and sets off to fetch the captain. The captain is taking prolonged leave of his sweetheart; having been briefed to ignore the fire alarm, he is at first uninterested in Charlie's tale of an emergency, even when distracted with the jab of a pin. Charlie finally gains the captain's attention by mimicking his amorous embraces with a nearby shrub. He explains about the visitor, and the captain sets off, allowing Charlie an opportunity to kiss the girl. At the station, they meet the householder, whose panic is renewed. The brigade is mustered, though Charlie knocks out the captain with a carelessly-slung axe. The captain is slumped on the engine as it sets off. Both he and the householder fall from the vehicle when it hits a bump in the road. They catch up with the engine at the burning house, where Charlie aims

the hose almost anywhere except the fire. Meanwhile, the father sets light to his own home, unaware that his daughter is upstairs. Discovering the truth too late, he calls the fire station but receives no answer. A bystander directs him to the other fire, where he begs Charlie to save his daughter. Charlie sets off alone with the engine, his comrades in pursuit. He arrives unaware that he has lost the business portion of the engine en route. Undeterred, he climbs to the upstairs window, retrieves the girl and brings her down to safety. The other firemen have arrived, and when Charlie collapses, the girl sends them for water. Once they have gone, Charlie instantly revives, kisses the daughter and walks off with her, arm in arm.

The Fireman is a Mutual that wants to be an Essanay. Second in the 'Lone Star' series, it shares with its immediate predecessor, *The Floorwalker* (*qv*), a preponderance of knockabout, but lacks that film's unified construction and spontaneity. Chaplin had, in fact, produced a 'crowd-pleaser', a film tailored to his own interpretation of the public's expectations. John McCabe has quoted a letter Chaplin received from an admirer in the Midwest, who enjoyed the film but believed Chaplin was becoming a slave to his public, adding, 'whereas in most of your pictures the audiences were a slave to you. The public, Charlie, likes to be slaves.' Chaplin took the advice, and thereafter adhered to his own judgment rather than attempting to speculate on

the preference of his spectators.

Taken in isolation, *The Fireman* is episodic but has many good gags and (unusually for Chaplin) some amusing trick work, as when Charlie puts the fire horses into reverse and when, through a joke in editing, the nightshirted firemen appear to dress in an instant. The supporting players contribute significantly to the fun: Eric Campbell (*qv*) portrays a first-class bully, whose antagonism towards Charlie has, for a change, some justification; Leo White (*qv*) provides some splendid comic panic, albeit ruined in a sound reissue that dubs in a French-accented 'Fire! Fire!' at every opportunity.

Part of that panic includes a two-shot of Chaplin and White seated on the engine, shouting 'Help, fire!' over and over. Many prints omit this section, among them a 'restored' video edition prepared in the USA. These shots are present in the author's print (a home-movie edition from a UK reissue of the 1920s) and the BBC's *Chaplin SuperClown* version. The author's copy has one or two minor cuts, including a curious printed-in splice excising the moment where Charlie, anxious to impress Edna Purviance (*qv*), pulls out his shirt to simulate a muscular chest. Given that Edna subsequently makes a coy gesture to her own impressive bosom, it is possible that a censorious mind construed Charlie's action as direct comparison.

(See also: Censorship; Essanay; Kelly, James T.; Mutual; Rand, John; Smoking; Television; Trick photography; Video releases)

FIRST NATIONAL 🎩

(Chaplin films *qv*)
The First National Corporation was an exhibitors' circuit, run by 25 theatre owners and thus ensuring distribution in North America (Chaplin's First Nationals were released in Britain by Western Import, which had earlier handled the Keystone comedies). The corporate structure is reflected in FN's logo, consisting of a map of North America encircled by a chain.

First National made a bid for Chaplin's services towards the end of his tenure with Mutual (*qv*). According to the *Moving Picture World* of 14 July 1917, renewal terms with Mutual consisted of a contract worth $1 million for twelve films, in addition to meeting all production costs. First National had

topped this by paying $1 million plus a $75,000 bonus, in addition to allowing Chaplin complete control and facilitating the building of a new studio (which Chaplin retained until after his final departure from America), located at 1416 La Brea Avenue, Los Angeles. John Jasper, business manager at the Mutual Lone Star studio, was to continue for the new series. In return, Chaplin was required to deliver eight two-reel films within sixteen months (i.e. one every two months), each at a negative cost of $125,000. Subjects running over the minimum two-reel length would bring the comedian an additional $15,000 per reel. A report in the *Motion Picture News* of 21 July 1917 specifies the boundaries of the two-reel length, in addition to tempering the amount to paid for longer subjects. According to this, Chaplin would 'receive the same sum for a film of 1,600 feet as he would for one of 2,300',

Chaplin built his studio, nominally disguised as English cottages, when commencing work for **First National***;*
Photo by courtesy and copyright of the Roy Export Company Establishment
Above:Chaplin shows a visitor around the lot

eliminating any excuse for padding. 'He has the privilege of making his pictures 3,000 feet long should he consider a scenario admits of this length, but only a fraction more will be paid by the Exhibitors' Circuit ... The whole idea of the contract is to do away with quantity and substitute quality.'

One of the circuit's initial acts was to combat, in the courts, a then-current spate of 'bogus Chaplins' (*qv*), using old clips bridged by Chaplin lookalikes. There was less to be done about the many reissues of his legitimate films, but Chaplin guaranteed his new 'million-dollar' comedies by signing the main title card of each (see also **Titling**).

Supporting players for the First Nationals remained similar to those at Mutual. Eric Campbell (*qv*) died before the series was under way, but Edna Purviance, Albert Austin, Loyal Underwood (all *qv*) and others remained. Added to the roster were Tom Wilson, Chuck Riesner (both *qv*) and, perhaps more importantly, Chaplin's half-brother Syd, who is believed to have made off-screen contributions at Mutual. Later FN entries reintroduced two former colleagues from Keystone (*qv*), Phyllis Allen and Mack Swain (both *qv*).

Chaplin did not like First National, considering them 'inconsiderate, unsympathetic and short-sighted'; in fairness to the company, it is possible that Chaplin's view was coloured by frustration, since his commitment to them meant that he was unable to take an active part in United Artists (*qv*) until four years after its inception. He was also unable to persuade the distributor to accept his semi-documentary subject, *How To Make Movies* (*qv*). First National were doubtless also worried: Chaplin had always been regarded a slow worker, but by this time he was even more in the mood to experiment, allowing the films to run more than the standard two reels, expending more time and raw stock than ever, and attempting to develop his characterization beyond the comparatively elemental slapstick of his previous films. When announcing the series to the press on 30 June 1917, he had stated his intention to destroy and restart any picture he believed was below standard. 'It is the comedian's avowed intention,' said *Moving Picture World*, 'with this series of eight pictures, to establish an artistic reputation rather than amass more money.' In the end, Chaplin took five years to complete the intended sixteen-month contract and, as

noted below, the results were mixed.

On 2 February 1918, the *Moving Picture World* announced that Chaplin had commenced work in his newly-constructed studio, despite giving all concerned a severe fright; he had decided to entertain the workmen with some impromptu clowning on the building's wire-framed roof, slipped and narrowly avoided plummeting forty feet to the hardwood floor. Suitably dusted down, he promised delivery of his first new comedy in the 'usual six weeks', or in other words, late in February.

That first film, *A Dog's Life*, did not appear until mid-April, but was considered by many to be Chaplin's best work up to that time; its immediate successor, *Shoulder Arms*, was an even greater hit, and would remain a critical yardstick for nearly a decade. After this, inspiration flagged somewhat, complicated in part by Chaplin's increasingly unhappy first marriage. Neither *Sunnyside* nor *A Day's Pleasure* were of his usual standard, and each remains somewhat overlooked today. Rick de Croix (in the January 1984 *Classic Images*) leaps to the defence of *Sunnyside*, which after its release prompted a *Theater Magazine* piece entitled 'Is The Charlie Chaplin Vogue Passing?', predicting (inaccurately) the comedian's obscurity within the space of five years. De Croix suggests *Sunnyside* to be a failure only in terms of its initial reception, its true value lying instead within the experimentation that would permit Chaplin's mature works of the 1920s.

It was one of those mature, feature-length subjects that restored Chaplin's reputation, in addition to calming FN's fears. *The Kid*, released in 1921, was seen as an important advance, both in Chaplin's work and for the cinema as a whole. It was after *The Kid* that Chaplin made one of his periodic attempts to buy himself out of the First National contract, to no avail. His remaining films for the company, *The Idle Class*, *Pay Day* and *The Pilgrim*, were the last to run less than feature-length. All have their moments, but it is easy to suspect Chaplin's lack of enthusiasm for what were essentially contractual obligations. It should be noted that Chaplin's reduced – and, by his high standards, lacklustre – output had, for a while, provided opportunity for his reputation to be compared alongside that of newer, more prolific comedians, notably Buster Keaton (*qv*), Harold Lloyd and, for a while, Larry Semon. Chaplin's subsequent work for United Artists would dispel any suggestion of redundancy. The First National Corporation was later absorbed into Warner Brothers.

(See also: *Bond, The*; Chaplin, Syd; Harris, Mildred; Impersonators; Marriages; Policemen; Prisons)

THE FLOORWALKER

(Chaplin film)
Released by Mutual, 15 May 1916. Written and directed by Charles Chaplin. Photographed by William C. Foster and Rollie Totheroh. Two reels. 1,734 feet.

With Charlie Chaplin (himself), Lloyd Bacon (the floorwalker), Eric Campbell (George Brush, the general manager), Albert Austin (counter clerk), Leo White (customer/shoplifter), Charlotte Mineau (detective), Edna Purviance (secretary), James T. Kelly (elderly lift boy), Frank J. Coleman (? cleaner).

In a busy department store, the floorwalker bears a strong resemblance to Charlie. In the office upstairs, the general manager, 'George Brush', reads a note from the store's owner, saying that detectives have been sent to investigate an $80,000 discrepancy in the accounts. He sends his secretary to fetch the floorwalker. They have a jarring ride up the store's escalator. In private, manager and floorwalker agree to disappear with the money. Charlie wanders into the store, trying out the drinking fountain and various goods before blundering into the moving stairway. He is playing with more of the stock when interrupted by a clerk, who fails to spot shoplifters at work. As the clerk bends to retrieve fallen goods, Charlie prepares to administer a kick, but is dissuaded when a detective walks over. The now-helpful Charlie takes his leave, stumbling briefly into the escalator. In the next aisle, he throws a quarter on the counter and carries off an empty rack marked '25¢'. He is apprehended by detective and clerk. Charlie retrieves his coin, and swoons on seeing the detective's badge. Charlie escapes first by hiding in a crowd of women, then behind a luggage display. Charlie plays a game of 'now-you-see-me-now-you-don't' with the detective before pushing a trunk on his foot. He then backheels the clerk into a

The Floorwalker: *Casual customer Charlie and confused counterman Albert Austin*

counter display. Upstairs, the manager gives the floorwalker half of the loot, keeping his own share in a briefcase. Charlie and an unsteady lady travel up the escalator. In the office, the floorwalker knocks out the manager using a desk drawer. Charlie, still eluding the detective, walks into an outer office just as the floorwalker enters. Each is startled to meet a near-lookalike, and they match gestures to ensure there is not a mirror present. When they touch, both flee the room but return, Charlie avoiding the detective, and the floorwalker deserting the manager. The floorwalker offers to switch identities with Charlie. After a change of clothes, Charlie is rewarded with a single note from the huge bankroll. Charlie passes as the floorwalker, but the suspicious detective follows him down in the lift. He is accepted by the clerk, even when the floorwalker is arrested in mistake for Charlie. The briefcase is left with the clerk. Charlie takes the briefcase, feels its weight and examines its contents with surprise. The manager regains consciousness, takes the lift downstairs and confronts Charlie in mistake for the floorwalker. Charlie dumps the briefcase, which travels up the escalator. The manager throttles Charlie when they are unobserved. Charlie, unaware of his identity, boots him into the upgoing escalator, from which the manager has difficulty climbing down. Charlie dusts both the luggage display and a customer. The manager returns to throttle Charlie, but ceases when spotted by a female

detective. Charlie, in mock bonhomie, delivers kicks amid the handshakes. The manager decides to kill him later. The secretary, finding the briefcase, takes it into the office. The manager takes the escalator upstairs as Charlie flirts with the statuesque sleuth. After an encounter with a doddery customer trying a toy trumpet, Charlie enters the shoe department, turning an electric fan on the line of stockinged feet. In the office, the secretary opens the case and finds the money. Charlie is at the millinery counter, where he sprays a floral hat with a borrowed watering can. The manager arrives in the office to take the briefcase. Charlie empties the water from the tray of hats. A pretty customer lifts her skirt to avoid the resultant pool; Charlie follows her into the shoe department, where he flirts outrageously on the mobile stepladder. The manager departs with the loot. As he reaches the ground floor, Charlie uses the task of shoe salesman as an excuse to massage the girl's ankle; by mistake, he grabs that of a man who has sat beside her. Charlie exits and is given a docket to sign and a package for despatch. Charlie places it in an overhead sliding basket, which first strikes a customer before knocking off the manager's hat. The manager shakes his fist at Charlie as the basket, on its return journey, knocks his hat off again. The basket narrowly misses the lady detective, who shadows the manager. He places the briefcase amid the luggage display. Charlie, dealing with the outraged customer, shows him the luggage. The customer chooses the briefcase left by the manager. The manager snatches it away, only to hand it back when the detectives arrive. The customer, deciding the case is too heavy, returns it to Charlie. Checking the contents, he makes for the escalator, trips and spends much of the journey lying flat. In the office, Charlie dives into the bag, but the manager catches up. Charlie avoids him by a series of balletic leaps, performed eventually for their own sake. At the finale, Charlie poses and is knocked flat. They are struggling while, downstairs, the floorwalker admits everything and is escorted away by the lady detective. Police burst into the office, and Charlie escapes both manager and detective, pushing the officer into the downward lift. Charlie tries to run down an escalator set to 'up', with, above him, the manager in equally fruitless pursuit. The detective awaits at ground level. The police open fire, sending the customers running. The detective throws the escalator into reverse, and Charlie descends. The manager hits Charlie, who lands on the escalator and is returned to the upper floor. Charlie enters the lift, where the detective is ready to grab him. Charlie sends the lift downwards, where it crashes over the manager's head. He too is caught.

First of the 'Mutual twelve', *The Floorwalker* is probably not the best of them, being reliant on a Keystone-like succession of knockabout gags; an exception is the central prop, an escalator, which was at that time a considerable novelty. Its use prompted a now-famous remark from Mack Sennett (*qv*), on the lines of 'Why the hell didn't *we* think of using a moving stairway?' Chaplin returned to the escalator idea for his much later *Modern Times* (*qv*). There is also some quite gentle humour, as when Charlie, examining the case of stolen money, thinks he has been arrested when a store dummy's arm drops to his shoulder. The ex-vaudeville 'mirror' routine – later reprised by Max Linder (*qv*) and the Marx Brothers – is performed skilfully, with Lloyd Bacon (*qv*) as a reasonably convincing lookalike in lieu of any trick photography.

The Floorwalker is above all Chaplin's best constructed film up to that time, displaying a unified scenario in place of the episodic nature characterizing most of the Essanay comedies that had preceded it. Another bonus is the standard of photography: even in poorer prints (though copies of *The Floorwalker* are often excellent), this film marks an immediate improvement over the Essanays, if only in

terms of lighting. It might be added that in 1916, film-makers were still employing diffused sunlight rather than exclusively artificial means, and the documentary *Unknown Chaplin* (*qv*) draws attention to the open-air breeze that disturbs the supposedly indoor shop display.

Available prints of *The Floorwalker* chop off rather abruptly on the closing scene, some slightly more than others. The otherwise very good *Chaplin SuperClown* edition cuts off directly; one of the best copies is that supplied for Britain's PolyGram video by David Shepard, which fades out as the manager is apprehended, an effect probably added to mask the abruptness. A tape issued by a different UK distributor, from a Canadian source, uses a frozen frame. There may originally have been a little more to the manager's arrest, but this will remain conjecture unless an undamaged original is discovered. The Canadian material, though inferior in quality, offers slight interest in that at least part of it seems to derive from a different negative; the same applies to the author's copy, which is from a silent-era edition with the 'illuminated initial' titles (see **Titling**). The difference is apparent in the store dummy gag quoted above: in most prints, we see the arm descending upon Charlie in long shot, after which the scene cuts away to the manager recovering from being knocked cold; next is a much closer shot of Charlie with the dummy. The Canadian edition shows the manager's recovery prior to the store dummy gag, which is played entirely in the closer shot and without interruption. Alternate takes in silent comedies are not unusual, owing to the industry practice of using two cameras to provide domestic and overseas negatives, but are seldom found in the Chaplin comedies (see also *The Count, Easy Street, A Dog's Life, Shoulder Arms* and *Pay Day*). One reason for this may be their continued revival in a single editions, ordinarily that prepared for domestic release.

(See also: Austin, Albert; Ballet; Campbell, Eric; Coleman, Frank J.; Essanay; Dual rôles; Kelly, James T.; Keystone; Marx, Groucho; Mutual; Policemen; Purviance, Edna; Reissues; Television; Titling; Trick photography; Video releases; White, Leo)

FLOREY, ROBERT
(1900–79)

French-born director, with early film-making experience in his native country.

Florey had become a movie journalist by the time Max Linder (*qv*) suggested he try his luck in the USA, where Florey arrived in 1921. He was found lodgings by French-Canadian Joe Bordeaux (*qv*), who was then making comedies for Fox and introduced Florey to his fellow-boarders, among them Leo White and Billy Armstrong (both *qv*). He was also introduced to Chaplin, with whom a friendship was formed. Florey became overseas press agent for Douglas Fairbanks and Mary Pickford (both *qv*); by the mid-1920s he was given work as an assistant director and, ultimately, director. In 1927, Florey wrote a biography of Chaplin, published in Paris (another such work, in collaboration with Maurice Bessy, followed in 1952). The same year, Chaplin assisted Florey's career by screening his experimental film, *The Life and Death of 9413 – a Hollywood Extra*. Among those present was Monta Bell (*qv*), who promised Florey directing work at Paramount's Long Island studio. It was at Long Island that Florey co-directed the first Marx Brothers feature, *The Cocoanuts* (1929); he also wrote the screenplay for *Frankenstein* (1931). Later work as director includes *Murders in the Rue Morgue* (1932), *The Beast With Five Fingers* (1946) and an assignment as associate director on Chaplin's *Monsieur Verdoux* (*qv*). Florey's later comments – as conveyed by Jack Spears' book *Hollywood: The Golden Era* – suggest their friendship to have ended after disagreements concerning this film; Florey believed Chaplin's methods often to be archaic and considered him reluctant to accept or acknowledge advice. Florey claimed that Chaplin tried to minimize his contribution, and was further embittered to see Wheeler Dryden (*qv*) billed above him on the credits, despite Dryden's lesser contribution. (It should be noted, however, that UA's French publicity release billed Florey above Dryden.) The irritation became magnified when advertising material in Paris reduced Florey's billing to 'assistant' rather than associate director, a distinction Florey was careful to emphasize in later interviews.

(See also: Abandoned projects; Books; Marx, Groucho)

FOOD 🎩

(Chaplin films *qv*)
Chaplin's impoverished childhood meant that food could be obtained either with the little money entering the family

purse or through the good graces of others. Charlie and Syd seem to have eaten better during their brief time with Charles Chaplin Sr (*qv*), whose habit of holding a knife in the manner of a pen was copied by the younger Charles for years after.

When touring with the Karno company (*qv*), Chaplin and Stan Laurel (*qv*) often broke lodging-house rules by preparing food in their room. Each room was supplied with gas, in an age before electric lighting had become the norm, but the two comedians employed it instead for cooking. 'I fried the chops,' recalled Laurel for *Film Weekly* in September 1929, 'while Charlie sat close to the door playing his mandolin, and so keeping the landlady from hearing the sizzling of the meat over the gas.' (A later account, as told to Laurel's biographer, John McCabe, describes Chaplin playing his violin to cover the noise.)

There are many food-related gags in the Chaplin films. Hot dogs seemed a particular favourite (though not for Charlie's dog in *The Champion*), as when one is taken by Charlie in mistake for a cigar in *His Favorite Pastime* and *Mabel's Busy Day*, the latter of which casts Mabel Normand (*qv*) as a hot dog vendor (there are other such characters in *A Dog's Life* and *In the Park*). A similar gag, with a salami sausage, may be found in *Pay Day*, which also contains an elaborate sequence in which Charlie grabs a free lunch from the food travelling up and down via a lift. He later returns home to find that cats have eaten every scrap of food in the house (one of their number returns to grab the salami he has brought home!).

Charlie's ability to transform objects manifests itself in the bread 'concertina' of *A Jitney Elopement*. More celebrated is his dance, using Oceana rolls speared with forks, in both *The Gold Rush* and one of the several home-movie clips in *Unknown Chaplin* (*qv*). When Charlie and Mack Swain (*qv*) face starvation in *Gold Rush*, Swain briefly visualizes his friend as a chicken. Their unorthodox feasting on a boot in the film was achieved by making the item from liquorice, the repeated consumption of which resulted in severe stomach problems for them both. When in London to record a new score for *The Kid* in October 1971, Chaplin attended a lunch but found there was another boot on the menu!

It is again Swain who is the noisy eater in *His Trysting Place*, an idea that resurfaced with Eric Campbell (*qv*) slurping soup in *The Count*. Subsequent servings of spaghetti and watermelon bring their own difficulties; Charlie guards his ears against the moist watermelon by tying a handkerchief around his head. Later, Charlie uses a chicken to knock out a footman and confounds his pursuers with a well-aimed cake. (Another cake has Syd Chaplin's bowler as its nucleus in *The Pilgrim*.)

Charlie's dexterity is apparent when, in *A Woman*, he scoops up doughnuts with a long knife, allowing them to slide the length of the blade before releasing them at the opposite end. This is an altogether more plausible feat than that in *The Rink*, when Charlie the waiter produces an egg from a roast chicken. Lunchtime in *Behind the Screen* sees Albert Austin (*qv*) munching on some asphyxiating spring onions, also Charlie's placing pieces of bread around Austin's main course, a meatbone. Eric Campbell tucks into a vast array of pies, leaving a pile of metal plates which Charlie plays like drums.

Charlie's varied duties in *Sunnyside* include the sale of food. *Easy Street* has him feeding a flock of children as if they are chickens, and *The Kid* is fed, initially, on milk dispensed from a suspended coffee pot (their later repasts seem to be from a cauldron of stodge or else some flapjacks prepared by the youngster).

When parcels from home arrive during *Shoulder Arms*, Charlie seems to have been neglected until he receives a consignment of hard biscuits and strong cheese, the latter of which is hurled into enemy lines. It lands on a German officer, who expresses comparable disgust to that shown a food vendor when Charlie becomes seasick in *A Day's Pleasure*.

The Circus has quite a few moments involving food. Charlie is seen cooking on an open fire, then goes off in pursuit of a chicken – but only to claim an egg. The heroine, deprived of food, shares Charlie's repast, and later has food thrown to her while on the trapeze. When Charlie auditions as a clown, he tries a William Tell act and takes a bite from the apple. Discovering a worm inside, Charlie produces a banana, eats half, then places its remains on his head.

Food looms large in times of desperate poverty, as in Charlie's foragings amid garbage in *A Dog's Life*. This is especially the case in *Modern Times*, which is essentially about the

Food: *Charlie's unorthodox repast from The Gold Rush ...*

... was relived at a lunch in October 1971

fight for survival. The *gamine* character frequently steals food, and Charlie's ex-colleagues are forced to become burglars through sheer hunger. Even when available, food remains a problem, particularly when administered mechanically or when Chester Conklin (*qv*) becomes trapped in a giant machine over the lunch break. One might add in passing that Chester's meal includes a whole chicken, which, in Britain at least, was a luxury during the 1930s, even for the comparatively well-off. Altogether more plausible is the wealthy-looking restaurant patron who, later in the film, orders roast duck, little suspecting it will become the object of an impromptu football game.

Although again in poverty, Calvero

of *Limelight* must acquire food for himself and his young charge, even if it requires him to pawn his violin. Elsewhere in Chaplin's talking films, one might recall *The Great Dictator* taking a banana, removing the peel, then throwing away the whole thing. His fellow-despot, Napaloni, carelessly pelts him with peanut shells, while his double, the barber, becomes embroiled in a conspiracy wherein lots are drawn using coins concealed within puddings. His last full-scale routine involving food, in the noisy supper club of *A King in New York*, compels an exiled monarch to mime both sturgeon and turtle soup.

(See also: Alcohol; Dreams; *Mabel's Married Life*; Mental illness; Smoking; Twists and Transformations)

FOR THE LOVE OF TILLIE

See: *Tillie's Punctured Romance*

FOSTER, WILLIAM C.

Shared camera duties with Rollie Totheroh (*qv*) for the Mutual series, up to and including *One A.M.* (*qv*). Biographical details are elusive, but other credits (mostly for Fox) include *American Methods* (1917), *The Blindness of Divorce* (1918), *The Man Hunter* (1919) and *The Silver Horde* (1920).

FRAWLEY, WILLIAM
(1887–1966)

Growling ex-vaudevillian who plays Jack, one of Mme Grosnay's party at her wedding to *Monsieur Verdoux* (*qv*). Prolific film career from the 1930s on, including Harold Lloyd's *Professor Beware* (1938), *Roxie Hart* (1942) and *Miracle On 34th Street* (1947). Subsequently a regular on Lucille Ball's TV series, *I Love Lucy*; latterly in the original cast of another TV perennial, *My Three Sons*, starring Fred MacMurray.

THE FUNNIEST MAN 🎩 IN THE WORLD
(1967)

(Chaplin films *qv*)
One of the more important Chaplin anthologies, *The Funniest Man in the World* is named after a publicity claim made by *Picture-Play* magazine at the height of the comedian's fame. *Funniest Man* is narrated by Douglas Fairbanks Jr, who, in an on-screen prologue, speaks of a childhood introduction to Chaplin via his father and of Chaplin's place in history.

The first clip introduces 'Charlie' by way of his first scene in *The Tramp*; next is a title sequence, much of it superimposed over the 'park' sequence of *A Woman*. The film proper begins with a résumé of Chaplin's early life, combining rostrum material with turn-of-the-century actuality footage, including a brief shot of two London newsboys who, at a pinch, might *just* pass for the young Charlie and Syd. A similar blend of stills and news film takes the story to the Karno tours, *Mumming Birds* being represented by extracts from Chaplin's filmed re-enactment, *A Night in the Show*.

There follows a little about Mack Sennett and Keystone (both *qv*) before presenting Chaplin's uncharacteristic debut in *Making a Living*. The disharmony between Chaplin and director Henry Lehrman (*qv*) is discussed during this and footage from *Kid Auto Races at Venice*. The latter is referred to as a rare film, presumably to excuse the comparatively poor quality, though in fairness it should be pointed out that prints of this film were somewhat harder to find in the 1960s. Much sharper is a lengthy extract from *Between Showers*, describing Chaplin's work with Ford Sterling (*qv*). Chaplin-as-Sterling is conveyed via *Mabel at the Wheel*, as is Sennett's promise to let Chaplin direct after clashing with Mabel Normand (*qv*). *Caught in a Cabaret* follows, from the version (described in the main entry) bearing gagged-up reissue titles. There follow sections from *Dough and Dynamite* (with the Syd Chaplin sub-titles), *His Trysting Place*, Chaplin's female impersonation from *The Masquerader*, the finale of *The Rounders*, highlights from *Tillie's Punctured Romance* and a summary of Chaplin's final Keystone, *His Prehistoric Past*.

Framing footage representing an early film theatre tells of the war in Europe and Chaplin's value as a morale-booster, permitting in turn a brief revisiting of the Keystones with the restaurant scene of *His Trysting Place*; a fragment of news film, presumably designed to represent an off-duty Chaplin of the period, seems instead to date from his 1921 British visit, but period detail returns with a trade advertisement by Essanay (*qv*) and extracts from *His New Job*. A chronological leap is made when using *Police* to illustrate the introduction of greater sophistication to the Essanay films, but the story is back on course with the debut of Edna Purviance (*qv*) in *A Night Out*. There are other clips from this film until Edna returns in her scene from *A Night in the Show*. Next are *A Jitney Elopement*, *The Tramp* and *Triple Trouble*, detailing Essanay's trickery by use of the kitchen scenes, and presenting almost the entire flophouse sequence.

An odd intermission presents some of the various Chaplin imitators: Billy West and Billie Ritchie plus Syd Chaplin, in the Charlie-like 'Gussle' character of his Keystone tenure. There are also artifacts representing the 'Chaplin Craze' (*qv*) of the middle of the second decade of the century, among them song covers, E.C. Segar's newspaper strip, the Sullivan studio's animated films and Minnie Maddern Fiske's Chaplin critique in the magazine *Harpers Weekly*.

A news photo shows Chaplin signing with Mutual (*qv*); films represented are *The Rink*, *The Immigrant* and *Easy Street*, perhaps an under-representation of the series, but doubtless imposed by a restriction in running time. A particular gem is a newsreel item of Chaplin and Fairbanks, out of make-up, clowning with boxer Jack Dempsey for the entertainment of the US Marines. They attempt a comic drill before Chaplin tries to conduct the Marine band. Fairbanks takes over the rôle, simultaneously functioning as referee when Chaplin and Dempsey pretend to square up to each other (a similar scrap with Benny Leonard appears in *Unknown Chaplin* [*qv*]). There are also scenes of Chaplin, Fairbanks and Mary Pickford (*qv*) at a War Bond rally. This leads naturally into sequences from *The Bond*, also newsreel footage celebrating both the Armistice and the formation of United Artists (*qv*). There is film of Chaplin with his co-founders and, from slightly later, extensive newsreel scenes of Chaplin from the 1921 trip.

The finale is a collage of gags from the hitherto somewhat neglected Mutuals, *Easy Street*, *The Floorwalker* and *The Count* (including, as noted in the main entry, an alternate take from the usual copies), also *Caught in a Cabaret*, *The Masquerader*, *Dough and Dynamite* and the final close-up of *Work*. There is one more brief shot of the real-life

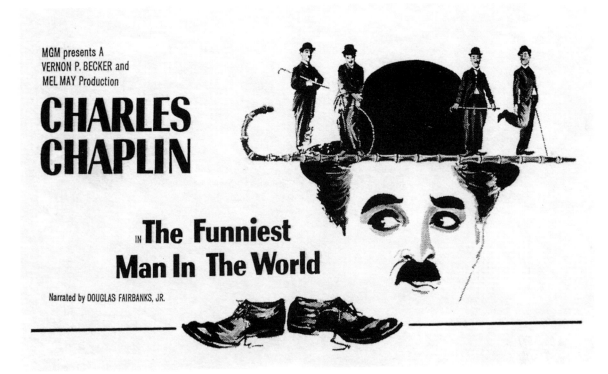

MGM presents A
VERNON P. BECKER and
MEL MAY Production

CHARLES CHAPLIN

in **The Funniest Man In The World**

Narrated by DOUGLAS FAIRBANKS, JR.

Chaplin before his screen equivalent bids farewell, via his famed walk into the distance from *The Tramp*.

Most of the footage derives from surprisingly good originals, a particular joy with the often fuzzy, contrasty Essanays. Despite evident wear to the source material, image quality tends to be sharp and possessed of good tonal range. There is a 'film restoration' credit for Rapid Film Techniques, Inc., whose contribution may have been the 'stretch-printing' to sound speed (though 'optical effects' are attributed to Film Formatics, Inc., and Cinema Research, Inc.). All but a few short scenes have been corrected in this way, mostly satisfactory, but producing jerkiness in some instances.

Narration is informative, avoiding the justly-despised facetiousness of some revivals. There are also appropriate quotes from contemporary sources and a general sense of appreciation of the subject matter. *The Funniest Man in the World* was released by M-G-M but produced by Funnyman, Inc., the type of name one associates with companies that exist for a single project (though a Keaton collection, *The Great Stone Face*, came from the same stable). Vernon P. Becker wrote, directed and (with Mel May) produced. Associate producer was Mitchell R. Leiser. Credited as

production consultants were historians John E. Allen, William K. Everson, Gerald D. McDonald and Chaplin veteran Edward A. Sutherland (*qv*). The pleasant musical score was composed by Albert Hague and arranged and conducted by Johnny Douglas (who later recorded an album of Chaplin's own compositions). Editor was William C. Dalzell. Publicity for the original UK release quotes a running time of 70 minutes; the print supplied for a UK video release and screening on Channel 4 clocks in at 87 minutes, which equates to 90 in theatrical presentation.

(See also: Animation; Caricatures; Chaplin, Syd; Documentaries, compilations; Fairbanks, Douglas; Female impersonation; Impersonators; Karno Company, The; Keaton, Buster; Music; Television; Video releases; Wartime)

GARCIA, ALLAN 🎩
(1887–1938)

(Chaplin films *qv*)
San Francisco-born actor; in *The Idle Class* he doubles up as both a party guest and the man on a park bench who wrongly suspects Charlie of theft; he is among Charlie's drinking buddies in *Pay Day*, and one of *The Gold Rush's* prospectors. His most prominent rôle in the Chaplin films is as proprietor of *The Circus*; he reappears as the millionaire's snooty butler in *City Lights* and the factory boss of *Modern Times*. This last rôle is vaguely reminiscent of one of his non-Chaplin films, *The Power God* (1925).

GARDINER, REGINALD
(1903–80)

British actor, a familiar face in films from both sides of the Atlantic; in Chaplin's *The Great Dictator* (*qv*) he plays Schultz, the barber's wartime comrade, and latterly aide to Hynkel, who defies the dictator out of loyalty to his old friend. Among Gardiner's many other films is the 1939 Laurel & Hardy comedy, *The Flying Deuces*, in which he portrays a Foreign Legion officer, and Warners' 1942 film adaptation of *The Man Who Came to Dinner*, with Gardiner as the Noël Coward figure, Beverly Carlton. Fans of comedy records revere Gardiner's eccentric classic, *Trains*, in which the actor describes his experience of railways while punctuating anecdote with his impersonations of various train noises. This party-piece first appeared as a Decca 78, and was considered worthy of reissue as a 45 r.p.m. single.

(See also: Laurel, Stan)

THE GENTLEMAN TRAMP 🎩
(1974)

(Chaplin films *qv*)
This 'authorized' documentary, made with Chaplin's participation, is narrated by Walter Matthau, with readings from the comedian's autobiography by Laurence Olivier. Film extracts range between those under Chaplin's ownership to representative segments from the Keystone and Mutual comedies, though, strangely, nothing from Essanay (Chaplin's own collection was less concerned with the earlier subjects). The clips are often designed to show the sometimes autobiographical nature of Chaplin's work; in turn, an opening collage of stills from various stages of his life is followed by new footage of Chaplin, punctuating the whole with understatement: 'I went through a hell of a lot.'

A collage from Chaplin's features precedes the story itself. Chaplin's childhood and eventual departure to the USA are chronicled mostly through rostrum material. Keystone's frenetic style, against which he rebelled, is represented by a non-Chaplin clip; this makes way for extracts showing the comedian's own work at the studio, using better-than-average quality extracts from *Kid Auto Races at Venice, CA* and *The New Janitor* (accompanied by Chaplin's composition *The Peace Patrol*). A chronological leap, bypassing Essanay, takes us straight into film of Chaplin's signing with Mutual. There are details of the 'Chaplin Craze' (*qv*) – comics, toys, and the like – and of a growing public awareness of Chaplin as an artist rather than simply a clown. The Mutuals are represented by extracts from *The Vagabond*, *The Adventurer* and *The Pawnshop*.

Evidence of Chaplin's escalating success is suggested in his acquisition of a brand-new, seven-seater Locomobile, complete with chauffeur. Further indication is found in the account of the building of his new studio, using stop-motion footage from what was identified later as *How To Make Movies* (*qv*). There are a number of scenes from this source, alongside more commonplace material from *A Dog's Life*, *Shoulder Arms* and *The Bond*. From the same period are scenes of Chaplin on tour in the Liberty Loan Campaign with Douglas Fairbanks and Mary Pickford (both *qv*) and, from peacetime, the announcement of United Artists (*qv*).

Chaplin's troubled first marriage is intertwined with the making of *The Kid*. An account of his 1921 trip draws extensively on news film, dubbed with effects and voices representing contemporary quotes. Back at the studio, there are more scenes from *How To Make Movies* and footage of Chaplin's visitors, among them Winston Churchill. Included also is Chaplin's trick film with the visiting

Reginald Gardiner plays the barber's wartime comrade in The Great Dictator

Naylor-Leylands (see **Trick photography**).

The Gold Rush and *The Circus* tie to the troubled period surrounding his divorce from Lita Grey (*qv*), repeating the technique of combining rostrum material with dubbed voices conveying comments and reports from the time. The same device is used to represent the debate as to whether *City Lights* would have dialogue. More news film and dubbing, from his 1931 tour, convey Chaplin's opinions on society, leading in turn to *Modern Times*. News film serves again to chronicle his years with Paulette Goddard (*qv*); also used is part of the item recording Chaplin's tennis game with Groucho Marx (*qv*).

The Great Dictator leads naturally into Chaplin's troubled 1940s, primarily the Joan Barry case and politics. Chaplin's court ordeal is compared to an equivalent scene in *Monsieur Verdoux*; in turn, his departure from America is juxtaposed with Calvero's surrender to an unamused audience in *Limelight*. A blend of home movies and news film covers Chaplin's barring from the United States and acceptance in Europe; this time the comparison is made with *A King in New York*. More home movies show the Chaplin family settled in Switzerland; other footage includes that of Chaplin conducting the orchestral accompaniment for *The Kid's* reissue, his return to America in 1972 and presentation of an Oscar. The final scenes were taken at Vevey for the documentary itself, with Chaplin and Oona in the company of Walter and Carol Matthau.

The Gentleman Tramp is a remarkably compact account of a busy life, clocking in at approximately 77 minutes theatrically. For an authorized piece, it is refreshingly frank – as Chaplin's memoirs often are – while access to the comedian's archive provided much rare material. If the film disappoints in any way, it is when specific items are not identified. Producer was Bert Schneider; writer and director was Richard Patterson.

(See also: Cars; Childhood; Documentaries, compilations; Keystone; Music; Mutual; Newsreels; Public appearances; Television; Video releases; Women)

GENTLEMEN OF NERVE 🎩

(Chaplin film)
Keystone Comedy released by Mutual, 29 October 1914. Produced by Mack Sennett. Written and directed by Charles Chaplin. Photography attributed to Frank D. Williams. Reissue titles include *Some Nerve* (see below) and *Charlie at the Races*. One reel. 1,030 feet (approximate UK length cited in *Bioscope*).

With Charlie Chaplin (Mr Wow-Wow), Mabel Normand (Mabel), Mack Swain (Ambrose), Chester Conklin (Mr Walrus), Phyllis Allen (Chester's other interest), Edgar Kennedy, Alice Davenport, Slim Summerville, Charley Chase, Cecile Arnold, (?) Vivian Edwards.

Mabel and Mr Walrus arrives at the motor races. At the barrier, Walrus fumbles for their tickets while Ambrose pesters Mabel. Walrus gives him a kick and escorts Mabel through the ticket barrier. Mabel sees the cars starting up, and they make their way to the stands. The drivers have first to engage in a 'tire changing race'. Walrus becomes interested in the woman sitting next to him, surreptitiously handing her his card. Ambrose is still outside the venue, evidently without a ticket; the same clearly applies to Charlie, alias 'Mr Wow-Wow, a disturbing influence', who tries to crash the barrier just the same. After an altercation with Ambrose, a truce is called, and both try to gain admittance through a gap in a fence. Ambrose goes first, and is stuck; Charlie crawls through beneath and tries to pull Ambrose inside. A policeman hits Ambrose's behind with his truncheon; Charlie has paused for a drink from a borrowed soda syphon, and turns it on the cop. Once Ambrose is freed, the policeman is sent away with further blasts of soda. On the track, Charlie meets Walrus and Mabel. Charlie strikes a match on the seat of Walrus' trousers and pushes him aside. Mabel is amused, Walrus less so, particularly when Charlie bites his nose. Walrus and Mabel return to their seats while Charlie has a skirmish with other spectators. Walrus resumes his flirtation with the other lady, this time in front of Mabel. Ambrose arrives, complaining to Charlie. He receives a cigarette burn to the nose, a kick in the stomach and a cane over the head. Charlie sits beside a pretty girl, taking sly drinks from her bottle of soda. She notices and gives him the bottle in disgust. Mabel is similarly disgusted at Walrus's faithlessness, and exits, tripping over Charlie's legs. Sitting with him, Mabel spots a peculiar racing car driven by a propeller. They go to investigate, but are blown around when it is started.

Mabel has already deserted Mr Walrus; now her attentions are divided between Mr Wow-Wow – alias Charlie – and Ambrose. A posed shot from **Gentlemen of Nerve**
BFI Stills, Posters and Designs

The cop catches up with Ambrose. Walrus falls out with his new girlfriend and returns to Mabel. He discovers her with Charlie, who, removing his jacket, limbers up and sends Walrus crashing into Ambrose and other spectators. He and Mabel watch, amused, as Walrus and Ambrose are escorted away by the cop. As they pass by, Charlie gives Walrus a whack with his cane. He tries to kiss Mabel, but she turns away, offering her hand instead. Charlie kisses her hand, but she tweaks Charlie's nose, making him sneeze.

Another of the impromptu Keystones shot during a single day, *Gentlemen of Nerve* is slight of construction and strong on violence. There are a few good gags – notably when Mack Swain (*qv*) is caught in the fence – but inspiration is otherwise lacking, although, as always, Chaplin's customary bits of business frequently enliven a commonplace idea. Robert Youngson, excerpting the film in his anthology, *When Comedy Was King* (1960), noted how Chaplin, instead of merely punching Chester Conklin (*qv*), paused first to lay down his cane, remove his coat and hat, feel his bicep, limber up, move Mabel out of the way, then place Conklin carefully before landing a devastating blow. Having dealt with Chester, he takes time to smooth the crease in his baggy trousers.

As with *Kid Auto Races at Venice*, *Mabel's Busy Day* and, to a lesser extent, *Mabel at the Wheel* (all *qv*), an authentic race meeting seems to have been used, verified by a scene with Charlie before a large crowd of spectators (surpassing the usual allocation of extras) and a shot of Chaplin and Mabel Normand (*qv*) examining an eccentric car beside the busy racetrack. One latter-day revival, with added sound, tacks on introductory motor racing footage of a much later vintage. From posterity's view, a major plus point is the film's availability in excellent prints. Youngson obtained crystal-clear material, and comparable originals were available to home-movie distributors in England and France. (British home-movie copies are titled *Charlie at the Races*. A re-edited theatrical revival was announced in August 1919; it saw release from the Tower Film Corporation in December of that year, under the name *Some Nerve*, itself inviting confusion with an earlier, non-Chaplin Keystone film of that title.)

There has also been a virtually mint-condition restoration in America, using a 35mm paper positive in the Library of Congress. This edition includes a few shots that are absent from some other prints, such as Conklin's falling-out with Phyllis Allen (*qv*) and resultant quarrel with spectator Charley Chase (*qv*), also such lesser omissions as one of the cutaways to Conklin and Swain as they are led away by the police. Just as importantly, the paper print retains full Keystone titles. These explain the tyre-changing race near the beginning and confirm Chaplin's reputed character name in the film, 'Mr Wow-Wow' (the direct legacy of an old Karno skit, *The Wow-Wows*). This version has been issued on laserdisc in America.

(See also: Arnold, Cecile; Cars; Davenport, Alice; Documentaries, compilations; Edwards, Vivian; Home movies; Karno Company, The; Keystone; Reissues; Smoking; Summerville, George 'Slim'; Titling; Video releases; Williams, Frank D.; Work)

GETTING ACQUAINTED 🎩

(Chaplin film)
Keystone Comedy released by Mutual, 5 December 1914. Produced by Mack Sennett. Written and directed by Charles Chaplin. Photography attributed to Frank D. Williams. Reissued by W.H. Productions as *A Fair Exchange*. One reel. 1,025 feet.

With Charlie Chaplin (himself), Phyllis Allen (Charlie's wife), Mack Swain

A posed shot of the principals in **Getting Acquainted**
BFI Stills, Posters and Designs

(Ambrose), Mabel Normand (Ambrose's wife), Harry McCoy (motorist), Cecile Arnold (blonde), Edgar Kennedy (cop).

Ambrose and his wife, Mabel, are taking a stroll in the park when Ambrose is called upon to help crank someone's car. Elsewhere, Charlie is sitting beside his sleeping wife when he notices an attractive blonde. She is evidently looking for someone; Charlie follows her, but is dissuaded when that someone turns out to be a knife-wielding, fez-wearing man. Mabel waits as Ambrose continues to crank the car. She is approached by Charlie, who taps her behind with his cane. Charlie's flirtation is returned with a slap in the face. Mabel's outrage grows when her skirt is hooked up by Charlie's cane. Charlie reprimands the stick for its behaviour. Ambrose returns, greets Charlie and introduces Mabel as his wife. Ambrose is called back to help once more with the car, but Mabel is reluctant to be left alone with Charlie. The car is started, and Ambrose is treated to a spin. Mabel continues to reject Charlie's attentions; Charlie persists until he realizes a cop is standing behind him. Mabel sets the officer after the fleeing interloper. Charlie is pursued into a bush, but he evades the policeman, taking time to stick a pin in the cop's behind. The chase takes them around Mabel and back into the shrubbery. Ambrose leaves the car and

takes a seat beside Charlie's wife. Charlie, meanwhile, has dodged the policeman but backed into the fez-wearing man, whom he places by a hedge so that the next blow from the cop's truncheon will strike him. Charlie ducks away. Ambrose annoys Charlie's wife with a flirtatious tweak of her nose. He exits, playing nonchalant as the cop passes by. Charlie is concealed in the bushes when his wife reports Ambrose to the cop. Ambrose blunders into the fez-wearer and is stopped; the policeman goes to strike him but hits the other man instead, allowing Ambrose to get away. The fez-wearer draws his knife and is struck by the cop, who continues after Ambrose. The two wives have met and are comparing notes. Unaware of Mabel's presence, Charlie sits by his wife and is aghast when she introduces him to Mabel. Charlie, hustling his wife away, makes a swift exit. Ambrose rushes past the knife-wielding foreigner and takes refuge in the bushes. The cop, still pursuing Ambrose, stops to give the knife-carrier another whack. The policeman fails to locate Ambrose, but sees Charlie with his wife. Ambrose sneaks away as the cop approaches Charlie, who now has to evade both the policeman and his foreign adversary. Ambrose finds Mabel; Charlie's wife, hitherto unaware of her husband's disappearance, sets out to look for him, but finds Mabel instead. When Mabel introduces her to Ambrose, she faints. Mabel wants to help, but Ambrose ushers her away. Charlie is nearby when the cop finally catches up with Ambrose; both take refuge in the same section of hedge. Mabel returns to Charlie's wife; the cop collars both men, leading them away past their wives, who reclaim their husbands. The cop abandons the whole effort, dealing instead with a quite different man who is pestering a woman. Charlie and Ambrose gesture for mutual silence; the couples settle their differences, but Ambrose earns another slap from Charlie's wife, whose husband in turn embraces Mabel rather too affectionately. Charlie's spouse frogmarches him home.

Some prints of *Getting Acquainted* (including the Blackhawk Films edition) omit the opening scenes of Mack Swain and Mabel Normand (both *qv*) prior to Charlie's first appearance. Chaplin's penultimate Keystone film is another of the shot-in-a-day 'park' comedies, pleasant enough individually, but unremarkable in the context of similar films, although in fairness the inter-shrubbery intrigues are better choreographed than usual.

(See also: Home movies; Keystone; Parks; Policemen; Risqué humour; Williams, Frank D.)

GIDDY, GAY AND TICKLISH
See: Keystone

GILBERT, BILLY
(1894–1971)

Burly, Kentucky-born comedian, real name William Gilbert Baron; plays Herring in Chaplin's *The Great Dictator* (*qv*). He is often recalled for many short comedies of the 1930s, particularly at Hal Roach; it was reputedly Stan Laurel (*qv*) who persuaded Gilbert to forsake the stage for movies. Feature film appearances are numerous, but among them are Wheeler & Woolsey's *Cockeyed Cavaliers* (1934), *A Night at the Opera* (1935) with the Marx Brothers, Laurel & Hardy's *Block-Heads* (1938), *Destry Rides Again* (1939), *Tin Pan Alley* (1940), *His Girl Friday* (1940), *Three of a Kind* (1944) and *Anchors Aweigh* (1945). Gilbert supplied the voice of Sneezy in Disney's *Snow White and the Seven Dwarfs* (1937).

(See also: Marx, Groucho)

GILLETTE, WILLIAM
See: Early stage appearances

GODDARD, PAULETTE
(c.1911–90)

Born Marion Levy (or Levee) in Great Neck, Long Island, Paulette Goddard reportedly had an uncle who knew stage producer Florenz Ziegfeld, thus securing her a job in his 1926 Broadway show, *No Foolin'*. Paulette was subsequently rehired for *Rio Rita*, after which she forsook both Broadway and an unsuccessful early marriage in favour of a trip west and extra work in Hal Roach comedies. She is reportedly in a 1929 Laurel & Hardy two-reeler, *Berth Marks*, and has also been spotted in *Young Ironsides*, a 1930 short starring Charley Chase (*qv*). Chaplin is believed to have acquired Paulette's contract from Roach, explaining her appearance at United Artists (*qv*) in Eddie Cantor's *The Kid From Spain* (1932). 'Charlie Chaplin appears very devoted to Paulette Goddard, the colony's latest platinum blonde,' claimed *Picturegoer* on 22 October 1932, noting both her recent appearance in the Cantor film and the way in which 'The gossips are already predicting a wedding in the near future.' The blonde hair had reverted to its natural brunette by her appearance as the *gamine* in Chaplin's *Modern Times* (*qv*); the gossips, at least temporarily deprived of the wedding itself, turned instead to attacking the couple's seemingly unmarried bliss. The circumstances of their legal marriage remained vague (and are *still* vague), but it took a divorce (in 1942) to produce the claim that they were married during a visit to China in 1936. Her second and final appearance with Chaplin was as heroine of *The Great Dictator* (*qv*).

Other notable films include two suspense-comedies with Bob Hope, *The Cat and the Canary* (1939) and *Ghost Breakers* (1940); also *The Women* (1939), *Reap the Wild Wind* (1942) and *Kitty* (1945). She was a considerable favourite to play Scarlett O'Hara in *Gone With the Wind* until Vivien Leigh was cast in the rôle. Paulette's divorce from Chaplin seems to have been amicable; she subsequently married actor Burgess Meredith, then novelist Erich Maria Remarque.

Paulette Goddard *was the third Mrs Chaplin*

(See also: *Countess From Hong Kong, A*; Hayle, Grace; Kono, Toraichi; Laurel, Stan; Marriages; Women)

THE GOLD RUSH

(Chaplin film)
Released by United Artists, 16 August 1925. Produced, written and directed by Charles Chaplin. Associate directors: Charles Riesner, H. d'Abbadie d'Arrast and A. Edward Sutherland. Photographed by Rollie Totheroh and Jack Wilson. Production manager: Alf Reeves. 9 reels, 8,498 feet (10 reels, 9,760 feet at première – see below). Reissued 18 April 1942 with added music, sound effects and narration by Chaplin (musical direction: Max Terr). Abridged to 72 mins (see below).

With Charlie Chaplin (lone prospector), Mack Swain (Big Jim McKay), Tom Murray (Black Larsen – spelled 'Larson' in reissue titles), Georgia Hale (Georgia), Betty Morrissey, Kay Deslys (two of Georgia's friends), Malcolm Waite (Jack [Cameron]), Henry Bergman (Hank Curtis), Tiny Sandford (large barman).

In frozen Alaska, many a brave prospector risks life and limb in the pursuit of gold. Among them is Charlie, who blithely trots through the mountains, unaware of the grizzly bear that is following him. Amid the icy wastes, Big Jim McKay stakes his claim

on 'a mountain of gold'. Charlie slides
down the snow-covered rocks, guiding
himself across a plateau with a compass
drawn on paper. All he finds is the grave
of one Jim Sourdough, who was lost in
the snow on 'Friday 1898'. An altogether
luckier Jim is Big Jim McKay, who has
struck gold. A storm erupts. In his cabin,
the unscrupulous Black Larsen keeps
warm by burning one of his own wanted
posters. Charlie, desperate for food and
shelter, enters Larsen's cabin. Larsen,
shotgun in hand, at first conceals himself
then confronts Charlie, who is helping
himself to the meagre supply of food.
Larsen orders Charlie to leave, but gale
force winds make this impossible. The
wind catches Big Jim's tent, and he is
blown through the cabin. Another
mighty gust sends Charlie out after him,
but he returns and sees Larsen blown
into the storm. Charlie resumes eating,
and Big Jim staggers in. Also desperately
hungry, Big Jim takes the food. Larsen
returns and, armed with the shotgun,
tells Charlie and Big Jim to leave. There
is a struggle between Big Jim and Larsen,
during which the gun barrels always
seem to point at Charlie. Eventually, the
gun goes off, but Charlie is not in its
path. Once Big Jim has commandeered
the weapon and the food, it is
understood that he and Charlie should
stay. Their food exhausted, the men grow
restless. Charlie eats the candle, but
denies it when challenged by Larsen,
despite a tell-tale case of hiccups. When
Big Jim walks in, smacking his chops,
Charlie wonders where the dog is. The
animal is alive, but Jim calls a meeting.
They cut cards to see who should go for
food; Charlie draws a three, believing
himself the loser until Larsen draws a
two. Larsen ventures into the storm,
where two lawmen are on his trail.
Larsen kills them both. In the cabin, a
dark-eyed Charlie has cooked one of his
boots as 'Thanksgiving dinner'. Big Jim
insists on taking the upper, though
eating with revulsion; Charlie makes the
best of what remains, treating the lace as
spaghetti and the nails in the sole as
bones from a Thanksgiving turkey. Later,
Charlie returns from a fruitless hunting
expedition. He places the bootless foot,
swathed in bandages, in the oven. Big
Jim can take no more, rejecting even the
other boot. Jim starts hallucinating. He
confides that, for a moment, he thought
Charlie was a chicken. Discreetly, Charlie
hides the breadknife. Jim sees Charlie as
a giant chicken and, armed first with a
knife then a shotgun, gives chase.

The Gold Rush: Charlie finds the grave of Jim Sourdough on location in snowy Truckee

Outside, Jim regains his senses. Charlie
understands his friend's lapse, but buries
the shotgun in the snow. Big Jim,
deciding that Charlie would make a
good meal even if he *isn't* a chicken,
grabs an axe. Charlie retrieves the gun,
and a stalemate is reached. They retire
for an uneasy night, Charlie lying
covered in bed with his footwear on his
hands, feigning slumber. Eventually a
fight breaks out, and Charlie, his head
beneath a blanket, fails to realize he is
grappling with a stray bear instead of Big
Jim. One shot and the bear becomes
breakfast. Larsen, meanwhile, has
deserted the others and stumbles across
Jim's claim. The storm over, Charlie and
Big Jim go their separate ways. Jim
returns to his stake, unaware of Larsen's
concealed presence. Larsen appears and,
in the subsequent fight, knocks Jim cold
with a shovel. Larsen moves on, but is
lost when a land fault gives way. A town
has been built, with the customary speed
of things in the Gold Rush. Its fairest
inhabitant, Georgia, is seen emerging
from the local photographer's studio.
Georgia is seemingly the only girl
resistant to the charms of Jack, the town's
ladies' man. At her place of employ, the
Monte Carlo dance hall, Georgia receives
the batch of photographs taken of
herself. Jack grabs one of them, which
becomes torn when Georgia tries to
reclaim it. The photo is discarded. Out
of the night, Charlie wanders into the
dance hall. Georgia, chatting to one of
the bar customers, sees a friend and
walks over to greet him. Charlie,
assuming the greeting to be for himself,
extends a hand but is bypassed. He
sneaks a drink from a waiter and, once

Georgia has returned, eavesdrops on her
conversation with another saloon girl.
Georgia, it seems, rejects Jack because he
is interested in *every* girl. She is bored
with the dance hall and would give it up
in favour of the right man. She turns,
looking straight through Charlie, who
walks away. He finds the torn
photograph and shyly examines it. Jack
tries to force Georgia to dance, but she
rejects him, choosing as partner the
shabbiest man in the house, Charlie. As
they waltz around, Charlie's belt becomes
dislodged and he soon has trouble
keeping his trousers up. His cane
provides temporary support until he
finds some rope. He ties it around his
waist, but there is a large dog at the
other end. Charlie notices the animal,
but does not realize his attachment to it
until a cat ventures in. He is freed using
a borrowed knife, then finds a rose on
the floor, which he presents to the
delighted Georgia. The girl retires
upstairs. Jack goes to follow, but Charlie
stands in his path. The frail tramp is
easily thrust aside, but Jack stays to
humiliate him, jamming Charlie's hat
over his eyes. Blindly, Charlie takes a
swing but hits a pillar; spectators in the
gallery, leaning over, dislodge a clock,
which lands on Jack's head. Charlie,
seeing the unconscious man, believes he
has landed a knockout punch and
departs as a conqueror. The next
morning, Charlie, still hungry, sees coffee
and beans being prepared in a cabin near
to the dance hall. He feigns
unconsciousness, and its kindly owner,
Hank Curtis, carries him inside for food
and warmth. Out in the snow, Big Jim
wanders aimlessly, a victim of amnesia.

Hank leaves with his partner on a long expedition, leaving Charlie to mind the cabin. Georgia and several girl friends are playing in the snow. Charlie, inside the cabin, fails to notice oil spilling on his bandaged foot while filling a lamp. When a snowball strikes the door, Charlie opens it to investigate. He is struck by both a snowball and the presence of Georgia. His moment's rapture is interrupted when a further snowball lands. Georgia steps inside the cabin. She is joined by her friends, to whom Charlie is introduced. While Charlie is away gathering firewood, Georgia discovers her photograph and the rose pressed beneath Charlie's pillow. The girls decide to have some fun at Charlie's expense, making rather a fuss of him; one of them lights a cigarette, carelessly allowing the match to fall on Charlie's oil-soaked, bandaged foot. Unaware of the flames, Charlie places his foot under the chair on which the girl is sitting. Eventually she jumps up, and Charlie must extinguish chair and foot. The girls facetiously suggest joining Charlie for dinner some time. They pretend to arrange a visit for eight o'clock on New Year's Eve. They exit, playing along with his old-world courtesy. Once they have gone, the jubilant Charlie leaps around the cabin, bursting open a feather pillow. Georgia, having forgotten her gloves, returns to see an embarrassed, feather-strewn Charlie. To finance his intended dinner party, Charlie clears snow. For a fee, Charlie volunteers to clear the front of a restaurant; the owner refuses, but Charlie is instead paid to clear the front of the neighbouring store. Charlie shovels the snow in front of the restaurant, sealing it in. The trapped owner is now willing to engage Charlie's services. The snow is shovelled in front of the *next* building; when Charlie realizes it is the jail, he decides not to enquire further. New Year's Eve, and the celebrants gather at the dance hall. Charlie, alone in the cabin, carefully lays places and tends to a roast. His first visitor is a stray mule, with whom Charlie reluctantly pulls a party cracker. It is nearly eight o'clock, and Charlie imagines his young lady guests, for whom he performs a miniature soft-shoe dance, 'The Oceana Roll', using forks inserted into bread rolls. He faints when Georgia kisses his cheek. When the fantasy concludes, we see that Charlie, alone, has drifted off to sleep. He remains so until just past midnight, when he is awakened by the

sound of celebrations at the dance hall. Georgia is with Jack and the girls. Charlie hears the party sing 'Auld Lang Syne', then walks to the dance hall. He observes the festivities through the window, then walks sadly away. Georgia remembers their invitation and, with Jack and her friends, decides to visit the cabin for a lark. The idea is for Georgia to enter first, then for Jack to follow, scaring Charlie with a gun. The joke pales when Georgia finds an empty cabin and carefully-arranged places with gifts. They depart, a chastened Georgia fighting off Jack when he forces a kiss. The next day, Big Jim is in town, visiting the recorder's office. He describes his gold mine, but the claim cannot be filed because the precise location has been erased from Jim's memory; all he can recall is that it was near the cabin. The officials believe Jim has gone mad, but he resolves to find the cabin. Charlie returns to the dance hall, where Jack trips him up. Ignoring the insult, Charlie brightens on receiving a note from Georgia, apologizing for her absence and asking to meet. Charlie rushes around in search of her, again ignoring Jack's habit of tripping him, but is intercepted instead by Big Jim, who has wandered into the bar. Jim promises to make Charlie's fortune in exchange for his help in finding the cabin. Charlie, seeing Georgia on the balcony, climbs up without bothering with the stairs. He promises to return as a wealthy man, ready to take her away, until dragged away by Jim. They reach the cabin, this time stocked with plenty of food. Charlie drinks deeply from an alcohol-loaded gourd, then brings in the supplies, unassisted. Big Jim tries to draw a map. When Charlie falls, exhausted, to his bunk, Jim blames the alcohol and decides also to retire. While they sleep, another storm brews up, depositing the cabin on a cliff edge. Awake, Charlie potters around the cabin, ascribing their evident tilting to stomach trouble. Charlie breaks off some icicles to melt down for water. He and Jim become aware of the tilt, but they only test the effect when standing at opposite ends of the cabin, thus cancelling it out. When both are at the cabin's far side, the resultant lurch suggests a lack in foundations. Charlie tries the back door, from which he finds himself dangling over a terrifying drop. Back inside, he and Jim cling for life as the cabin, anchored only by a rope caught on a rock, starts to slide. Big Jim escapes, to

The Gold Rush: *Black Larsen is supposedly going for help; Big Jim bids him farewell*

The Gold Rush: *Charlie fights off a hunger-crazed Big Jim*

discover he is by his gold mine. Distracted, he momentarily forgets Charlie, but throws him a rope just as the cabin slides to its doom. Jim declares them both millionaires; Charlie agrees, then faints. The wealthy and well-dressed prospectors leave Alaska on an ocean liner. Charlie has to be reminded that it is no longer necessary to pick up cigar butts. In their suite, Charlie removes an expensive overcoat – and the fur coat beneath it – before speaking to a journalist who is writing their story. Big Jim has a manicurist file the calouses on his hands instead of the nails. It is suggested that Charlie should be photographed in his old mining clothes. He pauses to look at Georgia's photograph. He does not know that Georgia is among the steerage passengers, where ship's officers are hunting for a stowaway. Back in his ragged clothes, Charlie gives Jim a playful kick with his bandaged foot before stepping outside to pose. At the photographer's request, he steps back, tumbling to the lower deck and blundering into a large, coiled rope.

By courtesy of Robert G. Dickson

Georgia, seeing him emerge, shares Charlie's astonishment at their sudden reunion. Believing him to be the stowaway, she tries to hide him, then, after he is discovered by an officer, volunteers to pay his fare rather than see him put in irons. The captain arrives, explaining Charlie's identity, and apologies are made. Charlie asks his valet to prepare another place for dinner. When the reporter asks about the lady, Charlie explains with a whisper. The reporter offers his congratulations, and Charlie takes Georgia off to a new life.

Chaplin described *The Gold Rush* as the picture by which he wanted to be remembered, and in a sense this has become true. Individual scenes – notably the 'dance of the rolls', the consumption of Charlie's boot and the perilous

The Gold Rush: *The Lone Prospector finds solace – and Georgia – at the dance hall*

teetering of the cabin – are recalled with justified affection, as are other worthy, but inevitably overshadowed, routines such as that reworked from *A Dog's Life* (*qv*), in which Charlie attempts to negotiate a dance floor while tethered to a large dog. Above all, the grandeur of the setting makes this the nearest to an 'epic' in the Chaplin canon.

The location was first suggested to Chaplin by some stereoscopic slides he had viewed at Pickfair, one of which showed the Chilkoot Pass, gateway to the fabled Klondike gold rush of 1898. Chaplin subsequently expanded this initial idea after reading a book about the Donner Party of 1846, who had resorted to cannibalism when stranded in the Sierra Nevada. In the film, Chaplin emphasized his character's hunger with the addition of heavy rings around the eyes. By the end of 1923 Chaplin had completed a play based on his new story, *The Lucky Strike*, which, as noted under **Reissues**, would later enable him to pursue a piracy case concerning the finished film.

Filming began early in 1924 with Lita Grey (*qv*) as female lead. On location in the snowy mountains of Truckee, California, Chaplin constructed both a gold rush town and a replica of the Chilkoot Pass (filled with hundreds of extras), which may be seen at the beginning of the film. It had been thought that the location work was confined to these brief moments, but stills provided for *Unknown Chaplin* (*qv*) by the Chaplin estate suggest all of the exteriors to have been shot initially in Truckee, an opinion confirmed by Lita's recollection of the harsh conditions. Other photos provide evidence of an extended, outdoor version of Big Jim's pursuit of Charlie when crazed by hunger.

Irregular conditions enforced a return to the studio, with the addition of Chuck Riesner (*qv*) as assistant director. The town was rebuilt on Chaplin's backlot, and all exteriors rephotographed, this time in artificial snow; the only readily identifiable survivors of the Truckee footage are the Chilkoot Pass scene, Charlie's slide down a slope and his discovery of a grave (illustrated). Further delay – and expense – were incurred when Lita fell pregnant, requiring both a replacement, Georgia Hale (*qv*), and the reshooting of Lita's scenes (which, fortunately, had been few). Production resumed, after a three-month gap, at the beginning of 1925,

The Gold Rush: *Charlie greets the New Year alone …*

and concluded in May.

The Gold Rush premièred at Grauman's Egyptian Theater, Hollywood, 26 June 1925, at a length of 9,760 feet; some idea of the last-minute nature of its cutting may be gained from the fact that Chaplin pruned the film to 8,498 feet prior to opening at the Mark Strand Theater, New York, on 16 August. After the Hollywood screening, *Variety* had reported an ecstatic reception, but by 19 August its editor, Sime Silverman, had evidently recalled his stance on Chaplin from a decade before. Sime regarded *Gold Rush* as 'just a good Chaplin comedy ... certain at the film theaters because of Chaplin's name', mentioning 'a lot of story with laughs spaced too far apart'. 'It can stand cutting with judicious cutting bringing the laughs closer together,' he decided, a view which, in the author's opinion, may be compared to the suggestion that a Rolls-Royce would be just fine if they'd only dispense with all the fancy stuff. Certainly, the view elsewhere was different. Mordaunt Hall of the *New York Times* (which, incidentally, voted *The Gold Rush* one of the ten best films of 1925) noted a triumphant late-night screening, complete with stage prologue, at which the somewhat nervous comedian 'was not insensible to the chuckles and shrieks of laughter provoked by his own antics on the screen'. 'There is more than mere laughter in *The Gold Rush*,' said Hall, seeing something of Chaplin's own background in the lone prospector's anguish. 'Throughout this effort there runs a love story,' he added, 'and one is often moved to mirth with a lump in one's throat.' *The Gold Rush*, in Hall's evaluation, was 'the outstanding gem of all Chaplin's pictures'. These views were shared by playwright Robert E. Sherwood, who, trailing the new Chaplin film in *Vanity Fair*, described *Gold Rush* as 'Chaplin's greatest picture', while also making mention of 'a sort of symbolical autobiography'. There was comparable reaction in London, where St. John Ervine of the *Observer* conquered his self-admitted tendency to melancholia by having 'laughed, not once or twice, but many times, and in an uproarious manner' when *The Gold Rush* opened at the New Tivoli. Regarding it as the funniest picture he or anyone else had seen, Ervine compared the blend of pathos and fun with the works of Shakespeare and Dickens (one of the most repeated remarks on Chaplin derives from Harriett Underhill's *New York Herald-Tribune* review of this film, in which she described praising Chaplin as like 'saying that Shakespeare was a good writer'). Ervine applauded the economy in presentation of gags (though believing one transformation into a chicken would have been sufficient) and, revealingly, cited the boot-eating as representative of 'the habit of performing supremely ridiculous things in a perfectly normal manner'. It might be said in passing that this approach, characteristic of British tastes in humour, made Chaplin and his UK contemporaries – not least Stan Laurel (*qv*) – of particular appeal when presented to American audiences. Ervine supplies comparable insight into Chaplin himself. 'Mr. Chaplin,' he said, 'is one of the few people whose personality survives the screen. The majority of us, when screened, are merely animated photographs, but Mr. Chaplin actually becomes more human.' After speaking of his single meeting with the comedian, Ervine concludes that, while each of us may project a powerful personality when first introduced, prolonged acquaintance is likely to reveal a less consistent fascination. Chaplin, by contrast, had 'the unique ability to enlarge himself. We cannot see the end of him. When we make his acquaintance we go on a journey which may be long, but is not exhausting, and has a great variety of views. Such men are rare. Mr. Chaplin seems to be one of them. He has made the whole world laugh.' David Robinson

... until he finds Georgia at the saloon

has cited records suggesting *The Gold Rush* to have been somewhat less popular in provincial America, but overall response was positive and, to say the least, profitable. The film's creation, over a period of more than 14 months, cost $650,000; it grossed $2.5 million in the USA and $5 million overseas, ultimately bringing Chaplin a profit of some $2 million.

The synopsis of *The Gold Rush* provided above is based mostly on his reissue version of 1942, in which a number of sections were either deleted, replaced or slightly rearranged. For this revival, Chaplin composed a new score and replaced the sub-titles with his own narration. It is believed that Georgia Hale was engaged to speak some of her own dialogue, but the idea was dropped. The reissue print runs for 72 minutes at 24 frames per second; original prints, at the same sound projection speed, clock in at around 81 minutes. Presentations in 1925 would have been at something like 20 f.p.s., which had become the average projection speed by the mid-1920s (Sime quotes the 8,498 feet as running for around 96 minutes).

In any version, *The Gold Rush* remains an undisputed classic. Ignoring the jokes surrounding Alexander Woollcott (*qv*) and his sometimes overly-effusive praise (Woollcott's often polarized views once earned him the nickname 'Old Vitriol and Violets'),

Chaplin dedicated the 1942 reissue to him, thanking the journalist for his appreciative comments on the original release. In *Time* magazine, James Agee, another of Chaplin's loyal supporters, greeted the revival as 'a sight for sore eyes', noting also an expenditure of $125,000 on 'refurbishing' the film. Agee remarked on the way in which Chaplin's narration 'kids the stylized exaggerations of Big Jim ... by referring to him as "the noble type ... Oh, how he loved to suffer."' Chaplin's decision not to have Georgia Hale speak her own lines is perhaps vindicated when Agee describes how the narrator 'anticipates Georgia's atrocious, kittenish, dated antics by introducing her to the audience with the single expletive: "Georgia!"' This, in fact, is direct replacement for the original title card, but it is easy to see Agee's point. By contrast, Bosley Crowther of the *New York Times*, in considering Chaplin's narration as replacement for 'those persons who used to read titles aloud', was impressed by the sincerity of his reading, without a trace of burlesque. 'And when he first recognizes the heroine,' continued Crowther, '... he utters the single name, "Georgia!" with such tenderness and affection that genuine sadness haunts his voice.'

Because of an oversight, copyright on the silent version of *Gold Rush* was not renewed after the initial 28-year

The Gold Rush: *Charlie helps Big Jim find his 'mountain of gold'*

The Gold Rush: *A wealthy Charlie, posing for pictures in his old costume, pauses to have fun*

period required by American law. In consequence, it has long been treated as public domain – at least in the United States – and thus is readily available for comparison with the reissue.

Aside from the deletion of sub-titles, it might be noted that the cast list changes the original's 'Larsen' to 'Larson' (though the original spelling remains visible on a wanted poster). Angles are slightly different throughout, owing to the use of negatives deriving from separate cameras; an article in the Winter 1995 *Limelight* magazine refers to Chaplin incorporating footage from the B, C and D negatives, which were intended to provide masters both for overseas and as protection material for the original (even the famous Chilkoot Pass scene is presented from a noticeably different angle). Charlie's discovery of

Jim Sourdough's grave is placed at a different point of the film and is an alternate take; as Charlie approaches, he may be seen twirling his cane in the reissue version, but not in the original. Big Jim, examining his discovery of gold, is seen in profile in the reissue, but from the back in the silent version. One of a few deleted shots from the original is that of Charlie staggering about in the storm; there is also slight re-editing at the time of Charlie's first meeting with Black Larsen, omitting the first shot of Big Jim's tent being blown away. The scene of Charlie serving his cooked boot derives from alternative cameras in the two versions. The earlier edit places Larsen's discovery of Big Jim's claim before the scene of Jim's hallucinations; a cutaway to Larsen, frying food while the others are starving, was removed entirely from the 1942 version. The reissue precedes a view of the town with what seems to be a new shot of snowy mountains, replacing that in which the townspeople are first seen. Also in the reissue is a longer introductory shot of Georgia, who is seen stepping out of a building, rather than already outside. In turn, the first shot of Jack, the 'Ladies' man', is omitted, as is a moment in which Charlie is seen pawning his mining gear. A title card identifies Georgia's workplace as the 'Monte Carlo' dance hall, unnamed in the reissue except by signs in the background. A close shot of Charlie amid the bar crowd is shortened; the scenes of Charlie raising cash by shovelling snow, originally divided by fades, are separated by more polished dissolves in the later edition. Jack's arrival at the dance hall on New Year's Eve, originally cut in while Charlie prepares table for his guests, was moved to midnight in the context of the story, using an entirely different take. The chorus of 'Auld Lang Syne' is led by an elderly Scot in the original cut, but this does not appear in the reissue. There are also variants in editing during the cutaways to Charlie, who is standing outside, and when Georgia suddenly recalls her forgotten invitation. Georgia's continued devotion to Jack is toned down in the revived edition by the removal of a scene in which, leaving the dance hall, Jack asks, 'Do you love me?', to which Georgia answers in the affirmative. Presumably reluctant to over-emphasize coincidence, Chaplin also decided to eliminate the moment in which amnesiac Jim, anxious to locate his comrade, narrowly misses him

outside the recorder's office. Nor does the reissue show Georgia writing the note that is ultimately delivered to Charlie: instead of a remorseful communication to the tramp, it is an apology to Jack for her rejection of him the previous night, concluding with 'I love you' (the later version substitutes an insert of a different letter). Jack is unconcerned and, because it is not addressed to him by name, he gives it to Charlie. It is to attract Charlie's attention that he trips him up, rather than merely for sport, as implied in the reissue. The deletion of this and Georgia's earlier avowal of love for Jack seems designed to make Georgia more compassionate, tempering her implied humiliation of Charlie and reducing the strength of Jack's competition, emphasizing his callous unconcern for one girl among many; her reason for leaving Alaska, alone, becomes all the more clear with the knowledge of Jack's rejection of her. As amended, Georgia's acceptance of Charlie seems rather pat, and her astonishment on Charlie's return to the dance hall less explicable. Chaplin made several cuts to this scene, including a close shot of Charlie with barman Tiny

The Gold Rush: *Charlie steps back for the camera, and soon falls back into Georgia's life*

The Gold Rush: *Lunch at the Truckee location, early in production; note the use of three cameras*

Sandford (*qv*) and his attempts to escape from a seemingly crazed Big Jim. When Charlie is dragged away, the reissue holds a mid-shot into the fade, omitting a long shot of Charlie trying to return to Georgia only to be dragged off again, as an amused crowd looks on. Chaplin tightened up the subsequent business with a cabin teetering on a cliff, removing several exterior and interior shots plus a close-up of Charlie and Jim after their rescue. There is a noticeable substitution of material when Charlie and Big Jim pose for a photograper on the ocean liner. The original has a jump-cut where a title card was inserted, whereas the reissue uses a different, uninterrupted take. There is slight decomposition in this and other shots, described below, where Chaplin obviously used out-takes to replace certain scenes. The original has a close-up of Georgia pleading for Charlie, offering to pay his fare, for which the reissue substitutes a mid-shot. Similarly, the reissue stays in mid-shot as Charlie whispers to the reporter, instead of cutting to a close-up as per the original. This is where the revival fades to a 'Finis' title, as Charlie escorts Georgia up the steps. The silent version continues as they reach the upper deck, where a photographer arranges Charlie and Georgia close together. He asks them to hold still, but they drift into a kiss. 'Oh! You've spoilt the picture,' says the photographer. Charlie waves away the complaint,

without interrupting the passionate kiss, as the film concludes. Georgia's concern for Charlie, believing him to be a stowaway, is supposed to convince us that she wants him for what he is; the fuller version suggests she is only on board because of Jack's rejection, and is willing to accept Charlie through fortunate circumstances. The final close-ups start with her willing to kiss Charlie, but she seems afterwards unresponsive, allowing Charlie to kiss her rather than taking some active part in the gesture. This places a slightly different edge on the conclusion than the unequivocal 'happy ending' of the revival. The general assumption is that Chaplin deleted the smooching finale because his then-current fling with Georgia Hale had passed. Equally possible is that he was aware of the implicitly compromised nature of the story's outwardly happy ending.

The silent version often surfaces in poor condition. Historians Kevin Brownlow and David Gill were able to present a restored copy for their 'Live Cinema' presentations, with the assistance of the Chaplin Estate (see **Reissues**), an effort that might have been spared; in the July 1983 *Classic Images*, correspondent Cliff Howe mentioned having found the 'complete tins' of a 35mm print of *The Gold Rush* in a neighbour's garage, only to find that decomposition had reduced the contents to brown powder.

(See also: Alcohol; Boats, ships; Caricatures; Children; Costume; *Count, The;* D'Abbadie d'Arrast, Henri; Dreams; *Easy Street;* Fairbanks, Douglas; *Floorwalker, The;* Food; Garcia, Allan; Home movies; Impersonators; *Kid, The; King in New York, A;* Mental illness; *Pay Day;* Pickford, Mary; Radio; Risqué humour; Sandford, Stanley J. 'Tiny'; Sickness; *Shoulder Arms;* Smoking; Sutherland, A. Edward; Swain, Mack; Television; Trick photography; Vagrancy; Video releases; Wood, 'Wee' Georgie; *Young Charlie Chaplin*)

GOLDEN, MARTA

See: *Adventurer, the,* Essanay and *Woman, A* and Work

GOODWINS, FRED

(1891–1923)

(Chaplin films *qv*)
British-born supporting actor, originally a journalist who worked as London correspondent for the *New York Times;* in January 1916, the *Motion Picture News* directory referred to him as a 'trick roller skater' whose stage career had been with Sir George Alexander and Tom Terriss prior to a season in stock with Charles Frohman (another source claims he was in Frohman's Broadway shows). Goodwins' earliest film work was at Edison and Imp (as an assistant director) before joining Chaplin's Essanay troupe. Both *A Jitney Elopement* and *The Tramp* cast Goodwins as Edna's father; *The Bank* places him both within the staff and amid the erstwhile thieves; he is one of the crew in *Shanghaied,* the hot dog vendor of *In the Park* and a theatre patron in *A Night in the Show.* He has been reported in *A Night Out* and cited as the fake preacher in *Police,* but this last may be an error; the preacher seems to be Wesley Ruggles (*qv*), and Goodwins is believed instead to be among the policemen. Quoted elsewhere (under **The Bank, Essanay** and **Shanghaied**) is a 1915 *Pictures and the Picturegoer* article drawn from a letter written by Goodwins, who also supplied illustrations. Goodwins is said to have returned to his native country for war service; certainly, his film work seems to have been interrupted after early 1916. Subsequent appearances are in films made variously in Britain and America:

examples are *Hitting the High Spots* (1918), *For Husbands Only* (1918) and *Mrs Leffingwell's Boots* (1919). Goodwins is also credited as director of several British films, such as *Chinese Puzzle* (1919), *Artistic Temperament* (1919), *Build Thy House* (1920), *The Scarlet Kiss* (1920), *Ever Open Door* (1920) and, as actor and director, *Blood Money* (1921). Goodwins' date of birth is uncertain, and that quoted above does not seem in keeping with his apparent age in the Chaplin films; his early death (in England) is reported to have been from bronchitis.

(See also: Camera-looks; Purviance, Edna)

THE GRAND ORDER OF WATER RATS

A charitable organization formed along masonic lines, the Grand Order of Water Rats draws its membership primarily from the entertainment profession. It was born from an informal outing of music-hall comedians in 1889, and formalized with a Constitution the following year. The name derives from the somewhat unkind nickname given to a trotting pony; 'rats', of course, also spells 'star' in reverse. According to a later account by 'Wee' Georgie Wood (*qv*) in *The People* of 1 January 1956, Chaplin had paid a visit to Bud Flanagan's dressing room at the Victoria Palace, where Flanagan was playing cards with Chesney Allen, and Fred and Charles Austin, of 'Parker P.C.' fame. Chaplin's head appeared around the door, greeting Charles Austin with a cheery 'Hello, Oats!' ('Oats and barley' being Cockney rhyming slang for 'Charlie'). Chaplin noticed Austin's Water Rats badge and recalled the time when, as a youth, he yearned for fame, 'so that they would invite me to be a Rat'. Charles Austin proposed Chaplin's membership, which was seconded by Wood (a later Chaplin-Austin communiqué is detailed within the **Keystone** entry). The initiation took place on the night of Sunday, 1 November 1931. According to a report in the *Performer* of 4 November, Will Hay, King Rat for that year, presided over what was 'one of the biggest attendances of officers and Rats ever experienced for such a ceremony'. The long list of those present reads like a directory of the variety profession – Flanagan and Allen, Teddy Knox, Robb

Wilton, Jimmy James, Harry Tate and Jack Hylton – are just a few names to stand out – while the *Performer* noted a large number of telegrams from reluctant absentees plus the embarrassing duty of having to turn away a great many others, owing to lack of space. (An oversight meant that three gatecrashers had witnessed Lodge ritual and, in consequence, were immediately initiated into the Order!)

The huge gathering was nearly in vain. Wood's recollection, in the *People* article and his book, *Royalty, Religion and Rats!*, is of Chaplin arriving very late. The assembled company was already growing impatient when, at nine in the evening, a telephone call was received from Charles Austin, who was escorting Chaplin and explained that he had been delayed but was en route. By ten, the grumbles had resumed, and eleven saw tempers more than frayed. 'In fact,' said Wood, 'had it not been for the efforts of Bud Flanagan, Chesney Allen and Clarkson Rose, there might have been a mass walk-out.' The trio had put on Chaplin-like moustaches and taken to 'bouncing in and out of the room every five minutes'. The joke had worn thin by midnight when, fortunately, an uncertain-looking Chaplin arrived. He described having spent four hours battling his way through crowds, which even the police had been unable to part. The *Performer* spoke of Chaplin entering into the occasion with 'zest and spirit, taking an active part in anything that happened', renewing acquaintance with those who were established names – some of whom he had met when a part of the 'Eight Lancashire Lads' – at a time when Chaplin was starting in the business. Chaplin was pleased to be himself amid a gathering of fellow-professionals, rather than a specified 'film star'. According to Wood, Chaplin eschewed the traditional initiation speech for an hour's impromptu performance, imitating past Rats and offering, as a 'party-piece', an impression of 'a girl undressing in a French hotel'. (A more discreet account, from *Film Weekly* of 5 December, refers to Chaplin's mute burlesque of a Spanish bullfight and a 'French mime comedy'!) The party adjourned first to Charles Austin's flat, then, at around 6 a.m., to Chaplin's old haunts in Kennington.

Chaplin remained proud of his connection with the Order, but declined to take part in the Rats' BBC TV programme, *This is Music-Hall*, in 1955.

*Chaplin joined **The Grand Order of Water Rats** in 1931; here he attends a Lodge meeting in the 1950s, as 'Wee' Georgie Wood acts as barker*
By courtesy of Roy Hudd and the Grand Order of Water Rats

His decision was based not on selfish reasons, but because he felt, probably correctly, that his presence would divert press attention from the other artists. Among the overseas members to supply film insert material were Stan Laurel (*qv*) and Oliver Hardy, in their final public performance. The programme has been preserved in BBC archives.

(See also: Early stage appearances; Karno Company, the; Leno, Dan; Public appearances; Riesner, Chuck)

THE GREAT DICTATOR

(Chaplin film)
Released by United Artists, 15 October 1940. Produced, written and directed by Charles Chaplin. Assistant directors: Dan James, Wheeler Dryden and Bob Meltzer. Music by Charles Chaplin, directed by Meredith Willson. Directors of photography: Roland Totheroh and Karl Struss. Art director: J. Russell Spencer. Film editor: Willard Nico. Sound: Percy Townsend and Glenn

Rominger. Original working title: *The Dictator* (see below). 124 mins (sometimes quoted erroneously as 126).

The People of the Palace: Charles Chaplin (Adenoid Hynkel, Dictator of Tomania), Jack Oakie (Benzino Napaloni, Dictator of Bacteria), Reginald Gardiner (Schultz), Henry Daniell (Garbitsch), Billy Gilbert (Herring), Grace Hayle (Madame Napaloni), Carter De Haven (Bacterian Ambassador). The People of the Ghetto: Charles Chaplin (a Jewish barber), Paulette Goddard (Hannah), Maurice Moscovitch (Mr Jaeckel), Emma Dunn (Mrs Jaeckel), Bernard Gorcey (Mr Mann), Paul Weige (Mr Agar). Also: Chester Conklin (barbershop customer shaved to music), Esther Michelson, Hank Mann (stormtrooper), Florence Wright, Eddie Gribbon (stormtrooper), Robert O. Davis, Eddie Dunn (stormtrooper), Nita Pike, Peter Lynn, Stanley J. 'Tiny' Sandford (Tomanian soldier in 1918), Leo White (Hynkel's barber), Max Davidson.

In 1918, the First World War is drawing to a close. Tomania's leaders seek peace while, on the battlefront, her troops anticipate victory with their powerful cannon, 'Big Bertha'. The job of firing the cannon is entrusted to a private, a barber in civilian life. The first shot demolishes an outhouse; the second, a dud, travels only a few feet. The private delegated to investigate, finds the shell's nose cone is following him around. He and his comrades have fled by the time the shell explodes. When they are attacked from the air, the private whirls around on the anti-aircraft gun. Word arrives of an enemy advance, and each man is sent to the front. The private loses a hand grenade inside his uniform, and retrieves it only just in time. In the mists of battle, he becomes lost and is soon amid the enemy. He takes cover in a ruined house, where he is ordered to man a machine gun. Outside, Schultz, a pilot officer, lies exhausted. He has urgent dispatches to deliver. The private helps Schultz to his plane and is asked to stay with him. They take off just before the enemy arrives. During the flight, the pilot loses consciousness but is revived; it takes them some time to realize they are flying upside-down. The fuel runs out, and they prepare for death; instead, they survive the crash, although the private – and the dispatches – have to be rescued from deep mud. The dispatches prove

useless when the pilot is told that Tomania has lost the war. Years pass, and the private, a victim of amnesia, remains in hospital. He is unaware of how much time has elapsed, or that Tomania has been taken over by his lookalike, the fascist dictator Adenoid Hynkel. The dictator delivers a speech to his people, relayed around the globe by radio. The English commentator delivers a bowdlerized version of Hynkel's fanatical splutterings in fluent, vehement Tomanian, which are aimed at his hatred of democracy, liberty, free speech and, above all, the Jewish people. Hynkel's style of oratory causes microphones to bend; his style of lunacy sees him pouring water in his trousers and placing the jug to his ear so that more water exits through his mouth. Hynkel's speech acknowledges his loyal advisers, Herring and Garbitsch; Hynkel is accidentally knocked down some steps by Herring's considerable bulk. Hynkel poses for photographers while holding an obviously damp baby, then exits in his staff car. He passes statues that deliver the fascist salute, and discusses matters of state with Garbitsch. Hynkel is advised that the Tomanian people might be distracted from their hunger by even greater persecution of the Jews. Hynkel agrees that things have been too quiet in the ghetto. In that ghetto, Mr Jaeckel receives a visit from Mr Mann. They discuss Hynkel and the absentee barber who writes every few weeks, expressing an intention to return to his shop. The barber shop has been derelict since the war, but the barber will not allow Mr Jaeckel to rent it out. They also discuss Hannah, an orphaned young woman lodging in his house. She toils mightily at various types of housework but cannot make enough to pay her rent. 'What can I do?' asks Jaeckel. 'I can't throw her out.' Hannah is to deliver a basket of laundry; Mr Jaeckel gives her some keys, because he is going out and plans to lock up in case the stormtroopers pay a visit. Hannah encounters the stormtroopers outside; when they steal fruit from a shopkeeper, Hannah alone stands up to them and is pelted with tomatoes. The laundry is ruined. At the hospital, the amnesiac's case is being discussed when word arrives that he has gone. The doctors, aware that little more can be done for him, are not interested in his return. The barber arrives at his shop, which is full of cats. Believing he has been away only a few weeks, he is surprised and horrified at the

The Great Dictator: *The Jewish barber dodges a wayward shell during the First World War*

Years of unrest allow Hynkel to become **The Great Dictator**

The Great Dictator: *Herring (Billy Gilbert) introduces the inventor of a compact parachute; it doesn't work*

accumulation of dust and cobwebs. When a stormtrooper paints the word 'Jew' on his windows, the puzzled barber starts to clean it off, and is soon in trouble. Hannah, wielding a frying pan, knocks out the two stormtroopers. She keeps the barber out of sight when reinforcements arrive. When the barber enters his shop, Hannah realizes who he is. She warns the barber that the stormtroopers will be looking for him. Two of them arrive, ordering him outside before putting on handcuffs; told to repaint 'Jew' on the windows, the barber hurls paint over them and runs. Again, Hannah tries to field the stormtroopers with her frying pan, but the barber is surrounded. He is about to be hanged when an officer arrives. It is Schultz, whose life was saved by the barber in 1918. Demanding to know what is going on, he is shown the prisoner. Schultz recognizes the barber, but had always thought of him as an 'Aryan'. 'I'm a *veget*arian,' comes the puzzled reply. When Schultz recounts the details of their crash, the barber's memory at last returns. Schultz is informed that the barber had resisted the painting of his windows. '*Any* brave man would resist,' replies Schultz, demanding the barber's release and guaranteeing less harassment in the ghetto. If the barber or his friends are in trouble, they should inform Schultz. Hannah drops a chimney pot on a stormtrooper's head. 'Who did that?' yells Schultz. 'Oh,' explains the barber, 'one of my friends.' At Hynkel's palace, the dictator attends to administration, fleetingly poses for increasingly frustrated artists, takes time to play piano, seduce a secretary and, at Herring's behest, witness spectacularly non-functional inventions, specifically a bullet-proof suit and a miniature parachute worn as a hat. Garbitsch informs Hynkel of unrest, based mainly on hunger and food mixed with sawdust (albeit from 'the finest lumber'); a diversionary tactic will be to invade Osterlich, before dictator Napaloni of Bacteria does so. The only one willing to loan money for the invasion is Epstein, a Jewish financier; to secure the loan, persecution of the Jews will be temporarily suspended. Mr Jaeckel brings the barber up to date with the news while his hair is being cut. He ponders moving to Osterlich, still a free country. As most of the men are in concentration camps, Mr Jaeckel suggests the barber might improve business by catering for women. Hannah, cleaning the shop, is used for practice. Absently, the barber tries to give her a shave, but eventually performs a first-class beauty treatment. Once finished, Hannah goes out to buy some potatoes, drops some in the street, and is astonished when the stormtroopers help to pick them up.

Hynkel, meanwhile, is dictating a letter. The typist records a few words for a long sentence and almost a chapter for a few syllables. Faced with non-functional pens, Hynkel abandons the letter. Hynkel waves aside Herring's announcement of a wonderful new poison gas, but is willing to see his female spy. Told of a strike at the arms factory, Hynkel orders them all shot, but is persuaded to postpone the execution until the strikers have taught their skills to others. Hynkel notices how all the strike leaders are brunettes; under Garbitsch's influence, Hynkel dreams of a fair-haired, blue-eyed world under a brunette leader. Left alone, Hynkel dances around his office, toying with an inflatable globe of the earth – until it bursts. The barber shaves a customer, accompanied by the *Hungarian Rhapsody* on the radio. As the ghetto contemplates better times, Hannah dresses for her date with the barber, who is busy polishing the scalp of a bald customer. At the palace, Hynkel receives word that Epstein has refused the loan. He orders Schultz to target the ghetto, but Schultz advises otherwise. Hynkel orders him sent to a concentration camp. Garbitsch hands the dictator his notes for that evening's speech, but they are rejected in favour of a diatribe against the Jews. Hannah and the barber set out on their date, but decide not to buy 'Hynkel buttons' when the dictator's voice bellows out over loudspeakers. Those in the ghetto take cover before the stormtroopers march through, vandalizing the streets. They break in on the barber and are about to lynch him when one of them remembers Schultz's orders to leave that house alone. They wander away, but the barber has to see off a stormtrooper who is determined to get Hannah. The barber cuts a brave figure until, intending to lean on the doorway, he falls over. The stormtroopers hear of Schultz's arrest and, believing he was corrupted, set out to kill the barber. He wants to fight, but is persuaded to hide on the roof. From the roof of Mr Jaeckel's home, Hannah and the barber watch as his shop is burned. Hannah comforts him with the idea of them starting a new life in Osterlich, then breaks into tears. As the barbershop burns, Hynkel plays piano. Night has fallen, and on the roof, Hannah contemplates a star that Hynkel can never extinguish. Mr Jaeckel announces that the coast is clear; even better news is that Schultz has escaped and is to preside

The Great Dictator: *The barber tries his hand as a beautician; Hannah (Paulette Goddard) makes it easy*

over a meeting in the Jaeckels' cellar. The barber will attend while Hannah assists Mrs Jaeckel in preparing a midnight supper. Lots are to be drawn by the placement of a coin in one of the puddings, seemingly an ancient Aryan custom; Hannah fixes it so that a coin is in *every* pudding. Schultz explains that one of their number must embark on a suicide mission to assassinate Hynkel. Schultz, claiming to be too well-known, abstains from the repast and leaves the room. The puddings are served, and each man, discovering a coin, nervously keeps the news from his comrades. The others dump their coins on the barber, who discreetly swallows them all. He hiccups and rattles. Mr Jaeckel finds a coin in his food and believes he has been chosen. When the barber begins coughing up coins, Jaeckel realizes something is amiss. Hannah, owning up, convinces them not to proceed with the plot. Schultz returns. 'What's this?' he asks, as Hannah and the men depart with a courteous 'Good night.' The morning's newspaper reveals suspicion of Schultz hiding in the ghetto and that the barber is wanted for questioning. Mr Mann visits with the news and nervously discovers Jaeckel to be harbouring Schultz and the barber. Outside, he sees the stormtroopers searching the street and returns to warn Jaeckel. Schultz and the barber pack hastily – the barber carrying Schultz's rather unnecessary set of golf clubs – and head for the roof. The barber will meet Hannah later. The barber crashes through a skylight and is apprehended; so is Schultz, who joins the barber in a prison camp. The barber's friends reach Osterlich and a peaceful life on the farm. Hannah sends the barber a food parcel, with a covering note promising a good life for him in Osterlich when he is released. While the barber eats, Hynkel presides over a banquet, celebrating the imminent invasion of Osterlich. He eventually finds room to pin yet another medal on Herring – only to confiscate them all, along with Herring's buttons, when told that Napaloni has already massed 60,000 troops on the Osterlich border. Hynkel declares war on Napaloni, until he hears from his rival dictator by telephone. Feigning hoarseness, he has Garbitsch take the call. Napaloni wants to discuss the invasion, and is invited to visit Tomania. Hynkel organizes a show for the visit. Napaloni's reception becomes a shambles when his train shifts to and fro along the platform. The dictators make a show of friendship but, trying to upstage each other for press photographs, stray too close to the locomotive and are blasted with steam. Napaloni points out that a huge clock, in Hynkel's likeness, is two minutes slow; getting into Hynkel's staff car, he fails to notice his wife and advisers roped off with the crowd. Garbitsch advises Hynkel that his interview with Napaloni is not to discuss Osterlich, but to establish psychological superiority: Napaloni is to sit in a lower-level seat; a bust of Hynkel is to face him constantly; and he will have to approach

Hynkel from a distance. Napaloni bursts in via a rear door, rejects the low-slung seat in favour of perching on the desk, and uses the bust to strike a match. Hynkel is soon spluttering in his attempts to apologize for the unfortunate treatment of Mme Napaloni. A party has been planned for that evening, so Napaloni suggests he and Hynkel should get a shave together. They sit in adjoining, adjustable chairs and, in their attempts to establish seniority, rapidly ascend towards the ceiling. Hynkel parades his armoured might before an unimpressed Napaloni. Napaloni thinks the aircraft flying over may be his own, but accepts they are Hynkel's once they have crashed. At the party, Garbitsch suggests Hynkel should seem to go duck-hunting, then cross over to lead the invasion of Osterlich. Napaloni has first to be persuaded to remove his own troops but, for the moment, Hynkel should dance with the ungainly Mme Napaloni. He breaks off when signalled by Garbitsch. In private, Hynkel and Napaloni discuss the border question; a stalemate is reached when Napaloni refuses to remove his troops until Hynkel signs a treaty guaranteeing that neither will invade Osterlich. Their argument leads to talk of war and – after each has nearly burned out his mouth with searing mustard – a food fight. A reporter catches some of the flying food, and Garbitsch, anxious to preserve the appearance of co-operation, advises

The Great Dictator: *Hannah and the barber are a match for the stormtroopers ...*

... but only for a while

Hynkel to sign but invade Osterlich. The dictators are reconciled. At the prison camp, Schultz and the barber escape in borrowed army uniforms. Nearby, Hynkel is in a boat, dressed for his 'duck-hunting' trip. He fires a shot, the recoil of which dumps him into the lake. Prison guards, alerted by the shot, investigate and mistake him for the escaped barber. He is knocked senseless and taken away. Schultz and the barber, keeping to the main road as part of their imposture, approach the Osterlich border. The stormtroopers mistake the uniformed barber for Hynkel and, with Schultz's guidance, the barber leads the Tomanian forces into Osterlich. The stormtroopers adopt their usual tactics in the Jewish ghettos and on the farm where Hannah and the others are living. 'Hynkel' is to address the conquered nation in public and over the radio. Herring and Garbitsch, seeing Schultz, assume him to have been pardoned, but a greater surprise awaits. The barber,

The Great Dictator: *Hynkel and Napaloni (Jack Oakie) compete for psychological superiority in elevated barbers' chairs; old-time foil Leo White stands behind Chaplin*

introduced as the 'future emperor of the world', speaks reluctantly. He announces that he has no wish to be an emperor, believing instead that people should work together for peace. 'Dictators,' he declares, 'free themselves but they enslave the people.' His speech for unity, peace and democracy earns a massive ovation. Hannah, listening to the broadcast, realizes who is speaking. The barber next addresses Hannah directly, wherever she may be. He asks her to look up, as the parting clouds signal a new world emerging from brutality. Mr Jaeckel emerges from the farmhouse. 'Hannah, did you hear that?' he asks. Hannah, who can hear something greater, bids for silence.

The Great Dictator is prefaced by an ironic sub-title, as follows: 'Note: ANY RESEMBLANCE BETWEEN HYNKEL THE DICTATOR AND THE JEWISH BARBER IS PURELY CO-INCIDENTAL.' This defiant non-disclaimer no doubt also refers to the frequently-held opinion that Hitler may have been partly Jewish. The more significant resemblance between Chaplin and Hitler of course needed no elaboration. It had been much discussed since the latter's rise to power and became the inspiration for a comic song, 'Who is That Man (Who Looks Like Charlie Chaplin)', sung by British comedian Tommy Handley. The Chaplin-Hitler parallels have been noted very frequently, but as a matter of record one must state that, by one of history's more extraordinary quirks, these erstwhile lookalikes – and polar opposites – were born in the same week of April 1889. As noted in the **Modern Times** entry, the Nazis had begun to suppress Chaplin's films in Germany even by the mid-1930s. The reasons became apparent to the comedian when Ivor Montagu, an Anglo-Jewish friend, sent Chaplin a Nazi propaganda book in which he was named, erroneously, as Jewish and, just as inaccurately, 'as disgusting as he is boring'. At this distance, it might seem obvious for Chaplin to respond by selecting Hitler as a target for his satire; he later recalled Alexander Korda suggesting a film based on the resemblance as early as 1937. Nonetheless, in 1947 Chaplin faced a plagiarism suit from a one-time friend, Konrad Bercovici, who claimed the use of his ideas. Chaplin was by that time under attack in the US over *Monsieur Verdoux* (qv) and his alleged political

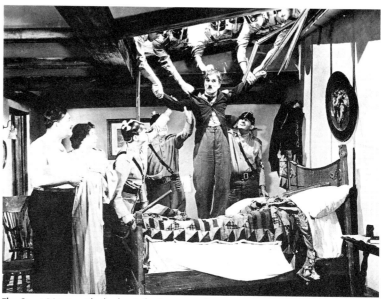

The Great Dictator: *The barber is finally captured*

leanings; this, plus the judge's stated wish to be with his dying father, persuaded Chaplin to make a quick settlement.

At the time, Hitler was more frequently ridiculed by members of the public than through official means. Governments favoured the notion of appeasing Hitler, and seemed anxious not to incur his anger. In consequence, Chaplin started to receive worried messages from United Artists (qv) on both sides of the Atlantic when his plans for a Hitler satire – tentatively called *The Dictator* – were made known at the beginning of 1939. He had registered a script bearing that name in November 1938, only to learn that Paramount claimed ownership, having acquired a play of that title by Richard Harding Davis. Since Paramount wanted $25,000 for its use, Chaplin inserted the word 'great' and proceeded as before. The amended title had been registered for a month when, on 22 July 1939, *Picturegoer*, after receiving a statement from Alf Reeves (qv), confirmed the casting of Paulette Goddard (qv) as leading lady and the construction of the first set, a large tenement street. This was of European design with, reportedly, all the shop signs in Esperanto. The set's completion was noted in a further report, from 12 August, less than a month prior to the outbreak of war in Europe. By 7 October, the magazine took some delight in learning that Chaplin had cast himself 'frankly and unequivocably as Hitler' and as 'an

The Great Dictator: *Hynkel takes to the floor with Mme Napaloni (Grace Hayle) .*

unknown Jewish tailor in Berlin'. In the end, the locale acquired a fictional name, 'Tomania' (a pun on 'Ptomaine', spelt 'Tomainia' on newspaper inserts), while Adolf Hitler became Adenoid Hynkel, and the tailor switched his profession to that of barber. Chaplin was reported as having spent hours listening to Hitler's speeches, developing a 'remarkable impersonation of Awful Adolf's hysterical public speaking manner, although not one word he utters is actually German' (one of the comedian's more celebrated private accomplishments was to replicate the *sound* of specific languages though in fact speaking gobbledegook, as in his comic song from *Modern Times* [qv]). Very little more was known by December, at which point *Picturegoer* described the refusal of Chaplin's press agent to answer calls and the comedian's reputation for working only when the mood took him. He had chosen to film a 'comedy dance' on an unusually hot day, at the end of which 'the dance was finished – and so, very nearly, was Chaplin'. (This may refer to a scene, deleted from the final version, in which the barber performs a Russian-style dance after the moment in which he is temporarily knocked senseless.) The general unreliability of this story is implicit within the claim that Chaplin's Hitler would be dressed as the tramp character, also that Henry Daniell (qv) would play Goering instead of Goebbels (Herring and Garbitsch in the eventual script); Picturegoer thought him better suited in the latter role, but as an interim measure recommended plenty of padding. Jack Oakie (qv) had already been announced as the fellow-dictator. 'There is always the danger that, by the time the picture is eventually completed and shown, we may all have forgotten

film had he been aware of the true horrors of the concentration camps. Such a camp, in highly sanitized form, is shown only briefly in the final cut; there exists at least one still suggesting further business in the camp, with Chaplin and Reginald Gardiner (qv) attempting to chew their way through the barbed wire. Also tempered was a greater measure of flippancy in the original script. Picturegoer described Chaplin's version of the Nazi salute as 'somewhat limp, with fluttery fingers', something not apparent in the completed film; John McCabe has detailed a lost joke in which even dachshunds are required to hail the dictator by raising their legs. Again according to McCabe, Hynkel's equivalent to 'Führer' underwent but scant alteration from 'Furor' to 'Fooey'; in turn, the Mussolini figure, 'Mussemup

actually manipulates Hynkel. By contrast, blustering comic Billy Gilbert (qv) fills Goering's uniform with the correct degree of corpulent buffoonery. Jack Oakie proved especially fortuitous as the Mussolini caricature, and indeed stole many of the reviews. His Napaloni is a vain, vulgar, jumped-up peasant with a jutting lip and Chico Marx accent, whose wife is a decidedly put-upon figure. Napaloni's bullish ways thoroughly undermine Hynkel's attempts at psychological warfare. He turns out to be smarter than Hynkel expects and,

By courtesy of Robert G. Dickson

... and little suspects his hunting trip will bring an end to his reign

who Hitler was,' said the magazine, combining a phoney-war optimism with foreknowledge of Chaplin's protracted methods. Production did indeed take a while, though not necessarily so by Chaplin's standards. Shooting began only days after war broke out, in September 1939, and concluded the following March, with post-production occupying the months prior to release in October. The arrival of war brought about Chaplin's decision to reduce his emphasis on the plight of Europe's Jews; he later said that he could not have made the

of Ostrich', became first 'Benzino Gasolini' before settling as Napaloni, Dictator of Bacteria. Just as Hynkel's equivalent to the swastika is a 'double cross', so Napaloni's fascist emblem is actually a seven at dice.

Doubtless in response to the project's scale and the demands of talking pictures, Chaplin assembled a supporting cast of established names rather than rely on his stock company or novice talents. Henry Daniell, as the Goebbels figure, is an impressively controlled, scheming creation, who in his effete insinuations

*Chaplin later admitted that he could not have made **The Great Dictator** had he known the true horrors of the concentration camps; this deleted scene with Reginald Gardiner, set in such a camp, suggests he may have become aware to some degree and curtailed the appropriate footage*

aware of the attempts to undermine his ego, consistently reverses the principle by a gentle criticism of everything he sees. When Hynkel tells a joke in Tomanian, Napaloni laughs, adding, 'That's-a very funny, I wish I understand it'; and, while watching a parade, he carelessly throws peanut shells at Hynkel. Charles Chaplin Jr noted a strong rapport between the two, although his father needed to feed Oakie vast amounts of food in order to combat the actor's then-current dieting.

The younger Chaplin also observed some of the new difficulties his father encountered when adapting to sound. One of these concerned Chaplin's reluctance to abdicate any duties to his freshly-hired sound effects man; the comedian tried unsuccessfully to obtain an aeroplane sound by vibrating various thicknesses of celluloid using an electric fan, prior to giving up (the sound technician simply went to an airport to record the genuine article). One of the several clever 'sound' gags takes place when the 'light infantry', off-screen, passes in complete silence. Another of Charles Jr's recollections concerns his brother, Sydney, laughing audibly during the filming of the 'Big Bertha' scene and thus ruining a $15,000 take. Chaplin's momentary fury was dispelled by the realization that even his own son found the scene funny.

Chaplin thought a dual rôle ideal for his first talkie, in that Hynkel, as a separate character, could have plenty to say, but his usual persona need not speak unduly (Chaplin's autobiography refers to 'the tramp' being allowed to remain more or less silent, refuting in some measure a frequent claim of the barber not being 'Charlie'). The barber's words are few and brief; when the barber tries to tell Schultz of the imminent arrival of the stormtroopers, he loses his voice through fear and has to mouth and gesture. Despite Chaplin's misgivings at the time of *City Lights* (qv), the voice is quite acceptable for the character, being a sort of soft, neutral 'everyman' voice, though one must allow that British ears would readily accept the accent.

Unusually, *The Great Dictator* premièred in New York in *two* theatres, the Astor and the Capitol, on 15 October 1940. Despite *Picturegoer's* speculation, Hitler was not only still around when the film was released, but the United States had also yet to enter the war. Chaplin had been advised not to make the film even before hostilities broke out in Europe, but in 1940

America was still officially neutral and, in some quarters, reluctant to accept a film of this nature (especially since its own pro-Nazi faction had yet to be silenced, something evident among those present when Chaplin was required to deliver his *Great Dictator* speech over national radio); nevertheless, Bosley Crowther of the *New York Times* had no qualms in speaking of '"Charlot" ... directing his superlative talent for ridicule against the most dangerously evil man alive'. '*The Great Dictator* may not be the finest picture ever made,' continued Crowther, 'in fact, it possesses several disappointing shortcomings. But, despite them, it turns out to be a truly superb accomplishment by a truly great artist – and, from one point of view, perhaps the most significant film ever produced.' Crowther was slightly uncomfortable with the barber's final speech, in which, for six minutes, 'Chaplin steps out of character and addresses his heart to the audience,' but found the tragic expression and sincerity of the message overpowering. This, for Crowther, threw into relief the prime virtues of *The Great Dictator*, 'the courage and faith and surpassing love for mankind which are in the heart of Charlie Chaplin'. An earlier draft of the barber's speech is said to bear some resemblance to a short story written by Chaplin, entitled 'Rhythm' (or '*Rhythme*'). This, his first public statement against fascism, was published in a French translation and, reportedly, also rendered into Spanish for the benefit of those opposing Franco in that country's Civil War. The piece is often thought to have been ghostwritten, but the style is difficult to determine in the available English re-translation (though Chaplin's authorship is implied by its parallels with the later text). Robert Florey (qv) included it in his study, *Monsieur Chaplin*. The key similarity is of Hynkel's forces abandoning their warlike ways as the barber speaks; it is probable that Chaplin realized how less effective – and, potentially, even corny – action of this sort might be when transferred into visual terms.

America's other metropolitan reviewers tended to express dissatisfaction with the speech (thought by some to be Chaplin's reason for refusing the New York Critics' Best Actor award) but *The Great Dictator* received unqualified praise in America's smaller cities. The same applied in wartime Britain, where its subject was of greater immediacy. The

film was screened privately for London's film trade and the press on 11 December 1940, prior to opening at three West End cinemas on the 16th. The *Daily Herald's* P.L. Mannock, much amused by Hynkel being saluted even by a statue of the Venus de Milo (!), considered it 'a good deal more than the grand little Cockney's greatest film' and applauded the 'electrifying' speech at its conclusion. Mannock thought that 'so much is behind the ghetto scenes that I feel Charlie (who has never denied it) must be a Jew himself'. Chaplin would never deny such claims, believing it would fuel the arguments of anti-Semites, but claimed to have made the film for the Jews of the world, to whom he felt especially close at that time. Seton Margrave of the *Daily Mail* seemed 'embarrassed' by the ghetto scenes, but otherwise enthused over the whole film. 'The paying public will vote it the biggest and the best comedy Charlie Chaplin has ever made,' he said. *The Times* made a worthwhile point in seeing *The Great Dictator* as 'a logical development of the mood of *Modern Times*', but suspected Chaplin's tilts at fascism were more effective through slapstick rather than 'preaching it in full canonicals'. The critic had gauged, however, Chaplin's realization of the inadequacy of comic mime in dealing with the persecution of the Jews, the concentration camps and the war in Europe, interpreting this as the reason why *The Great Dictator* 'moves unevenly and lacks the unity of a work of art'. Quibbling aside, mention was made of 'a wealth of wit and invention', including the 'brilliantly conceived and executed essays in caricature'. In the *Spectator*, film-maker and critic Basil Wright encapsulated the majority of contemporary observations: in the absence of a 'convenient sunrise towards which Charlie can walk', Chaplin needed to take the subject seriously, for 'the evils of dictatorship could not ... be conquered by a laugh, a flick of the stick, or a tilt of the battered bowler'; the closing speech, supposedly 'not well written', was delivered with enough sincerity to make it 'true and moving'; and, above all, Chaplin had surprised many in his depiction of Hitler, missing not one intonation or foible.

Jerry Epstein (qv) provided some indication of the accuracy in Chaplin's portrayal when recalling the comments of Albert Speer, Hitler's architect. After seeing the film, Speer thought Chaplin had got closer to representing Hitler than anyone else, remarking further that Hitler had also owned a balloon representing the earth – but a much larger specimen. There is also a story of Hitler, his curiosity presumably getting the better of him, having had a print of *The Great Dictator* smuggled in from Portugal. He insisted on screening the film – twice – in solitude, allowing his reactions to be seen by nobody. The tale reached Chaplin via an escapee from the Nazi Ministry of Culture. 'I'd give anything to know what he thought of it,' said the comedian.

(See also: Awards; Ballet; Birth; Cars; Children; Conklin, Chester; Costume; Dryden, Wheeler; Fairbanks, Douglas; Food; Hair; Home movies; Music; Politics; Prisons; Race; Radio; Religion; Risqué humour; Sandford, Stanley J. 'Tiny'; Struss, Karl; *Sunnyside*; Television; *Unknown Chaplin*; Video releases; Wartime)

GREY, LITA 🎩
(1908–95)

(Chaplin films *qv*)
Born Lillita Louise MacMurray (sometimes using 'McMurray'), Lita Grey first met Chaplin on her sixth birthday. She was in a restaurant with her mother, Lillian (1888–1985), who noticed the comedian sitting with a friend; after checking with the restaurant owner, Mrs McMurray took the reluctant child to meet the famous comedian. After a brief chat, Lita started to cry and had to be taken away. Lita had reached the age of twelve when a neighbour, Chuck Riesner (*qv*), informed Mrs McMurray that Chaplin needed youngsters for his new film, *The Kid*. Lita was taken to the studio and introduced once more to Chaplin, who, unsurprisingly, could only pretend to recall their first meeting. Hired as one of *The Kid*'s many child extras, Lita was soon singled out and given a screen test. Chaplin asked the hair and make-up artists to give Lita the appearance of an eighteen-year-old (Lita recalled, in any case, photographing as being older than she was), and as a result gave her the rôle of the 'flirting angel' in *The Kid*'s dream sequence. Her original agreement was torn up and replaced with a year's contract, during which Chaplin made only one more picture, *The Idle Class*, casting Lita and her mother as maidservants. The option was not picked up.

Lita re-entered Chaplin's story when it was made known that he required a new leading lady for *The Gold Rush*. Lita and a school friend, Merna Kennedy (*qv*), visited the Chaplin studio where, against all protocol, Lita confronted Riesner with her interest in auditioning for the film. Riesner, explaining how such things are normally done, dismissed the idea but invited the girls to watch the

Lita Grey eventually parted from Chaplin under the most acrimonious conditions; these pictures represent happier days, with Lita signing a contract to appear in **The Gold Rush**

studio's activities. When Riesner told Chaplin of Lita's enquiry, he was delighted and offered to make a test. Lita was duly hired, and in April 1924, taken on location to the snowy mountains of Truckee, California. In the ensuing months, their relationship became rather more than platonic; Lita's memoirs, *My Life with Chaplin*, claim that she was fifteen – and therefore under-age – when she became pregnant with Chaplin's child. Given that her sixteenth birthday coincided with the Truckee stint, and that, by her own admission, she and Chaplin did not consummate the relationship until some time thereafter, it seems fair to suggest that her memory – or arithmetic – may have been somewhat awry. Chaplin agreed to a hurried wedding, in Mexico, pretending to film additional scenes in this new locale.

As John McCabe has pointed out, Lita's highly unflattering record of events is not paralleled by an account from

Chaplin, whose autobiography brushes aside their association even to the extent of omitting her name. Chaplin's bitterness remains evident in his only slightly more detailed comments in *My Life in Pictures*. Thus, as McCabe concludes, it was left to Theodore Huff to speak for Chaplin, to the effect that the marriage took place only under threat of court action from

Lita's uncle, a lawyer.

According to Lita, Chaplin minimized potential scandal by not announcing the birth of their son, Charles Jr, until several weeks after his arrival in May 1925. Lita's pregnancy had meant that she could not continue in *The Gold Rush*. She was replaced by Georgia Hale (*qv*), in whom Chaplin began to take increasing interest. Much the same applied to her former schoolmate, Merna Kennedy, during production of *The Circus*. By the time of their marital split, Lita had borne Chaplin two sons; the second, Sydney Earl, was born in March 1926. At the end of that year, Lita returned to her family and instituted divorce proceedings. Her settlement demands included an injunction on all Chaplin's assets, including the uncompleted *Circus*, forcing Chaplin to flee to New York with the negative. Lita's divorce complaint ran to 42 pages, and there was much shedding of tears for the press, claiming not even to have money for the babies' milk. The newspapers carried lurid details of the couple's sex life and of Chaplin's alleged mistreatment of his wife. In a situation reminiscent of the fate that befell his friend Roscoe Arbuckle (*qv*), Chaplin was suddenly the target of protests from women's groups. The divorce was granted in August 1927. Lita's property settlement came to $650,000, not including a $200,000 trust fund for the children plus Lita's court costs, themselves totalling $950,000. As a consequence of the scandal, divorce and several unrelated difficulties with *The Circus*, Chaplin suffered a nervous breakdown, during which his slightly greying hair had turned white.

Lita pursued a modest showbusiness career of her own, working as a singer in vaudeville and cabaret (billed as 'Lita Grey Chaplin, sophisticated lady of song') on both sides of the Atlantic; on 19 October 1929, *Picture Show* referred to her forthcoming European tour, including a visit to London. According to this source, she had then been appearing in vaudeville for eight months. Lita remained there for seven years; she later ran a talent agency and appeared in a few minor films, one of them a discouraging-sounding drug 'exposé' film of 1949 called *The Devil's Sleep*. Chaplin prevented her from encouraging their sons into the profession until they had reached adulthood. Lita Grey was among those interviewed for *Unknown Chaplin* (*qv*); reportedly unhappy with her memoirs, Lita was, at the time of her death, preparing a new, updated work called *Wife of the Life of the Party*. This book, edited by Jeffrey Vance, has to be published at the time of writing.

(See also: Caricatures; Dreams; Hair; Marriages; Women)

GRIFFITH, D.W.
(1874–1948)

Director and producer, famed above all for inventing or defining many aspects of what became known as 'film grammar', also for his epic silent features *The Birth of a Nation* (1915), *Intolerance* (1916), *Hearts of the World* (1917), *Broken Blossoms* (1919), *Way Down East* (1920) and so on; he became one of Chaplin's co-founders in United Artists (*qv*) in 1919.

(See also: Fairbanks, Douglas; Normand, Mabel; Pearce, Peggy; Pickford, Mary; Sennett, Mack; Stockdale, Carl)

GRIFFITH, GORDON
(1907–58)

Child actor, born in Chicago. Appeared in several Chaplin Keystones, notably *The Star Boarder* (*qv*), following early stage experience. His later acting credits include Mary Pickford's *Little Annie Rooney* (1925). Graduated from Stanford University, then joined Monogram Pictures as an assistant director. He was later active in an executive capacity, becoming Production Manager for Columbia in 1941 and receiving Associate Producer credit on several features.

(See also: Keystone; Pickford, Mary; *Tillie's Punctured Romance*)

GUEST APPEARANCES

The majority of screen comedians make occasional contributions to other people's films, usually those of immediate colleagues or personal friends. Chaplin's rôle in *The Knockout* (*qv*) is, strictly speaking, that of a guest in a Keystone comedy starring Fatty Arbuckle (*qv*); in 1915 Chaplin paid a visit to his employer, G.M. Anderson (*qv*), in the latter's *His Regeneration* (*qv*). Anderson in turn may be seen in Chaplin's *The Champion* (*qv*). Similarly, Chaplin makes a fleeting appearance in *The Nut* (1921), a starring vehicle for his friend and co-founder of United Artists (*qv*), Douglas Fairbanks (*qv*). In this, Fairbanks retreats behind a screen, ostensibly to reappear in a series of impersonations. The appearances of Napoleon, General Grant, Abraham Lincoln and General Tom Thumb make it plain that Fairbanks is *not* doing the show unassisted. This is confirmed when the screen collapses,

revealing Fairbanks and a party of actors. One of these is a Chaplin lookalike, played by Chaplin himself. 'Charlie' hams it up for the crowd until escorted off. Intriguingly, Chaplin does not merely play his usual character, but actually seems to impersonate an *impersonator*, the moustache and costume being slightly wrong and the gestures exaggerated and obvious. A private film made that same year, *Nice and Friendly* (*qv*), seems to have been shot at the home of Fairbanks and his wife, Mary Pickford (*qv*). A 'Memories of Silent Stars' reel, subtitled *The Mirthmakers*, has footage of Chaplin seemingly planning a new film with Fred Newmeyer and Chuck Riesner (*qv*). A film of Chaplin directing is said to be from a 1923 feature, *Souls For Sale*; also in 1923, he contributed to James Cruze's *Hollywood*. In 1928, Chaplin did a walk-on, as his off-screen self, in King Vidor's *Show People*, starring Marion Davies. In this scene, Chaplin and an associate attend a screening of a new comedy. The associate tells Chaplin that the young female lead (Davies) is 'a real find', prompting Chaplin to seek her autograph. Her leading man recognizes the civilian-clad Chaplin but she does not, and is reluctant to supply a signature. She is persuaded to oblige, and Chaplin departs in his limousine. 'Who is that little guy?' she asks, and swoons on being told.

(See also: Impersonators; Swanson, Gloria)

HAIR 🎩

(Chaplin films *qv*)
Chaplin's natural hair was originally jet black with a tendency towards curls. His numerous imitators were required to replicate his distinctive, natural coiffure by means of curlers and, as appropriate, dye. Chaplin himself had to use dye when appearing in character from the mid-1920s on, as his hair turned prematurely white. It had begun to grey around 1921, but the process was startlingly accelerated at the time of his messy divorce from the perhaps appropriately-named Lita Grey. In *The Great Dictator*, his Jewish barber character returns to the ghetto somewhat greyer than in the opening scenes, suggesting considerable passage of time. Similarly, his characters in *Monsieur Verdoux*, *Limelight* and *A King in New York* are of sufficient maturity for the dark hair of youth to be unnecessary.

An amusing footnote: Colleen Moore's autobiography, *Silent Star*, makes reference to the widely-held belief that Chaplin, as ever cautious with money, dispensed with the need for a barber by learning to cut his own hair (he is earlier reported among the regulars at Helmens, a barber favoured by movie stars). Certainly, *The Great Dictator* offers a glimpse of his tonsorial skills (as does a deleted moment from *Sunnyside*), though with customary irony, the barber's own haircut is something of a mess. Charlie makes an altogether tidier job when playing barber to a bearskin rug in *Behind the Screen*.

(See also: Colour; Costume; Impersonators; Marriages; *Unknown Chaplin*)

HALE, GEORGIA 🎩
(1906–85)

(Chaplin films *qv*)
Actress, a former 'Miss Chicago', with stage experience. Georgia's appearance in Von Sternberg's *The Salvation Hunters* (see **Edna Purviance**) brought her to the attention of Chaplin, who hired Georgia to replace the pregnant Lita Grey (*qv*) as leading lady of *The Gold Rush*. They worked well together and formed an off-screen relationship, which endured in varying degrees of intensity for years thereafter; that their prolonged smooching at the end of *Gold Rush* was more than acting is evidenced by its removal from the 1942 reissue, by which time the romance had cooled. Georgia made no other films with Chaplin, but was brought in, temporarily, to replace Virginia Cherrill (*qv*) in *City Lights*. Footage of Georgia Hale in the rôle may be seen in *Unknown Chaplin* (*qv*), to which she also contributed as interviewee. Among her other films are *Woman Against the World*, *Gypsy of the North*, *The Rainmaker*, *Floating College* and *The Last Moment*, in a movie career that effectively concluded prior to the arrival of sound. She worked latterly as a dance instructor in Los Angeles, and was reunited with Chaplin when he received his special Oscar in 1972. A memoir, *Charlie Chaplin: Intimate Close-Ups*, was published by Scarecrow Press ten years after her death.

(See also: Awards, honours; Women)

HARRIS, MILDRED
(1901–44)

The young girl who was to become Chaplin's first wife made his acquaintance in late 1917 at a party at Sam Goldwyn's beach house. Without really intending to, Chaplin found himself courting her and, when Mildred believed she might be pregnant, married her on 23 October 1918. Chaplin was furious when Sam Goldwyn almost immediately signed her to a movie contract – but was willing to make a success of the marriage. The pregnancy was a false alarm, but Mildred eventually conceived a child who, born in July 1919, lived only three days.

Despite Chaplin's wishes, strenuous effort was made to promote Mildred's film career. *Picture Show* of 20 December 1919 announced her forthcoming starring film, *The Inferior Sex*, and a week later reported a 'strong supporting cast' for this, her first venture, namely Bertram Grassby, Milton Sills and Mary Alden. Some indication of Mildred's true drawing power may be gleaned from contemporary ads billing 'Mrs. Charlie Chaplin' in rather bigger type than 'Mildred Harris'. On 14 December 1919, the *Motion Picture News* suggested that Mildred's billing as 'Mrs. Charlie Chaplin' could have benefited both partners. The paper believed the first exhibitor to make the connection might have been a New Yorker with the appropriate name of Kashin, who

Mildred Harris became Chaplin's first wife; there is, of course, no suggestion that her film career owed anything to the Chaplin name Advertisement by courtesy of Robert G. Dickson

prepared a special wedding announcement and a trailer advertising a double-bill of Chaplin's *Shoulder Arms* (*qv*) alongside Mildred in the also aptly-titled *Borrowed Clothes*.

The marriage ended legally on 19 November 1920. Mildred, young and naïve, was hardly the ideal companion for such a complex man as Chaplin. She also saw Chaplin's moodiness as neglect, charging him with 'mental cruelty'. Rather late in the day, *Picture Show* of 20 November ran a syndicated story from Louella Parsons headed 'Charles Chaplin a Recluse'. The item described Chaplin as 'the most difficult man to see at the present time', ascribing his reluctance to give interviews to 'the recent trouble with his wife, Mildred Harris Chaplin'; Mildred had been giving interviews of her own, decrying her husband's 'penurious habits' and claiming she 'couldn't extract a cent from him with a vacuum cleaner'. Miss Parsons mentioned a 'mutual friend' having found Chaplin at his suite in the Ritz, playing classics on the violin and, on another occasion, scrutinizing Macaulay's *History of England*. There was speculation on Chaplin's desire to visit his native country – rumours that he had already sailed on the *Olympic* were swiftly discounted – but he did indeed embark on such a trip the following year. Chaplin had in fact escaped after a harrowing time; he had defended accusations of meanness, citing cancelled cheques totalling some $50,000, and had been willing not to contest the divorce. His main concern had been the possibility of Mildred's lawyers attaching the negative of his current project, *The Kid* (*qv*), forcing him to edit the film while in hiding.

Mildred's career quickly slid into oblivion. At the time of her divorce from Chaplin, she was in the employ of Louis B. Mayer; Mildred worked subsequently for Cecil B. DeMille, but by the end of the 1920s was among the fallen luminaries appearing in Hal Roach comedies. Mildred's early death, aged 42, was the result of pneumonia following surgery.

(See also: Children; Fighting; Marriages; Normand, Mabel; Women)

HAYLE, GRACE

Character actress who plays Mme Napaloni in *The Great Dictator* (*qv*). Other films include *Good-bye Love* (1933), *Bureau of Missing Persons* (1933), *Design For Living* (1933), *Sing and Like It* (1934),

Tovarich (1937), *Next Time I Marry* (1938), *Star Maker* (1939), *The Ghost Breakers* (1939) and *Maryland* (1940).

(See also: Goddard, Paulette)

HEIGH, HELEN (OR HELENE)

Plays 'Yvonne' in *Monsieur Verdoux* (*qv*); among her other films are *Undercover Woman* (1946), *Teenage Thunder* (1957), *What's the Matter with Helen?* (1971) and *Nine to Five* (1980).

HEIGHT

There are conflicting details concerning Chaplin's height. Some hold the view that Chaplin occasionally underestimated his stature, as a means of reinforcing his customary sobriquet, 'The Little Fellow'. Chaplin's true height may be gauged to some extent when examining photographs of him in the company of friends and colleagues; Stan Laurel (*qv*), for example, is believed to have been 5 feet 9 inches in height, and available pictures suggest Chaplin to have been three or four inches shorter. The *World Film Encyclopaedia* (1933) quotes Chaplin's height as 5 feet 6½ inches, a figure which ties into the comparison with Laurel, though it should be said that Alistair Cooke (in his book *Six Men*) estimated that neither Chaplin nor Alf Reeves (*qv*) 'could have been much over five feet'. Marilyn Nash (*qv*) told *Limelight* magazine that, at five feet six inches, she was 'a little taller' than Chaplin when she wore high heels, implying some confirmation of the *Encyclopaedia* data.

HELLO, MABEL

See: Keystone

HENDERSON, JACK
(1878–1957)

New York-born actor who plays the gypsy chief in Chaplin's *Carmen* (*qv*). His other screen work includes a 1926 serial, *The Mystery Box*.

HER FRIEND THE BANDIT 🎩

(Chaplin film)
Keystone Comedy released by Mutual, 4

June 1914. Produced by Mack Sennett. Screenplay and direction attributed to Chaplin or Mabel Normand. Photography attributed to Frank D. Williams. Reissued as *Mabel's Flirtation* and *The Thief Catcher*. One reel. 1,000 feet (UK length cited in *Bioscope*).

With Charlie Chaplin (the bandit), Mabel Normand (Mrs De Rocks), Charlie Murray (Count, or Mr De Beans).

A bandit intercepts a nobleman, Count De Beans, en route to a reception held by Mrs De Rocks. Wearing the victim's evening clothes and presenting a stolen invitation, the thief outrages those present until the arrival of the Keystone Cops, who initiate a free-for-all.

The above is based on accounts contained in contemporary reviews, for *Her Friend the Bandit* has the sad distinction of being the only lost Chaplin film. The fact that it was reissued at least twice (not counting foreign-language editions) suggests that a print may one day turn up from somewhere, albeit perhaps in truncated form; indeed, many Chaplin Keystones tend to circulate either in reissue versions or those prepared outside North America and Great Britain. The unavailability of *Her Friend the Bandit* is made doubly frustrating by its seeming influence on many of Chaplin's later comedies; although *Caught in a Cabaret* (*qv*) initiated the notion of Charlie gatecrashing society in the guise of nobility, *Bandit* seems to have been more in the direct line that includes, among others, *A Jitney Elopement*, *The Count*, *The Rink* and *The Adventurer* (all *qv*). It should be added that some doubt has been cast on *Her Friend the Bandit*'s authenticity as a Chaplin film. Chaplin scholar Hooman Mehran cites an often overlooked, pre-Theodore Huff filmography published by *Sight and Sound* in 1938, from which *Her Friend the Bandit* is omitted. Mehran notes also the absence of Chaplin's name from most contemporary reviews, the exception being that in the *Moving Picture World*, which even then misspells the name as 'Chaplain'. The point is amplified when inspection of a review in the British trade paper *Bioscope* again fails to disclose specific reference to Chaplin. One might add that, unlike many other Keystones, the film's first reissue incorporates 'Mabel' into the title rather than 'Charlie'. It may be that Chaplin was unrecognized, perhaps in a costume similar to that in

Making a Living or *Mabel at the Wheel* (both *qv*), but this must remain conjecture pending the film's rediscovery.

(See also: Keystone; Reissues; Williams, Frank D.)

HIS FAVORITE PASTIME

(Chaplin film)

Keystone Comedy released by Mutual, 16 March 1914. Produced by Mack Sennett. Directed by George Nichols. Photography attributed to Frank D. Williams. Reissued by W.H. Productions as *His Reckless Fling*; other reissue titles include *The Bonehead*. One reel. 1,009 feet (UK length cited in *Bioscope*).

With Charlie Chaplin (himself), Roscoe 'Fatty' Arbuckle (shabby drunk), Peggy Pearce (girl), Edgar Kennedy (tough).

Charlie is in a bar, where he takes one of a string of hot dogs from the lunch counter, thinking it to be a cigar. Pestered by a shabby drunk, Charlie pretends to let him have some beer, but eventually gives him the empty glass. Nearby, a society couple and their maid enter a taxi. In the bar, the weatherbeaten gent tries to get a handout, but Charlie, now obviously drunk, gives him a handful of squashed food from the counter. He departs in disgust. The cab pulls up outside as Charlie leaves the bar. He flirts with the young society woman,

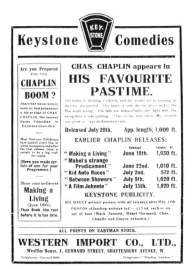

*A contemporary UK trade advertisement highlights **His Favorite Pastime**, its spelling suitably amended*

only to be sent away by her somewhat older husband. Charlie returns to the bar, and is pushed over by a tough. Charlie joins him for a drink but, when the man's back-slapping manner becomes too much, escapes into the washroom. Another customer, who is having his shoes polished by an attendant, accidentally kicks the swinging door into Charlie's face; Charlie retaliates by kicking him into the bar. The attendant, whose gratuity vanished with the customer, expects a sum from Charlie and turns his back, hands cupped; Charlie, lighting a cigarette, drops in a burning match instead of coins. Outside, the girl's father tells her to wait in the cab. Charlie, still in the washroom, dabs his face then, taking a towel, dries himself as though emerging from a bath. The husband enters the bar while Charlie, in the washroom, slumps into the shoeshine seat. Another customer enters to wash his face, but Charlie has taken the towel to polish his shoe. Blinded by soap, the customer dries his face and is covered in shoe polish. They argue, and Charlie kicks him into the bar, where he demands a clean cloth. Charlie, unable to negotiate the swinging door, crawls under it to re-enter the bar. Charlie's foot is caught in a spittoon; other customers help to free him, but Charlie blunders into the society man, who takes a swing at him. He is restrained while Charlie retaliates. Outside, Charlie sees the woman, still waiting by the taxi. She and her maid enter the cab, which drives off; Charlie, trying to catch up, falls in the road. He follows them home by streetcar, but has to clutch the outside of the vehicle. Having checked their address with the cabbie, Charlie enters the house. Charlie tries to climb the stairs but falls over the banisters, landing neatly on a chaise longue, where he calmly lights a cigarette. Charlie thinks he has found the girl, but is horrified to see the housemaid, who attacks him. The lady of the house returns to find a dazed, drunken admirer in the hallway. Her husband also arrives, and Charlie is pushed back into the room with the maid, who resumes her attack. Charlie is discovered, and the wife accused of infidelity. Charlie battles the husband as the servants look on; Charlie is pushed into them and fights the staff instead. Ejected from the premises, Charlie staggers on his way.

A contemporary review from the

*Charlie is treated royally in this posed still from **His Musical Career**; Charley Chase is at right*
Museum of Modern Art/Film Stills Archive

Syracuse Post-Examiner (reprinted by McDonald *et al*) describes a final scene with Charlie atop a telegraph pole which his rival is attempting to cut down. The print examined by the author, W.H. Productions' reissue entitled *His Reckless Fling*, includes no such conclusion: while there is the possibility of a reviewer's memory elaborating somewhat on the proceedings, it is far more likely that the film was trimmed on revival. The present ending, showing Charlie meandering away from the house, is rather a weak finale to the mayhem that has gone before. A clue may be found in the credits, which describe *His Reckless Fling* as being 'adapted' from *His Favorite Pastime*, generally a sign of greater mutilation than mere retitling. A similar statement may be found on the same company's edition of *The Rounders* (*qv*). When Dr F.C. MacKnight examined the film for his 'Collecting Chaplin' series in *Classic Film Collector*, he worked from a French-language print entitled *Charlot est Trop Gallant*, suggesting that, to the French, 'flirting is the "Favorite Pastime", rather than drinking!'. Content in this French edition seems to match the W.H. Productions reissue.

(See also: Alcohol; Arbuckle, Roscoe 'Fatty'; Cars; *Film Johnnie, A*; Food; Kennedy, Edgar; Pearce, Peggy; Race; Reissues; Smoking; Streetcars; Williams, Frank D.; Women)

HIS MUSICAL CAREER

(Chaplin film)

Keystone Comedy released by Mutual, 7 November 1914. Produced by Mack

Sennett. Written and directed by Charles Chaplin. Photography attributed to Frank D. Williams. Reissue titles include *The Piano Movers* (the working title) and *Musical Tramp* (sometimes misquoted as *Musical Tramps*). One reel. 1,025 feet.

With Charlie Chaplin (himself), Mack Swain (piano mover), Charley Chase (their employer), Fritz Schade (Mr Rich), (?) Alice Howell (Mrs Rich – see below), Joe Bordeaux (impoverished musician), Norma Nichols/Gene Marsh (his wife – see below).

Charlie applies for a job at a piano workshop. The piano mover examines Charlie's physique and teeth as though evaluating a horse. Charlie proves his strength by lifting a heavy can of beer; he takes a swig, but spits it out when slapped on the back. When the piano mover is not looking, Charlie switches the can for a similar one. When the piano mover takes a drink, he finds he has a mouthful of varnish. Charlie douses him with the first can. In the shop, Mr Rich orders a new piano. In the workshop, Charlie has been taken on as assistant and applies oil to his joints. In the shop, an impoverished, old musician paces nervously. The proprietor tells him that his piano will be repossessed if he cannot keep up the payments. Charlie busies himself in the workshop when the order comes through for him to help the piano mover with deliveries. They have two jobs in Prospect Street: to deliver the new piano to no. 666 and collect the other from no. 999. They take the new instrument from the shop to the cart outside, with interruptions when the piano mover becomes trapped beneath. They set off. At home, the sad musician tells his wife of the imminent repossession. En route, Charlie uses his clay pipe to scoop draughts of beer from the piano mover's supply. They pause when the heavily-laden cart tilts, leaving their mule hanging in mid-air. Reaching Prospect Street, they proceed to deliver the new piano to no. 999 by mistake, negotiating a long side staircase. This done, they set off to make their *second* mistake, collecting the piano from Mr Rich's home. 'They walked right in', says a title, suggesting the door to have been unlocked. The furniture is cleared and the piano removed, despite queries from Mrs Rich and a footman. The piano has been pushed into the street when Mr Rich arrives, asking where they are going

with his piano. The piano mover shoves him away, and is kicked in return. Thus the piano and the two workmen are sent cascading down a hill, coming to rest in a lake. Charlie valiantly plays the instrument as it sinks.

His Musical Career has frequently been cited as a prototype for the classic Laurel & Hardy short, *The Music Box* (1932), but in truth they share few ideas that were not essentially common property. Transporting the instrument on a cart was standard procedure at the time, and the idea of delivering to the wrong address was and is a staple of farce. The greatest similarities come in a brief gag when Charlie hitches a free ride as Mack Swain (*qv*) does the work and, more notably, in a comparatively underexploited scene of them hauling the piano up a flight of steps.

As with *Those Love Pangs* (*qv*), Norma Nichols has been cited in the cast, but the actress present seems instead to be the slightly chubbier Gene Marsh (thought to be the pretty patient in *Laughing Gas* and Charlie's Stone Age conquest in *His Prehistoric Past* [both films *qv*]). Similarly, Alice Howell (*qv*) has been credited with the rôle of Mrs Rich, but the actress playing the part looks more like Cecile Arnold (*qv*).

Prints of *His Musical Career* are unusual in that many retain their Keystone sub-titles despite evidence of considerable mutilation in length. Often part or all of the opening sequence is missing, while invariably the action concludes before the piano's final descent. Material from Europe is more likely to be complete than that available in the USA, though an American video edition from Grapevine fills out the missing scenes by combining the usual edition with footage transplanted from a reissue called *Musical Tramp*.

(See also: Animals; Keystone; Laurel, Stan; Reissues; Streetcars; Vagrancy; Video releases; Williams, Frank D.)

HIS NEW JOB 🎩

(Chaplin film)
Released by General Film Company, 1 February 1915. Produced by Essanay. Written and directed by Charles Chaplin. Photographer unknown. British title: *Charlie's New Job*. Two reels. Approx. length 1,996 feet (cited in Essanay's contemporary UK trade ads).

With Charlie Chaplin (himself), Ben Turpin (Charlie's rival), Charlotte Mineau (actress), Leo White (receptionist/actor), Gloria Swanson (typist), Agnes Ayres (extra).

In the office of the Lockstone film studio, Charlie awaits a job interview. The impatient receptionist tries to persuade Charlie to remove his hat, but Charlie remains stubborn. While young actresses are being interviewed in the office, the studio itself is making a costume drama. Charlie awaits his turn with the boss as an old-school actor is seen. Another applicant, Ben Turpin, tries to jump the queue, but Charlie gets the better of him. At the interview,

His New Job: *Charlie becomes a movie star at the 'Lockstone' studio*

Charlie can barely make himself understood via the boss's ear trumpet (through which Charlie manages to blow ink at himself!). A distinguished, statuesque actress (Charlotte Mineau) looks in, and Charlie is suitably charmed. Charlie is taken on as stage hand and sets to work, though not before a second crossing of swords – or, more accurately, a swinging door – with Turpin. Charlie reacquaints himself with the actress before walking through the set in civilian clothes. He is ordered off, but returns to create similar mayhem carrying props. Following a disagreement with the director, an actor storms off set and Charlie is instructed to 'make up as a hero'. Taking the star's dressing room, he begins to change into costume. A dazed Turpin is still awaiting interview. Regaining full consciousness, he kicks the office door but hits the boss. Turpin walks into the office and is promptly ejected. Back on set, the propman demands an assistant to replace Charlie. The director goes to the office and hires Turpin, dragging him into service without the formality of interview. In Ruritanian uniform, Charlie would make an impressive sight but for ill-fitting clothes and a shuffling walk. The image takes a further dent when he stops to play dice with the head propman. Separating the game from the set is a curtain; when Charlie suspects the propman of cheating, he jabs his sword through the curtain, catching both an actor and the director. By the time the director investigates, Charlie has handed the sword to the propman, who is duly ejected. Turpin has arrived on set, and hostilities are renewed. The star, meanwhile, enters his dressing room. Charlie attempts his first scene, but knocks himself half-unconscious with his sword. Partially recovered, he returns the now rather bumpy sword to its scabbard, gets into a scuffle with a fellow actor, and is suitably fortified to continue. In his dressing room, the star is enraged to find Charlie's street clothes instead of his costume. Before the cameras, Charlie proves an able player until pinned to the floor by a fallen pillar. Turpin sits on the pillar before helping to remove it. Once freed, Charlie continues into a heart-rending scene as the heroine takes leave of him, ascending a flight of stairs. Charlie accidentally tears off the train of her gown, making the best of things by using it to mop his tears. A fight breaks out between Charlie and his enraged director; the star arrives, demanding his costume, but a blow aimed at Charlie reaches the director instead. Armed with mallet and missiles, Charlie renders Turpin and the director unconscious. Turpin rallies enough to attempt a swing at Charlie, but the mallet reduces him to a twitching wreck. A final blow brings Charlie's new job to a devastating conclusion.

His New Job was Chaplin's first film for the Essanay company after leaving Keystone (*qv*), hence both its title and the friendly dig at his old employers in placing the action at the 'Lockstone' studio. The idea of such a location was hardly new, having been used in *A Film Johnnie* and *The Masquerader* (both *qv*); it would be employed again the following year, in *Behind the Screen* (*qv*), though without a hint of staleness. The humour in *His New Job* is slightly forced, being presented more methodically than its immediate predecessors at Keystone, but not as yet replacing speed with anything superior. Some of the gags are basic in the extreme, as when suggesting

that Ben Turpin (*qv*) has remarkably smelly feet. Turpin's long experience at Essanay made him a logical choice to partner the new arrival, but the Chaplin-Turpin association was to be brief. Even more brief was Chaplin's tenure at Essanay's Chicago facility; as noted elsewhere, he found the climate depressing and insisted upon a return to California after this one film. Although disappointing today, *His New Job* has a reasonable share of laughs, and at the time was greeted with enormous enthusiasm; shortly before its British release (as *Charlie's New Job*) in April 1915, *Pictures and Picturegoer* noted that one of its first American screenings had attracted 5,000 patrons in a single day. Essanay arranged trade showings of their first Chaplin film ('An irresistible absurdity in two acts') all around Great Britain between 18 March and 1 April 1915, prior to release on 20 May.

From posterity's viewpoint, *His New Job* retains particular interest for its use of a moving camera (despite Chaplin's reputation for static photography), a device seldom employed at the time, even in dramatic subjects.

(See also: Colour; Costume; Mineau, Charlotte; One A.M.; Policemen; Rink, The; Risqué humour; Smoking; Swanson, Gloria; Television; White, Leo)

HIS NEW PROFESSION 🎩

(Chaplin film)
Keystone Comedy released by Mutual, 31 August 1914. Produced by Mack Sennett. Written and directed by Charles Chaplin. Photography attributed to Frank D. Williams. Reissued as *The Good-For-Nothing*, *Helping Himself* and, *c*.1934, by Exhibitors Pictures Corporation under the original title. One reel. 1,015 feet (UK length cited in *Bioscope*).

With Charlie Chaplin (himself), Fritz Schade (uncle), Charley Chase (nephew), Norma Nichols (girlfriend), Roscoe 'Fatty' Arbuckle (barman), Cecile Arnold, Harry McCoy.

Charlie, in a park, examines the *Police Gazette* and its pin-ups. Nearby, a young man and his girlfriend sit beside a dozing uncle, whose gout has confined him to a wheelchair. The girlfriend sets off to find someone else to take care of uncle; she does not consider asking Charlie, who

*This scene, from **His New Profession**, is often misattributed to another Keystone, Recreation*
BFI Stills, Posters and Designs

picks up her dropped handbag as she passes. The nephew pushes uncle around the park, pausing by Charlie, whose foot is trapped beneath the wheelchair. The nephew engages Charlie to push uncle while he goes off to cavort with his girlfriend. Charlie is to be paid later. Another couple watch, amused, as Charlie clumsily attempts to negotiate the chair. On the pier, Charlie wants to call at a bar, but uncle will not advance him any cash. Uncle, dozing again, is parked beside another sleeping invalid, from whom Charlie borrows a collecting mug and a sign reading 'help a cripple'. A passerby donates enough change to finance Charlie's trip to the bar. In his absence, nephew and girlfriend return; the nephew is horrified to see the begging sign, but his fiancée is amused. Once they have gone, the sign's owner awakes and strikes uncle with his cane. Charlie arrives, drunk, returning the old man's cup but not its contents. Charlie, increasingly weary, pushes uncle along the pier but stops to show him his copy of the *Police Gazette*. The girlfriend, having fallen out with the nephew, sits beside them. Absently, she places her hand on Charlie's knee and he responds flirtatiously. Charlie pushes uncle out of the way, his wheelchair coming to rest at the very end of the jetty. The nephew returns to see Charlie canoodling with his girl. Nearby, the old man with the collecting cup is wheeling himself along. A fight begins, and Charlie collides with the old man. A policeman helps them both up. Uncle returns, but his nephew pushes him back to the jetty's end. The girl turns on the nephew, who is sent on his way by another policeman. Charlie, in a scuffle with the first policeman and the old man, gives the chair a shove, sending chair and occupant hurtling into the second policeman, who plummets into the sea. As uncle wheels himself back, Charlie gives the first cop a kick, dumping him in uncle's lap. Uncle is arrested. Charlie laughs, yawns and returns to the girl, whom he escorts away after booting the old man out of view.

His New Profession is one of the least-revived Chaplin Keystones, possibly owing to Charlie's callous attitude towards his elderly charge (see also **The Property Man**) and the bluntness of such things as the 'help a cripple' sign. Available prints are uniformly mediocre, making it difficult to spot Roscoe 'Fatty' Arbuckle (*qv*) as the barman. The comparative elusiveness of *His New Profession* may explain certain earlier accounts in which an early scene, with Charlie perusing the notorious *Police Gazette*, has been wrongly attributed to another rarity, *Recreation* (*qv*). The same scandal-sheet provides Charlie's reading matter in *The Kid* (*qv*), and is jokingly referred to as the source of Calvero's memoirs in a dream sequence of *Limelight* (*qv*).

The boozy, self-interested Charlie of Keystone days is given full reign on this occasion, though as always there are indications of better things. Charlie's emptying of the bar's various dregs (a gag repeated in *The Adventurer* [*qv*]) should be familiar to anyone acquainted with life's more enthusiastic drunks, and there is something engagingly child-like about his evaluation of the scandal-sheet, particularly when conspiratorially sharing the treat with uncle.

Charley Chase (*qv*), who appears in several Chaplin Keystones, is more prominent than usual. He later became a star comic at the Hal Roach studio, but was at this time being wasted portraying a succession of bland young men.

(See also: Alcohol; Costume; Dreams; Keystone; *Masquerader, The*; Parks; Sickness; Williams, Frank D.)

HIS NIGHT OUT

See: *Night Out, A*

HIS PREHISTORIC PAST 🎩

(Chaplin film)
Keystone Comedy released by Mutual, 7

December 1914. Produced by Mack Sennett. Written and directed by Charles Chaplin. Photography attributed to Frank D. Williams. Reissued by WAFilms under the original title, with new sub-titling by Syd Chaplin; also reissued as *A Dream*. Two reels. 1,945 feet.

With Charlie Chaplin (Weakchin), Mack Swain (King Lowbrow), Gene Marsh (wife), Cecile Arnold (another wife), (?) Fritz Schade (Ku-Ku), Al St. John (another of Lowbrow's subjects), (?) Syd Chaplin (policeman – see below).

Charlie settles on a park bench, where he drifts off to sleep. In Charlie's dream, King Lowbrow holds court in a caveman domain, entertained, if that is the term, by Ku-Ku, a decidedly epicene dancer. A lone caveman, Weakchin, wanders into view as Lowbrow sends the favourite of his several wives to fetch water. Weakchin, perhaps the only caveman to carry a cane and sport a bowler, breaks further with history by smoking a pipe, albeit filled with fur torn from his own costume and ignited with a flint struck in the same way as a match. Weakchin meets Lowbrow's wife. He is making progress when the dancer, seeing them, fires an arrow into Weakchin's rump. The woman obligingly removes the missile, and Weakchin hurls a rock at his attacker. The victim ducks, and the rock hits King Lowbrow. Weakchin is stalked around a boulder by both the dancer and Lowbrow. The dancer mistakenly jabs an arrow into the King. Weakchin knocks him out and, following an exchange of flint business cards, earns the King's friendship, cemented by a kick to the King's stomach and the rubbing of noses. Weakchin consolidates his favoured position by extracting a flea from Lowbrow's bearskin, extinguishing it with one mighty blow. Lowbrow's wives and their guard bow down in respect. Weakchin trips over the guard and gives him a thump, then accepts Lowbrow's offer of a drink. Having used a servant as foot-scraper, Weakchin displays all the skills of cocktail-mixer. His original attacker meanwhile regains consciousness. When the King becomes tipsy, Weakchin, borrowing a club from the servant, sneaks off to see his wives. Weakchin enjoys their company until they disappear with another caveman. Weakchin, at last noticing their absence, knocks the other man out and regains the women's attention. One of them

entices Weakchin into a beachside cave, where a sudden wave washes them into the sea. The King, angered by their apparent cavorting, is satisfied when Weakchin claims to have saved the woman from drowning. Weakchin and the King return to their drinking. Weakchin's rival for the women returns to consciousness, intent on revenge. Weakchin returns and sends him packing, before leading his sweetheart in a tango. Lowbrow catches them canoodling and, sending the girl away, takes Weakchin hunting in the hills. Weakchin would sooner pursue the flirtatious cavewoman, but manages to fire an arrow into a bird's nest, bringing down an egg onto Lowbrow's cranium. When Weakchin looks above, another egg – evidently bad – lands upon him. Lowbrow catches Weakchin with his wife once again; the resultant battle sees the King booted over a cliff. The others, alerted to what has happened, bow down again; Weakchin sends the girl to join the others. He lords it over them, unaware that King Lowbrow is alive. Lowbrow is helped back by Ku-Ku, who tells him what had happened originally. Weakchin is in Lowbrow's cave, enjoying his drink and the company of his wife, when the King sneaks up behind. When Lowbrow smashes a rock over Weakchin's head, he is suddenly the modern-day Charlie; the blow was actually from a policeman's truncheon, returning Charlie to consciousness on the park bench. The officer grabs Charlie's tie, pulling him to his feet before sending him on his way.

Stories set in the Stone Age – comic and otherwise – have always enjoyed something of a vogue. Parts of Keaton's *The Three Ages* take place in prehistory, as does an early Laurel & Hardy called *Flying Elephants*. The tradition has been

Charlie poaches the King's prize spouse in
His Prehistoric Past

continued with, among others, *The Flintstones*, and will probably survive another Ice Age. Chaplin later recalled the genesis of this, his final Keystone, as having been the single gag in which he filled his pipe using part of his caveman's fur. 'Genesis' is perhaps the operative term, since this is a parody of a D.W. Griffith drama, *Man's Genesis*, made two years earlier and featuring a hero called Weak Hands. The idea of the original was that Weak Hands, despite his lesser physical strength, had sufficient intelligence to vanquish a stronger opponent by means of weaponry. Charlie's name in *His Prehistoric Past*, Weakchin, comes to us via titles added to WAFilms' revival by Syd Chaplin (*qv*), but its similarity to that in the Griffith film suggests its presence in the original version.

Bo Berglund, in the August 1982 *Classic Images*, cites Syd Chaplin as the policeman who, at the conclusion, brings Charlie back to reality. Syd's tenure at Keystone is supposed to have begun after his brother's departure, but Berglund offers convincing evidence to the contrary. Examination of *His Prehistoric Past*, especially in better-quality prints, supports the notion of both Chaplins appearing in this scene.

Available prints of *His Prehistoric Past* tend to be the Syd Chaplin revamp, which circulates in copies of varying completeness (one, for example, has had many of its sub-titles deleted). Most copies omit the opening segment of Charlie settling down to sleep, with the 'dream' context revealed only at the film's conclusion.

When a reissue of *His Prehistoric Past* turned up at a 'comedy week' in New York's Rivoli Theater during March 1919, the *New York Times* found anachronism in more than the setting. The review described it as 'an early Keystone product of the time when, apparently, Chaplin's mastery of pantomime had not been developed or discovered ... those who relish Chaplin's artistry of today are glad that it belongs to his past, wishing only that it was prehistoric'. Posterity takes a gentler view of *His Prehistoric Past*, but this review provides insight into the degree to which Chaplin's methods – and those of the industry in general – were thought to have progressed in the intervening half-decade.

(See also: Documentaries, compilations; Dreams; *Funniest Man in the World, The*; Keaton, Buster; Laurel, Stan; Parks; Policemen; Reissues; Risqué humour; Swain, Mack; Vagrancy; Williams, Frank D.)

HIS REGENERATION
(1915)

During his time with Essanay (*qv*), Chaplin's relationship with G.M. Anderson (*qv*) seems to have been essentially one of *camaraderie*, at least until the time of parting. Anderson appears briefly in Chaplin's third Essanay film, *The Champion* (*qv*), and in return Chaplin may be seen in Anderson's *His Regeneration*, released in America on 7 May 1915 and in Britain on 30 August. In the introductory notes added to their prints of this subject, Blackhawk Films expressed a belief that Chaplin made guest appearances in several Essanay films, functioning also as associate producer under Anderson in a number of other projects. Blackhawk considered the rediscovery of *His Regeneration* to be substantiation of this claim, though at the time of writing no further examples have come to light. It might be added that Chaplin's involvement in the film should have been noted even prior to its recovery, if only on the strength of contemporary advertising in which he is billed quite prominently (an Essanay ad in *Bioscope* places it after the main list of current Chaplin films). The main title describes Anderson as 'slightly assisted by Charles Chaplin'; Chaplin's contribution to the film occurs near the beginning, where he attempts to flirt with a girl in a seedy dance hall. First, Charlie attempts to take her hand but grabs that of a man instead. Discovering his error, Charlie joins the girl's laughter, but turns his attentions elsewhere on the arrival of her giant boyfriend. Charlie is next seen in banter with the musicians, from whom he is dragged and kicked away. In a moment anticipating similar business in *Modern Times* (*qv*), Charlie is pushed and shoved by an army of dancing couples before making his exit. The rest of the film concerns Anderson, who, with an accomplice (Lee Willard), burgles the home of a beautiful young woman (Marguerite Clayton). On discovering her to be a society lady who helped him during trouble at the dance hall, Anderson decides they should abandon the robbery. His less scrupulous partner disagrees, and is shot dead in the ensuing struggle. The young woman permits Anderson to escape, assuming responsibility for the death on the

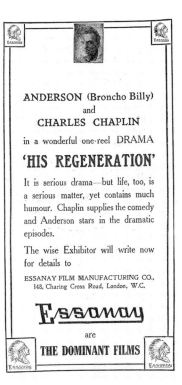

Chaplin's guest appearance in **His Regeneration** *did not go unannounced in the British press; also presented is a glimpse of his contribution to the film itself*

grounds of self-defence. She is subsequently reassured by a note left by Anderson: 'You saved me from a twenty year jolt. I'll try and make good.' Outside, Anderson assures himself of his security by stopping a policeman for a light. This established, he goes on his way as the scene irises out. Curiously, this is very much the story used in Chaplin's last *bona fide* Essanay, *Police* (*qv*), though of course Chaplin played it mostly for laughs and the final iris leaves Charlie with no sense of safety from the law.

(See also: Abandoned projects; Guest appearances; Home movies; Pollard, Harry 'Snub')

HIS TRYSTING PLACE 🎩

(Chaplin film)
Keystone Comedy released by Mutual, 9
November 1914. Produced by Mack
Sennett. Written and directed by Charles
Chaplin. Photography attributed to Frank
D. Williams. Also known as *His Trysting
Places*. Reissue titles include *The Henpecked
Spouse* and *Family House*. Two reels. 1,912
feet.

With Charlie Chaplin (himself), Mabel
Normand (his wife), Mack Swain
(Ambrose), Phyllis Allen (Mrs Ambrose).

Charlie, Mabel and their baby son enjoy
an uneasy kind of domestic bliss. Mabel
is outraged when Charlie knocks boiling
water from the stove and carries their
child by grabbing the back of his
clothing. While Mabel works in the
kitchen, Charlie hands the boy a genuine
revolver in lieu of a toy. Elsewhere, in a
hotel foyer, a young lady clerk examines
the letter she has written, arranging a
tryst with her gentleman friend. In one
of the rooms are the honeymooning Mr
and Mrs Ambrose. Ambrose goes out
and, passing through the foyer, meets the
attractive clerk. She asks him to post the
letter. At home, Charlie is again in
trouble when Mabel discovers their son
with his potentially lethal toy. Mabel
storms back into the kitchen, slamming
the door and dislodging a 'lucky'
horseshoe hanging from it. Mabel hurls
the horseshoe into the living room,
hitting Charlie. Outside the hotel,
Ambrose sets off for a stroll; at home,
Charlie puts on his coat, explaining that
he is going to buy a present for the boy.
Mabel gives Charlie a kiss and hands
him his overcoat. Pausing to trip over the
mat (which he uses as a handkerchief),
Charlie departs while Mabel stays to play
with the child. Charlie buys a baby's
bottle but, when outside the shop, his
purchase is noticed by a black youngster,
who makes fun of him. Charlie puts the
bottle in the pocket of his overcoat,
draped over his arm. Ambrose sees a
cheap, run-down café advertising a 25¢
meal. He goes in and hangs up his coat
and hat. Charlie, also seeing the
advertisement, walks in, hanging his coat
on the same rack. A bearded old man
occupies the seat beside Ambrose;
Charlie antagonizes him by using the
beard to wipe his hands. Charlie offends
the man sufficiently to ensure his
departure, and occupies the vacated seat.
While trying to eat, Charlie implies that

Ambrose is both a noisy eater and a
messy one, first by miming a violin, then
by covering his ears, then his face when
nibbling a hambone. Ambrose reaches
across the counter, interrupting Charlie's
meal; Charlie in turn dumps the bone
into Ambrose's soup dish. Their scuffle
develops into a free-for-all, with
Ambrose inadvertently grabbing Charlie's
coat when making his escape. Charlie
hurls a pie after him, which lands instead
on a top-hatted gentleman. Charlie,
taking what he believes to be his coat,
exits into the street. Tripping over the
splattered gentleman, he is challenged
but pushes the other man away. In the
park, an unnerved Ambrose meets up
with his wife. Mabel is ironing a pair of
Charlie's trousers when her husband
arrives home. Mabel greets him
affectionately and, while Charlie attends
to the child, looks in his overcoat pocket
to see what he has bought. Finding the
letter that was given to Ambrose to post,
Mabel assumes Charlie to be having an
affair. She turns on him, hurling
whatever is available before breaking the
ironing board over his head. Charlie
pushes her away and disappears through
the front door. Charlie slips on the mat
once more, landing firmly on his behind.
Mabel puts on her hat and coat and,
taking the child, sets off after Charlie. In
the park, Mrs Ambrose has comforted
her dazed husband, who sets off to buy a
drink from a nearby kiosk. Charlie passes
a policeman, pausing when his hat is

dislodged by a tree branch. The cop
queries Charlie's sanity as he mutters
over his fate. When questioned, Charlie
offers a discreet tip of the hat and swiftly
makes for a bench. Absently, he sits on
Mrs Ambrose. He is telling her of his
woes when Mabel arrives. Thinking he is
flirting, Mabel leaves her child with the
cop and takes a swing at Charlie. He
escapes, and Mrs Ambrose takes the
blow. Mabel leaves off throttling Mrs
Ambrose to catch up with Charlie, who
is resting against a dustbin, sobbing.
Mabel boots him into the receptacle.
Charlie emerges, is knocked back in
again, then stays put, ducking Mabel's
punches. Mrs Ambrose meanwhile
examines what she thinks is her
husband's overcoat; she discovers the
baby bottle and assumes he has an
undisclosed offspring. Ambrose, from
afar, observes Mabel's fury and goes to
offer help. Charlie appears from within
the dustbin, carefully arranging
Ambrose's coat-tails prior to delivering a
kick. Ambrose turns to see his attacker
and, recognizing Charlie, confronts him.
The two men slowly circle until Mabel
kicks Charlie, causing him to blunder
into Ambrose, who in turn is pushed
into the dustbin. Mabel renews her
attack until the policeman returns the
child, forgotten in the course of battle.
Charlie and Ambrose compose
themselves until the cop has gone. Mabel
returns to hitting Charlie, leaving the
baby with Ambrose. His wife sees him

Charlie, Mabel and son reunited for the finale of **His Trysting Place**
BFI Stills, Posters and Designs

with the child and faints. Mabel shows Charlie the letter; Mrs Ambrose challenges her husband about the baby's bottle. Charlie realizes he has the wrong coat, and calls Ambrose. The exchange is explained to everyone's satisfaction until Charlie hands Mrs Ambrose the letter. Ambrose receives a thrashing while Charlie, delivering the present at last, returns to his loving family.

The title of *His Trysting Place* is invariably quoted thus (and indeed makes more sense that way), but some sources, including home-movie distributor Blackhawk Films, have quoted the title as a plural. A main title for the Keystone edition quotes 'place', as do contemporary advertisements. The 'places' title is as per a WAFilms reissue, with titles rewritten by Syd Chaplin (*qv*). Some prints may not be relied upon for precise content, for the sequence of events seems to vary between copies of this film, and at least one source makes no mention of an early scene in which Charlie knocks hot water from the stove. Prints of Syd Chaplin's version can vary somewhat; in one copy, the author discovered a large section missing from the park sequence, which was present in an otherwise much shorter copy derived from the same master.

Collector and historian David Wyatt reports several reissue variations, one of them a 16mm silent print, called 'His Trysting *Place*', containing simple white-on-black titling. Text of sub-titles is brief and bears closer resemblance to the Keystone originals (e.g. 'Music' when Ambrose slurps his soup). In this version, the love note is signed 'Clarice', whereas others usually bear the sillier name 'Camomile'. This material suffers less from the usual peripheral cropping of image, so that the café's advertised menu is less obscured than usual. Wyatt also points out a continuity error, wherein Charlie's hat suddenly disappears during a close shot of him kissing the baby while saying goodbye to his family. Another reissue moves this shot to a different position but still does not mask the error. This appears in a British edition, with added sound, distributed by Adelphi Films and credited as 'Revised and re-edited by Horace Shepherd' (thus at least naming the culprit!). The main title reads 'His Trysting *Places*'; text throughout seems parallel to Syd Chaplin's, but sub-titles are adorned with stick-man illustrations differing from those in his version. Other

material, from Hollywood Film Enterprises, derives almost certainly from a WAFilms/Syd Chaplin print.

(See also: Allen, Phyllis; Children; Documentaries, compilations; *Funniest Man in the World, The*; Home movies; Keystone; Normand, Mabel; Parks; Policemen; Reissues; Religion; Risqué humour; Swain, Mack; Williams, Frank D.; Women)

HOME MOVIES 🎩

(Chaplin films *qv*)
Home movies have long been part of many people's lives, be they simple family documents or sometimes more elaborate efforts. Nowadays they tend to be on video, but in pre-war days even a simple ciné camera was available only to the comparatively well-off. For those to whom cinema was a profession, privately-made films were not only possible but quite often made on the full-sized 35mm gauge, a great luxury. Chaplin made a number of private reels which have survived the decades. In a sense, *How To Make Movies* (*qv*) was an elaborate home movie, albeit one that Chaplin hoped to persuade First National (*qv*) to release professionally. The best selection – primarily those taken on the *City Lights* set by Ralph Barton – may be found in the documentary series *Unknown Chaplin*; some, such as that showing Chaplin at Pickfair in a pre-*Great Dictator* ballet, preserve the origins of routines later used to considerable effect in his theatrical output. Perhaps the most famous privately-shot film is *Nice and Friendly* (*qv*), a spoof melodrama made with Lord and Lady Mountbatten. Doubtless similar in spirit is a trick film – preserved in Britain's National Film Archive – made at the Chaplin studio in 1923 with the visiting Sir Albert and Lady Naylor-Leyland. McDonald, Conway and Ricci's *The Films of Charlie Chaplin* notes home movie footage of Chaplin in a 1965 anthology, *Ken Murray's Hollywood*.

The long-time public domain status of Chaplin's early films has meant a proliferation of home-movie editions. To list every distributor would be impossible, for a book-length study could be devoted to this topic alone, but certain names stand out. As early as 1928, 16mm users in America could obtain a Kodak 'Cinegraph' edition of *Easy Street*. Similarly, Kodak-Pathé made

Chaplin films available on 8 and 16mm in Europe during the 1930s.

Again in the USA, Official Films maintained a useful selection of the Keystones on 8 and 16mm, some of them difficult to obtain elsewhere. For a while in the 1970s, Thunderbird offered many of the rarer Keystones, usually in W.H. Productions' reissues; there were also a number of Essanays (such as *The Champion*) and a complete set of the Mutual films, the latter from late 1930s prints. One of the most comprehensive lists was from Blackhawk Films, who offered on 8 and 16mm perhaps half the Keystones, all but one of the Essanays (*Carmen*), a complete run of Mutuals (latterly in restorations) and the silent original of *The Gold Rush*. For many years, Blackhawk had in release the four-reel abridgment of *Tillie's Punctured Romance*, but a restored edition was made available shortly before the firm's closure in the mid-1980s. Not all Blackhawk prints were particularly good, but most were superior, as in a version of *Mabel's Married Life* deriving from a Keystone original. Some effort was made to introduce new items or upgrade existing ones, as when the split-reel films *Kid Auto Races at Venice* and *A Busy Day* were paired from freshly-discovered originals in 1975.

Numerous smaller companies offered Chaplin subjects on both sides of the Atlantic, some films bearing unfamiliar new titles – particularly the four-minute extracts – while others retained their original names. In the UK, Chaplin releases came from firms such as Peak, Arrow, Mountain and Collectors' Club, to name a few. Capitol Films provided some comparatively uncommon films, notably the rarer Keystones (invariably from early reissues) and a good-quality, three-reel edition of *Carmen*. Walton Films' catalogue made the genteel boast that 'the quality of our Chaplin films is remarkably good', true at least until the company's last few years. The image quality of Chaplins could indeed be horrible, but Walton somehow managed to obtain good-quality masters on most subjects. Their original material on *Gentlemen of Nerve* (retitled *Charlie at the Races*) was truly remarkable for a Keystone; these comments apply also to the same subject as issued in France by Film Office, whose Chaplin range was similarly admirable. Latterly, some of Walton's one-reel abridgments were offered with synchronized music and effects tracks, that for *The Count* being

THE NEW OFFICIAL FILMS INC.

Charlie Chaplin

OLD-TIME COMEDIES

IN THE PARK

PEAK FILM PRODUCTIONS

Present

CHARLIE CHAPLIN

in his Famous Hilarious Antics

THE SCREENS GREATEST COMIC

8 mm

C.6. THE CURE.
Charlie at a Spa, empties his booze into the 'waters' and all the patients get 'lit up.'

8 mm

THE CHARLIE CHAPLIN CLASSIC COMEDY SERIES

CHARLIE CHAPLIN

8mm. 1 reel

Motion Picture Quality

ATLANTIS HOME MOVIES

Charlie Chaplin

8mm B/W

(approx. 160 ft)
52/6

CAT. No. 2

HAM ARTIST

Charlie tells how he was once a celebrated artist to an enthralled audience. His illustrations on the bar room floor nearly cause a riot.

ONE REEL
8 mm

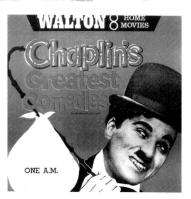

WALTON 8 HOME MOVIES

Chaplin's Greatest Comedies

ONE A.M.

Charlie the Perfect Lady

WITH CHARLIE CHAPLIN

particularly effective. Walton offered quality but, sadly, not necessarily completeness. The company's habit of pruning scenes marred several otherwise useful releases, even in nominally complete two-reel editions. For example, their two-reel version of *Easy Street* has been unnecessarily relieved of Chaplin's opening close-up plus a brief cutaway to his superior officer after the capture of the local bully. (In fairness, it should be noted that Walton was not alone in such editing; for example, quite a few Mountain editions were very heavily cut, particularly when offering two-reel versions that seemed closer to 1½ reels.) At various times, Walton offered prints in the two 8mm gauges in addition to 16mm and 9.5mm, though in time the formats were whittled down until only Super-8 remained.

An earlier generation was offered 9.5mm prints by Pathéscope Ltd, many of them short extracts of 30 or 60 feet, but several also in longer versions. The 300-foot one-reelers (termed 'Super reels') roughly equated to single 1,000-foot reels of 35mm and tended to be retitled: *The Property Man*, a Keystone two-reeler, became a one-reel abridgment called *Charlie on the Boards; The Vagabond* was cut to one reel as *Gypsy Life, The Rink* yielded a brace of one-reelers, known as *Waiter!* and *Rolling Around*, while *The Adventurer* was rechristened *Freedom For Ever.* The author's Pathéscope print of *Between Showers* (correctly titled for once) is sub-titled 'Charlie Chaplin as he was 20 years ago', a statement entirely true in 1934. There were also some two-reel editions, as in an above-average print of *The Bank*, retitled *Charlie Detective.* Pathéscope would remake the sub-titling, usually renaming Edna Purviance (*qv*) in the process; in *Charlie Detective* she becomes 'Helen'. There were occasional absurdities, as when 'Helen' types out a note only for the insert to be amended to a *handwritten* letter; but these are otherwise worthwhile editions. Shortly before the company's demise in 1960, Pathéscope realized that 9.5mm was being eclipsed, and started to offer 8mm releases. One of these was a two-reel version of *Shoulder Arms*, fine in itself until the conclusion, when the original 'dream' ending is replaced by library footage of a tickertape parade presumably intended for Private Chaplin, superimposing also a portrait of Chaplin in uniform plus the legend 'Charles Spencer Chaplin', rather as if he'd

captured the Kaiser in real life. Titling on this and other Pathéscope/First Nationals suggests origins in the contemporary – and illegal – British reissues from DUK, from whose edition this strange postscript seems to derive. It is likely that Pathéscope did not know of the films' true copyright status when acquiring them. Though long a specialist interest (as ciné in general is becoming), 9.5mm enthusiasts are a determined band, and a brief attempt was made in the 1970s to offer new releases under the name 'Novascope'. One of Novascope's releases at this time was version of *A Day's Pleasure*. A few other First Nationals were around – *A Dog's Life*, the aforementioned *Shoulder Arms*, a version of *Pay Day* chopped into separate, retitled extracts and a very rare six-reel 8mm version of *The Kid* – but of the latter-day features, only the public domain original of *The Gold Rush* (issued by various distributors) was available until the mid-1970s. In September 1976, Chaplin finally made some of his own package available (via RBC Films) in Super-8 sound, but initially on a 15-year lease, so that the prints would have to be returned after a fixed period (unless they wore out!). This idea, otherwise unheard of in the 8mm world (except for an earlier release of Griffith's *The Birth of a Nation*), seems to have been dropped soon after, to be replaced by outright sales on a no-strings basis, with the leasing agreements quietly forgotten.

Today, those seeking Chaplin films for home consumption have to rely mostly on second-hand prints or, more commonly, video releases (*qv*). On the subject of Chaplin issues not based on physical film, perhaps the most unusual release is a short clip from *The Champion* in the form of a do-it-yourself flicker book. This was published by the National Museum of Photography, Film and Television in Bradford, West Yorkshire, using frame enlargements supplied by the British Film Institute. The individual frames can be bolted together in sequence, so that Charlie is seen practising with barbells before pausing for a swig of beer.

(See also: Abandoned projects; Alcohol; Documentaries; Essanay; *Face On the Bar Room Floor, The; Fireman, The; His Regeneration; His Trysting Place;* Keystone; Kirtley, Virginia; Mutual; Reissues; Sound; Suicide; Television; United Artists)

HOW TO MAKE MOVIES 🎩

(unreleased Chaplin film)
When Chaplin began his association with First National (*qv*), a new studio was built for him at La Brea Avenue, Los Angeles. The comedian's own record of its construction, combined with footage taken on the set, formed the basis for a semi-documentary to be called *How To Make Movies.* Chaplin hoped to persuade First National to release the item as part of his contracted number of comedies, but they would not accept it; for this reason, the film remained unedited and untitled until historians Kevin Brownlow and David Gill, armed with cutting instructions and a title list, assembled a completed version for their 'Thames Silents' presentation at the 1982 London Film Festival. Chaplin had used extracts from the film in his introduction to *The Chaplin Revue* (*qv*) and within a much later documentary, *The Gentleman Tramp* (*qv*); not included was footage of Chaplin's golfing routine with Eric Campbell (*qv*), taken in 1917. According to Brownlow and Gill, this had been intended as the final comedy for Mutual (*qv*), tentatively called *The Golf Links*; it was remade later for *The Idle Class* (*qv*). Brownlow and Gill's *Unknown Chaplin* (*qv*) had been based initially upon this very footage, and much of it can be seen in this series; extracts also appear in *Chaplin's Goliath* (detailed in the **Eric Campbell** entry).

Scenes in *How To Make Movies* include a view of the undeveloped land, where Albert Austin (*qv*), as an Arabian-clad magician, causes the studio to develop (its swift construction being shown by stop-motion). The result, disguised as half-timbered English cottages, sets the scene for Chaplin's arrival. 'The boss' is driven to the premises by Kono, his Japanese chauffeur. Chaplin acknowledges the camera with a tip of his cap and enters the building. Secretary Nelly Bly Baker (*qv*) brings the mail (a significant amount), which Chaplin reads. In turn, valet Tom Harrington brings the tramp costume. The supporting players and technicians are sparked into action by an excited cry of 'He's here!'. Harrington brings Chaplin's 'greatest treasures', his boots, from a high-security vault, earning his employer's ire for treating them less than delicately. Having delegated the mail to his valet, Chaplin makes a hasty exit, pausing to pluck a lemon from one of the studio's many trees. He takes a

How To Make Movies *preserves this abandoned segment with Eric Campbell; the golfing idea was later to resurface in* The Idle Class
BFI Stills, Posters and Designs

bite of the sour fruit then offers it to his unseen audience. He narrowly misses a drenching as the pool is being filled, then startles his carpenters into action by suddenly appearing behind them. There follow glimpses of the laboratory (with manager Charles Levin), cutting rooms, and Chaplin himself inspecting the newly developed footage. Described under *The Chaplin Revue* is a scene in which Chaplin pretends to rehearse Edna Purviance, Henry Bergman and Loyal Underwood (all *qv*). The next scenes show Chaplin applying make-up and pretending to direct a young actress, with whom he exchanges flirtatious mannerisms. It was in part these scenes, amid the many other unfamiliar shots, that first alerted Brownlow and Gill to Chaplin's intended purpose for this footage. The actors are plainly seen reading scripts, something never employed by Chaplin in silent films, thus emphasizing a desire to stage such moments for a purpose outside of the studio's customary home movies. A return both to the studio pool and the technique of stop-motion shows Edna and some other young ladies change from their day clothes into swimsuits. Among those joining them at the pool is the large-framed Tom Wood, who provides an impressive display of diving. Chaplin, now in costume, is seen trimming his prop moustache. This leads into the golfing sketch, first with Albert Austin and John Rand (*qv*), then in the footage with Eric Campbell. At the end of the day, Chaplin returns to his studio bungalow, placing the priceless boots into a desk drawer. After changing back

into his street clothes, he enters the limousine but pauses to blow a farewell kiss prior to being driven away.

How to Make Movies has received several screenings over the years, but has never been made available to collectors. A transcript of the film, written by Jeffrey T. Vance, was published in the March 1993 edition of *Classic Times*. Vance points out that much of the footage was taken during Chaplin's creative lull around the time of *Sunnyside* (*qv*), as evidenced by the presence of the same supporting actors and costumes. He suggests also that Chaplin probably intended to use the earlier footage with Campbell as a tribute to his late colleague.

(See also: Abandoned projects; Bell, Monta; Costume; Documentaries, compilations; Home movies; Kono, Toraichi; Reeves, Alf; Reissues; Sport; Wilson, Jack; Wilson, Tom)

HOWELL, ALICE
(1888–1961)

(Chaplin films *qv*)
Petite, somewhat tubby comedienne, among whose trademarks were an eccentric mode of dress, a tall hairdo that compensated for a lack in height, and a willingness to do physical comedy that would put many of her male colleagues to shame. A profile in *Pictures and Picturegoer* of June 1917 expresses the opinion that Alice Howell was unique, regardless of such considerations as gender. Alice Howell was born in New York, of Irish stock, and according to her *Pictures* interview, was on the vaudeville stage as a child. Her entry in the *Motion Picture Herald*'s 'Blue Book' for 1930 mentions an appearance in musical comedy during 1907, then five years in the more downmarket area of burlesque (it also cites her year of birth as 1892, but the earlier date quoted above is believed to be correct). This was followed by three years in vaudeville with her husband, as 'Howell and Howell'. When her spouse was afflicted with tuberculosis, he was ordered to California for his health; Alice went along as nurse and, with the end of their vaudeville career, looked around for alternative employment. Alice was recruited by Keystone (*qv*), initially in minor bits. Kalton C. Lahue and Sam Gill (in their *Clown Princes and Court*

Jesters) note that she was rather wasted at Keystone, as evidenced by her rôles in the Chaplin films: she is among the rough café types of *Caught in a Cabaret*, a spectator in *The Knockout*, Mack Swain's wife in *Mabel's Married Life* and the dentist's disrobed spouse in *Laughing Gas* (she has been credited also as 'Mrs. Rich' in *His Musical Career*, but this is open to question). Of these, only *Laughing Gas* gives her very much to do; it is therefore unsurprising that she moved to Henry Lehrman's L-KO Comedies, playing alongside Billie Ritchie (see **Impersonators**) and soon becoming the star of the lot. Lahue records her having left L-KO to appear in her own Century Comedies, produced by L-KO's John G. Blystone; the *Pictures* interview refers to her moving from L-KO to her own series at Universal, billed as the 'Howl' Comedies (commencing with *Balloonatics*, featuring Alice taking flight in an airship!). A report in the *Motion Picture News* of 17 August 1917 suggests some experimentation in her screen persona, quoting Century's President, Julius Stern, to the effect that the forthcoming *Hey, Doctor!* would see Miss Howell's return to 'her former type of characterization'. Alice worked latterly with Reelcraft, Selznick and First National (*qv*); at least one of the Universal series, *One Wet Night*, was made available to collectors in home-movie form. Stan Laurel (*qv*), who had his own stint at L-KO after her departure (and whose later features *Swiss Miss* and *Block-Heads* credited Blystone as director) once cited Alice Howell among the greatest comediennes of the screen.

(See also: Home movies; Lehrman, Henry; Risqué humour; Swain, Mack)

THE IDLE CLASS

(Chaplin film)
Released by First National, 25 September 1921. Produced, written and directed by Charles Chaplin. Photographed by Rollie Totheroh. Working title: *Vanity Fair.* Two reels.

With Charlie Chaplin (tramp/rich man), Edna Purviance (Edna, the rich man's wife), Henry Bergman (sleeping tramp/stout guest), Lita Grey, Lillian McMurray (maidservants), Allan Garcia, John Rand (irate golfer), Mack Swain (large golfer, Edna's father), Rex Storey, Loyal Underwood.

A trainload of the Idle Rich arrives in Miami. One of them, Edna, expects her husband to meet her. Travelling in a baggage compartment is one of the Idle Poor, Charlie, equipped with hand luggage and golf clubs. Edna's husband – coincidentally, Charlie's double – has received her telegram asking him to be at the station for 10 a.m. It is 10:27, but her absent-minded spouse has yet to leave his hotel. 'Glad you're not drinking,' says the telegram. Edna and entourage, weary of waiting, set off in a cab. Charlie hitches a ride on the back, but has to catch up after the taxi hits a bump. The husband sets off, unaware that he has forgotten his trousers. Fortunately, his *déshabille* is concealed by the fortuitous passing of a man carrying curtains. He enters a telephone booth and, searching for change, suddenly realizes his dilemma. He tries to exit, but retreats when seeing a party of ladies. Using his cane as earpiece, he pretends to make a call. Edna's taxi pulls up outside. Charlie bids adieu to the driver while Edna and staff enter the hotel. The

husband swipes a newspaper from another guest and, posing as a midget, crouches behind it as a means of returning to his suite. Edna and the staff are present on his return, but he manages to leap into bed unnoticed. Husband and wife greet each other curtly. That afternoon, the husband receives a note: 'I will occupy other rooms until you stop drinking.' The husband turns his back, gazes at his wife's portrait, then seems to sob uncontrollably. Turning again, he is seen to be calmly shaking a cocktail. At this time, his wife goes horseback riding. Charlie, meanwhile, is at the golf course. He forms the tee, prepares his swing, then realizes he has no golf ball. He tries to obtain a ball through 'accidentally' kicking one along, but its owner is too vigilant. A more genuine accident is Charlie's acquisition of more clubs when one of his own hooks on to those of a passerby. A golf ball lands beside Charlie, who proceeds to use it himself. When its owner comes to protest, Charlie helps him to look for it. Another, much larger player hits a ball in their direction. Charlie convinces the other player that it is his. The delighted golfer plays it through. He and Charlie proceed as the best of friends, but the larger man follows irately. He catches them up, and Charlie continues along the links, unaware that his new acquaintance is being beaten to a pulp. Charlie hits the ball straight into the open mouth of a sleeping tramp. The ball bobs up and down as the tramp breathes. Charlie, noticing Edna riding by, absently treads on the tramp's stomach. The ball flies into the air and returns whence it came. Another tread to the stomach enables Charlie to retrieve it permanently. By the roadside, Charlie gazes at the elegant horsewoman. He fantasizes over rescuing her from a runaway horse, marrying her and starting a family. The dream concludes as Edna departs. The large man pauses to drink from a bottle of whisky. Charlie sets down two golf balls. His first swing hits the large man's face; the second smashes his bottle of booze. He is reduced to tears. Charlie meets the other golfer, who sports a swollen eye. Charlie hurries away, accidentally trampling the big man's straw hat. He does not see the culprit but, when the other golfer arrives to reclaim the ball, starts to throttle him. Another equestrienne dismounts for a rest. Charlie sees her reclining figure and, wondering if his fantasy has come true, goes to her 'rescue'. When she turns out

to be rather plain, Charlie continues with his golf. The swollen-eyed golfer insists on taking a shot ahead of Charlie; in consequence, he disappears down a mudhole. That evening, Edna is hostess at a costume ball. Her husband, dressed in medieval armour, has been sent a note promising Edna's forgiveness if he attends the party. Edna, dressed as Marie Antoinette, looks around for her absent husband. He is upstairs, trying to take a drink, but stymied when his visor becomes jammed shut. Outside, Charlie sits on a park bench. A pickpocket's arm appears from behind and tries to rob Charlie's neighbour. Charlie is blamed, and has to dodge a policeman. He escapes by stepping through a limousine, from which party guests are emerging. Charlie joins the party, unnerved at first by a stout policeman. Also present is the golfer with the swollen eye, who drops his invitation on entering. Charlie picks it up and thus gains admission. The stout policeman turns out to be another costumed guest. Edna's husband, his visor still trapped, blunders his way downstairs. Charlie receives a summons to see Edna, who takes him for her husband in tramp costume. Charlie is surprised by such affection from a stranger, and amazed once more when attacked by her unrecognized husband. The armour-clad man is led away. Edna introduces Charlie to her father, who is dressed in Scottish regalia. He is the large man from the golf course, and Charlie's instinct is to run, but the reception is cordial. Father introduces her daughter and son-in-law to some guests. When Charlie claims they are not married, father takes this as an insult to his daughter and proceeds to hit Charlie. Father chases him across the dance floor, but Charlie gives him the slip. Edna has fainted and been taken upstairs; a servant brings word for Charlie to join her. In their suite, the husband attacks Charlie once more, and is dragged away by her father. The husband explains who he is, and efforts are made to open the visor. Charlie finally achieves the task by means of a can opener. There is astonishment all round, and Charlie is ordered to leave. After he has gone, Edna has a change of heart, believing they owe Charlie an apology. Outside, the chauffeur, mistaking Charlie for the husband, offers to drive him. Charlie declines. Father catches him up, extending a hand of friendship. Charlie accepts then, pointing to something imaginary on the ground, persuades

The Idle Class: *a trouserless husband hides in bed ...*

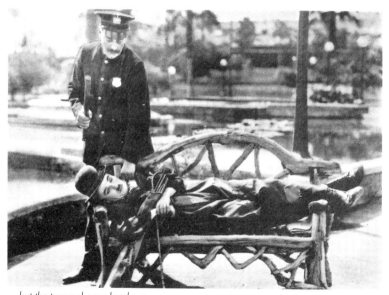

... but the tramp sleeps elsewhere

blanket aversion based on his 'crudities' meant losing an opportunity to savour the 'really fine things about Chaplin's acting' that lay in between. *The Idle Class* was considered 'not as penetratingly human as "The Kid" and "Shoulder Arms," but Chaplin does fine work in it, and it is more free from slapstick than some of his earlier productions'. Particular praise was earned by Charlie's wistful contemplation of the wealthy woman: 'Just watch for that, "O well, I'm a poor bum and she's a swell lady" expression when the girl on horseback rides away from him. There's philosophy in a flash.'

(See also: Abandoned projects; Alcohol; Cars; Costume; Dreams; Dual rôles; First National; Garcia, Allan; *Kid, The*; Left-handedness; Mutual; Parks; Policemen; Rand, John; Reissues; *Shoulder Arms*; Sport; Swain, Mack; Trick photography; Twists and transformations; Underwood, Loyal)

THE IMMIGRANT

(Chaplin film)
Released by Mutual, 17 June 1917. Written and directed by Charles Chaplin. Photographed by Rollie Totheroh. Two reels. 1,809 feet.

With Charlie Chaplin (himself, as the immigrant), Edna Purviance (girl), Eric Campbell (head waiter), Henry Bergman (large woman on boat/artist), Albert Austin (seasick Russian/diner), Loyal Underwood (pint-sized passenger), Janet Miller Sully (passenger), John Rand (crew member/drunk in restaurant), James T. Kelly (crew member/old man in restaurant), Frank J. Coleman (see below).

father to bend. Charlie delivers a swift kick, then runs into the distance.

Among the First National films, *The Idle Class* has most often been compared to Chaplin's Mutuals. The stylistic resemblance was explained somewhat when the never-released *How To Make Movies* (*qv*) and the subsequent *Unknown Chaplin* series (*qv*) revealed an earlier version of the golf routine that had been shot for an abandoned Mutual subject. Charlie's fellow-golfers were to have been Albert Austin and Eric Campbell (both *qv*), thus accounting for Campbell's presence in stills seemingly from a film released four years after his death.

In a rave review of 1 October 1921, Fritz Tidden of the *Moving Picture World* thought it 'hardly necessary to pick it to pieces' but singled out the golf scene as containing 'the most hilarious moments'. Tidden also felt obliged to record the total absence of 'vulgarity', a topic perhaps raised most frequently by the comedian's earlier detractors. The *New York Times* of 26 September 1921 reviewed not merely the film but Chaplin himself, being aware of both his huge following and of an admittedly large minority of dissenters. The reviewer did not take issue with those whose refined tastes excluded them from enjoying Chaplin's work, save to suggest that a

A steamship is ferrying impoverished folk to the New World. Among its passengers are an elderly, ailing widow and her daughter. Charlie is hanging over a ship's rail, apparently very ill but in fact hauling up a fish. The energetic fish is allowed to fall beside a seasick passenger, biting his nose. Charlie takes the air, countering the ship's swaying with his own sliding gait. Charlie dodges to the opposite side of the ship to avoid a Russian, who is martyred to *mal de mer*; once there, he is nearly in the firing line of another nausea victim, and returns whence he came. Charlie is unaffected until the Russian sits beside him. Fortunately, all this is forgotten when the dinner bell is rung. Charlie is among the last to reach the galley, tripping into and rolling along with a large woman passenger. Once seated, he shares with the Russian a plate of soup that slides to and fro. The girl, her mother asleep, enters the galley. Gallant Charlie offers her his place at the table, pausing to gaze at the girl before his stomach, and the rolling ship, dictate a swift departure. Charlie eases his nausea with a brisk stroll. 'More rolling' (according to a title) takes the form of a game of dice between Charlie and some of the grubbier passengers. Charlie's eccentric way with dice annoys his fellow-players but pays dividends; when Charlie scoops the pot, a burly gambler goes berserk and breaks up the group. The poor loser hurls a bucket, striking an innocent bystander who is engaged in protesting love to his lady friend. The burly man exits in fury (kicking the man who was flattened by the bucket), and the game resumes without him. He returns after stealing money from Edna's mother, who is asleep and unattended. Edna discovers the loss while the man is now risking all against Charlie's card skills. Charlie (who sneaks a look at his own cards when dealing) wins again, and the big man threatens trouble; Charlie, prepared, draws a revolver, keeping him covered by aiming the gun through his legs while retrieving his hat and cane. Charlie, combining a tip of the hat with a thumb to the nose, makes his exit, leaving his opponent to a futile rage. Charlie counts the money. The Russian he had met earlier is seasick again, having outstayed everyone else in the galley. To avoid the Russian's heaving, Charlie removes his hat from the firing lines and sits near Edna and her mother. Edna, in tears, tells Charlie of the loss of her mother's money. Without Edna's knowledge, Charlie places some money in her pocket. Concerned that he has put in perhaps a little too much, Charlie retrieves a small amount and takes his leave. He has been observed by a ship's officer, who accuses him of being a pickpocket. Edna is summoned and, on checking her pocket, is amazed to discover Charlie's cash gift. The officer, similarly baffled, returns to other duties while Charlie consoles the emotional girl. The Statue of Liberty comes into view; as the new arrivals ponder 'the land of liberty', they are abruptly roped back by the crew. An attendant, pushing people around, earns a carefully-delivered kick in the pants from Charlie. Edna and her mother are first past the barrier; Charlie, the next to go, bids them farewell. 'Later – hungry and

broke' (according to a title), Charlie finds a silver dollar outside a restaurant. Having determined that it is indeed a coin rather than an expectoration, Charlie pockets the money, unaware that it has gone straight through and returned to the pavement. He enters the restaurant, an artists' café, taking a seat beside another customer. As Charlie ponders the menu, the huge, sinister-looking head waiter expects him to remove his hat. The head waiter eventually does it for him (twice, no less) until Charlie, getting the idea, momentarily replaces the hat then makes it spring into the air. The hat stays off. Unknown to Charlie, Edna is sitting nearby. The head waiter brings Charlie's order of French bread, coffee and beans. As he bends, Charlie gives him a start by blowing his nose. He also startles his neighbour by reacting to the scalding hot meal. At first, Charlie ekes out his food by carefully eating one bean at a time, then fills his knife with beans and dunks the bread in his coffee. His outraged neighbour departs. Charlie notices Edna and, distracted, dumps a knifeload of beans in his coffee. He greets her joyfully until he notices her black-bordered handkerchief, indicating that her mother has died. Charlie expresses his sympathy, then attracts the attention of the indifferent head waiter. Edna is brought a plate of beans. Elsewhere in the café, a drunk becomes difficult and is given a thorough beating by the management prior to being ejected. Charlie enquires as to the problem, and is told he was ten cents short. Nervously, Charlie decides to check his own funds. Realizing the coin has vanished, Charlie practises his boxing technique, unaware that the head waiter is watching. Presented with the bill, Charlie stalls for time by ordering coffee for Edna. An old man takes a seat across the gangway, clutching Charlie's lost silver dollar. Charlie tries to approach him, but the head waiter returns with Edna's coffee. Charlie tries again, but once more the head waiter arrives, bringing coffee for the old man. The dollar is given as payment for the coffee. The coin slides to the floor through a hole in the head waiter's pocket. Charlie stamps his foot over the coin, briefly halting the restaurant's musicians. He has yet to retrieve it when the head waiter returns; fortunately, the head waiter stands on the dollar and thus cannot see it. Charlie is eventually able to distract his attention, grab the coin and pay his bill. The waiter, suspicious, tests the coin by biting it; it bends. Charlie buys more time with another order of

coffee. From another table, a flamboyant gentleman observes Charlie and Edna, framing them between finger and thumb. Charlie returns the scrutiny, using salt and pepper shakers as binoculars. The man joins them, explaining that he is an artist. The coffee is brought, and when the head waiter aggressively demands payment, the artist offers to pick up the tab. Charlie graciously refuses, but once too often; he settles the bill instead by using the generous tip left by the artist. They leave behind a head waiter fuming at the artist's supposed meanness. Outside, a sudden downpour is brightened by Charlie and Edna's new employment as artist's models. Charlie requests 'a couple of dollars on account', and leads Edna away to a registrar's office. Edna coyly demurs, but is carried, kicking and screaming, into matrimony.

Charlie dodges a seasick Albert Austin in **The Immigrant**

The Immigrant probably represents all the best elements of Chaplin, in a slapstick-punctuated comedy of situation and manners, allowing time for genuine, discreetly-placed emotion. An oft-repeated account maintains that Chaplin spent four days and nights without sleep, editing *The Immigrant* into around 2,000 feet from a massive 90,000. Detailed under the entry for *Unknown Chaplin* is how the ship's rocking motion was achieved and, more importantly, the manner in which this seamlessly constructed comedy was actually conceived in reverse.

As is usual with Chaplin's earlier work, *The Immigrant* circulates in many versions of varying quality and completeness. The sharpest available material derives from dupe negatives for a sound reissue, though height and the left of image are cropped owing to the smaller frame imposed by the sound track. The lateral trimming obscures the old man in the restaurant and the registrar's door at the finale, making it difficult to read the legend 'marriage licenses'.

Later versions are also subject to minor cuts, one of them a section in which Charlie, having fled from a seasick Albert Austin (*qv*), has to dodge an equally nauseous little man, Loyal Underwood (*qv*), being carried to the rail by his large wife, played by Henry Bergman (*qv*). The jump in continuity is filled by a cut back to Edna and her mother, probably trimmed from the end of the shot in which they are introduced. This applies to the 'Chaplin Festival' copy (bearing the 'silhouette' titles described elsewhere), both in American prints and an Equity-British copy in the author's collection. Another of the author's prints, from a full-frame copy with 'illuminated' titles, should ideally be closer to the original, but deletes the same gag and moves the whole introduction of Edna and her mother to this point. The opening scenes of ship and passengers are deleted entirely. Fortunately, the BBC *Chaplin SuperClown* copy seems to match the original version.

Stanley J. 'Tiny' Sandford (*qv*), who later appeared with Chaplin in *The Circus* and *Modern Times* (both *qv*), has long been credited with rôles in some of the Mutual comedies. One of these is the fierce, bearded gambler in *The Immigrant*'s first reel; in documenting Sandford for *The Laurel & Hardy Encyclopedia*, the author expressed the opinion that the gambler in this film is far too short to be Sandford and, through the facial fuzz, resembles instead Frank J. Coleman (*qv*). Coleman may be seen in reel two as the restaurant owner, where Henry Bergman reappears as the artist; others taking dual rôles are Albert Austin, John Rand and James T. Kelly (all *qv*).

(See also: Abandoned projects; Boats, ships; Bradbury, Kitty; *Day's Pleasure, A;* Dual rôles; Reissues; Sickness; Stamps, coins; Television; Titling; Twists and Transformations; Video releases)

IMPERSONATORS 🎩

(Chaplin films *qv*)
'Are you Programming CHARLES CHAPLIN, or a Deputy?' enquired an Essanay trade advertisement of March

1915, announcing the comedian in 'his original and laughable impersonations of HIMSELF'. The 'Chaplin Craze' (*qv*) brought a succession of imitators and impersonators, a few of them quite good, but the majority of whom paled drastically alongside the original. A famous story concerns the Crystal Cinema in New York, which ran Chaplin films exclusively for perhaps a decade. The theatre did good business until the week they decided to screen a film starring one his imitators. The resultant drop in patronage ensured an immediate return to the Chaplin-only policy.

A distinction must be drawn between Chaplin's 'imitators' and 'impersonators'. The former copied his style and appearance with no apparent claim, or stated intent, to deceive; the latter presented a facsimile of the sort designed to convince the public that Chaplin was genuinely on show, as with the lookalikes employed to provide linking footage for the 'bogus Chaplins' (*qv*). (This, of course, would not have applied to those offering an acknowledged impersonation as part of an act.) During an attempt to enjoin these spurious films in 1917, the *Motion Picture World* noted the absence, at that time, of any 'legal obstacle to a colorable imitation of an actor's screen personality' of the sort applicable to trademarked goods. 'Colorable imitations clearly meant to deceive,' it continued, 'are prohibited by law.'

When early cinema first began to be documented, the Chaplin imitators posed a interesting problem to historians. H.D. Waley's published list of known Chaplin Keystones, in the Spring 1938 *Sight and Sound*, included two frame enlargements with the question, 'Is this Charlie Chaplin?' The answer turned out to be 'no'. One picture was very obviously Billy West, of whom more later; the other presented either West or a similarly convincing Chaplin lookalike dressed in period costume. The latter was regarded as a possible fragment of *Tango Tangles*, unavailable at that time, but believed to include a sequence taking place at a costume party. The film's subsequent recovery destroyed that theory, but this example may serve to illustrate how much confusion these films have caused, both in the past and even today. During the 1980s, the author examined a reel identified by an internationally-respected archive as 'Charlie Chaplin 1917'. The year was presumably taken from the stock codes

Impersonators: Billy West was the most accomplished Chaplin lookalike
By courtesy of Claudia Sassen

in the film base itself, but the images contained on it were most definitely extracts from the Billy West comedies. Since that time, another of West's subjects (*His Day Out*, a.k.a. *The Barber*) has made its way into European TV distribution as a Chaplin comedy.

The vast majority of lookalikes were amateurs, whose existence did not trouble Chaplin, but served instead as a form of advertisement, particularly when – as for a screening of *The Kid* in Manchester during 1921 – such people were recruited by local exhibitors. According to a 1919 report in the *Motion Picture News*, a Chaplin lookalike was engaged by William Brandt, manager of Feltman's Open Aerodrome, Coney Island, to publicize *Sunnyside*. The impersonator led a cow along the busy Surf Avenue, using the animal's 'milk bag' to squirt away 'every noticeable chunk of dirt in the street'. The result was a huge crowd, and a request from the police for Mr Brandt to 'put the cow in a barn'. The *News* excused the absence of illustrations on the grounds that their photographer's camera had been overturned, and its plates broken, on each of his four attempts to take pictures within the frenzied gathering. Nor did Chaplin object to stage comedians presenting an imitation of his persona, as did Stan Laurel (*qv*) in his vaudeville days. One should add that, as Chaplin's former understudy, Laurel had a reasonable entitlement to perform such an imitation. Chaplin's objections were reserved instead for those who sought to compete directly in the medium of film. Of these, the most accomplished was the aforementioned Billy West (1893–1975), whose Chaplin imitation extended to the point of sleeping with his hair in curlers and, incredibly, replicating the original's left-handed violin playing. West, real name Roy Weissberg, was born in Russia but taken to the United States in childhood. He worked variously as a cartoonist and vaudeville comic until his convincing Chaplin act brought an offer to work in films. West's 'King Bee' comedies of 1917–18 are quite funny but, according to John McCabe, earned the contempt of trade papers, in which West's name would sometimes be printed entirely in lower case. West made no claim to be Chaplin. Indeed, a full-page ad in the *Moving Picture World* of 30 June 1917 announces his first five subjects with the comedian's name in gigantic type. (Rather cheekily, West is billed as the 'funniest man on earth', an uncomfortably similar claim to that recently made for Chaplin.) Apologists for West have suggested that his portrayal offered an alternate dimension of the 'tramp' character, and that his plots bore no resemblance to Chaplin's. The former point has some justification, but not the latter, as some of West's films are clearly modelled on situations in the Chaplin comedies. To the uninitiated, the easiest way to determine a West comedy is to look for a squarishness of face (quite apparent in close-ups) and, ironically, the presence of Stan Laurel's future partner, Oliver Hardy, as an equivalent to Eric Campbell (*qv*). Just to confuse matters further, West had also managed to obtain the services of ex-Chaplin foil Leo White (*qv*). Another King Bee player who worked with both Chaplin and Laurel & Hardy was Charley Chase (*qv*). Among the 'Funniosities From Charlie's Mail' recounted by Elsie Codd for *Pictures and Picturegoer* (29 November 1919) was a letter from someone who claimed to appreciate Chaplin's work, but would 'enjoy it more if you would be yourself and not always be trying to imitate Billy West'. Chaplin, it seems, was keeping the letter 'against the time when he notices symptoms of acquiring a swelled head'. West's later films saw his abandonment of the Chaplin image in favour of a straw-hatted *boulevardier*.

Two others were, in some quarters, believed to have had an at least partial claim to elements of the 'tramp' character: ex-Karno man Billie Ritchie, who made his films for Lehrman's L-KO studio, made some direct and doubtless overstated claims, essentially that he had worn a similar costume as long ago as 1887. Ritchie's persona was similar to Chaplin's, featuring the same large boots but with a slightly broader moustache, a snug-fitting frock coat rather than a tight cutaway, and somewhat narrower trousers. While the 1887 date is a trifle extravagant, there is evidence that at least part of Ritchie's ensemble may have dated back to around 1909. Some interest lies within a UK trade ad for Ritchie's L-KOs, placed in the *Bioscope* for 31 December 1914 by their British distributor, the Trans-Atlantic Film Company. It dubs Ritchie 'Our Own 'Ero of the 'Alls' (a strangely Cockney sobriquet for a Glaswegian), describing him also as having been 'Famed as the Drunk in Karno's "Mummingbirds" [*sic*]'. (Both Ritchie and Billie Reeves, brother of Alf Reeves [*qv*], have been cited as originators of the rôle.) *Vis-à-vis* Chaplin and Ritchie, one might ponder a likely sequence of connections in the public mind. An old song, 'The Moon Shines Bright on Billericay' (known to Americans as 'Red Wing', about a Red Indian maid), has been given colloquial lyrics (some of them clean) since the 18th century; the First World War in turn brought still another lyric, 'The Moon Shines Bright on Charlie Chaplin'. There seems no reason to connect 'Billericay' to 'Charlie Chaplin' unless one considers the vulgar children's lyric (sung by vulgar children) which goes: 'The moon shines bright on Billy Ritchie/His arse is itchy ...' At the risk of seeming fanciful, the punning reference to Ritchie seems to have progressed into a stylistic comparison with Chaplin. (In passing, Uno Asplund reports the Swedish censors of 1915 believing – incredibly – that *The Rounders* did not feature Chaplin at all, but Billie Ritchie!) Chaplin tried, unsuccessfully, to take legal action against Ritchie. Despite his court victory, Ritchie's story has a sad conclusion. Having continued with Lehrman after the latter's departure from L-KO, Ritchie died in 1921, the result – incredibly – of an attack by an ostrich while making one of his comedies. The author has been in contact with Frank Hill, a relative of Ritchie, who has made some interesting points. One is in verifying Ritchie's birthdate as 1874, rather than 1879 or 1877, as is sometimes quoted. Another is Ritchie's connection with the Hill family, which suggests some hitherto-unsuspected link with Chaplin through his mother, Hannah Chaplin (*qv*), *née* Hill. David Robinson notes that Ritchie's wife, Winifred, and her daughter, Wyn, were among Hannah's close friends after her move to America. This, and Chaplin's employment of Winifred as wardrobe mistress following her husband's death, may perhaps be explained by this implied family connection.

Probably not in the categories of imitator or impersonator was another Karno veteran, Fred Kitchen (1872–1951), whom many in the variety profession saw as the Chaplin character's true prototype, albeit in basic, undeveloped form. Though far from vociferous, Kitchen was drawn into conversation on the matter at least once, in a provincial paper, the *Nottingham Evening News*. In the edition of 8 December 1917, Kitchen recalled Chaplin having once arrived at the Leicester Palace, bearing a note from Fred Karno (*qv*) with a request to see what could be done with him. Kitchen wrote Chaplin a small part but, unimpressed, sent him back to London. Some time later, Kitchen heard that Chaplin had remained in America and gone into films. 'I went to see one of his pictures ... I was astounded; it was Charlie with my trousers, my boots, my coat and hat, and using all the mannerisms which I had for years affected. He must have a wonderful memory to have got them so perfectly in the short time that he was with me.' Kitchen went on to describe how he had posed in costume for a new photograph, which his four-year-old daughter had insisted was Charlie Chaplin. 'A few years ago,' he added, 'I had a very good offer to go to America for film work. It was very hard to have to refuse, but I have no doubt that if I had gone I should have been accused of copying Chaplin.' (It should be mentioned in passing that Kitchen was announced for a series of British film shorts for the Premier Agency, based in Manchester, in the early summer of 1914.)

Although it is fair to say that one or two comedians may have anticipated Chaplin in terms of superficial appearance, it was Chaplin who gave that image a character, thus investing it with the qualities that made it so attractive to would-be competitors.

Theodore Huff noted a brace of imitators in European films: a French comedian named André Séchan did a Chaplin routine as 'Monsieur Jack', while Germany, where the genuine Chaplin comedies would have been unseen at least after America's entry into the First World War, made do with the ersatz 'Charlie Kaplin', the pseudonym of Ernst Bosser. There are reports that Britain's National Film and Television Archive holds at least one film by a Russian Chaplin imitator who worked in Germany, named variously as Arkadi (or Arkady) Boytler (or Boitler). Closer in terms of name and geography was a Mexican, Carlos Amador, alias 'Charlie Aplin'. Chaplin eventually won a legal judgment against him in 1925, the only such action he pursued. He was advised not to sue Billy West, and seems to have ignored the smaller fish, among them one-time Keystone Cop Bobby Dunn and, more intriguingly, Ray Hughes (of the 'Pyramid Comedies'). As Kalton C. Lahue has noted, the Hughes films were regarded more as imitations of West's imitation; a contemporary UK advertisement, published in the *Kinematograph and Lantern Weekly* of 19 September 1918, deals Hughes the further blow of misspelling his name 'Hugh'. It is known that Chaplin, aware of his imitators' shortcomings, would parody them for the amusement of friends.

There was even less to be done about those who employed Chaplinesque elements but were not direct lookalikes. Syd Chaplin (*qv*), of course, did not offend his brother when adopting a similar costume at Keystone (*qv*). It is well known that Harold Lloyd, prior to adopting his familiar persona, portrayed a character called 'Lonesome Luke', whose costume was an inversion of Chaplin's (tight trousers rather than baggy, loose coat rather than snug); less often reported is that his 'Luke' plots tended to be lifted from Chaplin's recent releases. Larry Semon did not ape Chaplin's appearance, but sometimes copied his situations (see *A Night in the Show*). In fairness, it should be emphasized that Chaplin's influence on screen comedy was near-universal, and that few of its practitioners did not owe him at least a small debt.

In-house impersonators were, of course, a different thing. *Unknown Chaplin* (*qv*) has footage of Chaplin and Harry Lauder impersonating each other, commemorated also by a photo in Chaplin's book, *My Life in Pictures*. Mabel Normand, herself often called 'the female Chaplin', laments Charlie's mannerisms by way of mimicry in *Mabel's Married Life*. Lloyd Bacon (*qv*) plays Charlie's double in *The Floorwalker*, a function performed by Chaplin himself in *The Great Dictator*.

In the November 1989 *Classic Images*, Bo Berglund details a 'female Chaplin' who was active in pictures. Minerva Courtney, in her 'Metropolis Comedies', offered a Chaplin impersonation with no ambiguity: the first, a straight remake of Chaplin's *The Champion*, seems to have been called 'Minerva Courtney in her Impersonation of Charles Chaplin'. This was released in July 1915, as were at least two follow-ups, *Putting One Over* (later a reissue title for Chaplin's *The Masquerader*, in which the gender swap is reversed!) and *Her Job in the Laundry*. At around the same time, Essanay provided its own female Chaplin lookalike when Ruth Stonehouse impersonated him in *Angels Unaware*.

It is worth noting in passing that many Chaplin impersonators have been women, perhaps the result of the comedian's own slight build and delicate features (themselves the secret of his own successful female impersonations). As noted elsewhere, Gloria Swanson (*qv*) turned in a creditable Chaplin pastiche for both *Manhandled* and the much later *Sunset Boulevard*. More recently, TV's educational programme *Sesame Street* has employed a Chaplin lookalike called 'Maria'. One might also mention *Forces' Sweetheart*, an obscure British comedy of 1952 (with two far from obscure British comedians, Michael Bentine and Harry Secombe), which features a whole chorus line doing a Chaplin routine.

Detailed under *Carmen*'s main entry is a burlesque of the Chaplin film as enacted by children. This is mentioned by MacDonald, Conway and Ricci in their Chaplin study, as is a summer 1915 Pathé comedy, *When Charlie Was a Child*, with youngsters portraying Chaplin, Ford Sterling (*qv*), Mabel Normand (*qv*) et al. Another juvenile Chaplin imitation may be found in a Hal Roach 'Our Gang' comedy of 1923, *The Big Show*. According to Leonard Maltin and Richard W. Bann's history of the series, *The Little Rascals: The Life and Times of Our Gang*, the child in question, Andy Samuel, earned his place in the Gang by demonstrating his Chaplin act for producer Hal Roach. *The Big Show* was Samuels' first Gang appearance; he repeated his impersonation in a later entry, *Jubilo, Jr.* (1924). Samuel had earlier been an extra in Chaplin's *The Kid*; after seeing his impersonations in the 'Our Gang' films, the comedian gave him a gold watch inscribed 'From Charlie Chaplin to Andrew Samuel'.

There were many Chaplin lookalike contests organized for children in the 1910s. Milton Berle, later a famous comedian in his own right, once assembled a Chaplin costume in order to go trick-or-treating one Hallowe'en. Though only five, he did a good enough job for a theatre owner to suggest he enter a contest he had organized for youngsters. Young Berle entered and won the prize, a loving cup. Berle later claimed to have played a small rôle in *Tillie's Punctured Romance*. British comedian Sid Field, whose heyday was in the 1940s, idolized Chaplin from boyhood. In the *Leader* magazine of 29 November 1947, Ann Whitfield described how Field 'used to do imitations of him in the streets of Birmingham, and was often moved on by the local police for causing obstruction'. At the time of their conversation, Field had just been to see *Monsieur Verdoux*, and insisted upon quoting and acting out sections. (Field was one of many prominent comedians who, as youngsters, did Chaplin imitations. Eric Morecambe, who with Ernie Wise later formed Britain's top double-act, had early photos of himself with Chaplin hat and moustache.) In June 1917, *Pictures and the Picturegoer* ran a photograph of a ten-year-old girl, Doris Tickner, dressed as Charlie. She and a friend had gone 'egg-collecting' for wounded servicemen, raising £1 6s 9d plus 69 eggs for the hospital in Hendon. Their first trip was made in the costumes of 'ancient and modern jesters', while a subsequent effort saw them dressed as 'Prince Charming and Charlie Chaplin in *One A.M.*'

At around the same time, the magazine reported a full-scale Chaplin lookalike contest, for adults, around the comedian's old haunts in south London. In April 1917, the *Cinema* reported a music-hall comedian who, in a revue staged at the Cheltenham Hippodrome, was drawing large, appreciative crowds with his Chaplin impersonation, even down to the Chaplinesque backward tumble.

The trend was lampooned by the Marx Brothers in one of their stage sketches. In a 1921 skit, *On the*

Mezzanine, they targeted the numerous impersonators of Gallagher & Shean (a vaudeville act that included their uncle Al) in a scene where all four brothers offer that very impersonation for an increasingly bored theatrical agent. When performing the sketch for London audiences in 1922 (by which time it was called *On the Balcony*), they altered the impersonation to one of Charlie Chaplin, who was better known in England.

It is indicative of Chaplin's enduring image that impersonations have continued through the decades. Bert Wheeler does a Chaplin act in the last of his films with Robert Woolsey, *High Flyers* (1937). Sammy Davis Jr did a very creditable impression in one of Nat King Cole's TV shows of the 1950s, and as recently as 1991 ventriloquist Keith Harris appeared in a Chaplin-like costume for the Children's Royal Variety Show. In May 1978 there were reports of a touring company from the West Midlands presenting a 'Charlie Chaplin Show' at the Theatre Royal, Stratford East. Less reputable, in the author's opinion, is a photo-strip involving a Chaplin lookalike and a pin-up girl, published by *Titbits* in the 1970s.

A rather charming story appeared in a British newspaper, the *Sunday People*, on 20 July 1980. It concerned 89-year-old Charlie Delves, a Cornwall resident who had first performed a Chaplin act to amuse his fellow-soldiers in the First World War. Delves was called upon to perform at army concerts, one of them a 40,000-strong gathering at a football ground in Calcutta. He became a school caretaker on returning to civilian life, but continued to do his Chaplin imitation, at least after his retirement, for the benefit of schoolchildren on weekdays and when visiting hospitals on Sundays. In January 1997, some of Britain's tabloids carried a story about two teenagers who had been arrested after a security camera had recorded them doing impressions of Charlie Chaplin. Also of interest is an article from the *South London Press* of 4 October 1985, in which Lawrence Simmons, a 25-year-old trainee actor, was pictured revisiting Chaplin's old south London haunts while dressed in the appropriate costume. In the early 1990s, the author witnessed a young Chaplin lookalike performing a juggling act near London's Carnaby Street. Such things are invariably an act of homage, rather like the silent-comedy-obsessed character in the 1993 film

Benny and Joon, who duplicates Chaplin's 'Dance of the Rolls' from *The Gold Rush*.

Easily the highest-profile Chaplin lookalike of these latter days has been Robert Downey Jr in Richard Attenborough's *Chaplin* (*qv*).

(See also: Animation; *Bond, The*; Caricatures; Censorship; Chaplin, Hannah; *Chase Me, Charlie*; Children; *City Lights*; Dual rôles; Costume; *Funniest Man in the World, The*; Guest appearances; Jamison, William 'Bud'; Karno Company, The; Left-handedness; Lehrman, Henry 'Pathé'; Marx, Groucho; Smoking; Statues; Summerville, George J. 'Slim'; Swain, Mack; Television; Wartime)

IN THE PARK

(Chaplin film)
Released by General Film Company, 18 March 1915. Produced by Essanay. Written and directed by Charles Chaplin. Photographed by Harry Ensign. British title: *Charlie in the Park*. One reel. 994 feet (UK length cited in *Bioscope*).

With Charlie Chaplin (himself), Edna Purviance (nursemaid), Bud Jamison (her boyfriend), Leo White (French Count), Margie Reiger (Count's fiancée), Fred Goodwins (hot dog vendor), Lloyd Bacon (tramp pickpocket). .
In the tranquillity of a park, a top-hatted French Count and his lady love are, to use the old expression, 'spooning'. A nursemaid divides her interest between the couple's romance and that in a novelette. Nearby, Charlie is out for a stroll. He meets perhaps the world's least subtle pickpocket, a tramp who attempts to rifle Charlie's pockets while Charlie, unnoticed, steals a cigarette from the would-be thief. Charlie adds insult to injury by striking a match on the pickpocket's neck. Next, Charlie meets a policeman, recognizing his badge and uniform purely by touch. Continuing on his way, Charlie happens upon the Count and his beloved. He sits beside them on the bench, reacting to their passionate embraces. The nursemaid is joined by her boyfriend, who skips around in dandified contrast with his burly physique. The Frenchman and his girl, still cavorting, push Charlie from the bench. The nursemaid's beau departs for a drink of water. Charlie makes fun of the Count's romance and,

having toppled the man's hat, takes his leave. After bumping into a tree limb and knocking off his own hat with his cane, Charlie sees the nurse. After a brief flirtation, he sits beside her, pretending an interest in her book. The nurse seems unimpressed by Charlie's habit of crossing his leg into her lap. The pickpocket, still at large, helps himself to a purse belonging to the Count's fiancée. The nursemaid's boyfriend, still at the water tap, buys a

Essanay reissued **In the Park** *within a year of its debut*
By courtesy of Claudia Sassen

hot dog from a passing vendor, consuming it before returning to his girl. He finds her being pestered by Charlie, and boots him accordingly. Charlie moves on, to discover the hot dog vendor being robbed of his wares. Charlie intervenes, solely for the purpose of stealing them himself. He passes the Count, taking time to knock off his hat with the string of sausages. Charlie places the sausages in his top pocket, enabling him to make a game of swinging them up to his mouth. The nursemaid's boyfriend trips off to smell the flowers. The pickpocket reappears, removing the sausages from Charlie's pocket in what he believes to be a surreptitious manner. He is unaware that the hook of Charlie's cane is skilfully removing the stolen purse from his own pocket. Charlie walks away, the purse hanging from his cane. The boyfriend buys it from him as a present for the nurse; the thief observes and goes back to claim it. A scuffle breaks out for possession of the

Charlie meets Edna, a pretty nursemaid, **In the Park**

purse, interrupted briefly by the policeman. The nursemaid takes her pram and moves on. By this time Charlie and the pickpocket are hurling bricks at each other; Charlie avoids them but boyfriend, Count and fiancée are knocked cold. The battle over, Charlie hooks the purse on his cane once more. He passes the Count, whose legs kick at Charlie as he regains consciousness. Charlie uses the brick to knock him out again. Backing away from the scene, Charlie blunders into the nursemaid's pram. Her boyfriend awakes and takes a seat beside the sleeping Frenchman and his girl. Charlie presents the purse to the nursemaid, at last scoring a hit. He scores yet another when hurling a brick at her boyfriend, who is dozing beside the other couple. When the policeman arrives, Charlie, remembering the stolen purse, keeps his distance. The policeman gone, he goes back to the nurse, only to be confronted by her angry boyfriend. Charlie finds another bench while the furious man makes a fuss over the purse. The other couple, awakened, think the nurse is being robbed and the Count goes to her rescue. Duty done, he returns to his fiancée, who discovers her own purse is missing. She rejects him and storms off. The distraught Frenchman puts a gun to his head but decides on a different method of suicide. Charlie encounters the sausage vendor once more, who has obtained a new, but not fresh, stock. Charlie departs. The Count's lady has found the policeman, who investigates the theft. The suicidal Count asks for Charlie's assistance and is kicked into the lake. The purse is traced to the boyfriend, who tells the cop that it was bought from Charlie.

Boyfriend and cop confront Charlie, who kicks them into the lake prior to making a dignified exit.

A 'park' comedy in the Keystone mould, *In the Park* is better constructed and more incident-filled than its predecessors. It is sometimes believed to be a Keystone by the uninitiated, partly because of its format, but mostly owing to a reissue of *Caught in the Rain* (*qv*) bearing the same title. Its basic premise, that of a stolen purse or handbag, is essentially that of another Keystone, *Twenty Minutes of Love* (*qv*), but is handled here with greater finesse. The Keystone-like approach of this and the only other one-reeler in the series, *By the Sea* (*qv*), puts into relief the gradual change in Chaplin's style during his time with Essanay. While still selfish, violent and ruthless, the 'Charlie' character has acquired a modicum of grace, particularly apparent during his initial flirtation with the nurse. *Bioscope* of 20 May 1915 thought Chaplin to be 'seen at his best advantage in this riotous farce', pausing to note how Chaplin was, unlike many of his contemporaries, 'always amusing'. 'There seem to be no grey patches in his work,' decided the reviewer. The same cannot be said of many available prints of *In the Park*, which tend to be fairly fuzzy; that used in the BBC's *Chaplin SuperClown* series is better than most, the only serious flaw being a small cut, omitting the moment when a brick strikes the Count's fiancée. In consequence, she seems merely to snuggle beside him instead of being knocked cold. There exists in Britain a superb quality 35mm print (and 16mm reductions probably deriving from it), bearing what seems to be Essanay's original main title (for the UK market, where it was called *Charlie in the Park*). Sub-titles are from an early reissue. The opening scenes and final few seconds have been excised, but this copy would provide the basis for an excellent restoration. Sadly, this 35mm print has not surfaced for public scrutiny.

(See also: Bacon, Lloyd; Costume; Essanay; Goodwins, Fred; Jamison, William 'Bud'; Keystone; Parks; Policemen; Purviance, Edna; Reissues; Television; White, Leo)

INSLEY, CHARLES (A.K.A. INSLEE AND CHARLES E. INSLEY)

(Chaplin films *qv*)
Supporting actor, formerly with Edison, Bison, Kalem and Biograph prior to joining Essanay (*qv*), where he was described in 1915 by the *Moving Picture World* as 'one of the Pioneer West Coast players'. Known films from 1908 include *Skinner's Finish* (Porter/Edison), *The Adventures of Dollie* (Griffith/Biograph), *Where the Breakers Roar* (Griffith/Biograph), *Zulu's Heart* (Griffith/Biograph), *The Girl and the Outlaw* (Griffith/Biograph), *One Touch of Nature* (Griffith/Biograph, 1909), *Tribal Law* (Bison, 1913) and at least one of Kalem's 'Ham and Bud' comedies, *Lotta Coin's Ghost* (1915). With Chaplin, he plays a film director in *His New Job*, Charlie's boss in *Work*, the irate father in *A Woman*, the manager of *The Bank* and is among the audience of *A Night in the Show*. Later non-Chaplin appearances include *Good Little Bad Boy* (L-KO 1917) and *Cold Steel* (1921).

Charles Insley *plays Charlie's splattered boss in* **Work**

JAMES, SIDNEY
(1915–76)

South African-born comic actor, from the stage, Sid James settled in London, and was in turn adopted by Londoners as one of their own, a lovable rogue of near-legendary status. Early on, he was extraordinarily prolific in film character rôles; one of these, *The Lavender Hill Mob* (1951), led eventually to an invitation to support comedian Tony Hancock in his radio series *Hancock's Half-Hour*, starting in 1954. James continued with the show when it transferred to TV in 1956, and remained Hancock's regular sidekick until 1960. His later starring series for TV included *Citizen James*, *Taxi!*, *Two in Clover* and *Bless This House*. In films, he is perhaps best recalled for the long-running *Carry On* series. His contribution to Chaplin's work is as the hucksterish Johnson in *A King in New York* (*qv*)

JAMISON, WILLIAM 'BUD'
(1894–1944)

(Chaplin films *qv*)
Tall (6 feet), hefty supporting actor, born and educated in California; in vaudeville and stock before entering pictures. Jamison's first appearance with Chaplin was as a head waiter, the jealous husband of Edna Purviance (*qv*) in *A Night Out*; he appears in a number of subsequent Essanays, notably as Charlie's opponent in *The Champion*. *In the Park* sees him as an incongruously skittish suitor; in *A Jitney Elopement* he is one of the ineffective police officers; both *The Tramp* and *The Bank* place him among a band of thieves; in *By the Sea* he is again

Edna's jealous husband; he is a soldier in *Carmen*, and one half of the pelted singing duo in *A Night in the Show*. The flophouse sequence shared by *Police* and *Triple Trouble* depicts Jamison as an unexpectedly effeminate guest. He has been reported in the cast of *Shanghaied* but does not seem to be present. Like many others, Jamison spent time with Henry Lehrman's L-KO Comedies. He also worked at the embryonic Hal Roach studio, in its days as Rolin, as early as Harold Lloyd's *Lonesome Luke* series plus some of the first Stan Laurel films; later Roach appearances include the ZaSu Pitts-Thelma Todd short, *Strictly Unreliable* (1932), and *On the Wrong Trek* (1936) with Charley Chase (*qv*). He is also to be seen in some of Clark & McCullough's RKO shorts, and is the golfing buddy of W.C. Fields in his classic Sennett two-reeler, *The Dentist* (1932). Jamison worked sometimes in feature-length subjects, both silent and sound. Notables in the former category are *Dante's Inferno* (1924), Monty Banks' *Play Safe* (1927), also Harry Langdon's *The Chaser* and *Heart Trouble* (both 1928). He was one of the many silent veterans to find regular work in Columbia's sound shorts, including frequent appearances with the Three Stooges (one of which, the 1934 *Men in Black*, was nominated for an Oscar). Among numerous others are Buster Keaton's *Jail Bait* and *Love Nest On Wheels* (both 1937), Langdon's *A Dog-Gone Mix-Up* and *Sue My Lawyer* (both 1938) and Charley Chase's *The Heckler* (1940).

(See also: Essanay; Impersonators; Keaton, Buster; Laurel, Stan; Lehrman, Henry; Risqué humour; Sennett, Mack; Villains)

A JITNEY ELOPEMENT

(Chaplin film)
Released by General Film Company, 1 April 1915. Produced by Essanay. Written and directed by Charles Chaplin. Photographed by Harry Ensign. British title: *Charlie's Elopement*. Two reels. 1,968 feet.

With Charlie Chaplin (himself), Edna Purviance (Edna), Leo White (the Count), Fred Goodwins (Edna's father), Paddy McGuire (butler/policeman).

Edna returns home to discover that her father has promised her in marriage to a French count. Charlie, her sweetheart, is outside; from an upstairs window, Edna tells Charlie of her dilemma and persuades him to masquerade as the nobleman. Since he has never met either of Edna's suitors, father welcomes the bogus count, tolerating his seeming eccentricities for the sake of a profitable match. These foibles continue through

Bud Jamison (far right) surveys the havoc left by Charlie and Ben Turpin in A Night Out

A Jitney Elopement: Charlie impersonates the Count...

lunch, where Charlie cuts the bread lengthwise, turns it into a makeshift concertina and puts far too many sugar lumps into his boiling coffee; all these are accepted until a car draws up containing the real count, whose arrival prompts father to lead Charlie out by the ear. Charlie obligingly offers his rump for father to kick, returning the compliment by booting father into an armchair. Having disposed of the impostor, father suggests a drive into the country. Father leaves Edna and the Count, supposedly allowing them privacy to become acquainted, but observing from a slight distance. When her suitor gallantly brushes off a park bench, Edna is amused to see that Charlie has slashed and emptied the Count's pockets. She is equally convulsed by his heavy-handed attempts at romance; Charlie, nearby, tries to roll and light a cigarette, resorting to a ready-made one after its collapse. Seeing Edna and the Count, he approaches and is introduced. Battle commences when Charlie, having used the Count's hat as

an ashtray, tries to escort Edna away. Charlie pulls the Count's hat over his eyes, administering a kick that sends him blundering straight into Edna's father. Charlie savours the moment until followed by two policemen who have emerged from the shrubbery. These dim-looking lawmen are disposed of by the simple means of taking a few steps backward. Father and the Count are extricated from their physical tangle; Charlie and Edna rest on a tree limb, but tumble over. Father attacks Charlie, but to no avail; with the Count are the two policemen, who are also of no use. They are joined by a third officer, and set off in pursuit of Charlie and Edna. The fleeing lovers take the Count's motor car, which refuses to co-operate. Charlie tries putting a coin into the radiator cap, but a vigorous turn of the crank brings results. The car is in reverse, causing it to plough into its pursuers; Charlie gains control, and they set off. Father, the Count and the third cop commandeer another car. Each car is forced to travel in circles when passing a huge windmill; on the open road, the lovers gain sufficient lead for Charlie to stop and gather a supply of bricks. Back on the move, Charlie hurls the bricks at the pursuing car, but they are halted only when a mud puddle causes the policeman to fall out. The other officers create a road block by stretching out a rope, but are merely dragged along until forced to let go. The road ends at a jetty, where the two vehicles travel in a circle until Charlie shoves the other car into the water. Charlie and Edna survey what has happened and break into laughter. When Edna draws Charlie's attention to

the presence of an audience, they postpone a kiss until the moment of fade-out.

The 'Jitney' was one of several automotive nicknames then in popular use in the United States; 'flivver' was another, but only the term 'Tin Lizzie', used affectionately of the Model T, ever crossed the Atlantic. This, combined with a preference for incorporating 'Charlie' into each title, led to Essanay's UK office rechristening the film *Charlie's Elopement*. The basic situation, of Charlie masquerading as some sort of dignitary (usually a count), originated in the Keystone films *Caught in a Cabaret* and *Her Friend the Bandit* (both *qv*) and would recur through *The Count*, *The Rink* (both *qv*) and, to a lesser extent, *The Adventurer* (*qv*). The same premise, with a dual-identity twist, may be found in *The Idle Class* and *The Great Dictator* (both *qv*).

(See also: Camera-looks; Cars; 'Chaplin Craze', The; Dual rôles; Essanay; Fighting; Food; Goodwins, Fred; Jamison, William 'Bud'; McGuire, Paddy; Parks; Policemen; Smoking; Stockdale, Carl; Trick photography; Twists and transformations; White, Leo)

JOBS
See: Occupations

JOHNSTON, OLIVER
(1888 or 1889–1966)

British actor, who appeared in Chaplin's two UK films, *A King in New York* and *A Countess From Hong Kong* (both *qv*). In the former, he is Jaume, the King's ambassador; the latter casts the hero as Mr Clark, who introduces the hero to the 'Countess' of the title. Johnston died soon after filming this rôle. Other films include *Dr. Crippen* (1962) and *Cleopatra* (1963).

... and later confronts the genuine article

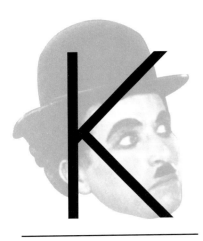

THE KARNO COMPANY

Chaplin's training with Fred Karno (*qv*) cannot be underestimated. As Stan Laurel (*qv*) told his biographer, John McCabe: 'Fred Karno didn't teach Charlie and me all we know about comedy. He just taught us most of it.' He went on to describe how Karno's own mental and physical flexibility, and insistence on precision, combined through endless rehearsal and performance to produce Chaplin, 'the most supple and precise comedian of our time'. He was also responsible, at least in part, for Chaplin's blend of laughter and pathos (*qv*), exhorting his comics to 'keep it *wistful* ... we want sympathy with the laughter'.

Karno based his touring companies at a Camberwell 'Fun Factory', comprising two houses (behind Coldharbour Lane by Southwell, Harbour and Vaughan Roads) knocked into one. Karno was always known to his comedians as 'the Guv'nor', even long after they had ceased to work for him. His companies were frequently given names such as 'Karno's Speechless Comedians', even though their sketches were by no means exclusively mute; further, 'Fred Karno' or 'a Fred Karno operation' fell into popular use as expressions for chaos or ineptitude. It should be stressed that 'Fred Karno's Army' was a humorous, self-deprecating soubriquet adopted by British troops during the First World War, not, as is sometimes claimed, the name of the troupe itself.

Syd Chaplin (*qv*) joined Karno in 1906, having been spotted by Karno in Wal Pink's knockabout sketch, *Repairs*, staged by Charlie Manon's troupe; Charlie, also in the sketch, was for the moment overlooked. Syd was sent briefly to America and, in February 1908, recommended Charlie again to Karno to replace a 'difficult' comedian in a sketch called *The Football Match*, written by Karno with Fred Kitchen. Charlie auditioned for Karno and was hired. (Although Charlie's audition for Karno seems generally accepted as being early in 1908, it should be mentioned that Sobel and Francis' Chaplin chronology cites an appearance as a rag-and-bone man in Karno's sketch *London Suburbia*, as early as 14 September 1907, barely a month after his disastrous solo outing at the Forester's, Mile End.) Initially, he was sent to Leicester, where Fred Kitchen tried to write him into a sketch called *G.P.O.* (which, for non-Britons, stands for 'General Post Office', the name of Britain's mail system at the time). Kitchen, who did not think greatly of Chaplin's abilities, promptly returned him to Karno, but later claimed to have cause to remember their brief acquaintance (see **Impersonators**).

In his book *Shake the Bottle* (1942), W. Buchanan-Taylor (a journalist who saw most of music-hall's greats) describes Chaplin at this time as '"on tap" for any fill-up job that came along ... hanging around Karno's headquarters for emergency jobs'. Chaplin was, it seems, 'a misfit in any part that demanded speech: his utility resided entirely in his singular ability to fill in and to interpret any part by gesture, grimace and manoeuvre'. Charlie made his London Karno debut when *The Football Match* played the London Coliseum for the week commencing 3 February 1908.

The plot centred around a final cup-tie between two teams, the names of which could vary; for example, in Manchester during Christmas 1906 it featured the 'Middleton Pie-cans' v. the 'Midnight Wanderers', while a 1924 London re-write (with additional material by Cyril Hemington) involved the 'Hotspuds' v. 'Bolting Wanderers'. Allowance must be made for the constant revision of Karno's sketches, but such changes may also have been designed to approximate the names of local clubs, for it was not unknown for prominent ex-footballers to be brought into the action. The first scene took place at the team's training headquarters, a pub called The Bull, where the dubious athletes went through their acrobatic paces. An attempt is made to bribe the goalkeeper; the second scene depicts the outside of the ground, with perhaps a hundred extras recruited from the local populace; the next is set in the dressing-room; while the fourth and final scene, on the football pitch, brings the match to a 0–0 score at half-time, and eventual abandonment owing to a downpour.

The star of this sketch was a north-country comedian, Harry Weldon, as 'Stiffy the Goalkeeper'. Weldon, who subsequently appeared on many gramophone records, made a disc recording based on this character around

The Karno Company: Chaplin's London debut with Karno, at the Coliseum in February 1908
By courtesy of Michael Pointon

The Karno Company: Wal Pink's sketch 'Repairs', in a photograph believed to depict both Charlie and Syd Chaplin
By courtesy of Tony Barker

the beginning of 1912. The main focus of the disc, made by the Columbia company, is a comic song written by Murphy and Castling. It is interspersed with patter, typifying Stiffy's achievements in goal:

... the Match of the Season. Stiffy the goalkeeper in wonderful form. 350,000 spectators. Ha! Thought there was more than that! Comes the time the match was started. All eyes were on the impossible Stiffy. The first chap sent in, was one that would've brained any *human* goalkeeper, but not the marvellous Stiffy. He calmly got the ball, carefully placed it at the opposing centre forward's foot, who immediately banged it into the net. Heh! Wants a bit of doin', y'know! Half time was called, and Stiffy was still alive. No sooner was the ball kicked off in the second half, than down came the forwards in a line towards Stiffy. But Stiffy rushed at the half back, and when he'd done with the half back, the half back couldn't get his jaw back. [laughs] I remember that! I did that with a hammer! Everybody shouted 'Penalty', Stiffy louder than anybody. The centre forward was entrusted with the penalty kick. He sent in a wonderful shot, but Stiffy brought off a marvellous save; but it is doubtful if he will ever get the front of his face round from the back of his neck.

The above preserves something of the spirit if not the actual letter of the sketch. Buchanan-Taylor's account continues with Chaplin's insertion into *The Football Match* by way of unscripted business, in a scene concerning attempts to sneak past the turnstile without paying. The routine had been played by Weldon with the other principal comic, Will Poluski, as provocateur. Both

comedians took umbrage when Chaplin completely stole the scene; Buchanan-Taylor, visiting Weldon's dressing-room, was present as Weldon and Poluski gave Chaplin the 'third degree', warning him about his future conduct. 'Charlie disappeared round the corner of the door into the corridor,' said Buchanan-Taylor, 'adroitly avoiding the toe of Weldon's boot and obviously puzzled as to why he should be skull-dragged for making the audience shriek.' Years later, Buchanan-Taylor met Chaplin at the Ambassadeurs in Paris, where he reminded him of the incident. 'Yes, I remember it very well,' said Chaplin. 'For the life of me I couldn't understand what it was all about. Karno had sent me out to "get the laughs", and all I got for getting them was a clip on the ear.' Chaplin used the turnstile routine in a 1914 film, *Gentlemen of Nerve* (qv).

Chaplin's own account of his contribution places him as a villain who tries to bribe Stiffy into losing the game, a motif used later in *The Champion* (qv). Armed with the Edwardian villain's top hat, frock coat, spats and cane – much as he later appeared on film in *Making a Living* (qv) – Chaplin entered, keeping his back to the audience, then scoring a huge laugh by turning to emphasize a dramatically-reddened nose. He continued with business such as tripping over a dumbbell, starting an unaccompanied fight by hooking his cane on a punch-bag, then, pretending to lose a button, dropping his trousers. A search for the button saw him rejecting the item picked from the floor with a disgusted 'Those confounded rabbits!'

Weldon, offstage, was used to the villain playing a 'straight' exposition, and made a swift entrance. Chaplin grabbed his wrist, ad-libbing 'Quick! I'm undone! A pin!' Their shared laughs were built upon this opening, which brought Chaplin the congratulations of his colleagues and a grudging 'That was all right – fine!'

Karno did not see Chaplin in *The Football Match* until the third night, by which time he was getting applause by simply making an entrance. This was enough to secure a year's contract at £4 per week. When *The Football Match* went on tour, Weldon, the slow-talking northerner, was appreciated in his native territory but less acclaimed elsewhere. A Belfast critic gave him a bad notice but praised Chaplin, leading to onstage retribution. Throughout the tour, Weldon had given Chaplin more than the simulated slaps required (the effect being enhanced by a handclap from the wings); in Belfast, Weldon gave Chaplin a bloodied nose, to which Chaplin, offstage, threatened to respond by 'braining' him with the prop dumbbell. Confronted by accusations of jealousy, Weldon merely scoffed. 'Jealous of you?' he said. 'Why, I have more talent in my arse than you have in your whole body!' 'That's where your talent lies,' replied Chaplin. Weldon died in 1930, aged 49.

Charlie and Syd took a flat at 15 Glenshaw Mansions, Brixton Road, near to Kennington Oval. In 1908 or 1909, Charlie was among those to appear when Karno received a Paris booking, at the *Folies Bergère*, for which his fee was increased to £6 a week. There followed a six-month period in which Chaplin

The Karno Company on board the Cairnrona bound for the USA in 1910: Chaplin wears the lifebelt; Stan Laurel is at left of centre row; Albert Austin to left of back row

worked as needed within the various Karno sketches; it is worth pausing to detail some of these, and the way in which they would recur in Chaplin's film work. *Skating*, written by Syd, was the prototype of *The Rink* (*qv*); *Jail Birds* seems a recognizable ancestor of *Police* (*qv*); *The Yap-Yaps* anticipated various boxing sketches, as in *The Champion* and *City Lights*; while *The Dentist* became *Laughing Gas* (*qv*). The most famous sketch – from today's perspective – is *Mumming Birds*, itself the basis of *A Night in the Show* (*qv*), and of which more anon. In later interviews, Hal Roach, who worked alongside Chaplin in 1915, expressed the controversial opinion that Chaplin's pictures started to 'go down' once he had exhausted the Karno backlog.

At the time, *The Football Match* was Karno's most elaborate presentation. Chaplin's big moment came when Karno chose him to replace Weldon in a second tour of the sketch, but the opening, at London's Oxford Music Hall, was marred when Chaplin was stricken with laryngitis. He was returned to *Mumming Birds*, after which there was a brief period when Chaplin's stock was low; theatres were reporting poor business and at least in part blamed Chaplin. Speaking to Karno, the comedian defended himself and even managed to secure a raise in salary. Chaplin declined the lead in a new sketch, *Jimmy the Fearless*, about a downtrodden lad who becomes a hero in his dreams. The part was taken by Stan Laurel, then known as Stan Jefferson. He was a great success, so much so that Chaplin, in the audience, decided to take the rôle after all. Laurel accepted the decision without rancour, and indeed kidded Chaplin later about the one occasion when Chaplin was *his* replacement. His eventual opinion was that Jimmy the Fearless 'one day grew up to be Charlie the Tramp'.

In passing, one might dwell on a rare glimpse of Chaplin from this period. In a 1984 Channel 4 programme about the Grand Order of the Water Rats (*qv*), *A Century of Stars*, veteran artist Nat Mills recalled appearing on the same bill as Chaplin at the Glasgow Empire in 1910. According to Mills, Chaplin was then receiving £10 a week; Mills, in a juvenile company, was paid 2s 6d plus 'keep'. 'He was a smart young fellow in those days,' said Mills, 'but very reserved ... a very reserved type of performer. Of course, he made headway so big, it's unbelievable.'

Chaplin's progress was hastened somewhat by his work in *Jimmy the*

The Karno Company tours the USA in 1911; Stan Laurel, with monocle and centre parting, is at the top of the picture, with Albert Austin to the right. Chaplin is sporting a similar prop moustache to that adopted later for the screen
By courtesy of John McCabe

Fearless, which restored his reputation with Karno. Chaplin was appearing in *Skating* when Alf Reeves (*qv*), managing Karno's American companies, sought a lead comic for a US tour. Chaplin, seeing greater opportunities in America, was both delighted and relieved to be chosen.

Their sketch, *The Wow-Wows* (billed as *A Night in a London Secret Society* for some US engagements), burlesqued the secret societies then proliferating in America. Karno, who had written it with Herbert Sidney, thought the premise singularly appropriate for the new tour; Chaplin, Reeves and Laurel (Chaplin's understudy for the trip) detested it, as did the other members of the troupe. Karno's word was final, however, and the company rehearsed the forlorn skit on board the *Cairnrona*, a cattle boat. This humble craft was chosen less through penury than from the absence of a regular steamer coinciding with the engagement. A text for *The Wow-Wows*, from a contemporary British presentation, survives in the Lord Chamberlain's Theatre Collection at the British Library. The script bears out the unfavourable recollections of those involved. It begins with Archibald Binks (Chaplin) having annoyed his friends by scrounging from them during their camping holiday. As a means of getting him to pay his way, they revive a practical joke that had worked on a similar character, namely dropping

hints about a secret society involving plenty of free food, then subjecting their victim to a tortuous 'initiation' into their fictitious lodge, the 'Wow-Wows'. Binks is duly persuaded to join and led to a club house, where hooded figures await. In the corridor, one of the group, disguised as a witch, asks Binks various questions, to which he supplies mostly facetious answers. Much the same takes place when he is admitted to the Inner Chamber, where the initiation requires shocks from an 'electric carpet' and a promise to pay his way in future. The promise secured, the 'Wow-Wows' remove their hoods, but Binks claims to have known their identities all along. A joker to the last, Binks extracts his revenge by waiting until all are assembled on the carpet, then switching on the current. In addition to the turnstile routine quoted earlier, Chaplin used the name 'Mr Wow-Wow' in *Gentlemen of Nerve*.

The *Cairnrona* arrived in New York, via Canada, in September 1910. Chaplin, concealing his nerves, placed his foot on the ship's rail, declaring loudly that he was to 'conquer' America, where every man, woman and child would have the name 'Charles Spencer Chaplin' on their lips. This prophetic remark was greeted by good-natured booing from his colleagues, Chaplin responding with a deep, formal bow before sitting down again. (Equally

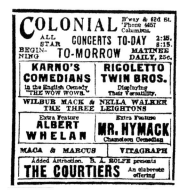

prophetic, if understated, was a *Variety* review of the Karno troupe, claiming 'Chaplin will do all right for America.') The New York *Times* of 2 October 1910 referred to them as 'the headline feature at the Colonial Theater'; when they opened the following night, 'It fell flatter than flat,' recalled Laurel for *Film Weekly* of 23 September 1929, 'so after eleven performances we returned to our old, sure-fire piece, "A Night in an English Music-Hall".' (It should be mentioned, however, that the *Times* review of 4 October thought the new sketch to be its equal 'in rapidity of action and lively knock-about comedy'.)

A Night in an English Music-Hall was the American title of *Mumming Birds*, which had served on earlier trips. *Mumming Birds* took the form of a show-within-a-show, consisting of a proscenium arch and boxes placed within the stage area. The 'acts', deliberately awful, were heckled by a rough audience, led by Chaplin (again as 'Archibald') in immaculate evening dress. On arrival, Chaplin tried to light a cigarette using a light bulb. A young boy, carrying a supply of food to use as ammunition, offered him a match, but Chaplin leaned too far and fell to the stage. He chased the first act, a comic singer and patter comedian, from the stage; the next, a female vocalist played by Amy Minister (soon to be the wife of Alf Reeves) endured first a stream of cracker crumbs spat out by Archibald, then a hail of oranges. There followed a lame magic act, a quartet and a patriotic singer of the Leo Dryden type; given the details related in the **Wheeler Dryden** entry, one can only speculate on Chaplin's delight in heckling such a character. The final victim, an emaciated wrestler called the 'Terrible Turk', undermined any claim to strength when diving for a bun hurled by the small boy. The

management offered £100 to anyone willing to fight the Turk; a 'plant' duly accepted, but found himself in combat with Archibald. By then stripped to his brightly-decorated underwear, Archibald saw off the challenger and brought the Turk to submission through the foul means of tickling. The sketch concluded amid general chaos.

Mumming Birds was much pirated, sometimes by comedians formerly in Karno's employ; there were occasions when the culprits would be in mid-performance, when, to their alarm, they would notice 'the Guv'nor' at the back of the house. Karno was able to halt unauthorized stage presentations, but failed in his legal action against Pathé Frères who, in 1907, made a film based upon the sketch. Coincidentally, it was Max Linder (*qv*) who played what was to become Chaplin's starring rôle on stage. The film exists, and was screened at London's MOMI theatre in January 1997, as part of a talk by Frank Scheide entitled 'Fred Karno's Music Hall'. There were unfounded rumours of Charlie and Syd filming *Mumming Birds* as a talkie in 1929; a British screen adaptation appeared in the early 1930s.

Available billing suggests *A Night in an English Music Hall* to have played less frequently than a hybrid sketch combining this and *The Wow-Wows*, known variously as *A Night at the Club*, *A Night in a London Club* and so on. The improved material was enough to secure bookings throughout America on the Sullivan and Considine vaudeville circuit. A week after the Colonial

engagement, they were at New York's Alhambra, after which they moved on to New York's American Music Hall. The week of 5 December billed *The Wow-Wows*; the next *A Night at the Club*, while the last week of 1910 saw *A Night in an English Music Hall* at the same venue. They were performing *A Night at the Club* at another 'American Music Hall', in Chicago, late in January 1911, as support to fellow-Briton Vesta Victoria. On her departure a week later, English *lion-comique* George Lashwood took over top billing, with Karno's 'London Comedy Co.' reverting to *The Wow-Wows*.

In the *Film Weekly* interview, Laurel recalled Chaplin receiving £12 a week, Laurel only £5, a problem given then-current living expenses in America. This aside, 'we had fun in those days, with Charlie always the life and soul of the party ... Charlie and I lived together, sharing the same room, for more than two years, [a slight inaccuracy, connected to a frequent misassumption that only one, lengthy tour was made] and many's the time we've cooked our dinners in our room' (see also **Food**). Laurel

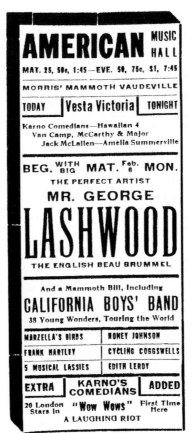

*When the **Karno Company** opened in New York in 1910 it was amid a flurry of British-based artists such as Albert Whelan, George Lashwood and, perhaps the most successful of all, Vesta Victoria. Much the same applied when moving on to Chicago.*
Advertisements by courtesy of Robert G. Dickson

remembered Chaplin as 'the ringleader in everything. Even then we all felt there was something in him which was different from other men. We didn't know what it was; we couldn't put our fingers on it; but it was there.' Laurel also told John McCabe of a time when he and Chaplin needed urgently to find a public convenience, only to find them non-existent in New York. The need was explained to a cop, who, on finally comprehending, directed them to a saloon. British courtesy compelled them to order a drink before making a dash for the facilities.

This first tour provided an opportunity to see virtually the whole of America, much of it still undeveloped. Intriguingly, a photograph taken in 1911 shows Chaplin wearing the type of prop moustache he was later to use in films, some three years prior to its accepted debut. The troupe arrived home in June 1912. Chaplin spent the rest of the summer working in France and the Channel Islands (see also **Newsreels**) prior to a return to America in October. It was in 1913, during this second visit, that

Chaplin was spotted by Keystone (*qv*); he signed with them, but was committed to remain with Karno until late in November. 'I missed him, I must say,' Stan Laurel told John McCabe. Laurel recalled Chaplin's unjust reputation for standoffishness as the result of chronic shyness, something most people refused to believe. Chaplin could socialize only with those who offered friendship or else among those unknown to him. One comedian who regarded Chaplin as 'haughty', 'cold' and 'superior' was Arthur Dandoe, with whom Laurel had worked in an act called *The Rum 'Uns From Rome* during the summer 1912 hiatus. After Chaplin's last Karno performance, at the

Empress, Kansas City, Dandoe prepared a farewell 'gift', comprising a fancy box containing greasepaint sticks, fashioned to resemble excrement. A bluntly-worded covering note compared Chaplin to the alleged contents. 'The so-called presentation never took place, however,' said Laurel to McCabe, 'and later Arthur told me why. First of all, Charlie stood the entire company drinks after the show. That fazed Arthur a bit but the thing that really shamed him into not going through with the so-called gag was this: just after his final curtain with us, Charlie hurried off to a deserted spot backstage. Curious, Arthur followed, and he saw haughty, cold, unsentimental Charlie crying.'

(See also: Armstrong, Billy; Austin, Albert; Boats, ships; Camera-looks; Campbell, Eric; Costume; Marx, Groucho; Music; Women; *Young Charlie Chaplin*)

KARNO, FRED
(1866–1941)

British comedy impresario, real name Fred Westcott; though born in Exeter, he was raised in Nottingham, a region perhaps at odds with the blunt Yorkshire voice by which he is represented in the 1992 biopic *Chaplin* (*qv*). Karno's early showbiz life consisted of acrobatics and adroit conmanship (see also *The Kid*), as when rigging up an early phonograph with air pumps in order to convince a naïve audience that he was in some way producing the sounds. His business skills, combined with a flair for both sketch-writing and talent-spotting, made him the leading comedy producer of the British music-halls. At the time, the terms 'Fred Karno' or 'a Fred Karno operation' were in everyday use to epitomize chaos or inefficiency.

Karno had several troupes on the road at any given time; the whole operation was run from his 'Fun Factory', described elsewhere. Though often billed under such names as 'Karno's Speechless Comedians', his sketches were by no means exclusively mute. There was, however, an unusual concentration on visual comedy, something that would equip more than a few Karno veterans for silent-film work. Among the many Karno comedians to make their names in films were, of course, Chaplin, his brother, Syd (*qv*), and Stan Laurel (*qv*); Karno continued to be known to his former stars as 'the Guv'nor', long after they had left his employ.

Karno's fortunes were in decline by the late 1920s, not least through an ill-advised venture on Tagg's Island in the Thames, the 'Karsino'. He visited the USA to seek work, claiming (implausibly) that he had been engaged to write and direct the second Marx Brothers talkie. Karno approached Chaplin, but it was Laurel who found him employment, as a gag writer at Hal Roach. Karno did not fit in at the studio, and departed swiftly. There were other attempts at a comeback in England (notably the show *Real Life*, which Roach attended), but Karno's last years were spent in obscurity, tending an off-licence. Karno's personal reputation has suffered considerably, owing to published details of his frankly lurid private life; professionally, he was revered by his various discoveries, whose gigantic contribution to popular entertainment might not have been made but for 'the Guv'nor'.

A footnote: Fred Karno Jr contributes to *Monsieur Verdoux* (*qv*) as 'Mr. Karno'.

(See also: Early stage appearances; Karno Company, The; Marx, Groucho; Public appearances)

KEATON, BUSTER
(1895–1966)

Joseph Francis Keaton acquired the nickname 'Buster' from Harry Houdini, during a childhood spent as

*Chaplin visits a rising contemporary, **Buster Keaton**; Alf Reeves stands between them. Behind Chaplin is the Comique Studio owner, Mr. Hockheimer; extreme right of group, Lou Anger*
By courtesy and copyright of the Roy Export Company Establishment

part of the Keaton family's vaudeville act. Buster would have become a star of musical comedy had he not been lured into motion picture work by Roscoe 'Fatty' Arbuckle (*qv*) in 1917. Keaton appeared in Arbuckle's short comedies (with a break for war service) until 1920 when Arbuckle, moving into feature films, passed the series on to Keaton. Also inherited was the location of Keaton's new studio. This was at Lillian Way, formerly the site of the Lone Star studio where Chaplin had made his series for Mutual (*qv*). Photographs of Chaplin visiting Keaton from around this transitional period are said to be from 1917, but Arbuckle does not seem to be present. Keaton quickly developed into one of the screen's top comedians, but by the 1930s had fallen victim to a mixture of studio politics, marital difficulties and alcohol. He later recovered his form, and was once again a busy man (albeit not in the millionaire bracket) when Chaplin invited him to play a fellow music-hall comedian in *Limelight* (*qv*). The two comedians worked well together; although Keaton might have been given more to do (Jerry Epstein [*qv*] denied claims of Chaplin having eliminated Keaton's best moments in the final edit), their evident rapport does much to dispel an occasional rumour of enmity. It is probable that Keaton would not have been allowed anywhere near the set of *Limelight* had he and Chaplin been anything less than friendly.

(See also: Bloom, Claire; Davis, George; *Funniest Man in the World, The*; Jamison, William 'Bud'; Keystone; Pearce, Peggy; Riesner, Charles F. 'Chuck'; Television; United Artists)

KELLY, HETTY

See: Women

KELLY, JAMES T.
(1854–1933)

(Chaplin films *qv*)
Small-framed, Irish-born actor and singer, from the stage. James T. Kelly (not Kelley) was a specialist in elderly or derelict characters, as in *A Night in the Show* (a doddering musician), *Police* (a drunk), *Triple Trouble* (ditto), *The Floorwalker* (an ancient liftboy), *The*

Fireman (an overage firefighter), *The Cure* (a geriatric bellhop) and *The Immigrant* (an elderly restaurant patron, also a ship's galley attendant). He plays yet another drunk in *The Pawnshop*, and has also been credited as the lady attempting to pawn a goldfish. The author doubted the latter credit until examining a very good quality print, in which Kelly's features may be discerned through the heavy white make-up. In *The Vagabond*, Kelly doubles up as both a member of the German band and as one of the gypsies. Early in *A Dog's Life*, he can be seen first buying a hot dog on a cold morning, then in the queue at the employment exchange. He was sometimes allowed to be a little more spruce: in *The Count* he is an uncharacteristically brisk footman, he portrays a cameraman in *Behind the Screen*, in *The Rink* he is an immaculately dressed old *roué*, while *Easy Street* provides him with the respectable – if hopeless – task of reforming a pickled John Rand (*qv*) in the mission hall. Other known appearances include a 1921 Harold Lloyd comedy, *Among Those Present*.

(See also: Dual rôles)

KENNEDY, EDGAR
(1890–1948)

(Chaplin films *qv*)
Burly, Monterey-born comic actor and sometime director (as 'E. Livingston Kennedy'), originally from vaudeville, and later distinguished by a 'slow burn' and famously bald head. Neither is particularly apparent in his early appearances for Keystone (*qv*), though the top of his scalp is starting to become visible in *The Knockout*. In this film he plays a prizefighter, recalling his true-life experiences in the ring (one of them, reportedly, against Jack Dempsey). He is also fairly recognizable in *Those Love Pangs*, but other Keystones see him disguised beneath bushy whiskers, such as *Twenty Minutes of Love*, *Getting Acquainted* (as the cop), *Caught in a Cabaret* (as the café owner), *Mabel's Busy Day* (another cop), *Dough and Dynamite* (a baker), *Tillie's Punctured Romance* (Uncle's butler and restaurant owner) and *Gentlemen of Nerve* (still another cop). Later worked at various studios, among them Fox, Universal

and Roach; many 1920s appearances include *The Better 'Ole*, starring Syd Chaplin (*qv*) and several of the earlier Laurel & Hardy comedies. In the 1930s, Kennedy commenced his own series of starring shorts at RKO, which continued until his death. He was also prolific in feature work during this period, as in the Marx Brothers' *Duck Soup* (1933), the 1937 version of *A Star is Born* and Harold Lloyd's final film, shot in 1946, *The Sin of Harold Diddlebock* (also known as *Mad Wednesday*).

(See also: Dual rôles; Laurel, Stan; Policemen)

KENNEDY, MERNA
(1908–44)

Born in Kankakee, Illinois, Merna Kennedy made her theatrical debut at the age of seven, and spent as many years on the Orpheum and Pantages vaudeville circuits, mostly in a song-and-dance act with her brother. She appeared in a musical comedy, *All For You*, in Los Angeles; at that time Chaplin was married to Lita Grey (*qv*), a childhood friend of Merna's who arranged for her to have dinner with the comedian. In this way it was contrived for Merna to become Chaplin's leading lady in *The Circus* (*qv*). A contemporary account suggests that, despite (or because of) this informal introduction, Merna was able to get away with giving Chaplin a kick during a bout of on-set temperament, a gesture to which the comedian reacted with amusement rather than anger. Just the same, her association with Chaplin lasted only for that one film. Among her

other appearances are *Broadway* (1929), Universal's revue film *The King of Jazz* (1930) and *Reputation* (1931). Her final film, *I Like it That Way* (1934), was followed by retirement on marriage to choreographer Busby Berkeley. Her real surname is said to have been Kahler, but Lita Grey, when questioned, insisted the 'Kennedy' to have been genuine; her forename is sometimes misspelled 'Myrna' in later references.

(See also: Marriages; Women)

KEYSTONE

(Chaplin films *qv*)

The name that has become synonymous both with its boss, Mack Sennett (*qv*), and the brand of slapstick in which it specialized, the Keystone Film Company was announced to the world on 12 August 1912. It was formed by Adam Kessel and Charles O. Bauman of the New York Motion Picture Company. Exactly *why* it was formed has become a matter of myth and legend; the most often quoted (and reportedly discredited) version is that Sennett persuaded Kessel and Bauman to finance the business as an alternative to claiming a gambling debt from him (Sennett's two creditors having been bookmakers). Less in dispute is that the company name and trademark were inspired by the logo of the Pennsylvania Railroad, although it should be stressed that the initial Keystone trademark was quickly superseded by a more elaborate design (resembling instead the Heinz label!). The New York Motion Picture Company had four studios in operation, all releasing via Mutual (*qv*); the other three were Kay-Bee, after the proprietors' initials; Domino, specializing in drama; and Broncho, producing westerns (see also *A Film Johnnie*). Contemporary trade advertisements would bill each batch of releases as 'four aces', with a film from each studio billed within the design of a playing card (shades of Kessel and Bauman's gambling heritage).

As noted elsewhere, Sennett had gained experience under D.W. Griffith (*qv*) at Biograph, in common with his leading lady, Mabel Normand (*qv*). The other founding members of the Keystone troupe were Fred Mace and Ford Sterling (*qv*). Mace, another Biograph veteran, had remained in California when Griffith took his company back to the east, and joined Keystone following a

Keystone announced its latest 'capture' with due satisfaction

brief tenure at Imp. The style of these earliest Keystones – and of the many to come – was, by Sennett's later admission, copied from the Pathé comedies made in France. They were essentially rough, farcical stuff culminating in a chase but, combined with the cutting technique learned from Griffith and Sennett's own vision, proved an instant success. Indeed, as Kalton C. Lahue has pointed out, Keystone became the first studio to thrive exclusively on comedy. Despite impressions to the contrary, written scenarios were used at Keystone, but only as a vague template that would make way for considerable improvisation; there were also a number of occasions when, as mentioned under *A Busy Day*, cameras would be rushed to a real-life event and the action improvised on the spot.

Production commenced on 28 August 1912 at the former 101 Bison studio at Edendale, California. Release was via Mutual (*qv*), the first of them being on 23 September. This was a split reel comprising two subjects, *Cohen Collects a Debt* (with Sterling as lead) and *The Water Nymph* (an excuse for Mabel to wear a tight swimsuit). A second unit was established early the following year, with Henry 'Pathé' Lehrman (*qv*) as director. Such immediate expansion provides a barometer to Keystone's impact. It might be noted that, at this time, Keystone's efficiency benefited immediately from the arrival of a new business manager, an ex-Universal employee named George Stout. The

Merna Kennedy was Chaplin's leading lady in The Circus

public's imagination was captured particularly by *The Bangville Police* (1913), which marked the debut of the Keystone Cops. Fred Mace was the original Chief, but departed later that year and was replaced Ford Sterling. Once Mace had gone, Sennett made up the troupe's numbers by hiring Roscoe 'Fatty' Arbuckle (*qv*).

By the end of 1913, Keystone was presenting full one-reelers and periodic two-reelers, and was expanding rapidly. Keystone's assembled company tended to be a mixture of ex-circus clowns (Sterling among them) and vaudevillians. Chaplin, from the latter category, was hired when Sterling began demanding more money and was ready to quit (Sterling would leave Keystone soon after Chaplin's arrival, only to return after an unsuccessful year elsewhere). Sennett had seen Chaplin on stage in New York with the Karno Company (*qv*), and arranged for Kessel and Bauman to wire Alf Reeves (*qv*) when the troupe was in Philadelphia. This famous telegram enquired as to whether there was a 'Chaffin in your company or something like that', a name sufficiently accurate for Chaplin to respond. Based on the number of lawyers based at the same address, Chaplin assumed some sort of mysterious legacy, and thus agreed to meet Kessel and Bauman in New York. Instead of an inheritance, Chaplin was offered $150 per week, double his Karno salary, to appear in Keystone comedies. Chaplin, not without misgivings, accepted the job, assuming that a year in pictures would provide enough publicity (and money) for him to return to the variety stage as a top-of-the-bill attraction. Chaplin's Karno commitments forbade the move until December 1913.

On Chaplin's arrival at Edendale, Sennett was surprised to see his youth – Chaplin was then only 24 years old – but was assured that the comedian could make up to any age required. Chaplin was given Lehrman as his director, and it would be understatement to suggest that they did not get on. After waiting around for his first film assignment, Chaplin donned a monocle and long moustache for his Keystone debut, *Making a Living*. Chaplin was at first baffled by the techniques of film-making, not least the practice of shooting at seemingly unrelated locations and editing them together. He was also of the opinion that Lehrman had, from spite, removed the film's genuinely funny

moments. Chaplin's initial bafflement applied also to Sennett, who remained unsure how this newcomer might be used. The assembly of Chaplin's 'Tramp' character, described under **Costume**, made for a more effective contribution to his next film, *Kid Auto Races at Venice*. Thus clad, Chaplin stole the third film, *Mabel's Strange Predicament*, from under the collective noses of its stars; this, and his final film with Lehrman, *Between Showers*, are good but still resemble the Keystone style rather than that of Chaplin. He started to gain some rapport with his new colleagues, especially when demonstrating how to do falls without sustaining injury. There was also some exchange of knowledge, in that Chaplin learned from them the business of film-making while at the same time instructing the studio in stagecraft. (Some Chaplin Keystones, particularly *The Masquerader*, see him engaging in friendly rivalry with his fellow comedians. Sennett's memoirs detail an offscreen practical joke where the men's toilet had been wired up for electricity, to which Chaplin pretended to succumb by feigning unconsciousness. As his worried colleagues surveyed the inert figure, Chaplin sprang back to life and walked away, blowing them a resounding raspberry.)

After the Lehrman experience, Chaplin seems still to have been ill at ease under director George 'Pop' Nichols, but even less willing to accept direction from Mabel Normand. Their quarrel during *Mabel at the Wheel*, detailed in the main entry, brought Chaplin a degree of temporary notoriety around the lot. Mabel was universally admired at Keystone, and Chaplin became unpopular among some of the veterans; one supporter was Chester Conklin (*qv*), who advised Chaplin not to quit. His departure might not have been voluntary, for Sennett was in any case ready to fire Chaplin. A reprieve came by means of a telegram from New York, requesting more of the very popular Chaplin films. Chaplin was allowed to direct himself (see **Caught in the Rain** and **Twenty Minutes of Love**), which led to an immediate improvement in the quality of his films.

This might be the moment to dwell upon the reception accorded Chaplin's first films in his native country. Impressions in Great Britain were essentially those of the continued success of an established Karno comedian, though his cinema reputation spread

among the general public before press awareness fuelled what was to become the 'Chaplin Craze' (*qv*). An article signed 'Edward Wood' in the *Picture Show* annual for 1931 reminisced over the British public's reaction at this time. Wood recalled having been art editor for the then *Sunday Graphic*, for whom he assembled a back page consisting entirely of Chaplin film stills. Though acquainted with Chaplin during Karno days, the journalist had not seen any of his Keystones, but incorporated the movie-like sequence of photographs purely for amusement value. He considered reducing the spread after a consultation with the managing editor, but the decision was reversed after they discovered the compositors in roars of laughter. 'They all seem to know him,' said journalist to editor, 'and if the pictures make all of them laugh they should be good enough for our readers.' Within weeks, large-sized Chaplin cut-outs were on display outside the theatres in London's West End. In Britain at least, Chaplin was being advertised alongside Sennett, Normand and Arbuckle as the 'Keystone Comedy Quartette'. Sennett's UK distributors, the Western Import Company, also offered a regular package known as the 'Keystone Night', by which exhibitors could book an entire evening's programme from the company's output.

Advertisements for the 'Quartette' depicted Chaplin with a growling face, reflecting the way in which the studio, in keeping with his intended function as Sterling's replacement, had often cast him as some sort of villain. The Chaplin character was extant only in primitive form, but was advancing quickly. Some measure of his status is that he was chosen to appear with Marie Dressler (*qv*) and Mabel Normand in *Tillie's Punctured Romance*, the first feature-length comedy (at least in America) and the film in which Chaplin drew the interest of prominent critics. By the end of 1914, Chaplin's Keystones had made him an international celebrity. Chaplin recalled having demanded an increase to $1,000 a week, and that Sennett, whose own salary was less than that amount, had refused. Sennett's version is that Chaplin declined his offer of half his stake in the company (i.e. one-sixth). Whatever the truth, Chaplin's demands were met instead by Essanay (*qv*), and he began 1915 with a new employer. On Charlie's recommendation, Sennett hired Syd Chaplin (*qv*) as replacement, but there would never be his equal at the studio. In consequence, the Chaplin Keystones were reissued with great frequency; some were in authorized editions, but others were not, for despite claims made on the main title cards, Keystone films were not copyrighted until mid-1914. Both the official and bootlegged prints were subject to retitling – sometimes by Keystone itself – particularly during a massive reissue campaign by W.H. Productions, who did at least quote original titles on their reissues. It was around this time (1920) that *Bioscope* published a trade advertisement listing the various aliases, designed to assist exhibitors but subsequently of considerable help to researchers. The accepted list of Chaplin Keystones totals 35, as per Theodore Huff's filmography published in 1945 by *Sight and Sound*. These are as follows:

Making a Living
Kid Auto Races at Venice, CA (or *Kid's Auto Race*)
Mabel's Strange Predicament
Between Showers
A Film Johnnie
Tango Tangles
His Favorite Pastime
Cruel, Cruel Love
The Star Boarder
Mabel at the Wheel
Twenty Minutes of Love
Caught in a Cabaret
Caught in the Rain
A Busy Day
The Fatal Mallet
Her Friend the Bandit
The Knockout
Mabel's Busy Day
Mabel's Married Life
Laughing Gas
The Property Man
The Face On the Bar Room Floor
Recreation
The Masquerader
His New Profession
The Rounders
The New Janitor
Those Love Pangs
Dough and Dynamite
Gentlemen of Nerve
His Musical Career
His Trysting Place
Tillie's Punctured Romance
Getting Acquainted
His Prehistoric Past

Huff's research into the Chaplin canon, since updated with the addition of such peripheral titles as *His Regeneration* (*qv*), has been questioned in

relation to the Keystone films. Perhaps the most intriguing debate of recent years concerns the status of the 'lost' Chaplin, *Her Friend the Bandit*. As noted in the main entry, only one contemporary review makes specific reference to Chaplin (misspelled, at that), and it may be significant that an earlier *Sight and Sound* list, compiled in 1938 by H.D. Waley, then Technical Director of the British Film Institute, omits this film completely. (Waley did, however, reach a total of 35 by including an erroneous title deleted from subsequent lists, Ford Sterling's *A Thief Catcher*.) Sennett's memoirs detail this among Chaplin's films, but it is evident that he had consulted Huff's listing.

Periodic suggestions of Chaplin 'helping out' as a Keystone Cop in 1915 may safely be disregarded, along with most claims of additional, 'unknown' Chaplin Keystones. It was once suggested that Chaplin might have appeared in a Mabel Normand film, *Hello Mabel*, but examination of a *Bioscope* review of 6 May 1915 produced no reference to a contribution by Chaplin; a print of the film has since been recovered, confirming Chaplin's non-involvement. In the August 1982 *Classic Images*, historian Bo Berglund speculated on a possible contribution to Syd Chaplin's first starring Keystone comedy, *Giddy, Gay and Ticklish*. Berglund cites a reference in Chaplin's admittedly unreliable memoirs, in which he describes cutting his last Keystone film, *His Prehistoric Past*, immediately prior to leaving at the end of December (which, in Berglund's opinion, has both Charlie and Syd in its cast). Given that this film had been completed and released weeks earlier, Berglund suggests that, as with Sennett and *Her Friend the Bandit*, Chaplin may have gleaned its name from an existing filmography and, in the process, overlooked the film's true title. Also cited is an interview with Chaplin from the March 1915 *Motion Picture* magazine, in which he describes having recently played a barber; when details of *Giddy, Gay and Ticklish* were tracked down, they revealed a barbershop setting with Syd Chaplin as customer. The barber in an accompanying still is recognizable as Edgar Kennedy (*qv*), though Charlie Chaplin may have been cast as his colleague. An alternative review, from *Bioscope* of 20 May 1915, offers a reasonably detailed description of the film but, despite noting extensively Syd's kinship with Charlie, makes no mention

of a contribution from both Chaplins. At the time of writing, *Giddy, Gay and Ticklish* has yet to be found, and the involvement of Charles Chaplin remains a point for debate.

Although Sennett continued to prosper into the 1920s, Keystone itself met a premature end. During 1915, crises within Mutual brought about the formation of the Triangle Film Corporation, its three sides being Sennett, Griffith and Thomas H. Ince. When Sennett left for Paramount in mid-1917, he was obliged to relinquish the Keystone name and trademark. After Sennett's own backlog had been exhausted, Triangle attempted some 'Keystone' comedies of its own, without success.

A postscript: the archives of the Grand Order of Water Rats (*qv*) preserve a comic account of Chaplin's entry into films, apparently written by the comedian himself in 1939 and sent to his sponsor in the organization, Charlie Austin (who, in 1944, sent it on to King Rat Tom Moss). Based loosely on the garbled telegram from Kessel and Bauman, it comprises a series of messages ostensibly within Universal Pictures (Keystone's rival at that time) concerning a Chaplin screen test of late 1913. Among the various in-jokes is that Chaplin was supposedly a potential replacement for Keaton, who was 'becoming difficult' (Keaton, of course, entered films some time after Chaplin). 'Karno' is given the customary misspelling 'Carno'; Chaplin's name mutates variously into 'Caplan' and 'Carl Chaplin'; he is considered 'better in sketches with dialogue than sight gags'; after being tested, Chaplin is deemed 'very disappointing', the recommendation being to delete use of the derby hat ('used by too many current comics'), the moustache (the type 'now being used by Charlie Chase'), the funny walk ('we must try to avoid offending people who are bow-legged or cripples') and even the name ('too easily confused with Charlie Chase ... Also Chaplin sounds Jewish'). Chaplin is told to return home, the entire business being dismissed as a 'fiasco' and Chaplin 'not outstanding enough to warrant either testing or sending to the coast'. This evident piece of self-mockery not only epitomizes the kidding that goes on between contemporaries, but suggests also that Chaplin may not always have taken himself as seriously as is often imagined.

THE KID

(Chaplin film)
Released by First National, 6 February 1921. Produced, written and directed by Charles Chaplin. Assistant director: Chuck Riesner. Photographed by Rollie Totheroh. Six reels (5,300 feet).

With Charlie Chaplin (himself), Jackie Coogan (the Kid), Edna Purviance (the Kid's mother), Carl Miller (the Kid's father), Chuck Riesner (bully), Tom Wilson (cop), Albert Austin (thief), Henry Bergman (Professor Guido, impresario/flophouse owner), Nellie Bly Baker (woman in slums), Lita Grey (flirty angel), Edith Wilson (woman with pram), Monta Bell, Jack Coogan Sr, Raymond Lee.

A young woman, 'whose sin was motherhood', leaves a charity hospital with her new-born baby. She sits in the park, distraught, while the man, an artist, is unconcerned when her photograph lands in the fireplace. The desperate mother decides to secure her child's future by leaving him in the back seat of a limousine, parked outside a mansion. She returns to the park. In her absence, the car is stolen. The thieves discover the child, dumping him in a slum area. The woman changes her mind and goes to reclaim the child. Charlie, out for his 'morning promenade' and trying – not always successfully – to avoid the rubbish that is being dumped from upstairs windows, finds the baby amid dustbins. He looks skyward to trace the source, then, seeing a woman with a pram, calls after her. It is not hers. Charlie tries to leave the baby, but a policeman arrives. He dumps the child on an old man and runs away. The old

The Kid: *'six reels of joy' became five reels of fun in Chaplin's reissue version*

man places it in the woman's pram. When Charlie passes by, she pursues him and returns the baby. Charlie sits by the kerb and, abandoning his idea of dropping the baby down the sewer, finds a note wrapped in the little bundle: 'Please love and care for this orphan child.' Charlie, warming to the rôle of parenthood, takes home his new charge. When a neighbour asks the youngster's name, Charlie momentarily disappears indoors. He returns to announce 'John', then climbs the stairs up to his dingy flat. The boy's mother, horrified to see the car has gone, calls at the mansion, and faints when told the car has been stolen. Charlie has fixed up a type of hammock for the baby, who is fed using a suspended coffee pot in lieu of a bottle. A commode is improvised by cutting the seat from a chair then placing it over a spittoon. Five years pass, and the Kid has acquired some of his adopted parent's street *savoir faire*. As Charlie lights the stove, the Kid places a quarter in the gas meter, retrieving the coin immediately thereafter. After a quick check of the Kid's cleanliness, Charlie and his assistant set off for work. The Kid's job is to break windows, setting the stage for the convenient arrival of Charlie, the glazier. The Kid manages two successful breakages before having to feign nonchalance in the presence of a cop. The Kid scurries off before the officer notices the broken window. The policeman watches, suspiciously, as Charlie replaces the glass. His suspicion turns to pursuit when Charlie is rejoined

by his accomplice. The policeman evidently shaken off, Charlie reaches the thirteenth job of the day without repercussion. His luck alters when flirting with the lady of the house; her husband arrives home and is none other than the policeman. Charlie and the Kid escape to the sanctuary of their flat and the comfort of a square meal. The boy's mother has by this time become a much-fêted theatrical star, given to visiting slum areas, where she distributes toys to the children. She is outside Charlie's flat, thinking of her own lost child, unaware that he is the urchin sitting beside her. She gives him a toy dog and an apple before continuing on her way. Back at the flat, the Kid cooks flapjacks while Charlie lies in bed reading the *Police Gazette*. Charlie joins the boy at the table, instructing him to eat using the *blunt* edge of the knife. Outside, a larger boy steals the Kid's toy dog and apple. The Kid fights back, and Charlie arrives to separate them; realizing the boy is coping adequately, Charlie turns ringside second, coaching the lad in fighting technique. The bigger lad is in tears, all the less fortunate for Charlie when his gigantic brother appears on the scene. Charlie pretends to admonish the Kid, but the big man insists that his brother should 'lick' the opposition. If the brother loses, Charlie will get a pasting from the big brother. Charlie tries to hamstring the Kid's progress, but to no avail; the big brother stalks him through the street, knocking out a policeman on the way, until the Kid's mother arrives to make peace. 'Remember,' she tells the bully, 'if he smites you on one cheek, offer him the other.' Charlie, armed with a brick, smites his opponent into insensibility. The menace seems over until the woman, carrying the Kid in her arms, tells Charlie that the boy has been taken ill and needs a doctor. She promises to return later on. The doctor arrives, a man of dubious skills who at first begins to examine Charlie. He takes a look at the child and asks Charlie if he is the father. Unconvinced by Charlie's 'well – practically', he demands further explanation. Charlie shows him the note left with the abandoned baby. The doctor insists the child should have 'proper care and attention' and departs, promising to attend to the matter. Days pass and the Kid recuperates, only for the 'proper care' to arrive in the shape of an orphanage wagon. The orphanage official speaks to Charlie only through a uniformed attendant. Charlie refuses to let them take the Kid, holding them at bay until the local policeman is brought. Charlie is held as the terrified, pleading youngster is loaded on to the wagon, where he is pushed brusquely by the doctor. Charlie breaks free and heads for the rooftops. After disposing of the cop, he is able to follow the wagon's progress and drop down to the wagon. Charlie wrestles the orphanage official, throwing him from the wagon and reclaiming the Kid. There is a tearful reunion and, when the wagon stops, Charlie chases away the driver. The woman calls at Charlie's flat, where the irate doctor tells her what has happened. He shows her the letter that was left with the baby, which she recognizes as her own. That night, Charlie enters a flophouse, locating with difficulty a coin for his own admission while the Kid sneaks in. Charlie is aware of a pickpocket's attentions and, when the thief locates a coin Charlie was unaware of possessing, encourages him to keep looking. Charlie and the Kid bed down, but the boy pauses to say his prayers. Despite some nimble manoeuvres, his presence is discovered by the flophouse owner. The proprietor collects the extra money and settles down to read the newspaper. An advertisement has been placed offering $1,000 reward for a five-year-old boy, last seen with 'a little man with large flat feet and small moustache'. The flophouse owner turns down the lights and carries off the sleeping youngster. Charlie awakens and, searching frantically, disappears into the night. The flophouse owner brings the Kid to the police station, while Charlie continues to search the streets. Dawn, and the woman collects her child from the station. Charlie, outside his home, sits down exhausted. In his dreams, the run-down street becomes Heaven, with all his residents – even a dog – sporting angelic wings. The Kid awakens Charlie, who is fitted with his own set of wings. All is well until the gatekeeper – the flophouse owner in celestial garb – falls asleep. Unobserved, demons creep in, persuading a pretty girl angel to 'vamp' Charlie, who is in turn encouraged to take interest. The girl's sweetheart – the large bully – arrives, his fraternal attitude swiftly turning to jealousy. A fight ensues, and the cop arrives, only for Charlie to escape. The winged Charlie flies past and is shot down, landing on his own doorstep. The policeman picks him up, and the dream concludes with the real-life cop shaking Charlie back to

Charlie and **The Kid** *think they have escaped policeman Tom Wilson*

Jackie Coogan proved a perfect miniature 'Charlie' in **The Kid**

*After editing the film in hiding, Chaplin was finally able to deliver **The Kid** to representatives of First National. Alf Reeves, third from left, looks unnerved by the large cheque he is holding; Charlie and, far right, Syd Chaplin, seem altogether happier*
By courtesy and copyright of the Roy Export Company Establishment

consciousness. Charlie is taken away in a car, uncertain of his fate. The cop takes him to the front door of a mansion, to be greeted by the Kid and his mother. The cop shakes Charlie by the hand as he embarks on a new life.

Sub-titled 'A picture with a smile – and perhaps, a tear', *The Kid* maintains its power to elicit both. The relationship between Charlie and Jackie has sometimes been viewed as less that of father and son, but rather Charlie alone, past and present; the window-breaking scam is, reportedly, based on an incident from someone *else*'s past, namely Fred Karno (*qv*). As Chaplin's first full-length film as both director and star, its protracted creation caused his employers at First National (*qv*) considerable anxiety. Chaplin's working pace – a matter of contention even during his Keystone days – had slowed even further, and the comparative weakness of his preceding shorts, *Sunnyside* and *A Day's Pleasure* (both *qv*), could have done nothing to salve their nerves. Consequentially, Chaplin invited them to his studio to witness his discovery, Jackie Coogan (*qv*), around whom the film was centred.

Production continued in secrecy until mid-1920, by which time Chaplin had spent twelve months on the project and was prepared to divulge selected details. 'It is time for Charlie Chaplin's

next picture,' reported *Picture Show* on 17 July 1920. 'The present rumour is that it will be a six reeler, and will contain more than the ordinary amount of the popular pathos in which Charlie, in his later plays, has liked to indulge. The title, if the report be true, will be "The Kid".' The report was 100 per cent true, and the negative of *The Kid* was formally delivered to First National towards the end of 1920. It had been a close thing: Chaplin's divorce battle with Mildred Harris (*qv*) had nearly resulted in the negative being attached by her lawyers, forcing the comedian and his assistants to flee with the endangered footage to Utah, where it was edited in secret. The formal end of the marriage enabled Chaplin to present his new film to First National, who, though doubtless relieved, were less happy with Chaplin's financial stipulations. According to Theodore Huff, his contract provided for an additional $15,000 for each reel exceeding two; reasoning that *The Kid* amounted to something more than the sum of its reels, Chaplin demanded and received a total of $600,000. First National's profits were in the end some $2.5 million, of which Chaplin received 30 per cent.

The Kid's first public showing, at Carnegie Hall on 21 January 1921, was to benefit the Children's Fund of the National Board of Review, a film industry body; the following day's *New York Times*, greeting Chaplin's first release in over a year, considered the comedian 'at his best, in some ways better than his previous best, and also, it is to be regretted, at his worst, only not with so much of his worst as has spoiled some of his earlier pictures'. Put plainly, Chaplin was thought funnier than ever, but marred, albeit to a lesser degree, by the vulgar aspects more beloved by patrons than critics. The article goes on to detail this point more succinctly, though admitting the supposedly vulgar sequences to be very funny. More significantly, Chaplin's decision to balance comedy and drama had paid off. 'There's nothing clumsy about the picture's continuity,' said the reviewer. 'Its "comedy relief" actually comes as a well-timed relief.' The film's opening at the Strand Theatre, on 6 February, was greeted again by the *New York Times* as (with a doubtless conscious understatement) 'The most important motion picture event of the week'. *The Kid* was rated as 'about the best' of Chaplin's work, 'as good as *Shoulder*

Arms in every way, and in some ways better'. Jackie Coogan was acknowledged as 'the best child actor on the screen ... a miniature Chaplin, as natural a pantomimist as Charles Spencer himself'. Once more, some regret was felt over Chaplin's seemingly characteristic 'vulgarity and witless horseplay', but the film was deemed to have 'many scenes of Chaplin and his company at their finest'. Above all, *The Kid* was seen as 'a real cinematographic work in the universal language of moving pictures', having little need of its few, succinct titles. *Variety* declared *The Kid* 'a corker' and Chaplin 'less of the buffoon and more of the actor', noting the continuing presence of his customary humour within the more polished context. *The Kid*, it was decided, 'has all the earmarks of having been carefully thought out and painstakingly directed, photographed and assembled. The cutting, in some places, amounts almost to genius.' The British reception was comparable and, as in the United States, followed considerable anticipation: in February 1921, coinciding with *The Kid*'s American release, *Pictures* had spoken of 'the new Charlie Chaplin', new both in the sense of providing a dramatic context for his comedy and in proving himself able to 'come back' after a lengthy absence from the screen. One British commentator later to offer criticism was J.M. Barrie, who questioned the suitability of the scene in which Charlie dreams of Heaven. Barrie's objection was based on artistic suitability rather than any similarity to his own *Peter Pan*; Chaplin listened, but defended his decision.

In a *New Republic* review of March 1921, Francis Hackett approved of the sequence, interpreting it as 'a simple man's version of the Big Change', but many of today's commentators concur with Barrie. Chaplin retained it when reviving the film in 1971, choosing instead to remove some of the more melodramatic plot footage with Edna Purviance (*qv*) (though he kept a heavy-handed title card in which the mother's burden is compared to Christ carrying the cross). These scenes have been reinstated in the laserdisc version issued in the USA; they exist also in old prints left over from an unauthorized British revival, via DUK, during the 1950s, and in a complete full-frame copy bearing Italian sub-titles that is known to have survived. The European material offers different camera angles; as was usual in the silent era, two cameras were employed in order to provide negatives for the domestic and foreign markets. David Robinson refers to the second negative having been destroyed by fire in 1938. The DUK version suffers from a degree of image 'cropping' to the left and in terms of height, the result of a sound track being added without reducing the full silent 35mm frame.

The scenes omitted from Chaplin's revival convey the experiences of the boy's parents, the first of them being when, soon after leaving hospital, the mother witnesses the marriage of a young girl to a rich old man. Symbolically, the groom treads on flowers that have fallen from the bridal bouquet; further symbolism is evident when the woman, cradling her baby, seems to acquire a halo when standing before a stained-glass church window. Presumably, this Madonna-like image is designed to suggest greater chastity in an unwed mother than in a bride whose motive is wealth. The scene introducing the father is abridged in Chaplin's revision; another cut takes place following the child's abandonment, in which the mother stands on a bridge, where a nursemaid is caring for an infant. She cradles the child, only for it to be taken away. It is because of this that she decides to reclaim her baby, rather than the simple change of heart suggested in the reissue. After the mother has become a successful actress, she meets the father – himself now somewhat eminent – at a party. There is an uneasy reunion as we see a book entitled 'The Past' and a page within it marked 'Regrets'. The father is remorseful, but the woman explains that she does not know of their child's whereabouts. Although Chaplin's reissue dispenses with this section, it includes a segment absent from DUK's print, in which the woman is greeted by an impresario (Henry Bergman [qv]) after a successful show. The DUK edition substitutes an amended title card to explain her rise to stardom. A further absentee from this copy is an effect by which a question mark appears on a window Charlie is repairing. There are also some variations in titling: although remade, the text seems to follow that from the original UK release. For example, the ironic reference to the unmarried mother's 'sin' becomes a 'mistake'; there is also preserved a substitute title card, made to appease the British censor in 1921, in which

Charlie's disappearance to establish the child's gender is unexplained and his comments are reduced to an innocuous 'It's mine, I found it.' Later on, Jackie is told to put a 'shilling' in the gas meter, though the reward offered towards the end of the film remains in American currency. Sub-titles in the available British copy make no reference to the unlucky '13th' house during the window-repairing scam. Oddly, when Jackie recuperates from his illness, the calendar reads 'September 1', which is then duplicated in at least two other languages before progressing to a monolingual 4th of the month.

(See also: Auctions; Baker, Nellie Bly; Censorship; *Chaplin*; *Count, The*; *Dog's Life, A*; Dreams; Dual rôles; *Easy Street*; *Floorwalker, The*; Food; *Gold Rush, The*; Grey, Lita; *His New Profession*; Home movies; Impersonators; Lee, Raymond; *Pay Day*; Policemen; Race; Reissues; Religion; Riesner, Dean; Sickness; *Shoulder Arms*; Smoking; Television; Titling; Trick photography; Vagrancy; Video releases; Wilson, Jack)

KID AUTO RACES AT  VENICE, CA.

(Chaplin film)
Keystone Comedy released by Mutual, 7 February 1914. Produced by Mack Sennett. Directed by Henry Lehrman. Photography by Hans Koënekamp and (?) Frank D. Williams. Split reel, released together with a factual film, *Olives and Their Oil*. 572 feet (UK length cited in *Bioscope*). Also known as *Kid's Auto Race* (see below). Reissued by W.H. Productions as *The Pest*.

With Charlie Chaplin (a pest), Henry Lehrman (film director) and Frank D. Williams (cameraman).

The film begins as a seemingly factual item, covering a push-car race with children. Charlie, a passerby, starts to hog the camera, walking to and fro past the lens. The camera catches part of the race without interruption, but Charlie is in evidence once more when the scene changes to the grandstand. Charlie follows the camera as it pans by the starting-ramp, despite periodic shoves from director Lehrman. From the point of view of a second camera, Charlie is seen again running along the track. Lehrman re-enters shot in order to push

the interloper out of range. The camera manages another unimpeded shot prior to 'Setting the camera at death curve', where Charlie continues to wander in and out of range. The viewpoint reverts briefly to that of the first camera, its view of the bend obscured again by Charlie. The director pushes him away once more. Back to the main view of the track and business as before. Though repeatedly removed from the action, Charlie returns to pose before the lens. The first camera records Charlie being moved from view by a burly spectator.

Charlie peers into the lens to conclude **Kid Auto Races at Venice**

The camera records another uninterrupted shot. Charlie is twice pushed away from the camera, only to return, knocking off his own hat with his cane. As a further excuse to get in the way, Charlie throws his hat on to the track and is nearly run over when retrieving it. Not content with this reappearance, he pops back into view a few more times. Posing grandly for the cameraman, Charlie exhausts Lehrman's patience and is booted to the ground. He protests, is ushered away but returns to make faces directly into the lens.

This slight, improvised piece is significant as the first appearance of Chaplin's 'tramp' character. Though Chaplin's autobiography attributes the character's debut to the next film, *Mabel's Strange Predicament* (qv), it is possible that Chaplin quite simply overlooked this impromptu half-reeler. It has sometimes been speculated that the two were switched in order of release; *Kid Auto Races* reached American cinemas two days earlier, though it should be noted that its British release, on 2 July 1914, was ten days after that of *Mabel's Strange Predicament*. Historian Bo Burglund, in the Spring 1989 *Sight and Sound*, has expressed doubt concerning the alleged reversal in release dates. Berglund confirmed the date on which *Races* was filmed (Saturday, 10 January 1914) by the simple expedient of checking the Venice, California, press for details of the children's car event. Previewing the article in *The Times*, David Robinson cited a local review of the film, in which the depiction of Venice and its townspeople took precedence over Keystone's 'Charlie Chapman'. (It has sometimes been suggested that the spectators, unacquainted with Chaplin's tramp character, may at times have construed him as a *genuine* nuisance; at one point, a young lad may be seen pulling a face at him!) Among Berglund's sources are accounts left by Henry Lehrman, Chester Conklin (both *qv*) and others, also Kalton C. Lahue's 1971 listing of completion/shipping dates for the Keystone films (from his book *Mack Sennett's Keystone: The Man, the Myth and the Comedies*) and, incredibly, weather reports of the period. Thus armed, Berglund suggests persuasively that *Kid Auto Races* was indeed made first; more importantly, the point is made that, irrespective of production sequence, the spectators at the race were the first public audience to see Chaplin in his tramp costume.

The exact title of this film presents something of a problem. It is generally referred to as *Kid Auto Races at Venice*, sometimes with the suffix 'CA.' denoting California. It was certainly advertised as such at the time, but an available Keystone print (from which Blackhawk Films struck copies in the mid-1970s) bears an original main title card with the ungrammatical name 'Kid's Auto Race'. This also appears on the print's sub-titles. The first of these sub-titles reads 'Kid Auto Race at Venice, Cal.', a virtual repetition of the alleged main title. The available Keystone copy is not quite a pristine version, omitting the final section by concluding after Charlie retrieves his hat from the path of the vehicles. A more common edition, the W.H. Productions reissue known as *The Pest*, continues into more business with Lehrman, concluding with the now-famous close-up of Charlie pulling faces straight into the camera lens. The main title card of this reissue cites 'Kid's Auto Race' as the original name. A later David Robinson work, *Charlie Chaplin: The Art of Comedy* (1995), reprints a sequence of frame enlargements from what purports to be an original Keystone print.

Included is a Keystone sub-title – missing from available copies – introducing the camera-hog and citing (at the top of the card) the main title 'Kid Auto Races at Venice, Ca.'. This suggests further unreliability in the rediscovered Keystone print. There is also a frame suggesting more extensive coverage of the start of the race. One might have expected a title change for the UK, where 'auto' should have become 'car', but contemporary trade advertisements refer to it as 'Kid Auto Races'. (*Bioscope*, incidentally, in the issue of 18 June 1914, said that 'sensational happenings are witnessed during contests between the baby cars, while the funny man persistently obstructs the eager camera men in their operations'.) A more probable explanation for the variant is an early reissue by Keystone itself. Theodore Huff noted that Keystone titles were not permanently inserted into the negatives and could sometimes be mislaid; it is therefore quite possible that an early reissue would have borne new titles offering variations in text.

(See also: *Busy Day, A*; Cars; Costume; Documentaries, compilations; *Funniest Man in the World, The*; Keystone; Newsreels; Reissues; Smoking; Williams, Frank D.)

A KING IN NEW YORK 🎩

(Chaplin film)
Released (in the United Kingdom) by Archway, 12 September 1957. An Attica Film Company production. Produced, written and directed by Charles Chaplin. Music by Charles Chaplin, arranged by Boris Sarbek and conducted by Leighton Lucas. Director of photography: Georges Perinal. Production controller: Mickey Delamar. Art director: Allan Harris. Assistant director: Rene Dupont. Camera operator: Jeff Seaholme. 110 mins (see below).

With Charles Chaplin (King Shahdov ['Shadov' on cast list]), Maxine Audley (Queen Irene), Jerry Desmonde (Prime Minister Voudel), Oliver Johnston (Ambassador Jaume), Dawn Addams (Ann Kay – TV Specialist), Sidney James (Johnson – TV Advertiser), Joan Ingram (Mrs Mona Cromwell – Hostess), Michael Chaplin (Rupert Macabee), John McLaren (Macabee Senior), Phil Brown (Headmaster), Harry Green (Lawyer), Robert Arden (Liftboy), Alan Gifford (School Superintendent), Robert

Cawdron (US Marshall), George Woodbridge, Clifford Buckton, Vincent Lawson (Atomic Commission), Shani Wallis, Joy Nichols, Lauri Lupino Lane (comic paperhanger), George Truzzi (his stooge).

The country of Estrovia stages a revolution. By the time the royal palace is stormed, its inhabitants have departed with the entire contents and flown to the USA. The deposed monarch, King Shahdov, is greeted in New York by pressmen, and his loyal ambassador, Jaume. Shahdov ignores the press, concerned instead with his securities. They have been turned over to his prime minister, Voudel, whom Shahdov considers a crook. The King greets his prime minister, who prefers to discuss privately the question of whose name the securities are in. The matter is raised at a press conference, at which Shahdov encourages Voudel to reveal that they are in his own name. Shahdov would like the securities back, but must first go through Immigration. He is curtailed in the middle of a speech, in which he attributes the revolution to his desire for nuclear power, as opposed to his ministers' preference for nuclear weapons. Shahdov, being fingerprinted, tells a reporter of America's hospitality towards those seeking refuge from tyranny. The King obliges for yet another photo call before withdrawing. At their suite in the Ritz, the prime minister shows the King details of their financial

A King in New York: *a jubilant king*

arrangements. Shahdov is horrified to learn there was so little in the treasury. The books have all been left behind. The securities are at the First National Bank; the bank has closed for the day, but Shahdov wants to see Voudel at ten the next morning. The King had not been informed that Voudel had taken the treasury funds; but for the moment, Shahdov wants to see something of the town. He is excited by America's freedom, 'its youth, its genius, its vitality'. The streets are crowded, so Shahdov and Jaume enter a movie theatre. As a curtain-raiser, there is a live and strident band playing. The King has to step over swooning teenage girls (one

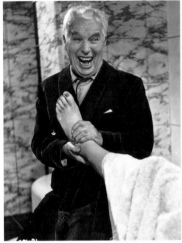

A King in New York: *the King indulges in a little massage; the foot belongs to Dawn Addams*

of whom bites his leg) to reach the front stalls, the best seats obtainable. The show begins with widescreen (*very* wide) trailers for a fatuous detective story, an exploitation picture about transsexuals and a childish western, whose spectators have to look to and fro across the wide screen. Shahdov decides to leave. A supper club proves quieter until a noisy swing band starts up. The noise is such that the King can order caviar only by miming a sturgeon, its capture and disembowelling and the subsequent spreading of eggs. The ambassador's turtle soup is ordered in like manner. That night, the King watches film of his own arrival on the TV news, hearing again the untrue claim that it was he, rather than Voudel, who took Estrovia's money. Jaume rushes in, announcing that Voudel has escaped to South

America with the funds. Nothing can be proved, and the King is penniless. All he has are his atomic plans, useless without backing. Shahdov's consort, Queen Irene, is on her way up to the suite. Jaume offers the King what little money he has, but Shahdov assures him that the nuclear project, on fruition, will solve their financial problem. Queen Irene has flown directly from Paris and wishes to return. They are friendly, but their marriage was a 'matter of State'; the demise of the monarchy allows Shahdov opportunity unselfishly to offer Irene a divorce, solely to give her happiness. Shahdov resists an invitation to dine with a Mrs Cromwell in order to share dinner with the Queen. They discuss their amicable divorce and their wedding, of which this is the anniversary. Shahdov explains that he will remain in the USA because, despite reports of his millions, he will need finance for his nuclear project. The King escorts Irene to the airport. At the hotel, Shahdov drinks champagne and wards off another invitation from Mrs Cromwell, a hostess who owns several women's magazines and a major TV network. Shahdov has no plans to write for the former or appear on the latter. Jaume believes both the King and Queen regret their parting, suspecting Irene is beginning to love her husband. 'Wishful thinking,' claims Shahdov. The King hears a woman singing from the adjoining bathroom. Amused, he has Jaume confirm there is a beautiful woman in the bath. She calls for help, and Shahdov, gallantly covering his head with a towel, obliges. She has donned a towel long before the King removes his. The young lady has hurt her ankle. Shahdov provides a massage, learning that she is Ann Kay, who had expected to meet him at Mrs Cromwell's dinner that evening. She is disappointed to know he will not attend. Jaume, spellbound, is sent to answer the telephone. Ann excuses herself, and the delighted Shahdov cavorts around, plunging fully clothed into the bath. While bathing, he watches a TV commercial for beer, then decides to accept Mrs Cromwell's invitation. Jaume prefers to stay home. At the soirée, the scheming Ann reveals that she persuaded Shahdov to attend by deliberately renting the suite next to his. She plans to get him on her TV show. Ann must get the King into party mood. Shahdov arrives, and is introduced. In the dining room, Ann's technicians have a concealed TV camera. She will try to 'get the King

A King in New York: *His Majesty orders a meal in mime*

going' and is to receive two buzzes as a commercial cue. The guests wait for Shahdov to sit, so they can follow suit; when he finally does so, dinner is served and they must rise again. Mrs Cromwell tries to build up Ann with the King. At dinner, Shahdov becomes amorous towards Ann, but she receives her commercial cue and turns her conversation to anti-perspirants. Shahdov nervously takes it as a hint, but is told Ann works in advertising. He is persuaded to recite the soliloquy from *Hamlet*. Jaume, dozing before the TV, is astonished to see his King performing Shakespeare. Ann congratulates the King, then, on her cue, rambles on about toothpaste. Shahdov, speaking of dentists, fills Mrs Cromwell's mouth with eating utensils to demonstrate their habit of leaving helpless patients while answering the 'phone. Shahdov returns to his suite, to discover he has been the unwitting star of *Ann Kay's Real-Life Surprise Party*. Unable to sleep, Shahdov takes Jaume to a night club. Jaume suggests they return to Europe, but Shahdov insists they need to remain in order to raise money. Jaume believes that no businessman will now take the King seriously, until they discover the TV appearance has made a positive impression on the Americans. The next week brings countless offers for the King to endorse various products. He rejects them all. An unexpected visitor, Mr Johnson, offers Shahdov $10,000 to say 'yum yum' for a cheese commercial. He is shown the door. There is a visit from Ann, delivering a note from Mrs Cromwell. The note, plus an enclosed cheque for $20,000, are torn up. Shahdov bids her a chilly goodbye. Shahdov is to visit a progressive boys' school. There is as yet no word from the Atomic Commission, and Shahdov thinks he may have to accept some of the commercial offers. On discovering he has a bank balance of $912, Shahdov hastily reassembles Mrs Cromwell's cheque. At the school, dedicated to encouraging genius by free expression, Shahdov meets a parade of spoiled brats. One of them,

A King in New York: *the TV girl persuades the King to pose*

A King in New York: *the King and his Ambassador (Oliver Johnston) are not at all unnerved by accusations of subversion ..*

Rupert, is a 10-year-old Marxist orator who will not allow the King a chance to speak. His obnoxious confrères make Shahdov sit in a cake. The hotel management sends reminders about the unpaid bill. There is still no word from the Atomic Commission, and social invitations have dried up. Jaume believes that Shahdov worried people at his first press conference, speaking of nuclear power bringing about a Utopia. Shahdov owes the hotel $11,000, but orders a lavish meal. Ann returns with Johnson,

who offers $50,000 for Shahdov to advertise whisky. Pretending not to need the cash, Shahdov accepts, and is photographed by Ann. He considers her sneaky, and takes revenge by making a play for her. Shahdov rehearses a TV ad without the whisky, then, on air, splutters over it. It is deemed a fiasco until Ann arrives, saying it has been taken as a deliberate joke. Offers flood in, and the ad is to be repeated across the nation, guaranteeing Shahdov an extra $20,000. A picture of Shahdov, choking, appears on billboards everywhere. Ann prepares a photo session for Shahdov to advertise hormones. To make it convincing, she persuades the King to have a face-lift, assuring him of an additional fee in consequence. The result is a waxen-looking Shahdov, with a turned-up nose. He is warned not to 'stretch' anything for a while. Shahdov is at first unrecognized at the hotel, while both Ann and Jaume are horrified by the overdone surgery. Shahdov is taken to a night club to cheer him up, but his shortened lip prohibits drinking, even through a straw. The house is in an uproar over a comic paperhanger and his well-dressed stooge, but Shahdov dares not laugh. Eventually, he succumbs and his stitches burst. Shahdov has the operation reversed and does the hormone commercial anyway. A blizzard grips New York. Shahdov meets the boy, Rupert, shivering in the street. The boy has 'graduated' from school. Shahdov takes him in, promising not to inform the police. Shahdov arranges a hot bath and food for the boy, informing Jaume that Rupert is obnoxious but a genius. He has run away from school as a result of being questioned about his family, who are evidently communists. Jaume reminds Shahdov that he has a broadcast in twenty minutes and cannot in any case become involved in defending communists. Shahdov refuses to turn the boy out in wet clothes. The boy, in loaned pyjamas and dressing gown, is questioned in mock-McCarthy style about his politics. Weary of being asked, Rupert settles for communism. In Shahdov's absence, the house detective queries the boy's presence; he claims to be Shahdov's nephew just as the King returns. Shahdov, surprised at the audacity, plays along. Rupert's clothes have yet to dry, so Shahdov orders new ones. There is at last a call from the Atomic Commission, whose delegates are en route. They arrive sooner than expected and meet the boy,

unaccompanied, while Shahdov and Jaume fetch their plans from the bank. Believing he is the King's nephew, they are startled by his fabricated tales of family history and radical ideas. Shahdov buys a suit for Rupert, unaware that he is scandalizing the visitors. On his return, they are told the truth about the boy and pacified. Shahdov, playing checkers with Rupert, insists he must return to school. On television, they see an 'Un-American Activities' trial at which Rupert's father admits having been a member of the Communist Party then is charged with contempt for refusing to testify against others. Learning that his father will be imprisoned, Rupert breaks down in tears. Comforting him, Shahdov promises to take Rupert back to school in his car and to visit him the next day. A US Marshal arrives to take Rupert back to school. Shahdov volunteers to take him, but orders must be followed. Rupert, though grateful, declines Shahdov's offer to accompany him. The charging of Rupert's parents with contempt does not excite newsmen, but Rupert's discovery in Shahdov's suite is another matter. Jaume thinks he is being followed; his seeming paranoia is justified when a radio broadcast speaks of an international atomic spy ring involving 'Royal communists'. They are tipped off about a man waiting to serve a subpoena. Shahdov and Jaume exchange hats as a ruse to fool him. Ann walks in, outraged at the news. She distracts the man long enough for Shahdov to attempt an escape. When Shahdov and the man are trapped in the hotel's revolving door, his pursuer turns out to be no more than an autograph hunter. Shahdov is besieged by a group of them and, while signing autographs, unwittingly accepts the subpoena. The committee tries to goad Rupert into 'helping' his parents by informing on their friends. Shahdov's lawyer advises him to use his Royal Prerogative when asked if he is a communist. Shahdov considers the question 'absurd', but is told there are many other absurd things going on. Leaving for court, Shahdov becomes entangled in the lift's fire extinguisher. Late, he arrives with the fire hose attached to his right index finger, causing hilarity when required to take the oath. Unaware of the situation, staff attach the hose to a hydrant and the resultant jet of water, though freeing the King, drenches the committee in front of millions of TV viewers. Shahdov, a 'friendly witness', is 'cleared of communism', but books a flight back to Europe. Ann, dressed in a fur coat, calls to say good-bye. Shahdov rejects her pleas to stay, even though the court appearance has made him vastly popular. She explains that America's apparent craziness is a 'passing phase', but Shahdov prefers to sit it out elsewhere. A telegram informs Shahdov that Irene has decided not to divorce. Shahdov's attraction to Ann is obvious but will not be pursued. He has time to visit Rupert, and is told the boy's parents were released from prison after their son 'co-operated'. The boy is deeply upset, but Shahdov promises to have Rupert and his family visit him once the 'hysteria' is over. He is warned there may be 'complications'. Shahdov and Jaume take their flight to Europe.

A King in New York, Chaplin's first film since leaving America, was also to be his last starring vehicle (he would take only a minor rôle in the subsequent *A Countess From Hong Kong* [*qv*]). Parallels between its story and Chaplin's contemporary position are, of course, easy to spot: an exiled monarch, his existence troubled by an American hysteria during which the unlikeliest people could be accused of dangerous sympathies.

On 25 February 1956, several weeks before shooting began, *The Times* published an interview in which Chaplin, denying the rôle of 'propagandist', claimed only a wish to make people laugh, albeit with an element of satire at the expense of general modern-day fads. Chaplin expected a filming schedule of ten weeks and, when asked if the New York scenes were to be shot in the genuine locations, laughed. 'I think they'd scalp me!' he said.

A King in New York was instead produced in England, at Shepperton studios. Consequently, most of the 'Americans' are portrayed by British actors, aside from a few genuine specimens (such as Alan Gifford) who were permanent residents. British actress Kay Kendall was first choice for the advertising girl, but the part went eventually to another Briton, Dawn Addams (*qv*), whom Chaplin had known since her unsuccessful audition for *Limelight* (*qv*); in turn, adopted Londoner Sid James (*qv*) replaced American expatriate Sam Wanamaker.

Chaplin's assistant, Jerry Epstein (*qv*) often spoke of an old-guard studio snobbery towards Chaplin, who tended to be looked down on as 'a mere music-hall comic'. Nothing like that ever happened in the USA, where, he felt, people are evaluated solely on ability rather than background. Chaplin was always aware that America had allowed him an eminence impossible within Britain's class structure of the day; fortunately, such barriers to mobility, and their accompanying attitudes, were broken down considerably in the decade separating this from his last UK production.

On 11 May 1956, Cecil Wilson of the *Daily Mail* reported heavy security around Shepperton's Stage 'C', where even the principal actors were required to produce an entry pass. Mention was made of the ten-week schedule – nine in the studio and one on location – allowing no time for personal interviews. Chaplin's day began at 8:30 a.m.; when others disappeared for lunch, Chaplin would be brought a snack to eat while viewing the rushes. After finishing at 9:30 p.m., he would spend his evening mulling over the day's work. Most of the scant details released concerned the advertising girl's ruse to have the King recite Shakespeare on TV, allowing Wilson an opportunity to compare the idea of concealed cameras with the genuine secrecy cloaking the film's set. A similar story – in the *People* of 27 May – spoke of Chaplin's ban on reporters and concern for potential 'sabotage' of his plans. The *Star* of 6 June managed to interview Dawn Addams, who offered a simple explanation for it all: '... comedy depends on surprise. What is more boring than a joke you have heard about before? So Mr. Chaplin is trying to keep the whole thing a secret.' Much as the surreptitious approach intrigued UK correspondents, speculation was even greater in America. As early as 19 May 1956, Felix Barker of the London *Evening News* reported that the film would not be shown in America; a week earlier, *Variety* had gleaned that Chaplin was specifically to attack McCarthyism, rather than the USA in general.

Looking back on the recent experience for *The Sunday Times* of 9 September 1957, Chaplin wrote of the difference in working outside his own studio. Although English himself, Chaplin felt like a 'lone stranger' among the all-English crew; he was used to a 'family' within which he was cosseted, by his own admission, rather like a 'spoiled brother'. Chaplin claimed to have enjoyed working at Shepperton, finding the people helpful and encouraging, if given to a 'wait-and-see attitude'. At a safe distance of time, Jerry Epstein was able to speak of a downside, consisting of a reluctance to provide props and, at one point, Chaplin causing a strike by the simple act of moving a chair, instead of asking a propman to do it. The French cameraman, Georges Périnal, had photographed Rene Clair's *Le Million*, but

His Majesty's pursuer turns out to be an innocuous autograph hound in **A King in New York**

A King in New York: Shahdov takes the boy genius (Michael Chaplin) under his wing

was, according to Epstein, more interested in fiddling with the dramatic lighting than in photographing the comedy.

On 31 August 1956, the *News Chronicle* reported Chaplin's hope to have finished the cutting by Christmas, claiming that he was at work from 9 a.m. to 7:30 p.m. each day. The film was edited in Paris, where Chaplin worked with one English editor and several French assistants. *The Times* of 1 January reported both this and the belief that editing was nearing completion. Music scoring was done after a return to

London, with the final mixing taking place again in Paris.

Chaplin relaxed his publicity ban on 31 May 1957, when the *Daily Mail* published an advance preview of the plot, accompanied by some then-exclusive stills. Two weeks before, he had startled the industry by choosing a minor distributor, Archway, established by two ex-servicemen only nine years earlier and known chiefly for dubbed imports or low-budget British efforts (noting a premature outbreak of American hostility to the film on 15 June, Anthony Carthew of the *Daily Herald* suggested that the same attitude might have spread to the major British distributors). The trade show, on 10 September, pre-dated release by two days. At his hotel that day, Chaplin was prompted by reporters to do his old comic walk, after which he explained why the tramp character could not be revived: 'The world in which he lived just doesn't exist any more. There is such a thing as an anachronism, and a satire about the tramp today would be just that.' Reaction to the film was, to employ the usual expression, mixed. The *Daily Film Renter* approved unconditionally, considering the 'old Chaplin magic' unimpaired. William Whitebait of the *New Statesman* implied praise for Chaplin himself rather than his latest picture, in the belief that it was 'better – a hundred times better – half-Chaplin than no Chaplin at all'. Kenneth Tynan, deputizing for the *Observer*'s C.A. Lejeune, regarded the film as 'never boring' despite its length and alleged weaknesses, the latter typified by Tynan's belief that Chaplin, 'flashes' of whose visual humour were to be seen, had not mastered verbal timing as opposed to its visual equivalent. Tynan decided it was for this reason that Chaplin allowed a child character to speak for him, suggesting a 'parental ventriloquism'; 'Even so,' Tynan continued, 'the points that are made – about the withdrawal of passports and the abject necessity of informing – are new to the screen, and it is about time somebody made them.' Exploring this topic, Donald Gomery of the *Daily Express* considered it 'disturbing' that Chaplin should use a child to express his views. After the screening, Gomery had asked Chaplin if he might have 'exaggerated the evil influence of the Committee on Un-American Activities – especially now that McCarthy is dead'. Instead of perhaps extending Gomery's logic by suggesting ironically that one might equally have forgiven Hitler after

1945, Chaplin instead replied that he made no apologies for the film and fully endorsed everything he had said in it. 'I make films to make people laugh,' added Chaplin, 'and I think this is a very funny film.' Gomery agreed that the first part of *King* was in this category, but likened the political attack to 'hitting a nut with a sledgehammer'. Dilys Powell of *The Sunday Times* saw *A King in New York* as a final stripping-down to 'Mr Chaplin' himself after the gradual discarding of the tramp via Hynkel, the Jewish barber and the new guises of Verdoux and Calvero. Left with 'nothing to be entertaining with except his own perpetually astounding gifts' and his own recent experience, Chaplin managed to be 'brilliantly funny' in guying his former host nation until getting to the real point, itself considered not unreasonable. In Powell's view, all the familiar Chaplin ingredients were present, save for the pathos, and *A King in New York* 'has the heaven-sent gift of making you laugh uncontrollably'. In *The Financial Times*, Derek Granger made it plain that he preferred the 'Charlie' of old to the latterly 'message-crammed' Chaplin, in whom he detected a measure of smugness. The *Daily Mail*'s Cecil Wilson appreciated the comedy scenes, but interpreted the result as 'Chaplin the matchless clown fighting a losing battle with Chaplin the pompous pamphleteer; a battle in which the clowning is repeatedly overrun by *thinking*'. Peter Burney of the *News of the World* offered some blunt advice: 'Get yourself a director and a scriptwriter.' Milton Shulman of the *Sunday Express* had been a Chaplin fan since boyhood but was 'bored with [Chaplin's] "sermonizing"'. Not surprisingly, the radical *Daily Worker* saw merit in an undisguised attack on America's far Right, citing *King* as 'one of Charlie's finest films' and relishing the moment when the 'witch-hunters are hosed'. That this was a sensitive picture did not go unnoticed. The French seem generally unworried by such matters, but the removal of certain 'anti-American' material was, reportedly, demanded by that country's distributor (Mexico and Italy screened it uncut). On 18 September 1957, *Variety*, from a distance, noted a good reception in Britain and 'raves' in France, but the film was widely attacked in the United States, sight unseen; Chaplin had kept to his decision not to release it there and, according to reports in *The Times* and *Daily Express* of 25 October 1957, had even barred US reporters from the French première. At

one press conference, he spent twenty minutes talking to a British TV news team, then snubbed a representative of NBC. Hostility in the USA had broken out in June, three months prior to the film's release.

At the time, Chaplin told the press that *A King in New York* 'is a non-political film. It is simply a fantasy on the adventures of an exiled European monarch who takes refuge in America.' This is not entirely true, but his widely-supposed 'bitter satire of the USA' is actually more a leg-pull at the expense of America's more vulgar trends of the period (Chaplin sings in a few broadly American-accented voice-overs in the early sequences), at least until the final attack on McCarthy-era absurdity, hysteria and the denial of liberty. Chaplin could have been far more devastating had he wished, but seems to have been widely construed as someone with an axe to grind. Among his targets are widescreen films (reportedly inspired by Epstein's comments after seeing *The Robe*), cosmetic surgery and 'progressive' schools of the type attended by at least one of his children, prior to the family's departure for Europe. (In this instance, the pupil is played by a son, Michael Chaplin. Michael's father wanted him to see the film and thus sent him to a private screening in London during November 1970.) Plenty of space was allocated to Chaplin's more familiar comedy of mime, notably his cavortings when first meeting the girl, and the silent conveying of his regret that the woman in his bath is visible only from the neck up. The slapstick paperhanging act (performed by veteran double-act Lauri Lupino Lane and his 'feed', George Truzzi) is both reminiscent of *Work* (*qv*) and slightly undercranked to simulate the received view of silent comedies. A later gag employing a revolving door has its roots in *The Cure* (*qv*) and works quite well; by contrast, the hose business in the courtroom is a more serious-minded echo of *A Night in the Show* (*qv*), but only serves to emphasize how Chaplin's latter-day adversaries required a more substantial means of retaliation.

For all his denial of a political motive, Chaplin's ban on an American release remained in force until its New York première at the Columbia University Cinematheque in December 1973. When finally made available in the USA, *King* provided a pleasant surprise to some people, who had hitherto been obliged to gauge the film by its reviews.

One of these was Scott Eyman in *Classic Film Collector*, who noted Chaplin's 'lack of accusatory shrillness' and 'amused bewilderment at what had happened to his adopted country'. Andrew Sarris of *Village Voice* offered great praise, allowing for Chaplin having been 'an unregenerate reactionary in the practice of his own craft' and the fact that the youth of Nixon's era might have wondered what all the fuss was over. 'As I write on and on about *A King in New York*,' mused Sarris, 'I seem to be developing excuses for not liking it. Actually, I love the film.'

A King in New York is generally cited to run 105 minutes; on British TV it runs 106 minutes at the increased speed of 25 frames per second, and this with a few obvious splices. Theatrically, it would run an additional four minutes. An American version, mastered for video at 24 f.p.s., seems to have been divested of perhaps seven minutes. Noticeable cuts are as follows: Shahdov's photo call on arrival at the Ritz; shots of Broadway theatres at night; footage of Shahdov and Jaume outside a movie house; a similar shot, after they have left; a brief section at the beginning of Mrs Cromwell's party; a turn by a cabaret singer (Shani Wallis [*qv*]), prior to the mimed dinner order; a scene where the hotel management discuss Shahdov's overdue bill; Shahdov and Jaume debating the idea of plastic surgery; a post-operative Shahdov failing to be recognized at the hotel; and Shahdov's meeting with Ann after the operation is reversed.

(See also: Alcohol; Awards; Children; Desmonde, Jerry; Food; James, Sidney; Johnston, Oliver; Music; Politics; Risqué humour; Royalty; Slapstick; Television; Trick photography; Villains; Walk, The)

KIRTLEY, VIRGINIA
(1883–1956)

The leading lady in Chaplin's first film, *Making a Living* (*qv*), and the heroine of the film-within-a-film that Charlie sees in *A Film Johnnie* (*qv*). A reference to the latter film, in the *Motion Picture News* of 14 March 1914, refers to the actress as 'Jickie Kirtely': the surname is one of a few published variants in spelling, while 'Jickie' is, presumably, a nickname. Prime source for her biographical details is an article in the November 1989 *Classic Images* by Billy Doyle, entitled 'Lost Players'. According to Doyle, Virginia Kirtley was born in Bowling Green,

Missouri, and made her stage debut in Los Angeles during 1910. There followed stock work until she entered films with the Imp Company in 1912. She joined Keystone in 1913, among her non-Chaplin appearances being a split-reel comedy with Roscoe 'Fatty' Arbuckle (*qv*), *A Flirt's Mistake* (1914) (once available to collectors from Blackhawk Films). During 1915 she was leading lady in a series of comedies under American's 'Beauty' banner, then moved to Selig during the autumn of that year. She appeared in a lengthy series of Selig shorts (varying between one and three reels) in addition to one feature, *Who Shall Take My Life?* (1918). In 1917 she had married Eddie Lyons, and went on to co-author some of the Nestor comedies in which her husband was teamed with Lee Moran. She retired after giving birth to a daughter, but made an unsuccessful comeback attempt in 1928, two years after Lyons' early death from appendicitis.

THE KNOCKOUT 🎩

(Chaplin film)
Keystone Comedy released by Mutual, 11 June 1914 (completed 29 May). Produced by Mack Sennett. Screenplay and director credits uncertain, the latter attributed variously to Sennett, Charles Avery or Arbuckle (see below). Photography attributed to Frank D.

Williams. Working title: *A Fighting Demon*. Reissue titles include *Counted Out* and *The Pugilist*. Two reels. 1,960 feet.

With Roscoe 'Fatty' Arbuckle ('Pug'), Minta Durfee (his girlfriend), Al St. John (her unwelcome suitor), Hank Mann (the fake Cyclone Flynn), Edgar Kennedy (Cyclone Flynn), Charlie Chaplin (referee), Mack Swain (cowboy), Mack Sennett (intimidated spectator in street), Slim Summerville, Charley Chase (spectators), the Keystone Cops.

Two hoboes are ordered off a freight car in the town of Dingville. Lacking money for food, and seeing prizefights advertised outside the town hall, they decide to 'pose as pugilists', one of them claiming to be 'Cyclone Flynn', the champion. At the local athletic club, 'Pug', an erstwhile boxer, proves his ability to fend off his girl's unwelcome suitor and his fellow-rowdies at the club. Outside the hall, the vagrants succeed in obtaining money from the contest's promoter, and proceed to buy a meal. Those from the athletic club persuade Pug to accept the challenge against Cyclone Flynn; Pug scribbles a note of acceptance, handing it to the promoter. When the promoter informs the vagrants of the beefy challenger, they disappear to watch him train. Unnerved, they send a forged note from the champ, offering to

The Knockout: *referee Charlie decorates the canvas while Arbuckle and Kennedy fight on*

split the purse in return for Pug taking a dive. From their hiding place, the tramps see Pug tearing up the note and promptly flee. They return to the hall just after the arrival of the real Cyclone Flynn, who, taking a dim view of being impersonated, sends the hoboes on their way. The time of the fight arrives. A crowd fills the auditorium, one of whom is Pug's girlfriend, disguised unconvincingly as 'one of the boys'. Pug, having met the true Cyclone Flynn, receives a visit from the MC, a gun-toting western type who has staked a large sum on Pug's victory. He is afforded unnerving proximity by means of a ringside box. The fight begins, and the referee is soon knocked to the ropes. His impartiality falls into question when he kicks Pug to the canvas; for part of the time it is the referee, rather than Flynn, with whom Pug is in the clinches. In time the dazed referee (who actually counts the stars he is seeing) uses the ropes to pull himself along, sliding across the wet canvas. The cowboy MC is aghast at the proceedings; so is Pug, who, grabbing the MC's guns, sets off on a rampage. He chases Flynn from the building, followed by the crowd. The police are summoned. Flynn's attempts to hide are futile; so are the efforts of the Keystone Cops. The chase continues over the rooftops, until Flynn ducks into one of the buildings, where the chase interrupts a sedate musical gathering. Pug, his ammunition exhausted, is lassooed by the cops but offers a creditable tug-of-war, dragging his pursuers to a jetty. Pug is first into the water, followed by the chaotic lawmen.

Though generally listed as a Chaplin film, *The Knockout* is in fact a starring vehicle for Roscoe 'Fatty' Arbuckle (*qv*), with Chaplin contributing briefly during the boxing sequence. Reissues (*qv*) have often billed Chaplin as star; one of these is from a series of revived Keystones, dubbed with sound in the early 1930s bearing the slogan, 'Charlie Chaplin as he was 20 years ago'. Available prints vary in completeness: that shown on British TV by Channel 4, though slightly marred by being 'cropped' for sound/film ratio, is substantially complete until the finale, which omits the cops' descent into the sea; the full ending is present in a version circulated on video in the US, although this edition lacks the opening scenes of the vagrants being ordered off the freight car (oddly, it is unique in having the main Keystone titles for parts

one and two, but is missing some of the sub-titles). The latter-day Blackhawk Films edition seems complete, albeit lacking the original main title.

Direction of *The Knockout* has often been attributed to Mack Sennett (*qv*) but, as Blackhawk's historical notes point out, Arbuckle is known to have directed his own comedies at this time. Several moments anticipate Arbuckle's subsequent work, among them an interesting shot of Arbuckle walking towards the camera into close-up, and a coy gag where he has the camera tilt upwards while he changes into boxing trunks (the latter idea resurfaces in Arbuckle's 1917 short, *Coney Island*). Harry M. Geduld, in his *Chapliniana*, expresses a belief that Chaplin choreographed the boxing scene, comparing it stylistically to later sequences in his own films and, from an earlier vintage, a Karno sketch called *The Yap-Yaps*. The basic idea of *The Knockout* was to resurface the following year in *The Champion* (*qv*). The sharp-eyed will notice a further Chaplin connection in the display of posters outside the town hall; one of these may clearly be discerned as an advertisement for Chaplin's *Caught in a Cabaret* (*qv*).

(See also: Bordeaux, Joe; Durfee, Minta; Fighting; Guest appearances; Home movies; Karno, Fred; Kennedy, Edgar; Keystone; Summerville, George J. 'Slim'; Swain, Mack; Television; Video releases; Williams, Frank D.)

KNOTT, LYDIA
(1866–1955)

Indiana-born character actress (mother of director Lambert Hillyer) who plays Jean's mother in *A Woman of Paris* (*qv*). Originally on the stage, she was taken to California and its film industry by Thomas H. Ince. Other films include *Crime and Punishment* (1917), *Common Law* (1918), *Danger – Go Slow!* (1918), *Marriage Ring* (1919), *Breaking Point* (1921), *Afraid to Fight* (1922), *Broadway Madonna* (1922), *Dynamite Smith* (1924), *East Lynne* (1925), *The Primrose Path* (1925), *Rose of the World* (1925), *Our Dancing Daughters* (1928) and *Men Without Law* (1930).

KONO (TORAICHI)
(1888–?)

Chaplin's Japanese chauffeur, valet and confidante for many years; appears on screen, as a chauffeur, in *The Adventurer* and *How to Make Movies* (both *qv*). Kono acted as intermediary for, and general organizer of Chaplin until ousted, it is said, by Paulette Goddard (*qv*). He is reported afterwards to have been given a job in the Japanese office of United Artists (*qv*). John McCabe records that, during the Second World War, Kono was among the many Japanese-Americans placed in the 'disgraceful relocation center' at Manzanar, California, on the eastern side of the Tehachapi Mountains; Alistair Cooke, translating the US government's 'relocation center' to 'concentration camp', met Kono there in 1942, 'sitting at the door of a wooden shack with a handkerchief over his mouth against the swirling dust storms of the Owens Valley'. There are reports of a 1993 Japanese-made programme about Kono, entitled *The Other Side of the Story*.

(See also: Cars; Documentaries, compilations; *Gentleman Tramp, The*)

LAMPTON, DEE
(1898–1919)

Born in Fort Worth, Texas, tubby Dee Lampton (who weighed 300lb) played the fat boy in Chaplin's *A Night in the Show* (*qv*); he entered pictures after a year's stage experience. Also worked at Keystone (*qv*) and Rolin, appearing in Harold Lloyd's early 'Lonesome Luke' comedies and the ironically-titled 'Skinny Lampton' series. Dee Lampton's early death was brought about by pneumonia.

LAUGHING GAS

(Chaplin film)
Keystone Comedy released by Mutual, 9 July 1914. Produced by Mack Sennett. Written and directed by Charles Chaplin. Photography attributed to Frank D. Williams. Reissue titles include *The Dentist* and *Tuning* (or *Turning*) *His Ivories* (see below). One reel. 1,020 feet (UK length cited in *Bioscope*).

With Charlie Chaplin (dentist's caretaker), Fritz Schade (Dr Pain, dentist), Alice Howell (dentist's wife), Joseph Swickard (frantic patient), Mack Swain (burly man), Slim Summerville (passerby struck by brick), Gene Marsh (pretty patient).

Charlie arrives at the dentist's surgery, authoritatively surveying the patients before setting to work as caretaker, taking cuspidors into the kitchen. After an altercation with a midget colleague, Charlie runs a carpet-sweeper over the waiting room, hitting a patient's foot. He returns to the kitchen and his argumentative colleague. Dr Pain, the

dentist, arrives to see his first patient who, frantic with toothache, is anaesthetized. At the dentist's home, Mrs Pain sets off for a stroll. Dr Pain extracts the patient's tooth, but finds he cannot be revived. He calls Charlie for assistance, though Charlie seems more interested in flirting with a pretty girl. Dr Pain leaves Charlie with the task of restoring the patient to consciousness. Charlie stimulates some life by means of a mallet; the patient, still under the gas, laughs uncontrollably, but is rendered dormant again with the mallet. Dr Pain returns with an urgent prescription for Charlie to have filled. Charlie blunders his way through the kitchen and waiting room, antagonizing colleague and patients. Outside the pharmacy, Charlie's cane accidentally strikes a large man, who complains. Back at the surgery, Dr Pain finds his patient laughing hysterically. Charlie, having obtained the prescription, gives the large man a kick, and battle commences. This is forgotten as the man stops to greet the dentist's wife, who is passing by. Charlie kicks his opponent in the stomach, and sets off after Mrs Pain. She rejects his attentions, climbing some steps to a doorway. Charlie makes a grab, pulling off her skirt. As she panics, the large man returns and, surprisingly, passes out. Mrs Pain runs, blundering into another passerby. Charlie gives the big man a kick and escapes. Mrs Pain rushes home. From his hiding place, Charlie hurls a brick at the large man, knocking out some of his teeth. A second brick misses its mark, but loosens the teeth of the other passerby, who does not see the culprit. Charlie scurries back to work while Mrs Pain collapses at home. Dr Pain receives a telephone call from his maid, asking him to hurry home because his wife has met with an accident. His patient regains consciousness and, puzzled, leaves the surgery. Charlie returns to work after Dr Pain has left, dumping the prescription into a cuspidor. The dentist is comforting his distraught spouse as Charlie takes the opportunity of 'treating' the pretty girl. Unknown to Charlie, the waiting room is now occupied by the two men whose teeth he sent asunder. Ushering the young lady out, he spots them but, hiding behind the door, brings in the second man. Charlie is using a giant set of pincers on the patient's teeth when the large man bursts in. As Charlie evades him, Dr and Mrs Pain enter the waiting room. Charlie throws a bag at his

adversary, knocking him into dentist and wife. Battles ensues between Charlie, the Pains, his colleague and the two patients. Believing he has vanquished them all, Charlie struts around until knocked down by Mrs Pain, who in turn collapses on the sofa.

Laughing Gas is said to owe much to an earlier Karno sketch, *The Dentist*. The outright sadism exhibited by Chaplin in this film (tempered by occasional romantic dalliance) is in the spirit both of Karno's presentations and the overall nature of Chaplin's work at Keystone (*qv*); while Charlie's brick-throwing seems gratuitous, the dental savagery is executed with the exaggeration and finesse that is essential to remove the sting from this kind of comedy (on 26 November 1914, *Bioscope* rather guardedly called it 'an uproarious farce of a kind which is likely to create unrestrained mirth for its particular class of audience'!). W.C. Fields managed a similar task in his 1932 short, *The Dentist*, as did Laurel & Hardy in *Leave 'Em Laughing* (1927) and *Pardon Us* (1931).

Many prints of *Laughing Gas* lack the opening and closing scenes, omitting most or all of Charlie's first appearance outside the surgery (greeting the new day with a yawn) and cropping off just as Mack Swain (*qv*) confronts Charlie for the final scrap. The 1920 British reissue copies were listed at the time under the title 'Tuning His Ivories', but at least one source quotes this as 'turning' (which makes less sense as a pun). Official Films' copy, retitled 'Laffing Gas', has the last few feet of the missing opening and a slightly choppy version of the often absent

Laughing Gas: *Charlie and two of 'his' patients*
Museum of Modern Art/Film Stills Archive

finale; the BBC *Chaplin SuperClown* edition is complete.

(See also: Auctions; Home movies; Karno Company, The; Laurel, Stan; Reissues; Risqué humour; *Rounders, The*; Sickness; Summerville, George J. 'Slim'; Television; Williams, Frank D.)

LAUREL, STAN
(1890–1965)

British comedian, from a theatrical family, born Arthur Stanley Jefferson in Ulverston, Lancashire (now Cumbria). Stan Jefferson (the name 'Laurel' was acquired in the USA) had a similar comic talent to Chaplin's, and was his understudy in the Karno Company (*qv*). Stan was never required to deputize in this way, but the two comedians became close friends, sharing lodgings while on tour. In 1929, Stan told *Film Weekly* of Charlie's habit of creating panic by arriving at the theatre at the last minute: '... many times I was dressed and ready. He always showed up just in the nick of time, smiling and unperturbed. His mind was usually a thousand miles away, dwelling in some land where the rest of us poor troupers could not follow.' He recalled the Karno people foreseeing Chaplin's move into films as a grave mistake, only to be proved wrong. Laurel spent several years in American vaudeville as a Chaplin imitator, but eventually abandoned the idea. A chance meeting on the street in 1917 saw Chaplin urging his former colleague to try the movies; a year later, Laurel made his picture debut under the auspices of a Los Angeles theatre

Stan Laurel's solo film comedies often recall his tenure as Chaplin's understudy; this film, The Egg *(1922), was made for G.M. Anderson, Charlie's former boss*
BFI Stills, Posters and Designs

Stan Laurel recalled never having deputized for Chaplin during Karno days; this congratulatory note, from Seattle in 1912, suggests otherwise

owner, Adolph Ramish. Chaplin attended its preview and, according to Laurel's biographer, John McCabe, promised to call with an offer of work. The call did not materialize, and Laurel went to work instead for Universal chief Carl Laemmle, who had also attended the screening. Laurel made his own way in films, including a series for G.M. Anderson (*qv*). His style at this time was an uneasy blend of his own and that of Chaplin. At the Hal Roach studio, he was teamed with Oliver Hardy (ironically, a former colleague of Chaplin lookalike Billy West), with whom he found both a distinctive screen character and a fame that is often compared to Chaplin's. Although it is believed that each was kept informed of the other's activities by Alf Reeves (*qv*), meetings between the two were usually brief and accidental. On one occasion, Laurel spotted Chaplin in a restaurant, whereupon he amused his guests with an overblown parody of Chaplin's elaborate method of mixing a salad. After touring Europe with Oliver Hardy during 1947–8, Laurel had the task of delivering a book to Chaplin on behalf of British journalist Hannen Swaffer. Instead of posting it, he visited Chaplin's home in person and was entertained for some eight hours. After extensive reminiscence, they decided to maintain closer contact, but Chaplin, never the most enthusiastic of correspondents, failed to answer Laurel's letters. Despite their numerous shared experiences, Laurel is referred to only

through a single photo caption in Chaplin's autobiography; its companion of a decade later, *My Life in Pictures*, adds little more.

(See also: Ayres, Agnes; Camera-looks; Campbell, Eric; Costume; Essanay; Food; Gilbert, Billy; Goddard, Paulette; Grand Order of Water Rats, The; Howell, Alice; Impersonators; Karno, Fred; Kennedy, Edgar; Left-handedness; Leno, Dan; *Mabel at the Wheel*; Music; Smoking; Stamps, coins; Sutherland, A. Edward; Turpin, Ben; Wood, 'Wee' Georgie; *Young Charlie Chaplin*)

LEE, FLORENCE
(1888–1962)

Plays the blind girl's grandmother in *City Lights* (*qv*); was married to Del Henderson (1883-1956), a comic actor who had been a director at Keystone (*qv*). Active at Universal, Pathé, FBO and elsewhere, her other films include *Top o' the Morning* (1922) and *Speed Mad* (1925).

LEE, RAYMOND
(c.1914-74)

(Chaplin films *qv*)
Child actor who is reported as playing one of Charlie's two offspring (the other being Jackie Coogan [*qv*]) in *A Day's Pleasure.* He has also been credited as the

younger brother of Chuck Riesner's character in *The Kid*, and the child who applauds Charlie's sermon in *The Pilgrim*. Latterly, he eschewed acting to become instead a prominent film historian.

(See also: Children; Riesner, Charles F. 'Chuck')

LEFT-HANDEDNESS

(Chaplin films *qv*)
Examination of the Chaplin films quickly reveals the comedian to have been left-handed. As an artist in *The Face On the Bar Room Floor*, he is seen wielding a paintbrush and, later, chalk, with his left hand; in *The Idle Class*, he takes a left-handed swing at a golf ball; but better known is his left-handed violin playing in *The Vagabond* and *Limelight*. Despite this predisposition, Chaplin tended to hold a pen in his right hand, something visible on-screen in the First National films in which he autographs the main title card. It is believed that Chaplin, in common with the majority of left-handed people at that time, was forced into right-handed penmanship during childhood. The same seems to have applied to his friend and one-time understudy, Stan Laurel (*qv*). Chaplin was in consequence ambidextrous, though with the usual result of neither hand producing an especially neat script. Although a more enlightened attitude prevails today, left-handedness was long regarded as undesirable and, on occasion, suspect; not for nothing does the word 'sinister' derive from the Latin word for 'left', while in heraldry a bar thus directed symbolizes illegitimacy.

(See also: Artists; *Chaplin Revue, The*; First National; Impersonators; Music; Titling)

LEHRMAN, HENRY 'PATHÉ'
(1883–1946)

Viennese-born director, reportedly a former streetcar conductor, Henry Lehrman is said to have acquired the nickname 'Pathé' after a fraudulent claim to D.W. Griffith (*qv*) that he had worked for the prestigious Pathé Frères company in France. A story from Mack Sennett's memoirs has Lehrman working as a cinema usher, whose acquaintance Sennett made when observing audience reaction to his screen performances. Sennett recalled Lehrman passing himself off to Griffith as a Frenchman, until the imposture was revealed. True or not, Sennett and Lehrman were colleagues at Biograph, an association that continued after Sennett founded Keystone (*qv*). Lehrman's reputation was essentially that of opportunistic ham; he soon rationed his acting appearances in favour of directing, and in fairness it should be said that he helped create the ultimate Keystone style. Because Lehrman ran Keystone's second unit, it was his job to ease in newcomers such as Roscoe 'Fatty' Arbuckle (*qv*) and Charlie Chaplin. As noted elsewhere, Lehrman and Chaplin clashed immediately, and their first project, *Making a Living* (*qv*), was not deemed satisfactory by either. Chaplin believed that Lehrman had cut all the comedy, but admitted in turn to having been baffled by the techniques of film-making, in which Lehrman was well-versed. In passing, one might note an essay by Hooman Mehran in the Winter 1995 *Limelight* magazine, speculating on Lehrman's possible influence on Chaplin as a director. Mehran compares Lehrman's strong ego with that of Chaplin, citing his consequent insistence on absolute control and willingness – on one occasion – to screen and edit films while in his sickbed. Chaplin seems also to have inherited both Lehrman's strictness and his practice of taking the cast through repeated rehearsal of his unscripted, on-set ideas.

Improvisation was facilitated more by their second effort, *Kid Auto Races at Venice* (*qv*), an informal location piece allowing, more importantly, the first glimpse of Chaplin's eventual screen persona. Chaplin stole the next film, *Mabel's Strange Predicament*, from its nominal star, perhaps because Sennett is alleged to have relieved Lehrman of the director's chair. Lehrman's final Chaplin film, *Between Showers* (*qv*), allocates almost equal prominence to his usual colleague, Ford Sterling (*qv*). Lehrman and Sterling departed from Keystone after receiving an offer from Universal – old enemies of Keystone's backers – to make a series called 'Sterling Comedies', employing Emma Clifton (*qv*) as leading lady. Sterling's defection was made known by the beginning of March 1914; Lehrman remained with the new unit only until October, when he formed a rival studio to Keystone, L-KO ('Lehrman Knock-Out') Comedies. L-KO's first star was Billie (or Billy) Ritchie, a Scots-born comic whose appearance approximated Chaplin's in the way that L-KO Comedies aped the Keystone output. As noted under **Impersonators**, Ritchie eventually died as a result of injuries sustained working for Lehrman, whose reputation for endangering his players was widespread. Lehrman's carelessness – to put it kindly – was compounded when, despite having promised to manage Ritchie's financial affairs, he failed to ensure an income for the comedian's widow and daughter. Lehrman had by then also abandoned L-KO, which was taken over by the Stern brothers, nephews of Universal chief Carl Laemmle. It was Julius Stern who, amid widespread industry contempt for the studio, uttered the famous defensive remark, 'L-KO Comedies are not to be laughed at.' Among those latterly employed by L-KO were Alice Howell and Stan Laurel (both *qv*). Lehrman's next berth was at Fox Sunshine Comedies, where he worked again with Keystone veterans Chester Conklin, Alice Davenport and George 'Slim' Summerville (all *qv*). Lehrman had entered the independent market when, in 1921, the Arbuckle scandal (described in **Arbuckle**'s entry) filled the newspapers. Although supported by the majority of his friends and colleagues – Chaplin among them – Arbuckle found a noteworthy exception in Lehrman. The girl who had died following Arbuckle's party, Virginia Rappe, was Lehrman's lover and almost certainly carrying his child. Lehrman was away on business at the time, but gave the press an account portraying Virginia as the epitome of virtue (which she most definitely was not) and Arbuckle as a sex maniac who, at Keystone, had needed to be warned against his molestations of women (an accusation verified by no other studio colleagues). Lehrman's activities in talkies were primarily as a screenwriter at Twentieth Century Pictures and its successor, Twentieth Century-Fox; credits include *Bulldog Drummond Strikes Back* and *Moulin Rouge* (both 1934). His career was over by 1935, and he was declared bankrupt six years later. Despite an accepted birthdate of 1883, his age at death in 1946 was given as 60.

(See also: Bergman, Henry; Mann, Hank; Nichols, George 'Pop'; Swain, Mack)

LENO, DAN
(1860–1904)

The premier comedian of British music-hall, Dan Leno's story is one of tremendous adversity in youth, unparalleled admiration in maturity and a tragically early death. In his autobiography, Chaplin refers to having seen Leno, but not in his prime. Leno and Chaplin scholars believe they were on the same bill as early as 1900, a time when Chaplin was one of the 'Eight Lancashire Lads' and Leno's abilities were virtually unimpaired; although Leno is known to have experienced occasional difficulties prior to his serious breakdown of 1903, there is the possibility that Chaplin, cautious of his reputation by the 1960s, was reluctant to admit to any influence in style. Chaplin's dictated account of his 1921 European trip (known variously as *My Trip Abroad* and *My Wonderful Visit*) makes reference to Leno as having been 'an idol of mine' during boyhood. At that time, Chaplin was prepared not only to lend his name to that statement but also to permit an amusing story at his own expense. When a teenager, Chaplin had been photographed at a studio in the Westminster Bridge Road. At the time, he had noticed a large portrait of Dan Leno in the window. Revisiting the premises in 1921, he found the Leno portrait still in place, but was told that his own negative had long since been destroyed. 'Have you destroyed Mr Leno's negative?' Chaplin asked. 'No,' he was told, 'but Mr Leno is a famous comedian.' More positively, it was during this visit that members of the Leno family presented Chaplin with a pair of Dan's old shoes, expressing the belief that he was the first comedian they had seen who was capable of filling them. To some extent, Chaplin is likely to have been influenced by Leno, if only indirectly (one might note that Dan stood with only *one* foot turned out!), and Lenoesque touches may be discerned in such as *The Floorwalker* (*qv*), in which Chaplin's dealings with customers recall those of Leno's sketch *The Shopwalker*. *A Busy Day* presents Chaplin as the type of comic female epitomized by the pantomime dame, a rôle in which Leno excelled. A gag in *One A.M.* (*qv*), where Charlie forgets his key, enters via the window and, on discovering the key, exits once more via the window in order to enter by the proper means, is said to have been used by Leno in Drury Lane pantomime; equivalent gags were later used by Stan Laurel (*qv*) in some of his films with Oliver Hardy, notably *The Music Box* and *Babes in Toyland*. As an aspiring comedian, Laurel modelled himself to some degree on Leno, albeit via imitators instead of first-hand observation. The similarity of Chaplin to the

determined sprite portrayed by Leno did not pass unnoticed by early British reviewers; on 1 July 1915, *Bioscope*'s review of *By the Sea* (*qv*) described Chaplin as 'the Dan Leno of the screen'. Dan Leno, who was a founding member of the Grand Order of Water Rats (*qv*), is portrayed in the 1989 TV drama series *Young Charlie Chaplin* (*qv*) by a present-day member of that organization, British comedian Roy Hudd.

(See also: Bell, Monta; Books; Caricatures; Documentaries, compilations; Early stage appearances; Female impersonation)

LIMELIGHT

(Chaplin film)
Released by United Artists, 23 October 1952 (premièred in London 16 October). Produced, written and directed by Charles Chaplin. Assistant director: Robert Aldrich. Assistants to Mr Chaplin: Jerome L. Epstein, Wheeler Dryden. Music and the ballet *Death of Columbine* by Charles Chaplin. Music arranged by Chaplin and Ray Rasch, conducted by Keith Williams. Choreography by Andre Eglevsky, Melissa Hayden and Charles Chaplin. Corps de ballet: Carmelita Maracci. The comic songs *The Animal Trainer*, *The Sardine Song* and *Spring is Here* written by Chaplin with Ray Rasch. Director of photography: Karl Struss. Photographic consultant: Roland Totheroh. Art director: Eugene Lourie. Sound: Hugh McDowell. Original working title: *Footlights*. 137 mins (sometimes reported as 143 mins and, at the London preview, 147 mins; the shorter running time is probably based on the film's eventual release length; see below).

With Charles Chaplin (Calvero), Claire Bloom (Thereza, 'Terry'), Nigel Bruce (Postant), Buster Keaton (Calvero's partner), Sydney Chaplin (Neville), Norman Lloyd (Bodalink), Andre Eglevsky, Melissa Hayden (dancers), Marjorie Bennett (Mrs Alsop), Wheeler Dryden (Thereza's doctor/clown in ballet), Barry Bernard (John Redfern), Stapleton Kent (Claudius – see below), Mollie Glessing (maid), Leonard Mudi (Calvero's doctor), Loyal Underwood, Snub Pollard, Julian Ludwig (street musicians), Charles Chaplin Jr (policeman in ballet), Geraldine Chaplin, Michael Chaplin, Josephine Chaplin

(children outside lodgings at start).

London, summer 1914. Calvero, formerly a great comic of the music-halls, returns drunkenly to his lodgings. He is sufficiently awake to detect the smell of gas from a downstairs room, where a young girl is attempting suicide. He breaks in and sees a bottle of tablets

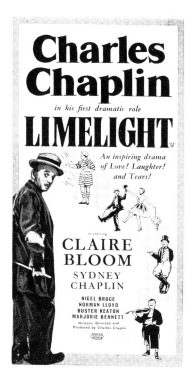

in her hand. He carries her into the hallway, and goes for help at the dispensary that supplied the tablets. The doctor opens the window in her room, turns off the gas and insists the girl be taken to another room. There is no time for an ambulance; an emetic must be administered. This done, he recommends she be allowed to rest. The hospital should not be informed, as questions may be asked and attempted suicide carries a prison term. The doctor leaves, telling Calvero there will be a prescription to collect in ten minutes. The girl regains consciousness and is told what happened. Calvero chides her for wanting to extinguish the miracle of human consciousness. 'Can the sun think?' he asks, 'Is it conscious? No, but you are.' The girl snores. 'Pardon me, my mistake,' concedes Calvero. Mrs Alsop, the landlady, assumes the worst of the girl. The broken door and the matter of back rent convince Mrs Alsop that she must be evicted. Calvero sneaks out to pawn his violin. The landlady calls for Calvero, who arrives, carrying a bag of groceries, just in time to stop her entering his room with the laundry. The groceries are left outside and the girl's presence is revealed when he emerges to fetch them. Mrs Alsop wants the girl out; Calvero explains about the suicide attempt, persuading her not to call an ambulance. The girl had moved in six weeks before. She described herself as 'a working girl'; 'That's what they all say,' sneers the landlady. The room has been rented, and Mrs Alsop does not want her staying with Calvero. She warns him that the girl is 'no good' and has been sick ever since her arrival; 'It wouldn't be dandruff, would it?' asks Calvero as the landlady departs. Calvero arranges discreet, separate sleeping arrangements. He drifts off to the sound of street buskers, transporting him into a dream of his former greatness. The Calvero of yesterday, dressed as a ringmaster, performs a comic song about an animal trainer who works with fleas. At its conclusion, he sees he is performing to an empty house. He awakens, distressed, then returns to sleep. Next morning, a housemaid calls on the girl, saying her husband had asked her to look in and warm up some soup. Calvero returns, with his violin out of pawn and some flowers. He explains the mysterious 'marriage' as a concession to the landlady's quest for decency. The girl is feeling better, but Calvero suggests she stay a little longer, partly because her room has been rented. The girl is destitute, ill; if the ailment is 'what Mrs Alsop thinks it is', Calvero suggests a new drug that has been developed. It has not been that kind of ailment but rheumatic fever, which has left her unable to work. Calvero is enchanted to learn she is a ballet dancer. She introduces herself as Thereza Ambrose, known as 'Terry'. She is intrigued to learn he is Calvero, the great comedian. 'I *was*,' corrects Calvero. Terry, if she wishes, can stay as the platonic Mrs Calvero (there have been five genuine specimens). That night, Calvero learns that Terry is the daughter of a disinherited aristocrat who married a housemaid. Her only living relative, a sister, is in South America. He asks if she attempted suicide because of ill health; he is told the other reason was a sense of futility. Calvero suggests a meaning to life isn't necessary, merely the desire, emphasizing his point by amusing Terry

with his mimed interpretations of trees and flowers. They settle down in their respective sleeping quarters. Again, the buskers lull Calvero into a dream of his old stage act, this time costumed as a hobo while singing 'Spring is Here'. The key differences this time are the presence of Terry as his foil, a comic twist on their earlier discussion and a more positive conclusion to their turn. The morning seems bright until Terry breaks into tears; she had tried to leave her bed but discovered her legs were paralysed. Calvero advises her to fight back, countering talk of hopelessness by recalling how, six months before, he had been given up for dead. Terry finds Calvero's philosophical views difficult to reconcile with those of a comedian; he admits that may be why he has had difficulty in obtaining work. He explains that age imposes a certain sad dignity, incompatible with a comic, and which, in his case, prevented him warming up to an audience. He warded it off with alcohol, became dependent on it for his performance, and in time suffered a near-fatal heart attack. Now, he only drinks when thinking about 'the wrong things'. A telegram arrives from Redfern, Calvero's agent; expecting a comeback, he dresses up and goes to the office, calling at the doctor's en route. After a considerable wait, he learns that his agent may possibly get him a week at the Middlesex music-hall, unbilled and purely as a favour. Calvero's name is

'poison' in the business. Calvero is defiant, but acquiesces to what are genuine efforts to help; ironically, he volunteers to use another name, but the agent, taking the suggestion seriously, agrees. Calvero returns home. The doctor has examined Terry and can find no evidence of rheumatic fever or any reason for the paralysis. He believes the paralysis to be psychological, the result of her failed suicide attempt. Turning psychologist, Calvero asks Terry about her sister. Terry's dancing lessons had been financed by her sister, who, unknown to Terry, earned her living on the streets. Terry learned the truth when, in the company of another girl, she saw her sister plying her trade. Terry first had trouble with her legs when the girl who had witnessed the disgrace joined the same ballet company as her. From here, it is deduced, the shamed Terry no longer wanted to dance. Calvero asks if Terry has ever been in love; the nearest is a young, impoverished composer, an American called Mr Neville. After leaving the hospital, Terry worked at a stationer's and would serve Neville his music paper. She was discharged after deliberately giving the starving man too much change. From there she attempted to return to dancing, but collapsed with the supposed rheumatic fever. She saw Neville again five months later, outside the Albert Hall, where his symphony was being played. Calvero predicts they will meet again, when Terry is a famous

Limelight: *Calvero receives a message at the bar*

ballerina. Terry is convinced she will never dance again, but Calvero insists otherwise; soon he is leading her in gentle steps, and Terry regains limited use of her legs. Calvero claims the Middlesex engagement is postponed. He has also benefited from his pep-talks to Terry, having stayed away from drink. He plans to remain sober for the Middlesex engagement. A letter arrives, informing Calvero of his opening at the Middlesex next Monday. Mrs Alsop, wanting both her rent and to know when Terry will be leaving, is fended off in mock-amorous fashion. Calvero keeps from Terry all knowledge of his opening at the Middlesex. He goes on,

Limelight: *Terry finds Calvero working as a busker*

performing 'The Sardine Song', but the audience walks out during his patter. Having failed, Calvero walks the night-time streets. Returning home, he confides the news to Terry and breaks down. This time it is Terry who offers encouragement, during which she automatically starts to walk normally. She realizes what has happened with delighted suddenness. They spend the night walking along the Embankment. Terry says she can keep them going by obtaining chorus work. Calvero is surprised when she thinks of them as a couple. Six months elapse. Terry is in the chorus of a show at the Empire. In the gallery, an expensively-dressed woman seeks the attention of wealthy gentlemen. Backstage, the dance director asks Terry to have Calvero come in for an audition the next morning. Calvero, violin in hand, is playing with the buskers when Terry returns home. Calvero is drunk. Terry is worried about them disturbing

Mrs Alsop with the music, but she has been drinking with them, the result of Calvero giving her a profitable racing tip. She escorts the buskers out and, expressing concern that Calvero has not eaten or taken his medicine, tells him of the audition for the part of Clown in a new ballet. Calvero is engaged as Clown at £2 per week and, still at the theatre, discovers that Terry is also auditioning. She is to be seen by Mr Postant, an impresario who had employed Calvero as a headliner in that very theatre. Terry is introduced to Postant and to the new show's composer, Mr Neville. 'Why, I believe we've met before,' says Neville. 'Really?' asks Terry. The audition is successful, Terry becoming prima ballerina. Calvero sits alone as the others go off to lunch. Terry finds him, moved to tears by her artistry. Terry proclaims her love for Calvero, asking him to marry her. He is touched, but laughs off the 'ridiculous' idea. Calvero feigns an appointment, directing Terry into a restaurant. In the background, a news vendor's papers announce America's entry into the First World War. In the crowded restaurant, Terry meets Neville and is offered a table with him. They make awkward conversation until they confirm their prior acquaintance. It is apparent that Terry's interest was returned, and that Neville had tried to seek her out at the stationer's after the success at the Albert Hall. Terry mentions her forthcoming marriage. At the theatre, the actors are briefed in the ballet, *The Death of Columbine*. The show opens after three weeks of rehearsal, showing Terry, as the dying Columbine, attended by her lover, Harlequin, two clowns and a policeman. Before the big finale, Terry asks Calvero to pray for her. He treats the request lightly. Terry's legs become paralysed, but Calvero snaps her out of it with a slap to the face. She is on stage when a propman catches Calvero praying to a non-specific, barely believed-in deity to keep Terry going. Terry, a resounding success, tearfully embraces Calvero. At a reception dinner, Calvero tells Terry to

wait, but does not appear. Instead, she sits between Postant and Neville. Postant mentions that Neville has been conscripted; Neville takes it with good humour, mentioning that he may be allowed to join up in England. Terry agrees to dance with him. Calvero is in the theatre bar, drunk. Receiving word that Terry awaits him in the dress circle, he sends back a reply that he has gone home and that Terry should remain and enjoy herself. The message is relayed, and Terry returns home. Calvero is inside the front door of their lodgings when Neville escorts her to the front door. He overhears Neville insisting that he and Terry are in love, believing her devotion to Calvero to be pity. Terry denies this, professing love for Calvero's 'soul ... his sweetness'. Calvero has already made his bleary way upstairs. Neville wishes Terry goodnight and goodbye. Next morning, Calvero reads out Terry's rave reviews. She cries, asking for them to marry soon and get away. Calvero believes it would be better for him to go away rather than for Terry to sacrifice her youth, nun-like, on an old man. In his last years, Calvero wants 'truth' instead of a false relationship. Despite Terry's protests, Calvero knows her true love is Neville. He understands, and reminds her of his prophecy. At the theatre, Postant has sent for another man to replace the Clown. On being told the Clown is Calvero under another name, he relents, calling to cancel the replacement. He is also surprised to learn of Terry's plan of marriage. Outside, Calvero meets the would-be replacement, an old friend, who innocently tells him of the offer to replace the Clown. Terry arrives home to find Calvero has moved out, leaving a note. Terry tours the Continent, to great acclaim; Calvero scratches a living with the group of buskers. Passing the hat inside a pub, he meets Neville, now in army uniform. Calvero accepts a coin, declines a drink, but welcomes a chat. He is gratified to learn that Terry and Neville have been seeing each other regularly. Postant walks in, and is astonished to see Calvero busking. Calvero would prefer that Terry was not told of his present occupation. Postant, wishing to help, invites Calvero to his office but, with humorous bravado, is told to speak to his agent. Terry finds him, and they stop to chat. Terry asks Calvero to come back, but he refuses. She tells Calvero that Postant wants to organize a benefit night for him. Once convinced it is not charity but a chance to prove himself, Calvero warms somewhat, speaking of a 'musical satire' act he has been developing with a pianist friend. Benefit night arrives, and Terry visits Postant in his office. She has been rehearsing a claque to laugh in the right places, believing that a failure would kill Calvero. The audience will be sympathetic, but Calvero wants a genuine triumph rather than sympathy. Terry claims she still wants to marry Calvero, but there seems more a sense of duty than love. Calvero and partner make up in their dressing room. 'If anybody else says it's like old times,' says his partner, 'I'll jump out the window.' Postant enters, saying it's just like old times. The partner exits to watch the other acts. Postant informs Calvero of an audience filled with luminaries, including Neville, then wishes him good luck. Calvero changes into the 'animal trainer' costume. Alone, he sneaks a drink just as Terry arrives. She knows what he has done, but he needs to calm his nerves. Everyone treats Calvero kindly, but he feels isolated in consequence. Terry cannot watch from the wings, but tells Calvero she loves him. Calvero goes on. The 'animal trainer' causes genuine uproar, with no need for a claque; Terry leaves her dressing room and hears the laughter. The 'Sardine Song' is similarly received, but Calvero is running three minutes late, with fifteen acts to follow, and has yet to do the new act. He is told to come off, but Postant insists he respond to the audience's cry for an encore. Calvero and friend, in ill-fitting trousers and tails, do their violin-and-piano act. Bits of business include Calvero's legs seeming to shorten and his partner having parallel difficulty with the sheet music. They tune up, the piano sounding better after the removal of its wires. Calvero's violin is discovered on his partner's foot. Fortunately, he carries a spare. They play a frenzied gypsy-style piece, pausing for a few tears, but continuing even after Calvero has fallen into the orchestra pit. As arranged, he is carried offstage, still playing, wedged in the bass drum. In the wings, Calvero believes he has hurt his spine. He complains of terrible pain in the back and chest, but refuses to allow the audience to know. Rather than spoil the evening, he has himself carried on in the drum to make a speech. He thanks the audience on behalf of self and partner. 'I'd like to continue,' he explains, 'but I'm stuck.' Calvero exits to rapturous applause. The doctor takes

Limelight: *Terry and Calvero at the benefit night*

him to the prop room. Postant arrives to congratulate Calvero, but is told that an ambulance is needed. Calvero has suffered a heart attack and may not last the night. Terry rushes in to see him. Bravely, Calvero speaks of touring the world with Terry but, looking at the uniformed Neville, repeats the words by which he prophesied Terry's eventual love for the composer. Terry must go on stage, but promises to return soon. Calvero knows he is dying, but is no longer in pain. He asks to be carried to where he can see Terry dance. The assembled figures recall those attending the death of Columbine, but this time it is the Clown, Calvero, who dies while Columbine dances on.

Limelight had been in release for slightly more than a year when Chaplin decided to eliminate one final sequence, that in which Calvero leaves the sleeping Terry and, downstairs, runs into Mrs Alsop. He is introduced to the new maid (whose arrival is unheralded in the final version) and warned that his 'wife' must forsake her room in favour of a new tenant. Calvero visits a theatre bar, where he orders milk. A small group of illustrious-looking gentlemen ponder Calvero's fall from grace. This becomes even more apparent during his conversation with a fellow-artist, Claudius, the 'armless wonder' (Stapleton Kent). Taking pity on Calvero's situation, Claudius invites his friend to take £20 from the wallet inside his jacket. Struggling to suppress his emotion,

Calvero accepts. The excision of this bizarre but touching segment – probably for reasons of taste – may perhaps account for the varying running times quoted for this film. It has recently been restored to the American laserdisc edition.

The story's original title, *Footlights*, was that of Chaplin's never-completed, unpublished, novel on which his screenplay was based. Filming was to commence in the autumn of 1951, following the selection of a leading lady. On 17 February 1951, London's *Evening News* printed a story from Reuter's describing Chaplin's quest for a suitable actress, in addition to outlining *Limelight*'s plot. It was believed that Chaplin might travel to England to produce the film, a theory overturned four days later when a follow-up reference appeared in the *Daily Mail*. After several unsuccessful auditions by New York actresses – one of whom became famous later on as Anne Bancroft – it became clear that a genuinely English actress would be needed to play Terry. In April, Chaplin auditioned Claire Bloom (*qv*), who had been recommended to him by playwright Arthur Laurents; until then, the comedian had despaired of finding a leading lady, even after placing a newspaper advertisement. In referring to the previous Spring's audition, the *Star* of 31 August 1951 stated that the actress was to be notified five days later through her agent, Olive Harding.

The audition was successful, and

once signed for the part, both Miss Bloom and Chaplin had to lose weight, to represent accurately the characters' penury; her costumes were researched by combining contemporary issues of *Punch* with Chaplin's memories of his mother's clothing. Chaplin took great care to

Limelight had been on release for months when Chaplin decided to eliminate this scene, in which Calvero visits a bar and meets an armless colleague

replicate the bars, agents' offices and dressing rooms he had known in youth – yet the ever-outspoken 'Wee' Georgie Wood (*qv*), visiting the set, protested, 'It was not like that!'. (While the authenticity of the music-hall sets is open to debate, one might instead query Tereza's ability to tour freely through Europe during the First World War.)

Chaplin recalled the Calvero character as being based on Frank Tinney, a vaudeville and Broadway droll of the type whose laughs came from personality rather than material, much of which was deliberately bad and delivered with a subtle double-edge. Tinney had lost the necessary touch and fallen from grace; the same was true of Calvero, who in a sense parallels Chaplin's own fall from favour with the great mass of Americans since the mid-1940s. Tinney was known to use blackface, something not essayed by Calvero, although his busker's outfit is of the banjo-top-hat-and-loud-jacket minstrel style. While Tinney was the main inspiration, it is difficult not to imagine him as an amalgam with Charles Chaplin Sr (*qv*),

Chaplin himself and, not least, Leo Dryden, whose son, Wheeler Dryden (*qv*), was present as both assistant and actor. Like Calvero, Dryden sang in the streets and was regularly construed as having fallen from public favour.

Rollie Totheroh (*qv*) started as

cameraman on the film, but Chaplin, dissatisfied, replaced him with Karl Struss (*qv*); Totheroh was credited in the end as 'photographic consultant'. Other technicians caused Chaplin considerable angst, actual or imagined; because of his then-current political harassment in America, any difficulties such as a lab problem with the negative would result in Chaplin fearing a conspiracy. One of Chaplin's assistants, Jerry Epstein (*qv*), often spoke of a camera loader who was suspected by Chaplin of wearing an American Legion ring, representing an organization very much opposed to the comedian. On examination, the adornment turned out to be no more than a college ring. Exteriors were shot at Paramount, using the set of William Wyler's *The Heiress*, while the theatre scenes were taken at RKO. Shooting began in November 1951 (after 'rehearsing behind closed doors for some time', according to *Reynolds News*) with, as noted in the *Daily Mail* of 2 December, a 36-day schedule. This was unusually brief for Chaplin, and proved to be over-optimistic, but even with

delays the filming was concluded in the space of eight weeks, in January 1952. On 16 December, the British *Sunday Express* carried one of the very few on-set reports, noting Chaplin's spontaneous amendments to the dialogue, and speaking of the project 'with the enthusiasm of a schoolboy discussing his end-of-term play'. 'I've written the script and the music for *Limelight*,' said Chaplin. 'I'm producing, directing, and playing the principal part. I'm having fun.' When asked about his new leading lady, he admitted to some initial misgivings, 'but now I know she is going to be great ... She had never been before the cameras previously, so I rehearsed her and trained her. She's an apt pupil. She's malleable.'

Perhaps in response to his American reputation at that time, and no doubt mindful of the film's location, Chaplin premièred *Limelight* in London rather than the United States. As noted elsewhere, the Chaplins left New York in September 1952 (after attending a Broadway press preview), and in two days Chaplin had been notified that his re-entry permit had been rescinded. It was a stunned but outwardly defiant Chaplin who attended *Limelight*'s première at the Odeon, Leicester Square, on 16 October, in the presence of Her Majesty Queen Elizabeth II. Proceeds from this charity screening were donated to the Royal London Society for Teaching and Training the Blind. The press saw the film two days earlier, after which Leonard Mosley of the *Daily Express* noted how everyone left the auditorium, Chaplin included, in 'unashamed' tears. Mosley took the cynical view that 'when you dry out *Limelight* to its real shape, it turns out to be a study in self-pity'. Aware of a likely allegory to Chaplin's own life, and laughing immoderately at the comedy material, Mosley felt ashamed of himself for 'blubbering' at 'outrageously old-time melodrama', but attributed much of the tale's palatability to Claire Bloom, 'full of heart and spirit, and as lovely to look at as a hidden pool in the forest'. Mosley's verdict on *Limelight* was as 'a strange film – but a film that only the great Chaplin could have made and well worth waiting for'. According to Campbell Dixon of the *Daily Telegraph*, many in the audience actually cheered at the screening, though 'many missed the inspired clowning of *The Gold Rush* and *City Lights*'. 'Mr. Chaplin's ability as a "straight" actor will surprise nobody,' remarked Dixon, 'handicapped though he is by dialogue (of his own invention) a shade too sententious.' Despite his further remarks in the *Telegraph* several days later (in essence recommending a tightening of the narrative and consequent tempering of the psychology), Dixon typified the general receptiveness to *Limelight*'s charm and comedy alongside modest discomfort with the drama. The *Observer*'s C.A. Lejeune, careful to isolate the film from any sympathy with its visiting creator and his apparent persecution, discerned a similarity of principle with *City Lights*, but saw the result as 'not altogether happy, and even occasionally embarrassing'. Lejeune thought that Chaplin's many words said less than his mime, delivering 'flowers of platitude which Charlie, the fastidious pantomimist, would have sniffed at delicately and tossed away'. Though 'imperfect' and sometimes 'uncomfortable', *Limelight* was considered 'a film of character; the character of something offered generously and after full consideration from one man's mind and heart'. By contrast, Richard Findlater of *Tribune* declared it 'A Triumph For Chaplin'; Fred Majdalanay of the *Daily Mail* was equally unequivocal, even though expressing a requirement for sympathy with Chaplin, the music-halls, *Pagliacci*, Hamlet and the tragedy of life itself; though 'beating relentlessly at our lachrimatory glands with sentiment that would be outrageous in lesser hands', *Limelight* 'ranks with the funniest Chaplin comedy *tours de force* ever ... It is the product of a true genius. And heaven knows there's little enough of that about.' Richard Winnington of the *News Chronicle* liked the film, even if it was not Chaplin's best. Winnington thought Claire Bloom as memorable as Virginia Cherrill (*qv*) had been in *City Lights*, and 'in a much more difficult part'. Jympson Harman of the London *Evening News* reported that Chaplin had reversed his original decision not to attend the press screening, slipping anonymously to his seat, ostensibly to 'check up on the sound'. Harman noticed, with amusement, Chaplin's difficulty in suppressing his own laughter at the film, while trying to remain inconspicuous. Afterwards, the comedian delivered a small speech, expressing his early 'doubts and difficulties' in deciding how the film should end, taking also the opportunity to thank Claire Bloom for her

contribution to the picture. Harman returned to the subject on the day of the première, conceding that a dramatic performance was 'the least we can grant him after the joy he has given so many millions', but thought, 'as a perfectionist', that the story might have been reduced in order to give 'a better shape to the film and throwing the hilarious comedy sequences to the front'. Harman, however, was 'still grateful ... for a film which stands out head and shoulders in the history of movies'.

Elsewhere, the *Sydney Morning Herald* remarked condescendingly upon *Limelight*'s great popularity, while simultaneously chiding the public for responding to it. Echoing Lejeune's comments to some degree, though one suspects for less constructive motives, a suggestion was made to the effect that *Limelight* had benefited from Chaplin's pillorying in America, 'for it is certainly a matter of considerable difficulty to find enough evidence within the film itself to warrant such praise'. In this lofty dismissal one might discern a willingness to follow the lead of the USA, where Chaplin and his film were decidedly unwelcome. There were exceptions: Bosley Crowther of the *New York Times* realized the core of *Limelight* to be 'the courage and the gallantry of an aging man', rather than any social struggle or implied political protest, his summation being that of 'a very moving film'. *Variety*, also less concerned with the star's supposed politics, considered *Limelight* 'deserving of stout b.o.' (i.e. 'box office', rather than anything less savoury). The period settings, music and supporting cast all received praise, while Chaplin himself 'is at times magnificent'. There was the expected grumble over pace, and although some of the dialogue struck the reviewer as 'tedious', it was perhaps no surprise that *Variety* found the stretches of showbusiness philosophy 'brilliant'. Otherwise, Chaplin's fears concerning the American Legion were fulfilled when that organization threatened to picket three Los Angeles theatres, thus forcing them to cancel *Limelight*. On 17 January 1953, the *Daily Worker* quoted Lewis K. Gough, national commander of the Legion, as stating that the action had taken place '"pending the outcome of the investigation by the Justice Department" on Mr. Chaplin's activities'. Twelve days later, the *Manchester Guardian* carried a report from Alistair Cooke in New York, where [RKO] boss Howard Hughes, whose studio facilities had been used in

the film, had boosted the Legion's cause by writing to their Hollywood Committee on Un-American Activities, detailing his 'most concerted effort to persuade the management of the [RKO] Theater Corporation to take necessary legal measures to cancel all bookings of *Limelight*'. Though a principal stockholder in the chain, Hughes was unable to make this a direct order, owing to a requirement under the anti-trust laws to keep studio and theatre management separate. According to Cooke, the Legion had tried unsuccessfully to halt *Limelight*'s release until the Department of Justice had decided if Chaplin was 'a fit person to come into the United States', and the film had been banned from the Fox West Coast and Loews circuits for that same reason. It had still managed to play in some fifty US cities, but Cooke thought it difficult to determine how many small towns, where 'the power of the Legion is more easily felt', had blackballed the film, pending a decision on Chaplin dependent on his return – should he decide to do so – to the United States. The same day's *Daily Telegraph* also carried the story of a 'US attack on Chaplin film', again detailing Hughes' letter and noting that *Limelight* had been booked into 32 of RKO's theatres in the New York area. On 25 February 1953, *Variety* quoted Lewis Gough's defence of the Legion's action, on the grounds that, irrespective of his art, Chaplin as an individual could not be separated from his politics. 'If we patronize those who are Communists or Fascists, or those who have been members of front organizations, we are inadvertently helping the

Limelight: *Calvero's benefit night is a great success – but his acrobatics have fatal consequences*

totalitarian causes.' Chaplin, of course, was not in those categories, and the Legion was accused of taking on the role of judge and jury. In response, Gough claimed, 'We have never endeavoured to judge or to clear anyone. We have given the facts to the public so that the people can judge.' That the people of Washington had judged in *Limelight*'s favour – despite pickets outside the Plaza and Little theatres during evening performances – is evidenced by reports of steadily building attendances elsewhere in *Variety*'s coverage. The paper also detailed opposition to the Legion's ban from two branches of the American Veterans' Committee, first in the Motion Picture Unit, then in the Brooklyn Bedford-Eastern chapter. Similarly, a New Orleans paper severely rebuked the Legion after the local RKO house had withdrawn the film, even though 'thousands of Orleanians' wanted to see it. Though aware that Chaplin might have left himself open to criticism in recent years, the paper condemned vigilante action on the part of private citizens while reminding all concerned that America considers a person innocent until formally convicted. More powerful, metropolitan publications expressed the same opinion, not least the *New York Times*, which, in an editorial headed 'Attack on Freedom', asked, 'If this whole business of pre-judgement, pressures, and – what is worse – knuckling under to those pressures – doesn't smack of un-Americanism, we would like to know what does.'

In the end, *Limelight* made a huge success around the world and, when permitted, in the United States. What is there in the film to arouse such negative passions? Very little. *Limelight*, in Richard Winnington's words, 'passes the one great test of a work of art – it stays with you and flourishes ... As you dwell on it the weaknesses dwindle and you know you cannot rest until you have savoured once more the sweetness and melancholy of its intuitive genius.' There is some sense of Chaplin's feeling of completeness in the film, suggested in part by the presence of several members of his family: Wheeler Dryden has been mentioned; Chaplin's son, Sydney, plays the juvenile lead, and his other elder son, Charles Jr, may be seen in the ballet; while three of his younger children play bits in the opening sequence (there are also those who believe that their mother, Oona, appears in long-shot). According to Charles Jr, his father encouraged such a gathering of the clan in the belief that *Limelight* might well be his final film. In keeping with an implied valediction, much of Chaplin's professional history is interwoven, such as the similarity between impresario Postant and real-life stage manager William Postance, whom Chaplin had known when appearing in *Sherlock Holmes* at the age of sixteen. The 'Animal Trainer' song recalls 'Prof. Bosco' and his flea circus from an uncompleted film, *The Professor* (see **Abandoned projects** and *Unknown Chaplin*), while one gag from this routine is actually recycled from as early as *By the Sea* (*qv*). The tramp character of 'Spring is Here' is a strong reminder of Chaplin's former persona; one might further recall a pleasant line where Calvero, as a busker, claims to enjoy working the streets; 'It's the tramp in me, I suppose.' Otherwise, there is an easy, informal charm, conveying rather the impression of the real-life Chaplin performing bits of business – such as his impersonation of a flower – in a style usually reserved for his friends.

Limelight also offers the singular pleasure of seeing Charlie Chaplin work with Buster Keaton (*qv*). In keeping with the Frank Tinney prototype mentioned by Chaplin, their act comprises the type of musical drollery more identifiable in Europe – as with Grock – than in English-speaking countries, among the notable exceptions being Max Wall, George Carl and the double-act cited in *Variety*'s review, William and Wolfus.

Limelight is undeniably old-fashioned, both in its plot and economy-minded special effects (its back-projection has long been the subject of derision). It is melodrama, but of the very best kind, the kind that can only be pulled off if played with the utmost conviction – which it is. Chaplin was uniquely qualified in this area, and one might add that, despite the carping of cynics, many of the attitudes to life expressed through Calvero's lips are not necessarily bad advice. Even so, Chaplin's speeches in the film can sometimes prove alienating, even to avowed supporters of his work. One such was Walter Kerr, who, in his *Theatre Arts* review (later reprinted in *Focus on Chaplin*), remarked on Chaplin's anticipation of his critics by having Terry say, 'To hear you talk, no one would ever think you were a comedian.' In Kerr's opinion, 'A profound clown – the greatest, most beloved we have – is seeking a second reputation as a sage. It is not likely to equal his first.'

(See also: Alcohol; Ballet; Bennett, Charles; Bruce, Nigel; Children; Costume; Early stage appearances; Left-handedness; *His New Profession*; Music; Parrish, Robert; Policemen; Politics; Purviance, Edna; Radio; Religion; Risqué humour; Royalty; Sickness; Smoking; Struss, Karl; Underwood, Loyal; Wartime; Women)

LINDER, MAX
(1883–1925)

French comedian, born Gabriel Leuvielle, originally from the stage. He adopted his more familiar name as a disguise when first working in moving pictures, which at the time (1905) were considered beneath most actors' dignity. Linder appeared prolifically in short comedies for Pathé until serving as a despatch rider in the First World War, during which he was injured and invalided out of the service. His Pathé comedies travelled the world in various languages, presenting him mostly as a top-hatted *boulevardier* engaged in a skilled balance of farce and knockabout. Much of the Linder approach is recognizable in Chaplin's work: several early Chaplin shorts, *The Rink* (*qv*) among them, are said to be based on Linder's Pathé films, one of which also employed the statue gag that opens *City Lights* (*qv*). Chaplin acknowledged the debt when Linder visited him at the Lone Star studio on 12 May 1917, where he inscribed a photo 'To the one and only Max, "The Professor", from his Disciple, Charlie Chaplin'. Linder in turn claimed to be 'glad enough myself to take lessons from him'. Linder had

Max Linder, Chaplin's friend and 'teacher'

recently returned to film work after his war experience, having been signed by Essanay (*qv*) for a series doubtless intended to replace Chaplin on the studio roster; it is probably no coincidence that Leo White (*qv*) was brought back from Chaplin's Mutual unit to participate in the Linder comedies. They were not an unqualified success. The same applies to the starring films Linder produced himself in America during 1919–22, *Seven Years' Bad Luck*, *Be My Wife* and *The Three Must-Get-Theres* (the latter kidding Fairbanks' *Three Musketeers*), though his work both in the USA and France continued to be worthwhile and, at times, highly imaginative. There is evidence of continued socializing between Linder and Chaplin during this period. On 6 May 1922, *Picture Show* ran a story (albeit the likely fabrication of a publicist) concerning a practical joke in which Chaplin, at a gathering, had presented Linder with a caged, singing bird. Linder tried to feed it before discovering the bird to be mechanical. These seemingly bright spirits had evaporated by 1925, when Linder and his wife died in what seems to have been a suicide pact; various attempts have been made to explain the tragedy, among them an upset of mind brought about by the war and the decline of his subsequent feature work (the latter unsubstantiated by extant feature work, including the very entertaining *Le Petit Café* and a truncated but prophetically-titled film, *Au Secours!*). Apart from an unusual devotion, none of these explanations account fully for his wife's decision to join him in death. As a mark of respect, Chaplin closed his studio for the day on hearing of the tragedy. The Linders left behind a small daughter, Maud, who grew up unaware of her father's eminence. On reaching adulthood, she learned of his status and set about restoring his films to public view. Maud assembled some of his American work into *En Compagnie de Max Linder* (a.k.a. *Laugh With Max Linder*), which did much to regenerate interest (Chaplin's inscribed photo is shown during the introduction). Linder's early Pathé films, most of them elusive at best, began to turn up (many on the obsolete 28mm gauge) and were compiled by Maud into a superb 1983 anthology, *The Man in the Silk Hat*.

(See also: De Limur, Jean; Documentaries; Fairbanks, Douglas; Florey, Robert; Karno Company, The; Mutual; Suicide; *Unknown Chaplin*)

LITTLE TRAMP: THE MUSICAL

See: Music

LONDON, JEAN 'BABE'
(1901–80)

Tubby comedienne, real name Jean Glover, Babe London was born in Des Moines, Iowa, but migrated to California with her family when still a child. She entered films at the age of 17 after reading a newspaper advertisement placed by a film company. She worked prolifically in silent comedies, notably with Al Christie, and may be seen in feature rôles such as that of switchboard operator in *When the Clouds Roll By* (1919), starring Douglas Fairbanks (*qv*). Talkie appearances were fewer, but she is remembered as Oliver Hardy's fiancée in a 1931 Laurel & Hardy short, *Our Wife*. In Chaplin's work, she may be seen as a seasick passenger in *A Day's Pleasure* (*qv*) (she is *not* the similarly large lady who becomes a human gangplank). Interviewed in 1972 by Anthony Slide for the magazine *Silent Picture*, she recalled having had 'quite a nice scene with him, close-ups and stuff', with Chaplin telling her, 'If you stick by this, you're going to make it.' Later in life, Babe London painted a series of oil portraits representing the silent greats, titled 'The Vanishing Era', which is now on display at the University of Wyoming.

(See also: Boats, ships; Laurel, Stan; Wilson, Tom)

LOREN, SOPHIA
(b. 1936)

International film star, born in Italy, whose celebrated career need not be detailed here save for its connection with Chaplin. Her experiences with the comedian are documented in a memoir transcribed for her by A.E. Hotchner, *Sophia, Living and Loving* (1979). In it she describes an initial call from Chaplin, arranging to meet the actress at her rented cottage at Ascot. He arrived, at least as shy as Miss Loren, bearing flowers and a copy of the script. As was usual, Chaplin acted out every part for her; she was 'captivated', and would have played the rôle 'if what he was reading were the London telephone directory'. Chaplin had decided upon Loren after

Sophia Loren helped Chaplin celebrate his 77th birthday on the set of A Countess From Hong Kong

seeing her in *Yesterday, Today and Tomorrow*; he repeated his enactment of the script at a further meeting at his home in Switzerland, with Loren and Marlon Brando (*qv*) in attendance. During filming, Loren's rapport with Chaplin survived rather better than did Brando's. She adored Chaplin and listening to his childhood reminiscences, which seemed akin to her own, and maintained a steady friendship with both Chaplin and his wife, Oona; indeed, it was Oona alone to whom she entrusted the knowledge of her secret wedding to Carlo Ponti.

(See also: Childhood; O'Neill, Oona; Rutherford, Margaret)

LUBITSCH, ERNST

See: United Artists

MABEL AT THE WHEEL

(Chaplin film)
Keystone Comedy released by Mutual, 18 April 1914. Produced by Mack Sennett. Direction and screenplay attributed to Sennett or Mabel Normand. Photographer unknown. Reissued (by W.H. Productions) as *His Daredevil Queen* and (by Exhibitors Pictures Corp.) with added sound as *Hot Finish*. Two reels. 1,900 feet.

With Mabel Normand (Mabel), Harry McCoy (her boyfriend), Chester Conklin (Mabel's father), Charlie Chaplin (villainous rival), Al St. John and William A. Seiter (Charlie's accomplices), Mack Sennett (foolish spectator).

Mabel greets her motoring boyfriend as Charlie, a villainous type, approaches on a motorcycle. Mabel and her boyfriend quarrel, and she accepts Charlie's invitation to ride on the back of his motorbike. They set off, the boyfriend in pursuit. Charlie fails to notice when Mabel is thrown from the vehicle into a mud puddle; she is picked up by the boyfriend and reconciled. Charlie, having noticed his lost passenger, has reached a halt and needs a start from a passerby. Seeing the couple, the furious Charlie vows revenge. He punctures one of the car's tyres, which, on discovery, leads to a prolonged battle with bricks. The day of the big motor race sees the boyfriend among the competitors. Charlie tries again to pierce a tyre, but succeeds in puncturing the rear end of a mechanic. In the stands, Charlie makes a menace of himself with Mabel, her father and, on his arrival, the boyfriend. Charlie departs, enlisting two thugs to help him abduct the boyfriend. He is tied up just

as the race is about to start. Mabel searches for him, but finds only Charlie, tugging at her coat. She bites his hand and returns to the track. In the absence of the driver, Mabel takes over the wheel, acquitting herself very well despite the bombs thrown by Charlie and his thugs. Mabel is in the lead when Charlie and comrades spray water on the track to create a mud patch. Mabel's progress is unimpeded, but the other cars are sent skidding back in the wrong direction. Eventually, Mabel's car is sent tumbling, but is soon back in the race. Her boyfriend escapes and, as Mabel continues to dodge her enemies' bombs, joins his girlfriend's father in the stands. They are on hand to congratulate Mabel when she wins the race, while Charlie and cohorts are blown over by one of their own bombs.

Available copies of *Mabel at the Wheel* seem to derive from an early 1930s sound reissue called *Hot Finish*. Again, Chaplin is costumed as per *Making a Living* and *Cruel, Cruel Love* (both *qv*), but with his usual toothbrush moustache. The addition of a rather obnoxious goatee and some notably vicious behaviour suggest his rôle to be as substitute for Ford Sterling (*qv*), who had recently left Keystone. Peter Cotes and Thelma Niklaus' *The Little Fellow* tells a story of Chaplin being asked if he could ride a motorcycle and, having

claimed to have cycled all around London, set off with Mabel Normand (*qv*) as passenger. The bike careered off out of control, losing Mabel en route and eventually crashing. Afterwards, Chaplin admitted not having realized the difference between a bicycle and a motorbike. The finished film shows the erratic journey (and Mabel falling from the motorcycle into a puddle!), but it is uncertain whether the genuine accident was captured on film. During production, conflict between Chaplin and Mabel Normand extended to psychological rather than physical bruising. The actress was also at least nominal director, and did not take kindly to Chaplin's ideas for improvement. Mack Sennett (*qv*) reprimanded Chaplin, who seemed destined to be fired. The following day, Sennett took him aside for an altogether friendlier chat, securing Chaplin's co-operation with Mabel in exchange for a chance to direct his own work. Detailing this in his memoirs, Chaplin recalled having taken several months to discover the reason for Sennett's change of heart; apparently reprimand had become reconciliation after Sennett had received a telegram from New York, requesting more of the sought-after Chaplin films. Chaplin's acquiescence to Mabel is implicit in the presence of a gag, originally disputed by Chaplin, in which he hoses down the race track in order to

A Sterling-like Chaplin menaces the eponymous heroine of **Mabel at the Wheel***; Chester Conklin is at left*
BFI Stills, Posters and Designs

send the cars skidding. Professional harmony was restored, and they quite happily shared direction of the subsequent *Caught in a Cabaret* (*qv*).

A footnote: one of Chaplin's hired thugs is played by William A. Seiter (1892–1964), a former cowboy double with Selig who was then serving something of an apprenticeship in silent comedy. Seiter moved into directing before the end of the decade, his later credits including Laurel & Hardy's *Sons of the Desert* (1933) and the Marx Brothers' *Room Service* (1938).

(See also: Cars; Caught in the Rain; Conklin, Chester; Costume; Her Friend the Bandit; Keystone; Laurel, Stan; Marx, Groucho; McCoy, Harry; Normand, Mabel; Reissues; St. John, Al; Sennett, Mack; Star Boarder, The; Twenty Minutes of Love; Video releases)

MABEL'S BUSY DAY 🎩

(Chaplin film)
Keystone Comedy released by Mutual, 13 June 1914. Produced by Mack Sennett. Screenplay and direction attributed to Chaplin or Mabel Normand. Photography attributed to Frank D. Williams. Reissued by W.H. Productions as *Hot Dogs*; other reissue titles include *Hot Dog Charlie* and *Charlie and the Sausages*. One reel. 998 feet (UK length cited in *Bioscope*).

With Mabel Normand (Mabel), Charlie Chaplin (a sharper), Billie Bennett (woman with handkerchief), Chester Conklin (first policeman), Mack Sennett (customer with note), Edgar Kennedy, Slim Summerville (policemen), Al St. John, Wallace MacDonald, Charley Chase (spectators).

Outside a motor-racing venue, Mabel, a hot dog vendor, has to bribe a policeman with a free hot dog in order to gain admission. Once inside, Mabel has to take violent action against a playful gentleman. At the main gate, Charlie, a sharp customer without a ticket, enters the stadium despite the efforts of the police. Mabel, too, has trouble with the law, when she is told to move way from a pitch near one of the cars. Business is poor. Charlie finds a discarded hot dog on the ground. Believing it to be a cigar, he tries to light the sausage before eating it. Mabel finds a customer, who at first tries to walk off without paying. He returns with a coin,

chucking Mabel under the chin while handing it over. Mabel resumes her sales cry. Charlie finds another hot dog and consumes it; Mabel finds another customer, but loses the sale when she cannot change a note. Charlie flirts with three women, but they are unimpressed. He seems to be stealing from a handbag belonging to one of them, but instead borrows a handkerchief to wave at the racing drivers. Mabel's latest customer is a bully who refuses to pay; Charlie goes to Mabel's rescue, seeing off the bully, comforting the tearful saleswoman, but ultimately making off with a stolen hot dog. Mabel gives chase and, failing to catch Charlie, enlists the help of the policeman who first let her into the stadium. Charlie disguises himself by adopting the rôle of hot dog salesman, and finds himself doling out the wares to an increasingly hostile crowd. Mabel returns to discover the tray has gone. When taunted by the crowd, Charlie fights back, doing so again when still another customer refuses to pay. Mabel notices the disturbance and confronts Charlie, kicking him in the rear as the cop looks on. Charlie spirits the officer's truncheon away and uses it to knock him over. The ensuing struggle sends the cop out of the running, leaving a fight between Charlie and Mabel. Eventually, Mabel breaks down into tears, as does a now genuinely sympathetic Charlie. He takes her arm and they depart together, Charlie doffing his hat to the crowd.

Mabel's 'business', explained *Bioscope* of 29 October 1914, 'consists of selling sausages on a racecourse, and, with the assistance of Mr. Mack Sennett and Mr. Charles Chaplin, it may be imagined that pretty Mabel's business is strenuous and mirth-provoking. The fun never flags, and is well up to the Keystone average.' *Mabel's Busy Day* is another of the Keystones in which Charlie portrays a villain, albeit ultimately a sympathetic one. His usual shabby attire has made way for a light-coloured bowler, sporty, double-breasted frock coat and a carnation, suggesting something of a racetrack huckster. The reissue titles quoted above serve as indication of Chaplin's speedy rise to pre-eminence, in that films nominally starring Mabel Normand (*qv*) soon came to be regarded as Chaplin vehicles.

(See also: Bennett, Billie; Cars; Conklin, Chester; Costume; Food; Keystone; MacDonald, Wallace; Policemen; Reissues; Summerville, George J. 'Slim'; Williams, Frank D.)

Mabel's Busy Day: *Charlie offers comfort amid chaos*
BFI Stills, Posters and Designs

MABEL'S MARRIED LIFE 🎩

(Chaplin film)
Keystone Comedy released by Mutual, 20 June 1914. Produced by Mack Sennett. Screenplay and direction attributed to Chaplin and Mabel Normand. Photography attributed to Frank D. Williams. Reissue titles include *When You're Married* and (from W.H. Productions) *Squarehead*. One reel. 1,015 feet (UK length cited in *Bioscope*).

With Mabel Normand (Mabel), Charlie Chaplin (her husband), Mack Swain (burly man), Alice Howell (his wife), Charlie Murray (bar patron), Hank Mann, Harry McCoy (barroom toughs), Al St. John, Wallace MacDonald (delivery men), Alice Davenport (neighbour).

In a park, a burly man and his wife kiss good-bye as he goes to play tennis. Elsewhere are Mabel and husband

Mabel's Married Life: *Charlie proves ineffective when confronted by a bullying Mack Swain*

Charlie, who hangs his hat over his shoe to cover the fragmented sole. Charlie lunches on a banana, from which he allows Mabel but one miserly bite. Charlie visits a bar, leaving Mabel behind. In his absence, the other man spots Mabel and begins to flirt. Charlie returns after a liberal intake of alcohol. The large man treats Charlie with contempt, and is impervious to repeated kicks in the rear. His attentions to Mabel grow more serious, but Charlie seems unable to assert himself; instead, the other man's wife breaks up the scene. She departs with her husband, but Charlie, disgusted with Mabel, returns to the bar alone. Mabel passes a sporting goods shop, where a boxing dummy is on sale. Hoping the dummy will enable Charlie to develop his fighting technique, she asks for it to be sent to her home. In the bar, Charlie is teased by one of a gang of roughnecks. At home, Mabel contemplates her hopeless spouse, imitating his shuffling walk. Charlie's problems in the bar escalate with the reappearance of his earlier adversary. Mabel, now clad in pyjamas, covers herself with a leopard skin rug when delivery men arrive with the dummy. She gives the dummy a shove, but is knocked over in return. At the bar, Charlie, fortified by drink, wearies of the teasing and fights back, sending the whole gang scurrying. On Charlie's return home, Mabel gets into bed. In his drunken state, Charlie mistakes the dummy for the bully he met before. The dummy is shown the door, but does not, of course, leave. Charlie launches an attack and, like Mabel, is knocked over when the dummy lurches back. Charlie is sent flying into the bedroom, where he confronts Mabel with her seeming infidelity. The noisy struggle between Mabel, Charlie and the dummy catches the attention of the neighbours. Charlie, convinced at last that it is only a dummy, falls with it to the floor. Mabel laughs until she, too, trips over.

'The mix up between Mabel, Charles and the dummy is extremely funny,' said *Bioscope* on 29 October 1914, 'and in the restaurant [*sic*] Mr. Chaplin gives a very excellent study of inebriation. This is certainly one of the best of the Keystone comedies.' *Mabel's Married Life* is one of those rare Chaplin Keystones that surfaces in unmutilated form. Although it was reissued several times, Blackhawk Films were able to make new prints from a Keystone

original. Blackhawk's material was lacking the main title card, which has been restored in facsimile for a recent American laserdisc release.

On this occasion, Charlie's appearance is somewhat altered by the use of a top hat instead of his usual headgear. Original publicity artwork, reprinted in a 1970s collection called *Fifty Years of Movie Posters* (though not identified by title) shows the comedian in his customary bowler.

(See also: Alcohol; Costume; Documentaries; Home movies; Impersonators; Keystone; MacDonald, Wallace; Normand, Mabel; Parks; Risqué humour; Sport; Swain, Mack; Video releases; Williams, Frank D.)

MABEL'S STRANGE  PREDICAMENT

(Chaplin film)
Keystone Comedy released by Mutual, 9 February 1914. Produced by Mack Sennett. Directed by Mack Sennett and Henry Lehrman. Photography attributed to Frank D. Williams. Reissued as *Hotel Mix-Up*. One reel. 1,010 feet (UK length cited in *Bioscope*).

With Charlie Chaplin (himself), Mabel Normand (herself), Harry McCoy (Mabel's boyfriend), Alice Davenport (elderly matron), Chester Conklin (her husband), Al St. John (hotel manager), Hank Mann (bellhop), Henry Lehrman (guest in opening scene).

Charlie, rather drunk, is in a hotel foyer when he meets Mabel and her dog. She rejects his advances and departs, as does another girl to whom Charlie turns his attentions. Outside, Mabel chats to a different gentleman friend and returns, gushing, to the foyer. As Mabel collects her key, Charlie tries to intercept by grabbing her dog but is pulled to the floor. Mabel goes upstairs to her room, greeting the elderly matron opposite, but is snubbed. In the foyer, Charlie, rejected by yet another girl, falls from his chair. Mabel, now wearing pyjamas, disturbs her elderly neighbours by noisily playing with her dog. Mabel opens her door slightly as the matron passes. The old woman goes to reception to complain, and is pestered by Charlie. Mabel throws a ball for her dog; the ball bounces into the hallway and in retrieving it she becomes locked out of her room, just as Charlie walks along the

A tipsy Charlie outrages Harry McCoy and horrifies the pyjama-clad Mabel Normand in **Mabel's Strange Predicament**
BFI Stills, Posters and Designs

corridor. Mabel tries to escape from the drunken stranger, who kisses a pyjama-clad man in mistake for the girl. Mabel takes refuge in the elderly couple's room, hiding under the bed. Charlie attempts to look through the keyhole, acting nonchalant when a bellboy arrives. Inside, the old man sits on the bed, unaware of his guest beneath. He is astonished as Charlie walks in, seeking Mabel in such unlikely hiding places as dresser drawers. Charlie abandons the search and departs. In the foyer, Charlie meets Mabel's beau, pulling a flower from the bouquet he has brought. After the man's departure, Charlie presents the flower to a girl. A bellboy shows the man into Mabel's room, but there is no sign of her. The dog trots into the corridor. The puzzled visitor goes to the room occupied by the old man, a friend; he is followed by the dog, who joins Mabel beneath the bed. The dog finally alerts the old man to Mabel's presence. The visitor, calling the animal, spots Mabel and pulls her out. He tries to throttle her, but the old man intervenes; unconvinced by his avowal of innocence, the boyfriend bites his ear. This is forgotten when the old man's wife returns with the manager. Mabel is hidden under the bed once more, and the boyfriend is escorted out. In the corridor, he meets Charlie and is unimpressed by his conspiratorial grin. Mabel is discovered by the matron, who, convinced of her husband's infidelity, attacks the girl. Mabel, attempting to cover herself with an eiderdown, is hustled into the corridor, bumping straight into Charlie. A struggle ensues between the old couple, the boyfriend, the girl and Charlie, whose kick sends the old man and Mabel into her room. The old man slams the door in Charlie's face; the old woman tries to open the door as Charlie fights the boyfriend. The elderly man, trying to pacify Mabel, is shown the door and taken back by his furious wife. The boyfriend tries to talk to Mabel as Charlie continues his protestations of love. The boyfriend sends him packing. The old man is slapped around by his wife as Mabel and boyfriend kiss and make up.

Once considered lost, *Mabel's Strange Predicament* had started to become generally available by at least the end of the 1960s (though, oddly, H.D. Waley's 1938 *Sight and Sound* article on Chaplin's Keystones reports a print in BFI hands even at that early date). A 1920 UK reissue, called *Hotel Mix-Up*, seems to have vanished along with the original prints. Available copies – including the author's – derive from a French edition called *Charlot à l'Hôtel*, which is probably incomplete; there is no sign of a reported opening gag with Charlie attempting to use a payphone, while the ending seems rather abrupt.

The rediscovery of *Mabel's Strange Predicament* ended considerable speculation as to the extent of Chaplin's contribution. Chaplin's *My Autobiography* attributes the first appearance of his 'tramp' character to this film (overlooking *Kid Auto Races at Venice* [*qv*]), while simultaneously recording the impact made on his fellow players while playing the lobby scene. Chaplin's account details an early cinema audience's slow appreciation of the film, building from modest reaction to the lobby scene up to hysterics during the climactic moments; yet certain chroniclers, writing before the film's rediscovery, were of the opinion that Chaplin appeared only in its first sequence. *Mabel's Strange Predicament* is in fact Chaplin's film almost throughout, thoroughly upstaging nominal star Mabel Normand (*qv*). Chaplin repeated its plot a year later in his second Essanay comedy, *A Night Out* (*qv*).

(See also: Alcohol; Conklin, Chester; Costume; Essanay; Keystone; Lehrman, Henry; Reissues; Risqué humour; Sennett, Mack; Williams, Frank D.)

MACDONALD, WALLACE
(1891–1978)

(Chaplin films *qv*)
Supporting actor, born in Nova Scotia; toured in stock in his native Canada, also California (San Francisco), Arizona (Phoenix) and Texas (El Paso). He is

present in a number of the Chaplin Keystones, as in the café scenes of *Caught in a Cabaret* and at the racetrack in *Mabel's Busy Day*. In *Mabel's Married Life*, he and Al St. John (*qv*) deliver the dummy ordered by Mabel Normand (*qv*); he patronizes a bar in *The Face On the Bar Room Floor*, and a restaurant in *The Rounders*; he is reportedly one of the strikers in *Dough and Dynamite*, and is among the Keystone Cops at the conclusion of *Tillie's Punctured Romance*. His later work in silent shorts also includes a stint as a director of Fox's Imperial Comedies. Prolific in features, among them the 1923 version of *The Spoilers*, *The Sea Hawk* (1924), *The Primrose Path* (1925), *Drums of the Desert* (1927), *His Foreign Wife* (1927), *The Rogue Song* (1930) and many talkie westerns, into the 1950s.

(See also: Keystone)

MAKING A LIVING

(Chaplin film)
Keystone Comedy released by Mutual, 2 February 1914. Produced by Mack Sennett. Directed by Henry Lehrman. Photography attributed to E.J. Vallejo. Reissued by W.H. Productions as *A Busted Johnny*. Other reissue titles include *Troubles* and *Doing His Best*. One reel. 1,030 feet (UK length cited in *Bioscope*).
With Charlie Chaplin (sharper), Henry Lehrman (Chaplin's rival), Virginia Kirtley (Lehrman's girlfriend), Alice Davenport (girlfriend's mother), Minta Durfee ([?] accused wife), Chester Conklin (policeman/tramp).

A 'sharper', played by Chaplin, ingratiates himself with a gentleman (Lehrman) before tapping him for a loan. Lehrman departs, dismissing the man as a 'bum'. The sharper, unconcerned, wins over Lehrman's girlfriend and her mother. An engagement is announced. Lehrman, spurned by the girl, does battle with his rival, but to no avail. Lehrman applies for a reporter's job at a newspaper office, but is turned down. Chaplin sees the position advertised and also applies. He uses his powers of persuasion on the editor, but Lehrman, recognizing him, tells the editor that Chaplin is 'a bum'. Their rivalry continues later that day, when Lehrman chances upon a 'scoop' in the form of a car accident. Lehrman

Making a Living: UK publicity for Chaplin's film debut, and a scene from the film itself

takes a photograph, but Chaplin, happening upon the scene, steals the camera. A chase takes them into the home of a married couple, with the wife wrongfully accused of infidelity. Chaplin is first to bring the story to the paper and a special edition is rushed out, with the sharper helping to load and distribute. Lehrman arrives and the pair do battle once again, even after they are picked up on the front of a streetcar.

Chaplin's first Keystone film was his nominal cinema debut but, as noted in John McCabe's Chaplin study and Harry M. Geduld's *Chapliniana*, the comedian is thought to have appeared in newsreels (*qv*) at an earlier date. Less credibility should be attached to an account in the early biography *Charlie Chaplin's Own Story*, a work which, though massively discredited, continues to entice even the most dedicated scholars. According to this, *Making a Living* had been preceded by a Keystone two-reeler considered too poor for release; this is unlikely, for the economy-minded Mack Sennett (*qv*) would not have permitted an obviously unsatisfactory project to continue even to a single reel, let alone two. Further, such a film – however awful – would somehow have found its way into release later in the 1910s, when every available scrap of Keystone-Chaplin footage was being recycled for reissue purposes. Academic points aside, *Making a Living* was the first entertainment film in which Chaplin was seen by the general public, and as such occupies a significant place in film history. His appearance is not at all typical, being that of a top-hatted type, sheathed in frock coat and sporting a drooping moustache. Contemporary audiences recognized this as the stereotyped villain of Victorian melodrama but, it should be noted, from Chaplin's English perspective it was equally the image of a gentleman on hard times. This same outfit had served Chaplin on stage in some of Karno's sketches, notably *The Football Match*, in which he made his debut with the company; it would reappear in *Cruel, Cruel, Love* (*qv*) and, without the drooping moustache, in *Mabel at the Wheel* (*qv*). Present-day commentators seeking parallels with Chaplin's familiar persona tend to cite his battle with Henry Lehrman (*qv*), in which a cane is used both as weapon and to keep an adversary at bay; but above all, *Making a Living* is representative only of the darker side of Charlie, the mercenary aspect which, for example, in *The Vagabond* (*qv*), enables him to collect money intended for the German band playing nearby. This is Hyde working independently of Jekyll, a ruthless Charlie untempered even by the limited degree of humanity found in subsequent Keystones. Sennett, Lehrman and Chaplin are known to have been dissatisfied with this first effort. From Chaplin's point of view, director/actor Lehrman excised any worthwhile comedy in the process of editing; similarly, Chaplin took a while to understand the technical process of film-making, be it the matching of shots taken in quite different locations or the need to shoot out-of-sequence. To make matters worse, there was a poor chemistry between director and star. Chaplin and Lehrman did not gel, and the brevity of their association was doubtless a relief to both parties. All concerned with the film would later dismiss it as a failure, despite a *Motion Picture World* review (possibly the most quoted in film history) marking out Chaplin as 'a comedian of the first water'.

Today's copies of *Making a Living* seem to derive virtually without exception from an early reissue, retitled *A Busted Johnny*. Content in each seems identical (except in retitling), although most tend to crop the final scene before Chaplin and Lehrman have disappeared completely from view. Original prints of the *Busted Johnny* version, distributed at that time by W.H. Productions, are identified on the main card by both original and reissue titles, and contain a few descriptive sub-titles. Such a version has been released on video in Europe. Most available prints dispense with the sub-titles, thus making the action sometimes difficult to follow. Most of the sub-titles are, however, dispensible things such as 'Break the news to Mother' when Chaplin proposes marriage, or 'Extra! Extra!' when the paper prints a special edition. Condition can also vary wildly, depending upon generations of duping or degrees of decomposition. Blackhawk Films had one of the better-quality editions, with the 'Making a Living' title reinstated (in a card of their own manufacture), but with the sub-titles remaining absent. This applies also to video editions from the USA. Curiously, Blackhawk's print shares with several others a fault in one sequence, where Chaplin is seen catching bundles of newspapers (one of several scenes reportedly taken on the premises of the *Los Angeles Times*); a printed-in frame line mars the beginning of the shot, which cuts and restarts with the fault corrected. This could only have occurred during the making of a duplicate negative, when such a fault would be pulled back in printing. This should have been cut from the new negative, but was evidently overlooked.

(See also: Abandoned projects; Conklin, Chester; Costume; *Her Friend the Bandit*; Home movies; Karno, Fred; Keystone; Kirtley, Virginia; *Monsieur Verdoux*; Policemen; Reissues; Video releases)

MANN, HANK (DAVID LIEBEMAN OR LIEBERMAN) (1887–1971)

(Chaplin films *qv*)
Comedian, born and educated in New York; according to Kalton C. Lahue and Sam Gill's *Clown Princes and Court Jesters*, Mann joined Keystone (*qv*) after experience as an acrobat in vaudeville, becoming one of the studio's celebrated Cops, as in *Tillie's Punctured Romance*. His other appearances in the Chaplin Keystones are as a bellhop in *Mabel's Strange Predicament*, Mabel Normand's father in *Caught in a Cabaret*, the bogus 'Cyclone Flynn' in *The Knockout* and one of the bar customers in both *Mabel's Married Life* and *The Face On the Bar Room Floor*. He has been reported as the sleeping man in *Twenty Minutes of Love*, but this seems instead to be Joseph Swickard (*qv*). Hank Mann was one of many Keystone comedians to be lured away by L-KO; after a subsequent return to Sennett he worked in Fox Sunshine Comedies, then for Morris Schlank in a starring series released by Arrow. Although he co-starred with Chester Conklin (*qv*) in a series of late 1920s shorts, Mann's later appearances were primarily supporting rôles in features, as when playing 'Ben Bates' in *Quincy Adams Sawyer* (1923), or the 1927 Fox film *Fazil*. Three such features were with Chaplin, playing a prize fighter in *City Lights*, one of the burglars in *Modern Times* and a stormtrooper in *The Great Dictator*.

(See also: Fighting; Lehrman, Henry 'Pathé'; Normand, Mabel; Risqué humour; Sennett, Mack)

MARIE'S MILLIONS

See: *Tillie's Punctured Romance*

MARRIAGES

Chaplin's first marriage was to Mildred Harris (*qv*) in 1918. It soon became clear to him that a mistake had been made, but there is no record of him attempting to take up a kind invitation from a Japanese fan, whose enthusiastic – but not entirely comprehensible – letter was published in the *Picture Show* of 29 September 1919:

Dear the comedy king:

I am very applaud your clever trick you have extraordinary feelings of community very very much in Japan, you are comedys authority of world indeed. May I trouble please give me your big photograph *and your wife*. Good bye.

H.T.

The marriage was terminated instead by the more orthodox means of divorce, in 1920. A syndicated column by Louella Parsons (which again reached Britain via *Picture Show*, on 21 May 1921) described the journalist as 'agog' over Chaplin's decision to marry May Collins as soon as the decree from Mildred was absolute; this did not happen, the comedian's next bride being Lita Grey (*qv*), who had appeared in *The Idle Class* and was in the cast of his then-current production, *The Kid* (*qv*). They were married in November 1924. Lita was to be leading lady of *The Gold Rush*, but became pregnant; she and Chaplin had two children before their highly acrimonious divorce, effective in 1927 and final in 1928. Chaplin's next marriage, to Paulette Goddard (*qv*), was, in Chaplin's later opinion, based on mutual loneliness. The exact circumstances of their wedding – in the Far East during 1936 – did not become apparent until their divorce, reportedly an amicable one, in June 1942. A year later, Chaplin married Oona O'Neill (*qv*), whom he had known for some eight months. This successful match endured until the comedian's death.

(See also: Children; Women)

MARX, GROUCHO
(1890–1977)

A friend and contemporary of Chaplin, Groucho Marx first made the acquaintance of his fellow-comedian in Canada during August 1913. The Karno troupe's engagement at Winnipeg coincided with a three-hour stopover for the Marx Brothers, who were bound for the west coast on the Pantages circuit. In a November 1935 newspaper interview with journalist Edward Lawrence, Groucho recalled having stopped at the Sullivan-Considine theatre to catch a friend's act, but his attention was taken instead by Chaplin, over whom 'People became hysterical. There never was such laughter.' Groucho visited him backstage, encountering both a dingy dressing room smelling of make-up and the fact that Chaplin owned but one shirt. Any dirt on the garment would be concealed by a wide tie until it was washed and re-worn, still wet (Chaplin, though comparatively well-paid, was already compulsively frugal). Groucho rejoined his brothers at the icy train depot, enthusing – to no avail – over the talented Englishman he

had seen. Although remaining on separate circuits, Chaplin and Groucho would socialize whenever their vaudeville commitments took them to the same town. A later version of their meeting, from a 1959 Groucho memoir entitled *Groucho and Me*, varies in that all four Marx Brothers were present at the meeting, which seems altogether less likely until one considers a story told by Chico Marx's daughter, Maxine (in her book *Growing Up with Chico*), in which Chaplin jokingly attended a Marx performance, prominently reading a newspaper instead of watching their act; in return, the Marxes sent four unsmiling rabbis to watch Chaplin (who mistook them for the Marx Brothers in disguise). From the same source derives an account of Maxine being placed on Chaplin's knee during a train journey, probably when the Marxes caught up with Chaplin after his success in films. At this time, Groucho noted the presence of both a butler and gold crockery as evidence of Chaplin's increased financial status. He was aware, too, of a diminished shyness with women, recalling the occasion when, escorted to a brothel, Chaplin elected to play with the madam's dog instead of one of the girls. The young vaudevillians followed the visit with a somewhat adolescent vaulting of dustbins in an alleyway. It is apparent that Groucho took some pride in his friend's success, the more so since a nervous Chaplin had sought his advice after accepting a contract with Keystone (*qv*). Chaplin returned the favour somewhat by lending his name to an endorsement of the Marx Brothers' stage revue, *I'll Say She Is!* In 1937 they were joined by Fred Perry and Ellesworth Vines in an England v. America tennis match, differing news clips from which may be seen in *The Gentleman Tramp* (*qv*) and a Marx documentary called *The Marx Brothers in a Nutshell*. 'I could play this game much better without the other three,' said Chaplin. 'How are you without a racket?' asked Groucho in reponse. 'Oh, marvellous,' replied Chaplin, adding, 'all I need is a shovel ...' before making appropriate downward scoops. Groucho disrupted the proceedings by first spreading out a picnic then producing a sleeping bag. Claims that Chaplin was annoyed by Groucho's clowning are not substantiated by the newsreel footage. When interviewed years later on TV's *Hy Gardner Show*, Groucho cited this as the occasion when Chaplin, perhaps mindful of his lapse into mime during their pre-game banter, had said, 'I wish I could

speak on the screen as well as you.' Chaplin, of course, had yet to make a talking picture, whereas the Marxes had gone straight into that medium while still performing on the Broadway stage. Chaplin did, of course, succumb to talking pictures, and in so doing abandoned his familiar screen character. When a completely transformed Chaplin appeared in *Monsieur Verdoux* (*qv*), Groucho (promoting his solo film, *Copacabana*, a contemporary United Artists release) defended Chaplin's position thus: 'I can just feel for Chaplin. How he must have wearied of those turned up shoes, that derby hat, that cane, that shuffle. It finally irritated him so much that he had to switch rôles in self-defence.' Long after each had established himself in the movie colony, Chaplin and Groucho discovered themselves sitting back-to-back in a Hollywood restaurant. They finished up comparing notes on a mutual insecurity about their lives and work. 'You would think,' said Groucho to Edward Lawrence, 'that by now Chaplin would be convinced of his own talent. But he was just as scared as he had been in the old days, when he came to me and asked my advice.' On their last meeting, at a party arranged by Carol and Walter Matthau when Chaplin visited the United States in 1972, it was Chaplin who offered the advice. 'Keep warm,' he suggested, possibly the best recommendation that one octogenarian could make to another. Groucho Marx died in August 1977; Chaplin, little more than a year Groucho's senior, followed him only four months after. The parallels between them were to continue in macabre fashion, in that both comedians' remains were stolen and recovered shortly after interment.

A footnote: Jerry Epstein's *Remembering Charlie* describes a meeting of Chaplin and another celebrated mime, Harpo Marx, after a charity screening of *City Lights* (*qv*) in the late 1940s. 'It's easy for you, all this pantomime,' said Harpo, to which Chaplin, who had laboured for years on the film, responded with a horrified '*Easy?*'

(See also: Abandoned projects; Bell, Monta; Camera-looks; Costume; Death; Documentaries, compilations; Impersonators; Karno, Fred; *Mabel at the Wheel*; Pickford, Mary; Politics; Raye, Martha; Religion; Riesner, Charles F. 'Chuck'; Sport; United Artists)

THE MASQUERADER

(Chaplin film)
Keystone Comedy released by Mutual,
27 August 1914. Produced by Mack
Sennett. Written and directed by Charles
Chaplin. Photography attributed to Frank
D. Williams. Reissue titles include *Putting
One Over, His New Profession* and *A
Female Impersonator* (see below). One reel.
1,030 feet.

With Charlie Chaplin (himself), Charlie
Murray (director), Roscoe 'Fatty'
Arbuckle (himself), Mabel Normand
(herself), Fritz Schade (villain), Minta
Durfee (heroine), Chester Conklin
(Charlie's replacement), Vivian Edwards,
Cecile Arnold (actresses with whom
Charlie flirts), Charley Chase, Harry
McCoy (actors).

Charlie arrives for work at the Keystone
studio. He is outside, talking to Mabel
Normand, when the director walks out
and leads Charlie in by the ear. Sharing
a dressing room with Fatty Arbuckle,
Charlie brushes down his costume. On
the set, a dramatic scene is being
rehearsed. In the dressing room, Charlie
tries to take a swig from Fatty's bottle of
beer, but Fatty switches it for petrol.
Charlie attempts to reach the correct
bottle, but has his knuckles rapped.
Both actors collide when standing up
simultaneously. Charlie blows face

powder at Fatty. Charlie is late, and the
actor playing the villain is sent to fetch
him. Fatty, in response to the face
powder, hurls an object in Charlie's
direction but strikes the other actor,
who retaliates in kind. Charlie enters
the set. He is instructed to foil a knife-
wielding villain but, distracted by two
pretty actresses, misses his cue.
Prompted, Charlie enters the fray but
makes a mess of the scene and is
replaced. Charlie insists on being part of
the action and, keeping his replacement
out of shot, rushes into the scene. He
boots not only the villain but also the
director. Back at the dressing room,
Charlie is fired by the director. Charlie
throws his valise at him, and is chased
through a neighbouring set before being
ejected into the street. Later, a beautiful
actress arrives at Keystone, attracting
much interest. She, of course, is Charlie
in disguise, but the director, taken in,
shows 'her' into his office. He makes a
play, but is gently repulsed. The
newcomer is offered the star dressing
room, much to the other actors'
discomfiture. The director chases the
visitor before departing. Charlie reverts
to his usual costume and admits the
imposture, prompting a chase with the
director and actors. Cornered, Charlie
hurls bricks, then takes refuge in a well,
where director and colleagues are
prepared for him to flounder.

Most copies of *The Masquerader*
omit the original opening of a civilian-
clad Chaplin chatting with Mabel
Normand (*qv*) outside the studio. The
author has examined three different
editions, only one of which (of
indeterminate origin) has this segment.
Also unique to this copy is a part of the
dressing room sequence, where Fatty
Arbuckle (*qv*) switches bottles so that
Charlie drinks some foul substance, then
raps his hand for trying to grab the
correct bottle. The next gag, also deleted
in most prints, shows Charlie fanning a
supposedly malodorous foot prior to
putting on a boot. This print is, however,
not complete, for it lacks the section
where Charlie is briefed on his part in
the film then misses his cue when flirting
with two actresses. Another version,
retitled *Putting One Over*, omits the early
scenes described above but includes the
footage of Charlie on set. The same is
true of a UK sound reissue from New
Realm called *A Female Impersonator*, a
title given to this film at least as early as
1920. Charlie's on-set disruption may be
seen in Robert Youngson's 1960
anthology, *When Comedy Was King*, and
during the opening credits of an
American TV package of Chaplin shorts.
It is possible that this sequence alone was
discovered in original negative form;
quality in both extracts is excellent,
whereas prints of the film itself tend to
be rather poor.

The main credits of the *Putting One
Over* reissue cite the original title as 'The
Masqueraders', but this is probably an
error. According to Theodore Huff,
another reissue went under the title *His
New Profession* (*qv*), actually the name of
Chaplin's next Keystone. Such cross-
pollination of titles caused confusion at
the time and has continued to annoy
collectors and historians.

(See also: Conklin, Chester; Female
impersonation; Keystone; *Recreation*;
Reissues; Television; Williams, Frank D.)

MCCOY, HARRY
(1894 or 1895–1937)

(Chaplin films *qv*)
Actor, educated in Philadelphia,
originally from the vaudeville and
Broadway stage before entering films
with American Flying 'A', Selig and
Keystone (*qv*); appeared with Chaplin –
usually as an outraged rival – in *Mabel's
Strange Predicament, Mabel at the Wheel*,

*Charlie Murray is unaware that the 'actress' is really the actor he dismissed, or in other
words,* **The Masquerader**

Caught in a Cabaret, Mabel's Busy Day, Mabel's Married Life, The Property Man, The Face On the Bar Room Floor, The Masquerader, His New Profession, Those Love Pangs, Tillie's Punctured Romance and *Getting Acquainted*. McCoy later joined Henry Lehrman (*qv*) at L-KO Comedies, worked as support to comedian Max Asher at Joker and, in 1920, appeared in the two-reel 'Hallroom Boys' series for the Cohn brothers, future executives at Columbia. McCoy eventually returned to Mack Sennett as a scenarist, as in the 'Smith Family' series. Before devoting himself exclusively to screenwriting, McCoy continued to play supporting rôles during the 1920s, as in Buddy Rogers' *Heads Up* (1925) and a 1928 vehicle for Syd Chaplin (*qv*), *A Little Bit of Fluff* (a.k.a. *Skirts*).

MCGUIRE, PADDY

(Chaplin films *qv*)
Supporting comic, with Chaplin at Essanay (*qv*): he appears in *A Jitney Elopement* as an inept cop, plays a farmhand in *The Tramp*, is one of the decorators in *Work*, a robber in *The Bank* and a press-ganged mariner in *Shanghaied*. McGuire is known to have left Essanay in 1916 for Vogue, where he sometimes worked with Ben Turpin (*qv*); later at Fox.

(See also: Trick photography)

***Paddy McGuire** shares Charlie's fatigue in* The Tramp

MENJOU, ADOLPHE
(1890–1963)

Born in Pittsburgh of French stock, Adolphe Menjou's early screen rôles were essentially minor, even in such comparatively high-profile things as Fairbanks' *The Three Musketeers* (1921, as King Louis XIII) and Mary Pickford's

Through the Back Door (also 1921, as 'James Brewster'). It was presumably the Pickford and Fairbanks films that brought Menjou to the attention of Chaplin, who, in giving him a prominent rôle in *A Woman of Paris* (*qv*), ensured the actor's lasting fame. (A later film, *A Gentleman of Paris* (1927), seems to owe its inspiration to Chaplin's work.) Menjou's niche became that of the ideal Frenchman, as evidenced by Chaplin's joky description of him as 'the perfect French tripe' when introducing the actor to Georgie Wood (*qv*). More seriously, Chaplin's evaluation of Menjou was 'an excellent actor in need of good direction'; Chaplin duly supplied it. Among others in Menjou's lengthy filmography are *Morocco* (1930), *The Front Page* (1931, for which Menjou was nominated as Best Actor), *A Farewell to Arms* (1932), Harold Lloyd's *The Milky Way* (1936), *A Star is Born* (1937), Hal Roach's *The Housekeeper's Daughter* (1939), *Turnabout* (1940) and *Road Show* (1941), also the Rita Hayworth vehicle *You Were Never Lovelier* (1942), Sinatra's *Step Lively* (1945), *State of the Union* (1948) and *Man on a Tightrope* (1953).

(See also: Bell, Monta; Fairbanks, Douglas; Pickford, Mary)

MENTAL ILLNESS

(Chaplin films *qv*)
As noted elsewhere, Chaplin's mother, Hannah, was a victim of mental illness for much of her life, and at one point had to be led to hospital by her young son. It was doubtless because of this that Chaplin often feared for his own sanity. There was unfounded press speculation on his mental health in one of several ridiculous stories published during the 'Chaplin Craze' (*qv*). In speaking of Chaplin's meeting with Nijinsky, who was then fast approaching madness, Isobel Quigly pointed out how Chaplin, unlike the dancer, 'did not crack', but survived the stresses and strains with the 'therapy' of humour. It was certainly enough to get him through the initial phase of his adulation, but did nothing to prevent the full-scale breakdown amid his divorce from Lita Grey (*qv*), during which Chaplin's hair turned white.

While silent comedy often employed stereotyped 'lunatics', this motif seldom appears in the Chaplin films, again probably due to the awful experiences of his mother (themselves perhaps inspiration for Terry's psychosomatic paralysis in

***Adolphe Menjou** achieved stardom in Chaplin's* A Woman of Paris

Limelight). Charlie is evidently worried that a cop thinks him odd in *His Trysting Place*, but, generally, insanity is confined to a realistic level, particularly to those in desperate circumstances. Examples are the crazy-looking flophouse types in *Triple Trouble*, among them a knife-wielding maniac. One might note how this Essanay-compiled film includes a character called 'Col. Nutt', an unsubtle name Chaplin would never have countenanced. More in keeping with Chaplin's style are Big Jim's hallucinations in *The Gold Rush* or Charlie's breakdown in *Modern Times*, despite a worryingly blithe title card announcing him as 'cured'. In *The Great Dictator*, Hynkel is portrayed as a madman, and is even called such by renegade assistant Schultz. There is also a suggestion in the dialogue that *Monsieur Verdoux's* murderous period was an aberration induced by the pressure of supporting his family during the Depression.

(See also: Ballet; Chaplin, Hannah; Childhood; *Circus, The*; Dreams; Food; Hair; Marriages; Sickness; Suicide)

MINEAU, CHARLOTTE
(1891–?)

(Chaplin films *qv*)
Statuesque actress, reportedly French-born and Sorbonne-educated, who was working at Essanay (*qv*) at the time of

In *His New Job*, **Charlotte Mineau** plays a movie actress who acquires an inexperienced leading man

Chaplin's arrival. In the first Chaplin Essanay, *His New Job*, she plays a movie actress, as she would again in a Mutual comedy with a similar setting, *Behind the Screen*. Also at Mutual, she plays an elegant store detective in *The Floorwalker*, and Edna's mother in both *The Vagabond* and *The Count*. In *The Rink*, she plays a friend of Edna's who, coincidentally, is an old flame of Eric Campbell's. Charlotte Mineau has been spotted in the downstairs audience of *A Night in the Show*, and is said to be the woman whom Charlie assists in stealing groceries in *Easy Street*. Other films include Mary Pickford's *Sparrows* (1926) and some Hal Roach comedies, among them two pre-teaming Laurel & Hardy appearances, *Love 'Em and Weep* and *Sugar Daddies* (both 1927). It is also the author's opinion that she appears in the Marx Brothers' *Monkey Business* (1931).

(See also: Campbell, Eric; Laurel, Stan; Marx, Groucho; Mutual; Pickford, Mary; Purviance, Edna)

MODERN TIMES 🎩

(Chaplin film)
Released by United Artists, 5 February 1936. Produced, written and directed by Charles Chaplin. Assistant director: Carter DeHaven. Music by Charles Chaplin, conducted by Alfred Newman and arranged by Edward Powell and David Raksin. Recorded by Paul Neal and Frank Maher. Photographed by Rollie Totheroh and Ira Morgan. Settings (art direction) Charles D. Hall and Russell Spencer. Nine reels, 87 mins (sometimes quoted as 85).

With Charlie Chaplin (himself), Paulette Goddard (gamine), Henry Bergman (café owner), Stanley J. 'Tiny' Sandford (Big Bill), Chester Conklin (the mechanic), Hank Mann, Louis Natheaux (Bill's fellow-burglars), Allan Garcia (president of company), James C. Morton (assembly line worker), Stanley Blystone, Dick Alexander, Cecil Reynolds, Myra McKinney, Murdoch McQuarrie, Wilfred Lucas, Edward J. LeSainte, Fred Malatesta, Sam Stein, Juana Sutton, Ted Oliver, John Rand, Lloyd Ingraham, Heinie Conklin, Edward Kimball.

This 'story of industry, of individual enterprise – humanity crusading in the pursuit of happiness' opens by contrasting herded sheep with the masses of workers leaving a subway, then entering a huge factory. One of them, Charlie, does a repetitive job tightening nuts on an assembly line. The President, by contrast, occupies himself with a jigsaw and the funny papers when not monitoring every corner of the building via closed-circuit television. Charlie finds the repetitive motion of his job difficult to shake off; so is the boss, who appears on screen when Charlie tries to sneak time for a smoke. Back on the assembly line, Charlie takes his time before resuming work. The president is shown a new device, a machine designed to save lost production hours by feeding his employees while they are working. That endangered institution, lunch time, arrives on the shop floor. Charlie is unable to shake off the motions of tightening; when the president's secretary walks past, Charlie applies his spanners to the buttons adorning her skirt. Charlie's burly colleague, Big Bill, pours soup from a thermos flask. Charlie avoids sitting in it but, in moving the bowl, twitches so badly that much of it is spilled. Distracted, Big Bill sits in the bowl. The feeding machine is wheeled in, and Charlie is selected to try it. Initial results are promising until a corncob holder shifts into hyperdrive, a soup dispenser splashes over his chest and face, a sliding arm feeds him metal components, a cake tray pushes its

Modern Times: *Better times have arrived with the girl's employment in a café ...*

contents into his face and a sponge napkin raps him in the mouth. Charlie slides to the floor as the idea is rejected. Late afternoon, and production is speeded up. Charlie tries to keep pace but, losing his mind, climbs on the conveyor belt and takes a trip through the gears of a gigantic machine. The machine is reversed, and Charlie reappears, dancing faun-like around the factory. Charlie, wielding the spanners, tightens everything in sight, including Big Bill's nipples (!) and nose. Once more eyeing the buttons on the secretary's skirt, he chases her into the street. Charlie pauses to tighten up a fire hydrant until distracted by a matronly woman, innocently sporting hexagonal buttons on her generous bosom. She is chased around the building until a cop comes to her rescue. Charlie returns to the factory – dutifully clocking in – then sets off all the controls, causing the generators to explode. Next, armed with an oilcan, Charlie goes on the rampage, swinging around Tarzan-like until he

... but terminate with the intervention of the authorities

sprays the president with oil. Still squirting oil, Charlie is taken away in an ambulance. Time passes, and a cured but unemployed Charlie is discharged from hospital. He finds there are no jobs. A red warning flag falls from the back of a passing truck; Charlie picks it up, attempting to alert the driver, and suddenly finds himself at the head of a communist protest march. The police intervene, and the crowd scatters; Charlie, yanked from a sewer, is accused of being the leader and arrested. On the dockside, a *gamine* is stealing bananas to feed herself and some children. At their shack, she distributes the food to her younger sisters and their father, a desperate, unemployed man. In jail, Charlie is unnerved to see his huge cellmate doing needlepoint. Ordered to take the upper bunk, Charlie pulls it down on his cellmate's head. He is saved from a throttling when the convicts are summoned to mess. There is a search for smuggled 'nose-powder', which is dumped into the salt cellar. Charlie gets some, and thus wanders off, dazed, instead of being returned to his cell. In consequence, he is both at large and suitably enlivened when a group of armed convicts hold the warden. Charlie overpowers them, and is congratulated. Outside, there is 'trouble with the unemployed'. The girl's father is killed in a street skirmish, and his orphaned daughters are taken in by the law. The younger sisters are taken away, but the eldest makes her escape. In prison, Charlie enjoys a luxurious private cell, insulated from the world's problems. His pardon is announced on the radio, and he is summoned to the warden's office. While the minister is making his weekly rounds, his wife, sitting beside Charlie, takes tea. The tea makes her stomach rumble; it has the same effect on Charlie, who switches on the radio to camouflage the noise. He hastily switches off a commercial for an indigestion remedy. The good lady departs with her husband, and Charlie is told he is free. He would prefer to remain, but is once again thrust into the outside world. Showing a potential employer a written reference from the Sheriff, Charlie obtains work in a shipyard. Asked to find a wedge, he removes one from beneath a partially-completed ship. The vessel sails into the distance, and Charlie, determined to return to jail, quietly takes his leave. The hungry, homeless girl steals a loaf of bread and runs straight into Charlie. When a policeman arrives, Charlie

Modern Times: *mechanic turns maniac ...*

claims to be the culprit and is led away. The girl is surprised at the seeming kindness. Charlie's name is cleared by a witness; disgusted at being free once more, he enters a cafeteria to order a giant meal for which he cannot pay. Outside, the girl is arrested. So is Charlie, who deliberately hails a cop when he cannot pay for the food. He compounds the felony by ordering things from a tobacconist while the cop makes a 'phone call. In the police wagon, Charlie encounters the girl again, offering her his seat and reminding her of their initial meeting. The girl begins to cry. The wagon makes a sudden swerve and they are thrown from the vehicle, landing on the ground. Charlie keeps their accompanying officer unconscious and tells the girl to run. She insists he should join her. Sitting by the roadside, Charlie asks the girl where she lives. 'No place – anywhere' he is told. Seeing a blissfully domesticated (and rather silly) couple, they contemplate a similar existence, fruit trees outside the doors and windows plus a cow on hand for instant milk. Charlie decides they will have a home even if he has to work for it; they make a discreet exit when a policeman appears. They chance upon a department store, to see the night watchman being carried out with a broken leg. Charlie's letter of reference is sufficient for him to obtain the injured man's job. Once alone in the store, Charlie brings in the girl via the staff entrance. They make themselves at

Charlie as the factory worker in **Modern Times**

home, obtaining food in the basement cafeteria and trying on roller skates upstairs in the toy department. Charlie is such an expert skater that he can even glide around blindfolded; unfortunately, he strays into a closed section where work is in progress, leaving a severe drop to the floor below. Charlie has several near misses before the girl helps him to safety. In the bedding department, the girl tries on a fur coat and, while Charlie is away punching the time clocks, settles in one of the beds. On his return, Charlie promises to wake her before the store opens,then continues to patrol the building, still on skates. In the basement, burglars are at work. Charlie discovers them, but is unable to stay put as ordered, having rolled over to an 'up' escalator while one of the gang fires shots at him. He is led over to some casks of wine; the burglar fires the pistol, and wine starts to cascade into Charlie's face. Upstairs, the girl sleeps on, oblivious. Charlie is very drunk by the time the other burglars have assembled. One of them is Big Bill, who, recognizing Charlie, greets him warmly then introduces him to his confederates. When Charlie asks why Bill has taken to crime, he is told, 'We ain't burglars – we're hungry.' There are tears all around before the foursome help themselves to the stock of alcohol. In the morning, the

Modern Times: *Charlie takes the blame for the gamine's act of theft, but is believed only momentarily*

Modern Times: *dreaming of an ideal home*

girl awakens just in time to escape before the store opens. There is no sign of Charlie until an assistant finds him on the counter, asleep, beneath a pile of clothes. Charlie is arrested, making sure the girl keeps her distance as he is taken away. Ten days later, the girl awaits

Charlie's release from custody. She greets him with a hug and some good news: she has found a home for them. It turns out to be 'no Buckingham Palace', being a shack in which everything threatens imminent collapse, but Charlie is content. Night, and the girl sleeps inside while Charlie rests in a kind of packing-case extension to the building. Charlie greets the dawn with a dip in the canal, into which a collapsing wall had dumped him the previous day. This time, the stretch of water is less deep than he had imagined. Dressed, Charlie settles down for breakfast – including an evidently filched ham – despite the continued danger of collapsing furniture. Charlie reads the newspaper, learning that the factories have re-opened. Determined to get them a real home, Charlie rushes off to the factory, beating a crowd of men to the last job before the gates close. He is put to work assisting a mechanic, who is repairing the long-dormant machinery. Charlie, operating a press, nearly flattens the mechanic's head, but squashes an oil can instead. Charlie suggests it might make a good shovel, then replaces it. When the press descends once more, Charlie retrieves the oil can, but not the mechanic's coat, resulting in a huge, flat pocket watch. Working on the mills, Charlie leaves the mechanic's toolbox in the wrong place, sending it through the gears. The same thing soon happens to its owner. Charlie pulls a lever, only for the mechanic to be trapped even further along inside the vast machine, leaving only his head visible. Charlie ceases his efforts when the lunch hooter sounds, but feeds the trapped mechanic. Lunch is over, and the mechanic is freed, only for he and Charlie to be told there is a strike. Outside, the police control the restless men. A cop gives Charlie an unnecessary shove on his way; Charlie reacts peaceably, but accidentally treads on a plank, causing a brick to fly into the air. The brick hits a cop, and Charlie is arrested. A week later, the girl dances to barrel organ music outside a waterfront café, whose proprietor takes her on as dancer. Another week has passed, and the girl, now making a good living and wearing a new outfit, meets Charlie as he is released. He is taken to the café and, despite his misgivings, agrees to try out as a singing waiter. Meanwhile, detectives are sent to retrieve the fugitive girl. That evening, the new waiter manoeuvres around the busy café, drilling holes in cheese and creating havoc when using the 'out' door to enter the kitchen. He tries to carry a tray of

food across the crowded dance floor, but a roast duck becomes hooked on the chandelier. The duck, once retrieved, becomes the object of a game between Charlie and some drunken college football types. Charlie returns it to the table, knocking it over. 'I hope you can sing,' says the proprietor, leaving Charlie to rehearse his number. As he cannot remember the words, the girl writes them on his cuff. Charlie takes the floor, but the cuffs fly off in an opening flourish. Charlie stalls, but the girl tells him to sing, irrespective of the lyric. Recalling the overall gist of the song, Charlie improvises a foreign-sounding but nonsensical lyric, conveying in mime the risqué tale of a young woman invited to share a cab with a rich old man. He is a sensation, and the delighted manager offers him a steady job. Their problems seem over until the girl, taking the floor, is apprehended by the authorities. The manager explains that she is employed by him, but acquiesces when shown the warrant. Charlie and the girl effect an escape, Charlie barring the officers' path by toppling over the chairs. At dawn the next day, they are at a country roadside. The girl despairs. 'Buck up – never say die,' Charlie tells her. 'We'll get along!' They set off, Charlie pausing to encourage a smile from the girl, then, hand-in-hand, walk away into the distance.

This famous ending provides a twist to earlier equivalents in that, for a change, Charlie at last has a companion, something long regarded as appropriate to the final appearance of 'Charlie' in undiluted form. *Modern Times* was inspired by tales of young men who had suffered breakdowns after moving from farm work into factories; at least as influential was Rene Clair's *A Nous la Liberté* (1931), to the point where its production company, Films Sonoris Tobis, later brought suit against Chaplin for his alleged borrowings, particularly of the conveyor belt sequence. Clair himself was quoted as being flattered; 'God knows,' he said, 'I have certainly borrowed enough from him.' The suit was dropped.

Modern Times was the first picture for which Chaplin used a shooting script, something he considered of sufficient importance to mention even when the project was first announced early in 1934. In an 'open letter' to Chaplin in *Picturegoer* of 10 February that year, Malcolm D. Phillips construed this – and a rumour that Paulette was in some

*Hundreds of extras for the **Modern Times** subway sequence arrive at the studio by bus*
By courtesy and copyright of the Roy Export Company Establishment

way 'collaborating' on the script – as a sign of faltering confidence, the result of having been left behind during the three-year gap since the release of *City Lights* (*qv*). Phillips believed that Chaplin needed to progress in his methods – presumably by adopting speech – and re-establish himself with 'a great picture, which *City Lights* undoubtedly was not'. Fortunately, Chaplin was seldom inclined to follow anyone's judgement save his own, and *Modern Times* made only limited concession to the increasing requirement for talk, retaining instead the customary sub-titles for narrative and dialogue. The use of a prepared script may have been prompted in some measure by the far tighter nature of the film's soundtrack, which, although ostensibly providing accompaniment for a 'silent' film, incorporated human speech via television screens, radio sets (including a commercial by Chaplin, adopting an American accent), a gramophone and the asynchronous chorus of singing waiters. In addition, Charlie sings a song, albeit in gibberish, to the tune of 'Titine', thus providing the tramp with a voice, but in a routine dependent almost entirely upon mime to convey its message (oddly, the song's final 'verse', concluding its risqué tale, is missing from the majority of prints, but has recently been included in restored video editions from the USA and Great Britain). For some reason, the song was omitted from a soundtrack album published in the 1970s. It might be noted that Chaplin, though silent, may be lip-read speaking his own dialogue in

this film, the absence of which had frequently been noted in his earlier works. When the film reached London's Tivoli Theatre in mid-February 1936, *The Times* appreciated a film using 'supplementary sound', with no submission to the tempo of theatre, likening it to 'relief from prolonged toothache'.

Filming occupied a ten-month period, commencing in October 1934. Assisting Chaplin in the direction were Henry Bergman (*qv*) and Carter De Haven (1886–1977), a vaudeville veteran who later played the part of an

ambassador in *The Great Dictator* (*qv*). Leading lady this time was Paulette Goddard (*qv*), who had been in Chaplin's life since 1932 and would become his third wife. Contemporary British publicity records an expenditure of £14,000 on the elaborate factory set, £11,000 for the building of three streets at the San Pedro waterfront (close to where Chaplin had shot *A Busy Day* [*qv*] back in 1914) and the employment of 400 people for the café set. Photographs (*illustrated*) exist of hundreds more extras being transported by coach for the opening crowd shot, and of their being directed by Chaplin himself – rather than delegating the task to an assistant – from the top of a high tower.

When *Modern Times* opened at New York's Rivoli in early February 1936, *City Lights* was exactly five years in the past. Frank S. Nugent of the *New York Times* welcomed Chaplin's return after an 'undue absence', acknowledging the comedian's unchanged genius before dismissing the rumour of *Modern Times* being 'preoccupied with social themes'. Nugent allowed for a possible 'sociological concept', but was no less delighted with this 'rousing, rib-tickling, gag-bestrewn jest', revisiting his earlier comedies (notably *The Rink* and, in its escalator routine, *The Floorwalker*) alongside the new routines, themselves taken as laughter-raisers with no political intent. Nugent was aware of a story to the effect that Chaplin had changed the ending on the advice of the head of Soviet Russia's

Extras for the subway sequence congregate outside the studio
By courtesy and copyright of the Roy Export Company Establishment

Chaplin – in costume and make-up – directs the subway sequence from on high
By courtesy and copyright of the Roy Export Company Establishment

film industry (actually an idle boast on that official's part), but was more pleased to say simply: 'Chaplin is back again.'

In the *Spectator*, Graham Greene glumly predicted how Marxists would 'claim it as *their* film', and it is perhaps unsurprising that *Modern Times*, with its concentration upon a little man at odds with authority, would in the 1930s be construed as as a treatise on Communism. In principle, it is little different from the early films in which Charlie did battle with employers and the police, but the greater sophistication of this film – and the period in which it was made – may have left such basic ideas open to misinterpretation. There has certainly been frequent misunderstanding of the joke in which Charlie, finding a red flag that has fallen from a passing truck, waves the flag in an attempt to alert the driver but finds himself unwittingly at the head of a Communist march. Oddly, this has often been cited as evidence of the comedian's supposed radicalism, even though the whole point of the gag is that Charlie is *not* connected with the organization. Even South Africa, long among the most conservative of countries, understood this gag, as quoted in the *Outspan* of 24 July 1936. The magazine thought *Modern Times* 'may have a Marxian [*sic*] intention, but in it sociology does not swamp the comedy'. The *Manchester Guardian* thought the film parodied Stalin's Five-Year Plans at least as much

as anything in the West; the *Era*'s Philip Guedalla in turn reminded his readers of the existence of 'just as much machinery and quite as many big policemen in the USSR'. C.A. Lejeune of the *Observer* saw irony in that Chaplin, as an enemy of regimentation, would be 'just as fierce an opponent of the Communist policy he endorses as of the Fascist authority he deplores', though one might query any specific 'endorsement' of any ideology in the film; a better point is made in regretting Charlie's use of outside devices in making chaos, rather than being an inherent source of disruption in himself. Robert Lynd in the *News Chronicle* favoured the 'glorious knockabout' over the reputed satire, in his view handled better in *A Nous la Liberté*. E.V. Lucas of *Punch* echoed Nugent by immediately dispelling rumours of 'sociology' in *Modern Times*, preferring to describe the comedy sequences of 'the most amusing film now being shown', albeit 'a little ragged and disjointed'. The episodic structure of *Modern Times* often drew dismissive comments, typified when Otis Ferguson of the *New Republic* suggested it to be no more than a collection of short subjects. G.A. Atkinson of the *Era* saw this as a virtue, to the point of asking Chaplin to produce three two-reelers a year instead of carrying through his stated intent to abandon 'Charlie'. The *Observer*'s Ivor Brown contrasted Charlie with the advance stills for *Things to Come*, evidently preferring his music-

hall figure with 'broken and bulging boots' to the Grecian-clad, machine-dependent citizens of an imagined future. Charlie was capable of making his flat-footed way not merely without mechanical contrivances but actually in opposition to them, for 'Charlie always is the symbol of Free Will.'

Free Will was not exactly in vogue within certain countries. On 18 February 1936, the *Manchester Guardian* carried a Reuter account of the ban on *Modern Times* in Nazi Germany. Doubt as to Chaplin's 'Aryan purity' had put an end to reissues of his earlier films and, when the Rivels clowns recently played a date in Berlin, one of their number had been obliged to drop his parody of the tramp character. Although Chaplin had not even submitted *Modern Times* for consideration by the German censors, it had earned the reputation of a 'Communist tendency' and was thus 'unacceptable'. The *Daily Telegraph*, also carrying the story, favoured the idea that the ban had less to do with the film's politics than the Nazis' belief that Chaplin was Jewish; the *Daily Herald* suggested various reasons, among them the similarity between Chaplin's moustache and Hitler's. Not unexpectedly, Mussolini followed Hitler's lead even though the film had been allowed into Italy. On 24 February 1936, the *News Chronicle* noted how the enthusiasm for *Modern Times* in Italian papers had 'petered out owing, it is believed, to the Duce's objection to the "Communistic" trend of the film. Efforts to screen it in its English version at the International Picture Theatre, which caters chiefly for foreigners, are meeting with the opposition of the Censorship Board, which wishes to cut the film drastically.'

Modern Times is rated highly in Chaplin's work – both as a comedy and for its theme tune, known eventually as *Smile* – and has mostly outlived any radical interpretations; Chaplin, however, may well have been unnerved by them, at least for a while. When he permitted a London revival late in July 1954, Arnold Russell of *Reynolds News* named the film as source for the comedian's political persecution in the USA, citing this as the reason why Chaplin had favoured other films for prior reissues. By the time of its widespread revival in 1972, technology was becoming unpopular and *Modern Times* was seen as nothing more than the very funny chronicle of a lone individual struggling against an increasingly mechanical, impersonal world. A much later British comedian, Marty Feldman, was heavily influenced by the silents and (in David Nathan's *The Laughtermakers*) said that in *Modern Times*, 'Chaplin said more about automation ... than anyone else has done since. People who invent machines expect you to take them very seriously and comics don't.' Feldman went on to speak of a comic's ability to 'bring life into proportion', using also *The Great Dictator* as an example of helping the world to understand a menace, even if 'you couldn't laugh Hitler out of existence'. Nor, it seems, can anyone threaten the existence of *Modern Times*. On 21 September 1989, the *Daily Telegraph* reported it among the 25 'untouchable' films considered by the United States government as worthy of 'eternal preservation'. 'If cut,' continued the story, 'they must carry notices that they have been altered.' Perhaps for this reason we might expect Charlie to complete his gibberish song in all future prints of *Modern Times*.

(See also: Abandoned projects; Alcohol; Camera-looks; Conklin, Chester; Costume; *Easy Street*; *Floorwalker, The*; Food; Garcia, Allan; Mental illness; Music; Policemen; Politics; Prisons; Rand, John; Radio; Reissues; Religion; *Rink, The*; Risqué humour; Sandford, Stanley J. 'Tiny'; Smoking; Stamps, coins; Television; Titling; Trick photography; United Artists; Vagrancy; Video releases)

MONSIEUR VERDOUX

(Chaplin film)
Released by United Artists, 11 April 1947. Produced, written and directed by Charles Chaplin, from an idea by Orson Welles (see below). Associate directors: Wheeler Dryden, Robert Florey. Music by Charles Chaplin, arranged and directed by Rudolph Schrager. Director of photography: Roland Totheroh. Operative cameraman: Wallace Chewning. Art director: John Beckman. Assistant director: Rex Bailey. Film editor: Willard Nico. Sound: James T. Corrigan. Artistic supervision: Curtis Courant. Working titles: *Lady Killer*, *Bluebeard*, *Bluebeard Rhapsody*, *Comedy of Murders*. 123 mins.

With Charles Chaplin (Henri Verdoux alias Varnay, alias Bonheur, alias Floray), Mady Correll (Mona, his wife), Allison Roddan (Peter, their son), Robert Lewis (Maurice Bottello, Verdoux's friend), Audrey Betz (Martha, his wife). The Ladies: Martha Raye (Annabella Bonheur), Ada-May Wells (Annette, her maid), Isobel Elsom (Marie Grosnay), Marjorie Bennett (her maid), Helene Heigh (Yvonne, Marie's friend), Margaret Hoffman (Lydia Floray), Marilyn Nash (the girl). The Law: Bernard J. Nedell (Prefect of Police), Charles Evans (Detective Morrow). The Couvais Family: Irving Bacon (Pierre), Edwin Mills (Jean), Virginia Brissac (Carlotta), Almira Sessions (Lena), Eula Morgan (Phoebe). Others in the cast: William Frawley, Arthur Hohl, Barbara Slater, Fritz Leiber, Vera Marshe, John Harmon, Christine Ell, Lois Conklin.

A gravestone reads 'Henri Verdoux 1880–1937'. Verdoux introduces himself in voice-over, confirming this as his real name, and explaining how, for three decades, he had been a law-abiding bank clerk until made jobless by the Depression in 1930. It was then that he embarked on 'liquidating members of the opposite sex ... a strictly business enterprise', to support a home and family. The story begins with the Couvais family, wine merchants of Northern France. Between bickering they find time to ponder one of their number, Thelma, who has drawn out all her money and disappeared with a new husband, after a courtship of only two weeks. They have not met the man, and have heard nothing from Thelma. If they do not hear from Thelma soon, the police will be called. All they know of the husband is a photograph, that of a man who, at that moment, is gardening at a villa in the South of France. Henri Verdoux – calling himself 'Varnay' – has had the incinerator burning for three days. He cuts flowers, and carefully removes a caterpillar who might otherwise be stepped upon. The postman calls with a registered letter for Mme Varnay; Verdoux takes it into the house and, pretending to summon the recipient from the bath, forges her signature. The letter is from Thelma's bank, enclosing 60,000 francs, thus closing her account. Verdoux counts the sum in swift, bank-clerk fashion. He has the telephone operator place a call to his stock market brokers in Paris, then sits down to play the piano. He is interrupted by an old lady, Louise, who has been sent as temporary housekeeper. Her job is to dust the drawers, clean everything, but initially to take down the curtains and put them away. Everything is to be left on the sideboard, to permit an inventory later. Verdoux's Paris call is connected, which he takes under his real name. He instructs his brokers to buy a large number of shares, the money to be wired to them the following day. The Couvais family visit the police. The photo of Verdoux has been destroyed, but they would recognize him again. The police promise to keep them informed. After the family's departure, Inspector Morrow, a senior detective, ponders the disappearance so far of twelve women, of similar types and in identical circumstances. He concludes there is at work a murderous bigamist, a modern-day Bluebeard, but his colleague is sceptical. An estate agent brings to the villa a potential buyer, Mme Marie Grosnay. Verdoux, seeing her instead as a potential *victim*, establishes her status as well-heeled widow and turns on the charm. His ardent pursuit becomes too much, and Mme Grosnay decides to leave. She may be contacted only via the estate agent. Verdoux travels to Paris. At a pavement café, he makes eyes at a suitable woman, but she has an escort. Verdoux acquires a *boutonnière* from a flower girl, and is joined at table by an old friend and his associate. Verdoux is queried over his recent business activities and, when seen to have a sizeable bankroll, is said to have made a 'killing'. He reacts slightly but, regaining his composure, bids the gentlemen good-day. His friend speaks of the poor deal Verdoux received on his redundancy from the bank. Verdoux arrives at his place of business, where he deals in antique furniture. He is greeted by a cat, for which he has bought food from the café. There is a phone call from his brokers, informing him of a drop in the market and the need to supply 50,000 francs by the next morning. Verdoux consults his little black book, deciding on Lydia in the city of Corbel. He can get there by train and still have 30 minutes before the local bank closes. Lydia, another bigamous wife, is furious at his three-month absence. Verdoux claims to be an engineer with business in Indo-China. He fabricates a story of an impending economic crash, and Lydia, against her better judgement, is persuaded to draw everything from her safe deposit box. At home, Lydia is suspicious and resolves to return the cash in the morning. Verdoux ensures she does not live to do so. Morning, and Verdoux counts the money at super-speed. Preparing two places for breakfast, he calls the stock exchange and arranges to send the necessary sum. His next call

Monsieur Verdoux buys a boutonnière ...

is to his true home, to see his wheelchair-bound wife and small son. Verdoux, determined to maintain a good home for his family, believes they may soon be able to retire. Mme Verdoux is concerned for her husband's health, particularly his state of mind. 'You seem so desperate about everything,' she says. Verdoux explains how these are 'desperate days'. He chastises his son for pulling the cat's tail; 'violence begets violence', he explains. They have company for dinner, the local druggist and his wife. Next morning, Verdoux is on a train to Lyon. He has Lydia's jewels and a naval tunic. As 'Captain Bonheur', he is awaited by the loud, brassy but rich Annabella. The 'captain', it seems, will stay for seven days before embarking on a six-week voyage. Annabella is with some shady-looking friends, one of whom reads her fortune in the cards. Annabella has such phenomenal luck that even the presence of the ace of spades should hold no

... and, at his nominal place of business, pauses to feed a cat

terror. A naval-clad Verdoux arrives and the friends depart. Verdoux makes slightly clinical love to Annabella before suggesting he might not need to be away so often if given charge of her financial affairs. Annabella refuses. He feigns hurt at her lack of trust, but Annabella has already resisted the scam that Verdoux used on Lydia. Verdoux insists she has been investing in worthless projects, and suggests jewellery. He is ready to produce Lydia's jewels when Annabella beats him to it. She has bought diamonds from the people who have just left, who deal in 'hot' goods. Suspicious of both people and price, Verdoux examines the jewels and declares them to be glass. Annabella faints. Later, Verdoux fabricates a tale of his ship being repaired, and announces his departure. Again he criticizes Annabella's business sense, but learns she has put the house in his name. She has also hidden the contents of her bank account on the premises. Verdoux decides to stay. They visit a nightclub and, while Annabella is cavorting, Verdoux slips out to the local druggist for two ounces of chloroform. He returns just in time to stop Annabella investing in a hare-brained scheme to convert salt water into petrol. That night, Verdoux prepares to administer the chloroform, but is interrupted by the maid, whom Annabella had dismissed that day but who has nowhere else to sleep. She is allowed to stay, and Verdoux's plans are postponed, the more so when the maid is reinstated. After breakfast, he decides to leave for 'that boat', hoping to return before sailing. In Paris, he finds Mme Grosnay in the phone book and arranges to be outside her residence on her return. She continues to resist his charm, so Verdoux calls at a florist, to arrange for flowers to be sent to her, the order to be repeated twice a week for two weeks. Back at his true home, Verdoux once more entertains his druggist friend, drawing from him a formula for the painless destruction of animals. The poison, banned by the authorities, simulates heart failure, works in an hour and is

undetectable, at least in animals. Verdoux suggests, hypothetically, that a criminal could test it on humans by taking a derelict from the streets, administering the poison then installing the victim in a hotel. There would be a post-mortem, allowing the criminal to learn the results from a safe distance. On his return to Paris, Verdoux obtains the ingredients and selects as guinea-pig a girl from the streets, whom he escorts to his *pied-à-terre* on a rainy night. Verdoux establishes that she is Belgian, originally a refugee from the war, and has just served a three-month sentence for a minor theft. He provides her with food and wine before she returns to her hotel. Her wine is poisoned. She and Verdoux discuss life and love. Verdoux is sceptical about women, believing their love for a man can turn to hatred when a more attractive specimen happens along. He assures the girl that he loves women, although he does not admire them. The girl thinks she knows very little about women, though Verdoux's ironic smile vanishes as he learns of the husband she selflessly adored. He had been crippled in the war, and died while she was in prison. Verdoux, pretending her wine contains some cork, disposes of it in favour of the non-poisonous variety. Verdoux gives the girl money to tide her over, a generous sum. She breaks into tears, this kindness having restored her faith. She has a more positive view of the world than Verdoux, who, jokingly suggesting she might corrupt him, sends the girl on her way. Next morning, Verdoux asks the florist if there have been any messages from Mme Grosnay. There have been none. Verdoux goes on his way, unaware that he is observed by the suspicious Inspector Morrow. At his flat, Verdoux is questioned by the suspicious detective. He has been tailing Verdoux and knows about Thelma Couvais, Lydia Floray and Annabella Bonheur. He has not yet informed his colleagues, but plans to hold Verdoux on bigamy charges until establishing those of murder. Verdoux agrees to come along peacefully, supplying a full confession, on condition of being allowed to see his wife one last time. On the train, the detective drifts off to sleep, unaware that Verdoux has given him poisoned wine. Verdoux quietly escapes and, at the pavement café, reads that Morrow has been found dead on a train, supposedly from heart failure. The poison's undetectability is established in practical fashion. Verdoux meets the girl again and, although he presses money on her, is abrupt and dismissive. Verdoux mixes the poison, places it in a bottle marked 'peroxide' and calls Annabella to announce his return home. 'Captain Bonheur' arrives to discover Annabella with baby's bootees – fortunately for the woman next door – and plans to have the house put back in her own name. She is persuaded to leave the matter for the weekend. The maid is dismissed, ensuring an intimate afternoon. That evening, they prepare dinner themselves. Preparing to add poison to the wine, Verdoux leaves the 'peroxide' bottle unattended; the maid uses it on her hair, accidentally drops the bottle and replaces it with a genuine one from the bathroom cabinet. Verdoux therefore laces the wine with harmless peroxide. He sticks to sarsaparilla while Annabella drinks wine. When their glasses become switched, Verdoux believes himself poisoned. The maid's hair starts to fall out. Verdoux drinks milk to try to counteract the poison. A doctor is summoned, supplying a stomach pump and medicine. He prescribes a few days' rest in the countryside. There, in a rowing boat, Verdoux plans to drown Annabella. While she is fishing, Verdoux waits in vain for his chance to place a weighted noose around her neck. Chloroform seems the answer, but Annabella's excited leapings send Verdoux toppling, the handkerchief over his face. Verdoux tries the noose again, supposedly to 'lasso' the fish. He demonstrates by placing the rope around Annabella's neck, but they are observed by a party of yodellers. Verdoux resolves to go back to his 'ship' and, amid all the fuss, tumbles into the water. At the home of Mme Grosnay, there is yet another delivery of flowers. A visitor advises her to respond, and a letter is sent care of the florist. Verdoux receives the note and calls Mme Grosnay from the shop. He arranges to visit, his poetic love talk causing the young lady assistant a few flutters. Verdoux mistakenly embraces the maid and a visitor before getting to Mme Grosnay, who this time returns his flirtation, but is nonetheless startled by his immediate proposal of marriage. They are to be married at the home of a friend of the bride. By chance, Annabella has been invited. She and Verdoux quite literally bump into one another without realizing it; later, he overhears her raucous laugh and becomes anxious, the more so after hearing her name. He tries to hide in the greenhouse, crouching down owing to an

Monsieur Verdoux and the family he supports by desperate means

invented attack of cramp. Annabella is recruited to assist the stricken bridegroom, but Verdoux remains elusive. He tries an escape beneath the buffet table, but is forced to return. Verdoux claims to feel better, but it is arranged for the ceremony to be delayed ten minutes while he lies down. Dodging Annabella, he enters a side room, climbs through the window, then dashes through the hallway in time to say 'see you later' to the bride before escaping from the house. The Couvais family pay a return visit to the police, this time with Mme Grosnay. It is agreed that 'Varnay' is their man, but there is little evidence. Their investigations are to be kept from the press; instead, the papers carry details of a stock market crash and bank closures. Verdoux hears from his bank; his family home will be foreclosed upon unless he can find some cash. Verdoux calls his brokers, instructing them to 'sell everything', but learns he was wiped out hours before. Time passes, and Europe's economic unrest leads to the rise of dictators. A visibly aged Verdoux leaves his customary pavement café and is nearly struck by a passing limousine. Its occupant is the girl he befriended years before, now evidently prosperous. He is invited into her car and driven to the Café Royale for lunch. She had tried to look him up at the furniture shop, but it had long been vacated. Her present affluence is due to having a met a munitions manufacturer, an industry that will be 'paying big dividends soon'. At the café, the girl notices how Verdoux has lost his 'taste for bitterness'. He explains that he has no further use for it, having 'given up the fight' after losing

his wife and child following the crash. Without being specific, he likens his years as a murderer to a strange dream from which he has awakened, clearly an aberration brought about by the loss of his protracted, mundane position at the bank. Life, it seems, is worth continuing, if only to fulfil one's destiny. The Couvais family arrive at the café, and Verdoux is recognized. The police are summoned. The girl offers to take care of Verdoux but, as they are leaving, Verdoux becomes aware of the Couvais' interest in him and cleverly locks them into a side room. Outside, he bids farewell to the girl, prepared to meet his 'destiny'. When she drives off, Verdoux discreetly tears up her visiting card as he awaits the police. He is ignored in the crowd while the police mistakenly attack Monsieur Couvais. Verdoux remains unrecognized until helping the swooning Mlle Couvais to her feet. The newspapers carry details of the Verdoux trial. Before sentence, he offers a comparison between his activities and those of organized warfare, by which certain concerns profit from the mass destruction of innocent people. 'I shall see you all very soon,' he claims. Verdoux refuses to appeal against the sentence of the guillotine. In the condemned cell, the good-humoured Verdoux expands on the nature of war as big business, believing that 'numbers sanctify' the business of murder. He expresses an opinion that evil is necessary for the existence of good, the former being a shadow cast by the latter. He continues in similar vein when visited by a priest. Verdoux is led away, at first refusing rum, then accepting it on the grounds

Monsieur Verdoux entertains the druggist and his wife; this seemingly deleted shot, from early in the film, suggests Chaplin to have intended their discourse on an undetectable poison to have occurred sooner than in the final version

that he has never tried it. Henri Verdoux, breathing deep of the morning air, continues on his way to the guillotine.

Sub-titled 'a comedy of murders' (one of its working titles), *Monsieur Verdoux* is widely acknowledged to be based on Landru, the French mass-murderer, though Chaplin's own publicity cites also Thomas Wainwright, 'forger and murderer who was the friend of Charles Lamb and other literary celebrities of the early nineteenth century ... who cheated the gallows to become a distinguished, if involuntary citizen of Australia'. Oscar Wilde's portrait of Wainwright had, according to this source, long fascinated Chaplin. 'Landru, the French Bluebeard whose life I also studied,' he added, 'was a much less subtle and aesthetic character. Monsieur Verdoux is a tragi-comic projection of these two strange men.' The film's main titles acknowledge Orson Welles with the original idea. Welles, in conversation with Peter Bogdanovich (published in *This is Orson Welles*), recalled having got to know Chaplin through Aldous Huxley and King Vidor. Welles had been inspired by a subway advertisement for an anti-dandruff treatment, in which a 'hairdresser type', employing an archetypal gallic gesture to represent 'something too exquisite for human speech', posed some such question as '*Avez-vous Scurf*?' Welles conceived the idea of Chaplin playing Landru, approached the comedian and, on

securing his interest, wrote a script. The intention had been for Chaplin to take an acting rôle at Welles' company, Mercury Productions, for RKO, but in the end Chaplin preferred not to be directed by someone else. Instead, he offered to buy *The Ladykiller*, as it was then titled, to which Welles agreed. 'An awful lot was his,' claimed Welles, though one survivor from Welles' draft was the early scene of Verdoux tending his garden while the incinerator belches black smoke. One of Welles' intended scenes had Landru taking a mountain trip with, unknown to him, a woman whose murderous tendencies equalled his own; Chaplin's script replaced this idea with Verdoux attempting to dispose of the indestructible Annabella. Chaplin also updated the tale from the First World War setting favoured by Welles. According to Welles, Chaplin denied that a complete script had been written for the original version; 'but I've still got a copy of it,' he added. (Chaplin is known to have written, re-written and extensively revised his script up until the actual shooting, leading one to query how little Chaplin might eventually have owed to Welles' original text.) The final script takes up the story in 1932 – as established by a letter to Thelma Couvais dated 6 June of that year – by which time Verdoux has eradicated twelve victims. The market failure detailed towards the end of the film is conveyed in a newspaper dated November 1932, suggesting only five months to have elapsed during the bulk of the film; in turn, the murder verdict is dated as January 1937, implying that Verdoux managed to avoid capture for some four years after ceasing his career of murder.

The story had evidently taken recognizable shape by the autumn of 1942. In a letter to Thornton Wilder dated 22 October, Alexander Woollcott (*qv*) spoke of having dined with Chaplin in New York, after which the comedian 'lavishly acted out every scene of his coming Landru picture which, as you

may know, is going to be called *Lady Killer*'. Woollcott went on to describe how each victim should be sufficiently obnoxious for the central character to be cheered by every man in the audience and meet his execution as something of a hero. 'I suppose the picture, when released, will inspire a few throat-cuttings here and there,' concluded Woollcott, 'but on the whole its effect should be beneficial and it will improve the home life of several million Americans.' Woollcott did not live to see either the finished picture (under its revised title) or a partial vindication of his words. As things turned out, it was Chaplin who alone fell victim to the throat-cutting, much of it by the millions of Americans – or at least those purporting to represent their opinions – who did not exactly take *Monsieur Verdoux* to their hearts.

Chaplin continued to work on his script during 1943, albeit with the pleasant interruption of marrying Oona O'Neill (*qv*) in June; the following year brought a less pleasant hiatus when Chaplin's involvement with a woman named Joan Barry led to him being hauled into court over Mann Act, conspiracy and paternity charges (see **Women**), all of which dragged on into the middle of 1945. Chaplin was exonerated, but the bad publicity was to have repercussions later on. The *Verdoux* script was finally completed in 1946, with shooting taking place over 83 days between May and September. For the rôle, Chaplin spent six weeks cultivating a genuine moustache, suitably wax-tipped; at times his appearance and manner are vaguely reminiscent of Adolphe Menjou (*qv*), whom Chaplin

Monsieur Verdoux: 'Captain Bonheur' is rightly suspicious of Annabella's friends

had given an important break in 1923. There were, at the time, some well-publicized censorship difficulties; on 6 July 1946 *Picturegoer* reported that Chaplin, 'whose script of *Comedy of Murders* (new title of *Bluebeard*) has not been approved by the Breen Office, is going straight ahead with its production'. He was quoted thus: 'If necessary I can do without any release in the American market; I can get all I need to make a profit from foreign distribution alone.' (Chaplin eventually reached a truce with the US censors, though not without much nit-picking, ranging between an overall implication of 'illicit sex' to Verdoux's ironic tone with the priest.) He was soon willing to trail the film for the UK market, for on 17 August 1946 the British magazine *Leader* published an interview with Chaplin conducted by Ivar Ohman. After recommendations by director Jean Renoir and actor Fritz Kortner, the temporarily-moustachioed Chaplin invited the journalist to his home, where they discussed war, art, politics, Chaplin's background and, especially, music, particularly that for the new film. Chaplin handed Ohman 'a book bound in blue with 157 yellow pages inside. The title on the cover is *Bluebeard Rhapsody; or the Life of Mr. Verdoux*.' As in his meeting with Woollcott, Chaplin acted out much of the story for his visitor. This account details something of Verdoux's introduction to bigamy and murder, activities in which he is already engaged when first seen in the film. Having been made redundant from his job as bank clerk during a slump, Verdoux 'starts dealing in furniture. He is married but meets another woman who can help him in his business. He marries her and so commits bigamy. But this manoeuvre helps him for only a very short while. Then his marriage begins to threaten his business. The little man is determined not to give in. Rather than that he will commit murder. He kills one of his wives.' Charles Chaplin Jr, another witness to the comedian's private performances of scenes from *Verdoux*, recalled his father having discarded most of the sequences he had tried on his guests. 'I always regretted this,' he claimed, 'for I thought those spontaneous episodes far funnier than anything I saw on the screen.'

Chaplin hired Robert Florey (*qv*) – whom he had known since the 1920s – as an associate director and, informally, technical adviser on authentic French detail. According to Jack Spears, Florey directed some of the non-Chaplin footage, wrote a continuity and suggested such things as the condemned Verdoux being offered rum (an idea claimed also by Welles in the Bogdanovich interview). Florey was delegated the task of casting the smaller rôles, including, it is said, an ultimately unsuccessful test with Edna

Monsieur Verdoux picks up a waif as guinea pig for his poison, but soon changes his mind

Purviance (*qv*) for the rôle of Mme Grosnay. Opinions differ as to whether she is present in the final film, as one of the wedding guests; the author's opinion is that she is first seen standing directly behind William Frawley (*qv*), and is in the immediate background when Verdoux and Annabella unwittingly back into each other. Florey's recollections of working with Chaplin are sometimes unflattering and, one suspects, coloured by subsequent events; despite Florey's accounts of Chaplin's alleged temperament, John McCabe has quoted Bernard J. Nedell – who plays the Prefect of Police – to the effect that Chaplin was not a tyrant, but instead a hard worker who expected the same from others. Nedell, stating clearly that 'the cast loved him' (a view shared by Martha Raye [*qv*]), cited as example a scene in which Chaplin, though almost physically ill with exhaustion, insisted on the endless repetition of a scene with an actress until it was exactly right. 'He had that curious mixture of a hot temper and very great patience,' Nedell believed.

Henry Bergman (*qv*) was considered for a rôle in the film, but Chaplin thought the actor looked too ill (he died prior to the film's release); ominously, Bergman, who considered himself Chaplin's good luck charm, predicted *Verdoux*'s consequent failure. Bergman's vision was correct, at least in the USA. Chaplin's recent bad publicity – essentially over the Joan Barry case and his alleged radicalism – was enough to secure considerable hostility for a film dealing with a bigamous murderer who queries the link between war and business.

An advertising page taken out in the *Hollywood Reporter* quoted D.J. McNerny, executive vice-president of the Blumenfeld chain of theatres, as expecting *Verdoux* to top a $20 million gross within one year. This proved to be rather optimistic. A somewhat disastrous press conference took place in New York on 12 April 1947. Chaplin, knowing what to expect, invited journalists to 'proceed with the butchery'; they did. When asked about his story's likeness to the Landru case, he admitted only to a similarity in the central character. There followed questions concerning his insertion of a 'message' into his pictures, his opinions on possible changes in audience taste and, more directly, whether he shared Verdoux's conviction that civilization was turning the public into mass-murderers. In reply, Chaplin expressed a horror of violence, and the view that the atomic bomb would make people 'grow up a bunch of neurotics'. He claimed never to have approached his work from the point of view of audience taste, believing in the public's preference for him to be 'honest and sincere' with himself. The next question anticipated what was to come. Asked if *The Great Dictator* (*qv*) had played in the Soviet Union, Chaplin said there had been interest, but that no arrangements had been made. The question had been put because of a newspaper comment claiming Chaplin to have been involved in a combine aiming to screen Soviet films in America or vice versa. This was also denied. The same reporter got into stride by asking about Chaplin's alleged status as 'fellow-traveller' and Communist sympathizer. Chaplin claimed never to have belonged to any political party or to have voted at any time in his life. This was not good enough for the reporter, who asked, directly, 'Are you a Communist?' 'I am not a Communist!' was the response, to which the journalist (evidently afflicted with momentary amnesia) countered, 'A Communist sympathizer was the question.' Chaplin defined 'sympathizer' only in terms of supporting Russia as a wartime ally. Led in some degree by a representative of New York's Catholic War Veterans, the questioning soon degenerated into queries about Chaplin's nationality, his income from abroad, an alleged failure to answer Britain's call in the First World War, and his personal friendship with composer Hanns Eisler, whose brother had been accused of being a Soviet spy. Virtually the only friendly voice – and that sometimes inaudible – was of critic James Agee, who, his voice trembling in anger, expressed doubt concerning those who supposedly care

about freedom and congratulate themselves on living in a free country, 'when so many of the people in this country pry into what a man's citizenship is, try to tell him his business from hour to hour and from day to day and exert a public moral blackmail against him for not becoming an American citizen – for his political views and for not entertaining American troops in the manner – in the way that they think he should. What is to be thought of a general country where these people are thought well of?' Chaplin, quietly grateful, offered Agee his thanks, but claimed to have 'nothing to say to that question'. When finally asked for his reactions to New York's reviews of his new film, Chaplin said, 'Well, the one optimistic note is that they were mixed.' This at least brought a laugh. 'Incidentally,' said Chaplin, reminding those present of the gathering's intended purpose, 'I hope you've all seen *Monsieur Verdoux*.'

Agee proved to be one of Chaplin's main defenders within US critical circles. The *Nation* granted him space for a lavish, three-part review of *Verdoux*, published on 31 May, 14 June and 21 June 1947. 'Disregard virtually everything you may have read about the film,' warned Agee. 'It is of interest, but chiefly as a definitive measure of the difference between the thing a man of genius puts before the world and the things the world is equipped to see in it.' He took issue with those who claimed it was 'not funny', morally questionable, badly cast, poorly written, poorly directed and so on, answering each accusation point-for-point. To those who missed the 'tramp' figure, Agee remarked on the way in which children object to the slightest variant in a retold story, an 'extreme conservatism' not respected in 'older boys and girls'. The thought that Martha Raye 'stole' all her scenes with Chaplin was explained as a deliberate move on the comedian's part, aware that his character could not 'properly get many of the big laughs; that

is what Raye is there for'. The second part of Agee's review dwelt on extensive character analysis; the third did not appear until, to his chagrin, the film had been withdrawn, pending a new campaign by United Artists (*qv*). Agee promised to inform his readers of the film's return and of any alterations. Apologizing for being overdue – or even premature – with his review, the critic believed *Verdoux* had in any case a long life ahead of it. 'It is permanent,' he said, 'if any work done during the past twenty years is permanent.'

Within a round-up of comments from elsewhere, Theodore Huff quoted Howard Barnes in the *Herald-Tribune* as calling it 'something of an affront to the intelligence'. When reviewing Chaplin's next film, *Limelight* (*qv*), Walter Kerr recalled Parker Tyler's comments on *Verdoux* in the *Kenyon Review*, to the effect that Chaplin's main point, that Verdoux treats murder as an extension of business just as war is supposedly an extension of diplomacy, was 'stated verbally by Chaplin in the bluntest possible terms and with a bitterness of intonation carrying with it, astonishingly enough, a grain or two of smugness'. In *Remembering Charlie*, Jerry Epstein (*qv*) wrote bitterly of the way in which Bosley Crowther of the *New York Times* slaughtered *Verdoux* on its first release, only to applaud it on a 1964 reissue, mentioning how few people had seen it originally! Crowther, in Epstein's view, had done little to encourage the film's widespread showing in 1947, but he was far from alone. It has often been claimed that much of *Verdoux*'s adverse reception was directed at Chaplin personally, instead of his film; there was, as noted elsewhere, talk of Chaplin being questioned by the House Un-American Activities Committee. The early withdrawal of the film mentioned by Agee was due in part to many theatres being forced to cancel the film because of picketing by, again, the Catholic War Veterans and the American Legion. Ten years after the film's release, Richard Griffith and Arthur Mayer's book *The Movies* viewed Chaplin's intent with perspective. It was realized that Chaplin had set out to shock, 'but to shock us to our senses'. '*Monsieur Verdoux*,' it continued, 'managed to shock the American middle class, but not in the way its maker had intended.' Another factor cited was the way Chaplin's recent personal experiences and alleged radicalism had combined to alienate the

Monsieur Verdoux receives a visitor, unaware that he is a detective

American public.

Monsieur Verdoux is said to have grossed only $325,000 domestically but, true to Chaplin's earlier prediction, made a more than reasonable success overseas. On 3 May 1947, Britain's *Leader* magazine returned to *Verdoux* with a front-page photo of Chaplin's 'discovery', Marilyn Nash (*qv*) and, within, a two-page spread conveying the film's plot in stills. Alongside the photo-strip were the reactions of composer Ivor Novello after seeing, privately, a rough-cut of the film. To compensate for the unfinished music track, Chaplin would frequently dash to the piano to accompany the screening as appropriate. Novello, conscious of his friend's usual diffidence ('Charlie is so completely lacking in the grand manner'), found him unusually nervous when seeking an opinion of *Verdoux*, primarily because 'he is doing something utterly different from anything he has ever done before ... I can only compare it to *Arsenic and Old Lace*, and it should be just as successful.' (A closer parallel appeared in Britain two years after *Verdoux*'s release, the justly-celebrated *Kind Hearts and Coronets*.) The front cover of *Everybody's Weekly* (25 October 1947) directed readers to 'A Letter to Mr. Charles Chaplin', in which Ronald Hilborne expressed astonishment at the thought of the comedian being 'a threat to America'. Quoting Chaplin's remark that 'the little tramp has been put on the shelf until the golden days arrive', Hilborne advised him to reverse the decision, believing this to be 'just the kind of statement to make Congress suspicious, aware as they are of the overtones in your clowning'. The UK critics, less affected by Chaplin's supposed personal misdemeanours, were able to appreciate *Verdoux* more objectively. Jack Davies of the *Sunday Graphic* had read the American reviews and was 'prepared for the worst', but instead 'got a very pleasant surprise indeed'; Leonard Mosley of the *Daily Express* could not see anything in the film to justify America's reaction, noting mixed reactions after the trade screening, but mentioning the many funny scenes and praising the performances of Chaplin and Marilyn Nash; *The Times*, sensibly 'wiping from the table' all memory of Chaplin's former character, questioned the film's premise and thought the point insufficiently conveyed, but found a surprising degree of humour – though perhaps underdeveloped – in the macabre subject; Stephen Watts of the *Sunday Express* believed some might find the comedy

Monsieur Verdoux: Annabella unwittingly attends the 'wedding' of her supposed husband

aspect limited for its subject, 'But the best of it is brilliant'; the *Daily Worker*, with a left-wing brief, evaluated it as 'the most grown-up film ever to have come out of America'; London's *Star* thought the loss of the tramp to have been compensated by 'a new revelation of Chaplin's superb artistry'; similarly, Dilys Powell in *The Sunday Times* agreed with the change in character, the tramp having become 'too restricted for what he has to do'; Patrick Kirwan, of London's *Evening Standard*, did not mourn the tramp unduly, realizing how Chaplin's advancing age did not 'take kindly to knockabout'; Richard Winnington of the *News Chronicle* thought *Verdoux* to be 'the most exciting thing that has happened to the screen for years; very probably it is his greatest film'; the *Sunday Dispatch* agreed it was 'certainly among Charlie's best'; Joan Lester in *Reynolds News* claimed that, 'In a spate of pictures which you forget before you have left the cinema, this is one which will keep you arguing for hours, and which you will want, I as I do, to see again'; in the *Observer*, C.A. Lejeune acknowledged the 'gusts of outrageous laughter', but did not consider the film funny, its merits lying instead in its star's exact, perfect and individual portrayal; Elspeth Grant of the *Daily Graphic* said Chaplin 'asks too much' in requesting sympathy for a mass-murderer; C.A. Lejeune, writing this time for the *Sketch* magazine, may perhaps have supplied the answer in defending Chaplin's blend of slapstick and the macabre with a comparison to the Porter's scene in *Macbeth*; P.L. Mannock

of the *Daily Herald* found the film 'disfigured by intrusions of pompous, phoney philosophy', but also possessed of 'brilliance, hilarity and fascination'; the *Daily Mirror*'s Reg Whitley enjoyed the 'mixture of comedy and drama', sometimes recalling the earlier 'Charlie', but would have preferred Chaplin to 'cut out some of his philosophical platitudes and cease being one of those comedians who insist on being tragedians'. In a review published on 26 November 1947, *Punch*'s critic considered *Verdoux* 'the usual rag-bag of slapstick and showing-off and sententiousness', but admitted there was plenty to laugh at. One may not necessarily concur with the reviewer's evaluation of Chaplin as 'undoubtedly a great man, even though he is not precisely the sort of great man he believes he is'. As philosopher, Chaplin was considered 'on a rather simple and obvious level', his speeches on the world's ills failing to enthral those who 'reached similar conclusions almost as soon as they were old enough to argue', especially once the principle had been established and the audience felt no need for laboured explanation. The reviewer admitted making 'too much of these didactic passages', citing as compensation 'long stretches of good, old-fashioned, perfectly timed, unbeatable slapstick farce'. Any notions of the rowing boat scene being considered unfunny because it involves attempted murder were promptly dismissed; there was also reiteration of the film's 'old-fashioned' quality, both in terms of Chaplin's stereotyped Frenchman and in his techniques, the sets having 'that dark, flat, crowded, artificial look one associates with the short comedies of thirty years ago'. (Another frequent objection has been to the hackneyed use of train wheels as a linking device.) A key to Chaplin's appeal – of which the comedian himself was quite aware – lies in the opinion that 'Perhaps nobody but Charlie Chaplin could make all these points seem finicking and irrelevant.'

Not surprisingly, *Monsieur Verdoux* was particularly well-received in French-speaking countries – Belgium advertised it as his *chef d'oeuvre* – despite the name's alleged translation (of which Chaplin had been unaware) to 'sweet worm'. Charles Chaplin Jr recalled a time when Martha Raye visited France to entertain the Occupation troops. She stopped in Paris to buy an outfit from Dior's, only to be told there was a fashion show in progress, during which nothing would be sold. The ban was lifted when Dior's assistant, Pierre Balmain, took a closer look at Miss Raye; exclaiming 'Madame Verdoux!', he embraced the actress, planting a kiss on both cheeks. Miss Raye was thereafter given *carte blanche*. An intriguing postscript concerns the dilemma of a real Paris bank clerk, also named Henri Verdoux, to whom the film was far from a joke. Weary of being called 'Landru' and 'Bluebeard', and of people enquiring as to his women, the other M. Verdoux sought first to take out an injunction against the film, then to sue for damages. In March 1948, a Paris court found against him, awarding costs to the defendants, producing organization United Artists,

French distributors Nouvelle Gaumont and two Paris cinemas.

One might agree with those critics who found the film's moral rather pat, and the view of Chaplin sometimes tending to bite off more than he could chew when it came to philosophy. There is also the opinion that the film, though set in the 1930s, makes clear reference to the upcoming World War, and it may have been too soon after that war for Chaplin's sentiments to be acceptable. Away from his homicidal practices, Verdoux is concerned for the welfare of a caterpillar, chastises his son for cruelty to a domestic pet and favours a vegetarian diet; as a parallel, Isobel Quigley pointed out that society had yet to absorb the horrifying truth concerning some of those who ran Hitler's concentration camps, people who were discovered to be capable of leading normal family lives despite committing the worst atrocities.

The author's opinion is that Chaplin, as social commentator, was far better at understanding people than concepts or ideologies. The strength of the film lies instead in the ingenuity of its central character, though he forgets himself when re-introducing himself to Mme Grosnay as 'Bonheur' and, when believing himself 'poisoned', asks for his wife to be called. At the time of release, the *Daily Mail*'s Fred Majdalany remarked on the speed at which this 'new Chaplin' becomes less of a shock, whereupon one discovers 'there isn't so much difference between Charles and Charlie after all'; as Charles Silver has said, 'Verdoux is the Tramp grown old and forced by the responsibility of family to participate finally in the games of life.' This is particularly apparent when, flirting with Mme Grosnay, Verdoux conceals the effort from the estate agent by pretending to catch a bee, employing a 'silly me' expression prior to falling backwards through the window. Even more in keeping is the moment where Annabella, in the boat, almost sees Verdoux wielding a noose; her would-be assassin promptly switches to a coy, wide grin, hands clasped around crossed knees. 'Charlie' was always a ruthless survivor, and *Monsieur*

Monsieur Verdoux and the former street waif visit a nightclub, where his liberty comes to an end

Verdoux is something of a harking-back to the comic villains he often essayed at Keystone (*qv*); indeed, the aforementioned scene where Verdoux thinks he has been poisoned is reminiscent of parallel business in *Cruel, Cruel Love* (*qv*).

(See also: Bennett, Marjorie; Cars; Censorship; Children; Costume; Dryden, Wheeler; Frawley, William; Heigh, Helen; Karno, Fred; Keystone; Parrish, Robert; Policemen; Politics; Prisons; Religion; Risqué humour; Smoking; *Young Charlie Chaplin*)

MORRISSEY, BETTY
(?1908–44)

(Chaplin films *qv*)
New York-born actress who plays 'Fifi' in *A Woman of Paris*, one of Georgia's friends from the dance hall in *The Gold Rush* and 'the Vanishing Lady' in *The Circus*. Her other films of the period include *Skinner's Dress Suit* (1925).

MOSCOVITCH, MAURICE
(1871–1940)

Russian-born actor who plays 'Mr Jaeckel' in *The Great Dictator* (*qv*). His other films include *Winterset* (1936) and *Suez* (1938).

MURDER ♟

(Chaplin films *qv*)
As noted in the main entry, Chaplin's 'comedy of murders', *Monsieur Verdoux*, was often misunderstood in its day, but has since been recognized for its adroit treatment of a macabre topic. Among the attempted homicides in Chaplin's films are those in *The Floorwalker*, *The Count* (as Charlie's former employer fires a gun) and, in *The Great Dictator*, the barber's near-lynching and later involvement in a plot against Hynkel.

Chaplin himself occasionally brushed against what is sometimes termed 'unlawful killing': his friend and former Keystone comrade, Roscoe 'Fatty' Arbuckle (*qv*), found his career in ruins after a trial for manslaughter; the reputation of another ex-Keystone colleague, Mabel Normand (*qv*), was also tarnished by a peripheral connection with one of Hollywood's murder scandals. Chaplin's own life was threatened during his tour of the Far East in 1932, reportedly by a Japanese secret society; while there has also been much speculation over the death of producer Thomas H. Ince in 1924, following a party on board a yacht owned by newspaper proprietor William Randolph Hearst. A story persists that Ince had been shot by Hearst in mistake for Chaplin, whom Hearst had caught with his mistress, Marion Davies. Hearst was supposedly able to have the whole business suppressed, not least by granting considerable power to gossip columnist Louella Parsons, who was on board. John McCabe has cleared up this story by stating clearly that neither Chaplin nor Louella Parsons was present. Ince, suffering from stomach ulcers and heart trouble, ignored medical advice by filling up with alcohol and salt-laden food. He spent the night vomiting and, after being removed to shore and taken home by his wife, was diagnosed by the family doctor as suffering from gastric upset and a heart attack. He died the following day; Chaplin was among those who attended the funeral three days later. In his memoirs, Chaplin took great pains to settle any rumours, describing a subsequent visit to the ailing Ince, who assured his friends that he would soon be well. In so doing Chaplin, in McCabe's view, only added to the confusion. 'Chaplin's statement in the autobiography,' wrote McCabe, 'is typical of his vagueness on chronology there. Likely Chaplin confuses this with a time when he, Hearst, and Marion visited Ince some weeks before when the producer had also been ill.'

(See also: Boats, ships; Keystone; Politics; Public appearances; Suicide; Women)

MURRAY, CHARLIE 🎩
(1872–1941)

(Chaplin films *qv*)
Indiana-born comedian, in travelling shows from the age of eleven. Murray teamed with Oliver Trumball, alias Ollie Mack, as vaudeville's 'Murray and Mack', an association lasting more than twenty-one years. After their break-up, Murray entered films at Biograph with D.W. Griffith (*qv*), as did Mack Sennett (*qv*). Murray spent some two years with Biograph before joining Sennett's Keystone Comedies (*qv*) in 1913. One of his best for the studio is *The Plumber* (1914), in which Murray applies his inexpertise at the home of Josef Swickard (*qv*). In Chaplin's *Her Friend the Bandit*

(now lost), Murray is the aristocrat whose place is taken by Charlie, the 'bandit' of the title; *Mabel's Married Life* casts Murray in the rôle of bar customer; *The Masquerader* sees him as Charlie's boss at Keystone, on whom the tables are briefly turned; while in *Tillie's Punctured Romance* he is the detective in the film-within-a-film that so unnerves Charlie and Mabel Normand (*qv*). Murray has also been credited as the sailor in *Recreation*, but the actor does not resemble him. For Sennett, Murray often appeared as 'Hogan', an Irish stereotype similar to that in his vaudeville act with Ollie Mack; he was to repeat the experience as 'Kelly' in the long-running series of 'Cohen and Kelly' films opposite George Sidney, which ran through the 1920s and into the next decade. Perhaps his best latter-day work for Sennett is a two-reeler of 1924, *The Hollywood Kid*. Other films include *The Wizard of Oz* (1925, as the spurious Wizard), the Colleen Moore vehicle *Irene* (1926), and Paul Whiteman's Technicolor revue film, *The King of Jazz* (1930).

(See also: Allen, Phyllis; Conklin, Chester; Edwards, Vivian; Murray, Tom; Thatcher, Eva)

MURRAY, TOM
(1875–1935)

Burly actor who plays the ultimately kind-hearted Sheriff in *The Pilgrim* (*qv*) and the altogether less benign Black Larsen (or Larson) in *The Gold Rush* (*qv*). His other comedy work of the period includes Harry Langdon's *Tramp, Tramp, Tramp* (1926). His wife, Louise Carver, appears in many comedy films of the period, among them Charlie Murray's *The Hollywood Kid*.

(See also: Murray, Charlie)

MURRAY, WILL

See: Early stage appearances

MUSIC 🎩

(Chaplin films *qv*)
On various occasions, Chaplin recalled the childhood moment when he was first impressed by music. He had been left alone in the Kennington Road, and was sitting, alone and miserable, at Kennington Cross when music came

Music: a song identified as from The Gold Rush, *but seemingly not part of the original score*
By courtesy of Mark Newell

from the vestibule of the nearby White Hart pub. A blind harmonium player ('harmonica' in *My Wonderful Visit*) and a clarinettist were playing *The Honeysuckle and the Bee*, a sentimental music-hall ballad. These turn-of-the-century buskers are commemorated somewhat in the equivalent characters of *Limelight*.

As a young man, Chaplin took up the violin, which he plays in both *Limelight* and (silently!) *The Vagabond*. His left-handed playing – with the strings reversed – is mentioned elsewhere. He also posed for photographs with a cello but, as he admitted in *My Life in Pictures*, could not really play the instrument. In a September 1929 interview with *Film Weekly*, Stan Laurel (*qv*) recalled this as an example of Chaplin's frequent adoption of unusual pastimes: 'He knew nothing about the instrument ... he bought a second-hand 'cello and lugged it home to our room in the hotel. After the matinée he did not join the party for dinner. When it was time to go back to the theatre for the evening performance and he had not yet shown up at our favourite restaurant, I went over to the hotel to look for him. I opened the door of the bedroom and, coming from behind the closed door of the bathroom, I heard terrible whines and moans and scrapings. There I found him with his 'cello, posing in front of the full-length mirror in the bathroom. He had tousled his hair into a mass of curls.

With grandiose gestures he was pulling the bow back and forth across the strings while he admired his reflected self! His imitation of one of these high-brow artists of the concert stage was so ridiculously funny that I simply stood there and howled ... the next day he forgot all about his musical career, and turned to something else.'

In a BBC discussion programme of 15 October 1952 (see **Radio**), Chaplin acknowledged the Karno Company as an influence on his use of music as counterpoint to the action. 'They had splendid music,' he recalled. 'For instance, if they had ... squalor ... with a lot of comedy tramps working in it, then, you see, they would have very beautiful boudoir music, something of the eighteenth century, very lush and very "grandioso", just purely as satirical and as a counterpoint; and I copied a great deal from Mr. Fred Karno in that direction.' Long before attempting to score any of his films, Chaplin recalled pacing the action of *Twenty Minutes of Love* to a popular hit, 'Too Much Mustard'; the author has tried matching the film to a December 1913 recording of the tune by Jim Europe's Society Orchestra, with mixed results. Chaplin also recalled a folk song called 'Mrs. Grundy' setting the mood for *The Immigrant*. By this time Chaplin had already established the Charlie Chaplin Music Publishing Company for his own songs; in April 1916, *Pictures and the Picturegoer* announced that 'the Chaplin Music Company already has three of the talented artiste's compositions on the market'. Capital for the new company had been provided by his bonus from Mutual (*qv*); the three published songs were 'Oh! That Cello', 'There's Always One You Can't Forget' and 'The Peace Patrol'. While still in New York, at the Hippodrome on 20 February 1916, Chaplin conducted John Philip Sousa's band in the last-named item, plus the overture to 'Poet and Peasant'.

At the height of the silent-film era, it

was usual for prestigious feature films to have specific scores, to be played by a full orchestra in the larger theatres (a 1920 reissue of *Carmen* brought the publication of a new comic song tied to the film, with Chaplin and Edna Purviance [*qv*] pictured on the cover).

Chaplin supplied three themes for *The Kid*, and prepared a full score for the original release of *The Gold Rush*; two songs, published at the time, were suggested to be from this score but are now thought not to have been included (nor, despite claims to the contrary, are they in the 1942 reissue). These were 'With You, Dear, in Bombay' and 'Sing a Song'. The former was written entirely by Chaplin, the latter in collaboration with Abe Lyman and Gus Arnheim. In 1925, Chaplin appeared as guest conductor when Lyman's orchestra recorded the two songs (film of which may be seen in *Unknown Chaplin* [*qv*]). The disc was issued on Brunswick 2912 ('the Brunswick BLKE Bollender Co.') in the USA and Brunswick Cliftophone 2912 in the UK, the latter bearing a label suggesting exclusivity to Chappell's music stores.

The Circus was first released with a score compiled by Arthur Kay, under Chaplin's supervision. Kay's diverse source material ranged from *Lohengrin* to the 'Charleston', via *Pagliacci*, *Carmen* and Scott Joplin's 'Maple Leaf Rag'. A particular irony was the use of Irving Berlin's *Blue Skies* when Charlie remains, alone, as the circus moves on. This, and the scores for *The Gold Rush* and *A Woman of Paris*, were retrieved from Chaplin's archive by Gillian Anderson, Music Specialist at the Library of Congress. On 20 January 1995, she conducted the Manhattan School of Music Orchestra for a performance of the film at the Metropolitan Museum of Art in New York. The *Circus* score had been deciphered with great difficulty; it also proved impossible for musicians to keep pace with the film at its now-standard projection speed of 24 frames per second, suggesting original screenings to have been at around 20. Chaplin composed an entirely new score for *The Circus* for its eventual reissue,

incorporating a title song, 'Swing Little Girl', sung by the octogenarian Chaplin.

The pre-recorded accompaniment of *City Lights* brought forth Chaplin's first complete, self-composed score. Perhaps in recollection of the sometimes bizarre score for *The Circus*, he made the decision that his music should not be consciously humorous, but should instead contrast with the comic visuals, a decision adhered to for the rest of his career. Phil Posner, in *Limelight* magazine, has mentioned Chaplin's awareness of the concept of *leitmotif* as acknowledgement of specific characters, recurrent events and pivotal moments. As Theodore Huff noted, Chaplin's composer credit brought wry comments when Padilla's 'La Violetera' was used as motif for the blind girl, but the score was otherwise Chaplin's own (it was perhaps with this in mind that Chaplin credited the use of a theme from Balfe's *The Bohemian Girl* within his 1970s score for *Sunnyside*). It is of course accepted practice to incorporate familiar themes from the classics, as when the barber in *The Great Dictator* shaves a customer to Brahms' 'Hungarian Rhapsody'. When the score for *City Lights* was to be performed live in 1989, conductor Carl Davis encountered an unexpected difficulty with the orchestra parts, which proved more elaborate in comparison to the soundtrack recording. It became clear that Chaplin had simplified the arrangements as the music was recorded, the alterations being made to the score by means of additional sections which were pasted over the individual sheets. These had become detached and lost, necessitating transcription work from the film track.

In common with many composers of popular song, Chaplin was unable to write out music in sheet form and, consequentially, required the assistance of arrangers. His score for *City Lights* was arranged by Arthur Johnston and conducted by Alfred Newman, one of the film industry's top musical names. Newman worked on the next Chaplin film, *Modern Times*, for which the 23-year-old David Raksin was also recruited. Raksin, who had taught himself orchestration and put himself through university on his earnings as a musician, had already made something of a name in radio and recordings when George Gershwin heard his arrangement of 'I Got Rhythm'. On Gershwin's recommendation, Raksin was employed by the Harms/Chappell organization that dominated the Broadway stage, a connection that led to an invitation to work with Chaplin. Raksin established a rapport with Chaplin, but was fired after only one week. Raksin had expressed his own opinions in an environment where Chaplin's word was considered law. He was about to return home when Newman approached him, expressing approval of the young arranger's sketches. Alf Reeves (qv) offered to reinstate Raksin, who demurred until speaking privately to Chaplin, insisting that he should be allowed to do his best work instead of merely functioning as a yes-man. Chaplin agreed, and work resumed. Raksin has described the use of a projection version of the movieola, allowing flexibility in the re-running of scenes. He recalls further an atmosphere of improvisation, the two singing the themes as they were created, with Raksin providing basic piano accompaniment. By necessity, Raksin's notation would be made swiftly, then written out in full after returning home at night. He mentions Chaplin being involved throughout, contributing ideas from an instinctive, if untrained, knowledge of how the various instruments would suit specific effects. Chaplin would also draw upon his extensive recollection of musical styles and compositions, ranging from the music-halls to more recent works. The scene where Charlie is released from prison is underscored by a momentary pastiche in the style of 'Rhapsody in Blue', the result of Chaplin's request for some Gershwin-like music. When he wanted 'a little Puccini', it led to the creation of the tune known ultimately as 'Smile' (after the addition of a lyric by John Turner and Geoffrey Parsons). Among the more successful commercial discs of 'Smile' are those by Nat 'King' Cole and Frank Chacksfield's Orchestra. The recording of *Modern Times* occupied slightly more than four months, part of which saw the 60–70-piece orchestra removed to a larger space than that permitted by UA's normal recording studio. Raksin went on to a distinguished career in film music, his most famous composition probably being the title theme for *Laura* (1944). An American soundtrack LP of *Modern Times* was published to coincide with the 1972 reissue, on United Artists UAL-4049 and, later, UAS-5222.

In some respects, Chaplin's score for *The Great Dictator* overlaps with that for his 1942 reissue of *The Gold Rush*, though for *Dictator* he wrote music and

lyrics for a piece called 'Falling Star'. In turn, *Monsieur Verdoux*'s music is often similar to that written before and after by Chaplin. (There are rumours of at least privately-pressed 78 r.p.m. discs of the score.) Altogether more distinctive within Chaplin's music is *Limelight*, the theme from which – with lyrics by Geoffrey Parsons – became a standard under the title 'Eternally'. Frank Chacksfield's orchestral recording of the song, on Decca F 10106, reached number two in the UK charts in 1953. In addition to this composition – itself developed from incidental music in the restaurant scene of *Modern Times* – Chaplin, in collaboration with Ray Rasch, devised the comic songs 'Spring is Here', 'The Animal Trainer' and 'The Sardine Song'. These were issued on an HMV 78 in, surprisingly, Denmark. Most impressively of all, Chaplin choreographed a ballet, 'The Death of Columbine'.

A promotional film exists of Chaplin conducting 'Mandolin Serenade' from *A King in New York*, which he is reported to have planned as a musical. Other songs from the film – complete with lyrics – include 'Now That It's Ended', 'Without You', 'Park Avenue Waltz', 'Weeping Willows' and 'The Spring Song'. The last three, plus 'Mandolin Serenade', were recorded by Boris Sarbek and his Orchestra on a British EP, Philips BBE 12146. 'Mandolin Serenade' and 'Spring Song' were recorded by Mantovani and his Orchestra on Decca F10918; still another 'Mandolin Serenade', this time by Kenneth McKellar, was released on Decca F10920.

A Countess From Hong Kong was not a successful film, but one of its themes, 'This is My Song', provided UK hits at numbers one and two for, respectively, Petula Clark (Pye 7N 17258) and Harry Secombe (Philips BF 1539). The soundtrack album was issued on Decca DL 1501 in the USA and Brunswick AXA 4544 in Great Britain. Each contained a souvenir booklet, inserted separately into UK copies, but stapled inside a gatefold sleeve for the US market.

Several commentators have suggested Chaplin's use of uncredited ghostwriters for his compositions. This is not borne out by the recollections of his collaborators – among them David Raksin, as noted above – or through stylistic analysis of his musical work as a whole. In evaluating the 'Chaplinesque' approach, Theodore Huff wrote of 'a fondness for romantic waltz hesitations played in very rubato time, lively numbers in two-four time which

might be called "promenade themes", and tangos with a strong beat'. Jerry Epstein (qv) recalled Chaplin admitting to certain borrowings from earlier tunes, suitably altered or inverted; the 'Countess From Hong Kong Waltz' was, in Chaplin's words, '*The Merry Widow* transposed'. (One theme in the reissue of *A Day's Pleasure* resembles, in the author's opinion, the joint offspring of 'For He's a Jolly Good Fellow' and 'The Man Who Broke the Bank at Monte Carlo'.)' According to Epstein, Chaplin would watch the on-screen action and sing to a pianist or, at least later on, into a tape recorder. His piano work was confined to the beginning of the scale, comprising the four notes C, D, E, F and G. It took only as many notes to create trouble; there was a court case following Charles Trenet's accusation that a theme in *A Countess From Hong Kong* utilized the first four notes from Trenet's 'La Romance de Paris'. The result of this case is unclear, but on 27 June 1968 the London *Evening News* reported a ruling in which the judge agreed that, while the first four notes were the same, Trenet had composed a waltz whereas Chaplin had written a gondolier's song.

As detailed under **Reissues**, Chaplin's remaining silent backlog, at least from 1918, saw gradual re-release during the 1970s with new scores. From this period, the composition to gain most attention was the title theme from *The Kid*; another piece in this film employs an incidental theme from *Limelight*. Certain compositions from these 1970s versions looked back to the scores for *A Countess From Hong Kong* and others. His chief musical associate of later years was Eric James, a British pianist whose association with the comedian began with *A King in New York*, continuing into *The Chaplin Revue* (qv) and subsequent reissues. According to the contemporary press, it was James who persuaded Chaplin to sing on *The Circus* reissue track. Several months after the *Revue's* completion, Weston Taylor of the *News of the World* provided a glimpse at their working methods, in the issue of 12 June 1960. The music was created over a two-month period, occupying six days of each week from 10:30 a.m. until 6 p.m. Chaplin would send a car for James, who had travelled to Switzerland. A white-coated butler would answer the door, but it was Chaplin himself who greeted James in the 40-foot hallway. Settling to work, Chaplin would try humming a melody, with James attempting frantically to write it down. Considering a scene from *Shoulder Arms*,

Chaplin said, 'We want a ponderous rhythm – like this,' before giving James a 'ta-da-di-dum' rendition. As the always-mobile Chaplin crossed the room, James touched the piano keyboard, making a 'tentative correction'. 'No, that isn't what I'm looking for,' said Chaplin. As Chaplin sought perfection, Oona preferred lunch. After a meal supplied by Joseph, the butler, work resumed until the evening; 6:30 p.m. saw the chauffeur's return with the evening papers from Lausanne, followed by dinner and conversation. James asked why such a well-read man as Chaplin never bothered to learn to read music. Chaplin explained that, had he embraced the 'academic' side, he would have become 'hemmed in by all the rules'. Chaplin told James that he and his colleague, Eric Spear, could write their own screen credits. 'How about: "Music composed *in spite of* Charles Chaplin"?' suggested James. Chaplin laughed loudly. James' tongue-in-cheek suggestion is in keeping with his summation of the experience. 'Sometimes I thought I would go mad,' he claimed, 'but I learned more from Chaplin than in the rest of my life.' A record album of *The Chaplin Revue* was issued on Brunswick LAT 8345 in Britain and Decca DL 4040 in America; there are reports of a recent CD edition from Japan.

There have been many commercial recordings of Chaplin's music, but among the albums are *Chaplin: The Warm Strings of Stan Butcher* (Fontana SFL 13207), *Great Chaplin Film Themes* by Johnny Douglas and his Orchestra (RCA Camden CDS 1114), *Music From the Films of Charlie Chaplin* by Michel Villard and his Orchestra (Pye International NSPL 28173) and *The Chaplin Collection* (Windmill WMD 205). Special mention should be made of the German musician Thomas Beckmann, whose cello recordings of Chaplin's music – from all periods – are a delight. *Oh! That Cello* was issued on Jaro 4125 in 1986; another, *Play! That Cello* on Jaro 4135; while *Charlie Chaplin: Music For Cello and Piano* (with Kayoko Matsushita on piano) was released in 1989 on Jaro 4143. In November 1995, Carl Davis – who has conducted at many 'live cinema' Chaplin screenings – recorded a CD, *The Film Music of Charles Chaplin*, with the German Symphony Orchestra. The disc comprises selections from *The Kid*, *The Gold Rush*, *The Circus*, *City Lights* and *Modern Times*.

As noted elsewhere, Chaplin's final completed work was the preparation of a reissue score for *A Woman of Paris* in

1976. A BBC radio documentary of 1997, *Charlie Chaplin – Composer* (detailed again under **Radio**) includes a theme, titled 'Love Song', written by Chaplin for his never-completed film, *The Freak* (see **Abandoned projects**). A collection of twelve Chaplin compositions, with words and music, was published in 1992 by the Bourne Co., New York, under the title *The Songs of Charlie Chaplin*. One of these, 'You Are the Song', was written by Chaplin (with lyrics by Glen Anthony) for the documentary film *The Gentleman Tramp* (*qv*).

A footnote: in 1992, a cast album was recorded of a new musical based on Chaplin's life, entitled *Little Tramp: The Musical*. Music and lyrics were by David Pomeranz; book was by Pomerantz and Steven David Horwich. In an intriguing Anglo-American cast, Richard Harris played Chaplin, aged 82; Petula Clark played Hannah Chaplin (*qv*); Peter Duncan was Chaplin in mid-life; Mel Brooks played Mack Sennett (*qv*); Lea Salonga was cast as Oona; Johnny Logan was Syd Chaplin (*qv*); Tim Curry played Tippy Gray, FBI agent; Treat Williams was cast as J. Edgar Hoover; David Pomerantz portrayed a 'fan club president'; Mel Smith was 'Mr. Blackmore'; Leonard Smith and Jonathan Rudoe were Charlie and Syd, as children, and Jacquie Toye was 'Mrs Henley'.

(See also: Ballet; Early stage appearances; Food; Left-handedness; Parrish, Robert; Reissues)

MUTUAL 🎩

(Chaplin films *qv*)
Chaplin was growing uncomfortable during his last days at Essanay (*qv*). George K. Spoor (*qv*) offered him $350,000 for a dozen two-reelers but Syd Chaplin (*qv*), who had taken over Charlie's business affairs since leaving Keystone (*qv*), demanded a bonus of $150,000. When Spoor refused, Syd departed for New York to solicit other offers, leaving Edna Purviance (*qv*) on guard to prevent Charlie signing for anyone in his absence. Syd began negotiations with Mutual, and was horrified when his brother, who had decided to join him in New York, demanded an advance of $100,000. Syd doubted Mutual's ability to survive the expenditure, but Charlie is believed to have said, 'Well, even if the bubble bursts – and I agree it probably will – they can't take the

hundred thousand away from me.'

The origins of Mutual were in the partnership of John R. Freuler and H.E. Aitken, who in 1906 formed the Western Film Exchange of Milwaukee. In March 1912 they launched the Mutual Film Corporation from an address in Wall Street, with the backing of several prominent businessmen. Mutual acquired distribution of the New York Motion Picture Company's products – soon to include the new Keystone films – after its proprietors, Kessel and Bauman, fell out spectacularly with Universal. As a consequence, Mutual was the distributor of Chaplin's comedies during his time with Keystone. According to Terry Ramsaye, it was the fast-dwindling supply of Mutual's old Keystone prints that drew the corporation's interest in signing Chaplin for a new series.

Chaplin signed the Mutual contract (which ran to 20,000 words) on Saturday 26 February 1916. Syd was in attendance, as were Freuler and a gigantic entourage of attorneys, notaries and photographers. At least one newsreel was shot of the occasion, in which Charlie may be seen examining the cheque. He reacted with a comic blinking of the eyes, a gag he sometimes used when feigning shock (this extract may be seen in *The Gentleman Tramp* [*qv*]). The reason was that Syd had extracted from Mutual the then-astronomical sum of $670,000, which translated to £134,000 a year in British currency. The money was broken down into $10,000 per week, plus a bonus of $150,000 on signature, a 50 per cent increase on the requested advance that had unnerved Syd. The *Moving Picture World* of 11 March 1916 published the details, remarking upon the unprecedented amount while adding how, unusually, its recipient would not be required to take any part in the business side of production. A new production entity had been established for the Chaplin films, the Lone Star Corporation, giving him the autonomy of an independent producer but with none of the financial concerns.

Pictures and the Picturegoer of 8 April 1916 spoke of 'the world and his wife' being 'open-mouthed' at the huge figure, noting also that Chaplin claimed not to have given it much thought. Naturally, Chaplin was aware of the vast sum, but financial responsibility was in the hands of Mutual, who in turn had to deal with Syd. 'Money and business are very serious matters, and I have to keep my mind off them,' said Charlie at the time, '... in fact, I do not worry about money at all; it would get in the way of my work.' Perhaps that is why his money started to accumulate from this point; put simply, Chaplin was comparatively frugal and did not spend his vast income. Chaplin did not want the public to think that life was a joke to him, but stressed that he enjoyed 'working on the funny side of it'. 'What this contract means,' he said, 'is simply that I am in business with the worry left out and with the dividends guaranteed. It means that I am left free to be just as funny as I dare, to do the best work that is in me, and to spend my energies on the thing that the people want. I have felt for a long time that this would be my big year, and this contract gives me my opportunity. There is inspiration in it. I am like an author with a big publisher to give him circulation.'

Studio premises had yet to be finalized at the time of signing. Freuler claimed that two sites were under consideration, but in the end a studio was built in Los Angeles for Chaplin's exclusive use. This was the Lone Star Studio at 1025 Lillian Way, Hollywood, encapsulated by a special logo on contemporary advertising and, seemingly, the original titling of the films themselves. *Pictures and Picturegoer* said: 'The total operations in forming the Chaplin Producing Company involved the sum of £310,000,' reputedly 'the biggest operation centred about a single star in the history of the motion-picture industry.'

The intention was to produce a total

of twelve two-reel comedies on a monthly basis, but minor delays for illness – and Chaplin's increasingly slow methods – saw them delivered over a period of seventeen months. The extensive Mutual out-takes in the series *Unknown Chaplin* (*qv*) reveal Syd's presence during the making of at least some of these films. (The out-takes provide above all a singular glimpse at the comedian's working methods of the time. The same applies to a 1917 article written for *Pictures and the Picturegoer* by his publicist, Elsie Codd, which is detailed under *The Adventurer*.)

Edna Purviance (*qv*) continued as leading lady for the Mutual films, while other former Essanay colleagues included John Rand, Leo White, James T. Kelly, Lloyd Bacon and Charlotte Mineau (all *qv*). Frank J. Coleman (*qv*) has been credited in some Essanays, but seems instead to have joined Chaplin for the Mutual series; another newcomer was an ex-Karno colleague, Albert Austin. Also new to the roster were Henry Bergman (*qv*), who remained in Chaplin's employ for the rest of his life, and a further Karno veteran, the giant Eric Campbell (*qv*), who became resident villain of the series. Assisting Chaplin in the writing and directing were Maverick Terrell and sketch writer/librettist Vincent Bryan.

Chaplin's Mutual comedies are as follows: *The Floorwalker*; *The Fireman*; *The Vagabond*; *One A.M.*; *The Count*; *The Pawnshop*; *Behind the Screen*; *The Rink*; *Easy Street*; *The Cure*; *The Immigrant*; and *The Adventurer*. In his autobiography, Chaplin recalls his tenure with Mutual as the happiest of his career, something that is apparent when seeing the bright results on screen. He was also comparatively settled in private life: on the suggestion of Julian Eltinge, the most celebrated female impersonator of his day, Chaplin forsook the downmarket neighbourhood in which he had lived, moving instead to the Los Angeles Athletic Club. His

relationship with Edna brought a measure of emotional stability, while his professional and domestic routines were organized by his trusted Japanese chauffeur-cum-valet, Kono (*qv*).

Although not as sophisticated as his later full-length works, the Mutuals are remarkably polished and display Chaplin's comic talent at its most consistent. For many people, Chaplin's name remains synonymous with perhaps nine or ten of these twelve films. On the completion of his contract, Mutual attempted to secure Chaplin's services for a further period, but were outbid by First National (*qv*). Mutual did not long survive the comedian's departure; the Lone Star premises themselves were taken over by Buster Keaton (*qv*).

Of the later Chaplins, *The Idle Class* bears the closest resemblance to the Mutual films, probably because a central sketch – a golf routine – had originally been intended for one of the Mutual comedies. *Modern Times* takes as its inspiration several ideas from the Mutuals; *The Rink*, for example, may be seen as prototype for the scenes with Charlie on skates and in his later attempts to wait at table.

(See also: Abandoned projects; Auctions; Home movies; *How To Make Movies*; Policemen; Prisons; Reissues; Television; Titling; Video releases; Wartime)

MYERS, HARRY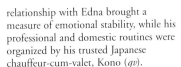
(1886–1938)

Actor, born in Connecticut but educated in Philadelphia; nine years' stage experience preceded film comedy work, which included stints with the Lubin Company and its successor, Vim. In the 'teens, Myers was often paired in comedies with his actress wife, Rosemary Theby. Myers was much in demand by the big studios during the 1920s: his films include *A Connecticut Yankee in King Arthur's Court* (1921), *Zander the Great* (1925) with Marion Davies (*qv*), *Up in Mabel's Room* (1926) and *Exit Smiling* (1926) with Beatrice Lillie. By the latter part of the decade, Myers' career was faltering, as evidenced by a stint with Hal Roach as one of the 'fading stars' appearing in the studio's short comedies; his career revived somewhat when he was chosen to replace Henry Clive as the drunken millionaire of Chaplin's *City Lights* (*qv*).

Harry Myers took over the rôle of drunken millionaire in City Lights

NASH, MARILYN
(b. 1926)

Actress in *Monsieur Verdoux* (*qv*), as the waif whose life Verdoux decides not to take. Detroit-born Marilyn Nash was a pre-medical student at the University of Arizona until holidaying in California. She and a party of friends visited the Chaplin home, wishing to use the tennis court, whereupon the comedian noticed her and arranged an audition, reading from *King Lear*. A screen test was postponed until she had taken her college exams. Miss Nash had no previous acting experience except for amateur theatricals with a college group, but was trained by Chaplin. She was also involved in productions at the Circle Theatre (see **Epstein, Jerry**). By the time *Verdoux* was released, she had married playwright Philip Yordan. Marilyn Nash made something of an impact at the time – her portrait adorned the cover of Britain's *Leader* magazine on 3 May 1947

Marilyn Nash was Chaplin's new discovery for Monsieur Verdoux

– but she voluntarily left Chaplin's employ. Before retiring, she made a large number of TV appearances plus one more film, *Unknown World* (1951).

(See also: Height; Raye, Martha)

NEGRI, POLA
See: Smoking and Women

THE NEW JANITOR

(Chaplin film)
Keystone Comedy released by Mutual, 24 September 1914. Produced by Mack Sennett. Written and directed by Charles Chaplin. Photography attributed to Frank D. Williams. Reissued by W.H. Productions as *The New Porter*; other reissue titles include *The Blundering Boob*. One reel. 1,020 feet (approx. UK length cited in trade press).

With Charlie Chaplin (himself, as the new janitor), Fritz Schade (president), Jack Dillon (manager), Minta Durfee (typist), Al St. John (lift operator).

Charlie, arriving for his new job as office janitor, chats to the lift operator before being denied access to the lift. Charlie ascends the stairs to the top floor, where the manager has received a disturbing letter. If a gambling debt is not settled, his creditor will make the matter public. His mood worsens when Charlie, collecting waste paper, spills most of the litter and places a dropped book into the bin. Charlie enters the president's office (despite barring the way with his own broom), where he flirts with the typist and dusts everything from the safe to the typist's bottom. The manager receives a visit from his creditor. In the corridor, the typist overhears the manager's promise to obtain the money by five o'clock. She continues on her way, and the angry creditor leaves. Charlie, perched on the window he is preparing to clean, nearly falls to the street. Unaware that the president and two ladies are standing beneath, Charlie squeezes out his cleaning cloths then, clumsily, drops the bucket. The drenched employer takes the lift to his office to find Charlie peering through the window frame. Charlie receives a swift kick and equally swift dismissal. In the corridor, Charlie once again sees the lift disappear and must take the stairs. He is on the ground floor when the manager begins

his surreptitious activities. He attends to business with the president then, satisfied the office is empty, starts to open the safe. The typist, having forgotten something, returns and nearly catches the manager in the act of embezzlement. The manager returns to his office. When he returns, carrying a gladstone bag, the typist is concealed beside a desk and witnesses the theft. The typist confronts the manager and attempts to call the police, but is thrown to the floor. During a struggle, the typist is pushed against an intercom button connected to the janitor's room. After some consideration, Charlie responds to the call, climbing back to the top floor. The typist has fainted after seeing the manager brandish a revolver. Using his cane, Charlie knocks the manager's gun to the floor and kicks him away. Charlie bends to pick up the gun, keeping the manager at bay by aiming the revolver through his legs. Charlie, having ordered the manager to put the unconscious typist in a chair, tries to telephone for help but, with only one hand free, puts the base of the receiver to his ear. He fends off the manager by firing the gun through the window; a further shot scrapes Charlie's foot. The shots alert a nearby policeman, who rushes to investigate. Charlie knocks over the manager using the safe door. The cop reaches the top of the stairs, but the president arrives first; misinterpreting the sight of a gun-wielding Charlie, the president pushes Charlie into the corridor. Charlie briefly eludes the cop, but is dragged into the president's office. He is freed when the manager is named as the true culprit. As a parting shot, Charlie aims the telephone at the manager as though pointing a gun. Charlie almost declines the president's cash reward, but accepts the money, offering the telephone in lieu of a handshake.

Some prints of this comedy partially obscure the plot by omitting the opening scenes, commencing instead with Charlie in the manager's office. Fortunately, the Blackhawk Films copy seems complete, but most available material tends to be rather fuzzy (a rather superior print is excerpted in *The Gentleman Tramp* [*qv*]). According to Chaplin's autobiography, *The New Janitor* convinced him of his ability to 'evoke tears as well as laughter'. Chaplin recalled Alice Davenport (*qv*) breaking down in tears when observing a scene in which, pleading for his job, he mimes a large family. This does not

The New Janitor *keeps the villain covered*
BFI Stills, Posters and Designs

occur in available prints, and it is possible that Chaplin's recollection, half a century later, had confused the moment with a parallel scene in *The Pawnshop* (*qv*); one might add that he misremembered the actress's first name as 'Dorothy'. Detail aside, Chaplin's dismissed janitor displays a hitherto unseen vulnerability and grace – he bows to his former employer when taking his leave – and this new dimension, though seldom explored in subsequent Keystones, would be further developed in the following year's series for Essanay (*qv*). One of these, *The Bank* (*qv*), is essentially an expansion of *New Janitor's* premise. Even later, in *The Immigrant* (*qv*), Chaplin would repeat the gag in which, bending down, he holds a villain at gunpoint by pointing the revolver between his legs, stepping over it in order to regain a standing position. At this time, Chaplin's work was perhaps earning a swifter reputation than the man himself; a review in the *Motion Picture News* of 26 September 1914 said *The New Janitor* 'will arouse peals of laughter from any audience', but named its star as 'Charles Chapman'!

(See also: Home movies; Keystone; Smoking; Williams, Frank D.)

NEWSREELS

It is believed that Chaplin may have made his first appearance before a movie camera when still a child. Harry M. Geduld's *Chapliniana* quotes a *New York Times* article of 2 September 1921, which claims he was caught on film (while playing truant in St. James' Park!) by a newsreel cameraman. Geduld is one of a few sources to mention a further chance

appearance in newsreels, when Chaplin was engaged with the Karno Company (*qv*) at St. Helier, Jersey, during 1912 (there is a parallel story of a newsreel cameraman who later claimed to have filmed Chaplin on stage in Britain during that year, which may or may not tie in to this account). Chaplin observed a cameraman filming the annual 'Battle of the Flowers' event and offered some impromptu mime for the benefit of cinemagoers. Neither of these items is known to have survived. It is said that Chaplin and company manager Alf Reeves (*qv*), inspired by the Jersey experience, agreed to club together to buy a camera, the plan being to make short comedies starring the Karno troupe. Their idea was, reportedly, stymied by rehearsal commitments, but Chaplin's encounter with the newsreels evidently stayed with him; two of his earliest film comedies, *Kid Auto Races at Venice* and *A Busy Day* (both *qv*) show him supposedly interrupting the work of a newsreel crew (there is also a bogus newsreel in a much later film, *The Great Dictator* [*qv*]).

As noted elsewhere, news film survives of Chaplin signing with Mutual (*qv*) in 1916 and of the public announcement, with his colleagues, of United Artists (*qv*). There are also extensive scenes of Chaplin addressing rallies during the First World War and entertaining troops (see **The Funniest Man in the World**). One of the better-known silent newsreels is the Topical Budget item covering his journey to Britain in 1921. This and several later examples are mentioned under **The Gentleman Tramp**.

Unknown Chaplin (*qv*) has news film of *City Lights*' US première. The UK opening, with Chaplin present, is covered similarly. Several news items are known to exist, as is a collection of out-takes reportedly in the Visnews collection. Perhaps the most accessible examples are those in the Pathé News archive, some of which have been released on home video. From later in the decade is a 1937 appearance in *Hollywood, USA* (*March of Time*, 3rd year no. 5).

Several news clips preserve Chaplin's return to Britain in 1952; there are also some later BBC reports, as when receiving an ovation in America in April 1972, and speaking to reporters after being dubbed 'Sir Charles' nearly three years later.

The UCLA archive preserves several Chaplin news items from the Hearst collection, one of which shows Chaplin,

Fairbanks, Pickford and Griffith (all *qv*) signing the UA contract. Another comparatively early example features Chaplin's departure from the USA in 1921. Several clips date from later in Chaplin's life: the UK première of *Limelight* (*qv*); the Chaplin family arriving in Cherbourg in 1952; Chaplin with his wife, Oona, in Switzerland during 1954; Anthony Asquith presenting Chaplin with Honorary Membership of the British Film Academy in 1956; a Variety Club luncheon in Chaplin's honour, from the same year; mute footage of the 1965 *Countess From Hong Kong* press conference, with Sophia Loren (*qv*); and Chaplin's 77th birthday celebrations, in London.

(See also: Awards, honours; *City Lights*; Countess from Hong Kong, A; *Making a Living*; O'Neill, Oona; Public appearances; Sport; Video releases; Wartime)

NICE AND FRIENDLY

A private film shot in 1921 at Pickfair, the home of Douglas Fairbanks and Mary Pickford (both *qv*). *Nice and Friendly* is in fact an elaborate home movie, lasting approximately one reel. It was made for the benefit of the visiting Lord Louis and Lady Edwina Mountbatten, who are given star billing in this production of the 'Accidental Film Company'. They are supported by Chaplin and Jackie Coogan (*qv*); also participating are Colonel Robert M. Thompson, Eulalia and Frederic Neilson and Sara and Stephen Pell. The slender plot has Lady Edwina as *ingénue*, whose pearl necklace attracts the interest of gun-toting thieves 'Picking Pete' and 'Nora "The Nip"'. Another of the villains is Chaplin, in civilian clothes but sporting a pencil moustache (jettisoned later on). Jackie, the first to notice anything amiss, is half-throttled for his trouble and laid out on the ground, covered over. Lord Louis, the hero, has an ally, but the heroine's rescue is delegated to Charlie the tramp, who sets to the task clumsily but effectively. Aided by a mallet, he knocks out the villains one by one. Their dazed condition is conveyed by 'pixilation', i.e. using live figures for single-frame animation. The crooks are laid out in a neat line beside Jackie. Charlie and his friends shake hands all round – though Charlie absently taps himself with the mallet – and he joins the Mountbattens as they walk off into the grounds. As a Fairbanks home movie, *Nice and Friendly* is stylistically more in his idiom than Chaplin's. According to Pickford/Fairbanks biographer Gary Carey, the Mountbattens were reprimanded by King George V when stills from the film began to appear in magazines, though the welcome extended Doug and Mary by the British aristocracy remained unimpaired. *Nice and Friendly* is sometimes excerpted in documentaries (*qv*), among them a late 1960s series called *The Life and Times of Lord Mountbatten*. It has been released in its entirety on laserdisc in the USA.

(See also: Animation; Dual rôles; Guest appearances; Home movies; Royalty; Trick photography; Video releases)

NICHOLS, GEORGE 'POP'
(1865–1927)

(Chaplin films *qv*)
A veteran of movies' earliest days, George Nichols – known as 'Pop' – served briefly as Chaplin's director at Keystone (*qv*) following his unhappy association with Henry Lehrman (*qv*). Nichols is credited with directing *A Film Johnnie* and *His Favorite Pastime*; Chaplin's autobiography conveys his opinion of Nichols' outmoded ideas, which, in Chaplin's words, consisted of 'one gag, which was to take the comedian by the neck and bounce him from one scene to another'. Although Nichols has been cited as director of *Cruel, Cruel Love* and *The Star Boarder*, recent scholars suggest that Mack Sennett (*qv*) may have taken over their supervision. 'Pop' Nichols was among the many who left Keystone for Lehrman's L-KO Comedies; he was occasionally seen as an actor, as in Mabel Normand's Sennett features, *Molly O'* (1922) and *The Extra Girl* (1923). His son, George Nichols Jr, also became a director, but died in 1939, aged only 42.

(See also: Normand, Mabel)

NICHOLS, NORMA

See: *Dough and Dynamite*; *His Musical Career*; *Property Man, The*, and *Those Love Pangs*

A NIGHT IN THE SHOW

(Chaplin film)
Released by General Film Company, 20 November 1915. Produced by Essanay. Written and directed by Charles Chaplin. Photographed by Harry Ensign. British title: *Charlie at the Show*. Two reels. 1,735 feet.

With Charlie Chaplin (Mr Pest/Mr Rowdy), Edna Purviance (attractive lady in stalls), Dee Lampton (fat boy), John Rand (conductor), May White (dancer), Leo White (Frenchman/black patron in gallery/magician), Bud Jamison (large singer), James T. Kelly, Paddy McGuire (musicians), Wesley Ruggles (in gallery audience), Carrie Clark Ward (in downstairs audience).

Mr Pest, a well-dressed drunk, arrives at the theatre. He jumps the queue but is told to wait his turn. From behind a buxom statue, Mr Pest admires a pretty theatregoer. The scruffier but no less intoxicated Mr Rowdy takes his seat in the gallery, nearly tumbling into the stalls. Mr Pest dozes behind the statue. An attendant places by it a notice reading 'Coming: Madame De Milo' and dusts the sculpture. Mr Pest, awakened, moves away, planting a kick on the attendant. In the auditorium, Mr Pest is shown to his seat, forcing a row of people to stand before realizing it is the wrong one. He sits in the front row, lighting a cigarette with a match struck on the tuba player's bald head. When the musician turns around, Mr Pest hurls the match and his gloves into the instrument. An usher informs Mr Pest that he should have been seated in the second row. The first and second rows are disrupted before Mr Pest returns to the front. Arguing with the lady sitting behind, Mr Pest falls into his neighbour's lap. Neighbour and friend move elsewhere. Mr Pest meets more of the band, among them a tremulous trombonist and the conductor, with whom Mr Pest has a scrap. Struck by the conductor's baton, Mr Pest knocks him over and a fight breaks out. Mr Pest grabs the trombonist's slide, and is led away to another seat. The trombonist reclaims his slide. Mr Pest grabs it back, pulls it away and is propelled into the foyer, pushing a *grande dame* into the fountain. He helps her out, but when she slaps him, Mr Pest pushes her back in. Mr Pest returns to his seat as the lady, complaining to the management, departs. Mr Pest competes for elbow room with the lady beside him.

A Night in the Show: *Mr Pest eyes conductor John Rand …*
BFI Stills, Posters and Design

He notices a particularly attractive woman further along the row, and takes an adjoining seat. He tries to settle but opts instead for the seat on her opposite side. She expresses disdain. In the gallery, Mr Rowdy opens a bottle of beer, spilling it into the stalls. The woman tries to shelter as she and Mr Pest are doused. Her husband arrives, and she takes his hand; Mr Pest, his eyes closed, takes the husband's hand by mistake. The husband pushes up his sleeves, a cue for Mr Pest to find yet another seat. He is placed in a box, shared by his former neighbours. He sits on one gentleman's hat; moving to the next chair, he does as much for the second topper. The irate patrons take their leave. The show begins. The first act is a chubby harem-girl dancer whom Mr Rowdy tries to pursue over the balcony. A society couple are seated in front of Mr Pest, obscuring his view. He extracts the gigantic plumes from the lady's hat. Shocked by the dancer, the lady leads her husband away. Mr Pest replaces the plumes unnoticed, only to withdraw them again to throw at the stage. The dancer's act concludes with her blundering into a turbanned assistant. Mr Pest takes the stage, lifting her off the unfortunate stooge. She falls again, pinning Mr Pest to the stage; freed, he dives at her before she flees backstage. The stage manager, pushing Mr Pest back to his seat, is flattened by the falling curtain. A fat boy, laden with sweets, arrives in the foyer with his hapless father. They are seated behind Mr Pest, at whom the boisterous lad pushes his messy confectionery. Mr Pest turns on them before the next act, a woman snake charmer. She reclines on cushions placed stage right; attendants light her cigarette, from which Mr Pest tries to obtain a light for himself. Rejecting his advances, she reverses her position, but Mr Pest strikes a match on her bare foot. A basketful of snakes is brought on. She dances with the snakes around her shoulders, then replaces them. The basket tips over, its occupants causing panic by slithering into the orchestra pit. Some of them slide over Mr Pest, who calmly brushes them away. The next act comprises two male vocalists. Mr Pest makes known his contempt, and the audience soon agrees. Mr Rowdy leads the others in throwing fruit; there is amusement in the stalls, even when some of it lands in their midst. The larger vocalist makes an exit. The boy provides Mr Pest with a plate of goo, which, at length, is pushed into the remaining singer's face. Mr Pest kicks him off. The stage manager intervenes, but receives a pie in the face. Curtain down, curtain up and the singers take a bow, to be splattered once again. Next is a sinister-looking fire-eater, capable of making props appear from nowhere and causing fire to roar. Mr Rowdy, alarmed, grabs the fire hose, drenching the stage, balcony, stalls and box. Mr Pest makes a futile attempt to shelter beneath a broken umbrella.

Amid the progression in his work characterizing the Essanay series, Chaplin took a deliberate step back by filming the stage sketch in which he became famous, *Mumming Birds* (see **The Karno Company**). Though perhaps an easy option in its day, the film provides a service in preserving Chaplin's performance, and was doubtless useful when re-enacting the skit in the 1992 film *Chaplin* (*qv*). Unlike the stage original, the technique of film enabled Chaplin to play both his usual rôle of elegant drunk and that of the unruly monarch of the gallery. Larry Semon later employed a similar device in two theatre-set films, *Between the Acts* (1919) and *The Show* (1922).

It is something of a surprise that Chaplin was able to make the film at all, as Fred Karno (*qv*) was notoriously protective of his sketches (though, as noted elsewhere, his action against an earlier film version proved futile). One can only surmise that Chaplin, in a sense Karno's prize pupil, was granted special dispensation.

The film often circulates with replacement titling designed to resemble the original Essanay cards. That they are not original versions is betrayed by the presence of one sub-title deriving from

... and, in the box, combats a lady's headdress

the usual reissue plus the absence of several shots, most of them in the foyer scenes, but also including Mr Pest's striking of a match on the snake charmer's foot. The BBC's *Chaplin SuperClown* edition, also with remade Essanay titles, reinstates these sections in lesser but adequate quality.

The title 'A Night *in* the Show', rather than 'at', suggests the degree to which Chaplin, the nominal spectator, takes part; the BBC's title card reads 'at', but is evidently listed in programme files under the correct name. This was suggested when it was once advertised and announced as 'A Night in the *Snow*', presumably in vague homage to *The Gold Rush*!

(See also: Alcohol; Costume; Dual rôles; Goodwins, Fred; Jamison, William 'Bud'; Kelly, James T.; *King in New York, A*; McGuire, Paddy; Race; Rand, John; Ruggles, Wesley; Smoking; Television; Vagrancy; Ward, Carrie Clark)

A NIGHT OUT

(Chaplin film)
Released by General Film Company, 15 February 1915 (see below). Produced by Essanay. Written and directed by Charles Chaplin. Photographed by Harry Ensign. Also known as *His Night Out* and (in a UK home movie edition) *Charlie's Drunken Daze*. Two reels. 1,961 feet (approx. length cited in UK trade ads). With Charlie Chaplin (himself), Ben

Turpin (Charlie's drinking pal), Bud Jamison (head waiter), Edna Purviance (head waiter's wife), Leo White (French count).

Charlie prepares for a night out. He meets up with Ben Turpin and, greeting him, inadvertently knocks the top hat from a French count. The resultant scuffle is interrupted by a passing cop. Charlie and Ben repair to a saloon while the Count enters a plush downstairs restaurant. Charlie and Ben emerge from the bar very drunk and go on to the same restaurant. Charlie annoys the Count, and when he retaliates, Ben insists on getting involved. Charlie and Ben squabble among themselves, and Ben has to be retrieved from a fountain. The Count complains to the head waiter, who promptly beats up and ejects Ben as Charlie keeps a low profile. Charlie is still at his table when the now-pacified Count greets a lady friend, who makes idle chatter while absently swinging her handbag in Charlie's direction. This is halted when Charlie traps the bag between his knees, but she goes on to slap *Charlie's* thigh when amused by conversation. Amused, Charlie dodges the last slap and offers in return a hearty blow to her back. The furious Count confronts Charlie, but receives a pie in the face. Charlie is engaged in an impromptu wash-and-brush-up at the fountain when the head waiter orders him to leave. Outside, Charlie slips over and joins Ben on the pavement. Charlie knocks Ben flat, and sets off for the

Charlie and Ben Turpin spend **A Night Out**. *They are monitored by* Bud Jamison *and flanked by* Leo White *and his lady friend*

saloon. Ben follows, asking a policeman if he has seen his friend. Charlie drags Ben into the saloon with his cane. The head waiter quits work for the night, passing the saloon en route. Charlie is half-way out of the place, and promptly retreats inside. The Count and his lady friend observe from a nearby park, and go on their way. Leaving the saloon, Charlie and Ben are even more drunk, so much so that Charlie has to be dragged to the hotel where he and Ben are to stay. They stagger up to their room as a beautiful young woman checks in. Ben attempts to unlock the door, when they are observed by the woman, whose room is across the corridor. She is amused to see Charlie perched on Ben's crouched figure. Both men flirt with her, but Charlie kicks Ben into their room. Charlie's attempt to perch on the woman misfires, and he is pitched to the floor; Ben in turn collapses on their bed. Charlie attempts to spy on the woman through the keyhole, but is interrupted by a bellhop carrying a soda syphon. Charlie unwittingly sprays the soda into his trousers, and makes for his own room, only to strike Ben with the door. Returning across the corridor, Charlie knocks the door, but it is answered by the woman's husband, who turns out to be the head waiter. Under his stern gaze, Charlie soberly packs and makes his exit. The presence of a policeman dissuades Charlie from returning to the saloon, and he checks in at another hotel. In the foyer, Charlie's foot reaches automatically for a bar rail while its owner sips at a bottle of ink. As Charlie attempts to sign in, he is distracted by a pretty girl and slides to the floor, where he continues to sign his name. Charlie's foot is caught in a spittoon, and he is sent reeling back into the street. The head waiter and his wife, dissatisfied with a cheeky bellhop and some damaged laundry, leave the hotel in disgust. Charlie is seen taking a rest on a park bench. Ben

awakens and goes off in search of his pal. The head waiter and his wife check into the second hotel. Ben is required to pay for the room he was sharing with Charlie. Catching up with him in the park, Ben demands half the money, and is knocked cold for so doing. Charlie staggers back to the hotel, meeting in the foyer a buxom, veiled woman. His pursuit is welcomed, but he loses interest when the veil is lifted. Charlie enters his room to prepare for bed, tucking in his cane. He is unaware that the head waiter and his wife are located across the hallway. The head waiter goes out. Abandoning his attempts to extract soda from a telephone, Charlie changes into pyjamas (inadvertently dumping his trousers through the window). Charlie is in the bathroom, seemingly applying toothpaste to his slipper, when the head waiter's wife, also pyjama-clad, chases a pet dog across the hallway and under Charlie's bed. Charlie returns from the bathroom and, sitting on the bed, notices a disturbance. He investigates, and slides to the floor, to discover his unexpected guest. The woman's husband has reappeared, but she has a chance to return when he goes to the foyer in search of her. Charlie and the woman sneak across the hallway, and are both in the room when the head waiter comes back. Charlie is discovered hiding in the bed, and is forced to leap from a window when the husband draws a gun. Ben regains consciousness in the park and makes his way to Charlie's hotel. He is outside his room by the time Charlie has made his way back through the foyer. They start to scrap, but most of their blows miss the mark. Charlie kicks Ben across the hallway; he rebounds off the head waiter and pushes Charlie into the filled bath. Charlie, spitting water, climbs out, only to fall in again.

A reworking of *Mabel's Strange Predicament* (*qv*), *A Night Out* takes on some importance in Chaplin history through being the first appearance of Edna Purviance (*qv*) as leading lady. It is also Chaplin's second and last extensive work alongside Ben Turpin (*qv*), who would reappear only as a bit player in *The Champion* (*qv*) and in the non-Chaplin footage added by Essanay (*qv*) to *Carmen* (*qv*).

Chaplin's second Essanay comedy, *A Night Out* was his first West Coast production since leaving Keystone (*qv*) late in 1914. The first in the Essanay series, *His New Job* (*qv*), had been made in Chicago, but Chaplin preferred the Californian climate. All subsequent

Essanays were made at their studio in Niles, California.

As is often the case with early Chaplins, available prints offer only a partial idea of the film's original impact and are, at best, an unreliable guide to intended content. At least one source has claimed that the order of sequence has been amended in reissues (*qv*). In this account, the original version would have shown (a) Charlie and Ben on the town, (b) Charlie at his hotel, signing in, (c) Charlie retiring early, receiving an unexpected visit from a woman, (d) the husband chasing Charlie from the hotel, (e) Ben finding Charlie outside, the two heading for a restaurant, (f) the head waiter turning out to be the husband and (g) Charlie returning to the woman at the hotel, meeting her husband again and making his exit. This is unlikely, partly because it ignores the progression of Charlie and Ben from sober acquaintances to drunks then, finally, to bitter enemies. On their first, sober, meeting, they encounter Leo White (*qv*), which progresses logically into their second altercation with him in the restaurant; the head waiter clearly does not know Charlie in the restaurant scene, and is prepared to tolerate him even after ejecting Ben; further, when Charlie escapes from the head waiter's hotel room he is wearing pyjamas, rendering it impossible for Ben to discover him dressed and ready to continue their evening out; in addition, the alternate account makes no mention of the head waiter and his wife moving to a separate hotel, or of Charlie having done likewise; while the finale, with Charlie falling into the bath, fades to black, just as the opening scene had faded up.

Today's prints of *A Night Out* adhere to the accepted sequence, but vary considerably in content. The author's copy, slightly rechristened '*His* Night Out', is virtually complete but omits the final shots of Turpin in the hall and Charlie falling back into the bath. A version circulated on video in the UK has Essanay-style titles, but these are probably remakes, as the titling is of reasonable quality and properly centred, while the picture element itself is quite poor and 'cropped' in the manner of a sound reissue. There are also a number of deleted moments, most noticeably Charlie's flirtation with the veiled woman. Titling in this edition is of some use when comparing it to other prints, such as that shown on BBC Television. The BBC copy also has remade Essanay titles, but of different text; missing altogether is a card in which Turpin demands half of their room rent, partially obscuring his motive for attacking Charlie in the park. Otherwise, this BBC edition is as complete as is possible today; a small jump cut in the restaurant scene – just before the arrival of Leo White's girlfriend – seems to occur in all surviving material and cannot be replaced.

The title variant noted above parallels another in a contemporary Essanay announcement, from the *Moving Picture World* of 13 February 1915. Here the title is given as '*One* Night Out'; also slightly at odds with usual histories is a release date of 11 February, rather than the 15th as is usually cited.

(See also: Alcohol; Costume; *Funniest Man in the World, The*; Goodwins, Fred; Jamison, William 'Bud'; Parks; *Pay Day*; Policemen; Risqué humour; Television; Titling; Video releases)

NORMAND, MABEL
(1894–1930)

(Chaplin films *qv*)
Comedienne, usually cited as the finest of the silent screen and, with comparable frequency, 'the female Chaplin'. Born in Boston, Massachusetts, Mabel entered movies after working as an artists' model. Her first appearances were made at Vitagraph's New York studios, among the survivors being two John Bunny films of 1911, *The Troublesome Secretaries* and *The Subduing of Mrs. Nag.* Next came a stint working for D.W. Griffith (*qv*) at Biograph, where she made the acquaintance of Mack Sennett (*qv*). Biograph used her in dramatic stories such as *A Squaw's Love* (1911) and, more in keeping with her eventual image, the type of light-hearted action seen in *A Dash Through the Clouds* (1912). Mabel's relationship with Sennett developed into a romance; she left Biograph with Sennett when he established his own company, Keystone (*qv*). Much early publicity refers to her simply as 'Keystone Mabel' (often misspelled 'Mable'). Her forename was often incorporated into the titles, as with her first appearance with Chaplin, *Mabel's Strange Predicament.* The same applies to their next film together, *Mabel at the Wheel*, which nearly brought about Chaplin's dismissal from the studio. At least nominally her own director, Mabel insisted on things being done her way, and took umbrage when Chaplin disagreed over specific business. Mabel was beloved around the lot, and Chaplin was suddenly

very unpopular; as noted elsewhere, it was only a timely request for more Chaplin films that saved his job. Sennett re-established harmony between his stars, who are believed to have shared direction of their next joint appearance, *Caught in a Cabaret. The Fatal Mallet* is little more than an impromptu effort from Chaplin, Normand, Sennett *et al*, while their next, *Her Friend the Bandit* is unavailable for viewing. *Mabel's Busy Day* and *Mabel's Married Life* are thought to have been directed jointly by Normand and Chaplin, but *Gentlemen of Nerve* was entirely Chaplin's work, as suggested by the absence of Mabel's name from the title and a concentration on Charlie in the film's action. Mabel's new status as Chaplin's supporting player, rather than the reverse, is implicit in the title of their next film, *His Trysting Place.* Mabel was considered very much third in interest, after Marie Dressler (*qv*) and Chaplin, in *Tillie's Punctured Romance*; her final appearance with Chaplin was in his penultimate Keystone, *Getting Acquainted.*

Mabel's romantic involvement with Sennett was terminated when she found him under embarrassing circumstances with another Keystone actress, Mae Busch. Sennett later claimed the whole matter to have been a misfired joke, but Mabel at least seems to have been unconvinced. She continued to work for Sennett, and of her later Keystones, some of the best-known are those with Roscoe 'Fatty' Arbuckle (*qv*), notably *Fatty and Mabel Adrift* (1916). Sennett, still in love with Mabel (as he would remain for the rest of his life), directed her in a feature-length film, *Mickey*, in 1917, after which Mabel left to work for Sam Goldwyn. Most of her feature-length work has been allowed to vanish – one exception being from a brief return to Sennett, 1923's *The Extra Girl* – leaving only memories of the scandal that tarnished her name during that period. She had become less than dedicated to her work when at Goldwyn, often arriving late for work or absenting herself altogether. She was thought to have become a drug user and, in 1922, was the last person to see director William Desmond Taylor before his murder. Although absolved of any involvement with the killing – which remains officially unsolved even today – Mabel's reputation had been severely damaged. More was to come when, at a gathering attended also by Edna Purviance (*qv*), Mabel's chauffeur drew a revolver, with which he shot and wounded the host.

It is not true to suggest that Mabel never again acted in films after the Taylor

Mabel Normand, queen of the Keystone lot

scandal. *The Extra Girl* was one of at least two features released after the affair, and Mabel's withdrawal from Hollywood to the Broadway stage was a voluntary move. She returned as one of Hal Roach's 'fading stars' in a series of featurettes, among them *Raggedy Rose* (1926), directed by Stan Laurel (*qv*).

Mabel's health – probably affected by the stresses and scandals of 1922–3 – had been in decline as much as her career, something which in part had decided her initial withdrawal from the film capital. She recovered from double pneumonia early in 1927, but developed tuberculosis, from which she died in February 1930. Towards the end of her life she had married actor Lew Cody, a match viewed by some as purely for companionship.

(See also: *Chaplin*; Edwards, Vivian; Female impersonation; Nichols, George 'Pop'; Sport; Women)

NORTHRUP, HARRY (S.)
(1877 or 1880–1936)

The valet in *A Woman of Paris* (*qv*); birthplace reported variously as Paris or, more plausibly, New York City. Educated in San Francisco, he spent 15 years playing villains on the dramatic stage. He appeared in films from 1911, among them Vitagraph's production of *Vanity Fair*, produced that year; many others include *The Four Horsemen of the Apocalypse* (1921), *The Christian* (1923) and Theda Bara's penultimate film, *The Unchastened Woman* (1925).

(See also: Swickard, Joseph)

OAKIE, JACK
(Lewis D. Offield) (1903–78)

Comedian who plays 'Napaloni', the Mussolini equivalent in Chaplin's *The Great Dictator* (*qv*), for which he received an Oscar nomination as Best Supporting Actor. Numerous films from the late 1920s onwards, among the earlier talkies being Leo McCarey's *Let's Go Native* (1930). Oakie's films of the period sometimes overlapped with those of W.C. Fields, as in *Million Dollar Legs* (1932), *If I Had a Million* (1932) and the 1933 version of *Alice in Wonderland* (as Tweedledum). His later films include *The Big Broadcast of 1936*, *Hitting a New High* (1937), *Hello, Frisco, Hello* (1943) and *Around the World in Eighty Days* (1956).

(See also: Awards, honours)

Jack Oakie (right) made a memorable 'Napaloni' in The Great Dictator

OCCUPATIONS 🎩

(Chaplin films *qv*)
Chaplin's autobiography mentions a few childhood jobs, notably a stint helping a gang of woodcutters. Otherwise, he was drawn largely towards the entertainment profession, within which he would depict many other occupations.

Although ostensibly a tramp, 'Charlie' is very often in gainful employment. Several of the earlier films are titled after their occupational themes: *The Property Man*, *The New Janitor*, *The Floorwalker* and *The Fireman* come to mind, while *Making a Living*, *His New Profession* and *His New Job* bespeak the process of earning, if not the precise method. Other occupations are as a waiter in *Caught in a Cabaret*, *Dough and Dynamite*, *The Rink* and *Modern Times*, a caretaker in *Laughing Gas*, *The Bank*, *Triple Trouble* and, again *Modern Times*, an artist in *The Face On the Bar Room Floor*, a comedian in *The Masquerader*, *The Circus* and *Limelight*, an assistant deliveryman in *His Musical Career*, a decorator's assistant in *Work*, a reluctant mariner in *Shanghaied*, a soldier in *Carmen* and *Shoulder Arms*, a busker in *The Vagabond* and, once more, *Limelight*, a tailor's assistant in *The Count*, a general dogsbody in *The Pawnshop*, *Behind the Screen* and *Sunnyside*, a policeman in *Easy Street*, a glazier in *The Kid*, a builder in *Pay Day*, a prospector in *The Gold Rush*, a mechanic in (yet again!) *Modern Times*, a barber in *The Great Dictator* and a ship's steward in *A Countess From Hong Kong*. Interestingly, both *Monsieur Verdoux* and *A King in New York* present Chaplin as a redundant man, respectively a bank clerk and monarch. In *City Lights*, Charlie anticipates the job-hopping of *Modern Times* by trying his hand as road sweeper and, as in *The Champion*, a prizefighter.

Although frequently sacked for ineptitude, Charlie tackles each job with enthusiasm and panache. Theodore Huff wrote of Chaplin's way of performing each task with super-human dexterity, so that his 'super-waiter' of *The Rink* mixes a cocktail with gusto as, by a logical progression, his 'super-bank clerk' of *Monsieur Verdoux* is able to count banknotes and scan telephone directories with bewildering rapidity. In similar vein, publicist Elsie Codd (in *Pictures and the Picturegoer* of 21 April 1917) evaluated two Chaplin scenes, the measuring of a lady customer in *The Count* and the alarm-clock examination of *The Pawnshop*, as 'the tailor and the distinguished physician to the life ... each plus the personality of Charlie Chaplin is just what the latter would have been, had he been a member of either profession'.

(See also: Artists; Boxing; Childhood; Costume; Early stage appearances; Female impersonation; Hair; Policemen; Royalty; Vagrancy)

ONE A.M. 🎩

(Chaplin film)
Released by Mutual, 7 August 1916. Written and directed by Charles Chaplin. Photographed by William C. Foster and Rollie Totheroh. Two reels. 2,034 feet.

With Charlie Chaplin (himself), Albert Austin (taxi driver).

Charlie, a man-about-town, arrives home very late and very drunk. Initially, he cannot find the door handle to leave his taxi; trying to ascertain the fare, he encounters a meter turning at a rate of knots. The cab driver gets a burning cigarette in his hand before receiving the fare. Having extricated his cloak from the taxi door, Charlie reaches his front step. In the absence of a key, he climbs through a window, placing his foot in a goldfish bowl. Once inside, he finds the key and returns through the window, determined to come in the proper way. Inside again, he competes with a swinging door and sliding mat; despite steadying himself on a coat rack, he slides to the floor. In his daze, Charlie mistakes the animal-skin rugs for wild beasts. Out of their way, he tries to obtain a drink, placed on a revolving table; his cloak is caught and the table revolves, keeping the booze out of reach. He removes the cloak but catches it with his foot, keeping the table in motion. He trips and, fortuitously, the table comes to rest in the desired position. Charlie attempts to spray soda into a glass, but is unaware it is pointing in the wrong direction. Blaming the glass for its limited capacity, he tries a larger receptacle, a resolutely non-watertight stand for the syphon. Again he sprays soda in the wrong direction; next he pours his drink into the syphon stand, succeeding only in dampening his shoe. Charlie, giving up the effort, lights a cigarette, but absently keeps the match and throws the cigarette into a spittoon.

It's **One A.M.** *and Charlie is trapped behind his own bed*
BFI Stills, Posters and Designs

After burning his fingers on the match, he takes another cigarette from the floor, making much of dropping it into the spittoon. Charlie tries to light a third cigarette, but extinguishes the match before doing so. He tries to hang his cloak on a downward-pointing arm of the coat-rack, abandons the effort and tries to climb a staircase to the right of the room. He slips on the mat and returns to the table, dumping the cloak. Charlie falls to the table in just the right position to reach a drink. Tossing his hat on to a stuffed ostrich, he makes for the left-hand staircase, only for his leg to be seized in the jaws of still another stuffed animal. Once freed, he makes two attempts to climb the stairs, only to totter back to another drink. He slides over, depositing glass and decanter on the floor. He climbs the stairs again, sliding back down the banister to where he left the bottle. Two more unsuccessful ascents later, Charlie improvises mountaineer's equipment to make the climb, but is pulled back by the rope attached to his waist. A further attempt, clinging to the banisters, brings success until Charlie is knocked downstairs by a gigantic clock pendulum. He tries the opposite staircase but is frightened away by a stuffed bear. Through all this, Charlie has continued to try lighting his cigarette; having used all the matches, he gets on the table in order to reach an overhead lamp. Soon he is running atop the revolving table. Hitting the floor, he renews his assault on the staircase, only to roll down inside its carpet. He lands in the right spot to obtain another drink. Charlie bypasses both stairs and stuffed bear by climbing the coat-rack. Charlie is about to enter the bedroom when the clock pendulum knocks him downstairs, taking the stuffed bear with him. A second climb up the coat-rack brings the desired result, though Charlie is struck repeatedly by the pendulum before crawling under its path. In the bedroom, Charlie braves more odd-looking animal trophies en route to his bed. The bed, mounted in the wall, is operated by push-buttons; Charlie is whirled around but halts its progress; then the bed decides to come to rest on the floor, pinning Charlie beneath. Charlie clambers out to find his hat trapped under one of the legs. Trying to pull it free, he tears off the brim. He stands up, allowing the bed to retract; he sits down and plummets to the floor. Pressing another button brings the bed back down on Charlie. Clambering out, he tries to push the bed down into position, but is bounced up and down then trapped as the bed folds back into the wall. The bed is flattened again, but decides to turn itself upside-down. Charlie prepares to sleep on the inverted bed, which pops back into the wall. He settles for sleeping on the floor until the bed decides to drop into the correct position. Charlie reclines on the bed, but the frame disappears into the wall, leaving only mattress and bedclothes. The frame reappears just in time to trip Charlie. He makes for the bathroom. Trying to obtain a glass of water, Charlie is drenched in the shower. He settles down to sleep in the bath, using a towel as blanket.

One A.M. holds a singular place in the Chaplin canon, being a solo performance save for a brief bit by Albert Austin (*qv*) as the cab driver. (An edition prepared for European video and TV distribution misidentifies him as Albert 'Martin'!). Otherwise, in lieu of a supporting cast are several bizarre props, some of them perhaps the customary decor of the period (such as the animal rugs), but others, one suspects, not. One of these presents a small continuity error (at least in available material), when Charlie places his hat on a stuffed ostrich then, mysteriously, seems to have the hat when he has climbed upstairs. Chaplin's performance is again a revisiting of his drunken swell from *Mumming Birds* (*qv*), who this time not only fails to get the better of the world around him but is actually helpless in the face of his own possessions. The film overall is characterized by a large set and the frequent use of a moving camera, a device used by Chaplin with greater frequency than his detractors would admit.

TV, video and theatrical revivals tend to be from sound reissue prints, even when shown at silent speed with new music added. Reductions from a full-frame silent edition sometimes surface in Britain, with sub-titles of a slightly ornate but otherwise anonymous design. Prints vary somewhat in the number of sub-titles retained. A problem with such revivals is that the opening exteriors, supposedly depicting the small hours, were very obviously shot in broad daylight. In the silent era, night scenes were usually taken in the daytime but tinted blue in the release prints, creating a convincing illusion of night. (Much the same is often done today, darkening the image by means of filters or in the grading.) Original prints of *One A.M.* probably would have been tinted in this fashion, but the only modern-day edition to have followed suit seems to be a version supplied for UK video distribution by historian David Shepard.

(See also: Alcohol; Animals; Cars; Colour; Costume; Leno, Dan; Mutual; Smoking; Television; Titling; Vagrancy; Video releases)

O'NEILL, OONA
(1925–1991)

Chaplin's fourth and final wife, with whom he found lasting happiness, Oona was born in Bermuda, the daughter of playwright Eugene O'Neill and his wife, writer Agnes Boulton. She met Chaplin late in 1942 when, as detailed elsewhere, the comedian planned to cast her in a film called *Shadow and Substance* (see **Abandoned projects** and **Women**). Oona was 17 and Chaplin 53. There seems already to have been a split between Oona and her father. In her book *Among the Porcupines*, Carol Matthau, a lifelong friend of Oona's, recalled Oona's attribution of the rift to O'Neill's anger at Oona and her older brother having decided not to go to college. In Los

*Chaplin found lasting happiness with his fourth wife, **Oona O'Neill**; this photo sees them leaving the US in 1952, immediately prior to Chaplin's exile*

Angeles, Oona wrote to Carol about the famous people she'd met, among them Orson Welles; all, it seems, wanted to take her out, give her jobs – and sleep with her, something Oona found unnerving. The letter ended 'P.S. I just met Charlie Chaplin.' They married on 1 June 1943, a move which, reportedly, consolidated the break with Eugene O'Neill. Carol Matthau met the couple at lunch in June 1944, after which she described Chaplin as 'the most in-love man I ever saw'.

Despite their considerable difference in age, Chaplin's marriage to Oona brought him a domestic serenity of the type seemingly absent at any other time in his life. Such a firm relationship was particularly fortunate when Chaplin's reputation was being dragged through the mud in the 1940s, both with the court case (see again, **Women**) and subsequent accusations of Communist subversion. When Chaplin was exiled from the USA in 1952, Oona not only remained with him but, early in 1954, renounced her American citizenship in favour of British. At the time of their departure from the US, they had four children; another four were to follow over the next ten years.

It was often believed that Oona had subverted her own considerable talents in favour of her marriage, but she seems to have regarded it all as a fair exchange. Some believe she gave Chaplin the love she couldn't give to her father, while he in turn made her feel safe. The latter probably worked both ways, for her presence would always be required on the set of his later films; Chaplin even grew noticeably uncomfortable if Oona left the room for too long a period. Margaret Rutherford (*qv*) described how Oona's 'stillness and gentleness pervaded the room like pot-pourri. She rarely spoke, but you felt that she was there to protect her husband from any strain.' Candice Bergen (in *Knock on Wood*) recalls having met Oona and Charlie at a revival of *Modern Times* (*qv*) in France. She remarked on the absence of Chaplin 'holding court' in any sense, he and his wife seeming not to have 'acquired the protective finish of social shellac'. In Bergen's view, 'Their love for each other was palpable; it was good to see them together, impossible to imagine them otherwise.' During her husband's last, frail few years, Oona told people that he had looked after her, and she was doing as much for him. Chaplin's absolute devotion to her is clear in an interview conducted by Harold Clurman in 1962 for *Esquire* (later reprinted in *The Sunday Times*): 'Oona jokingly issued some stern command to Charlie about how and where he was to sit at the table while coffee and pastry were being served. "What!" I cried mock-seriously, "You let her browbeat you!" "Well, you see, I'm in love with her," Charlie said almost childishly.' Much of the interview concerns Chaplin's then-forthcoming autobiography, which concludes with what was, in effect, a brief love letter to Oona. He said much through very little, as 'perfect love is the most beautiful of all frustrations because it is more than one can express'.

After her husband's death, Oona, always diffident, withdrew increasingly into private life. Alexander Walker's book, *It's Only a Movie, Ingrid*, speaks of Chaplin's neighbours in Switzerland; those they would visit included James Mason and, unexpectedly, rock star David Bowie. After Chaplin had gone, Bowie dared Oona to take a part in a film, with Bowie in return offering to face his own horror by accepting a rôle in a Broadway production of *The Elephant Man*. Oona did not accept the challenge. As time progressed, Oona's brave public face came to conceal an escalating private sadness. This did not start to become known publicly until after her own, premature, death in 1991. Carol Matthau believed Oona was born with a broken heart and eventually died from one. Oona O'Neill's birthdate is sometimes given as 1926, apparently in error. The earlier date appears in a biography, *Hidden Star: Oona O'Neill Chaplin*, which was written by Patrice Chaplin (former wife of Charlie and Oona's son Michael). The book was published in 1995.

(See also: Children; *Limelight*; Marriages; Politics)

THE PAPERHANGER

See: Reissues and *Work*

PARKS

(Chaplin films *qv*)
During Mack Sennett's attempts to keep Chaplin's services at the end of 1914, he expressed doubt at the comedian's ability to function at another studio. 'All I need to make a comedy is a park, a policeman and a pretty girl,' retorted Chaplin. On another occasion he described the sadness and loneliness associated with public parks.

Certainly, Chaplin found such a setting useful either as a starting point or, in many instances, the location for an entire film. This proved invaluable when a one-reeler had to be created swiftly – sometimes in a day or less – in order to meet Keystone's shipping dates. In addition, trees and shrubbery provided natural concealment for comic intrigues, just as doors, windows and curtains do for theatrical farce. Many of Chaplin's Keystones take place in Westlake Park, close to the studio at Edendale. *Between Showers* was shot there, as was his possible debut as a director, *Twenty Minutes of Love*. The other contender for this accolade, *Caught in the Rain*, begins in a park but soon relocates to a hotel, making its reissue title of *In the Park* (actually the title of his Essanay remake of *Twenty Minutes of Love*) all the less appropriate. Similarly, the early scenes of *Mabel's Married Life* have a park location, as do those in *A Woman*. Conversely, *Those Love Pangs* begins at Charlie's lodgings prior to his departure for the open spaces. Other fully-fledged 'park' comedies are *His New Profession*,

Getting Acquainted and *Recreation*. One source suggests *Recreation* to have been filmed around left-over footage from *Twenty Minutes of Love*, but this seems unlikely; their similarities are no greater than those between most other park comedies, and one must also consider for their separation in terms of chronology.

Numerous films take Charlie into a park at some stage in the action, among them *Caught in a Cabaret*, *His Trysting Place*, *The Rounders*, *The Face On the Bar Room Floor*, *Tillie's Punctured Romance*, *His Prehistoric Past*, *A Night Out* and *A Jitney Elopement*. *The Fatal Mallet* is similar in approach but has more of a barnyard setting, just as *By the Sea* is a 'park' comedy relocated to the beach.

The device was employed less frequently as time progressed, but in *The Rink* a park serves once more as social contact point, as Edna's party invitation is extended to various individuals. *The Bond* has Charlie and Edna meeting – seemingly at night – in a park. In one of his last short comedies, *The Idle Class*, Charlie takes a seat on a park bench, where he finds himself unjustly accused of theft.

On 16 April 1997 – the 108th anniversary of Chaplin's birth – the London *Evening Standard* quoted the comedian's son, Eugene, regarding plans to construct a £30 million Chaplin theme park in Vevey, Switzerland. Eugene stated that the park was to include ten cinemas showing Chaplin films, and would 'boost the economy' of a region where his father spent some of the 'happiest years of his life'.

(See also: Essanay; Keystone; Policemen; Sennett, Mack)

PARRISH, ROBERT
(b. 1916)

(Chaplin films *qv*)
Director, whose filmography includes *Cry Danger* (1951), *Assignment Paris* (1952), *Fire Down Below* (1957), *The Bobo* (1967), *The Marseilles Contract* (1974) and many others; his autobiography, *Growing Up in Hollywood*, attributes his interest in film-making to Chaplin, for whom he appeared when still a child. Parrish and another boy, Austin Jewell, were selected to play the newsboys in *City Lights* (*qv*) when Chaplin's casting director visited their schoolroom. The main requirements were to be up to date with

schoolwork and to possess a modicum of skill with a peashooter. On the set, Parrish noted one of the assistant directors shouting at everyone through a megaphone until quietly interrupted by Chaplin, who said, 'If you are through yelling, we'll make the shot.' The two boys had developed two misconceptions, one being that the director always used a megaphone to issue instructions, the other that D.W. Griffith (*qv*) directed every film ever made but was allowing Chaplin to deputize on this occasion. Word of this got back to Chaplin, who, for the boys' amusement, borrowed the megaphone to parody the image of a director, speaking into the wrong end and getting the instrument stuck on his foot. Chaplin explained how he preferred to explain – and, better still, *demonstrate* – action rather than yell at his actors. He coached the boys through their scenes, which were duly shot; the process had to be repeated after a break in production, because the youngsters had grown, meaning that any new scenes would not match those taken earlier. Before graduating to the director's chair, Parrish worked as a film editor, in which capacity Chaplin asked him to look at some rushes for *Monsieur Verdoux*; Chaplin also invited him to hear *Limelight*'s score before the picture was shot, acting out his story to the music. They met again years later, in Ireland, when Chaplin drew Parrish's attention to a successful revival of 'our' *City Lights* in New York.

(See also: Births; Children; *Unknown Chaplin*)

PATHOS

(Chaplin films *qv*)
Much misunderstood and misinterpreted (often by people who, the author suspects, have never actually sat through a Chaplin film in its entirety), Chaplin's use of pathos – instilled early on by Fred Karno (*qv*) – is invariably tempered by its context. Such moments are usually maintained long enough to establish the point, but deflated immediately by a gag; in *City Lights* the tramp gazes adoringly at the blind girl, who, unaware of his presence, unwittingly hurls water into his face. An earlier example, from *The Immigrant*, has the gallant Charlie signifying his love, only to ruin the effect by realizing, belatedly, that his 'heart' is located on the opposite side of his chest.

Chaplin's use of **Pathos** has often been misunderstood

On 23 August 1919, *Picture Show*, in trailing the forthcoming *Sunnyside*, described his 'inimitable way of turning his sad eyes in pained endurance when he has committed a more than usually funny mistake', thus acknowledging the link between Chaplin's frequent melancholy and its comedic setting. One might compare this restraint to equivalent scenes in the works of others who, especially when unchecked by an objective hand, consciously aped Chaplin's pathos to nauseating lengths.

It may be this type of imitation that has brought about a popular confusion of pathos with self-pity. Chaplin's screen character was not one to surrender when wounded; his first recognizable foray into this area, *The New Janitor*, depicts a resourceful employee whose bravery is ultimately rewarded. It is this same resourcefulness that provides balance to the pathos of *The Gold Rush*, in which elements of triumph and defeat are alternated in equal measure. The justly-famous ending of *The Tramp*, later repeated with variants, allows Charlie only a brief moment of despair prior to recovering his usual spirit.

This and comparable scenes have been excerpted on numerous occasions, obscuring the fact that Chaplin rationed them. When *A Woman of Paris* was revived in 1978, Vincent Canby of the New York *Times* observed that 'the

Tramp comedies are, upon close inspection, much less sentimental than they originally appear to be', noting that despite Charlie's adoration of his leading ladies, 'there's something quite perverse about his romantic vision of women. Idealizing them is a backhanded way of calling attention to the ways in which most women fall short.'

Posterity, it must be allowed, has not necessarily favoured Chaplinesque pathos. This is a less sentimental age – or, more to the point, an age in which people are more reluctant to admit sentiment – wherein undue displays of emotion are likely to induce discomfort. Often overlooked is that Chaplin's introduction of a convincing emotional aspect to his films was considered innovatory, in a period when drama, much less knockabout comedy, often failed to convey anything as realistic.

(See also: Abandoned projects; Karno Company, The; Slapstick; Women)

THE PAWNSHOP

(Chaplin film)
Released by Mutual, 2 October 1916. Written and directed by Charles Chaplin. Photographed by Rollie Totheroh. Two reels. 1,940 feet.

With Charlie Chaplin (himself), Edna Purviance (pawnbroker's daughter), Henry Bergman (pawnbroker), John Rand (clerk), Albert Austin (customer with clock), Eric Campbell (crook), James T. Kelly (old drunk in street/lady with goldfish).

At the pawnshop, the proprietor paces angrily in the shop as his daughter works in the kitchen. We learn the reason for the pawnbroker's impatience when Charlie arrives for work, 'late – as usual'. At the rear of the premises, Charlie dusts his hat and the birdcage in which it is placed. This enthusiastic dusting and consequent clouds of dust disturb his colleague, the clerk, especially when dusting the blades of a moving electric fan. They come to blows, but the other man is trapped in a ladder which Charlie is taking outside. Outside, Charlie enlists a small boy to hold the ladder while he spars with his trapped colleague. Suddenly aware of a policeman behind him, Charlie returns to the shop. He sees the proprietor, and returns to work outside. Dismissing the boy, he frees the

By courtesy of Robert G. Dickson

clerk and, after bashing the ladder into colleague and employer, climbs it in order to clean the shop's business sign. The clerk staggers into the shop, dazed, after Charlie has dropped one of the sign's enormous brass spheres on his head. He returns with a bucket just as Charlie, attempting to clean the 'money lent' sign, has started to teeter on the ladder. A policeman looks on, horrified, as Charlie starts to overbalance. When he finally plummets, the ladder falls over the clerk, and Charlie, unhurt, checks to see if his watch is intact. Charlie takes the ladder inside, knocking over clerk, policeman and boss. Outside, the policeman blames the other man and takes a swing; escaping into the shop, he and Charlie flip a coin to decide who should go out to fetch the bucket. The coin disappears, but is inside Charlie's palm; still the loser, he manages to elude the officer. Inside, the coin business is repeated, and the clerk has to carry the ladder through to the back. He trips over the bucket placed down by Charlie; they spar at each other, but swiftly return to their working positions when the pawnbroker walks in. Charlie washes not just the floor but also a violin; he is fired, but reinstated after miming a group of variously-sized offspring. The pawnbroker departs, and Charlie renews his attack on his fellow employee. Charlie has the best of the scrap, but feigns otherwise when the pawnbroker's daughter emerges from the kitchen. Charlie is taken out to help her, sampling cakes that can shatter crockery and putting dishes through a mangle. He stages an impromptu serenade, using a wooden spoon as ukelele and dough as

Hawaiian garland, until the clerk arrives and battle is renewed. Again, the pawnbroker's presence terminates the fight, Charlie using the mangle to flatten out pastry. Charlie retires to the safe to fetch his lunch. He is at the counter when an elderly customer enters, evidently an actor of the old school. Tragically, he must pawn 'her wedding ring' or face starvation. Charlie, reduced to tears, spits his lunch in the customer's direction. Charlie, refusing the item, rings up $5 and hands the man a $10 bill. 'Ten?' replies the aged thespian. 'You want five change,' he adds, peeling off five bills from a huge bankroll. Charlie slaps his own face before thumping himself with a mallet. The next customer is a shifty-looking gent, who is about to steal the cash register until the girl and her father appear at the counter. He asks to be shown some diamonds. Charlie is sweeping the back room. Arranging some rope into a straight line, he plays at being a tightrope walker. Still sweeping, Charlie moves the chair intended for the dubious customer, who falls to the floor. Charlie is sent to serve another customer, who hopes to raise $2 on an alarm clock. Unconvinced of its worth, Charlie examines it with a stethoscope, investing in the task the professional *élan* of an eminent physician. This is in stark contrast with his next assault, using first a brace and bit then a can opener. He smells the contents as though evaluating sardines. Borrowing the telephone's mouthpiece in lieu of a jeweller's glass, Charlie inspects the contents (using the wrong eye) before adding liberal quantities of oil. Using pliers, hammer and wirecutters, he slowly disembowels the clock, as its astonished owner looks on. There is, not surprisingly, no sign of ticking. Charlie winds the clock, only for its displaced viscera to dance around on the counter. Taking the oilcan, Charlie drowns them into immobility. Sweeping the works back into the clock, Charlie returns the item with a firm shake of the head. The customer protests, but is silenced by a blow with the hammer, which, fortunately, has a rubber head. Outside, the customer pushes away an old drunk who asks the time. At the back of the shop, the pawnbroker is showing diamond rings to the disreputable customer. At the counter, Charlie serves a lady who wants to pawn a fish bowl, complete with live goldfish. The pawnbroker arrives in time to stop Charlie using acid to test the 'gold'; he shoves Charlie into the back room,

Charlie upsets the cop, his colleague and the owner of **The Pawnshop**

where his head becomes caught in a bass fiddle. Charlie blunders into the clerk, receiving a kick in return; in the shop, the woman is sent away; attempting to free himself, Charlie hits his colleague again, and is kicked several times. Once out of the instrument, Charlie hurls it at his rival, but hits the shady customer instead. The fight spreads to the kitchen, from where Charlie hurls a plate of pastry, splattering his boss and the customer. Aiming for his rival, Charlie hits his boss with a rolling-pin; the crook, meanwhile, disappears into the safe while Charlie takes refuge inside a trunk. The crook reappears with the jewellery, keeping all at bay with a revolver – all, that is, except Charlie, who pops out of the trunk to flatten the thief with the rolling pin. Charlie leaps into heroic stance, embraces the pawnbroker's daughter, and permits himself one final devastating kick to the clerk.

Impossible though it is to choose a 'best' Chaplin Mutual, *The Pawnshop* would have to be considered in the top three. It is so well-constructed, and filled with memorable bits of business, that most people have probably seen at least part of it. This applies especially to a scene, described above, in which Charlie dissects a clock, a virtuoso routine often selected as a self-contained extract for home-movie use. Among the many other notable scenes are Charlie's triumphant stance when conquering the villain (the nearest visual equivalent to a fanfare) and those of opportunistic Charlie gaining the sympathies of others, as when seeking 'protection' by Edna Purviance (*qv*) or miming several offspring in order

to persuade employer Henry Bergman (*qv*) to reinstate him. Bergman, who made his first appearance with Chaplin in this film, was to remain part of the comedian's unit for thirty years. Many revival prints of *The Pawnshop* are slightly marred by damage at the conclusion, when Charlie gives John Rand (*qv*) a final back-kick. Despite the comparatively large number of copies bearing this fault, this moment exists undamaged, and may be seen intact in *The Gentleman Tramp* (*qv*).

(See also: Campbell, Eric; Fighting; Home movies; Kelly, James T.; Mutual; *New Janitor, The*; Reissues; Television; Titling; Twists and transformations; Video releases; Villains; *Young Charlie Chaplin*)

PAY DAY

(Chaplin film)
Released by First National, 2 April 1922. Produced, written and directed by Charles Chaplin. Photographed by Rollie Totheroh. Two reels.

With Charlie Chaplin (himself), Mack Swain (foreman), Edna Purviance (foreman's daughter), Phyllis Allen (Charlie's wife), Henry Bergman, Syd Chaplin, Allan Garcia, John Rand, Loyal Underwood (builders).

Charlie arrives late for work on a busy building site. He tries to appease the foreman by the gift of a lily. Charlie sets to work in a trench, jabbing his pick-axe into a colleague's behind. The foreman, observing how little earth Charlie is digging, reminds him he is being paid by the hour – not the ounce. The foreman's daughter arrives, bringing lunch for her father. Charlie accompanies her in the site lift, then bobs up and down on the lift, admiring the young lady. Still aloft, Charlie collects and stacks bricks as they are hurled up by his fellow-builders. Charlie treads on a nail and sits on a barrel placed on the lift. The lift continually descends and reascends as Charlie, unaware of its periodic absence, sits down. Lunch time, and Charlie, having nothing to eat, resorts to picking up the foreman's scraps. The lift reascends, this time with a hot poker resting on the barrel. Charlie sits and gets a scorched rear. He hands the poker

Charlie greets cheerless boss Mack Swain in **Pay Day**
BFI Stills, Posters and Designs

to the foreman, sitting above, who drops it to the ground. Another builder sits on it. Still another worker places his lunch on the lift, which ascends. Charlie gets a free lunch as its owner ponders the disappearing food. The food consists of a small loaf of bread and a hot dog. Charlie makes a 'frankfurter sandwich' by drilling through the bread and hammering in the hot dog. The lift rises to the foreman, who leaves a banana on it. The banana is delivered to Charlie, and its empty skin returns to the foreman. Lunch over, Charlie resumes catching and stacking bricks. At the end of the day, the builders receive their wages. Charlie, 'underpaid on his overtime', complains, but the foreman sends him on his way with a rap in the mouth. Outside, Charlie's wife awaits. Charlie, calculating four times two as 'nine', returns to the pay office. He goes

through the figures with the foreman, and seems pacified when given a dollar *less*. In the street, Charlie is counting his money when his wife appears from behind. Unaware that she is following, Charlie pauses to admire a pretty girl. Placing part of his money in his hat, Charlie prepares to pursue the young lady, but turns to see his glowering spouse. Dutifully, he takes some money from his pocket and hands it over. His wife takes the remaining sum from his hat as Charlie swipes back the first amount from her bag. Ordering him to follow, the wife sets off for home; Charlie disappears in the opposite direction. Late that night, Charlie's colleagues, very drunk, emerge from a bar. Charlie, the last to leave, tries drunkenly to light a cigar. Having given up, he rests on his cane, which manages to perch on the bars of a sewer grating without slipping between. Eventually, Charlie's luck runs out and he tumbles over. Some of the party leave for home. The remaining four sing 'Sweet Adeline', earning them a soaking from an irate neighbour. Charlie puts up a friend's umbrella, but the next missile is a more solid washing bowl. They prepare to leave, but Charlie's overcoat is buttoned into that of a fellow-reveller. As he is dragged along the street, Charlie acknowledges a puzzled policeman. Charlie is separated from his friend and finishes up wearing both overcoats, buttoned together. Charlie notices rain, and puts up the man's umbrella once more. Charlie gives the other man his cane to hold aloft, and departs with the umbrella. Charlie waits for a streetcar but, on its arrival, is beaten in the rush. He misses the next when a limousine stops in his path. Charlie staggers back to the pavement, losing both overcoats and treading over them. The owner of coat and umbrella returns, and Charlie swaps the umbrella for his cane. Trying to light his cigar, Charlie strikes a match on the man's behind. There is a rush for another streetcar. Charlie gains admittance by climbing over the crowd, but is pushed out at the vehicle's front

entrance. The last car of the night is rendered barely visible by the numbers of passengers clinging to its exterior. Charlie hangs on, but must relinquish half his grip when the conductor demands his fare. Charlie holds on to a fellow-passenger's trousers, but these are torn off, leaving Charlie to run behind the vehicle. Charlie, abandoning the pursuit, drunkenly mistakes a lunch wagon for another streetcar, 'strap-hanging' on a suspended salami. The proprietor throws him out. Charlie, still gripping the salami, tries to light it, then carries the sausage in his back pocket. Chancing upon one of his friends, Charlie asks him for directions, then drunkenly proceeds in the wrong direction. Charlie finally reaches home at five in the morning. His wife is sleeping, but with rolling-pin at the ready. Charlie places his remaining coins under the doormat and, entering their apartment, puts out the cat. Switching on the light, Charlie has to shoo away a host of other felines, who have consumed whatever food may have awaited him. Charlie does at least have some bread and the salami, the latter of which is stolen by yet another cat. Charlie thinks there may be another kitty when he treads on a child's squeaking toy. He tries the bedroom door, but develops hiccups. After a drink of water, he creeps into the bedroom, pausing to oil his creaking boots. He sits, unbuttons his coat, then quickly replaces it as his wife is woken by the alarm clock. Pretending to have been to bed, he sets off, ostensibly to work, but goes instead to the bathroom. He intends to sleep in the bath, but inadvertently steps into a full tub. To make himself comfortable, he turns on the 'hot' tap. His wife follows him into the bathroom. Charlie, fully clothed, goes through the motions of bathing then is ordered out. He tries to re-enter the bedroom, but is told to leave. Thinking the coast is clear, Charlie reclaims the money he left under the mat, but has to hand it over when his wife returns with the milk. She nags at Charlie as he sets off for another day.

Chaplin's last two-reeler resembles a more polished Essanay, its two-half structure combining echoes of *Work* and *A Night Out* (both *qv*). Its technique, however, is several leagues ahead of these earlier comedies, particularly in the impressive night photography dominating its latter scenes. It had begun as a story entitled *Come Seven*, with Charlie and Mack Swain (*qv*) in a different line of business (see **Abandoned projects**).

'A new Chaplin comedy, of course, is an event in the motion picture world,' declared the *New York Times* on 3 April 1922. It was decided that a reviewer's duty extended no further than announcing the film, a belief indicative of Chaplin's as yet unimpaired invulnerability to criticism. *Pay Day* was considered 'one of his best', even though it had long become standard practice to compare everything unfavourably to *Shoulder Arms* and *The Kid* (both *qv*). Singled out was Chaplin's ability to expose 'the irony of life' by means of a 'refreshing treatment of the commonplace'. This was illustrated by the scene in which Charlie's devotion to Edna Purviance (*qv*) is interrupted by the sudden appearance of limburger cheese; the review's comparison of this motif to the pranks played on mortals by the gods of classical mythology, while perhaps tenable, may serve in its turn to typify the sometimes over-extravagant interpretations being placed on Chaplin's work in the early 1920s.

With or without malodorous dairy products, there seems to have been a definite sense of not knowing how to cast Edna by this time. She has little involvement in *Pay Day*, and Charlie's ambitions towards her are doomed by her status and his own loveless marriage, in this film, to Phyllis Allen (*qv*). From today's perspective, *Pay Day* is not an outstanding Chaplin film and, as his last two-reel subject, is typical of the way many comedians would not put their best into short subjects that preceded more ambitious feature-length projects. His next film, *The Pilgrim* (*qv*), was to be a featurette and would represent his final link with the short comedies in which his reputation had been made.

Chaplin's reissue version of *Pay Day* derives from a crystal-clear master; as with several other films, there is, in addition, surviving material deriving from an entirely different negative, taken with a separate camera. This is particularly apparent in the scene where Charlie, counting his pay, is unaware of his wife standing behind. The long-defunct home-movie extracts distributed in Britain are evidently from this second version.

(See also: Alcohol; Animals; *Count, The*; *Dog's Life, A*; *Easy Street*; Essanay; First National; *Floorwalker, The*; Food; Garcia, Allan; Home movies; Occupations; Policemen; Rand, John; Smoking; Streetcars; Titling; Trick photography; Underwood, Loyal)

PEARCE, PEGGY
(1894 or 1896–1964)

Keystone actress, formerly with D.W. Griffith (*qv*), Peggy Pearce was Chaplin's first real-life romantic involvement after arriving in Hollywood. She is the leading lady of Chaplin's *His Favorite Pastime* (*qv*); other Keystone films include Arbuckle's *Help! Help! Hydrophobia!* (1913) and *'Twixt Love and Fire* (1914). Peggy Pearce became known later under the name 'Viola Barry'. Among her post-Keystone films are *Ace of the Saddle* (1919), *Sex* (1920) and *Good Loser* (1921). She is reported as one of Buster Keaton's erstwhile brides in *Seven Chances* (1925).

(See also: Arbuckle, Roscoe 'Fatty'; Keaton, Buster; Keystone; Women)

PICKFORD, MARY
(1893–1979)

Born Gladys Smith in Toronto, Canada, Mary Pickford became known ultimately as 'America's Sweetheart'. She entered pictures in 1909, working, like many others, for D.W. Griffith (*qv*) at Biograph. By 1913 she was starring in features for Famous Players-Artcraft (Paramount), and was among those whose demands forced movie stars' salaries up to high levels, mainly in parity with Chaplin; Richard Griffith and Arthur Mayer's *The Movies* states that each time Chaplin was paid more by a new studio, she demanded a corresponding salary raise from Adolph Zukor. As detailed elsewhere, this trend led to a move to First National (*qv*) and, ultimately, to her formation in 1919 of United Artists (*qv*) with Chaplin, Griffith and Douglas Fairbanks (*qv*). Pickford and Fairbanks also entered into the partnership of marriage the following year, a ceremony numbering Chaplin among its guests.

Mary's child-like image, topped with blonde ringlets, belied an astute business brain. She enforced her views when, in 1922, Chaplin and Fairbanks opposed her by supporting Griffith's desire to sell *Orphans of the Storm* to an outside

*With Douglas Fairbanks and **Mary Pickford** at the couple's home, Pickfair*

distributor; she was similarly impatient for Chaplin to contribute a big moneymaker to United Artists, following the delay imposed by his First National contract and the financial disappointment of *A Woman of Paris* (*qv*). Chaplin's *My Life in Pictures* recalls, with amazement and sadness, her familiarity with intricate market terminology and the phrase with which she once addressed her partners: 'It behoves us, gentlemen.'

Griffith eventually departed, but otherwise the United Artists partnership endured. The same was not true of the Pickford-Fairbanks marriage, which broke up in 1933 and ended legally in 1935; Mary later wed actor Charles 'Buddy' Rogers. Like Fairbanks, Mary Pickford survived somewhat as a talkie attraction, but in modified form; her last starring film, *Secrets*, was released in the same year as her split from Fairbanks. Among her final credits was that of executive producer for the Marx Brothers' unmemorable *Love Happy*, in which she took no active part. Neither she nor Chaplin retained an interest in United Artists after the mid-1950s. They had long since become estranged, not least owing to business differences, culminating in Chaplin's 1943 legal action against David O. Selznick, who was by then a partner in UA. Scott Eyman's 1990 Pickford biography, with access to released papers, suggests that by 1948 the actress may have been volunteering information to the FBI concerning Chaplin's alleged political leanings. Publicly and privately, it seems, her views on Chaplin veered between defence and condemnation; in the mid-1950s, she defended him against the political smears that were being made in his absence, despite having possibly contributed to his persecution in the United States. Eyman quotes a Pickford associate of the late 1940s, Malcolm Boyd, to the effect that she maintained an underlying affection for Chaplin, in remembrance of their shared experiences in movies' fledgling days. She declined to meet Chaplin on his return to America in 1972, issuing a statement (via business manager Matty Kemp) to the effect that she 'shares the opinion of many of the people here that Chaplin sympathised with a country that was a great threat to our country'. Several commentators have speculated that Chaplin and Pickford had only ever tolerated each other's presence for the sake of Fairbanks; perhaps more cogent is Mary Pickford's own much-quoted summation of Chaplin as 'that obstinate, suspicious, egocentric, maddening, and lovable genius of a problem child'.

(See also: Abandoned projects; Austin, Albert; *Bond, The*; Campbell, Eric; De Limur, Jean; Documentaries, compilations; Female impersonation; Florey, Robert; Guest appearances; Marx, Groucho; *Nice and Friendly; Pilgrim, The*; Politics; Religion; Swain, Mack; Wartime)

THE PILGRIM

(Chaplin film)
Released by First National, 25 February 1923. Written and directed by Charles Chaplin. Associate director: Chuck Riesner. Photographed by Rollie Totheroh. Four reels, 4,300 feet.

With Charlie Chaplin (himself, as the 'pilgrim'), Edna Purviance (Miss Brown), Sydney Chaplin (eloper/train conductor/little boy's father), 'Dinky' Dean (Riesner) (bratty little boy), Mae/Mai Wells (his mother), Chuck Riesner (crook), Tom Murray (sheriff), Kitty Bradbury (Mrs Brown), Mack Swain (large deacon), Loyal Underwood (small deacon), Henry Bergman (sheriff on train), Raymond Lee (applauding boy in congregation), Jack Wilson (swimming clergyman at beginning).

Charlie, an escaped convict, borrows a suit of clothes while its owner is bathing. The outfit is that of a clergyman and it is thus attired that the convict arrives at the railroad station. Charlie is seen by an eloping couple who, taking him for a real parson, want him to perform an

impromptu marriage ceremony. Suddenly pointed out by the anxious groom, Charlie runs away, but heads back in the opposite direction on the approach of the girl's angry father. The girl is returned home, and the clerically-attired escapee, unnoticed by two policemen, chooses a random destination. Covering his eyes, Charlie stabs a pin into a printed route but chooses Sing Sing. His next attempt accidentally punctures the rear end of a passerby. The final effort, *sans* pin, lands upon Dallas, Texas. There is sufficient money in the stolen clothes to finance a ticket; the ticket, a lengthy affair, is caught in the door, but Charlie catches his train. Initially, Charlie adopts the customary hobo's seat, beneath the coach, but is shown to a place within the train. Coincidentally, one of the towns en route to Dallas, Devil's Gulch, is expecting the arrival of a new minister, the Rev. Philip Pim. Sunday morning, and as the train enters Devil's Gulch, the good townspeople are waiting at the station. Charlie is sitting beside the man he had jabbed with a pin. The man is reading a newspaper containing a photo of Charlie and details of the reward offered for his capture. Charlie, eating crackers, splutters on seeing the article. He is even more nervous to see his neighbour sporting a sheriff's badge. Charlie disembarks, but is alarmed when

meeting still another sheriff. Instead of being arrested, he is greeted as the Rev. Pim and introduced to his congregation. As they head for the church, Charlie swipes a bottle of whisky from the back pocket of a heftily-built deacon. A telegraph boy hands the Deacon a message; being without his glasses, he asks Charlie to read it. The message is that Rev. Pim has been delayed a week. Charlie pretends it is a misdirected telegram that reads 'Am feeling much better – Lizzie.' The telegram is torn up and discarded. Charlie and the deacon proceed in an identical, self-consciously saintly manner until a young lad drops a banana skin so that they will slip over. The whisky bottle, in Charlie's back pocket, is smashed; the deacon assumes it has broken in his own pocket, and both men are too embarrassed to mention it. They continue their journey, now walking rather awkwardly. In church, the 'Reverend' must hold a service, but at first reacts as if in court. He is unsure whether to rise or sit in accord with the congregation, and busks his way through the first hymn. He has to be prodded into organizing the collection, and nearly forgets himself when taking out a cigarette. Pressed into giving a sermon, he presents a vividly-mimed account of David's battle with Goliath. Charlie earns applause from the young lad, takes 'curtain calls', then offers around the collection boxes once more. The Deacon eyes Charlie incredulously as the nonplussed congregation files out. Charlie tries to escape via the back window, only to meet the sheriff. Charlie pretends to pick flowers from around the window, and retreats inside. The deacon entrusts to him the collection, and they depart, again in synchronous, pious-looking strides. Outside, Charlie is introduced to the widowed Mrs Brown and her daughter, with whom he is to lodge. Elsewhere, at the nearby saloon, arrives 'Howard Huntington – alias "Nitro Nick" – alias "Picking Pete"'. Pretending to ask directions, he picks someone's pocket. Charlie and his new-found friends pass the saloon, and the thief, recognizing the 'Reverend', goes to greet him. Charlie, preferring to maintain his imposture, passes him by. The villain contemplates the time he spent as Charlie's cellmate, then watches him enter Mrs Brown's home. Mrs Brown shows Charlie the family album as her daughter serves tea. Visitors arrive, a cheerless-looking couple with a small but boisterous son. Discouraged from pawing his parents, the boy decides to punch Charlie in the face. He is passed between Mama, Papa and Charlie, the while punching Charlie and his father, whose glasses are knocked to the floor. He jabs a knitting needle into Charlie's posterior then explores the goldfish bowl, from which he scoops water over Charlie. Removed from the bowl's proximity, the boy is seen to have sticky paper attached to his knees. Once this is peeled away, he jams it into Papa's face. The boy's father goes away to clean up, leaving his wife to chastise the infant. This she does, ineffectively, leaving the room with the paper adorning her behind. After an exchange of smiles, Charlie detaches the child from his coat-tail with a gentle boot. In the kitchen, Charlie tries to help the young Miss Brown by placing a rolling-pin on a high shelf. He secures it after it has landed on his head. Miss Brown has prepared a dome-like cake. While she and Charlie attend to the cooking, the boy places his father's bowler hat over the cake. Charlie, distracted by the youngster, unwittingly glazes, ices and decorates the hat. The two deacons are present when the cake is brought in, as are the boy's parents (once his mother has removed the sticky paper). The parents are invited to stay, but politely decline; father cannot find his hat, and refuses to leave without it. His headgear is discovered after Charlie attempts to cut the 'cake'. Father, huffily, departs with his family. That evening, Charlie and Miss Brown are by the front gate, chatting, when Charlie's old cellmate arrives. Shaking Charlie by the hand, he introduces himself to Miss Brown as an old college chum of the minister. He is invited in, and very soon relieves the large deacon of his wallet. Charlie swipes it back, telling the Deacon he had dropped it. There is a discreet scuffle between Charlie and the thief, who manages to steal the wallet a second time. As the deacons make to leave, Charlie shows them a 'trick' by which he makes the deacon's wallet supposedly disappear into the thief's pocket. Charlie returns the wallet. Mrs Brown offers the deacon a payment on the mortgage; as it is the Sabbath, he asks her to wait until the following day. The deacons leave the house. The thief pretends to have missed his train, and is invited to stay the night. Once alone with Charlie, the thief tries to grab the money, but is fought off. Mrs Brown returns with candles and, despite another

attempted theft, the villain accompanies the others upstairs. Charlie foils the thief's attempt to return downstairs by summoning Miss Brown, ostensibly to fetch a glass of water. Charlie thinks he has locked the thief in, but he has already sneaked out of his room. Downstairs, Charlie leaps on to the thief's back, kicking shut the dresser drawers as he tries to steal the money. The thief dislodges Charlie by holding him over a lighted candle, then knocks him cold. The villain has escaped with the money by the time Miss Brown discovers Charlie. Once revived, Charlie sets out, promising to retrieve the cash. The thief enters the saloon, heading straight for the gaming table. The sheriff arrives at Mrs Brown's home and, having seen Charlie's picture in the newspaper, is convinced the 'parson' will not return. At the saloon, a hold-up is taking place. Charlie converts his clerical outfit into a desperado's costume and, while the gunmen have their victims covered, comes in and frisks the thief. Outside, a sheriff spots him and gives chase. Next morning, Charlie brings the money back to Miss Brown. The sheriff catches up with him and explains to Miss Brown that the prisoner must return to jail. The sheriff escorts Charlie to the Mexican border. He asks Charlie to pick him some flowers; Charlie obliges, but the sheriff wants some from 'over there'. Again Charlie obliges, but fails to get the message. Once the sheriff boots Charlie over the border and rides away, Charlie finally understands that he is free. He savours the moment until, seeing some Mexican bandits fighting it out, he continues on his way with one foot on each side of the border.

'Charlie Chaplin's next picture has been titled "The Pilgrim",' reported *Picture Show* on 25 November 1922, 'and is about an escaped convict who turns preacher. Now that this film is finished, it is expected that Charlie will join Mary Pickford, D.W. Griffith and Douglas Fairbanks as a member of the Big Four in the United Artists.' In addition to being Chaplin's final release for First National (*qv*), *The Pilgrim* also marked the end of his

shorter films. At four reels, it is really more of a featurette, but has seldom been listed among the comedian's full-length productions. It was also something of a farewell to Edna Purviance (*qv*), whose last appearance this was as Chaplin's leading lady. Chaplin tried to launch her as an independent name in his next production, *A Woman of Paris* (*qv*), and the later, unreleased *Sea Gulls* (or *A Woman of the Sea*), but Edna's film career was effectively over.

When embarking on the film, Chaplin risked offending religious sensitivities, particularly in America. As Dr F.C. MacKnight pointed out in *Classic Film Collector*, the choice of title was discreet, 'pilgrim' having the necessary theological connotations without being too specific. Despite this caution, there were objections to the film, either wholly or in part, from various regions in the USA, notably Pennsylvania. It is easy to see why: the suggestion of hypocritical intemperance on the part of a deacon might have caused outrage in certain quarters, ditto the notion of a convicted criminal proving to be at least the moral equal of a 'respectable' community (though the film is as much about the convict's adopted position bringing about his rehabilitation). Some, indeed, might have construed Chaplin's mimed version of David and Goliath – however lauded as a virtuoso piece – as sacrilege.

When *The Pilgrim* was reissued as part of *The Chaplin Revue* (*qv*), much of the footage was 'stretch-printed' in order to adapt it to projection at sound speed. Although its companion pieces, *A Dog's Life* and *Shoulder Arms* (both *qv*), were

The Pilgrim *delivers a stirring account of David and Goliath*

also subjected to this treatment in some degree, the effect is altogether more damaging to the flow of this film. An American laserdisc edition has been transferred at the correct speed, using an 'unstretched' copy.

Chaplin assembled a cast list for the *Revue*, but seemed unable to identify the actress playing the small boy's mother. This must have been rectified soon after, for the actress in question – Mai Wells – was named in the *Revue*'s promotional literature. Mai (sometimes known as 'Mae' or 'May') was a former stage actress, prolific in character parts during the 1920s. She died in 1941, aged 79. Among her other films are *Excuse Me* (1925) and *Blondes By Choice* (1927). (She is, incidentally, credited in *The Pilgrim* among the '500 Famous Casts' in a 1933 UK reference work, *The World Film Encyclopaedia*.)

The Pilgrim has always had something of a mixed reputation. The present generation may perhaps find the stretch-printing a disadvantage, but there were conflicting reviews even in 1923. The New York *Times* thought it less worthy than *Shoulder Arms* or *The Kid*, but reported a crowd laughing at each of the film's eight daily screenings at the Strand theatre. The opinion was that Chaplin had neither repeated himself nor 'played low to the mob with haphazard slapstick. He has aimed at something in his new work and hit it.' By contrast, the *Times* in London all but dismissed it as 'aimless in story and formless in structure', a retrogression to the 'primitive' methods of his 'early manner', from which the reviewer had found welcome relief in *The Kid* (*qv*). *Variety*'s Sime Silverman, never an unconditional admirer, thought it 'not sensationally funny, not as much so as expected from Chaplin in four reels'. Sime, who would have preferred the film at half the length, singled out Charlie's absent-minded climbing on the train's undercarriage as the 'nearest approach to genuine humor'. The mimed sermon was 'illogically done in very broad if not uncouth style'. By contrast, Robert E. Sherwood, admittedly a Chaplin devotee, included *The Pilgrim* in his survey, *The Best Movies of 1922–23*; Sherwood considered it not Chaplin's funniest, but the most typical, 'a dramatization of Chaplin himself – an exposition of his point of view, a recitation of his creed'. Chaplin, in Sherwood's view, had fooled clergymen, intellectuals and revolutionaries into believing he was one

of their number, while remaining in fact 'an agnostic, in the most inclusive sense'; consequently, Charlie as bogus cleric was nothing less than autobiography.

Sherwood regarded the obnoxious youngsters in *The Pilgrim* as 'atonement for his glorification of childhood' in *The Kid*. Chaplin admitted 'Dinky Dean' Riesner (*qv*) to be the Kid's antithesis, as the boy who so irritates both the preacher and the child's own father, Syd Chaplin (*qv*). In various interviews, as for *Unknown Chaplin* (*qv*) and the enthusiasts' magazine *Limelight*, Riesner has explained that, as a normally well-behaved child, he had to be convinced that Charlie and Syd really *enjoyed* being punched.

Just as *The Pilgrim*'s 1926 UK reissue was punningly described as 'the great revival', so has there been a more recent reappraisal of its position within the Chaplin canon. Jeffrey Vance, writing in *Limelight*, quotes director Lewis Milestone's observation of the way *The Pilgrim* establishes its premise and destination within three brief cuts, the whole being presented in a disciplined four reels rather than as a full-length feature. Vance compares its plotline to Molière's *Le Tartuffe* – also about an escaped convict posing as a religious man – and its routines, the mimed sermon in particular, to the acts Chaplin would have known in British music-hall. Vance considers the satirical content more than evident, albeit not as pronounced as in the later features, while making an interesting point by citing the finale – in which Charlie straddles the international border – as anticipation of Chaplin's future political difficulties. (Elsewhere in the same issue, Dr Constance Kuriyama notes how *The Pilgrim* is set in 'an imaginary Texas with no Rio Grande on the Mexican border'!)

A sidelight: during February and March 1996, an exhibition of the works of photographer James Abbe was presented at London's National Portrait Gallery. Among the film stars represented were Douglas Fairbanks, Mary Pickford, Ben Turpin (all *qv*) and Chaplin, in a character portrait from *The Pilgrim*.

(See also: Alcohol; Bradbury, Kitty; Children; Costume; Dual rôles; Fairbanks, Douglas; Griffith, D.W.; Lee, Raymond; Music; Pickford, Mary; Policemen; Politics; Prisons; Purviance, Edna; Religion; Reissues; Swain, Mack; Television; Underwood, Loyal; United Artists; Video releases; Wilson, Jack)

POLICE 🎩

(Chaplin film)
Released by General Film Company, 27 March 1916. Produced by Essanay. Written and directed by Charles Chaplin. Photographed by Harry Ensign. Also known as: *Charlie in the Police* [*sic*]. Two reels. 2,050 feet.

With Charlie Chaplin (Convict 999, alias 'Charlie'), Edna Purviance (girl in burgled house), Wesley Ruggles (crooked preacher), James T. Kelly (drunk/flophouse vagrant), John Rand (policeman), Leo White (greengrocer/flophouse owner/? policeman), Bud Jamison (prissy flophouse customer), Fred Goodwins (policeman), Billy Armstrong (policeman/? miser – see below).

Charlie, released from prison, places a small gratuity in his waistcoat pocket. He meets a preacher who, reducing him to tears, persuades Charlie to 'go straight' while surreptitiously picking his pocket. When Charlie sees a drunk, his new resolve prevents him from the stealing the old man's pocket watch. Charlie passes a greengrocer's. The tubby proprietor looks on with increasing impatience as Charlie samples the wares. Charlie finally decides to buy something, but discovers his money has been taken. Charlie meets the preacher again, who this time is talking to the drunk. The preacher excuses himself, and Charlie notices that the drunk has also been robbed. He sets off in search of the crooked 'preacher', but meets instead a genuine example. Once more offered help to 'go straight', Charlie loses his temper and chases the unfortunate man through the streets, knocking over a policeman in the process. The cop gives chase; Charlie loses the preacher, but takes to his heels once more on seeing the policeman. That night, Charlie arrives at a flophouse. There is one man waiting to go in; Charlie tries to jump the queue. While they are arguing, a long procession of customers make their way in. Charlie is eventually left arguing by himself. The flophouse owner admits the sorry parade of derelicts, taking a coin from each; one entrant gains free admission by a toss of the coin, another, a tubercular type, is accommodated free out of compassion. Charlie searches for a coin and, having none, feigns a cough and sunken cheeks. He is thrown out, though not before yanking the proprietor's beard. On the street, he meets a policeman; they exchange indignities, concluding with Charlie tripping the officer with his cane. Exit Charlie, policeman in pursuit. In an alleyway, Charlie is accosted by a hold-up man. He searches through Charlie's pockets while Charlie picks the pocket of the would-be thief. The robber, recognizing Charlie as his former cellmate, engages him as accomplice in a burglary. They are spotted by a policeman, who shadows them as they approach the house. At the front door, Charlie makes plain his inexperience as housebreaker; the policeman saunters up, playing along with them prior to making an arrest. He even passes a mallet to Charlie, who drops his pretence of idiocy by knocking the policeman unconscious. After giving up his attempt to prise open the window, Charlie tries the door, which was open all along. They make their way from hallway to lounge, where Charlie's cane pulls over a stand filled with ornaments. The burglars hide, Charlie opting for a space beneath the rug. He offers up a small prayer. Disturbed by the noise, a girl descends the stairway. Unaware of her presence, the thieves continue their business, Charlie drilling open the piano lid. The girl quietly phones the police. Charlie's partner queries the point in opening the piano; Charlie emphasizes his purpose by crashing his hand noisily upon the keys. There is an even greater noise when the other burglar sits him down on the keyboard. Charlie scurries into the kitchen, and becomes entangled in a wicker basket. Once freed, he attempts to open the stove as if it were a safe. Panic returns when an alarm clock in his pocket sounds off. The other burglar gets him back to work; Charlie, having filled the basket with such things as flower vases, exits into the hall only to meet the girl. He rushes back to the lounge, and his partner goes to investigate. The girl begs the thief not to go upstairs, where her mother is seriously ill. She offers to help them 'go straight', and provides them with a meal. At the kitchen table, the second thief's gaze is concentrated on the rings adorning the girl's hand. He resumes looting while the girl persuades Charlie to reform. The burglars prepare to leave, one with a sack, Charlie with his arms full of unwieldy items. Charlie decides he cannot carry the piano, and cordially shakes the girl's hand before leaving. The other burglar decides to look upstairs; the girl begs him not to,

and stands in his way. Charlie intervenes just as his colleague is about to use violence; he suggests they have enough and should leave, but the other man disagrees. When Charlie prevents him going upstairs, they come to blows. The police, meanwhile, are on their way. The cop who was knocked out earlier regains consciousness, but when Charlie raises the sack of loot to strike his partner, the cop is caught on the backswing. Reinforcements arrive, and the unscrupulous thief heads for the kitchen, firing a revolver. The first cop rushes around to the back of the house. Charlie, at the piano, leaps up and down to dodge the gunfire. The thief climbs through the window, startling the cop with a final gunshot, and makes his escape. Charlie, panicking, runs around the kitchen table, grabbing a drink en route. The police are ushered in, and Charlie, having emptied the bottle, leans out of the window, grabs the policeman's truncheon and knocks him cold. The other officers arrest Charlie, but the girl tells them he is her husband. Charlie escorts them out, but hurries inside when the first cop reappears. Charlie returns the stolen items and is rewarded with a silver dollar. The cop, determined to catch him, disappears around the back once more. Charlie has now resolved to go straight. Outside the house, he instinctively bites the dollar to check its authenticity, then goes on his way. Arms outstretched, he greets a new life, only to turn hurriedly when the cop returns. The scene irises out on the scowling officer.

Police is essentially a comic reworking of *His Regeneration* (*qv*), a G.M. Anderson film in which Chaplin had made a guest appearance several months earlier; in turn, its inept housebreaking probably owes something to an old Karno sketch, *Jail Birds*. Chaplin's last official Essanay film, *Police* is in many ways the most mature entry in the series. While there is still too much in the way of frenetic action and unbelievably silly policemen, Chaplin's comedy is increasingly whimsical (clapping in time as his partner hops up and down with a sore foot) and contrasted with authentic drama. There

is social comment of a sort, and the photography – mostly functional in the Essanay films – is sometimes genuinely impressive, as when the two burglars are seen approaching the house only in shadow, or in vignetted close-ups that cut from the villain to the girl's ringed hand, panning slowly up to her face. None of these finer points were noticed by the New York *Times* which, on 22 May 1916, acknowledged Chaplin's final Essanay by referring to his 'familiar tricks', suggesting it to be a matter of opinion as to whether it was funny: 'If one likes Chaplin, it is; if one doesn't, it closes the bill and one may leave.' One may in addition suspect a reluctance to express an opinion that might have offended either the New York *Times*' pro- or anti-Chaplin readers.

Police: Edna tells the law that housebreaker Charlie is her husband
BFI Stills, Posters and Designs

It is believed that Essanay amended Chaplin's final edit prior to release. Chaplin had left the studio, and was thus powerless to prevent the removal of an extended scene in the flophouse. This had been shot for an intended feature film, *Life*, itself abandoned for reasons of time; the sequence was finally released in 1918, when the studio assembled a 'new' Chaplin comedy, *Triple Trouble* (*qv*), using a mixture of old footage and newly-shot bridging scenes. Comparison with the flophouse scene in *Triple Trouble* poses the question of how it could fit into *Police*: in *Police* Charlie, penniless, feigns illness to obtain a bed but is thrown out; in *Triple Trouble* he has enough money to afford a cigar, and enters the establishment unchallenged. It may be surmised that Chaplin filmed alternate versions of his arrival at the flophouse, and that Essanay may have substituted the rejected version when re-editing *Police*. Either way, *Police* does not seem an especially short two-reeler, despite the apparent deletion. An extended version of *Police*, incorporating both the flophouse and kitchen scenes of *Triple Trouble*, has been assembled and incorporated into a documentary, *The Chaplin Puzzle*. The implication is that Chaplin had intended an extra-length comedy running some three reels; the sequence of events in this version has Charlie making *two* visits to the flophouse, on the nights before and after his employment as kitchen hand. This edit suggests that Edna, as the lady of the house, recognizes Charlie as her former colleague in the kitchen; the author is not convinced by this reasoning, and does not believe the kitchen scenes to have been in Chaplin's original cut.

The author's print of *Police*, from a silent-era reissue, has titling that seems to adhere to the original text. It also provides a cast list, offering some clue as to which scenes were originally included. Billy Armstrong (*qv*) is identified as a 'miser', although his character appears only in the 'Life' segment of *Triple Trouble*, suggesting the inclusion of this scene at least until the cast list had been compiled. No mention is made of any characters from the kitchen sequence.

The video restoration mentioned above has yet to be seen in Britain at the time of writing. The UK Palace video release crops the finale, but retains the short section missing from the BBC copy, that in which Charlie turns and flees from a cop after chasing away the preacher. Titling in the latter is also slightly confused towards the end.

(See also: Abandoned projects; Anderson, G.M.; 'Bogus Chaplins'; Costume; Documentaries; Essanay; *Funniest Man in the World, The*; Goodwins, Fred; Guest appearances; Jamison, William 'Bud'; Karno Company, The; Kelly, James T.; Policemen; Pollard, Harry 'Snub'; Rand, John; Reissues; Religion; Risqué humour; Ruggles, Wesley; Smoking; Television; Vagrancy; Video releases)

POLICEMEN 🎩

(Chaplin films *qv*)
Chaplin's screen character is by nature an outsider, and consequently at frequent odds with the law; it is therefore no surprise to see him as a convict (see **Prisons**) or in direct conflict with policemen. There are plenty of cops in the Keystone films as in *Twenty Minutes of Love*, *Those Love Pangs*, *Recreation*, *His Trysting Place* and many others especially *Tillie's Punctured Romance*. The policeman who appears at the end of *His Prehistoric Past* has been named by one source as Syd Chaplin (*qv*). Chester Conklin (*qv*) makes an archetypal Keystone lawman in *Making a Living*, *Between Showers* and *Mabel's Busy Day*; Edgar Kennedy (*qv*), in a sense the perfect comic officer in later Hal Roach comedies, performs this function in *Getting Acquainted*. The fame of the Keystone Cops has sometimes led to them being miscredited whenever comic policemen appear, as in a *Radio Times* billing for Chaplin's first Essanay, *His New Job*. The second Essanay, *A Night Out*, includes a cop who seems remarkably indifferent to drunks Chaplin and Turpin, despite the protests of Leo White (*qv*). *A Jitney Elopement* casts Bud Jamison and Paddy McGuire (both *qv*) as a pair of officers whose imbecility sometimes eclipses that of their Keystone counterparts. Charlie has no trouble in disposing of them or other troublesome cops; examples here include *In the Park*, *A Woman* and, especially, *Police*, though in the latter film John Rand (*qv*) seems more persistent than most. For all their absurdity, comic cops in Chaplin's films do tend at least to present a plausible opposition, something that becomes all the more apparent in juxtaposition with the officers in *Triple Trouble*, whose unduly silly antics were not of Chaplin's creation. In the Mutuals, Charlie eludes cops in *The Count* and *The Rink*, but joins their number in *Easy Street*. The series concludes with prison escapee Charlie pursued by uniformed officers in *The Adventurer*. Such pursuit continues into the First National films, with the suspicious local officers in *A Dog's Life* and *The Kid*, also a puzzled policeman in *Pay Day*. According to contemporary publicity, Chaplin researched the difficulties of a traffic cop for *A Day's Pleasure* while in New York, where he observed Patrolman Larry O'Toole on duty at Broadway and 42nd Street. Charlie is chased again, though innocent, in *The Idle Class*, and is again unnerved when seeing Henry Bergman (*qv*) in police uniform at a costume ball. Bergman is a civilian-clad sheriff in *The Pilgrim*, while another, Tom Wilson (*qv*) proves a kindly specimen at the conclusion. In later comedies, another vigilant cop joins Charlie for an inadvertent clown act in *The Circus*, while there are frequent arrests in both *City Lights* and *Modern Times* (the latter of which sometimes depicts what became known later as 'police brutality'!). *Monsieur Verdoux* falls foul of the French *gendarmerie*; among other guardians of the law are the store detectives in *The Floorwalker* and, indirectly, Charles Chaplin Jr as the policeman in *Limelight*'s Harlequinade sequence.

(See also: Children; Essanay; First National; Keystone; Mutual; Parks; Statues; Television; Wood, Tom)

POLITICS 🎩

(Chaplin films *qv*)
Chaplin's much-cited status as 'little man' might be construed as inevitably placing him on the side of the oppressed, if not the outright revolutionary. This is true to an extent, the underdog rôle carrying with it an implied wish to reverse the odds, but to expect political consistency within the frenzied activity of Chaplin's earliest comedies is to dignify basic knockabout with an intellectual level it was never designed to possess. There are those who see the terrorist-style strikers of *Dough and Dynamite*, or Charlie's strike-breaking in *Behind the Screen*, as incompatible with his supposed later sentiments. The truth is that *anything* new, as assertive industrial protest most certainly was at that time, was considered ripe for kidding. Radical sentiments were then chiefly associated in the public mind with the stereotype of a bomb-throwing, foreign subversive, an image that recurs in many comedies of the 1920s. For example, a proposed union of the International Workers of the World, known as the IWW, was lampooned in a short comedy of 1916 called *Bill Joins the W.W.W.s* (it starred Tammany Young, later a stooge for W.C. Fields). The strikers of *Dough and Dynamite* fit the violent category, while those in *Behind the Screen* have more in common with the assumption that withdrawal of labour is motivated chiefly by laziness (a concept underlying the Boulting Brothers' 1959 satire *I'm All Right, Jack* and much subsequent British comedy of the next two decades). Chaplin did not begin to think of himself as especially political, or indeed profound in any way, until certain critics of the early 1920s told him so. Not that this was without foundation, though it seems fair to suggest that he was better when allowing

Winston Churchill and Chaplin were long-time friends

such ideas to be implied than specifically stated. In January 1972, he told the *Daily Mail*: 'When I was making all those films as the little man in the bowler hat I didn't want to change the world. My idea was to please the boss – and if he grinned I was happy.' The simple days when Charlie could blithely masquerade as the 'Prime Minister of Greenland' (in *Caught in a Cabaret*) had departed long before Chaplin was accused of taking politics seriously.

In the September 1983 *Classic Images*, Dr F.C. MacKnight wrote: 'I agree with Chaplin that there is no great social message in any film of his. But some Chaplin commentators are always looking for social criticism in his works because they think it ought to be there.' Chaplin was long acquainted with Winston Churchill, whose several meetings with the comedian included a visit to the set of *City Lights* (see *Unknown Chaplin*). Although Churchill was a knowledgeable and enthusiastic comedy fan, he was also a staunch Conservative, and it is difficult to imagine his friendship with Chaplin to have survived had the comedian displayed overtly left-wing sympathies. Indeed, Churchill seems to have been vaguely annoyed with Chaplin only once, after the comedian had sent him a print of one of his latter-day films; Churchill had written a letter of thanks and praise, to which the comedian had not responded. Chaplin, who had no idea of his friend's discomfiture until they met for lunch a year or two later,

was much taken with the fact that Churchill should have been so concerned over such a matter.

As noted in the main entry, *Modern Times* has sometimes been cited as the origin of Chaplin's political troubles in the USA, yet, as Theodore Huff was aware, the comedian was being asked if he were a 'Bolshevik' even in the early 1920s, not least after being accompanied on his 1921 European trip by a known radical, Max Eastman. David Robinson's *Chaplin: His Life and Art* publishes details of the extensive FBI file on Chaplin, dating back to Chaplin's reception of a visiting labour leader in 1922, and continuing even into the theft of his body after burial. This sometimes baffling, and frequently absurd, chronicle tries to give credence to the myth that Chaplin was really Israel Thonstein, offspring of an East European Jewish family who emigrated to England in the mid-19th century.

Chaplin swiftly became *persona non grata* in Nazi Germany, which banned *Modern Times* on its reputation alone, in addition to discouraging the screening of his earlier comedies. Chaplin publicly opposed fascism during the Spanish Civil War and, when replying to Hitler in *The Great Dictator*, encountered some resistance in America. According to Chaplin's 1962 *Esquire* interview with Harold Clurman (who, incidentally, regarded Chaplin as never politically-minded and, by then, 'avowedly apolitical'), one person who disagreed with the idea was William Randolph Hearst. When Hearst asked Chaplin to explain his antagonism to Hitler, he listened for a while before saying, 'Oh, I understand; it's because you're Jewish.' Chaplin was not, but did not believe in denying it. 'That,' he told Hearst, 'has nothing to do with it; I'm against Hitler because he's anti-people.' Opinions in the USA changed after that country's entry into the war; Jerry Epstein (*qv*) mentioned General Eisenhower having requested prints of *The Great Dictator* to show the troops in Europe.

In *Six Men*, Alistair Cooke wrote that Chaplin's 'much-abused "radical philosophy" was no more than an automatic theme song in favour of peace, humanity, "the little man", and other desirable abstractions – as humdrum politicians come out for mother-love and lower taxes'. He described also how Chaplin, 'in a single act of misjudgement, laid up years of grief for himself'. The act in question was to

deputize for the former US Ambassador to the Soviet Union by addressing a rally in San Francisco promoting Russian War Relief. This was followed by another address, via long-distance telephone, to a gathering at Madison Square Garden sponsored by the Congress of Industrial Organizations. The campaign was to encourage the Allies to open a Second Front in the war, as a means of reducing the burden on the Russians. This, at the time, was endorsed by several far-from-radical political figures, but later became a weapon in the hands of Chaplin's opponents. One might note further how America's post-war Communist hysteria brought with it a curious lapse in memory concerning the several wartime films praising the Soviet Union as an ally – a type of amnesia which did not apply when Chaplin's reputation was under discussion.

Chaplin's growing reputation for Communist leanings was noted around the world; an insert to the Italian *Film Rivista* of December 1946 ran a small column headed 'Charlie Chaplin *comunista*', in which the distinction was made between Chaplin's art and his millionaire status. During the next year, Chaplin – whose personal reputation had already taken a severe beating over a Mann Act trial – found himself under attack for both moral and political reasons. As detailed in the main entry, the New York press conference for *Monsieur Verdoux* became instead a kangaroo court in which Chaplin was asked directly if he believed in Communism. Chaplin denied it. Contrary to expectation, he was not summoned by the House Un-American Activities Committee, but the press conference had in any case performed much the same task. Among the issues brought up was that of Chaplin's citizenship; he was often criticized for 'refusing' to become a US citizen, even though a great many British subjects have lived, worked and paid taxes in America without feeling the need to take out papers (one might add that Chaplin consequently paid the US government a fortune in taxes, without receiving in exchange the right to vote or any guarantee of residency, thus posing the question as to who might be the injured party). Chaplin was British but, as he said to Ivar Ohman of *Leader* magazine in 1946, 'I am an American because I love America. I don't have to take out registration papers for that. But I know only one country; that is the world.'

Chaplin's frequent claim to be 'a citizen of the world' was idealistic but, to Cold War ears, sounded suspiciously Marxist. He was in any case soon glad he had his British passport, as detailed below.

Monsieur Verdoux was sometimes picketed by representatives of America's far right, as was his next picture, *Limelight*. The main entry describes something of Chaplin's fears concerning his political status during its creation, fears which turned out to have considerable foundation. Certainly, Chaplin was made to feel uncomfortable during his last days in America. In *Leaving a Doll's House*, Claire Bloom (*qv*) describes her first meeting with Chaplin, in a New York restaurant where other diners were 'commenting audibly, and far from kindly, about his political opinions'. Chaplin ignored them. When Chaplin planned to take Oona to see England, his application for a re-entry permit brought a visit from FBI men, demanding information concerning his politics, sex life and even ethnic origin. Despite having assured the FBI that, with a business worth $30 million, he was hardly a Communist, the trip was postponed. Once satisfied of his re-entry permit, Chaplin prepared to set sail. Jerry Epstein had dinner with him shortly beforehand, when the comedian expressed his love for the USA, which had provided him with opportunities of the sort totally unavailable in England. Chaplin, with his family, sailed for England on board the *Queen Elizabeth* on 17 September 1952; suspecting trouble, he had persuaded a reluctant Oona to agree to a joint account at the Bank of America. His decision was vindicated when, two days later, a cablegram from Attorney-General James McGranery announced that Chaplin's re-entry permit had been revoked and that he would need to go through the usual immigration procedures at Ellis Island – with no guarantee of acceptance – should he wish to return. The *Daily Mirror* of 20 September screamed the news with a banner headline: 'CHAPLIN SENSATION – Ban on return to U.S. until court of inquiry decide'.

The United States authorities planned to interview Chaplin when or if he returned to America. Chaplin, though upset, put on a defiant face and made his decision to stay overseas. At one gathering, he was asked if he had anything to say to America and, in a creditable imitation of the grouchy Calvin Coolidge exiting from the presidency, replied 'Yes – goodbye!' Chaplin's welcome in Britain combined the hospitality of a nation greeting one of its own with an implied condemnation of his expulsion from America. The London première of *Limelight* on 16 October attracted much favourable publicity, as did Chaplin's meanderings around former haunts (something he repeated, in various stages of incognito, for the rest of his life). The *Daily Mail* of 1 October 1952 reported Chaplin visiting a house in Lancaster Gate where, it was claimed, he was once a houseboy. One of his chief grumbles was the replacement of Waterloo Bridge, the old – and in his view, superior – bridge having vanished since his last visit in 1931.

Oona made a discreet return to America in November 1952, drawing all their money from the Bank of America and grabbing everything she could in the way of stocks and paperwork, which were crammed into a small suitcase. The domestic staff were paid off, and the Chaplin home, at 1085 Summit Drive, closed down. Chaplin was widely expected to live in Britain – in 1953, he was rumoured to be buying a house in London – but the family settled instead in Switzerland, at the Manoir de Ban in Corsier-Sur-Vevey. Even here, the United States government continued to pursue Chaplin for tax reasons, which prompted his swift withdrawal from United Artists (*qv*) in the mid-1950s. On 11 December 1958, *The Times* reported a forthcoming legal action against Chaplin from the US government, which planned to sue Chaplin for $1,242,532 (around £440,000), the main issue being 'whether Mr. Chaplin, a British subject, was entitled to claim status as a non-resident alien before April, 1953, when he moved to Switzerland' (to compound the pain, he was presently in the London Clinic to be operated on for an abscess on a wisdom tooth). The *Daily Mail* of 30 December recorded a settlement having been reached, by which the US was prepared to accept £150,000. In January 1959, Chaplin was photographed while in London to pay the American tax officials; he travelled, unrecognized, on the London Underground from Leicester Square to Bank. The settlement meant that, technically at least, Chaplin could apply to re-enter the United States, but he remained unmoved.

Chaplin's most public comment on contemporary America was, of course, his 1957 film *A King in New York*, produced in London. Neither this nor his 1959 anthology, *The Chaplin Revue* (*qv*), were screened in the United States until many years later. There were indications of a thaw in US opinion as the 1950s drew to a close. Richard Griffith and Arthur Mayer's mammoth film chronicle, *The Movies*, was published in 1957 and takes a strongly favourable and balanced view of Chaplin. There is even a section headed 'the greatest star of them all', defending *Monsieur Verdoux* and *Limelight* – both rejected by Americans at the time – through comparisons with Sophoclean irony and, in more immediate terms, Von Stroheim's doomed masterpiece, *Greed*. The only curious exception involves a different comparison, this time with the Marx Brothers, who were said to 'create the kind of anarchy Chaplin yearned for. He would have been happier in their world than in that to which another Marx beckoned him.' This is quite restrained by contemporary US standards, and the use of such a shopworn pun suggests an unwilling concession to then-current sensitivities. An equally reluctant disclaimer may be found in the narration of Robert Youngson's 1960 anthology, *When Comedy Was King*, which refers to its early Chaplin footage as 'blameless' in relation to the latter-day controversy surrounding the man.

In 1962, Chaplin told *The Times* that it was 'nonsense' to describe him as a Communist, though he spoke out against nuclear weapons and repeated his claim to have 'always been a peacemonger'. On 2 July of that year, the *Daily Telegraph* quoted the New York *Times*' opinion that the US government's immigration ban on Chaplin should be lifted. It is believed that President Kennedy – on whom the Ogden character in *A Countess From Hong Kong* was based – planned to do something about Chaplin's exile from the United States, but was assassinated before it could happen. Not everybody shared Kennedy's view. On 11 July 1962, *Variety* reported the previous day's press conference in East Berlin, to which Western journalists had been invited. The Communist bloc countries were complaining over the unavailability of Chaplin's films; 'The statement was immediately greeted with jeers by some of the Western journalists, with such remarks as "Isn't Chaplin a communist or a Socialist or a fellow traveller?" And that earned the retort: "It isn't Chaplin, it's United Artists. They hold the rights and are asking impossible prices." It's believed the real demand comes from Chaplin.'

Contrary to legend, the USSR did not accept Chaplin unconditionally: *Monsieur Verdoux* was not screened in Russia, on the grounds that its protagonist would have done better to use socialism as the solution to his economic difficulties; it was probably Chaplin's ejection from the USA that encouraged the Soviets to claim him for their own purposes, for on 22 June 1954 the *Daily Mail* published details of Moscow Radio having broadcast 'elaborate tributes' to the comedian. 'He came into our camp as simply and naturally as a tributary falls into a river.'

One doubts Chaplin inviting or encouraging such remarks, but they would have done nothing for his reputation in America. After visiting Hollywood in 1964, British historian Kevin Brownlow noted (in issue 40 of *Film*) that 'Chaplin is still an explosive topic,' before going on to quote an unnamed production executive, who called Chaplin 'just a tax-dodging Communist'.

America had undergone considerable social and political change by the time Chaplin was invited to return in 1972. Richard Nixon, who had earlier been one of Chaplin's more vociferous opponents, was still president (having yet to be massively discredited over the Watergate scandal), but had no involvement with the proceedings. On 29 November 1971, London's *Evening Standard* had quoted his comments to *Life* magazine about the forthcoming reissues and his attitudes towards America: 'I like America. I always did. I have no ill feelings. That's politics and when you live as long as I have, all politics looks pretty foolish'; yet when Chaplin was in London for the revival of *Modern Times* in January 1972, he was quoted by the *Daily Mirror* as 'emphatic' that he would not be returning to America. Chaplin is said to have changed his mind primarily through a desire to promote the reissues of his films. As noted under **Awards, honours**, Chaplin's 83rd birthday – on 16 April 1972 – was spent in Hollywood, where he received a special Oscar. Although Chaplin was made welcome, it is tempting to believe that he feared to some degree for the safety of his family; although his younger children also made the trip, Chaplin left them in Bermuda instead of bringing them into the United States.

Most of the people who knew Chaplin deny any strong radicalism on his part, merely a sympathy with the underdog and an overall belief in fair

play. Clurman's interview quotes him as saying, 'I can't stand Communists with their *system* and systems ... I hate systems.' Nevertheless, his political reputation continues to arouse controversy. During 1996, the more conservative sections of the British press noted the appearance of a new book from America, which was interpreted as offering positive proof of Chaplin's alliance with Communism and the Soviet Union. Among the startling 'revelations' was Chaplin's amendment of *Modern Times*' finale on the advice of a Soviet representative, a 'secret' so well kept that the New York *Times* made mention of it in its review of the film in 1936. When reviewing another such book in the Los Angeles *Times* the following year, David Robinson explained that Chaplin had amended the film's 'mawkish' ending – in which the *gamine* becomes a nun – on his own initiative, following a preview. He added that neither the FBI nor Chaplin files make mention of any such meeting with the visiting Russian.

A footnote to the subject of Chaplin and politics: casual examination of *Punch* for 22 September 1915 reveals a story concerning loud laughter in parliament at the mere mention of the Opposition leader, a Mr Chaplin. 'The only inference we can draw from these mysterious outbursts of merriment,' said *Punch*, 'is that the Members of Parliament had confused the Leader of the Opposition with another person of the same name.'

(See also: Boats, ships; Childhood; Documentaries, compilations; *Pilgrim, The*; Public appearances; Reissues; Women)

POLLARD, HARRY 'SNUB' (1886–1962)

(Chaplin films *qv*)
Slightly-built, Australian-born comedian (real name Harold Fraser), characterized by a drooping moustache. Pollard's heyday was in the 1920s at the Hal Roach studio, having graduated to his own series after supporting Harold Lloyd. It is likely that Pollard made Roach's acquaintance when both were working at Essanay (*qv*) during 1915. Less well known is that Pollard may be seen in some of the Essanay-Chaplin comedies. Though difficult to identify without the famous moustache, he is recognizable as the ice cream vendor in *By the Sea* and has been identified among

the flophouse types in *Police* and *Triple Trouble*. He is reported also in *His Regeneration*. Pollard's starring career was in trouble by the late 1920s, by which time he had descended to Weiss Brothers shorts; sound relegated him to minor supporting rôles, typified by his contribution to *Limelight* as one of the street musicians.

(See also: Chase, Charley; Underwood, Loyal)

POLO, MALVINA

Daughter of actor Eddie Polo, Malvina Polo plays 'Paulette' in *A Woman of Paris* (*qv*). Her other rôles include that of 'Marietta' in Erich von Stroheim's *Foolish Wives* (1922).

PRISONS

(Chaplin films *qv*)
It may be significant that each series for Essanay, Mutual and First National (all *qv*) ends with a film in which Charlie – legitimately or, more usually, otherwise – leaves jail. *Police* begins with Charlie rejoining the harsh outside world after being released; *The Adventurer* sees him on the run from the authorities; while *The Pilgrim* repeats the idea, with Charlie adopting clerical garb as temporary disguise. The related films *Police* and *Triple Trouble* show Charlie wearing what seems to be a striped

Prisons: *Charlie's mug shot in* The Adventurer

waistcoat, though this may be instead merely the striped longjohns of the period (Gus Elen, a boyhood idol of Chaplin's, was often seen with such striped sleeves). Charlie lands back in jail in both *City Lights* and *Modern Times*; the consequences are altogether more serious when *Monsieur Verdoux* is executed in prison, and there are hints of incarceration in other films. *The Great Dictator* has a scene taking place in a concentration camp and, as noted elsewhere, Chaplin evidently toned down this section in his final edit. In real life, Chaplin was once taken on a grisly tour of Sing Sing by writer Frank Harris; nearly three decades later, Chaplin found himself being fingerprinted like a criminal, during the notorious Joan Barry case (see **Women**).

(See also: Costume; Early stage appearances; Policemen)

THE PROPERTY MAN 🎩

(Chaplin film)
Keystone Comedy released by Mutual, 1 August 1914. Produced by Mack Sennett. Written and directed by Charles Chaplin. Photography attributed to Frank D. Williams. Reissue titles include *Getting His Goat* and *The Roustabout*. Two reels, 2,118 feet (UK length cited in *Bioscope*).

With Charlie Chaplin (the property man), Fritz Schade (Garlico, the strong man), Gene Marsh (Mrs Garlico), Phyllis Allen (Ham Lena Fat, tragedienne), Joe Bordeaux (her husband, a ham tragedian), (?) Norma Nichols (one of the 'Goo-Goo Sisters'), Mack Sennett (excited spectator), Charles Bennett, Lee Morris, Harry McCoy.

Charlie is propman in a vaudeville theatre. His idea of work is taking a swig from a jug of beer, spitting it over his elderly assistant, then sending him out to replenish the stock. Outside, 'Ham Lena Fat', a tragedienne, is enraged to see that she and her actor husband have not been billed. Inside, she confronts Charlie over the omission, but he simply puts cotton wool in his ears. Charlie enforces a backstage 'no smoking' rule despite the clay pipe in his mouth, but he makes a further exception for Garlico, the strong man. The tragedienne decides to take the star dressing room, and thus immediately antagonizes the strong man's wife. While

they are arguing, Charlie, carrying Garlico's prop trunk, blunders into the tragedienne's husband. The actor takes a swing at Charlie, hits the strong man by mistake and is, in return, knocked down. The actor is carried out, leaving the star dressing room to Garlico and spouse. Charlie delegates the task of toting the strong man's trunk to his assistant. He is carrying a jug of beer, which he conceals within his spacious trousers when chatting to the lovely 'Goo-Goo Sisters'. When one of them drops her bag, Charlie bends to retrieve it; the resultant spillage of beer creates an unfortunate impression. Once they have gone, Charlie takes a drink, only to be returned to his task by the strong man. Charlie allows the old man to carry the heavy trunk, and is of no assistance when his colleague is trapped beneath. The Goo-Goo Sisters protest at finding the tragedienne and her husband in their dressing room. Charlie, meanwhile, is chatting to Mrs Garlico, whose husband throttles him before bouncing him away. Charlie lands on the trunk, beneath which his elderly colleague remains pinned. Charlie, atop the trunk, calls for help; the other players rally to assist, but it takes the strong man to do the job. Charlie gives his assistant a thump and kick before going about the business of scene-shifting. Garlico and wife change into costume. The strong man's tights need a repair, and his wife takes them to Charlie. He uses them to wash the floor. The first act, a singer, is onstage; Charlie strikes his assistant, causing him to allow a backdrop to descend on the vocalist. Charlie takes a broom onstage to sweep him up. The backdrop descends once more, hitting Charlie. Backstage squabbles are interrupted as the Goo-Goo Sisters commence their dancing act. The old man tries to ogle their limbs, but Charlie blindfolds him, taking him behind the scenes. They try to move Garlico's props. The old man pulls a mat on which Charlie is standing; Charlie slides over, and the old man tumbles into the rear of the curtain, bumping into one of the dancers. Mrs Garlico, sent to retrieve her husband's tights, asks Charlie for them, but gets a sheepish

response. The propmen miss the cue for the dancers' change of backdrop, and have to rush. Charlie hurls the discarded tights at his colleague, but they land onstage. One of the dancers hurls them into the audience. Offstage, the Goo-Goo Sisters complain to the old man while Mrs Garlico enquires again over the missing tights. The strong man, now due onstage, approaches and the old man raises the curtain, treating the audience to an argument between Charlie, Mrs Garlico and the strong man himself, the last-named clad in leopard skin and long johns. Garlico continues his act but, in a backstage scuffle, Mrs Garlico is accidentally knocked cold. Charlie takes her place as the strong man lifts barbells, making Garlico fear the worst by tearing a handkerchief behind him; on Garlico's final attempt, he drops the weights on Charlie's foot. Exit Charlie, to face a complaint from the tragedienne and her husband, whose turn has been delayed. Charlie blows smoke in the actress's face, and carries Mrs Garlico to her dressing room. Garlico's act concludes when another backdrop lands upon him. In his dressing room, the strong man misconstrues the propman's attentions to his wife. The dramatic scene commences, and is immediately too much for one excited spectator. The play is disrupted by the backstage fight between Garlico and Charlie, all the more so when they chase each other around the stage. In the wings, Charlie takes the barbells to hit the strong man, but his backswing strikes the actor onstage. Having thumped Garlico, Charlie turns the fire hose on him. Soon he has drenched the stage,

The Property Man: *some early Chaplin savagery that was considered strong even at the time*
BFI Stills, Posters and Designs

wings and, ultimately, the audience.

Contemporary reviewers thought *The Property Man* sadistic even by the standards of Chaplin's Keystone films, mainly on the strength of Charlie's cavalier attitude towards an elderly assistant. This, aside from an alleged inadequacy in the theatre set, was the only serious quibble in an extensive *Bioscope* review, which otherwise claimed that audiences 'will simply shriek with laughter, loud and unrestrained'.

The Property Man is revived quite often, probably owing its show-within-a-show plot. As is usual for a Keystone, such revivals have involved varying degrees of trimming; the author has seen BFI material that is evidently the subject of much reconstruction from different elements. Another copy is lacking a few sub-titles plus much of the action, including the opening section prior to Charlie plugging his ears with cotton wool and, later, the scene where the strong man discovers his wife with Charlie in the dressing room.

(See also: Alcohol; Bennett, Charles; Caricatures; Davenport, Alice; Early stage appearances; *His New Profession*; Home movies; Risqué humour; Smoking; Williams, Frank D.)

PUBLIC APPEARANCES 🎩

(Chaplin films *qv*)
As noted under **Childhood**, **Early stage appearances** and **The Karno Company**, Charlie Chaplin began his showbusiness career in live theatre. He moved almost exclusively into film work from the end of 1913 but was to be seen in person, for professional or recreational purposes, on numerous occasions.
When in 1915 Chaplin was offered $25,000 to appear for two weeks at Madison Square Garden in New York, Essanay (*qv*) paid him an identical bonus to prevent him doing so, ostensibly (according to the house journal, *Essanay News*) so 'the exhibitor will not be deprived of any Essanay-Chaplin comedies'. According to the *Moving Picture World* of 29 May 1915, the offer had come from I. Presburg of the Arena Amusement Company, New York, who had approached George K. Spoor (*qv*) by telephone. Chaplin knew his Essanay contract would permit him to make the trip, which would be by 'special train, with observation platform appearances

Public appearances: a rapturous reception in London, 1921

and a circus parade on arrival in New York'. Spoor had seen Presburg in New York, and after returning to Chicago, travelled to Oakland, California, for a meeting with partner G.M. Anderson (*qv*). Spoor and Anderson paid the $25,000 bonus directly into Chaplin's bank account, and the matter was settled. Chaplin's autobiography claims that the company which had made the offer went bankrupt two weeks later. 'Such was my luck,' he concluded.

En route to New York to negotiate with Mutual (*qv*) early in 1916, the comedian found himself mobbed when the train reached Amarillo, Texas; he was shaving at the time, and thought the welcome was for someone else (similar things occurred in Kansas City and Chicago). Having reached New York, Chaplin appeared on stage for a benefit at the New York Hippodrome on 20 February. *Pictures and the Picturegoer* reported a nervous Chaplin, in the wings prior to going on, saying, 'Oh, God, if only it was over!' Jerry Epstein's *Remembering Charlie* records Fred Karno (*qv*) having invited Chaplin back to London in 1916, offering him £1,000 per week to appear in a revue Karno was staging with C.B. Cochran. As noted elsewhere, Chaplin was contractually forbidden to leave the USA but, replying to 'the Guv'nor',

explained that he was committed to film work for several years, promising Karno the first option should he become available. It may have been this offer that brought about an unsubstantiated rumour from late September 1917, whereby *Pictures and the Picturegoer* believed Chaplin might be 'coming to England soon, and may appear for one week only at a certain West End variety house'. Instead, Chaplin's public appearances were made in America, promoting the sale of Liberty Bonds (see **Wartime**).

Chaplin did not revisit his native country until September 1921. Of the newsreels (*qv*) taken at this time, the best of them is from the British 'Topical Budget', which had exclusive coverage of the entire transatlantic journey. The reel exists today, and shows Chaplin in New York, where he was waved off by Douglas

Public appearances: Chaplin, in top hat, visits the night composing staff of a now long-defunct periodical, the Weekly Dispatch, *while in London, September 1921*

Fairbanks and Mary Pickford (both *qv*) prior to embarking on the White Star liner *Olympic* on 3 September. Shipboard scenes include Chaplin signing autographs (one for a small boy who evidently asked where the moustache had gone!) and witnessing a 'circus' put on by the crew, with whom he can be seen clowning and practising baseball pitching. The film shows the *Olympic's* arrival at Southampton on 9 September, and the subsequent crowds at Waterloo Station and outside the Ritz Hotel. His arrival at the Ritz was much anticipated, and considered newsworthy enough for the press to photograph a maid preparing his rooms. Of the Waterloo arrival, the *Daily Telegraph* spoke of the 'noisy and boisterous scene' as the astonished comedian was borne to his car on the weight of the crowd. One group of people to make Chaplin's acquaintance consisted of children from Hoxton, who had travelled to the Ritz to present him with a box of cigars and a bouquet of flowers. Chaplin revisited his own childhood scenes – which had started to vanish, even then – only to draw an unwelcome crowd in Kennington. He also spent time with such literary figures as H.G. Wells, J.M. Barrie (see also *The Kid*) and Thomas Burke, author of the Limehouse novels (one of the East London areas to which Chaplin accompanied him on a night-time visit, an excursion detailed in Burke's *The London Spy*). When Chaplin moved on to the Continent, the reception was just as enthusiastic. He saw Paris, then Berlin (where he first met Pola Negri [see **Women**]), prior to returning once more to London via Paris. He returned again to Paris for the opening of *The Kid*, meeting up with Pickford and Fairbanks. It was on this occasion that Chaplin was first decorated by the French government (see **Awards, honours**). There was time to visit a cousin, Aubrey Chaplin, in London prior to rejoining the *Olympic* for the journey back to America, reaching New York on 17 October.

Several of Chaplin's trips were in the nature of holidays rather than through any professional connection. In 1922, Douglas Fairbanks invited Chaplin and Pola Negri to join a party of fifty friends on a chartered six-month cruise, at a cost of $250,000, but the trip was cancelled. Otherwise, Chaplin was more likely to be seen at the premières of his films, as detailed under *A Woman of Paris* and *The Gold Rush*. Three weeks after attending the US screenings of *City*

Lights, Chaplin was in London for the film's opening at the Dominion Theatre. Among those travelling with Chaplin on the *Mauretania* was the artist Ralph Barton, whose home movies from the set of *City Lights* today provide a singular glimpse at Chaplin's directing methods. Part-way through Chaplin's trip, Barton returned to New York, where he committed suicide.

Accompanying Chaplin to the opening of *City Lights* was George Bernard Shaw, whom Chaplin had rather shied away from meeting during his visit of a decade before (they met again at a Hollywood lunch in March 1933). He had also demurred from revisiting the Hanwell School, but on this occasion made the trip (recounted again by Thomas Burke, in *City of Encounters*). He promised to return to present the children with gifts, but drew adverse comment when he left the task to others.

Chaplin spent the remaining months of 1931 travelling between England, France, Algiers, Berlin, Vienna, Venice and, at the end of the year, the Swiss resort of St.-Moritz, where he spent the winter season with Fairbanks. During his various engagements in England he was introduced to the Prince of Wales, the Duke and Duchess of York (later King George VI and Queen Elizabeth), Lady Astor, Lloyd George and the Prime Minister, Ramsay MacDonald. As noted elsewhere, there seem to have been plans for Chaplin to make a film for the British government, alongside heavy hints of a knighthood; nothing came of it, though reportedly not through

Chaplin's failure to keep a subsequent dinner engagement with the premier. In September 1931 he was introduced to Gandhi, who, genuinely unaware of the comedian's reputation, asked, 'Who is Mr Chaplin?' Chaplin was honoured by the music-hall profession when he joined the Grand Order of Water Rats (*qv*) on 1 November. He was also in fairly august company when Winston Churchill introduced him at a reception at the Carlton Hotel, and when meeting Albert Einstein (who had attended the Los Angeles première of *City Lights*) in Berlin. In Paris, the French honoured Chaplin once more, this time with the Légion d'Honneur (see **Awards, honours** and **Royalty**). While in France, there was opportunity to visit brother Syd, who was living in Nice.

It was arranged to meet up with Syd for a Far East tour in the spring of 1932. Chaplin travelled through Italy, where he failed to meet Mussolini (though his subsequent caricature in *The Great Dictator* seems adequately researched despite) before meeting Syd in Naples. Their itinerary took them to Japan via Ceylon, Singapore, Java and Bali. According to Eric Lister's chronicle of S.J. Perelman reminiscences, *Don't Mention the Marx Brothers*, it was humorist Perelman who had recommended Bali to Chaplin as a place where he could visit unrecognized and unharried. Instead, the boat was instantly besieged by canoes with an invitation to meet the King. Chaplin weakened, was entertained ashore, and suitably entranced. The moment was spoiled when, having been presented with a large, gift-wrapped metal dinner service, Chaplin was expected to pay for it. He returned to his vessel in great fury. Japan proved to have been a more hazardous trip than had been anticipated; a right-wing group, the Black Dragon Society, had planned to kill Chaplin as a means of triggering war with the United States. Chaplin was aware of trouble but, according to his memoirs, the full story did not become known to him until long after. He envisaged the assassins' reaction had they been successful, only to discover their target was not an American after all: 'Oh, so sorry!'

Chaplin returned to California in June 1932. His troubled time in Japan did not seem to discourage a further jaunt east, for that is exactly where he headed after the release of *Modern Times* in February 1936. Accompanying him this time was Paulette Goddard (*qv*). The intention had been to visit Honolulu, but Chaplin's yacht, the *Panacea*, was taken on instead to Hong Kong, China, Indo-China and Japan. In Tokyo, more than a hundred police were required to escort him from the docks to the Imperial Hotel. It was believed that he and Paulette were married during this trip, something not verified until their eventual divorce; completely unfounded was a report that Chaplin had been killed, as evidenced by his safe arrival back in California in June.

Detailed under **Politics** are some of Chaplin's public speeches during the Second World War. The last years of that conflict, 1944–5, saw Chaplin reluctantly under the public gaze in the court case instigated by the accusations of Joan Barry (see **Women**), an ordeal he was able to endure not least through his happy marriage to Oona O'Neill (*qv*). They were sometimes seen on trips to New York but, as noted under **Politics** and elsewhere, it was an intended trip to England that brought about their exile from the USA in 1952. Chaplin had intended taking Oona to see his homeland during the previous year. A contemporary edition of *The Performer* details a party held in London to celebrate Chaplin's birthday in 1951; though working on *Limelight* and consequently unable to attend, Chaplin sent a cable expressing a hope to visit during the summer.

Although barred from the United States, Chaplin was welcome in England; for example, the London première of *Limelight* attracted much favourable

publicity, and on 10 October 1952, the Critics' Circle Film Section gave a luncheon in his honour. Contrary to expectation, the Chaplin family settled in Switzerland rather than London, but the comedian was seen often in England for business purposes or, as was often the case, to visit the fast-vanishing scenes of his youth (noting that, despite the frequent demolitions, the workhouse gates always managed to survive). This he tried to do in secret, though nevertheless attracting attention. Chaplin and his wife were photographed visiting the Old Kent Road when *A Countess From Hong Kong* was in production. A friend of the author once related having seen Chaplin peering into the window of a butcher's shop in south London; the second man walked over, pretending to examine the window display but saying quietly, 'Excuse me. Are you Charlie Chaplin?' 'Sh!', replied Chaplin conspiratorially, 'Don't give me away!' Some indication of Chaplin's doomed attempts at anonymity may be gauged from a visit by the author to Brixton, shortly after Chaplin had been in London to score his reissue of *The Kid*. A small shop had a selection of 8mm Chaplin films on sale. When interest was expressed in the films, the shopkeeper was quick to point out that Chaplin himself had visited the immediate area just a couple of weeks before. A later visit to the Kennington Road brought interest not only among the locals but also from representatives of the *Evening News*, which published the story on 13 January 1975.

The press continued to take notice of Chaplin wherever he went, including family holidays to Kenya in March 1958 and, closer to home, Ireland in 1960 and 1965 (in 1957, he visited Southend, where, as a child, he had first seen the sea). There was similar coverage of him in Oxford, receiving an honorary degree in 1962, flying into London from Paris a year later, and arriving again by air when preparing *The Circus* for revival in 1968. When in London for the re-première of *Modern Times* in January 1972, the *Daily Mirror* quoting him as saying, 'There's no laughter any more. That's the truth. Honestly, I'm not interested in laughter.' There was, however, satisfaction, as when finally revisiting America later that year to collect a special Oscar, or receiving his knighthood at Buckingham Palace in 1975. He was last seen in Britain in 1976, for an award from BAFTA in March, and when scoring *A Woman of Paris* in July. His final public appearance, less than three months before his death,

Edna Purviance with Charlie in a posed shot for 1915's A Woman ...

was among the audience at the Knie Circus in Switzerland, which he had attended periodically from the mid-1950s.

(See also: Abandoned projects; Auctions; Awards, honours; Bloom, Claire; Boats, ships; Books; Chaplin, Syd; Death; Food; Home movies; *King in New York, A*; Marriages; *Monsieur Verdoux*; Suicide)

PURVIANCE, EDNA
(1895–1958)

(Chaplin films *qv*)
Chaplin's most fondly-remembered leading lady, Edna's surname is correctly pronounced with a second-syllable emphasis, to rhyme with 'reliance'. Her beauty was considerable, of the slightly plump variety favoured in the early 20th century, but timeless for all that. Terry Ramsaye (in his 1926 history, *A Million and One Nights*) regarded Edna as the perfect counterpart to Chaplin, 'as blond as he was dark, as placid as he was mercurial'; these contrasts proved as fortunate as Edna's natural good humour, which again complemented Chaplin's.

Edna was born in Paradise Valley,

Nevada. Accounts vary somewhat concerning her early life; much was clarified by an Internet article by Nevada author David W. Toll, *Edna Purviance, Nevada's Forgotten Star*, which in turn inspired Gerald Smith to write his own Website piece, *Edna Purviance, Charlie's Leading Lady*. Edna's full name has been quoted as Edna Olga Purviance; according to documentation unearthed by Smith, her forenames seem instead to have been in reverse order, with the actress using her middle name. Her birthdate, often quoted as 1894 or 1896, has been confirmed as 21 October 1895. She was the third daughter of Madison G. Purviance and his English-born wife, Louise. The family moved to nearby Lovelock (a town sometimes quoted as Edna's birthplace) on acquiring the Singer Hotel in 1900. Madison and Louise parted two years later; Louise subsequently remarried, to a Robert Nurnberger, who died soon after. Louise and her daughters continued to run the hotel and Edna grew into something of a local celebrity, appearing in amateur stage presentations while in her mid-teens. Shortly after graduating from high school in 1913, Edna left Nevada to share a flat with her married sister, Bessie, in San Francisco. According to Toll, Edna obtained an office job in Market Street after taking a business course, spending her off-duty hours amid

'the Bohemian life of the city'.

Terry Ramsaye describes Edna's first meeting with Chaplin as having been at a party, during the comedian's tenure at Essanay (*qv*). Chaplin's autobiography concurs with the timing (if not the venue), though elsewhere in the text he recalls having attended a reception at the Alexandria Hotel, Los Angeles, given in 1914 by flamboyant millionaire 'Diamond Jim' Brady. Chaplin's later memoir, *My Life in Pictures*, includes a photograph of the gathering, with Chaplin, Mack Sennett (*qv*), Mabel Normand (*qv*) and Edna Purviance present. The picture is again dated 1914 and, although the presence of his Keystone colleagues may have caused Chaplin to misdate the picture, it seems equally possible that Edna may have been within the comedian's social circle rather earlier than he would eventually recall.

According to Chaplin, he and G.M. Anderson (*qv*) were in San Francisco searching for a leading lady while the café set for the second Essanay comedy, *A Night Out*, was under construction. Edna, though not in showbusiness, was recommended to them, and an interview was arranged at the St. Francis Hotel. On returning to Essanay's facility at Niles, Chaplin found the new set inadequate and requested improvements, notably a fountain. The day before

production commenced, Chaplin attended a supper party, with Edna also among the guests. Chaplin claimed to possess hypnotic powers, and chose the sceptical Edna to be his subject. Despite having accepted a $10 wager against Chaplin's ability to hypnotize her, Edna played along when the comedian whispered for her to 'fake it'. This, in Chaplin's view, 'won her my esteem and affection and convinced me that she had a sense of humour'.

Edna made her film debut as leading lady for *A Night Out*, remaining not only throughout the Essanay series but in all of Chaplin's films (barring *One A.M.*) until 1923. As noted elsewhere, Gloria Swanson (*qv*) had previously auditioned as *ingénue*. There is the vague possibility that Edna was regarded initially as only a stop-gap, for she had already appeared in five Chaplin films when, on 17 April 1915, the British magazine *Pictures and the Picturegoer* announced that Leona Anderson, sister of G.M. Anderson (*qv*), was to be Chaplin's leading lady. There is, of course, the possibility that news had taken time to travel, or that Edna had been permitted time to prove herself.

Although Edna had only pretended to be hypnotized by Chaplin in 1915, she was very soon under his spell in quite a different way, for it is apparent that their on-screen romances were duplicated in private life. When asked, around March 1916, if he was married, Chaplin laughingly described himself as 'kind of semi-detached', an evident if oblique reference to his involvement with Edna. On completing the series for Mutual (*qv*) in 1917, the couple took a short break in Honolulu, nominally chaperoned by Chaplin aide Tom Harrington and press agent Rob Wagner. The romance was soon to founder as a result of Edna's parallel friendship with actor Thomas Meighan, but their professional association continued unimpaired.

After 1922's *Pay Day*, it had become apparent that Edna had outgrown the rôle of *ingénue* and should be groomed for other things. Chaplin attempted to launch her as a dramatic star in *A Woman of Paris*, which earned its share of plaudits but did not establish Edna as a name in her own right. Her reputation suffered further after an incident, detailed under the **Mabel Normand** entry, in which Edna was the guest of an oil magnate wounded when Miss Normand's chauffeur fired a revolver. Despite the bad publicity, there was no connection with the decision to replace

... and sharing a bed – ghastely – on the set of A Woman of Paris

Edna with Lita Grey (*qv*) then, ultimately, Georgia Hale (*qv*), as leading lady of Chaplin's next starring vehicle, *The Gold Rush*. Chaplin had stated his intention to retain Edna at the studio and, on 27 June 1925, the British magazine *Picture Show* reported that *A Woman of Paris* would now be followed by 'a series of Society dramas', again with Chaplin directing Miss Purviance (see also **Abandoned projects**). None of these entered production. Instead, Chaplin engaged Josef von Sternberg to direct her in a 1926 film known variously as *The Sea Gull, Sea Gulls* and *A Woman of the Sea*. Chaplin's enthusiasm for von Sternberg's *avant-garde* film, *The Salvation Hunters* (with Georgia Hale [*qv*] in the cast), is known to have caused some puzzlement at the time. Douglas Fairbanks (*qv*) had acquired the low-budget production for United Artists (*qv*) but, according to Richard Griffith and Arthur Mayer's *The Movies*, Chaplin felt compelled to retract his endorsement when the picture failed. 'I was only kidding,' said Chaplin. 'They all take everything I say so seriously I thought I'd praise a bad picture and see what happened.' Why Chaplin should have employed an outside director – and one whose UA debut had been unpopular – is unclear; as demonstrated by the Mutual out-takes in *Unknown Chaplin* (*qv*), he was used to coaxing a performance from Edna by his usual means of extensive retakes. Perhaps the dissolution of their personal liaison had rendered such an approach difficult, or Chaplin may have felt in some way responsible for her supposed failure in *A Woman of Paris*. Von Sternberg's memoir, *Fun in a Chinese Laundry*, emphasizes that the story (written by Chaplin from an original by von Sternberg) was in no way an adaptation of Anton Chekhov's *The Sea Gull*; John McCabe describes it as having been a love story set in a Monterey fishing village comprising, according to eye-witness John Grierson, beautiful images of 'net patterns, sea patterns and hair in the wind'. Co-starring in the film were Gayne Whitman and Eve Southern. The director found Edna 'the most willing woman that ever faced my camera', but incapable, at least by that time, of performing before that camera without the various stimuli of alcohol and the playing of kettledrums on the set. The account in von Sternberg's book describes her as being hampered by extreme timidity, of which Chaplin was

aware but which he had hoped von Sternberg could overcome. The director believed he had succeeded in this respect, and was therefore unhappy when Chaplin withdrew the film after a single screening and, eventually, destroyed the negative. David Robinson's explanation is that it allowed Chaplin to write off the film's expense. No trace was thought to survive of the film until David Totheroh, grandson of cameraman Rollie, found a 35mm positive fragment among the family effects. The Summer 1996 *Limelight* magazine reproduces these few frames which, according to Totheroh, are of leading man Gayne Whitman. The film's withdrawal was somewhat detrimental to the director's reputation, but his friendship with Chaplin continued, perhaps because neither party mentioned the matter again. In the same year as this ill-fated project, Edna Purviance made one final appearance, in a French film called *Education du Prince*. There has long been controversy as to whether she played extra rôles in *Monsieur Verdoux* and *Limelight* (both *qv*). In February 1997, Gerald Smith placed a further Internet item claiming Edna to be the grand-looking 'Miss Parker', who, aside from Calvero, is the only client not to be dismissed from the agent's office in *Limelight*. Another historian, Hooman Mehran, thus armed with Edna's latter-day image, identified her as a wedding guest in *Verdoux*. The author's opinion is that both sightings are correct: the wedding sequence places Edna behind William Frawley (*qv*) and, later, behind Chaplin and Martha Raye (*qv*) at the moment where they unwittingly back into each other.

Chaplin clearly had difficulty in finding a replacement for Edna Purviance as his leading lady; as noted elsewhere, it was a resemblance to Edna that first drew his attention to Virginia Cherrill (*qv*). In turn, Edna seems to have found Chaplin impossible to replace in her personal life. Some commentators have suggested how less troubled Chaplin would have been, personally, professionally and even politically, had he married Edna in 1918 and left it at that. One suspects that Edna – who, though inactive, remained in his employ until her death – would probably have welcomed such a marriage. She continued to write to Chaplin even after he had settled with his new family in Switzerland. His autobiography reprints some of her final correspondence, to which Chaplin

admits not having replied. Her letters, alternately humorous, wry and undeniably touching, were written at a time when Edna was undergoing drastic and, ultimately, unsuccessful treatment for cancer. It is generally believed that Edna Purviance never married, but at least one source, an obituary in the *New York Times*, claims otherwise. The Humboldt Museum at Pioneer Park, Winnemucca, Nevada, preserves the silk dress worn by Edna in *The Adventurer*, also a wooden jewellery box bearing her pencilled autograph.

(See also: Camera-looks; Children; Death; Dryden, Wheeler; Marriages; Risqué humour; Women)

RACE

(Chaplin films *qv*)
Chaplin worked in an era when the subject of race was not in any way sensitive. The stage – comic and otherwise – used stereotypes without compunction, and early film comedy followed suit, though it should be said that the better silent-film comedians seldom resorted to this or any other easy form of laugh.

Chaplin's work is mostly devoid of directly racial material; for example, a doorman in *The Rounders* is obviously a white actor in blackface, though nothing is made of it, and his presence seems no more than an ingredient of Keystone's rather surreal landscape. The same may be said of a blacked-up Leo White (*qv*) in the audience of *A Night in the Show*. (A genuine black actor is cast as one of the prizefighters in *City Lights*, again without undue attention being drawn.) Another Keystone, *His Favorite Pastime*, shows a white actor in blackface playing a washroom attendant; once more, there is no significance attached to it, Charlie's mistreatment of him being that meted out to almost everyone in these Keystones; some audiences may, however, be uncomfortable with the white woman playing a black housemaid in this film, especially when Charlie is horrified to learn he has mistaken her for the lady of the house (a joke commonplace at the time). Otherwise, virtually the only 'black' joke in Chaplin's output occurs in *A Day's Pleasure*, when a black jazzman turns pale owing to seasickness. It may be significant that this dates from a brief period when Chaplin, by his own later admission, was having trouble in developing ideas.

The depiction of Jewish characters in the earlier films tends towards their casting as shopkeepers in downmarket areas, in truth a not uncommon rôle for them in the early 20th century. Examples here include *Police* and *A Dog's Life*. Charlie's dream of Heaven in *The Kid* shows him being outfitted in angelic garb by a Jewish tailor. In *The Vagabond*, Leo White (again!) plays a bearded, bowler-hatted Jewish stereotype whom Charlie observes taking ham from the free-lunch counter of a bar. Charlie, helpful as always, switches the 'ham' sign to 'beef' in order to render it kosher. It is perhaps unsurprising for Henry Bergman (*qv*) to portray a stereotypical Jewish pawnbroker in *The Pawnshop*, but *Sunnyside* has him rather obviously reading a Hebrew newspaper, for no apparent reason other than to convey that Edna Purviance (*qv*) has a Jewish father. Once again, this film dates from the period in 1919 when Chaplin's creative flow was in temporary suspension.

The series *Unknown Chaplin* (*qv*) incorporates unused footage of Chaplin with Harry Lauder, intended for a film promoting the sale of War Bonds; Lauder is seen drawing a chalk caricature of Chaplin, who objects to the shape of the nose, implying through mime that it is 'too Jewish'. Chaplin sometimes claimed to be Jewish, or at least partly so, and was often assumed to be (particularly by the Nazis), but his complex family history offers no evidence (see **Religion**). His brunette cast and curly hair have often been attributed to partial Spanish and Romany descent. In his dual rôles for *The Great Dictator*, Chaplin played a Jewish barber as direct counterpoint to his fascist *alter ego*, Adenoid Hynkel.

(See also: *Bond, The*; Dual rôles; Keystone; Politics; Wartime)

RADIO

(Chaplin films *qv*)
For the bulk of his career, Chaplin was, of course, a non-speaking performer. In consequence, radio documentaries on his work have been few, though BBC Radio 4 broadcast a sound profile after the comedian's knighthood in 1975. Fifty years earlier, the BBC (then still a 'company' rather than a 'corporation') had broadcast audience laughter from a screening of *The Gold Rush* at London's Tivoli Theatre. At the time of writing,

Race: *City Lights has a black boxer, but no real attention is drawn to the fact*

the most recent radio documentary on Chaplin is BBC Radio 2's *Charlie Chaplin – Composer*, introduced by the comedian's daughter, Josephine, and broadcast on 13 April 1997.

Chaplin was persuaded to appear on radio in the autumn of 1934, when Alexander Woollcott (*qv*) presented a series of radio 'serenades' (sponsored by Cream of Wheat for CBS) to his 'ten favourite Americans'. Chaplin, though British, was included among those who were asked which song they would prefer to have sung under their window. This appearance was as a favour to a friend, but otherwise Chaplin's broadcasts were designed to serve a specific purpose, such as a 1933 speech on CBS to support Franklin D. Roosevelt's National Recovery Act, the national hook-up when repeating the closing speech from *The Great Dictator* (reaching an audience of 60 million), his 1943 message to the people of Lambeth (see **Wartime**), or a BBC discussion programme, broadcast on 15 October 1952, concerning Chaplin's new film *Limelight*. Among those joining Chaplin in the studio were John Mills, Michael Balcon and critic Dilys Powell. The programme still exists in BBC Sound Archives; other recordings preserved thus include a broadcast from *The World Tonight* in 1965 and four news items from the time of Chaplin's knighthood a decade later.

The introduction of recorded sound into Chaplin's films – albeit only music and effects at first – facilitated such things as the gag in *Modern Times* in which stomachs start to rumble, complemented by a radio commercial for an indigestion remedy. *The Great Dictator*, with dialogue, enabled the barber to shave to the radio's musical accompaniment and, ultimately, deliver his speech over the airwaves.

(See also: Awards, honours; Documentaries, compilations)

RAND, JOHN (F.) 🎩
(1872 or 1878–1940)

(Chaplin films *qv*)

Former circus clown whose association with Chaplin began at Essanay (*qv*). Contrary to some listings, he is neither the top-hatted man leading the robbery in *The Bank* nor the Captain in *Shanghaied* (both are played by Lawrence A. Bowes [*qv*]), but Rand does appear as the cook in the latter film (see also **Billy Armstrong**). Rand conducts the orchestra in *A Night in the Show*, plays the matador in *Carmen*, and in *Police* portrays the officer who is consistently on Charlie's tail. In the Mutuals, Rand may be seen as one of the brigade in *The Fireman* and among the party guests in both *The Count* and *The Adventurer*. He leads the German band in *The Vagabond*, and is perhaps best recalled as Charlie's unfriendly colleague in both *The Pawnshop* and the restaurant scenes of *The Rink*. Rand plays dual rôles in both *Easy Street*, as a drunk in the Mission Hall and as one of the beleaguered constabulary, and in *The Immigrant*, in which he plays a ship's officer and the drunken customer who is beaten up by a gang of waiters. His contribution to *The Cure*, as an attendant at the spa, is known to have been Chaplin's own intended rôle at the commencement of shooting. This has sometimes been claimed as a dual rôle, with Rand appearing also as a masseur, but this seems merely to be the same character serving in different capacities at the resort. The same might be said of *The Idle Class*, in which Rand's irate golfer is among those reunited at a party following an altercation at the links. Rand has been reported among the doughboys in *Shoulder Arms*, and is one of Charlie's fellow-builders, with whom he goes on the town, in *Pay Day*. He returns to his pre-Chaplin milieu as an assistant to property man Tiny Sandford (*qv*) in *The Circus*, plays a tramp in *City Lights*, and also appears as a convict in *Modern Times*.

(See also: Dual rôles; How to Make Movies; Mutual)

RAYE, MARTHA
(1916–94)

Comedienne, born to the vaudeville song-and-dance act of Pete Reed and Mabelle Hooper, Martha Raye continued that robust tradition with her energetic, large-mouthed performances in several movies of the late 1930s and 40s, among them *The Big Broadcast of 1938*. During the Second World War, she toured extensively with the USO, an experience re-enacted on film in *Four Jills in a Jeep* (1944). When Chaplin saw the movie, he knew she was ideal casting as the awful 'Annabella' in *Monsieur Verdoux* (*qv*), whose vulgarity rendered her invulnerable to the suave murderer's attempts on her life. In a 1980 interview, British documentary-maker Michael Pointon asked her about the comedians with whom she had worked. 'Well,' she replied, 'I loved W.C. Fields, Milton Berle ... of course, my favourite of all was Chaplin.' Miss Raye recalled having been working in a Chicago nightclub when a call arrived from Los Angeles. 'This is Charlie Chaplin,' said the voice. 'Sure it is,' replied Miss Raye, who, believing it to be a joke, hung up. Her agent called back, asking why she'd hung up on Chaplin. Once convinced that he really *did* want her to be in his new film (an accolade she described as 'the highest that you can ever get'), she quit the nightclub and departed for Los Angeles. Although an established star, Miss Raye was 'scared to death' of meeting 'the genius of all'. Chaplin, sensing her anxiety, put her at ease. 'Call me Charles,' said Chaplin, and before long they were addressing each other as 'Chuck' and 'Maggie'. Speaking to *Limelight* magazine in 1994, Marilyn Nash (*qv*) laughingly described her displacement from the star dressing room on the arrival of Martha. 'He loved Martha Raye,' she said. 'They worked so well together, were so compatible. Whatever she wanted to do, they would do it ... and they would start laughing so hard that they'd have to stop the shooting and wait until they got themselves together.'

Because her nerves were still a problem on the first day's work, Chaplin suggested they should instead rehearse for a week, in full costume and with lighting. The scene chosen was that in the boat, during which, according to Marilyn Nash, they continued to break each other up while Rollie Totheroh (*qv*) and the crew waited to shoot. Although

the scene was eventually accomplished in only one take, the participants were drenched and thankful for the warm weather. Amid the water and hilarity, Martha observed the comedian's timing. 'I think I learned most of my timing from that man,' she said, as he explained how he had written the part expressly for the actress and wanted her to be herself. He also offered advice on the physical comedy she did at personal appearances, recommending immaculate clothing, hair and make-up as contrast to the knockabout humour. 'Don't wear earrings,' he added. When asked why not, he explained that anything dangling around the face would detract from the facial expressions on which she depended. Miss Raye took the advice, and noticed a marked improvement in her performance. During filming, she often benefited from moments in which Chaplin pulled her up for being 'plastic', or in other words, not honest with herself.

She described rehearsing for the party sequence over a period of some four days. Chaplin had a stand-in to act with the others while he stood behind the camera, after which he would step in for filming. In addition to constantly dashing to and from the camera, Chaplin also designed Miss Raye's gowns and did her hair and make-up. She was consistently amazed by his ability to do everything, including writing music, while maintaining a 'beautiful, rich, warm off-screen humour'. In contrast to the recollections of some others on the *Verdoux* set, Martha Raye saw Chaplin as 'a very lovable man', loved and respected also by the crew. 'He tolerated no nonsense,' she added, 'everybody knew their job and they did it, and if they did

Martha Raye made a superbly vulgar foil in Monsieur Verdoux

their job that was fine with him ... and they could do anything they wanted to do'. She recalled that Chaplin believed in 'disciplined freedom'.

Monsieur Verdoux was not filmed in continuity. Although standard industry practice, Miss Raye believed that in Chaplin's case it was the result of his preference to film whatever scene suited his mood on the day. Chaplin would sometimes commence a scene but interrupt it, requesting the set for a different segment of the film. She felt also that he 'lived' the character. 'His comedy was so believable ... so beautiful,' she said, adding that Chaplin, who had never needed to deliver dialogue throughout a film (he had spared himself dialogue through much of *The Great Dictator* [*qv*]) was at least as nervous as she was.

It has been suggested that Martha Raye's association with Chaplin brought about an unofficial blacklisting from movies lasting some sixteen years. Instead, she appeared frequently on television, resulting in an Emmy nomination for her work in *McMillan and Wife*. Chaplin and Martha Raye were reunited in 1972, when the comedian visited America to receive a special Oscar. They met at the home of Carol and Walter Matthau, whose other guests that day included Groucho Marx (*qv*). Miss Raye was latterly a regular on the *Alice* TV series.

(See also: Awards, honours; Politics; Women)

RECREATION

(Chaplin film)
Keystone Comedy released by Mutual, 13 August 1914. Produced by Mack Sennett. Written and directed by Charles Chaplin. Photography attributed to Frank D. Williams. Split reel, released with a travelogue, *The Yosemite*. 462 feet.

With Charlie Chaplin (himself), (?) Norma Nichols (girl).

A young girl leaves her sailor boyfriend asleep on a park bench. Charlie, out for a stroll, makes her acquaintance, but has to do battle with the mariner once he awakens. From a distance, Charlie hurls a brick at the sailor; unfortunately for Charlie, the sailor is equally skilled at throwing them back. Charlie's next two bricks hit a policeman and the girl. He

plays nonchalant when a second officer arrives, but the sailor, about to return fire at Charlie, is arrested by the first cop. Charlie is allowed on his way, but the sailor, under arrest, accuses him of the crime. Meanwhile, the second cop makes time with the girl; Charlie escapes from the other officer, and returns to the bench. Seeing the girl's new, uniformed beau, Charlie makes a discreet exit. The sailor, still protesting his innocence, throws a brick at Charlie, but instead strikes the second cop. When the officer enters the fray, the girl wanders over to the lake. She bends over the edge, but Charlie resists the temptation to tap her with his cane. They are getting along well until the sailor, escaping the two officers, arrives for a fight. Charlie, dodging his blows, kicks him into the water; the cops, realizing they have been struggling with each other rather than their prisoner, walk to the scene and are also kicked into the lake. Charlie seems to have won but the girl, disgusted, boots Charlie into the water with the others. Unexpectedly, Charlie drags the girl in along with him.

Recreation is sometimes confused with a reissue of *Tango Tangles* (*qv*) called *Charlie's Recreation*. Just to add to the confusion, the author's collection includes a genuine oddity called *His Recreation*, a half-reel subject using *Recreation* as its middle section, but topped and tailed by footage from *Laughing Gas* (*qv*). Such hybrids of Chaplin Keystones are not uncommon (see also *A Busy Day*).

A sequence of Charlie in the park reading the *Police Gazette* (the most salacious scandal-sheet of its day) has sometimes been attributed to *Recreation*, but appears instead in a subsequent film, *His New Profession* (*qv*). Quite an uncommon subject, *Recreation* sometimes turns up in disappointing prints, though an excellent-quality extract may be seen in an episode of the TV series *Silents, Please*, sub-titled *The Clown Princes of Hollywood*.

(See also: Keystone; *Kid, The*; Murray, Charlie; Parks; Policemen; Reissues; Television; Williams, Frank D.)

REEVES, ALF
(1876–1946)

Acted as business manager to the Karno Company (*qv*) during its tours of North

Chaplin employed former Karno stalwart **Alf Reeves** *at his studio*
By courtesy and copyright of the Roy Export Company Establishment

America; it was he who received the telegram requesting Chaplin's presence in New York when he was offered a job by Keystone (*qv*). Reeves was later hired to repeat his Karno duties within the Chaplin Studio, at which he remained employed for the rest of his life; he appears in his real-life rôle of studio manager in *How To Make Movies* (*qv*). He has been spotted in at least two of the Chaplin films, as a bar patron in *A Dog's Life* and as the desk sergeant in the deleted army medical of *Shoulder Arms* (both *qv*).

(See also: Abandoned projects; Height; Wood, 'Wee' Georgie)

REIGER, MARGIE

See: *By the Sea*; Essanay, and *Woman, A*

REISSUES

(Chaplin films *qv*)
Chaplin's continued popularity ensured the frequent reissue of his earlier films. To an extent this helped keep his name in the public eye at a time when his output became less prolific; it was more of a nuisance when such revivals competed with new product. Although the reissue prints are largely responsible for preserving almost his entire output,

such versions tend to be unfaithful to the originals.

Such mutilation can take the form of re-editing, deletion of scenes and changes to titling (*qv*). The reasons for cutting films are varied: sometimes it can be the result of negative damage, but more often it derives from conscious tampering, either by someone attempting to 'improve' upon the original, or through the even lower motive of saving upon raw stock in the length of release prints.

The Keystone Chaplins were much bootlegged, even at the time, for many of them were not copyrighted despite on-screen notices to the contrary. A number of Chaplin hybrids are noted within the films' main entries, but a few other oddities are worth detailing here. Theodore Huff cites *The Perils of Patrick*, a 30-reel 'serial' assembled from the Keystone films; the AFI Catalog notes also a four-reel subject of 1915 called *Mixed Up*, which seems to have been precisely that. The AFI list suggests it may have been compiled from Chaplin shorts including *Those Love Pangs* and *His New Job*, but one doubts any Essanay subjects were used. Although probably not extant, a report survives of a screening by Kansas State Censors on 4 October 1915. According to this, the film contained a 'bad egg scene', 'two barroom scenes' and a scene in which Charlie pulls off a girl's skirt (this last occurs in *Laughing Gas*). Apparently, certain cuts were made to the film, released by a firm calling itself Wichita. Even the most famous Chaplin Keystone, the six-reel *Tillie's Punctured Romance*, generally appears in versions cut to five or even four reels.

Many Keystone Chaplins circulate in the legitimate revival versions – 'taken from original negatives' – prepared by a firm calling itself W.H. Productions ('Wonderful Hits'). On 29 December 1917, the company placed a full-page advertisement in the *Motion Picture News* announcing 28 Keystone reissues, among them '3 of the funniest Charlie Chaplins'. Other artists named were Syd Chaplin, Chester Conklin, Mabel Normand, Mack Swain, Mack Sennett, Charlie Murray, Ford Sterling and Fatty Arbuckle (all *qv*). It is not known which three Chaplins were considered the funniest, but by 1920 W.H. Productions had reissued at least 26 of them, as listed in a trade advertisement by a British distributor, the Unity Film Company. This source again guaranteed the use of 'original negatives',

THE BIG REVIVAL

THE GREAT PILGRIM-AGE

to the theatres will commence on DEC. 27, 1926 to welcome **Charlie** again in his brilliant masterpiece. **FOUR RIOTOUS REELS.**

The Pilgrim

Note the London Release Date— December 27, 1926

Trade Show at the New Oxford Theatre, April 27, at 3 p.m. PEARL FILMS. LTD., 86-88, WARDOUR STREET, W.1.

but claimed they were printed in Britain. As noted elsewhere, W.H.'s prints took care to credit the films' original names, but were often edited in some way, particularly when titling described the new edition as having been 'adapted from' the original. Another 1920 British advertisement, placed by Western Import, announced 're-edited' Keystones featuring Chaplin, Arbuckle, Swain *et al.* Some of the new titles are easy to identify (*Doughnut Designers*, formerly *Dough and Dynamite*), others less so; the author admits at least temporary defeat over a two-reel Chaplin Keystone renamed *The Hula Hula Dance*. During 1919–20, some Keystones were revived in the USA on a State Rights basis by the Tower Film Corporation, under whose auspices *Cruel, Cruel Love* became *Lord Helpus*, while *Gentlemen of Nerve* was amended to a perfunctory *Some Nerve*.

Syd Chaplin (*qv*) re-edited and retitled several of the Keystones for WAFilms at some time around 1923. *Dough and Dynamite*, *His Trysting Place* and *His Prehistoric Past* frequently circulate in these versions, characterized by overly-punning sub-titles. The rationale for these is conveyed in a poem on *Dough and Dynamite*'s opening credits:

> Old songs grow sweeter with the years
> Old wines improve with age
> And Shakespeare with his smiles and tears
> Still dominates the stage.
> Old masterpieces of the screen
> Will stand the test of time
> When walks the master on the

scene
The King of Pantomime.

Essanay were quite adept at mutilation without any outside help. Their anthologies – such as *Chase Me Charlie* (*qv*) – are detailed elsewhere, as are the sad stories concerning *Carmen*, *Police* and *Triple Trouble*. Chaplin's Essanays were revived by the company itself within twelve months, and would resurface throughout the silent period. In April 1919, George Klein and the World Film Corporation took over all prints, contracts and advertising materials from Essanay's old distributor, General Film, with an initial announcement of the re-availability of *The Bank*, *A Night in the Show*, *Shanghaied*, *Police* and the patchwork film *Triple Trouble*. In reporting the deal, the *Motion Picture News* described how 'within 72 hours telegraphic returns are said to have indicated a complete wiping out of all existing records for fast selling and results obtained in distributing pictures'. The following year saw Victor Kremer providing reissues of *Burlesque on Carmen*, *The Champion*, *A Jitney Elopement*, *By the Sea* and *Work*. Many UK copies tend to be from the 1932 added-sound prints distributed by Bernard Smith of Equity-British.

The Mutuals made an early reappearance from a company using the name Chaplin Classics, which were announced to the trade in the first week of December 1919. Less than a year after the series' completion in 1917, British distributor J.D. Walker placed a full-page ad in the *Kinematograph and Lantern Weekly* with the declaration 'Walker's Mutual Chaplins are the Best Chaplins Charlie ever made ... Theatres all over the country are doing record business again re-booking these Twelve Wonder Comedies.' At this stage the prints were substantially intact, but damage started to be inflicted on revivals during the 1920s. Further trimming was done in 1932, when RKO added sound effects and music scores by Gene Rodemich and Winston S. Sharples (the latter of whom, perhaps significantly, later applied his musical skills to cartoon films). These scored versions were in turn resurrected in 1938 by Guaranteed Pictures, who collected the twelve films into blocks of four, the *Chaplin Carnival*, *Chaplin Cavalcade* and *Chaplin Festival*. For these editions, the sub-titles were remade with a Chaplin silhouette in one corner. The author has examined a combined, nitrate dupe negative of Guaranteed's edition of

The Immigrant, with a 'Bernard Smith' main title spliced in. The soundtrack is printed in throughout, but the 'silhouette' sub-titles have been physically cut into the material. Once again, UK copies of the Guaranteed Films package distributed from Equity-British, who in the 1940s also circulated a number of Chaplins with narration dubbed by comedian Tommy Handley. In many cases, the added-sound copies provide the best-quality material, despite 'cropping' to the left of picture where a track has been printed. There were, in addition, dubbed versions of some of the Essanay and Mutual films which had been 'converted to sound speed'. This referred to the process, described elsewhere, in which every other frame is printed twice. Some of these came from a New York distributor calling itself the King of Comedy Film Corp.

Chaplin's First National films were less often revived. Pathé reissued them at intervals during the 1920s, as with *Shoulder Arms* in October 1923 and again, five years later. Pathé's reissue posters for *A Dog's Life* and *Sunnyside* are sometimes reproduced today, and much was made of *The Pilgrim*'s UK reissue by Pearl Films (*illustrated*) in 1926. Several of the First National films reappeared in Britain from 1958, via a distributor called DUK. Picture quality suggested dupes from old release prints (possibly from Europe), and they were subject to varying degrees of amendment. *The Kid* was much as the original British release except for the omission of a scene where Henry Bergman (*qv*) appears as an impresario. *Shoulder Arms*, oddly, incorporated *A Day's Pleasure* as a dream sequence (which the bulk of the film was intended to be!) and was given a new finale, using library footage and stills, in which war hero Charlie was given a tickertape parade (see **Home movies**). These reissues were not authorized, and Chaplin took legal action. The *Daily Mail* of 10 August 1958 reported Chaplin arriving unexpectedly in London, where he checked into the Savoy Hotel. He told reporters, 'I am here to hunt pirates,' after receiving several letters informing him of the re-edited prints. Lawyers had estimated a necessary outlay of $100,000, but Chaplin was more concerned over the damage to his artistic reputation; 'it reflects on me,' he said. Oddly, during the case, DUK took its own action against Chaplin, seemingly claiming slander in his comments that the

mutilated versions were detrimental to his artistic reputation; DUK, while admitting liability as distributors, were thought to have acquired these versions in good faith from a third party. The case was settled in June 1962. Other such actions included a German firm which had used the silent edition of *The Gold Rush*, which has long been treated as public domain in America. According to *Variety* of 26 June 1963, Chaplin was able to claim otherwise on the grounds that he had written a never-produced play (*The Lucky Strike*) on which his screenplay was based. *Variety*'s report adds that Chaplin was taking further action in Switzerland, Finland and Japan over infringement of *The Gold Rush*; mentioned also are the withdrawal, after threats of legal action, of a 1961 German release of *The Kid* and 'an Italian mishmash of parts of four old Chaplin silents' called *The Laugh Parade*. There had also been a French decision regarding an unauthorized revival of *The Kid*, in which Chaplin was awarded symbolic damages of only one franc, but confirmed as sole legal distributor of the film. Another disagreement over *The Gold Rush* had taken place in May 1955, when London's National Film Theatre had included it in a season of early United Artists films. Chaplin had agreed to a single showing but, in an apparent misunderstanding, the theatre had construed use as part of the 'opening programme' as meaning more than one night. Chaplin relented in part, allowing it to be screened on three other advertised nights, but insisting on the cancellation of further showings.

Chaplin established the Roy Export Company, through which to distribute his films; the name is said to originate in his Anglicized pronunciation of *A King in New York*'s French title, *Un Roi à New York*. In 1959 the comedian assembled *A Dog's Life*, *Shoulder Arms* and *The Pilgrim* into *The Chaplin Revue* (*qv*), for which the films were slightly abridged. It was at the time of *The Circus*'s belated reissue, over 1969–70, that Chaplin initiated a new distribution outlet, Black Ink, with the assistance of Jerry Epstein (*qv*).

Chaplin's 1971 reissue of *The Kid* – paired with *The Idle Class* – was cut by a total of one reel, as detailed in the main entry. Chaplin prepared new editions of *A Day's Pleasure*, *Pay Day* and *A Woman of Paris* (paired with *Sunnyside*) during the years up to 1976.

A Woman of Paris was Chaplin's first United Artists film, but the last to be

revived for a modern audience. As detailed in the specific entry, Chaplin presented *The Gold Rush* with music, effects and narration as long ago as 1942. *City Lights* received particular acclaim when revived in 1950, and there were periodic revivals of this film, also *Modern Times* and *The Great Dictator* (though *Monsieur Verdoux* remained unseen, at least in the USA, for many years).

On 29 November 1971, London's *Evening Standard* quoted a *Life* magazine article concerning the imminent reissue of Chaplin's films, in a deal bringing him $5 million plus 50 per cent of the net income. Eight films were to be seen in ten countries, with screenings in forty US cities to commence in Christmas week.

Modern Times was on view in the USA and Britain during 1972, when Vincent Canby of the New York *Times* claimed that '"Modern Times" is a very, very funny movie. It is also an extremely loving one. If, for some ridiculous reason, you haven't seen it, you cannot afford to delay.' The film was still on the road into 1976, when Mike Harris of *The Australian* said, 'Seeing his films helps one understand how he has become legendary: they are his immortality.'

The same year, 1976 also saw *Monsieur Verdoux* and *The Great Dictator* back in London. *A Woman of Paris*, prepared at this time, did not reach US theatres until 1978, several months after Chaplin's death.

The most recent theatrical revivals have been in the 'live cinema' format pioneered by historians Kevin Brownlow and David Gill. Their restored version of the original silent *Gold Rush*, presented in co-operation with the Chaplin Estate, was screened thus at the Royal Albert Hall on 31 October 1993. When the occasion was first announced on 13 May, Robin Stringer of the London *Evening Standard* quoted the theatre's director, Patrick Deucher, to the effect that the Albert Hall was in use as a cinema during 1925, the year of the film's release. Sponsored by American Express, this charity 'première' was intended as the first stop in a world tour, with only one performance in each country. Seats were priced up to £250, the proceeds to benefit research into muscular dystrophy and to contribute towards the restoration of the venue itself. The film was accompanied by the Royal Liverpool Philharmonic Orchestra, conducted by Carl Davis, whose new score was based on surviving fragments of Chaplin's original. A less expensive event, for the afternoon, was a 'live cinema' presentation of *City Lights*, 'augmented by live performances from clowns, stilt-walkers and other entertainers'.

The 'live cinema' presentation of *City Lights* was repeated at London's Dominion Theatre, where the 1931 UK première had taken place, for Chaplin's centenary in April 1989. The supporting programme consisted of *How To Make Movies* (*qv*) and, in a print supplied by historian David Shepard, *Kid Auto Races at Venice*. Carl Davis again conducted the orchestra from 16–18 April, with Bramwell Tovey taking over for the remaining four nights. The gibberish noises at the radio microphone were provided by comedian Spike Milligan.

Since then there have been numerous 'live cinema' screenings of Chaplin films, many with Carl Davis as conductor. The repertoire includes *The Kid*, *The Idle Class*, *A Woman of Paris*, *The Gold Rush*, *City Lights*, *Kid Auto Races at Venice*, *How To Make Movies* and others; venues have been all around the US and Canada, also Australia, Austria, Belgium, Colombia, Finland, France, Germany, Holland, Israel, Italy, Northern Ireland, South Africa and Switzerland. A presentation of *Shoulder Arms* took place at the doubly appropriate Imperial War Museum in Kennington, London. These presentations have sometimes been interspersed with revivals of sound films, such as *The Great Dictator* and *Monsieur Verdoux*.

(See also: *Bank, The*; *Between Showers*; 'Bogus Chaplins'; *Caught in a Cabaret*; Documentaries, compilations; Dreams; Essanay; *Face On the Bar Room Floor, The*; *Fireman, The*; First National; Home movies; Keystone; *Kid Auto Races at Venice*; *Making a Living*; Music; Parrish, Robert; *Pawnshop, The*; Television; United Artists; *Vagabond, The*; Video releases)

RELIGION 🎩

(Chaplin films *qv*)
Chaplin's upbringing was not essentially of the religious kind, although his mother, in common with many people facing adversity, acquired a Christian faith. She and her father were baptized at Christchurch, Lambeth North, in 1898. Chaplin acquired a brief interest in Roman Catholicism during his stint with the 'Eight Lancashire Lads', the other

members of which were of that faith. His autobiography records a childhood illness when his mother spoke of religion in such a way that he wanted to die that night in order to meet Jesus. The boy's mother explained that he should instead remain on earth to fulfil his purpose. Accounts of Hannah's mental condition suggest an unfortunately misplaced zeal, as when travelling to the USA and telling a customs official that he was Jesus Christ; perhaps it was this aspect that alienated Chaplin from organized religion, to the point where he would frequently declare himself an atheist. Something of Chaplin's attitude towards religious preoccupations may be gauged from the dull society girls in *A Countess From Hong Kong* (one of them played by his daughter, Geraldine) who share a preoccupation with the question of 'the immortality of the soul', the implication being that they have little else to ponder in their leisured lives.

Colleen Moore's autobiography, *Silent Star*, describes a startling moment when meeting Chaplin with Robert Leiber, the president of First National (*qv*), who had acquired the film rights to Papini's *Life of Christ*. To everyone's amazement, Chaplin expressed a wish to play the lead, arguing, with partially obscure logic, 'I look the part. I'm a Jew. And I'm a comedian,' by which he referred to the slender division between comedy and tragedy. Chaplin insisted that his atheism would enable him to treat the character objectively, then issued a direct challenge to the Almighty to prove His existence by striking the comedian dead. Nothing happened. Miss Moore further recalled a parallel scene as told to her by Mary Pickford (*qv*), when Chaplin leapt, fully-clothed, into the swimming pool at Pickfair. A non-swimmer, Chaplin once more declared his non-belief, challenging God to save him. Douglas Fairbanks (*qv*) did the job instead, as Mary called out, 'Let the heathen drown!'

Chaplin's claim to be Jewish was one he made occasionally, though when asked once if he was, his reply sidestepped implied anti-Semitism by stating, 'I have not that good fortune.' Sometimes he professed to be part-Jewish, difficult either to prove or disprove; biographer John McCabe puts the matter into perspective by believing that Chaplin simply liked the idea of being part-Jewish, a preference to which he was quite entitled. David Robinson's meticulously-assembled Chaplin family tree suggests no Jewish

ancestry on either side.

There are occasional tongue-in-cheek references to religion in the Chaplin films. One of these, from *A Day's Pleasure*, involves Loyal Underwood (*qv*) as an old man whose language is clearly under-represented by a sub-title reading 'Stupid ass!' Charlie at first covers his ears, then gestures to the effect that the man's assumed blasphemy will eventually cause him to travel 'down' rather than 'up'.

Clerics in the films tend to receive no less savage treatment than any other establishment types, even when genuinely benign. When Charlie encounters a conman posing as a preacher in *Police*, his wrath is turned to an authentic example who simply has the misfortune to appear immediately thereafter. The depiction of a mission hall in *Easy Street* was controversial in its time, even though its minister is not lampooned in any way; while it is the parson's wife who, in *Modern Times*, is subjected to the embarrassment of a gurgling stomach. In *The Pilgrim*, Charlie, as an escaped convict in clothes stolen from a clergyman, proves himself worthy of the rôle by risking life and liberty for the sake of a good cause. Although *The Pilgrim* raised a few contemporary eyebrows, nothing seems to have been said about the moment in *Sunnyside* when a runaway farm animal disrupts a church service. Surprisingly, the Hays Office permitted a moment in *The Great Dictator* in which Hannah asks the barber if he believes in God, then expounds her own views without waiting for an answer. There seems to have been a slight tempering in the Hays Office's theological objections by 1940. When *Room Service* was adapted as a screen vehicle for the Marx Brothers two years earlier, a play-within-the-play had to be renamed 'Hail and Farewell' because the censors forbade the original's 'Godspeed'; yet in 1940, the play *Susan and God* was permitted to reach the screen under its original title (though, untypically, the UK insisted on a renaming).

Any querying of Charlie's dream of heaven in *The Kid* seems to have had more to do with aesthetic suitability than any presumed blasphemy. Early in the film is an illustrated title card in which an unmarried mother, treated as an outcast, is compared to Christ carrying the cross; later, she attempts to quell a street fight using a reference to scripture. Religion plays some part in the plot near the film's conclusion, when the flophouse owner is alerted to the Kid's presence as the lad kneels to say his prayers.

The defiance suggested in Colleen Moore's recollections finds a parallel when *Monsieur Verdoux*, in the condemned cell, is visited by a priest. When the priest asks God to have mercy on the prisoner's soul, Verdoux replies, 'Why not? After all it belongs to Him.' For all this insistent bravado, Chaplin seems to have been less an atheist than an agnostic. Jerry Epstein (*qv*), in his book *Remembering Charlie*, speaks of Chaplin's 'Calvero' character in *Limelight* being an atheist, implicit in the final version though all scripted references to it were abandoned during shooting. Epstein notes Chaplin being persuaded to retain a touchingly humorous scene where Calvero, in momentary doubt, is caught praying for Terry's success and pretends to be searching for a lost button (the earlier Charlie sometimes offers brief prayers for deliverance, as in *Tillie's Punctured Romance*, *His Trysting Place* and *Easy Street*, or in purely token fashion when settling down to sleep in *Triple Trouble*). Perhaps similarly, Epstein repeated to Chaplin an account of Kay Kendall's death, as told by her husband, Rex Harrison. The bereaved actor was convinced his wife had seen God at the moment of death, something which fascinated Chaplin. Certainly, by his mid-eighties, Chaplin had begun seriously to reflect on death, as suggested by a brief moment in a latter-day interview. Soon after his passing, the *Evening Standard* of 15 February 1978 described 'London's first memorial' to Chaplin in the shape of a gift to a 14th-century Lambeth church. Two months before his death, Chaplin had donated £500 and his support to a trust planning a memorial to the 17th-century gardeners John Tradescant and his son, also named John. The project aimed to raise £250,000 for the restoration of the church and the planting of a memorial garden. Mrs Rosemary Nicholson, one of the trustees, explained that she had written to Chaplin, 'simply asking for his support and the use of his name. I was delighted to get a cheque from his lawyers, who told me how keen Sir Charlie was on the idea.'

A footnote: the Winter 1997 *Limelight* magazine mentions Neil Hurley's book, *Religion in Film*, which makes theological comparisons with Chaplin's tramp character. Also described is a controversial-sounding novel by Gorman Bechard, *The Second Greatest Story Ever Told*, in which the Almighty sends a daughter to earth after having already sent a son – 'once as Jesus and once as Charlie Chaplin'.

(See also: Abandoned projects; Censorship; Chaplin, Hannah; Death; Documentaries, compilations; Early stage appearances; Marx, Groucho; Race)

RIESNER (OR REISNER), CHARLES F. 'CHUCK' (1887–1962)

(Chaplin films *qv*)
Minneapolis-born actor, director and sometime song lyricist, a former prizefighter who spent a decade in vaudeville then graduated to musical comedy for Charles Dillingham. His early film experience was at Keystone (*qv*), Vitagraph, Astra and elsewhere, prior to joining Chaplin's unit in 1918. Riesner had evidently joined Chaplin's circle of friends during the previous year, for the *Motion Picture News* of 26 January 1918 notes his presence at the comedian's all-stag New Year gathering at the Alexandria Hotel. *A Dog's Life* casts Riesner as both the employment office clerk and the café's drummer, whose tears Charlie mistakes for laughter; he appears also as the neighbourhood tough in *The Kid* and Charlie's villainous old acquaintance in *The Pilgrim*. Riesner became an assistant director for the First National series, and is also credited thus on *The Gold Rush*. He later directed Syd Chaplin (*qv*), as in *The Man on the Box* (1925) and *The Better 'Ole* (1927); other directing credits include *Hollywood Revue of 1929*, Keaton's *Steamboat Bill, Jr.* (1928), Marie Dressler's *Reducing* (1931), *The Big Store* (1941) with the Marx Brothers and 1944's *Meet the People*, starring Lucille Ball and Dick Powell. Chuck Riesner was one of several American members of the Grand Order of Water Rats (*qv*).

(See also: Dressler, Marie; Dual rôles; First National; Grey, Lita; Guest appearances; Keaton, Buster; Marx, Groucho; Riesner, Dean)

RIESNER, DEAN ('DINKY DEAN') (b. 1918)

(Chaplin films *qv*)
Son of Charles F. 'Chuck' Riesner (*qv*), Dean Riesner was billed as 'Dinky Dean', a variant of his family nickname, 'Dink', for his childhood rôle in *The Pilgrim*. He has also claimed to be among the young extras in *The Kid*. The younger Riesner appeared subsequently in a few other silent films (such as *A Prince of a King*), but became known later as screenwriter 'Dean Franklin' (his two forenames). Dean Riesner is among the interviewees in *Unknown Chaplin* (*qv*).

(See also: Austin Albert; Children)

THE RINK

(Chaplin film)
Released by Mutual, 4 December 1916. Written and directed by Charles Chaplin. Photographed by Rollie Totheroh. Two reels. 1,881 feet.

With Charlie Chaplin (himself), Edna Purviance (Edna, the girl), James T. Kelly (her papa), Eric Campbell (Mr Stout), Henry Bergman (Mrs Stout/diner), John Rand (second waiter), Albert Austin (chef/skater), Frank J. Coleman (restaurant manager), Charlotte Mineau (friend of Edna), Lloyd Bacon (cleaner in kitchen).

Papa is awakened by a playful kitten and his equally playful daughter, Edna, who tells him she is going to the skating rink. Papa leaves the house with Edna. At a restaurant, Charlie the waiter makes up Mr Stout's bill by examining him for food stains. Mr Stout pays up, but is enraged when Charlie keeps all the change without permission. He is pursued, and the money retrieved. Charlie's next customer requests a cocktail; entering the kitchen through the 'out' door, he collides with a fellow-waiter. Re-entering by the correct doorway, he bumps into him a second time. A plate of food has been knocked to the floor; rearranging it, Charlie includes the cleaner's implements. Charlie mixes the cocktail, counteracting a malodorous egg with a flower. Before leaving the kitchen, he pauses to water down the mixture, then shakes the drink once more, his whole body vibrating. The other waiter's customer is outraged to find a scrubbing brush, soap, rag and sponge on his plate. In the kitchen, Charlie's elaborate cocktail mixing continues, some of it landing on the chef. He goes to hit Charlie, but strikes the cleaner instead. The chef is wielding a carving knife while, in the restaurant,

*An off-duty waiter disrupts **The Rink**: note Chaplin's preference for showing havoc in long-shot*

the customer storms off and the manager investigates. In the kitchen, the manager chastises waiter and chef while Charlie makes an exit, discreet except in knocking over a fellow-waiter. Outside, Mrs Stout is nagging her husband, who walks away in disgust. Mrs Stout enters the restaurant, followed by Edna's Papa. Charlie gives Papa the chair intended for Mrs Stout, allowing her to fall to the floor. When a second chair is provided, Charlie thoughtfully removes its arms so that she can fit inside. Again, Charlie enters the kitchen by the wrong door, hitting the manager in the face. Skilful use of the double doors enables Charlie to avoid being seen. Papa joins Mrs Stout after an exchange of flirtatious glances. Mr Stout enters the rink, where he flirts with an unresponsive Edna. At the restaurant, Charlie continues his rivalry with the other waiter. Clumsily serving a roast chicken to Papa and Mrs Stout, he produces an egg from within the bird, which lands on Papa's face. Charlie unwittingly strikes the other waiter, who, hitting back, mistakenly lands a punch on Mrs Stout. He is dismissed. At the rink, Mr Stout continues to pursue Edna. Fetching his hat, coat and cane from the oven, Charlie goes for lunch. Entering the foyer of the rink, Charlie meets a girl who sits with her pretty ankle bobbing up and down. In response, he flirtatiously does a trick by which his hat seems to rise. Mr Stout is still blundering after Edna when Charlie glides into the rink, narrowly missing him a few times before their eventual collision. A suddenly unsteady Charlie makes his way to the spectators' enclosure. Back on his feet, Mr Stout continues to annoy Edna,

who, tripping up, puts her arms around Charlie. When she requests Charlie's help in disposing of Mr Stout, he trips the man with his cane and escorts Edna away. Charlie clears the way by booting a fellow-skater; Mr Stout issues a direct challenge. The two men bounce off each other before going into a kind of waltz; next, Charlie holds Mr Stout at bay with his cane before dragging him around, eventually launching him into the neighbouring cafeteria. Charlie falls over. Charlie and Edna have removed their skates in the foyer when Mr Stout, still on wheels, arrives. Charlie is able to topple the big man with strong breaths. Outside, Charlie presents Edna with a calling card, fraudulently identifying him as 'Sir Cecil Seltzer, C.O.D.' In return, he is invited to Edna's skating party that evening. Soon after, Edna invites a woman friend to the party, asking her to bring a friend of her own. She bumps into 'an old sweetheart', Mr Stout, who is duly invited along. Charlie returns late to work, to be reprimanded by the boss in addition to renewing hostilities with the chef. At home, Mr Stout informs his wife that he will be working late that evening. Edna excitedly tells her father that 'Sir Cecil' will be at the party. Papa calls Mrs Stout with an invitation to attend. Another mix-up at the restaurant, and Charlie serves a customer with a live cat. At the party, the various individuals are embarrassed to meet each other, not least Mr Stout, sporting a black eye acquired in the earlier scuffle. The arrival of 'Sir Cecil' completes a line of guilty people who agree that 'Mum's the word.' The skating begins, and Charlie, escorting Edna, blunders straight into the Stouts. Mrs Stout cannot be lifted, and a fight begins between Charlie and Mr Stout. Charlie gradually gains his footing, as does Mrs Stout, who aims for Charlie but hits her husband instead. Many of the guests depart, and soon Charlie is pursued by a line of irate skaters, led by Mr Stout, whom Charlie manoeuvres into the cafeteria, where they crash into a table. Mrs Stout is

booted after them, causing general collapse. The police arrive, but Charlie, eluding them and the partially-recovered guests, makes his way into the street. His escape is complete when, hooking his cane on to a passing car, he allows himself to be towed away. Charlie watches with glee as the skaters trip over.

Chaplin's autobiography cites this film as an example of camera placing, in that the tramp, surveying the havoc he has caused, is funnier through being seen in the distance rather than in close-up. It is this type of detail that is often overlooked by critics who accuse Chaplin of merely pointing a camera as a means of recording his performance. Chaplin refers to the film as being called *Skating*, probably a working title, but also the name of a Karno sketch that was its probable inspiration. Chaplin later employed another such routine in *Modern Times* (*qv*), which also revives some of the business with Charlie as waiter.

The Rink is one of the most popular Chaplin films, despite frequent mutilation in its many reissues. Some prints are missing brief sections, such as that in which a lady orders a cocktail (rendering Charlie's mixing of same a purely arbitrary act). Another frequent casualty is a scene in which chef Albert Austin (*qv*) hurls items of food backwards over his shoulder, which Charlie catches on plates; still another is an exterior shot of John Rand (*qv*) being ejected from the restaurant and Charlie's subsequent reaction; while most prints are missing the gag where Charlie, flirting at the rink, makes his hat rise by leaning back so that its brim pushes against the wall. In addition, some of the concluding shots are often omitted, after Charlie has hooked his cane on to the car. The BBC *Chaplin SuperClown* copy seems complete but, as with a parallel insert during *The Count* (*qv*), has unnecessarily remade inserts of Charlie's oddly made-out bill and bogus visiting card.

(See also: Alcohol; Cars; Costume; Food; Home movies; Karno Company, The; Kelly, James T.; Parks; Policemen; Skating; Television; Titling; Video releases)

RISQUÉ HUMOUR 🎩

(Chaplin films *qv*)
One of the more frequent early

complaints about Chaplin was his supposed fondness for vulgarity and 'dirt'. Such grumbling tended to come from journalists with highbrow aims

Charlie's reputation for **risqué humour** is reflected in this early Belgian postcard, based on that country's most celebrated statue
By courtesy of Michael Pointon

(actual or assumed) rather than from the general public. Many contemporary reviews suggest a reluctant tolerance of Chaplin's earthier moments in order to savour his more refined material. As Julian Johnson wrote in a 1915 edition of *Photoplay*: 'Mr. Chaplin is funny with a funniness which transcends his dirt and vulgarity.'

Chaplin's frequent use of lavatorial humour – as with his reluctance to sweep up after animals in *City Lights* – is characteristic of his native Britain. *The Property Man* has a gag in which Charlie, concealing a jug of beer in his trousers, absent-mindedly bends and appears to have had a mishap. When, in *A Dog's Life*, a woman cries copious tears, Charlie thinks his dog has left a puddle. *The Great Dictator* is dampened by a baby he is given to hold (shades also of *The Kid*), and one might mention a sequence from earlier in the film, wherein a shell from 'Big Bertha' demolishes an outhouse. David Yallop's Arbuckle biography tells a Keystone anecdote in which Chaplin's colleagues neglected to mention the electrification

of a toilet seat he was about to use; the studio joke was that this startling occasion brought about the Tramp's distinctive walk.

There is a certain amount of innuendo throughout Chaplin's work, invariably of the modest cheekiness associated with children. This applies in some degree when, in *Easy Street*, Charlie congratulates a frail old man on his prolific fatherhood. In *His New Job*, Charlie is sufficiently taken with the rounded rump of a statue for him to mime its contours to the head propman. This gag is sometimes ruined in reissue prints, where the statue, to the left of frame, has been obscured to accommodate a soundtrack. Similarly, a much-quoted gag in *Work* has Charlie providing a statuette with a lampshade 'skirt', which he manipulates into doing a bump-and-grind dance.

Both *Caught in the Rain* and *A Night Out* see Charlie caught in bed with another man's wife, albeit not necessarily through choice; this was very risqué for the time, especially given that Hollywood's later censorship forbade even married couples to share a bed. The whole idea of pyjama-clad women in *Mabel's Strange Predicament*, *Mabel's Married Life* and the aforementioned *A Night Out* would again have seemed outrageous in an era still accustomed to ankle-length dresses and heavy corsetry. The applies to Charlie's hooking up of Mabel's skirt in *Getting Acquainted* and the removal of Alice Howell's skirt in *Laughing Gas*. The notion of Ambrose fathering an illegitimate offspring in *His Trysting Place* would also have raised eyebrows in 1914.

It has been suggested that *Mabel's Strange Predicament* depicts Mabel as prostitute, implicit of the dance hall girls in *The Gold Rush*, and also possibly the case with Vivian Edwards and Cecile Arnold (both *qv*) in *Those Love Pangs*. As Charlie watches Vivian Edwards' undulating walk in *Dough and Dynamite*, he makes a comparison by glancing at a sign reading 'assorted French tarts'.

Direct sexual references are few and, inevitably for the period, usually understated. One example is a throwaway gag in *The Champion* when Leo White (*qv*) aims a gun at Charlie, who lifts the barrel so that it no longer points down the front of his trousers. There are a surprising number of homosexual gags, notably that in *Behind the Screen* and, to a lesser degree, Charlie's coy reaction in *The Cure* when

mistakenly believing Eric Campbell (*qv*) to be making eyes at him. In the flophouse scenes of *Police* and *Triple Trouble*, Bud Jamison (*qv*) contrasts his burly appearance with a manner suggesting effeminacy, as does the rather camp dancer in *His Prehistoric Past*. There are hints of something similar in *Modern Times* when Charlie becomes nervous of a huge cellmate, engaged in needlepoint. There is a flamboyant party guest in *Tillie's Punctured Romance* who, after trying to ingratiate himself, turns to leave, whereupon Charlie is persuaded not to land a kick on his behind. Charlie's equivalent attempts to ingratiate himself with boxing opponent Hank Mann (*qv*) in *City Lights* are misinterpreted, so much so that the fighter goes off to change in a curtained cubicle.

The woman whose apron is filled with stolen food in *Easy Street* looks heavily pregnant, and seems to be taken as such by Edna Purviance (*qv*); it may be that the inappropriate sub-titles added on reissue were designed in part to obscure this reference.

Modern Times revisits the child's concept of the risqué when a crazed, spanner-wielding Charlie tightens the buttons on the bottom of a secretary's skirt, does as much for the nipples of a male colleague, then sets out – unsuccessfully – to tighten the buttons on a matronly woman's breasts. Altogether more subtle is his gobbledegook song in the film, which, according to the accompanying mime, is clearly about a girl who acquiesces to a rich man's desire in exchange for a diamond ring, the payoff being that a pawnbroker pronounces the gift worthless, sending the girl into a panic (this final 'verse' is omitted from most prints, but has recently been restored on video in the USA and Britain).

Contemporary censors seemed at least as concerned over *Monsieur Verdoux*'s sexual activities as his systematic murders; it may be revealing that his match was met in the graceless Annabella, who, it is implied, has a fondness for coarse jokes. Again from the later works, *Limelight*'s Calvero, speaking of the advantage human consciousness has over anything else, claims that the stars can do nothing but 'sit on their axes', one of several lines to have escaped censorship (the 'Animal Trainer' song provides a misleading moment, until we learn that 'Phyllis' and 'Henry' are merely fighting rather than engaging in any other physical contest).

A King in New York took Chaplin into another era, a latter-day world with concerns unheard of only a few years before. When the exiled King visits a cinema, the trailers advertising 'forthcoming attractions' are designed to lampoon then-current trends in the American way of movies. One of these is for a deathless epic called *Man or Woman*, an exploitation film about transsexuals (quite recent news in 1957) in which a beautiful woman speaks in bass tones while her gentleman friend replies in falsetto. 'We can go to Denmark,' he suggests. Though daring at the time, this is fairly obvious material to a modern audience, and may suggest why *A King in New York* lacks the timelessness of Chaplin's major works. The same may be said of *A Countess From Hong Kong*, whose heroine admits directly to being a prostitute, and which incorporates gags relating to an oversized bra. Another product of relaxed censorship is the preoccupation of Hudson, the valet, with the non-consummation of his bogus marriage, to the point where he absently refers to 'consummated soup'.

(See also: Arbuckle, Roscoe 'Fatty'; *Bank, The*; Censorship; Howell, Alice; Normand, Mabel; Statues; Swain, Mack; Video releases; *Walk, The*)

THE ROUNDERS

(Chaplin film)
Keystone Comedy released by Mutual, 7 September 1914. Produced by Mack Sennett. Written and directed by Charles Chaplin. Photography attributed to Frank D. Williams. Reissue titles include *Oh! What a Night* and *Revelry*. One reel. 1,010 feet.

With Charlie Chaplin (Mr Full), Roscoe 'Fatty' Arbuckle (Mr Fuller), Phyllis Allen (Mrs Full), Minta Durfee (Mrs Fuller), Al St. John (bellboy), Fritz Schade (diner annoyed by Chaplin and Arbuckle), Charley Chase, Wallace MacDonald (other diners).

Mr Full, an elegantly-dressed drunk, staggers into his hotel. In the foyer, he surveys an attractive girl and absently bumps into Mr Fuller. Upstairs, a bellhop assists the wavering Mr Full to his room. A furious Mrs Full awaits. Coolly, she offers a chair, but sits upon it herself, allowing her husband to hit the floor. Mr Full makes it to his feet, one of which pins his cloak to the floor. The cloak is removed. Mr Fuller, also drunk, ascends the stairs to his own room. The bellhop finds him amusing until Mr Fuller pulls the chair from under him. In his room, Mr Fuller ignores his distraught wife. Across the corridor, Mrs Full catches her husband by the neck, using his own cane. He recoils from her diatribe, but is pulled back. When he staggers back on the bed, Mrs Full uses the cane to whack his behind. Because reason has failed, Mrs Full beats her husband with pillows. Mr Fuller, meanwhile, is also being beaten up by a desperate spouse. Mrs Full, hearing the noise, sends her husband to investigate. Mr Fuller, retaliating, is throttling his wife when Mr Full is thrust into the room, knocking over Mr Fuller in the process. Mrs Fuller attacks Mr Full, incurring the wrath of Mrs Full. During the quarrel, Mr Full is bumped back and forth between Mrs Full and Mr Fuller. The two men exchange lodge greetings and set off together, Mr Fuller carefully stealing his wife's handbag with the crook of his cane. Mr Fuller empties the bag of money, while Mr Full, fetching his hat, plunders his own wife's handbag. The two inebriates prepare for synchronized drinking by putting on their hats with a peculiar twining of arms. They are already on the street, Mr Fuller dragging Mr Full, by the time the two women notice the theft of their money. The angry wives depart. At a café, Mr Fuller tries to restore his friend to his feet by lifting him with their canes. They annoy a diner, and make themselves too comfortable on the premises. Their wives enter the café to see their husbands in a scrap. Mrs Full swings at her spouse with an umbrella, but strikes the innocent diner instead. The two drunks flee the establishment, pursued by angry wives and diners. Reaching a lake, they commandeer a rowing boat and sail into what they consider a safe distance. They settle down to sleep, unaware that the

The Rounders, *Arbuckle and Chaplin, seek refuge in an open boat*

boat is leaking. Their tearful wives can only watch as they sink slowly into the lake.

There is a story to the effect that this finale was contrived by Fatty Arbuckle (*qv*), who, aware of Chaplin's aversion to water, decided to play a joke on his friend by deliberately removing the bung from the boat; Chaplin, placed on the spot, had no choice but to incorporate it into the action. If this is true, Chaplin's reactions are remarkably smooth and display an ability to take a joke, for he has evident difficulty in keeping a straight face when disappearing beneath the surface. This very effective teaming of Chaplin and Arbuckle was, sadly, their only such excursion, their other collaborative appearances being rather less focused. Arbuckle, who maintained his friendship with Chaplin after their professional separation, later expressed regret over the comparative insignificance of their collaborative work at Keystone (*qv*). *Bioscope* of 18 February 1915 offered praise, though believed its success depended 'more upon vigorous action than upon story'. In *The Rounders*, the two comedians complement each other perfectly, even to the point where it is Arbuckle rather than Chaplin who uses a cane to steal a handbag. The now mostly obsolete term 'rounders' (vaguely synonymous with 'rogues' or 'scoundrels') has sometimes been mistranscribed as the more familiar 'bounders'. In turn, the comedians' character names in this film are usually quoted as 'Mr. Full' and 'Mr. Fuller', though present copies – all of which seem to have come back from a W.H. Productions reissue called *Oh, What a*

Royalty: Her Majesty Queen Elizabeth II attends the UK première of Limelight

Night – do not offer these in the subtitling. The same applies to the remade Keystone titles in the BBC's *Chaplin SuperClown* version. On this occasion, *The Rounders* is paired with *Laughing Gas* (*qv*), the only other Keystone film to be represented in this series.

(See also: Alcohol; Allen, Phyllis; Boats, ships; Chase, Charley; Costume; Durfee, Minta; *His Favorite Pastime*; MacDonald, Wallace; Parks; Race; St. John, Al; Schade, Fritz; Smoking; Television; Video releases; Williams, Frank D.; Women)

ROYALTY

(Chaplin films *qv*)

In June 1917, *Pictures and the Picturegoer* reported that Prince George of Battenburg had written to Film Booking Offices, requesting copies of the forthcoming Essanay-Chaplin anthology *Chase Me, Charlie* (*qv*) to screen on board his ship. Thus, Chaplin was by Royal Appointment at a time before he was required to meet them in person. It was only a year later that, on screen, he did battle with the Kaiser in *The Bond* and *Shoulder Arms*; ultimately, of course, Chaplin became a deposed monarch in *A King in New York*.

As noted in the main entry, King George V was reportedly less than pleased when his kin became involved

with Chaplin in a 1921 home movie, *Nice and Friendly* (*qv*); it was Chaplin's turn for discomfort when presented to King Albert of Belgium, when visiting Paris a decade later. The King, in any case much taller than Chaplin, was seated in a much higher position, an idea Chaplin later put to use in *The Great Dictator*. Conversation proved difficult; Chaplin, having heard that the King had travelled by air, expounded his own enthusiastic views on aviation, to no avail. The King, at length, proved himself an able conversationalist, but the meeting remained a gentle embarrassment.

Chaplin's experiences with British royalty were less fraught: Her Majesty Queen Elizabeth II attended the UK première of *Limelight* in 1952 and, in 1975, dubbed the comedian 'Sir Charles'. They met again the following year, when the Queen, Prince Philip and Princess Anne congratulated Chaplin on having been made a Fellow of BAFTA, the British Academy of Film and Television Arts.

(See also: Aircraft; Awards, honours; Public appearances)

RUGGLES, WESLEY
(1889-1972)

(Chaplin films, *qv*)

Los Angeles-born actor, brother of Charles Ruggles. Wesley Ruggles began his a career on stage but entered pictures at least as early as 1914 (one contemporary source claims 1912) and worked at Keystone (*qv*) during that year. He does not seem present in any of the Keystone Chaplins but is known to have worked there with Syd; he joined Charlie's company at Essanay (*qv*), appearing in *The Bank, Shanghaied, A Night in the Show, Carmen* and *Police*. He is sometimes credited with two rôles at Mutual (*qv*), one of them as an actor in *Behind the Screen*. The other cited rôle, that of the elderly theatrical type in *The Pawnshop*, is, in the author's opinion, questionable. Ruggles had become a director at Vitagraph by 1917; the following year saw him as an Army Signals Corps cameraman. He resumed directing following the Great War. Talkie credits include *Cimarron*, (1930), *I'm no Angel* (1933) and *True Confession* (1937). Ruggles functioned also as producer; his last effort was a pleasant but unsuccessful British-made Technicolor musical starring Sid Field, *London Town* (1946).

(See also: Chaplin, Syd; Desmonde, Jerry; Goodwins, Fred; Impersonators)

RUTHERFORD, MARGARET
(1892–1972)

British character actress, frequently in comedy, as in *The Happiest Days of Your Life* (1950); remembered also as Agatha Christie's 'Miss Marple' in a series of comedy-thrillers made during the 1960s. She modestly dismissed occasional comparisons with Chaplin and Jacques Tati as a 'natural clown', but was nevertheless a formidable comedienne. In Chaplin's *A Countess From Hong Kong* (*qv*), she plays Miss Gaulswallow, a hypochondriac whose identity is assumed by glamorous stowaway Natascha. Jerry Epstein (*qv*) later conveyed the impression that he had recommended her, but that Chaplin, reluctant to engage too many stars, agreed to see her only under sufferance. Regardless of this, Chaplin treated her with extreme cordiality. In her memoirs, the actress spoke warmly of Chaplin, recalling his invitation to meet at London's Savoy Hotel, where he dispelled any nervousness on her part by making her feel like an old friend. Typically, Chaplin gave the actress 'a one-man performance' of the part he wanted her to play, describing also his own rôle as steward while emphasizing its insignificance compared to hers. Also present was her husband, actor Stringer Davis, who had brought along the copy of Chaplin's autobiography given to him by his wife. She had autographed it to him for 'my favourite "Clown", Guide and Counsellor, Friend and Husband with the everlasting love of Eternal Things'. Chaplin offered his own addendum, endorsing the statement. In making *Countess*, Margaret Rutherford claimed that Chaplin 'was always considerate, never raised his voice and was one of the most helpful people I have worked with'. It was, in her opinion, 'one of the most enjoyable films that I have ever made. And all because of the genius of Chaplin.' She also enjoyed working with Sophia Loren (*qv*), who insisted on a photograph together while Miss Rutherford was tucked up in bed as the eccentric invalid. She did not meet Marlon Brando (*qv*) but, on his insistence, was provided with his dressing room on the days when she was filming (as a pleasant footnote, Brando left her a tiny love letter on the first day!).

(See also: Bloom, Claire; O'Neill, Oona)

SANDFORD, STANLEY J. 'TINY' 🎩
(1894–1961)

(Chaplin films *qv*)
Born in Osage, Iowa, the good-humoured, giant (6 feet 5 inches) Sandford spent four years in repertory with the Daniel Frawley Company in Seattle (where he was educated) and Alaska. Known to have been in films from at least 1910, Sandford has been named as the whiskered gambler in *The Immigrant*, but this is clearly a different – and far shorter – actor (see also **Frank J. Coleman**). He plays the bartender in *The Gold Rush*, but editing has rendered him barely visible in the reissue version. Sandford's next rôle with Chaplin was as the property man in *The Circus*. He is the operator of a pavement lift, with whom Charlie decides not to argue, in *City Lights*. *Modern Times* sees him on the assembly line as Charlie's co-worker, who is later forced into crime by unemployment. His final Chaplin rôle,

in *The Great Dictator*, is as one of the barber's comrades-in-arms during 1918. Sandford was a familiar face in Hal Roach comedies, among them *Movie Night* (1929) with Charley Chase (*qv*) and several Laurel & Hardy comedies, notably *The Second Hundred Years* (1927), *Their Purple Moment* (1928), *Big Business* (1929), *The Hoose-Gow* (1929), *Pardon Us* (1931) and *Our Relations* (1936). Other films include Erich von Stroheim's *Blind Husbands* (1922) and, as Porthos, Fairbanks' *The Iron Mask* (1929).

(See also: Fairbanks, Douglas; Laurel, Stan; Rand, John)

SHANGHAIED 🎩

(Chaplin film)
Released by General Film Company, 4 October 1915. Produced by Essanay. Written and directed by Charles Chaplin. Photographed by Harry Ensign. Sometimes known in Britain as *Charlie Shanghaied*. Two reels. 1,771 feet.

With Charlie Chaplin (himself), Edna Purviance (the daughter), Wesley Ruggles (her father, owner of the ship), Lawrence A. Bowes (captain), John Rand (ship's cook), Billy Armstrong, Paddy McGuire, Leo White, Fred Goodwins (crew).

A ship's owner instructs his captain to destroy the vessel for insurance money. The Captain informs the mate that a crew is needed; some dockside layabouts are approached but are not interested. Charlie calls on Edna, his girlfriend. Edna's father, the ship's owner, sends Charlie packing. Charlie meets the ship's mate, who offers money in exchange for help in shanghaiing a crew. The mate is to entice each man with the promise of a drink; Charlie then pops out of a barrel, knocking the victim cold with a mallet. Three men are recruited before the Captain arrives. Charlie bops the Captain, offering a left-handed, thumb-on-nose salute as apology. Charlie is paid as promised, then knocked unconscious. The men are brought round, and given the choice of work or physical violence; Charlie eagerly opts for work. In the hold, a cabin boy tries to get tough with Charlie; he is saved from a pasting by the arrival of the Captain, kicking and whipping the new mariners into activity. Charlie, ascending steps towards the deck, finds time to boot the

*Charlie is **Shanghaied** ...*

cabin boy. Charlie is put in charge of a grappling hook, to be used to unload cargo. Charlie's signals to the crane operator send the cargo plummeting into the hold, flattening the Captain. The load descends a second time, landing not just on the Captain but also on some of the crew. The hook, minus its burden, reappears with a crew member clinging hard. He drops to the hold; on the next descent, the hook picks up the Captain. He is returned below, then reappears, knocking the mate overboard. Captain and mate are fished out of the sea, only to plummet back. Charlie and another crew member attempt to haul them in; to obtain leverage, Charlie places his foot on the man in front, pushing him over the side. The other deckhands throw them a line, but in attempting to haul them up are themselves dumped over the opposite side. All are eventually brought to safety. Back on land, the owner finds a note left by his daughter. She has stowed away aboard the boat. The panic-stricken father departs for the quayside. In the hold, Edna hides in a sack. Her father arrives at the dock, where, hiring a speedboat, he sets off after the doomed vessel. On board, soup is being prepared. Charlie, now in sailor's rig, is to serve soup to the Captain and mate. As Charlie has used it for washing dishes, it is swiftly returned, and the cook blamed. The cook discovers what has happened, and a fight ensues. The furious cook is also unimpressed by Charlie's dancing an impromptu sailor's hornpipe, twirling a hambone like a baton. Charlie serves the next course as the ship rolls mightily. Between galley and table, he turns several somersaults, but keeps the tray level. Once served, the tray slides to the floor. Meanwhile, the owner is on the way by speedboat. In the crew's quarters, pork is

'Tiny' Sandford (centre) plays Charlie's colleague in Modern Times

served. Charlie attempts to eat, but is hampered by a neighbour's elbow. Before long, seasickness has overtaken Charlie, who departs for some fresh air. On his return, Charlie pretends he had merely gone outside for a smoke. Salad is next, with oil borrowed from a lamp. Charlie, queasy once more, retreats outside and falls into the hold. He meets Edna, who, pointing to their cargo of explosives, tells Charlie of the plot. They hide on the approach of Captain and mate, who light the fuse to a barrel of gunpowder. As they board a lifeboat, the cook is seen nearby. The Captain gives him a start, and the cook jumps overboard. Captain and mate have escaped, but Charlie throws the barrel of gunpowder into their boat. It explodes just as Charlie and Edna board the owner's speedboat, which has pulled alongside. The Captain and the mate disappear beneath the waves. Edna and Charlie embrace, but father

... and gives Captain Lawrence Bowes an unusual salute

intervenes. Charlie, threatening suicide, makes a dramatic leap overboard; as father looks for him, Charlie clambers into the other side of the boat, and kicks him into the sea. Exit the lovers, jubilant.

Shanghaied moves quickly, and is among the better-constructed of Chaplin's Essanay comedies. Sime Silverman, in *Variety* of 22 October 1915, approved of the strong storyline and seemingly reduced vulgarity: 'The

Essanay has the right idea now for that film comedian, if it keeps along the "Shanghaied" lines.'

The shipboard scenes are anticipatory of Chaplin's later *The Immigrant* (*qv*), both in terms of gags and the means by which the illusion of a rough sea is obtained. It is evident that the interior set is built on some type of rocking apparatus, moving in opposition to a tilting camera fitted with a pendulum. The illusion fails on exteriors, where the swing of the camera also takes in a completely static horizon. This said, a contemporary report from Fred Goodwins (*qv*) to the British *Pictures and the Picturegoer* suggests some initial desire for authenticity; according to this source, the company sailed for some 'distant islands out in the Pacific', encountering rough seas overnight. In common with most of the party, Chaplin fell prey to severe nausea and, when slumber came, periodically recited poetry in his sleep. 'The boat will *not* go out to the island again, methinks,' continued Goodwins. 'Charlie has changed the story so that it can be taken at the dockside for the most part!'

Today's copies of *Shanghaied* tend to be rather murky and seldom vary significantly in content, although the opening scenes of conspiracy and Charlie's arrival at Edna's home are sometimes transposed. A version frequently in UK distribution has, in common with several other Essanays, rewritten sub-titles containing such inappropriate puns as 'They always had Pork on Sundays, so Charlie made a pig of himself.' The original text confined itself, mercifully, to the simple description 'Pork!'

(See also: *Bank, The*; Boats, ships; Bowes, Lawrence A.; Costume; Essanay; Jamison, William 'Bud'; McGuire, Paddy; Rand, John; Reissues; Ruggles, Wesley; Smoking; Television)

SHOULDER ARMS

(Chaplin film)
Released by First National, 20 October 1918. Produced, written and directed by Charles Chaplin. Photographed by Rollie Totheroh. Three reels.

With Charlie Chaplin (himself, as a doughboy), Edna Purviance (French girl), Syd Chaplin (Charlie's comrade/the Kaiser), Henry Bergman (Fat, whiskered

German soldier/the Kaiser's General/bartender in flashback), Albert Austin (doughboy in drill scene – see below/American officer/clean-shaven German soldier/bearded German soldier/doctor in deleted sequence – also see below), Loyal Underwood (small German officer), Jack Wilson (Crown Prince), Tom Wilson (German woodcutter), Park Jones.

Charlie, a new recruit, is the most awkward of the 'awkward squad'. After making a mess of drill, Charlie flops down on his bunk. 'Over there', Charlie arrives in the trenches, shells landing perilously nearby. Charlie, allocated no. 13, is equipped for any eventuality, carrying such things as mousetrap and cheese grater, the latter serving as back-scratcher. Behind enemy lines, a diminutive but bullying officer inspects his men. Charlie pauses for lunch. Belatedly, his colleague suggests he should make himself at home, as Charlie does sentry duty with shells exploding behind him. A retaliatory shell explodes in the German trench. Standing in the rain, Charlie dreams of home and a friendly bar-room. Charlie is relieved, the new password being 'It's wet'. Mail arrives from home, but Charlie receives none. Some of his comrades have been sent food, so Charlie makes do with the cheese from his mousetrap. Charlie begins to read a letter over the recipient's shoulder, but it is taken out of his view. There is a package left over, its name indecipherable, which is assumed to be for Charlie. It contains hard biscuits and Limburger cheese, for which Charlie dons a gas mask. The cheese is hurled away with great force, coming to rest on the German officer just as he proposes a toast to victory. Charlie retires to his bunk, in a now flooded dug-out. He plumps up a soaking pillow before settling into a submerged bed. His comrade, barefoot, is asleep in the water. Charlie disturbs him by making a wave. A lighted candle floats past on a piece of wood, which Charlie directs so that his comrade gets a singed foot. Charlie settles down in the water, using a gramophone horn as snorkel. Next morning, Charlie tries to massage his feet back to life, but grabs one belonging to his comrade. The men are suddenly ordered to go over the top. Charlie nervously contemplates his number, 13. He lights cigarettes for himself and two comrades, but relinquishes his own when reminded of the poor luck attending

Shoulder Arms: *Charlie on parade*

'three on a match'. Charlie strikes a brave pose, but obligingly lets the others go first. The German trench is captured, and no. 13, 'not so unlucky', brings in a crowd of thirteen prisoners. Charlie gives them cigarettes, and when their tiny officer refuses the gesture, Charlie wins the prisoners' cheers by spanking the officer. Charlie is asked how he captured so many men; 'I surrounded them,' comes the reply. Charlie, ironically indicating the sign 'Paris 1918', leads his captives away. A caption, 'Poor France', precedes a ruined cottage and a desolate French girl sitting outside. In the trenches, Charlie shows his buddy a technique for opening bottles, in which the bottle is held aloft until decapitated by a passing shell. Charlie surveys the battlefield with a periscope, then takes pot-shots at the opposition. He chalks up a few victims, then erases one that fires back. He corrects this, and notches up even more, one from overhead. A volunteer is required for a dangerous mission; Charlie finishes up behind enemy lines, camouflaged as a tree. The arrival of a squad of Germans brings an unexpected hazard, when one of them prepares to chop Charlie down for firewood. He is knocked out with a well-aimed branch. Charlie deals with two others in like fashion, and goes on the run. Nearby, Charlie's comrade is signalling back to the Allies. He is apprehended and about to be shot when Charlie, standing by the firing squad, launches his own attack. They both escape, Charlie being pursued through the woods then through a water pipe. He seems to be trapped, but the Germans put a bullet through what turns out to be an empty tree costume. A fat German tries to follow Charlie through the pipe, but becomes stuck; his comrade with the axe smashes him free. Charlie takes refuge in the ruined cottage, using the door and window as if not exposed to the open air. He has collapsed on the bed

upstairs when the French girl returns. She tends to a wound on his hand. Having established his rôle as an American soldier (by making himself 'see stars' and underlining them with stripes), Charlie wins her confidence. Downstairs, Germans approach with a machine gun. Charlie confronts them, and momentarily turns the gun on them. The situation is reversed once more, and Charlie makes his escape, leaving the Germans in the collapsing house. The French girl, arrested for aiding the Allies, is at the mercy of an unscrupulous officer; Charlie climbs into the building through a hole in the wall, emerging through the fireplace. Using a hot poker, he overpowers the officer, locking him inside a cupboard. Another German climbs in, but is sent away with a jab from the poker. Outside, the troops have lined up to receive a visit from the Kaiser, Crown Prince and a general. The French girl hides Charlie in the closet as another German climbs in through the fireplace. Kaiser and entourage enter by the comparatively prosaic means of a doorway. The Kaiser demands to see the officer. The French girl pretends he isn't there, but the Kaiser hears noises from the cupboard, from which Charlie emerges buttoning a borrowed uniform. Misbehaviour is assumed; 'We will discuss your case later,' says the Crown Prince. Charlie and the girl are ordered outside, where a chauffeur complains when Charlie strikes a match on the Kaiser's car. Charlie's comrade has been captured once more. For the benefit of the Germans, Charlie slaps him around then dismisses the guards. While the Kaiser and entourage plan their campaign, the drivers are overpowered and their uniforms stolen. Charlie's comrade makes his own way; the French girl, with a moustache painted in grease, becomes a German soldier. She kisses Charlie, leaving a moustache imprint on his cheek. The Kaiser and his party enter the car and are driven to the Allied lines; Charlie's comrade telegraphs the news in advance. The Kaiser is captured, Charlie and the girl are fêted, and the war seems to be over – until Charlie, still on his bunk, is awakened by two doughboys.

Shoulder Arms was Chaplin's greatest success up to that time, and was to remain a yardstick for his work for years to come. The New York *Times* noted that people who attended solely to find fault remained instead to laugh, and considered Chaplin 'even more enjoyable

Shoulder Arms: *in the trenches, ready for anything ...*

... except despair

A French girl discovers an exhausted doughboy in **Shoulder Arms**

than one is likely to anticipate because he abandons some of the tricks of former comedies and introduces new properties

Stage star Ina Claire visits the set of
Shoulder Arms

into his horseplay'. Chaplin had, of
course, been prolific over the preceding
four years, and was to some extent being
taken for granted by critics.

During production, visitors to the set

Shoulder Arms was reduced from feature-
length prior to release. The deleted scenes
of Charlie's home life and army medical
have recently been restored to an
American laserdisc edition
BFI Stills, Posters and Designs

included opera singer Nellie Melba and
the actresses Ina Claire and Marie Dressler
(*qv*). A screening was attended by the deaf
and blind Helen Keller, for whom an
interpreter conveyed the action through
touch. The film was not completed until
near the end of the First World War, and
was considered daring by many, partly
because of an assumed sensitivity over
humour in this situation, but also owing
to controversy over Chaplin's non-
participation in the fight. The film was,
however, approved by contemporary
troops – most of whom seem to have
preferred Chaplin to remain a laughter-
maker rather than a soldier – while the
supposed sensitivity evaporated because, as
Isobel Quigley has noted, there is a certain
acceptability in jokes made at the time of a
crisis that cannot apply later on.

Syd Chaplin, who had joined his
brother's unit for the preceding film, *A
Dog's Life* (*qv*), here portrays both Charlie's
army pal and the Kaiser; he may also be
seen as the latter in *The Bond* (*qv*). Henry
Bergman and Albert Austin (both *qv*) also
contribute multiple rôles, though one of
Austin's characters (as a soldier in the
opening drill sequence) was overlooked
when the film was revived as part of *The
Chaplin Revue* (*qv*). The *Revue* version,
sometimes screened as a separate entity,
derives from a negative quite different
from other surviving material. For
example, when Syd Chaplin faces a firing
squad, the soldiers walk somewhat across
camera instead of directly towards it, as in
other material. In the same scene, a close-
up of Syd is taken from different angles,
and the choice of close and long-shots
varies as he hitches up his trousers. This
variation of material was the result of
domestic and overseas negatives being
obtained using twin cameras, in an age
before adequate duplicating negative stock
was available. Similar variants are noted
under **The Floorwalker**, **The Count**, **Easy
Street**, **A Dog's Life**, **The Kid** and **Pay Day**.
There are a number of small trims in the
Revue copy, such as the 'three-on-a-match'
business and a later moment when
Charlie, posing as a German officer, can
easily be lip-read during his attempts to
say '*Jawohl.*'

Much of *Shoulder Arms* was deleted
before its initial release. Chaplin had
planned a five-reel film (it was announced
as such by *Pictures and the Picturegoer* less
than three weeks before its American
release) showing Charlie's exploits before,
during and after the war, but he had
settled for the middle section alone. Even
this seems to have been trimmed prior to

release; a clue to some of the deleted
footage comes again from *Pictures and the
Picturegoer*, to the effect that 'his juggling
with hand-grenades is said to rank
amongst the funniest things he has ever
done'. Stills from a deleted early sequence,
showing Charlie's army medical, were
widely reprinted as general publicity over
the years, seemingly in ignorance of their
origins. The footage itself was rediscovered
and used in part for *Unknown Chaplin*
(*qv*), presenting Albert Austin (again!) as
the doctor, and employing a gag in which
Charlie, shown in silhouette, appears to
swallow a lengthy wooden spoon and
other implements, which are retrieved only
with some difficulty. Other footage from
this sequence shows Charlie, stripped to
the waist, attempting to hide his semi-
nakedness from two female clerks; one of
these is Edna Purviance (*qv*), who
plays the French girl in the final edit. It is
unlikely that Edna would have played such
an undisguised dual rôle in any released
version, even though Charlie's wartime
exploits are eventually revealed as a dream.
Both this and the film's intended opening
sequence, with Charlie as a family man,
have been issued on laserdisc in the United
States. This section, again used partially in
Unknown Chaplin, was copied only after
decomposition had become fairly
advanced. It begins with Charlie and a trio
of small sons, whose respective ages are
suggested by height ratio. Each son copies
his father's walk. When they walk past a
bar, Charlie excuses himself momentarily,
to reappear after evidently consuming the
speediest of drinks. At home, Charlie must
cook and clean for his wife, an off-screen
character whose dimensions and
temperament are suggested by some
gigantic underwear and an unerring way
with missiles. It comes as no surprise when
Charlie, receiving a circular extolling the
virtues of army life, departs swiftly for the
recruiting office.

(See also: Alcohol; Animation; Caricatures;
Costume; Dreams; Food; Home movies;
Idle Class, The; Jones, Park; Left-
handedness; Music; Rand, John; Reeves,
Alf; Smoking; Titling; Underwood, Loyal;
Video releases; Walk, The; Wartime;
Wilson, Jack; Wilson, Tom)

SICKNESS

(Chaplin films *qv*)
The early 'Charlie' – particularly at
Keystone (*qv*) – could often be an
unsympathetic character. This is

particularly apparent in his cavalier attitude towards infirmity, a legacy of the macabre humour often prevalent in Chaplin's native Britain. An extreme example is the mistreated invalid of *His New Profession* and the tortured dental patients in *Laughing Gas*. Chaplin's screen image gradually acquired greater compassion, but the savagery continued when deserved by the recipient, notably a gout-ridden Eric Campbell (*qv*) in *The Cure*. When *The Kid* is taken ill, Charlie treats the matter with due seriousness, his parental manner anticipating that of Calvero towards Terry in *Limelight*. There are also severe consequences – ultimately resolved – of Big Jim's amnesia in *The Gold Rush*; altogether less severe are the attacks of *mal de mer* in *The Immigrant* and *A Day's Pleasure*.

Chaplin himself proved unusually resilient in terms of physical illness, despite – or perhaps because of – the severe deprivations of his childhood. Aside from periodic colds and similar commonplace ailments, he remained agile until October 1966, when, aged 77, he fractured a leg during production of *A Countess From Hong Kong*. Although Chaplin recovered from the injury, there are those who believe that his gradual decline in health began with this accident. Similar concern was expressed when, as reported in the *Evening Standard* of 11 July 1975, he was forced to return home from London after injuring his ankle in a fall.

(See also: Alcohol; Boats, ships; Childhood; Death; *Easy Street*; Mental illness; Villains)

SKATING 🎩

(Chaplin films *qv*)
As a comic device, skating is known to have been in the Chaplin repertoire at least as early as his stint with the Karno Company (*qv*). The troupe had both a sketch entitled *Skating* and a company hockey team, of which Chaplin was a member. There is a story concerning Chaplin's mastering skates after being caught in a situation where it was required; an alternative account, as noted under **Caricatures**, is a perhaps apocryphal tale related by an article in the *Performer* of 31 May 1951. This version records a 16-year-old Chaplin, then touring in *Sherlock Holmes*, making friends with George Cooke, a caricaturist, and his wife. The Cookes

had a roller-skating rink, where, if the story is true, George taught the youngster how to skate. However they were acquired, Chaplin's impressive roller-skating forms an integral part of *The Rink*, and would be employed once more, two decades later, in *Modern Times*.

(See also: Early stage appearances)

SLAPSTICK 🎩

(Chaplin films *qv*)
The term 'slapstick' derives from an instrument in which two slats of wood make a noise quite out of proportion to the impact made through wielding it. Its frequent use by knockabout comedians has led to the name being applied to an entire genre of physical comedy, within which it is sometimes confused with the altogether more intricate principle of the sight-gag.

There is a tendency to classify all silent film as slapstick, inappropriate when considering how much of it situational. Chaplin was certainly a slapstick comedian, but interspersed the motif with gentler gags and, as time progressed, much more in the way of situation comedy and emotion. Some of Chaplin's roughest stuff is in the Keystones, such as the hurling of bricks in *Between Showers*, *Laughing Gas*, *Recreation* and others, also the excessive violence in *The Fatal Mallet* and *The Property Man*. Though gradually introducing subtler elements, his Essanays were very similar in this regard, continuing the Keystone-like scraps and a degree of vulgarity that served to alienate certain commentators. By the time of his Mutual films, Chaplin, and to some extent the industry in general, has progressed to the point where early slapstick methods could be lampooned. The Keystone brand of pie-throwing (itself not as dominant as folk memory insists) was considered old-fashioned even in 1916, hence Chaplin's parody of it in *Behind the Screen*. The Mutuals still retain their share of violence, albeit within a more organized context (Chaplin, in the direct fashion of a Londoner, customarily spoke of 'arse-kicking'), the gradual phasing out of which was noted by critics as the First National series progressed.

The mature Chaplin films ration slapstick somewhat, allowing it to serve as punctuation to subtler techniques;

there was, however, always room for slapstick when blended with an ingenious setting, as in the feeding machine of *Modern Times*, or the sequence in which *Monsieur Verdoux* tries in vain to drown Annabella.

Much of Chaplin's knockabout style was inherited from the Karno Company (*qv*). He retained elements of this training throughout his career, even when delegating the task to others; the messy business of decorating, a Karno idea revamped in Chaplin's *Work*, was revisited as a nightclub act in *A King in New York*, performed by George Truzzi and Lauri Lupino Lane. This segment, effective enough in isolation, is enlivened further by cutaways to Chaplin's own reactions; less satisfactory is the sequence in which the King turns a hosepipe on the courtroom, suggesting the horrors of McCarthyism to require more potent belittlement than a simple reversion to the baser slapstick of *A Night in the Show*.

(See also: Essanay; Keystone; Mutual; First National; Pathos; Politics; Risqué humour; Trick photography)

SMOKING 🎩

(Chaplin films *qv*)
In keeping with the majority of adults in his day, Chaplin was a regular smoker, and remained such until at least well into middle-age, after which he abandoned the habit (*Monsieur Verdoux* refuses a cigarette prior to his execution). Pola Negri, with whom Chaplin had a well-publicized affair during the 1920s, recalled that 'the only physically attractive thing about him were his hands, which were never without a cigarette'. It was usual for Chaplin to favour cigarettes, though Stan Laurel (*qv*), in a 1929 *Film Weekly* interview, recalled Chaplin's interest when someone in the Karno troupe had acquired a beautifully-coloured Calabash pipe. Chaplin immediately bought a similar pipe, brand new and white. Chaplin, 'always terribly impatient and nervously active', smoked tenaciously in order to colour the pipe, lighting up first thing in the morning and continuing into the night. The pipe took longer than expected to colour, and was eventually hurled through the window, at which point Chaplin returned to his customary cigarettes.

The cigarette was an early trademark of Chaplin's screen character (he was usually depicted with one in the *Funny Wonder* comic strip, for example), even from the tramp's first outing in *Kid Auto Races at Venice*. It was certainly considered an essential ingredient for the mutual impersonation, detailed elsewhere, in which Chaplin and Harry Lauder swapped pipe and cigarette along with their distinctive hats and walking sticks.

A pet gag, as in *The New Janitor*, consisted of discarding a cigarette butt, hurling it over his shoulder then back-kicking it away (a gag reportedly taught to him by Karno comic Fred Kitchen); a variant, as in *Those Love Pangs*, sees him making a pointless back-kicking gesture, as if sending the spent match on its way. Perhaps the most adept manoeuvre is that in *Triple Trouble*, wherein Charlie, arriving at the flophouse, casually flips a cigar up to his mouth. In another bit of business, he would take a mouthful of smoke, blowing it out while simultaneously twisting an ear. This gag makes an early appearance in *The Rounders*, and may be seen again when Charlie contrives his own arrest in *Modern Times*. Home-movie footage of this gag appears in *Unknown Chaplin* (*qv*).

In *A Film Johnnie*, Charlie uses a revolver to light his cigarette. Equally hazardous is the moment in *Easy Street* when he causes an explosion by lighting up beside the ruptured gas lamp. (After a later victory in the film, he stops for another smoke, but tumbles backwards in a chair from which the back is missing!) Less dramatic is the scene in *His Favorite Pastime* where Charlie takes a hot dog from a bar-room lunch counter in mistake for a cigar. Later in the film, he lights a cigarette, dropping the burning match into the hand of an attendant who is expecting a tip; still later, Charlie staggers upstairs and, cigarette in mouth, tumbles over the banisters but lands on the settee, where he calmly strikes a match in order to light up (a moment sometimes misattributed to *The Star Boarder*).

Despite his private failure with the pipe, Chaplin sometimes used one in films when wishing to seem workmanlike, one example being *Behind the Screen*. In *The Property Man*, Charlie, clay pipe in mouth, otherwise enforces a backstage smoking ban, but turns the appropriate sign to the wall when the strong man ignores the rule. A clay pipe in *His Musical Career* is used to scoop mouthfuls of beer from a can; as a gesture of contempt towards Albert Austin (*qv*) in *The Fireman*, Charlie places the stem of his pipe to his nose, in the manner of a substitute thumb.

Similar contempt is evident when, in *Gentlemen of Nerve*, Charlie strikes a match on the seat of Chester Conklin's trousers (he also blows smoke at the crowd during a subsequent altercation). A savage variant occurs in *A Night in the Show* and *Triple Trouble*, where he strikes a match on someone's bare foot. In *His New Job*, Ben Turpin (*qv*) places a cigarette in his mouth, only for Charlie to steal it by biting the opposite end (in those pre-filter days when cigarettes were reversible!). *In the Park* sees Charlie flicking cigarette ash into the open mouth of a rival. In *A Jitney Elopement*, Charlie rolls a cigarette, burning himself while lighting it, only for the home-made cigarette to fall apart in his mouth (a gag re-used in *A Dog's Life*); he tries chewing the tobacco before replacing it with a tailor-made cigarette found in his pocket. Also employed is the oft-repeated gag of flicking ash into an opponent's hat. *The Cure* sees Charlie reprimanding an elderly bellhop for smoking, as if to suggest he is too young. Later in the film, he drops a cigarette end into Eric Campbell's coffee, while another scene, including a close-up of Chaplin lighting up, seems to have been trimmed from at least one health-conscious revival.

Shanghaied includes a seasick Charlie explaining his temporary absence from lunch by pretending to have gone out for a smoke. A different kind of imbalance, induced by alcohol (*qv*), impedes Charlie's smoking habit on several occasions. Early in *One A.M.*, an intoxicated Charlie drops a lighted cigarette into a cab driver's hand; much of the subsequent action deals with his attempts to light another, at one point using an overhead lamp. The nightclub scene of *City Lights* shows the millionaire thrusting his cigar across Charlie's face as he tries to light his own (there is also a gag in which a discarded cigar burns a woman's bottom!). Altogether similar are his efforts to light a cigar in *Pay Day*; later on, he strikes a match on Henry Bergman's behind, and later still tries to light a salami. In *Limelight*, a drunken Calvero mistakes the smell of gas for either a bad cigar or, worse still, some unfortunate addition to the sole of his shoe.

Smoking could sometimes be used to indicate Charlie's financial circumstances. When we first see him in *The Kid*, he pauses to select, fastidiously, one of a collection of dog-ends placed inside a tin. His city rival in *Sunnyside* has a lighter in the handle of his walking stick, something Charlie tries to emulate by lodging matches in his own humble cane. Charlie's borrowed wealth in *City Lights* leads to the

spectacle of a man diving for a cigar butt despite being at the wheel of a Rolls-Royce. Charlie concludes *The Gold Rush* with a fortune of his own, but has to be checked when instinctively reaching for a discarded cigar. (At another point in the film, Kay Deslys [*qv*] lights a cigarette, igniting Charlie's bandaged, oil-soaked foot!)

Chaplin's own revival of *Shoulder Arms* omits a gag concerning the taboo against lighting three cigarettes on a single match. This is of particular interest, for this superstition is believed to have originated during that war (the idea being that offering three lights was long enough for an enemy sniper to home in on the flame). This may perhaps serve as further tribute to the accuracy brought by Chaplin to the film, despite his controversial non-involvement in the fighting.

An interesting sidelight: the female snake-charmer of *A Night in the Show* makes rather an elaborate display of smoking, this having been a time when respectable women were not expected to indulge in such habits. This becomes evident also in *The Masquerader*, when a female-clad Charlie has to sneak a smoke.

(See also: Bergman, Henry; Campbell, Eric; Caricatures; *Chaplin*; Conklin, Chester; Impersonators; Karno Company, The)

SPOOR, GEORGE K.
(1872–1953)

Illinois-born film pioneer and producer, originally a railroad 'caller' who took a second job in an opera house. He helped finance an inventor who was developing a motion picture projector, and eventually made short films to use as demonstration. In 1907, Spoor became a co-founder of Essanay (*qv*) with G.M. Anderson (*qv*). Later activities included experiments in 3-D and 70mm films, the latter represented by *Danger Lights* (1930).

(See also: Struss, Karl)

SPORT

(Chaplin films *qv*)
Tennis loomed large in Chaplin's off-duty hours, often with Douglas Fairbanks (*qv*), who, incidentally, created a variation of badminton known as 'Doug'. Chaplin was photographed on the courts at Nice when visiting France in April 1931. As noted in the **Groucho Marx** entry, film exists of the

Sport: Chaplin (right) and Fairbanks at a 1923 event

Sport: Tennis in Nice, 1931

two comedians in an England v. America match of 1937. On screen, Charlie displays an eccentric brand of tennis in *The Star Boarder*, while in *Mabel's Married Life*, Mack Swain (*qv*), racquet in hand, invites Mabel Normand (*qv*) to join him on the courts. Mouth organ virtuoso Larry Adler, whose exile from the USA came about for similar reasons to Chaplin's, once recalled (on BBC TV's *Good Morning* of 16 February 1996) a time when Chaplin, then a near neighbour, invited him to make up a foursome at tennis. On arrival, Adler discovered the other participants were Greta Garbo and Salvador Dali, forming perhaps the least likely doubles match in history.

Other sporting activities include a publicly-staged, comic boxing match with Eric Campbell (*qv*), with whom he participated in a comedians v. tragedians baseball game in March 1917. In April

1923, Chaplin and Fairbanks – dressed in their street clothes – joined runner Charles Paddock in a hurdling event (*illustrated*), as part of an athletic meeting connected with the University of Southern California. In describing his love for deep-sea fishing, Chaplin's *My Life in Pictures* reprints a photograph of the comedian with a giant marlin he had caught at Catalina Island in October 1918. *The Idle Class* features a golf routine which, as noted elsewhere, was planned both for a Mutual short and the abandoned *How To Make Movies* (*qv*). The earlier footage may be seen in *Unknown Chaplin* (*qv*).

(See also: Abandoned projects; Cars; Fighting; Newsreels; Public appearances; Wartime)

ST. JOHN, AL
(1893–1963)

(Chaplin films *qv*)
Nephew of Roscoe 'Fatty' Arbuckle (*qv*), Al St. John (pronounced 'Saint John' and not 'Sinjun', as has once happened) trained himself as a trick bicycle rider, but was discouraged from a film career by his parents. They prevailed upon Arbuckle not to offer any help in this regard, but his wife, Minta Durfee (*qv*) arranged a 'chance' display of trick riding for Mack Sennett (*qv*) while Roscoe was away. Al was in the movies and portraying a succession of rural and other boisterous types by the time Chaplin joined Keystone (*qv*) late in 1913. In *Mabel's Strange Predicament*, Al has the (for him) upmarket occupation of hotel manager; he is Arbuckle's rival for Minta's attention in *The Knockout*, and is a bellhop in *The Rounders*, again with both Arbuckle and Chaplin. *The New Janitor* gives him a similar rôle, that of a sassy liftboy, and he is one of the many Keystone Cops in *Tillie's Punctured Romance*. Al continued with Arbuckle in his Comique series for Joe Schenck, joined by Buster Keaton (*qv*), and was on hand for one of Roscoe's 'comeback' sound shorts, *Buzzin' Around* (1933). In between, he starred in many silent comedies for Educational, and in sound films became known for 'sidekick' rôles in westerns, using the nickname 'Fuzzy'.

STAMPS, COINS

(Chaplin films *qv*)
Charlie Chaplin is among the many

people whose achievements have been commemorated in postage stamps. When the Royal Mail celebrated British Film Year in 1985, Chaplin, though active primarily in the USA, was one of several British-born film talents honoured with a postage stamp. The portrait chosen, a photograph by Lord Snowdon, depicted the comedian late in life rather than in his familiar character. Other countries to issue Chaplin stamps are India, Guyana (adapted from a poster for *The Circus*, Spain and Czechoslovakia. The USA eventually issued its own Chaplin stamp in 1994, as a part of the 'Legends of the Silent Screen' series. The stamp shows Chaplin as the 'tramp', in a caricature by Al Hirshfeld. There has since been a movie-collage stamp from Norway incorporating a scene of Chaplin in *Modern Times*. Other images used include those of Stan Laurel (*qv*) and Oliver Hardy. Commemorative coins are less common; the first, and to date only, legal Chaplin coin seems to be a crown (face value 25p) issued in Gibraltar to mark the centenary of cinema in 1995. The head bears the likeness of Queen Elizabeth II, while the reverse shows Chaplin in his usual screen costume. Infinitely preferable, of course, to the tinplate coin bitten by Eric Campbell (*qv*) in *The Immigrant*!

(See also: Caricatures)

THE STAR BOARDER 🎩

(Chaplin film)
Keystone Comedy released by Mutual, 4 April 1914. Produced by Mack Sennett. Directed by Sennett or George Nichols. Written by Craig Hutchinson. Photography attributed to Frank D. Williams. Reissue titles include *A Hash House Hero* and *The Landlady's Pet*. One reel. 1,020 feet (UK length cited in *Bioscope*).

With Charlie Chaplin (himself), Minta Durfee (landlady), Edgar Kennedy (her husband), Alice Davenport (lady friend), Gordon Griffith (boy).

Charlie, as favoured lodger or 'star boarder', is more of a hit with the landlady than with her husband or small son. Escorting her out, Charlie plays an eccentric game of tennis; when they go to fetch a stray tennis ball, the landlady

The Star Boarder has helped himself in the kitchen

adjusts Charlie's tie, unaware that her son is taking their photograph. Their playfulness is interrupted by the arrival of her husband. When climbing steps to pick apples, the landlady topples, falling onto Charlie as he tries to assist. The boy obtains another incriminating photograph. Landlady and star boarder return home, but the child remains, secretly photographing his father with a lady friend of his own. Back at the house, Charlie helps himself to the stock of drink. The boy prepares to give a magic lantern show. The assembled residents are treated to innocuous views until one appears of the father and his lady friend; the landlady's annoyance turns to horror when the next few shots are of her dalliances with Charlie. Amid the pandemonium, Charlie successfully fights off his knife-wielding landlord, while the landlady gives her son a well-earned spanking.

Dr F.C. MacKnight, in part one of his 'Collecting Chaplin' series for *Classic Film Collector* (Winter 1974), notes *The Star Boarder* as one of the earlier Keystones in which Chaplin is permitted a more sympathetic rôle. Many of the Keystones present Chaplin in either a ruthless prototype of his tramp character or, as in *Mabel at the Wheel* (*qv*), an out-and-out villain. Rick De Croix, in one of a series of Chaplin reappraisals for *Classic Images* (July 1983), contrasts the subtler, slower pace of Chaplin's work in *Star Boarder* with the otherwise frenetic Keystone output of the period. Even under the direction of others, Chaplin was already finding his own style, and would soon be permitted full control of his starring vehicles.

(See also: Alcohol; Children; Keystone; Reissues; Sport; Williams, Frank D.; Women)

STATUES

(Chaplin films *qv*)
Charlie's first scene in *City Lights* shows his dormant, homeless figure being unveiled atop a new sculpture, ironically named 'Peace and Prosperity'. Later in the film, always with an eye for beauty, he pauses in the street to evaluate a nude statuette in a shop window. Another nude statue, a film studio prop in *His New Job*, induces coyness; when revisiting this line of work in *Behind the Screen*, Charlie observes decency by turning two unclad statues to face in opposite directions.

Possibly the furthest-flung Chaplin tribute is the statue of him gracing the Bulgarian town of Gabrovo. Altogether closer to his long-time home is the statue gracing the lobby of the Hollywood Roosevelt Hotel. In Chaplin's native Britain, a commemorative statue was mooted early in 1978, shortly after the comedian's death. Behind the idea was Illtyd Harrington, former deputy Labour leader of the Greater London Council. In the London *Evening Standard* of 31 January, John Munch speculated on the site of such a memorial, quoting Harrington's recommendation of the Elephant and Castle or possibly the South Bank. Opinions were sought from local residents at Kennington (who suggested it should replace a public convenience at Kennington Cross), but the journalist thought Leicester Square likely to gain 'the best audience ratings'. In the end, that is where the statue was placed, but not without considerable delay. The project met with opposition from certain quarters, and it took a rather vociferous group of prominent arts figures to fight the cause. Another difficulty arose when support was withdrawn by the original sponsor; by this time, sculptor John Doubleday had completed the bronze figure of the 'Tramp' character, slightly larger than life-size, which remained in a Fulham store room for a year. On 14 January 1980, *The Financial Times* reported the bizarre police 'arrest' of a 10-foot fibreglass statue of Chaplin that had been placed in Leicester Square the previous day. A spokesman for those attempting to raise money for the memorial denied any knowledge of this 'monumental waste of police time'. Evidently *someone* was determined to see

Chaplin so honoured, as evidenced six days later when the *Sunday Telegraph* announced the statue's financial rescue by the Bristol and West Building Society. It was finally unveiled (by Sir Ralph Richardson) in Leicester Square on 14 April 1981, but even then did not find permanence; subsequent renovations to the square saw the statue's removal to a slightly different position. In 1982, an identical statue was placed in Parc Charles Chaplin, created in 1980 near his former home in Vevey.

Another Chaplin figure, in wax, was on full view to Londoners in 1985 as it travelled from its home in Madame Tussaud's to the National Portrait Gallery. The occasion was an exhibition of rare Chaplin material furnished by his estate, featured in David Robinson's book *Chaplin: His Life and Art*, published in March that year. The comedian's youngest children, Annette and Christopher Chaplin, were photographed with the wax figure when attending the opening ceremony.

(See also: Artists; Childhood; Children; Death; Policemen; Risqué humour)

STERLING, FORD
(1880 or 1883–1939)

Wisconsin-born comedian, real name George Ford Stitch, who eventually reached movies through the varied routes of circus (as 'Keno, the Boy Clown', according to Kalton C. Lahue), repertory, the Broadway stage and vaudeville. He met Mack Sennett (*qv*) when both were working at Biograph, and joined Keystone (*qv*) at its inception in 1912. Sterling became known especially (though not exclusively) as a 'Dutch' comedian, America's then-current term for a German characterization. The image was complemented by a goatee beard, in which guise Sterling came to personify the Chief of the Keystone Cops. According to Chaplin's memoirs, Sterling would complete his portrayal with a strong, gutteral accent, seemingly redundant in silent films but creating much amusement on set. Sterling appeared alongside Chaplin in only three films, *Between Showers*, *A Film Johnnie* and *Tango Tangles* (all *qv*) before leaving Keystone for his own series, 'Sterling Comedies', under the auspices of the ubiquitous Henry Lehrman (*qv*), and taking with him Emma Clifton (*qv*) as leading lady. At least one of this series, *Sergeant Hofmeyer*, was made available to collectors by Blackhawk Films. Although there is probably no truth in the oft-held view that Chaplin was hired specifically to replace Sterling, the latter's departure saw Chaplin functioning as an interim substitute. Chaplin was given a number of unsympathetic rôles in the Sterling mould, even to the point of sporting a goatee in *Mabel at the Wheel* (*qv*). The defection of Ford Sterling gave rise to considerable rumour within the industry, as evidenced by a statement issued to *Bioscope* by Keystone's UK distributors, the Western Export Company, published on 5 March 1914. 'We wish to contradict in the most explicit manner,' it began, 'the statement widely advertised in the Trade papers last week that "practically the entire Keystone Company" has been engaged by another producing organization. The statement in question has naturally led a large number of our customers to imagine that the Keystone films would in future appear without any of the artistes who have become so popular with the British public, whereas, in fact, *only one prominent artiste* has left the Keystone Company, and the organisation will continue as before ...' There followed the denial of further rumours, to the effect that Sennett and Mabel Normand (*qv*) had gone, but it is indicative of Sterling's fame that the resignation of 'one prominent artiste', albeit in the company of a regular director and leading lady, could alone provoke such speculation. Keystone absorbed Sterling's loss quite efficiently, Chaplin's portrait replacing his in trade ads depicting him alongside Sennett, Normand and Fatty Arbuckle (*qv*) as the 'Keystone Quartette'. After filling in briefly for Sterling, Chaplin, of course, found his own character, the success of which enabled him to leave Keystone for greater opportunities; Sterling, by contrast, did not fare so well, and by 1915 was back with Keystone. His frantic, one-dimensional style was appropriate to Sennett's mayhem, but could not foster star billing elsewhere; instead he continued as head of the Cops into the 1920s, in addition to playing supporting rôles in the feature films of others, as in several of Colleen Moore's vehicles at First National (*qv*), the 1923 version of *The Spoilers*, the 1924 Lon Chaney classic,

He Who Gets Slapped and the 1928 version of *Gentlemen Prefer Blondes*. One of Sterling's more notable talkie appearances was with W.C. Fields in Warners' *Her Majesty, Love* (1931) (See also: Conklin, Chester; Costume; Edwards, Vivian; Hair; Home movies; Swain, Mack; Villains)

STOCKDALE, CARL 🎩 (CARLTON)
(1874–1953)

(Chaplin films *qv*)
Minnesota-born actor who plays 'Charles', Charlie's cashier rival in *The Bank*; he is one of the sparring partners in *The Champion*, and has been spotted as a policeman in both *A Jitney Elopement* and *By the Sea*. Following education at the University of North Dakota, Stockdale embarked on a theatrical career, variously in repertory and vaudeville. Stockdale entered films in 1912, working for many studios including Fine Arts, Essanay (*qv*), Universal, First National (*qv*), Sennett (*qv*), Fox, Paramount, PDC and comedy independent Jess Robbins (supervisor of Chaplin's Essanay unit in Los Angeles). Among his important early films is Griffith's *Intolerance*; other 1920s films include *Molly O'* and *The Extra Girl*, both with Mabel Normand (*qv*); *The Half Breed*; *Oliver Twist* with Jackie Coogan (*qv*); *Twinkletoes* with Colleen Moore; and DeMille's *King of Kings*. Stockdale continued into talkies, one of them a 1930 two-reeler with Charley Chase (*qv*), *Whispering Whoopee*; he also appeared in features, such as *Abraham Lincoln* (1930), *The Vampire Bat* (1933), *Dr. Socrates* (1935), *Lost Horizon* (1937) and *All That Money Can Buy* (1941).

STREETCARS 🎩

(Chaplin films *qv*)
Streetcars (trams in the UK) have long been eclipsed in America and Great Britain, but seem set to make a return. In the early 20th century they were commonplace, and may sometimes be observed in the background of Chaplin's films, as in *Between Showers* and *His Musical Career*. Charlie narrowly avoids being struck by them in *Caught in the Rain* and *Work*, ditto Marie Dressler (*qv*) in *Tillie's Punctured Romance*. Charlie rides on the outside of a car in *His Favorite Pastime*, a

mechanical stunt of the sort to which Chaplin objected and would not repeat once in total control of his films. Rather more in keeping is the elaborate scene in *Pay Day*, wherein Charlie battles the crowds in an attempt to board a late-night streetcar.

STRUSS, KARL 🎩
(1886–1981)

(Chaplin films *qv*)
New York-born cinematographer whose 1920s work includes *Something to Think About* (1920), *Fool's Paradise* (1921), Mary Pickford's *Sparrows* (1926), Murnau's *Sunrise* (1927) and the Pickford-Fairbanks *Taming of the Shrew* (1929). Struss also photographed the Technicolor footage for the 1925 version of *Ben-Hur*. Among numerous talkies are *Danger Lights*, a 1930 film originally shot in an experimental 70mm process (see also **George K. Spoor**); the 1931 *Dr. Jekyll and Mr. Hyde*; Mary Pickford's final film, *Kiki* (1931); *Island of Lost Souls* (1932); DeMille's *The Sign of the Cross* (1932); the Mae West vehicles *Goin' To Town* (1935), *Go West Young Man* (1936) and *Every Day's a Holiday* (1938); Hal Roach's *Zenobia* (1939), with Oliver Hardy and Harry Langdon; and *Tarzan's Magic Fountain* (1948). Struss shares 'Director of Photography' credit with Rollie Totheroh (*qv*) on Chaplin's *The Great Dictator*; he is credited alone in this capacity, with Totheroh as consultant, on Chaplin's final American production, *Limelight*.

(See also: Fairbanks, Douglas; Pickford, Mary; Williams, Frank D.)

SUICIDE 🎩

(Chaplin films *qv*)
Much of Chaplin's comedy is based upon adversity and tragedy, a legacy of his childhood and, in no small part, the often macabre humour of his native Britain. Detailed under its main entry is a reputed alternate ending to *The Vagabond*, in which Charlie tries to end his own life; other attempts are seen in *Cruel, Cruel, Love* and *Sunnyside*. Charlie spends part of *City Lights* persuading a millionaire not to commit suicide, while the finale of *Carmen*, with Don José's suicide after murdering his love, provides a moment of authentic drama prior to its farcical conclusion.

The most serious portrayal of suicide in Chaplin's films is that of Jean in *A Woman of Paris*; noted under **Abandoned projects** is Chaplin's intention to film *The Suicide Club* (or *The Club of Suicides*). This made way instead for *The Circus*, at a troubled period in Chaplin's life during which a statement was issued, denying rumours that the comedian was being guarded against suicide attempts. Chaplin was strong-minded and resilient, and one doubts the urge for self-destruction to have been strong, irrespective of his then-current disasters.

Sadly, some of Chaplin's real-life friends and associates took their own lives. Among them were Max Linder (*qv*) and illustrator Ralph Barton, whose home movies taken on the set of *City Lights* provide rare glimpses of Chaplin at work. Barton accompanied Chaplin for the first part of his 1931 European trip, but committed suicide after returning to New York.

(See also: Abandoned projects; Childhood; Murder; Public appearances)

THE SUICIDE CLUB ♟

See: Abandoned projects and Suicide

SUMMERVILLE, GEORGE J. 'SLIM' (1896–1946)

(Chaplin films *qv*)
Lankily-built comedian, real name Somerville, quoted variously as hailing from Albuquerque, New Mexico and, more probably, Calgary, Canada; Summerville became an all-purpose talent at Keystone (*qv*), capable of filling any number of supporting rôles in addition to functioning as one of the Keystone Cops. He was for a while paired with a fellow-cop, Bobby Dunn, who at one time was one of the many Chaplin imitators. Summerville is among the cops in *Tillie's Punctured Romance* and *Mabel's Busy Day*, and is one of the bakers in *Dough and Dynamite*; he has greater prominence in *Laughing Gas*, as a passerby who becomes a patient after a brick – hurled by Charlie – hits him in the teeth. Summerville is also in the crowds of spectators in *Gentlemen of Nerve* and Arbuckle's *The Knockout*. Summerville's later Sennett films include work with Ben Turpin (*qv*) and Syd

Chaplin (*qv*), with whom he later appeared in the film *Skirts*. Summerville spent much of the 1920s as a comedy director at Fox, FBO and Universal, but was reunited on screen with Keystone colleague Mack Swain (*qv*) in John Barrymore's 1927 version of *The Beloved Rogue*. Of his talkie appearances, the best-remembered is that in *All Quiet On the Western Front* (1930); the remainder of his career was spent in such feature rôles, along with a series of short comedies of the early 1930s.

(See also: Arbuckle, Roscoe 'Fatty'; Impersonators; Lehrman, Henry 'Pathé'; Schade, Fritz; Sennett, Mack)

SUNNYSIDE ♟

(Chaplin film)
Released by First National, 15 June 1919. Produced, written and directed by Charles Chaplin. Photographed by Rollie Totheroh. Three reels.

With Charlie Chaplin (himself), Edna Purviance (girl), Tom Wilson (the boss), Albert Austin (village doctor), Henry Bergman (Edna's father), Loyal Underwood (small old man), Tom Wood (his overweight son), Park Jones.

Sunday morning in the village of Sunnyside. Charlie, 'the farm hand, etc. etc. etc.', is awakened at dawn by his boss, the local farmer/grocer/hotel keeper. The boss returns to bed, as does Charlie; suspecting his employee of laziness, the boss hurls a shoe into his room to ensure re-activity. Charlie removes his nightshirt, beneath which are his day clothes. Charlie dozes off again, and the boss returns to shake and kick him into life. Charlie exits through the door, the boss returns to his room, and Charlie sneaks back to his bed via the window. The boss catches Charlie, whose exit is made through the same window. In the reception area of the 'Hotel Evergreen – etc. etc. etc.', Charlie mows the grass growing from between the flagstones. Being the Sabbath, the boss is upstairs contemplating the Good Book, but Charlie must continue working, waiting for a hen to produce an egg while sitting in the frying pan and pouring vast numbers of sugar lumps into teacups. Milk is dispensed into the cups directly from a cow. The boss makes his way downstairs, to be greeted by doorsteps of bread. He notes Charlie's sugar-solidified tea. The good citizens of Sunnyside set off for church,

among them a diminutive father and his gigantic son. Charlie would like to attend, but must instead read from suitable texts while outside, herding the cattle. While he is reading, the cattle stroll off elsewhere, and Charlie absently jabs his stick into a matronly woman. He goes off in search of the stray animals, discovering one of them emerging from a house and another causing panic in the church. He rushes in, only to emerge riding the uncontrollable animal into the street. His journey ends when he is thrown into a ditch. Unconscious, Charlie dreams of dancing with wood nymphs. When he falls once more, he imagines being pulled up by the ladies of his dream, but regains consciousness to find the townspeople hauling him from the ditch. The boss kicks Charlie from the scene. Later, Charlie calls upon Edna, his beloved, having waited for her father to leave the house. He disposes of a bratty youngster with a game of Blind Man's Buff, then places a ring on Edna's finger. Charlie tries his skills at the piano, but his flat notes are complemented by the bleating of a goat and offspring. The goat bites a chunk from the sheet music, appropriately entitled 'The Lost Chord'. Charlie tries 'The Gallant Bandelero' instead, but exits swiftly on the return of Edna's father. Outside, Charlie gives the blindfolded youth a kick before arriving, late, for duty at the hotel. Charlie upholsters the seat of his trousers with leaves, but the expected boot from his boss does not arrive. Instead he is put to work while, outside, a city type staggers from his overturned car. He is carried to the hotel desk and, being unconscious, fails to notice Charlie holding up the register for him to sign. The local doctor arrives, opening a black bag filled with everything needed to treat a horse. Charlie borrows the patient's watch, placing it in his mouth while taking the man's pulse. The doctor's main achievement – with Charlie's assistance – is to find his pencil, enabling him to write out a bill for $10. The visitor duly pays up and is installed in a room. Charlie is unable to extract a tip. Various of the locals sprawl within the lobby while Charlie mops up around them. They move with reluctance, but are repaid when struck with the dripping mop. The city visitor, recovered from his ordeal, arrives at reception. Charlie is despatched to serve Edna with groceries. She cannot remember what they were, and after Charlie suggests several items of varying likelihood (among them a man's razor), Edna settles for woollen socks wrapped as a bouquet. The city visitor, noticing Edna, follows her into the street;

Dancing with the nymphs in **Sunnyside**

Charlie looks on, aghast, as he seems to make an impression. The boss kicks Charlie back to work, but the saddened assistant can only sit in a chair, pondering the cruelty of fate. The city type is made welcome by Edna and her father. Charlie, bearing flowers for Edna, surveys the scene through the window. His suave rival lights a cigarette using a lighter built into the handle of his cane. Charlie, seeing Edna showing him the family album, walks away dejectedly. As a last resort, Charlie puts on what he imagines to be his Sunday best, including spats made from heavy socks placed over his shoes. As he passes, a rascally neighbour steps on a rogue strand from one of the socks, causing it to catch and unravel. At Edna's home, Charlie tries to impress in the same way as his rival (lighting up with matches fixed into his cane), but Edna returns the ring he gave her earlier. When the new boyfriend reappears, Charlie takes his leave and stands in the path of an oncoming car. Instead of a speeding roadster, the impact he feels is, again, a kick from the boss. Charlie has been dozing again. He is ordered to fetch the city gent's luggage. Edna walks in and, when the visitor seems interested, Charlie makes a point of establishing his claim by smothering Edna with hugs and kisses. He momentarily squares up to the visitor before taking his bags out to the car. Charlie receives a generous tip from the visitor, who drives off as Charlie and Edna embrace once more.

Interpreted by some as a consciously peaceful post-war effort, *Sunnyside* has comparatively little slapstick, favouring a gentle whimsy in a pastoral setting. Although his 1922 book, *My Trip Abroad*, refers to it as one of his favourites, Chaplin was not at peace during its creation, and later compared the experience to 'pulling teeth'. Probably due to an increasingly complex personal life, his inventiveness was frankly in hiatus during 1919, and neither *Sunnyside* nor its immediate successor, *A Day's Pleasure* (*qv*), was particularly outstanding. Not that Chaplin's skills were totally absent: there is some pleasant comic business, and his dance with the nymphs has been justly celebrated over the years. There is also some good photography, notably as the camera tracks to and fro across the hotel reception. When first released, *Sunnyside* received due attention despite any alleged shortcomings: *Picture Show*, for example, devoted a full-page picture spread to this 'third Million Dollar Chaplin' on 23 August 1919. *Sunnyside* was something of a gift to the highbrow element who sought, at least for a while, to claim Chaplin away from the masses. For example, on 12 July 1919, the *Motion Picture News* reported the efforts of S.B. McCormick, manager of the Circle Theater in Indianapolis, seeking the patronage of 'the most elite local society', albeit alongside 'dyed-in-the-wool Chaplin fans' by presenting *Sunnyside* as Art, emphasizing in his advertising the depiction of Chaplin as the god Pan within

the setting of classical dance. 'McCormick's campaign,' said the report, 'was based on the psychology that the regular Chaplin fans would attend regardless of the kind of exploitation, but that to reach the society element of Indianapolis it would be necessary for him to lift his exploitation into the "society" stage.'

Sunnyside would probably have been a more satisfying effort as a two-reeler. It might also have benefited from the retention of a sequence deleted prior to release, in which Albert Austin (*qv*) falls victim to Charlie's dubious skills as barber. First, Austin is helped into the chair, a piece of furniture threatening disintegration. Once settled, he is blinded by soap, convinced – in error – that his throat has been cut, then is burned around the feet and head as the chair is swung into the vicinity of the shop's boiler. Ultimately, Charlie ploughs a wide furrow through the back of Austin's hair. The disgruntled customer leaves as soon as he is able. The obviously genuine sacrifice of Austin's locks was all in vain, for this sequence – possibly the funniest from the film – remained unseen until excerpted in *Unknown Chaplin* (*qv*). The complete section has since been issued on laserdisc in the United States. *Sunnyside* itself remained out of public view – at least in legal prints – until 1976, when it was paired with *A Woman of Paris* (*qv*). It is probably confusion between literature for the two films that has led to some TV listings erroneously crediting Adolphe Menjou (*qv*) in the cast of *Sunnyside*.

(See also: Ballet; Bergman, Henry; Dreams; First National; Hair; Impersonators; *Limelight*; Music; Race; Reissues; Religion; Smoking; Suicide; Television; Titling; Underwood, Loyal; Vagrancy; Video releases)

SUTHERLAND, A. EDWARD
(1895–1974)

Assistant director on *A Woman of Paris* and *The Gold Rush* (both *qv*); in a 1959 interview (excerpted in *Unknown Chaplin* [*qv*]), Sutherland admitted having contributed in only a functional way to *Gold Rush*, emphasizing that Chaplin had directed himself. Sutherland has, however, been quoted as having devised the teetering-cabin idea in *The Gold Rush*, a gag initially rejected by Chaplin. According to Sutherland, Chaplin returned to it a few days later, genuinely convinced that it was his own suggestion. 'I planted it in his mind,' recalled Sutherland, keen to ward off accusations of theft on Chaplin's part. 'He probably didn't hear it consciously. But subconsciously it stuck there.' Sutherland had earlier been an actor with Sennett (*qv*); director credits in the sound era include Eddie Cantor's *Palmy Days* (1931), W.C. Fields' *Mississippi* (1935) and *Poppy* (1936) and Laurel & Hardy's *The Flying Deuces* (1939). Sutherland also functioned as a producer, as in Hal Roach's *Zenobia* (1939).

(See also: Laurel, Stan)

SWAIN, MACK
(1876–1935)

(Chaplin films *qv*)
Born in Salt Lake City, Mack Swain entered pictures in October 1913, after a career on the legitimate stage lasting some twenty-two years. At Keystone (*qv*), Swain became known for his 'Ambrose' character, distinguished by heavily-darkened eyes, a large, Germanic moustache plus an incongruous kiss-curl amid an otherwise receding hairline. He may be seen thus in Chaplin's *Caught in the Rain, His Trysting Place, The Fatal Mallet, Laughing Gas, His Musical Career, Getting Acquainted, Gentlemen of Nerve* and *His Prehistoric Past. The Knockout* varies his persona, being superficially 'Ambrose', but sporting cowboy gear and displaying a murderous temperament. In *A Busy Day*, he appears without his customary make-up and is almost as unrecognizable as the female-clad Chaplin; much the same applies to Swain's thuggish image in both *Caught in a Cabaret* and *Mabel's Married Life*, also his

Mack Swain becomes crazed by hunger in The Gold Rush. *This startling pose created a furore when it was selected for a British display poster in 1925*

comparatively straight rôle in *Tillie's Punctured Romance*. Swain continued as 'Ambrose' even after departing for L-KO in 1917; he worked subsequently with Chaplin imitator Billy West, then starred in a minor series, the 'Poppy Comedies', one of which (*Heroic Ambrose*) was once available from Blackhawk Films. He continued from one lesser studio to another until an alleged disagreement with a producer saw him blacklisted by the entire industry. His career was restored by Chaplin, who hired him to replace Eric Campbell (*qv*). Swain's 'comeback' in *The Idle Class* was sufficiently effective for him to be used again in *Pay Day, The Pilgrim* and, best of all, *The Gold Rush*. Swain's Chaplin work brought offers from elsewhere; other appearances include Mary Pickford's *My Best Girl* (1927), John Barrymore's *The Beloved Rogue* (1927), the 1928 version of *Gentlemen Prefer Blondes* and *The Sea Bat* (1930), and also in some of Sennett's sound shorts of the early 1930s.

(See also: Conklin, Chester; Costume; Female impersonation; Food; Home movies; Impersonators; Lehrman, Henry 'Pathé'; Pickford, Mary; Risqué humour; Sennett, Mack; Sport; Sterling, Ford; Summerville, George J. 'Slim')

SWANSON, GLORIA
(1899–1983)

Legendary in the sense of being a major star from the comparatively early days of silents until the 1980s, Gloria Swanson was an unknown bit player with Essanay (*qv*) when Chaplin joined the studio early in 1915. She appears briefly in *His New Job* (*qv*), when Charlie awaits an interview in the 'Lockstone' offices. Her rôle is that of a typist in the background. Later on, both Chaplin and Swanson denied her presence in the film, but were forced to admit a lapse in memory after seeing it together in the 1960s. The actress's subsequent autobiography, *Swanson On Swanson*, makes no mention of this appearance, detailing only a morning's work in which she auditioned as a potential partner to Chaplin. Miss Swanson describes Chaplin's soft-spoken, encouraging attempts to involve her in knockabout routines, to which she could not respond. This seems unlikely, given that any prominent female rôle would have been that of *ingénue*; there is of course the possibility of Chaplin having been in search of someone closer to Mabel

Normand (*qv*) than the passive type soon to be represented in his films by Edna Purviance (*qv*). Miss Swanson admitted to finding nothing amusing in Chaplin's routines, and was relieved when word arrived that the comedian did not consider her suitable. Ironically, it was in the wilder environs of Mack Sennett's studio that Gloria Swanson began to draw attention, prior to graduating to higher drama with Cecil B. DeMille; a 1924 feature, *Manhandled*, sees her offering a brief impersonation of Charlie Chaplin (as does the much later *Sunset Boulevard*, released in 1950. The story of her elevation was lampooned in Marion Davies' *Show People*, in which Chaplin makes a brief appearance. Although a party to this prank, and despite a discouraging introduction at Essanay, Chaplin had been on good terms with Gloria Swanson and would remain so; she was among those to visit the set of *A Countess From Hong Kong* (*qv*). The actress may be heard as narrator of Harry Hurwitz's Chaplin documentary, *The Eternal Tramp*.

(See also: Anderson, G.M.; Ayres, Agnes; Documentaries, compilations; Guest appearances; Impersonators; Sennett, Mack; United Artists)

SWICKARD, JOSEPH (OR JOSEF, ALSO JOE)
(1866–1940)

(Chaplin films *qv*)
Born in Coblenz, Germany, but long in America, where he completed his education, grey-haired, gaunt-looking Joseph Swickard entered the theatrical profession (as did a brother, Charles) in or around 1898. He was based variously in Chicago, New York and Toronto. Swickard's first film was in 1912; by 1914 he was a regular at Keystone (*qv*), where he appeared with Chaplin in *Twenty Minutes of Love, Caught in a Cabaret* and *Laughing Gas*. Among many other Keystones are *Love, Loot and Crash* (1915) and *Ambrose's Cup of Woe* (1917). His 1920s features include *The Four Horsemen of the Apocalypse* (1921), Larry Semon's *The Wizard of Oz* (1925) and *Stop! Look! and Listen!* (1926), *Don Juan* (1926) and *King of Kings* (1927). His talkie work was primarily in serials.

(See also: Chase, Charley; Mann, Hank; Murray, Charlie; Northrup, Harry; Schade, Fritz; Stockdale, Carl; Swain, Mack)

TANGO TANGLES 🎩

(Chaplin film)
Keystone Comedy released by Mutual, 9 March 1914. Produced by Mack Sennett. Written and supervised by Mack Sennett. Photography attributed to Frank D. Williams. Reissued by W.H. Productions as *Charlie's Recreation*, other reissue titles include *Music Hall*. One reel.

With Charlie Chaplin (himself), Ford Sterling (bandleader), Roscoe 'Fatty' Arbuckle (clarinettist), Minta Durfee (hat-check girl), Edgar Kennedy (man who helps Charlie to his feet), Chester Conklin (one of the costumed dancers).

At a dance hall, a pair of professional dancers display their skills prior to the start of the masked ball. A title introduces 'One of the early arrivals, a little the worse for wear'; this is Charlie, who joins two girls in a high-kicking dance before falling over. Charlie checks in his hat and cane; after he has gone, the hat-check girl receives a visit from her boyfriend, the bandleader. He has a rival, the clarinettist, whom he tries to warn off. The large musician, unimpressed, picks up a smaller man to use as a club. The bandleader makes a swift exit, pushing Charlie out of the way en route to the dance floor. The clarinettist catches up with the bandleader, scowling, but is sufficiently appeased to continue playing. Charlie returns to the hat-check girl and takes her up to the dance floor. The bandleader, observing Charlie's progress, eventually leaves his post to stake his claim on the girl's affections. A fight breaks out, with the bandleader as apparent victor; the clarinettist notices what has happened and is standing behind him when a challenge is issued to

anyone who would care to try stealing the girl. The bandleader is pushed out of the running by the clarinettist, who claims his prize. The bandleader and Charlie meet again, and hostilities resume. At the cloakroom, they try to put on the same large overcoat; they hit each other with coats then, exhausted, try to deliver blows while in a clinch. The rivals collapse to the floor, Sterling telling Charlie that he can have the girl. Charlie delivers one final knockout blow before losing consciousness himself.

Tango Tangles' immediate predecessor, *A Film Johnnie* (*qv*), shows Ford Sterling and Fatty Arbuckle (both *qv*) out of make-up and in their street clothes. In the earlier film, they are supposed to be their off-screen selves; by contrast, *Tango Tangles* presents Sterling, Arbuckle and Chaplin in off-duty garb while playing their usual screen characters. The most striking aspect is seeing the young Chaplin, smartly-attired and without the prop moustache and oversized shoes. His appearance in this film conveys something of the shock Mack Sennett (*qv*) must have felt when Chaplin first arrived at the studio. Sennett had expected someone much older, prompting Chaplin's use of a disguising moustache. Opinions are divided as to whether *Tango Tangles* was filmed at Keystone (*qv*) or at a genuine dance hall; Harry M. Geduld's *Chapliniana* cites the former, based on the familiar checked floor tiling, though the size of the dance floor itself suggests at least partial location work.

As with most Chaplin Keystones, *Tango Tangles* often turns up in a reissue from W.H. Productions. This version, renamed *Charlie's Recreation* (not to be confused with *Recreation* [*qv*], a quite different Keystone), quotes the original as having been called 'Tango *Tangle*' (as does H.D. Waley's 1938 *Sight and Sound* filmography), rather than the plural generally accepted elsewhere. Sub-titles in this release seem to have been slightly updated, as in the reference to 'The Darktown Strutters Ball'. The print issued to collectors by Blackhawk Films has a similar text, though in different cards and with a few deletions, one of them the final dialogue card in which Sterling abandons competition for the girl. Neither version is of especially good quality, that from Blackhawk being particularly disappointing; fortunately there exists at the BFI superb, crystal-clear 35mm material, of the sort rarely

encountered with the earliest Chaplins.

(See also: Conklin, Chester; Durfee, Minta; Home movies; Impersonators; Kennedy, Edgar; Reissues; Williams, Frank D.)

TELEVISION 🎩

(Chaplin films *qv*)
As a concept, television dates back into the 19th century, but it only began to assume practicality during the 1920s. Its expected ubiquity was regarded as a potential boon in some quarters, an insidious intrusion in others. That Chaplin fell into the latter category is evidenced by much of *A King in New York* and, from its pioneering days, a pre-Orwellian application in *Modern Times*, a film which, coincidentally, saw release only nine months prior to the launch of BBC Television. The comedian's attitude was certainly unmodified into the early 1950s. Buster Keaton (*qv*) recalled a conversation around the time of *Limelight* when he and Chaplin were discussing the new medium. Chaplin made his total disdain apparent but, when asking Keaton what he had been doing 'of late' – doubtless expecting the answer 'not much' – was told 'television' (Keaton had in fact done some very worthwhile live shows on the West Coast, at least one of which has been recovered).

Chaplin did not exactly encourage the screening of his films on television. Leslie Halliwell (in *Halliwell's Hundred*) described a time when, anxious to make a British TV programme tied into *The Chaplin Revue* (*qv*), he contacted Chaplin for permission to use extracts. Negotiations were cordial until a fee of £20,000 was proposed. It is therefore no surprise that Chaplin was long represented on British TV by the earlier films not under his control, with the exception of a one-off screening of *The Gold Rush*. Programmes based on silent-film extracts – notably *Mad Movies* and *Golden Silents* in Britain, and Paul Killiam's anthologies from America – had to rely on pre-1918 material. Several of the Mutuals, with their added soundtracks, were shown by the various ITV regions during the 1960s. BBC 1 offered a different package to commemorate Chaplin's 80th birthday, via early-evening screenings of the American 'Charlie Chaplin Comedy Theatre' series. The BBC listings magazine, *Radio Times*, described them as 'special sound versions with intelligent and informative commentaries which don't score off the material'. This was certainly true from the perspective of a young viewer (as the author was at that time), for whom the narration provided dates, production companies and, perhaps most importantly, the names of the supporting players. The series was in some respects tailored for children (or at any rate the contemporary kindergarten standards of US television), as evidenced by the amendment of *Easy Street*'s drug addict to a more innocuous 'mad scientist'. Although stretch-printing was used extensively to approximate the original projection speed, each programme occupied a slot of only 22 minutes. The title sequence relied heavily on the early sequences of *The Masquerader*, with the main title illustrated by a cartoon Charlie standing before a theatre curtain. A batch of six – *The Rink*, *The Immigrant*, *The Cure*, *The Tramp*, *The Adventurer* and *The Floorwalker* – were shown between 28 March and 2 May 1969; the remaining titles, among them a two-part version of *Tillie's Punctured Romance*, were allocated varying slots over the next two years.

This was perhaps a worthwhile series for the novice admirer, but not for the purist. Aware of the unsatisfactory versions in circulation, BBC Television announced a series of restored Chaplin shorts under the title *Chaplin SuperClown*, made in association with Chaplin's company, Black Ink. The films were transferred at the correct speed, with titling remade in the original design. Contemporary publicity suggested a global scouring for material, though only Britain's National Film Archive received screen credit; *Radio Times* devoted a two-page spread to the series, which began on 5 April 1973. It was a laudable act to schedule the films at peak time (8 p.m.) on the mass channel, BBC 1, given the unfashionable nature of silent films plus the fact that colour had by then started to dominate. First to be shown was *The Immigrant*; in all, 26 half-hours were made, covering all the Mutuals, every Essanay except *Carmen* (though *Triple Trouble* was included) and two Keystones, *The Rounders* and *Laughing Gas*. Half of these remained unseen until the series was quietly resurrected for a Saturday morning slot, commencing in August 1975. The implied failure of *Chaplin SuperClown* may be ascribed to several factors. One frequent objection was to the music scores, under the direction of Dennis Wilson and played by the Goed Nieuws Orkest. Many were composed by Wilson himself, with several by Keith Amos and others. Such things are, of course, a matter of taste, but the majority view of *aficionados* in the author's acquaintance was that the scores were inappropriate. Subsequent letters to *Radio Times* expressed both this view and its opposite, but widespread disapproval is implicit in a BBC response defending the music as being similar in style to Chaplin's own. The author's view is that it was not; Chaplin avoided flippancy in his music, to provide contrast with the comic action, but still maintained a light touch, whereas much of *Chaplin SuperClown*'s accompaniment seemed better suited to drama. This said, Wilson's scores for *The Immigrant*, *The Vagabond* and *Laughing Gas* (and that for *The Rink* by Max Harris) are quite worthy of praise. One correspondent applauded the whole enterprise, thanking William Fitzwater (the Executive Producer) and his team for 'restoring the films to their former glory', and continuing with a request for similar treatment of the remaining subjects. In fairness, it should be said that much in the way of rare footage was reinstated (detailed within the films' main entries), some of which continues to be absent from other attempted restorations; on the minus side, there were occasions when easily-obtainable shots were missing, and the series often disappointed in terms of print quality; *The Adventurer* was inferior to material sometimes seen elsewhere. In many instances, an attempt seems to have been made to reduce the harshness of 'duped' material by softening focus and flattening the contrast, to the point where the image looks discouragingly grey. (*The Rounders* undergoes a disturbing adjustment in contrast part-way through a single shot.) One journalist believed that viewers, accustomed to seeing Chaplin moving either at hastened speed or in stretch-printed jerkiness, could not accept the smooth transfer, a point which may perhaps be dismissed. Grumbles aside, *Chaplin SuperClown* was a brave effort which receives periodic repeats even to this day.

Chaplin SuperClown pre-dated the appearance of Chaplin's own package on television. He had announced a TV deal late in 1971, but nothing happened for some two years, presumably to avoid conflict with a theatrical reissue of *Modern Times*. It was this same film that commenced BBC screenings late in 1973, to be followed by the other titles – including the assorted truncations of *The Chaplin Revue* (*qv*) – in the remaining years of the decade. (*A Countess From Hong Kong*, not under Chaplin's control, also surfaced in 1973.) The BBC retained Chaplin's films until the mid-1980s, but they were with Channel 4 at the time of his centenary. Channel 4's commemorative season included the documentary *Our Charlie*; the station has also shown the Mutuals with their Van Beuren tracks, somewhat restored in terms of picture, but still at the wrong speed (despite an impossible claim to the contrary in at least one listings magazine). There have been satellite showings of Chaplin's package on both sides of the Atlantic. *Sunnyside* has been ignored by UK terrestrial TV, but has been screened several times on satellite. In addition to those mentioned above, there have been numerous TV screenings of documentaries and compilations relating to Chaplin. These include Robert Youngson's anthologies, also *The Funniest Man in the World* (*qv*) and the invaluable *Unknown Chaplin* (*qv*). Mention might be made of an American series, *Hollywood and the Stars*, bought in by BBC TV and screened during spring 1965. One episode – 'The Funny Men, Part 1' – promised footage of Chaplin, in civilian clothes, rehearsing a scene for *City Lights*; this was presumably that in which Charlie contemplates a nude statue, a segment also used in *Unknown Chaplin*.

(See also: Animation; Documentaries, compilations; Mutual; Reissues; Titling; Trick photography; Video releases)

THATCHER, EVA
(1862–1942)

Born in Omaha, Nebraska, Eva Thatcher plays Charlie's somewhat mature girlfriend, the cook, in *The Count* (*qv*); other rôles include that of wife to Charlie Murray (*qv*) in Sennett's first Paramount release, *A Bedroom Blunder* (1917); also *Thirst* (1917), *Yankee Doodle in Berlin* (1919), *Dangerous Fists* (1925) and *Blazing Days* (1927). Some of her credits are believed to be as 'Eve' Thatcher.

(See also: Keystone; Sennett, Mack)

A THIEF CATCHER

See: Keystone

THOSE LOVE PANGS

(Chaplin film)
Keystone Comedy released by Mutual, 10 October 1914. Produced by Mack Sennett. Written and directed by Charles Chaplin. Photography attributed to Frank D. Williams. Reissued by W.H. Productions as *The Rival Mashers*; other reissue titles include *Busted Hearts*. One reel. 1,010 feet (approx. UK length cited in contemporary press).

With Charlie Chaplin (himself), Chester Conklin (rival), (?) Norma Nichols/Gene Marsh (landlady – see below), Cecile Arnold (Chester's blonde girlfriend), Vivian Edwards (her brunette counterpart), Harry McCoy (policeman).

Charlie and Chester Conklin are rivals for their landlady's affections. All being fair in this combination of love and war, Charlie interrupts Chester's moments with the landlady by jabbing a fork into his behind. There are more skirmishes until a dubious truce takes the two men outdoors. Charlie borrows money to buy a drink, while Chester sets off to meet his girlfriend in the park. Instead of entering the bar, Charlie decides instead to follow a passing brunette. She is waiting on a corner as Charlie flirts, but he makes a strategic exit on the arrival of her hefty boyfriend. Seated on a bench, Charlie is confronted by the couple, but he ducks under the man's arm, crawls along the bench and, as a parting shot, takes a shot at the man's hat with his cane. Charlie, looking on from beside a tree, sees Chester and his girlfriend. He watches, disheartened, as Chester seems blasé about the girl's devotion. The couple take their leave, and Charlie prepares to end it all by jumping into the lake. A cop prevents this rash move by grabbing the seat of Charlie's trousers. Charlie, seated on a bench, watches again as Chester's girl gives him money amid her embraces. Chester and his girl take a seat beside the other couple. Charlie fastidiously dusts off a brick and, pausing for a drink at a fountain, drops it on the foot of the brunette's boyfriend. Charlie is pursued to the lake. The other man chastises Charlie, but still prevents him falling into the water; as a reward, he is sent plunging in by the hook of Charlie's cane. The cane is turned on Chester, who by now is enjoying the attentions of both girls. Chester tries to retaliate, but is knocked cold. The young ladies have fled by the time Charlie perches on his victim, counting the loot rifled from his pockets. Charlie follows the girls into a movie theatre, using the stolen money to buy a ticket. In the park, Chester and the other man recover and set off for revenge. They arrive at the theatre, where Charlie is seated between the girls. While he is dozing, they take the girls' places, and Charlie awakens to find himself surrounded. He tries to flee, but is sent flying through the cinema screen, from which his head emerges as the two rivals hurl bricks.

According to Mack Sennett's memoirs, *King of Comedy*, production of *Those Love Pangs* was suspended after a few takes while Chaplin and Chester Conklin (*qv*) searched for a more substantial story than simply pursuing the landlady. Sennett recalled the two comedians finding a new milieu for their on-screen rivalry when their streetcar paused near a bakery. The resultant sequence grew into a quite independent two-reeler, *Dough and Dynamite* (*qv*); the cast is similar, even to the point of Vivian Edwards (*qv*) wearing the same dress (!). The latter film remains one of the best Chaplin Keystones, but *Those Love Pangs* is by comparison unremarkable, overlapping as it does with numerous other 'park' comedies while also containing moments similar to *The Star Boarder* (*qv*) and the opening scenes of *A Film Johnnie* (*qv*). Intriguingly, *Those Love Pangs* contains the intimation that both girls may be prostitutes. When Charlie decides to follow the brunette instead of buying a drink, he examines his money as if to decide which commodity to purchase. Similarly, one might query Chester's status with blonde Cecile Arnold (*qv*) (herself sporting a stereotypical 'streetwalker' kiss-curl) when she gives him a sum of money retrieved from her shoe. Such references appear in several non-Chaplin Keystones of the period, and must have been quite shocking to contemporary audiences. The rôle of the

A short-lived truce between rival boarders Chester Conklin and Charlie in **Those Love Pangs** *BFI Stills, Posters and Designs*

brunette's boyfriend has sometimes been ascribed to Edgar Kennedy (*qv*), but the actor in question seems much slimmer. Similarly, Norma Nichols has been credited as the landlady, but once more seems to be a different player, Gene Marsh (see also *His Musical Career*).

(See also: Conklin, Chester; Edwards, Vivian; Keystone; McCoy, Harry; Parks; Policemen; Risqué humour; Smoking; Williams, Frank D.)

TILLIE'S/TILLY'S LOVE AFFAIR

See: *Tillie's Punctured Romance*

TILLIE'S PUNCTURED ROMANCE

(Chaplin film)
Keystone Comedy released by Alco Film Corporation, 14 November 1914. Produced and directed by Mack Sennett. Written by Hampton Del Ruth, from the stage play *Tillie's Nightmare* (book by Edgar Smith). Photography: various. Released in Britain Spring 1915 by Globe Film Distributors. Six reels; reissues sometimes abridged to five or, more commonly, four reels. Reissue titles include *Marie's Millions*, *For the Love of Tillie* and (from Equity Films in the UK) *Tilly's Love Affair*.

With Marie Dressler (Tillie Banks), Charlie Chaplin (city slicker), Mabel Normand (Charlie's girlfriend), Mack Swain (Tillie's father, John Banks), Charles Bennett (Tillie's Uncle, Douglas Banks), Edgar Kennedy (butler at Banks

Tillie collars her crooked husband and his accomplice in **Tillie's Punctured Romance**

home/Tillie's restaurant employer), Chester Conklin (waiter at first restaurant/Mr Whoozis, a party guest), Alice Davenport (another guest), Minta Durfee (upstairs maid), Charley Chase (detective in cinema), Charlie Murray (detective on screen), Al St. John, Slim Summerville, Hank Mann, Edward Sutherland (Keystone Cops), Phyllis Allen (prison matron), Harry McCoy (cinema pianist), Gordon Griffith (paper boy), (?) Rev. D. Simpson (clergyman), Wallace MacDonald, Joe Bordeaux.

Charlie, a 'city slicker' conman lying low in the countryside, saunters past a farm. The farmer, John Banks, has a heavyweight daughter, Tillie, who inadvertently hurls a brick in Charlie's direction while playing with the dog. The battered stranger is invited home, where Mr Banks takes a poor view of Tillie's flirtation with the visitor. Tillie's boyfriend calls to collect the mortgage payment; Mr Banks takes some money from a well-filled wallet, which the city slicker eyes greedily. Charlie woos the unlovely lass, acting as protector when, in their cavortings, she inadvertently throws a brick at her father. While the farmer tends the land, Charlie persuades her to steal the wallet and accompany him to the big city. While she is doing so, Charlie deals with the jealous boyfriend. In the city, Mabel, Charlie's old girlfriend and accomplice, sees Charlie trying to keep Tillie out of the traffic. She catches up and confronts Charlie at a street corner. Charlie is horrified, and a squabble breaks out between the two women, terminating only on the arrival of a policeman. Tillie leads Charlie away. Mabel follows as Charlie escorts Tillie into a restaurant.

Tillie has her first taste of strong drink and spits it out, creating a disturbance. There are further ructions when Mabel arrives to confront Charlie once more, arousing Tillie's wrath. Taken aside, Charlie explains the scam to Mabel, while Tillie, rather drunk, begins dancing with strangers. Having taken the wallet, Charlie exits with Mabel. They watch from afar as the drunken Tillie is ejected and led away by the police. Tillie makes a playful prisoner, biting the custody sergeant's finger when asked her name. While Charlie and Mabel live it up on the stolen money, a more contrite Tillie tells the prison matron her identity, claiming to be the niece of a wealthy man. Uncle is telephoned, verifying her story, but expressing no wish to see her. Charlie and Mabel buy expensive new clothes with the stolen money, then, witnessing Tillie's release, promptly hide. They enter a cinema (to see a Keystone film advertised as 'Double Crossed' but bearing the on-screen title 'A Thief's Fate'!). On screen, they watch a story very similar to Charlie's recent betrayal of Tillie. Charlie and Mabel, unnerved to see the culprit's arrest (and by the presence of a detective sitting beside them), make a hurried departure. Meanwhile, Tillie's uncle leaves his mansion for a mountaineering expedition. Tillie, penniless, takes a job as waitress in a restaurant. Tillie's uncle sets off through the mountains, accompanied by a guide. In the restaurant, Tillie is startled to see Charlie and Mabel among the diners, and goes berserk, but the villains escape. They enter a park, but keep moving when they see a policeman. In the mountains, Uncle loses his footing and takes a nasty spill. The guide reports the accident, and a telephone call is made to the millionaire's home, announcing his demise. Uncle's secretaries decide that Tillie is sole heir. Charlie buys a newspaper from a small boy. The paper announces the death of Tillie's uncle and her inheritance of $3,000,000. Before Mabel even notices his departure, Charlie has rushed back to Tillie, protested his devotion and rushed her to a minister for instant wedlock. Tillie

remains unaware of the legacy until they return to the restaurant, where the secretaries await. Once informed, Tillie understands Charlie's haste but, after eyeing him suspiciously, embraces her new spouse. Mabel, who has been waiting for Charlie, finally examines the newspaper and sets off after her boyfriend. In the mountains, Uncle is discovered to be alive. The newlyweds arrive at Uncle's mansion, installing themselves with lack of grace and total disregard for the staff. The servants acquire another to their number when Mabel takes a job as maid. In the mountains, Uncle is helped back to the cabin. Tillie and Charlie make their society debut by throwing a lavish ball. Among the guests is Mr Whoozis, a friend of Tillie's uncle. Host and hostess are clumsy, Charlie all the more so when confronted by Mabel. Unaware of what is happening, Uncle is nursed back to health in the mountain cabin. Charlie takes a reluctant trip around the dance floor prior to sneaking off to square things with Mabel, who is by the punch bowl. Tillie tracks him down and, failing to notice Mabel, drags her reluctant husband back to the dance floor. They sit back to watch another couple dance and, Tillie, impressed, disappears upstairs to put on her own special dancing frock. Mr Whoozis has seen through Charlie, and a fight ensues. At its end, Charlie turns to Mabel for consolation. Mr Whoozis returns for more, and is disposed of appropriately. Atop the main staircase, Tillie calls Charlie to escort her down to the dance floor. Charlie and Tillie essay an ungainly tango; Mabel, passing, gives Charlie a kick before returning to the punch bowl. Charlie, leaving Tillie to her cavortings, goes off to console Mabel. Noticing Charlie's absence, Tillie embarks on a search, and catches him smooching with Mabel. Everyone scatters as Tillie, firing a revolver, pursues Charlie through the house, disturbing a lady who is upstairs changing her dress. Charlie takes refuge in a giant vase. The chase is interrupted by the return of Tillie's uncle, far from dead and furious to see his home invaded. Tillie smashes the vase, revealing Charlie; she is astonished to see both Charlie and her uncle, who orders everyone from the house. Outside, Tillie embraces Charlie, but he kicks her away, preferring to disappear with Mabel. Uncle, furious at the damage to his home, instructs a servant to call the police, demanding Tillie's arrest. Tillie, firing more shots, pursues Charlie and Mabel to a jetty. The police blunder onto the scene, knocking over a passerby. They commandeer a car, in which they push Tillie into the sea. Car and cops soon join her. Charlie phones the Water Police for assistance. A speedboat loaded with officers is dispatched, joined by others in a rowing boat. More police throw Tillie a rope, but the arrival of their colleagues sends them tumbling over, and Tillie falls back into the water. The rowing boat loses a man as its motorized equivalent rushes to the scene. Charlie helps a cop haul Tillie to the surface, but he accidentally boots the policeman into the sea. The speedboat sinks the rowing boat. Tillie, at last brought to safety, returns her wedding ring to Charlie. He is also spurned by Mabel, and collapses, to be dragged away by the police. Tillie chastises Mabel but, on discovering how she, too, is Charlie's victim, embraces her. They agree that Charlie 'ain't no good to neither of us' as Tillie starts to wail.

The Keystone Film Company had been in business for less than two years when Mack Sennett (*qv*) decided to embark upon a feature-length subject. Such things were still uncommon even for dramatic pictures, and by 1914 there had yet to be a full-length comedy, at least in America. Sennett is believed to have been inspired by news of his former mentor, D.W. Griffith (*qv*), working on a full-length film known initially as 'The Clansman' but released eventually as *The Birth of a Nation*. It was thought that Keystone's regular players, however popular, could not in themselves secure bookings at the first-run theatres. In consequence, Sennett approached stage star Marie Dressler (*qv*), whose advice he had once sought when first embarking on a theatrical career.

Sennett later claimed that Marie Dressler took a house in California specifically to make the film. The actress, in her own published account, suggests it to have been pure coincidence that she was in the Los Angeles area. After a recent professional disaster (of the sort that periodically dogged her career), Dressler had been ordered to the West Coast for the sake of her nerves. She had visited a movie theatre, and was accosted by Sennett, accompanied by Charles Bauman, who had waited for her outside. They arranged a meeting at her hotel, where the film project was explained. According to her memoirs,

Miss Dressler agreed to participate for the sum of $2,500 per week, a stark comparison to the $200 then being paid Chaplin. There was also a verbal understanding that the film was to be leased, rather than sold outright, that she would also own half the film, and that a weekly financial statement would be sent. Distribution was to be handled by Dressler's husband, James Dalton, rather than through Keystone's usual arrangement with Mutual (*qv*). Sennett's book, *King of Comedy*, states that scenario editor Craig Hutchinson had suggested a film version of the play *Tillie's Nightmare* (1910), in which the actress had earned national fame. The stage original is best recalled for a song, *Heaven Will Protect the Working Girl*; its plot, the Cinderella-like dream of a 'boarding house drudge', was, again according to Sennett, used by scenarist Hampton Del Ruth and his team as no more than a slight basis. The essential ingredient was to be the 'Tillie' character herself.

Sennett poured all his resources into the film, engaging virtually every player and technician at the studio's disposal. He later recalled slight delays during shooting, which took place over a fourteen-week period commencing in late April 1914 and concluding late in July. The main difficulty lay in Miss Dressler's memory of him as an unknown, rather than the boss of the studio, and consequent unwillingness to take direction until baffled by the techniques of film-making. According to Harry M. Geduld's *Chapliniana*, Sennett encountered further problems with his star over the matter of distribution. Instead of honouring their verbal commitment to allow Dressler's husband to distribute the film, Kessel and Bauman sold the appropriate rights to the Alco Film Corporation. This prompted Dressler to instigate a series of legal actions against Keystone, none of them successful. Neither Sennett's nor Dressler's memoirs make mention of the case, the latter claiming instead (and inaccurately) that Keystone was unable to find a distributor for some nine months.

Tillie was reissued on many occasions, as in this 1920 revival; note Chaplin's promotion to top billing
By courtesy of Claudia Sassen

Tillie's Punctured Romance was released in the UK by Globe Films

Trade ads for *Tillie* appeared on 7 November 1914 (one week prior to release), at this stage offering the film on a State's Rights basis, or in other words covering US release by allocation to various local bidders. Marie Dressler's name, in large type, dominated the copy, which described her as 'America's Greatest Box Office Attraction' and *Tillie* as 'The "Impossible" Attained — A SIX

REEL COMEDY'.

Tillie was played broadly, as one might expect from a Keystone farce, and today seems more than a trifle overdone. *Variety*, comparing the film favourably to the concurrent stage farce (*A Mix Up*) in which Miss Dressler was opening, also picked up on her furious mugging and tumbling, but considered them more of a virtue; 'she makes gestures and distorts her face in all directions, which help all the more,' it was said. 'Mack Sennett directed the picture,' noted *Variety*, 'and right well has he done the job.' Chaplin was named among the Keystone players by whom the star was 'splendidly supported'. In the author's opinion, Chaplin's visual impact in this film seems diminished, his youthful features being perhaps under-disguised by a slight, pencil moustache. Posterity's quibblings aside, the film was considered a breakthrough at the time, and did enormous business (Marie Dressler later recalled eight showmen having told her that *Tillie* 'built their theatres'). Clifford H. Pangburn of the *Motion Picture News* (14 November 1914) conceded the difficulty in doing justice to visual humour on the printed page, especially in relation to 'this masterpiece of the slapstick art'. Unlike the *Variety* scribe, who thought the picture 'a trifle too long', Pangburn considered the revolutionary six-reel length 'amply justified' (subsequent abridgers, please note), the result being 'six thousand feet of undiluted joy', at which 'case hardened reviewers, trained to sigh at ordinary humor, laughed until the tears streamed down their careworn faces'. Marie Dressler 'even surpasses her work on the stage', while Chaplin, 'nearly an equal factor in the laugh making', brought roars 'wherever he really extends himself'. Mabel Normand received doubtless unintentionally faint praise: 'Of almost equal importance is Mabel Normand, who also has a leading part.' Sennett's inclusion of many 'excellent scenes' and top-notch photography (generally lost in today's dupes) contributed to 'the longest and at the same time one of the best comedies yet seen on the screen'. (It might be noted, incidentally, that Pangburn cites Mutual as distributors, perhaps more through an assumption than any conflicting data.)

As with most Chaplin Keystones, *Tillie* has been reissued on numerous occasions, easily outliving a purely nominal – and seemingly lost – remake from 1928, starring Louise Fazenda,

W.C. Fields and Chester Conklin (*qv*). Despite its survival, the film often surfaces with a different title, and is invariably mutilated. There was a four-reel abridgement in circulation by 1922, or possibly even two years earlier; another revival, as *Tillie's Love Affair*, ran to only three. The six-reeler is reported to have been reissued in 1928. There are a number of silent, five-reel copies in circulation; one of these incorporates a sub-title referring to Prohibition, evidently in an attempt to revitalize the subject, but serving only to date this particular revival. Possibly the only complete, original version is that held by the British Film Institute; among those available to collectors, by far the most worthwhile is the American laserdisc of David Shepard's six-reel restoration, most of which derives from an original of truly remarkable image quality.

Sub-titling on the BFI and Shepard copies reveals the standard Keystone design, though minus the company logo in each lower corner. Significantly, the full title, as quoted at the top of the screen, reads 'Marie Dressler in Tillie's Punctured Romance', emphasizing her original top billing. Reissue titles, in addition to those noted above, include that a UK variant, *Tilly's* (*sic*) *Love Affair*, *For the Love of Tillie* and a 1929 sound revamp, *Marie's Millions*. Shepard's copy incorporates a pleasant closing touch, invariably trimmed from revivals, in which *Tillie's* stage origins are acknowledged when curtains close over the final shot.

The majority of today's prints derive from a later four-reel edition, from Burwood Pictures, which reverts to the original title. This version, with added sound, creates a new title sequence by introducing the cast with their names superimposed over shots from the film or still frames. Ford Sterling (*qv*) is listed in the cast, but he is not present, having embarked on his sojourn away from Keystone by this time; he is, however, visible in one of the display posters when Charlie and Mabel visit a cinema, and one might note that one of the party guests has been made up to resemble him. A lengthy text sequence makes a bold citation of *Tillie* as 'the world's oldest living motion picture', which is total nonsense given the existence of films dating back to the first half of the 1890s. This sound reissue was among the shortest to be released theatrically (a one-reeler, *The City Slicker*, was long circulated in home movie form).

Ironically, when International brought it to the UK in the early 1950s, one evidently uninformed reviewer said 'the only alteration is that it now has a sound track'. Blackhawk Films offered a four-reel edition for many years until superseding it with more complete material. Among other copies, the author has compared a silent five-reeler with the four-reel sound edition. The latter has numerous small cuts, but contains the cinema sequence, absent from the longer print; it also includes a shot, again missing from the five-reeler, of Mabel entering Tillie's mansion via the servants' entrance, when taking a job as maid.

Trivia note: the rôle of the newsboy is usually credited to child actor Gordon Griffith (*qv*), despite a claim by comedian Milton Berle, in his 1974 memoirs, to have played the part himself. Berle's other childhood screen appearances included films with John Bunny, Pearl White, Mabel Normand (*qv*) and Mary Pickford (*qv*). Berle met Chaplin again 52 years later, when *A Countess From Hong Kong* (*qv*) was being shot in England. Berle approached Chaplin, describing their scene together. Instead of the anticipated pleasured surprise, what he got was, 'Oh, I see ... exposition,' before Chaplin turned away to resume business with his technicians.

Although it brought him international exposure in a feature-length subject, Chaplin later had as much time for *Tillie's Punctured Romance* as he seems to have had for Berle. During its creation, he was more concerned with developing both his own talent as director and the 'tramp' character he had created. After its release, other studio bosses expressed such interest in Chaplin's services that Sennett had to place guards on him while at the studio. For Chaplin, however, the rôle of a Keystone villain, once more under Sennett's direction, must have seemed a retrograde step.

(See also: Bennett, Charles; Boats, ships; Camera-looks; *Carmen*; Cars; Costume; Dual rôles; Impersonators; Kennedy, Edgar; Keystone; MacDonald, Wallace; Parks; Policemen; Reissues; Risqué humour; Streetcars; Summerville, George J. 'Slim'; Swain, Mack; Television; Video releases; Villains)

TITLING 🎩

(Chaplin films *qv*)

Titling has always been important in the presentation of film. In silent days, this was all the more so, as the image was everything, and it was normal for subtitles to provide both narration and dialogue. Design for main titles and, frequently, sub-titles, often favoured elaborate artwork, and much time and expense would be invested.

The better silent film-makers strove to minimize sub-titling, and Chaplin's work, in its original form, avoids them where possible. The New York *Times* believed that *The Kid* 'could be understood, which means mightily enjoyed, anywhere in the world without a single sub-title, and those it has are few, far between and brief'. *Pictures and the Picturegoer* singled out a title card from *One A.M.* when reviewing the film in April 1917. Amid Charlie's attempts to reach his bed, the action pauses to observe, drily and tersely, 'you can't keep a good man down', a remark taken to summarize the man's own early, real-life struggles in addition to those of his screen character.

It was usually when the films were reissued by unsympathetic hands that additional sub-titles began to appear, some of them employing unnecessary verbal jokes or an inappropriate brand of vulgarity (examples, detailed elsewhere, include **Caught in a Cabaret** and **Shanghaied**). On occasion they were both primitive in appearance and inaccurate in tone, such as those added to a later incarnation of *Easy Street*.

Theodore Huff was among the few Chaplin commentators to make the effort to describe the correct titling for Chaplin's early films. As he has noted, main titling for the Keystone comedies, based on Biograph's house style, should present the company name in an arc, forming part of a scrolled ellipse within which the title itself is written (with the description 'farce comedy' beneath). Keystone sub-titles place the name of the film, underlined, at the top of the screen, with a Keystone 'K' symbol at each lower corner. If the film is two reels in length, then 'part one' or 'part two' appears between these logos. The text itself is written in italicized capitals, with quotation marks for dialogue. They read as white-on-black, having been shot in negative form. Keystone 'end' titles take the form of the company trademark; during Chaplin's tenure their releases

Titling: *Chaplin authenticates the main title of* Sunnyside

were via Mutual, though this distributor's closing title is seldom present on those occasions when an original Keystone Chaplin is shown. This would bear the slogan 'Mutual Movies Make Time Fly', accompanying a winged clock face with rapidly-turning hands.

Essanay's main titles, again white-on-black, enclose the design within a large square, formed by four white lines. The name 'Essanay', in chunky, closely-set, back-slanted letters, is itself enclosed within a rectangular border interrupting the upper side of the square. The company's Indian-head logo is placed within a smaller square at each corner. The title itself, incorporating Chaplin's billing and the copyright date, are placed centrally. Huff said the studio's sub-titles were undecorated, but they are in fact distinguished by the standard back-slanting 'Essanay' name in the lower right-hand corner. Sometimes, as in Blackhawk's print of *The Champion* (though these might be facsimiles), the film's title plus 'Act 1' or 'Act 2' appears at the lower left. 'Act Two' and 'The End' titles are based on the opening cards.

The Mutual films present something of a mystery. Huff considered the original sub-titles to have been those distinguished by a large initial within an illuminated box (scrolled rather than floral); the author has seen nothing earlier in full-framed silent copies, yet the BBC restorations remake these cards in a quite different design, placing the film's main title within a double-lined rectangle with the Mutual logo at the lower right corner. Sub-titles present the text in italic capitals, quoting the title of the film in similar, smaller lettering at the foot of the picture. To the lower left corner is the Mutual-Chaplin 'Lone Star' symbol. It is possible that the illuminated-initial titles derive from an

early reissue of the series, via a distributor calling itself Chaplin Classics; a clue is provided by an appearance of the company's 'end' title on an available print of *The Pawnshop* bearing these distinctive sub-titles. Some newer copies have these illuminated titles remade, as in the restored versions issued on video. The author has seen a print of *The Count* with authentic 'illuminated' titles, in addition to another in which these appear with different typography plus horizontal borders placed at the top and bottom of the card.

Reissues of the shorts tended to bring replacement designs. Some of the Essanays turn up in British revivals with their sub-titles decorated by landscapes. Certain Keystones have silly cartoons plastered over the titling, while the author's print of *The Fireman* has subtitles superimposed over a full-faced portrait of Chaplin. Guaranteed Pictures, which reissued the Mutuals with added sound, inserted main and end titles that were superimposed over a design showing Charlie's hat, cane and shoes. Sub-titles in the late 1930s editions take the form of angular lettering with a Chaplin silhouette placed to the lower left; those in the 'Chaplin Cavalcade' version of *The Rink* shown on Channel 4 incorporate a full-length Chaplin caricature in all four corners. One edition of *A Dog's Life*, presumably from the 1920s UK revival via Pathé, employs a cloudy sky as background for its titling.

Some reissues retained earlier titling alongside new cards, generally providing unnecessary comment on the action; for example, a version of *The Immigrant* released to 16mm (from which some 8mm reductions have been made) preserves both the full-frame area and the illuminated titling, but also adds narrative titles of a different design, telling us such things as 'Alas! Edna is now an orphan' when Chaplin's images convey the fact unassisted. Such titling, generally designed to bolster footage, can usually be identified by a tedious fading in and out rather than straight cutting.

By the time of Chaplin's First National series, such revivals – and, especially, the 'bogus Chaplins' (*qv*) – had proliferated to the point where Chaplin's new product needed to be distinguished in some way. On 27 October 1917, the *Moving Picture World* reported how 'Chaplin's signature will play an important part in the promotion and exhibition of all the comedian's future releases.' 'In future,' said *Pictures and the Picturegoer* on 17 November, 'Charles Chaplin's signature is to be his trade-mark. So that all can distinguish the difference between his earlier comedies and those he is now producing, the title of every new release will bear the comedian's autograph.' When the series commenced, *Photoplay's* advertising section published 'A Letter From Charlie Chaplin', asking the public to look for his signature both on posters and on the main titles of the films themselves. Chaplin was actually filmed signing the main title cards of these 'Million Dollar' productions, crouching below camera range with only his hand visible to the audience. In present-day revivals, only *Shoulder Arms* circulates with its 'autographed' title. Sub-titling on the First National films takes the form of square-ish lettering surrounded by a chain border (a reference to First National being a theatre chain); the company logo itself appears centrally within the lower part of the frame. In authorized reissues, the First National subjects are retitled in a different white-on-black style.

Chaplin's later work tended towards titling unique to each subject and seldom elaborate. It is evident that *City Lights*, in its planned silent version, would have opened with the neon-style presentation that in the eventual release is preceded by a very plain credit sequence. Its sub-titles are of the cloth-background look favoured by the industry in the 1920s. By the time *Modern Times* was produced, silent films were even more of a memory, and its sub-titles have a consciously updated look. Its main credits are superimposed over a clock face with moving hands (shades of Mutual!), a sequence marred on reissue when one title (bearing updated copyright details) was remade as a frozen frame. Fortunately, a more recent video edition has corrected this slipshod detail.

The sound reissue of *The Gold Rush* remakes main and end titles, dispensing entirely with sub-titling in favour of narration. Chaplin's reissue of *The Circus* retains its sub-titles, but a new credit sequence has been added, duplicating shots of Merna Kennedy (*qv*) from elsewhere in the film, and accompanied by Chaplin's own vocal rendering of the theme song.

(See also: *Chase Me Charlie*; Costume; Essanay; *Immigrant, The*; *In the Park*; Keystone; Left-handedness; Mutual; Reissues; *Shoulder Arms*; *Sunnyside*; Television; *Tillie's Punctured Romance*; Video releases)

TOTHEROH, ROLAND H. 'ROLLIE'
(1890–1967)

Cameraman, brother of actor/director/writer Dan Totheroh; a former cartoonist, Rollie Totheroh was working as a cameraman at Essanay (*qv*) prior to and during Chaplin's tenure, but was for many years miscredited with photographing his comedies for this studio. Recent sources have instead named Harry Ensign as cameraman for the Chaplin Essanays, although it is possible that Totheroh may have functioned as assistant. (Ensign's details are elusive, but *Variety* reported the death of a Harris Newton Ensign, a former Paramount laboratory head, on 13 October 1943, aged 60.) Rollie Totheroh became Chaplin's full-time cameraman at Mutual (*qv*), initially in tandem with William C. Foster (*qv*), and has long been regarded as functioning as an assistant director when Chaplin was before the cameras. Foster's departure saw the appointment of George C. ('Duke') Zalibra as Totheroh's assistant. Totheroh remained in the job – graduating eventually to Director of Photography – until Chaplin's departure from the USA. As noted under *A Dog's Life* (*qv*), Rollie functioned also as Chaplin's film conservator and archivist,

in which capacity he fortunately chose to ignore Chaplin's instructions to destroy his out-takes; it is thought that Totheroh wanted them as back-up material should negative repairs become necessary. This decision led ultimately to the invaluable series *Unknown Chaplin* (*qv*).

(See also: Politics; Purviance, Edna; Raye, Martha; Struss, Karl; Wilson, Jack)

THE TRAMP

(Chaplin film)
Released by General Film Company, 11 April 1915. Produced by Essanay. Written and directed by Charles Chaplin. Photographed by Harry Ensign. British title: *Charlie, the Tramp*. Two reels. 1,896 feet.

With Charlie Chaplin (the tramp), Edna Purviance (farmer's daughter), Lloyd Bacon (her sweetheart), Leo White (thief), Paddy McGuire (farmhand).

Charlie, a wanderer, finds his progress through a country lane impeded by passing motorists. Nearby, a farmer hands his daughter some money, in order to run an errand. Charlie sits beneath a tree, preparing to eat, but a tramp swaps the food in Charlie's handkerchief for a brick. Charlie makes do with handfuls of grass. The same thief sets out to rob the farmer's daughter; pursued, she runs past Charlie, who overpowers the tramp but nearly

Rollie Totheroh was Chaplin's cameraman for over thirty years

The Tramp: *nursing a tender rear end, Charlie prefers to eat while standing*

keeps the girl's money for himself. Charlie relents and becomes her protector, seeing off both the first thief and his two comrades. The thieves are pelted with flying bricks; in return, Charlie is knocked into the thieves' camp fire and has to rush to a water pipe to extinguish his smouldering rear. The girl takes Charlie home to meet her father. A meal is prepared, but Charlie, his behind still tender, places the food on the mantelpiece so he can eat while standing. Charlie has barely started to eat before he is put to work, which in Charlie's case consists of guiding a fellow employee with a pitchfork. His colleague, trying to carry a large sack of flour up to a hay loft, first bashes it into Charlie before dropping it on to the farmer. A poet stands surveying the beauty of the fields; his expression changes when Charlie and comrade walk by, having obviously trodden in something highly organic. Much the same applies to the eggs; on his return journey, Charlie dumps one particularly malodorous specimen into the poet's book of verse. By the time the farmer emerges from beneath the sack, Charlie and friend are in the loft, from where Charlie drops two smaller sacks on his employer. Charlie is descending the ladder with a third sack when the farmer kicks him. Another sack is dropped on the farmer's head. The farmer, seeking revenge, arms himself with a large piece of wood. Charlie blames his colleague, who in being whacked unwittingly drops a sack on Charlie's head. The farmer returns to his house, where the trio of thieves watch as he counts his money. Charlie is occupied elsewhere, using a watering can in a fruit orchard, when the daughter rings a bell to summon him. Charlie is given a bucket and the task of milking a cow. After first approaching a bull, Charlie reaches the correct animal, but tries to produce milk by using her tail as a pump. After collecting eggs and setting to work with a wheelbarrow, Charlie is intercepted by the trio of

robbers. He is offered part of the take if he co-operates, and seems to agree. Bedtime arrives on the farm. Charlie and colleague retire upstairs, Charlie's candle leaving the farmer with a burning newspaper. In their room, Charlie helps the other farmhand remove a boot, and promptly opens a window to clear the air. Charlie takes a rack from the wall, forming makeshift

The Tramp *settles down to eat, but his meal is stolen almost from under his nose*

tongs in order to dispose of the farmhand's sock. Charlie, intent on foiling the robbery, remains dressed and is poised by the open window with a mallet. A blow from the weapon ensures the farmhand's slumber. The first head to appear belongs to the farmer, who is duly conked. When the farmer investigates, Charlie ensures the other man is holding the mallet. Charlie explains all to the farmer, and when the robbers try to climb the ladder to the window, Charlie is ready with the mallet while the farmer goes to fetch his shotgun. The thieves make a swift exit, disappearing over a fence; Charlie, climbing after them, is accidentally shot in the leg. Charlie's convalescence is made all the more pleasant by the daughter's pamperings. His dreams of a future with the girl are terminated by the arrival of her sweetheart. Charlie retires to compose a heartfelt, if semi-literate note: 'i thort your kindness was love but it aint cause i seen him XXI Good-bye.' The note is left in the kitchen as Charlie collects his meagre belongings. Outside, Charlie bids the young couple farewell, politely refusing the newcomer's offer of money. In the kitchen, daughter and friend greet the farmer. All is bright until the girl discover's Charlie's note. By this time, Charlie is walking dejectly into the distance. He pauses, then brightens, continuing jauntily as the iris closes behind him.

This famous ending contributes mightily to *The Tramp*'s status as the first 'Chaplin classic'. Although still heavily dependent on slapstick and a measure of sometimes startling vulgarity, this endowment of 'Charlie' with an emotional dimension is both a turning point within the increasingly sophisticated Essanay series and a forerunner of the intelligent knockabout characterizing the Mutual films. Oddly, Chaplin's *My Autobiography* draws no attention to this comedy, attributing the advance in his technique to later subjects.

Surviving material on *The Tramp* seems to derive from a common, if early, source. Inherited scratches and other minor damage recur in every print, the key difference being in the number of generations from the original. Although the film sometimes turns up in very poor prints, there is – unusually for an Essanay – some very good material in existence. Video editions have often derived from that issued by Blackhawk Films, whose print was of indifferent quality despite the presence of authentic-looking (but probably remade) Essanay title cards. Theodore Huff described a mutilated reissue in which Charlie seems only to fall from the fence instead of being shot; this does not apply to a reissue version common in the UK, from Williams & Ivey Films, a firm who had several Essanays and Mutuals in release. The author's copy of this edition is, however, lacking the scene of Charlie eating grass and the business with the farmhand's boot and sock. The BBC's *Chaplin SuperClown* print is very acceptable (though it cuts rather abruptly prior to the scene of Charlie's convalescence), but the prize must go to that excerpted in *The Funniest Man in the World (qv)*, which utilizes material of an exceptional standard.

(See also: Cars; Colour; Costume; Essanay; Documentaries; Goodwins, Fred; Jamison, William 'Bud'; McGuire, Paddy; Mutual; Reissues; Television; Trick photography; Vagrancy; Video releases)

TRICK PHOTOGRAPHY

(Chaplin films *qv*)
The practice of using the camera to deceive may be traced back at least as far as Georges Méliès in the 1890s. Among the more elementary techniques is that of undercranking, or in other words reducing the camera speed in order to accelerate movement on projection.

This has sometimes been confused with the fact that silent films, at least until the late 1920s, were usually made at a slower linear speed than their talking counterparts (the Chaplin films of around 1914–22 would have been made at a nominal 16 frames per second). Projection speed was also slower and, consequently, would have presented the action at a normal pace. The slapstick nightclub act of *A King in New York* is undercranked, as a means of simulating the received idea of silent comedies. Such cases of deliberate undercranking – i.e. creating action that would seem unduly hastened even at the original projection speed – are comparatively rare in the Chaplin films. Much of *A Jitney Elopement* is undercranked, most noticeably when Edna arrives at the park with her father and suitor and, especially, when the cars circle beside the jetty. Similarly accelerated motion is used for Charlie's attempts to work on the farm in *The Tramp*, at least in the scenes with Paddy McGuire (*qv*). In *A Dog's Life*, many of the early scenes are undercranked, though this becomes less obvious in the copies that have been stretch-printed, or in other words converted to sound speed by printing every other frame twice.

City Lights was shot mostly in the late-silent speed of around 20–22 frames per second, and seems only slightly fast at the sound speed of 24 f.p.s. It has been suggested that Chaplin liked the resultant added energy, and deliberately retained it for *Modern Times*, except in the few scenes shot with synchronized sound.

It is not true to suggest that Chaplin willingly accepted the increased speed in his reissues. He sometimes employed the stretch-printing technique mentioned above – as in *The Chaplin Revue* and *The Idle Class* – but was clearly unhappy with its jerky result. He left most of *The Kid* 'unstretched', probably as the lesser of two evils. (A number of the short comedies not under Chaplin's control were printed thus in the 1930s.) Subsequent 1920s films – *A Woman of Paris*, *The Gold Rush*, *The Circus* – were, like *City Lights*, shot at higher speed and are therefore less exaggerated by the increased projection rate. TV's *Chaplin SuperClown* (see **Television**), *Unknown Chaplin* (*qv*) and other more recent projects have benefited from the comparative ease in transferring film to videotape at the correct speed, as have

the restored versions issued on laserdisc in the USA. Unfortunately, there have been a number of commercial video releases in which this facility has been ignored.

Another staple of trick photography is the use of stop-motion, either in the sense of single-frame animation or of simply stopping the camera while a person or object is substituted. *The Gentleman Tramp* (*qv*) incorporates a trick film reportedly made at the Chaplin studio in 1923, with visitors Sir Albert and Lady Naylor-Leyland. When another couple bring drinks for his guests, Chaplin gestures magically to make them disappear; once he starts to pour, the table vanishes; and after his visitors shake hands and depart, Chaplin also disappears. Other peripheral subjects to use stop-frame are *How To Make Movies* and *Nice and Friendly* (both *qv*). Again in the elementary category is reverse photography, employed in *The Bond*, *Pay Day* and a deleted segment of *Behind the Screen*.

Double-exposure provides the opportunity to create ghostly and similarly unreal effects, as when Charlie steps out of his body during moments of fantasy in *Sunnyside*, *The Kid* and *The Circus*. One might expect some trickery when Charlie has a lookalike in *The Floorwalker* and *The Idle Class*, but the former uses Lloyd Bacon (*qv*), while the latter is achieved by means of editing and the use of an unidentifiable stand-in.

It has to be admitted that Chaplin did not exactly overspend on technical effects, even though much money was expended both on numerous retakes and in retaining his supporting players over many idle weeks. The model cabin in *The Gold Rush* can pass muster to some extent, and the matte work providing a giant TV screen in *Modern Times* is very acceptable; the example most frequently cited, however, is the poor back-projection work in *Limelight*. Chaplin, of course, was unworried. In various interviews, Jerry Epstein (*qv*) explained the comedian's belief – true, as it turns out – that an audience had come to see a Chaplin performance rather than any technical niceties.

(See also: Documentaries, compilations; Dreams; Dual rôles; Home movies; Reissues; Television; Video releases)

TRIPLE TROUBLE 🎩

(Chaplin film)
Released by V-L-S-E, 11 August 1918. Produced by Essanay. Written and directed by Leo White, incorporating footage written and directed by Charles Chaplin (see below). Original source footage photographed by Harry Ensign. Two reels. 1,460 feet.

With Charlie Chaplin (himself), Edna Purviance (laundry skivvy), Leo White (foreign count), Wesley Ruggles, Bud Jamison, James T. Kelly, Billy Armstrong (cook/miser).

At the home of an eccentric inventor, Charlie is hired as assistant to the cook. The cook alternates between supervising the girl scrubbing the laundry floor across the hallway and keeping Charlie's ineptitudes in check. The butler is also kept on his toes by the inventor's experiments with a new explosive. A group of top-hatted subversives are addressed by a sinister-looking count. He exits, in agitation. In the kitchen, Charlie fills a bin with kitchen waste and, in transporting it outside, dumps half the contents over the girl and her freshly-scrubbed floor. The bin is emptied over a fence, just as the Count is passing beneath. Charlie returns to the kitchen and the stone-faced girl. Realizing what he has done, Charlie bends to collect the rubbish and is kicked in the behind. The girl lectures him then breaks down in tears, mopping her eyes on the hem of her voluminous skirt. Charlie, similarly moved, absently dries his tears on a piece of the rubbish. The Count enters the professor's home. The girl aims a wet rag at Charlie, hitting the Count instead. The Count hurls it away, striking the cook, who responds with a kick. Charlie and the girl look busy. The Count explains what happened; the cook approaches Charlie, who finishes his elaborate peeling of a potato; the girl is reprimanded instead. In the corridor, the butler knocks his tray against the Count's hat. The furious Count departs. The cook kicks the girl's behind, and thus receives the same from gallant Charlie. The cook produces a knife, which Charlie renders useless by placing a potato on the end. Their scrap continues as the Count approaches the inventor. The Count offers money, and is keen to examine the explosive's ingredients. The inventor has him thrown out. Charlie, out of a job, arrives at a flophouse,

Supplying a hotfoot in **Triple Trouble**
BFI Stills, Posters and Designs

pausing to strike a match on someone's bare foot. He places the burning match between the victim's toes, causing them to singe. Charlie reaches a cot, using his neighbour's foot as a stand for his cane, and hanging his hat on the end of the man's bed. Opposite is an elderly drunk, gibbering a song through gaping mouth. Charlie observes before silencing him by flicking cigar ash into the man's mouth. Charlie leans him forward and boots him over, but the drunk bounces back, still singing. Charlie retires to bed. Outside, the Count meets with a hired assassin to discuss stealing the formula. A hyperactive cop listens in and goes for reinforcements. This eccentric band overruns the inventor's house, looking for assassins and clues wherever they go. The inventor is baffled until he learns they are his guardians. The assassin arrives at the flophouse. He receives a playful shove from the drunk, but gives him a heftier push in return. The assassin retires to bed, fully clothed. The drunk's singing disturbs the other vagrants; when one of them throws a pillow, the drunk responds by hurling back a boot, which strikes Charlie's head. Charlie delicately puts the drunk to bed, rendering him unconscious with a bottle over the head. He is warmly congratulated by his neighbour. When all seem asleep, a miser creeps in to rob the vagrants. Charlie, seeing him, conceals his coat beneath the mattress and puts what little money he

has into his mouth. On reaching Charlie's cot, the miser sees a blanket beneath which Charlie seems curved ninety degrees. The miser pushes Charlie's rear end down flat, only for it to spring back up. This happens twice before the blanket is removed. The miser selects another victim. The assassin is awake and sees what is going on. The miser counts his loot. Charlie awakes, going automatically into poker-dealing mode. He sees the miser counting cash and, believing he has swallowed his own modest hoard, taps his body to find out if it clinks. Charlie reverses his position in bed, placing his boots on his hands and concealing himself beneath the blanket. When the miser is not looking, he reaches over and takes the money. The assassin tips off the miser, who plunges a knife into what he thinks is Charlie's heart. The blow has, of course, missed and Charlie springs to life, taking on the miser, assassin and others. He escapes both the flophouse and the police, who arrest the miser and the drunk. The assassin, who has also escaped, holds up Charlie in an alley. He decides Charlie would be useful, and persuades him to assist in burgling the inventor's home. When they reach the front door, the inventor hears them and hides upstairs. His police bodyguards are sitting around when the assassin breaks in. They hide when he fires a shot. One officer is in another room with the butler; on seeing

the intruder, the butler flees and the officer whistles for his comrades. The assassin grabs the officer by the neck, hurling him into the other policemen's path. He is pursued and runs upstairs; the inventor hides in bed while his daughter, in the corridor, goes downstairs for help. The policemen rush upstairs, save for one who remains to hug the terrified girl. The police descend upon the bed containing the inventor while the assassin, who was behind the door, makes his escape. Downstairs, the girl rejects the other policeman's advances and pushes him into the assassin's path. Upstairs, the police realize their mistake and rush back to the ground floor. Charlie, in the kitchen, falls from the table into a laundry basket. The assassin fends off the police with gunshots as Charlie runs around the kitchen in panic. A bullet strikes the inventor's explosive device, which detonates. Policemen descend through the air, breaking through the floor into the plotters' hideout. The assassin stirs amid the debris; Charlie's head peeps out through a stove door. Charlie surveys the scene, smiles, only to retreat inside when the assassin hurls some debris.

Question: when is a Chaplin film not a Chaplin film? Answer: when he didn't make it ... with one exception. In August 1918, almost three years after the conclusion of Chaplin's association with Essanay (*qv*), George K. Spoor (*qv*) placed a trade advertisement (published in Britain by the *Kinematograph and Lantern Weekly*), as follows:

To the Exhibitor:–

If you bought a piece of real estate and foresaw that its value would quadruple if you held it a certain length of time, what would you do?

Certainly you would hold it. That's just what we did with 'Triple Trouble.'

Essanay made this picture with Charlie Chaplin when he was at the zenith of his laugh-making powers. We knew its value then. We knew there would come a time when it would be worth many times its weight in gold.

We held this negative in our vaults for the most opportune time of release, which we believe is NOW.

There has been only one new Chaplin film in several months. The public is eager for a NEW Chaplin comedy and will welcome 'Triple Trouble' with open arms.

Were we right in holding this laughing-nugget back for the propitious moment?

We were!

Yours truly,
ESSANAY FILM MFG. CO.

(signed) George K. Spoor
President.

A shorter version of this message, also bearing Spoor's name, appeared for the benefit of US exhibitors in the *Moving Picture World* for 17 August, proclaiming *Triple Trouble* as 'NOT a Reissue – NOT a Rehash But a NEW Film'. One doubts if Spoor himself wrote a word of either statement, but whoever did was lying spectacularly. Virtually the only authentic claim was that relating to a contemporary lack of new Chaplin films; he had issued only one since the previous October, *A Dog's Life* (*qv*), though *Shoulder Arms* (*qv*) was nearing completion.

Triple Trouble was assembled by Leo White (*qv*) from a combination of leftovers and new footage. White had left Chaplin's unit and returned to Essanay, working also at the King Bee studios with Chaplin lookalike Billy West. White filmed a new plot, with topical wartime implications, to supply bridging material for the available Chaplin scenes. One of these, the flophouse sequence, had been withheld from Chaplin's final Essanay, *Police* (*qv*), and was itself a leftover from an abandoned feature called *Life*. Also from *Life* were the scenes of Charlie, Billy Armstrong (*qv*) and Edna Purviance (*qv*) in the kitchen and laundry. Other scenes were duplicated from the released version of *Police*, as in Charlie's encounter with the 'assassin' and their attempt to break into the house (though these were disguised by 'flopping' the image to read right-to-left!). Also from *Police* are the shots of Charlie rushing around the kitchen, while the concluding moments of *Work* (*qv*) yielded the finale with Charlie in the stove. The new footage employed a double for the assassin/housebreaker character (on whom the suit looked rather tight), while unknown arms, in a striped, prison-style

undershirt, approximated Charlie's when dumping rubbish over a fence.

Essanay must have assumed a phenomenally short memory and/or supreme gullibility on the part of critics and public alike. They were, to some degree, proven right, for some contemporary reviewers seemed oblivious to the trickery. Others, however, were more than aware of what had been done: in August 1918, the *Moving Picture World* reprinted a cutting from the *Chicago Daily News*, headed 'Don't Blame Chaplin For This Film Crime', adding a description of *Triple Trouble* as an 'Atrocious Patch Quilt of Ancient Slapstick Reels'. 'Do you want to run a picture which the newspapers of your town will "pan" like this?' it asked. The response appeared towards the end of September, reprinting some of the more positive reviews with the question 'Don't you want to run a picture which the newspapers of your town will <u>praise</u> like this?'

Theodore Huff, while explaining *Triple Trouble*'s genesis, chose to incorporate it into his Chaplin filmography (as others have done since then). It was perhaps on the strength of this that Chaplin included *Triple Trouble* in the filmography accompanying his memoirs; another reason may be that this, unlike the numerous other 'bogus Chaplins' (*qv*), incorporates genuine Chaplin material to be found nowhere else. Indeed, the main distinction of *Triple Trouble* is that it preserves what there was of *Life*, Chaplin's first attempt to direct himself in a feature-length comedy.

(See also: Abandoned projects; Alcohol; Costume; *Funniest Man in the World, The*; Impersonators; Jamison, William 'Bud'; Kelly, James T.; Policemen; Pollard, Harry 'Snub'; Reissues; Religion; Risqué humour; Ruggles, Wesley; Smoking; Television; Vagrancy; Wartime)

TULLY, JIM

See: Vagrancy

TURPIN, BEN 🎩
(1874–1940)

(Chaplin films *qv*)
Cross-eyed comedian, with Essanay (*qv*) from its beginnings; paired with Chaplin in *His New Job* and *A Night Out*, in

addition to playing a small part in *The Champion* (he was also used in the additional footage tacked onto *Carmen*). It is known that Chaplin and Turpin did not get on, Turpin having no time for Chaplin's formal methods. It is perhaps significant that Turpin's heyday was with Mack Sennett (*qv*) during the 1920s, when 'impossible' gags tended to carry the films; after a brief defection to Weiss Brothers in 1928, and the introduction of sound, the wealthy Ben Turpin entered semi-retirement. His occasional talkie appearances concluded with a brief bit in Laurel & Hardy's *Saps at Sea*, made shortly before Turpin's death.

(See also: Laurel, Stan; McGuire, Paddy; Summerville, George J. 'Slim')

TWENTY MINUTES 🎩 OF LOVE

(Chaplin film)
Keystone Comedy released by Mutual, 20 April 1914. Produced by Mack Sennett. Direction attributed variously to Sennett, Joseph Maddern or Chaplin. Screenplay latterly attributed to Chaplin. Photography attributed to Frank D. Williams. One reel. 1,009 feet (UK print cited in *Bioscope*). Reissued as *Cops and Watches*, *He Loved Her So* and *The Love-Fiend* (sometimes misquoted as *Love-Friend*).

With Charlie Chaplin (himself), Edgar Kennedy (young lover), Minta Durfee (his fiancée), Chester Conklin (lover turned pickpocket), Emma Clifton (second girl), Joseph Swickard (sleeping man), Gordon Griffith (boy).

In the park, Charlie is amused by the young lovers embracing on a bench. He joins them, but is bounced off the seat by the boyfriend. Charlie forces his attentions on the girl, but is sent on his way, albeit with a defiant back-kick to his rival's stomach. Nearby, another couple are canoodling on a bench. When the girl demands a present as evidence of her fiancé's love, the lovesick man departs to see what he can find. He notices a sleeping man and steals his pocket watch; Charlie, meanwhile, has returned to the other couple, but is distracted when the second girl wanders by. He pursues her, but she disappears amid the greenery. She has settled at a different bench while her boyfriend and Charlie seek her out. Charlie blunders across a third couple but takes his leave, meeting the pickpocket. Charlie espies the watch, taking it without the thief's knowledge. The thief returns to his girl, discovers the watch has disappeared, and sets off to retrieve it. When a policeman asks him the time, Charlie tries to sneak off, but the watch is returned to him without question. The thief continues searching for the watch while Charlie presents it to his girl. Charlie and the girl are kissing when confronted by the irate pickpocket. Charlie rushes away, only to slow down when passing the policeman. The girl tries to complain to the policeman, but is dissuaded by her boyfriend. Charlie sits beside the watch's slumbering owner and, unaware of the truth, awakens him in order to offer the timepiece for sale. Charlie has to make another hasty exit. He meets the pickpocket again and battle commences, complicated when the watch's owner reports the theft to the policeman. Everyone finishes in the lake except Charlie and the girl, who depart together.

When smoothing out Chaplin's disagreements with Mabel Normand (*qv*) during the filming of *Mabel at the Wheel* (*qv*), Mack Sennett (*qv*) promised Chaplin the opportunity to write and direct his own films. Chaplin's autobiography cites *Caught in the Rain* (*qv*) as his first effort, a claim long accepted as fact (indeed as long ago as a brief reference in *Picture Show* of 3 April 1920); however, David Robinson's *Chaplin: His Life and Art* refers instead to an early filmography compiled by the comedian himself, detailing *Twenty Minutes of Love* as the first of Chaplin's 'own' pictures. The point continues to inspire debate, but the absence of Mabel Normand suggests this to be the film in which Chaplin was first granted autonomy. Chaplin recalled having made this film in a single afternoon, suggesting further a 'test' piece dashed off in minimal time. For all its slightness, the film was well received. 'The comic element is given especial prominence,' said *Bioscope* on 17 September 1914, 'and is quite safe in the hands of this well-known comedian.' Although similar to his many other 'park' comedies (both earlier and later), Chaplin's authorship of *Twenty Minutes of Love* is implied by the reappearance of its basic premise a year later, as *In the Park* (*qv*).

The author's print of this subject is of above-average quality, bearing what seem to be the original Keystone titles. There is a probability that these are remakes, being of unfamiliar typography; they become particularly suspect when a Keystone 'the end' title has been modelled on the house sub-title design instead of the company's usual single trademark. The print's authenticity is again called into question when a shot of Charlie twirling the stolen watch is removed to the *beginning* of the film, long before he has ever seen it; worse still, a lengthy section has been removed in which the pickpocket's motives are established when his girlfriend demands a gift (its absence bridged by a slight rearrangement of footage). Another available print presents the action in correct sequence and retains the missing section described above, but typifies a collector's frustration in being of far lesser quality.

(See also: Conklin, Chester; Costume; Kennedy, Edgar; Keystone; Mann, Hank; Music; Parks; Policemen; Titling; Williams, Frank D.)

TWISTS AND TRANSFORMATIONS

(Chaplin films *qv*)
One of the techniques to impress Chaplin's early audiences was that of surprise, wherein Charlie would fool them by an unexpected twist. One of the best of these opens *The Immigrant*, when Charlie seems to be suffering from *mal de mer* but turns out to be hanging over the ship's rail merely to catch fish. A later equivalent is the celebrated joke in *The Idle Class* where, back to camera, he seems to be in tears but, when he turns, is revealed as vigorously shaking a cocktail. Parallel to this motif is a gift for transforming objects, endowing them with an alternate existence based, again, on unexpected similarity. Again *The Immigrant* yields a prime specimen, as Charlie uses salt and pepper pots in lieu of binoculars. *The Pawnshop* offers particularly fertile ground for such ideas, as when turning a piece of string into a tightrope (an idea tried later for *The Circus*). Detailed under **Food** is a gag in *A Jitney Elopement* wherein a loaf of bread becomes a makeshift concertina. People too, were subject to transformation by comparison, as with the masseur who becomes a wrestling opponent in *The Cure*.

UNDERCRANKING

See: Trick photography

UNDERWOOD, LOYAL
(1893–1966)

(Chaplin films *qv*)
Diminutive supporting actor, born in Illinois. Underwood is among the party guests in *The Count*, *The Adventurer* and *The Idle Class*; he plays the tiny father of a huge brood in *Easy Street*, doubling also as one of the police officers; he is a patient in *The Cure*, the tiny émigré with a giant wife (Henry Bergman [*qv*]) in *The Immigrant*, and the similarly tiny German officer who receives a spanking in *Shoulder Arms*. There are echoes of *Easy Street* when he is the father of a giant offspring in *Sunnyside*. Underwood plays a boat passenger (and has been cited also as an irate character in the street) in *A Day's Pleasure*. In later films he plays one of Charlie's co-workers in *Pay Day*, the 'small deacon' in *The Pilgrim* and, after a seeming gap, one of the buskers in *Limelight*. Underwood is reported also in *A Dog's Life*, and may be seen in gag footage intended for the abortive *How To Make Movies* (*qv*) and used instead in *The Chaplin Revue* (*qv*). This sequence shows Chaplin supposedly demonstrating a point by lifting Underwood and shaking him vigorously.

(See also: Dual rôles; Pollard, Harry 'Snub'; Religion)

UNITED ARTISTS

(Chaplin films *qv*)
In 1919, Chaplin, alongside Mary Pickford, Douglas Fairbanks and D.W. Griffith (all *qv*), took the revolutionary step of founding United Artists, a production and distribution organization entirely in the hands of its stars. One version attributes the idea to B.P. Schulberg, who, suggesting a partnership with himself and Griffith, advised the stars that their ever-increasing salaries were eating into their films' profits, to the point where studios might conceivably abandon them. Another account – favoured by the author – is that Mary Pickford had taken literally a vague suggestion by William G. McAdoo – the US Secretary of the Treasury who had organized the Liberty Loan tour with Pickford, Fairbanks and Chaplin – to the effect that the stars should make and distribute their own films. The idea blossomed through necessity, after Mary Pickford left Paramount for the newly-established First National (*qv*) as producer-star, where she confounded the predictions of Paramount head Adolph Zukor by continuing her success. In consequence, there was talk of the various studios merging into a few large entities as a means of limiting the stars' negotiating power. The announcement of United Artists – after a meeting at Syd Chaplin's home in January, 1919 – rendered such a move pointless. Contracts were signed on 5 February, each founding artist agreeing to contribute $125,000 to the company.

McAdoo declined an offer to become UA's president but, opting instead to become general counsel, recommended Oscar A. Price for the job. George Clifton was appointed secretary and treasurer.

Adolph Zukor managed to bid sufficiently high to prevent western star William S. Hart joining the renegades, but otherwise it was left to Metro chief Richard Rowland to utter his now-famous summation, 'The lunatics have taken charge of the asylum.' Of those 'lunatics', only Fairbanks, without an existing contract with another studio, was able to contribute immediately. Chaplin's commitment to First National meant that he needed to wait four years until his initial UA release, *A Woman of Paris*. This was not a starring vehicle for him, but the next, *The Gold Rush*, was not only centred around the Tramp but remains, for many, his finest work.

By the 1920s, UA's roster included each of its founders plus some of the decade's most prestigious talents, among them Buster Keaton and Gloria Swanson (both *qv*) and Ernst Lubitsch, the German-born director (and former star comic) whose American career was fostered by the UA partners. Chaplin's remaining American films, *The Circus*, *City Lights*, *Modern Times*, *The Great Dictator*, *Monsieur Verdoux* and *Limelight*, were all produced for United Artists release. Chaplin eventually sold

Ernst Lubitsch (centre) was among the talents fostered by **United Artists**

out his interest in UA in 1955, after his exile to Switzerland, but retained ownership of the films he had made for them. Publicity material suggests that UA handled *The Chaplin Revue* (*qv*) in at least some territories. After severe financial setbacks of the early 1980s, United Artists merged into M-G-M, an ironic move given the reasons for its origin.

(See also: Chaplin, Syd; Kono, Toraichi; Newsreels; Politics; Wartime)

UNKNOWN CHAPLIN 🎩

(Chaplin films *qv*)
Perhaps the most important Chaplin documentary to date, the nucleus of *Unknown Chaplin* was the footage assembled by historians Kevin Brownlow and David Gill into Chaplin's intended film *How To Make Movies* (*qv*). Added impetus was gained from the availability of the Mutual out-takes – at that time in the possession of Raymond Rohauer – plus home movies (*qv*) and existing out-takes from the Chaplin Estate, representing scenes deleted from the First National and United Artists films. As they did for their silent-film history, *Hollywood*, Brownlow and Gill wrote and produced this three-part series for the ITV company Thames Television, from whom it was networked. Carl Davis provided the music, using Chaplin's theme for *The Kid* over the main titles. James Mason narrated.

The first episode, 'My Happiest Years', was screened on 5 January 1983. It opens with Chaplin playing piano, between takes of *The Cure*, which is intercut with tasters from the programme, essentially goofs from *The Cure*, *One A.M.*, *The Count*, *The Idle Class*, *The Pawnshop* and *The Immigrant*. The programme explains the usual practice of destroying the out-takes, a loss compared here to that of an artist's sketch-books. What survived conscious destruction was imperilled further by decomposition, as illustrated by a ruined negative section from *The Vagabond*. The otherwise pristine nature of these out-takes, and of the later films in Chaplin's ownership, is emphasized by juxtaposition with extracts from dupes of *Easy Street* and *The Cure*. Unusually poor copies were used for this purpose, presumably to reinforce the point, and it should be noted that far better material exists on these and the other Mutuals.

Extracts from the release versions – distinguished by framing the image – are used throughout as punctuation to the rushes.

Explained also is Chaplin's secrecy concerning his methods, which, combined with the absence of any surviving colleagues of the period, means that the out-takes alone serve as eye-witness. Established early on are his signing with Mutual and working conditions at the Lone Star studio. Out-takes from the first Mutual, *The Floorwalker*, demonstrate the use of on-camera slate numbers to differentiate takes, also the overhead diffusing cloths to combat glare and shadow – though not a strong breeze! – on what were then exclusively outdoor sets. Chaplin's publicist Elsie Codd, writing for *Pictures and the Picturegoer*, had perhaps singular access to Chaplin's on-set methods but was clearly stymied by the comedian's ability to view his own performance objectively. In April 1917, she rejected all notion of Chaplin rehearsing before a mirror, believing instead that 'the secret lies in his marvellous faculty of sinking his own identity into the part he has assigned himself for the moment to play'. This is true enough, but Chaplin did indeed have a 'mirror' in the form of his rushes; perhaps the most important discovery in *Unknown Chaplin* is that Chaplin rehearsed his material on film, enabling him to evaluate the results.

The Floorwalker's rushes provide shots of Chaplin directing and Rollie Totheroh (*qv*) at the camera, but a more intriguing tale concerns the genesis of *The Cure*. Chaplin's original intention was to provide the sanitorium with attendants of a comparable frailty to the ailing proprietor. Charlie, despite his slightness, is the fittest of them, but still has considerable difficulty in pushing Eric Campbell (*qv*) in a bath chair. Chaplin varied the sequence, shifting the emphasis from the chair to Campbell himself and, in the process, lightening the colour of his uniform to ensure clarity. Another jettisoned moment has Charlie in the lobby, directing various chairbound patients in the manner of a traffic cop. Realizing the need for a centrepiece, Chaplin replaced an ornate fountain with a well. John Rand (*qv*) was tried as a well-dressed drunk, whereupon Chaplin realized where the problem lay. He and Rand switched rôles – the attendant's uniform looks a little small on Rand! – and the film began to take shape, particularly after the addition of a

revolving door. The main casualty was the traffic cop routine, its impact diminished when tried by a civilian-clad Charlie. Sidelights include a stuntman replacing Campbell for his descent into the well, signalling a need to be retrieved by placing his legs together; Campbell himself is seen among those coming to his rescue. A contortionist, seen in the final version as one of the masseur's victims, was evidently tried out doing his usual act without much context; also of interest is an alternate take of the final scene, rejected because Chaplin, facing the camera, could not see the shadows cast when the overhead diffusers were caught in the wind. There follows an extended shot of Chaplin amusing Edna Purviance (*qv*) by clowning in the well.

A beautiful camera test of Edna for *The Cure* precedes a series of out-takes from *The Adventurer*. The first of these show Chaplin coaching Edna through a scene in which she repels Campbell's advances, employing repeated takes in order to extract the correct degree of boredom from the actress. Edna's natural sense of humour is conveyed through her continued breaking up during this scene, as also in a clip where she confronts, unscheduled and unannounced, her long-lost 'mother' in *The Vagabond*, Charlotte Mineau (*qv*). A *Behind the Screen* out-take reflects their probable working relationship as Charlie, in character, teaches Edna how to act. Something of their private intimacy at that time permeates other byplay, in the segments in which Edna, disguised as a boy, is seen playing first a harp then the more masculine guitar of the final edit.

Also from *Behind the Screen* is Chaplin being hit by a pie, something avoided in the release version, also a rejected idea – since employed by others – in which Charlie parodies a ballet troupe by leading an ensemble of prancing cleaning ladies. By far the most elaborate is a gag in which Charlie, wheeling a trolley, walks into the path of a falling axe. Scrutiny of the footage reveals that the apparent risk was eliminated by the simple means of shooting the action in reverse.

As also noted under the main entry, *The Immigrant* began life as a *Trilby*-like tale set in an artists' café. This was jettisoned in favour of a disembodied restaurant scene with Albert Austin (*qv*). Edna was added as a penniless customer, and Henry Bergman (*qv*) was cast as the waiter. Extra menace was provided by substituting Campbell in the rôle, with

Bergman recast as an artist. This brought the bohemian café idea full circle, but did not provide enough for a two-reeler. A context was found by providing a context for Edna; the answer was a ship laden with immigrants to the New World, thus facilitating also a background for Charlie. A photo reveals the camera to have been mounted on a pendulum when photographing the boat scenes, while out-takes betray in turn the pivoting set used for the teetering galley. The programme shows a few deleted moments on shipboard, and demonstrates how the whole was tied together by linking footage of Charlie finding a coin. All that was needed was a retake of Charlie and Edna's meeting in the café – to suggest their prior acquaintance – plus a charming coda for the finale. Ironic mention is made of a contemporary review in which *Photoplay*, unaware of its reverse construction, believed that 'no farce ... has been more adroitly, more perfectly worked out'. (When looked at today, *The Immigrant* clearly suggests itself as two single-reelers, and was split that way by at least one home-movie distributor.)

Rehearsal footage from *The Pawnshop* provides opportunity to acknowledge the importance of such seasoned veterans as John Rand. Another in that category, Syd Chaplin (*qv*), is shown juggling on the set, suggesting his presence as adviser. Syd's juggling ultimately goes wrong, providing *entrée* to a collection of Charlie's mistakes from *The Count*, *The Adventurer* and *The Cure*. *The Adventurer*'s out-takes show Chaplin improvising and developing gags in the vestibule of the mansion and, in the ballroom with Edna, indulging in palmistry. The programme assembles the rushes of a deleted section of this ballroom scene, showing him growing hot in the presence of a sexy Spanish dancer, unaware that he is sitting above the radiator. This gag is hinted at in the final version (detailed under the main entry), but remains unresolved. Considerable interest lies within a unique, somewhat decomposed *Adventurer* fragment with Chaplin pacing on the set, discussing ideas with Bergman and Austin. This solitary scrap bears witness to the comedian's own recollection of spending long hours brooding over ideas. The episode draws to a close with a collage of high-pitched moments from *The Adventurer*, *Behind the Screen* and *The Count*, before quoting Chaplin's contemporary musing on the

necessity of a chase to climax every film. His exit from Mutual is marked by footage from *How To Make Movies* (*qv*), showing his arrival at a new, independent studio.

Episode 2, 'The Great Director', was transmitted on 12 January 1983. For the First National period there were survivors to be interviewed, among them Dean Riesner (*qv*) who speaks of playing a brat in *The Pilgrim*. Extracts from *How To Make Movies* are used to parallel interview footage in which Lita Grey (*qv*) recalls the customary cry of 'He's here!' – unique among film studios – when Chaplin arrived for work. Other extracts from the film depict backlot scenes, Albert Austin in the laboratory section, Chaplin in a cutting room and, above all, the studio's leisurely pace, contrasting with the rapid production at Mutual. The cast are shown clowning in and around the studio pool, followed by the comic 'rehearsal' (excerpted in *The Chaplin Revue* [*qv*]) in which Chaplin pretends to throttle Loyal Underwood (*qv*).

Chaplin's protracted creation of *The Kid* is examined, though hamstrung by the absence of all but one of the rushes (in which the child is seen cooking flapjacks). In an interview, Jackie Coogan (*qv*) speaks of entertaining visiting First National bosses as a means of winning them over to Chaplin's feature-length project, accompanied by film of him performing a dance of pure vaudeville hokum. Lita Grey speaks in turn of being added as the 'flirty angel', and of her introducing Merna Kennedy (*qv*) to the studio.

At this stage there is an abrupt chronological leap to the United Artists films, presumably through the unavailability of out-takes from the remaining First National subjects. The story behind *The Gold Rush* is told via stills and footage with the assistance of interviewees Lita Grey, Georgia Hale (*qv*) and, via a 1959 recording, Eddie Sutherland (*qv*). As noted in the main entry, Chaplin constructed both a Rush Town and a replica of the Chilkoot Pass when in Truckee, California; it had been thought that these were the only location shots, but *Unknown Chaplin*, aided by Lita's recollections and photographs from the Chaplin archive, was able to establish otherwise. Almost all the exteriors – including an extended version of the 'chicken' sequence – were abandoned after a return to the studio, where Chaplin rebuilt the town. Lita, being pregnant, was replaced by Georgia Hale,

forcing Chaplin to reshoot his leading lady's scenes. Interviewed for the programme, Georgia described how Chaplin acted for his supporting players, instilling into them the minutest detail, and countering any tendency to overact with the instruction 'walk through it'. In a parallel to Edna Purviance in *The Adventurer*, Chaplin continued to shoot the scenes of Malcolm Waite (*qv*) forcing his attentions on Georgia until she was genuinely angry. She described also his poor mood when struggling for ideas, keeping the cast waiting, sometimes abandoning the effort for a week before calling everyone back. Similarly traumatic was the necessity to eat a liquorice boot, which, according to Lita, made Chaplin and Mack Swain (*qv*) genuinely ill. Lita's marriage to Chaplin had foundered by the end of filming. Chaplin had fallen for Georgia and, again according to Lita, their final on-camera smooch required a large number of takes. The programme includes this finale, which, as detailed below, was deleted from the 1942 reissue.

For *City Lights*, the programme features home movies (*qv*) taken on the set. Robert Parrish (*qv*), himself later a director, describes his rôle as a sassy newsboy, and the way in which Chaplin, typically, acted it out for him. Parrish sensed that Chaplin wanted to be everywhere, even behind the camera, a view with which fellow-interviewee Virginia Cherrill (*qv*) concurred when recalling, 'You found yourself feeling he was you.' Chaplin's inability to be on both sides of the camera was remedied by his old method of rehearsing on film. The programme shows footage of Chaplin in street clothes, save for hat and cane, rehearsing the routine involving a platform in the pavement. This is skilfully dubbed with equivalent music from the film's soundtrack before cutting to the final version for its conclusion. Further home-movie footage shows Chaplin – in what is described as the only film of him directing while wearing the tramp costume – guiding Virginia Cherrill through her first scene. As noted in the main entry, Chaplin, in the absence of a script, tried various means to work out the action so that the blind girl would mistake Charlie for a millionaire; the sequence was postponed until Chaplin devised the necessary motif near the end of shooting. Another interviewee, Alistair Cooke, worked with Chaplin later (see **Abandoned projects**), and was told that Virginia was incapable of holding up a flower (!). Both Virginia Cherrill and Robert Parrish describe the long periods of idleness, during which there were such distinguished visitors as Douglas Fairbanks (*qv*) and Winston Churchill. The programme shows film of Chaplin performing a ballet to enliven the film of Churchill's visit, also a fantasy sequence of the girl's vision of him as a prince in the Von Stroheim mould. In contrast to their on-screen harmony are tales of their off-screen discord. Chaplin's son, Sydney, explains how his father 'went crazy' when Virginia, due to attend a party, wanted to leave early in order to have her hair done. As detailed elsewhere, she was eventually fired and replaced – though only temporarily – by Georgia Hale (*qv*), who is seen in an alternate take of the film's final scene. The episode concludes with news film taken at the première and, indispensibly, the famous conclusion of *City Lights* with Cherrill restored to the rôle.

Transmission of the final episode, 'Hidden Treasures', was on 19 January 1983. The first rarity, a 1929 Fairbanks home movie, pinpoints the origin of Hynkel's ballet in *The Great Dictator*, as Chaplin – in classical Greek costume, topped by a spiked German helmet! – dances with a globe. A film of Chaplin conducting the Abe Lyman Orchestra in 1923 is carefully synchronized with the record made at that session, a version of Chaplin's song 'With You, Dear, in Bombay'. Another home movie, this time from 1926, shows Chaplin posing as a mystic, using his hand as a puppet and performing his trick of blowing out smoke after twisting his ear (see **Smoking**). He also performs another favoured party piece, the bread roll dance from *The Gold Rush*.

There is a return to the comedian's more public endeavours with rejected footage from the Chaplin vaults. *How To Make Movies* is explored again, in footage of Albert Austin as an Arabian magician causing the studio to grow, and more everyday business around the lot, Chaplin guying his rôle as boss. There are also reels commemorating 'Visitors', among them actress Maxine Elliott, for whom Chaplin does his comic walk; the former Chief of Staff, General Wood, with Chaplin clowning in civilian clothes but wearing his moustache, hat and cane; and the Bishop of Birmingham, in army uniform, evidently when shooting the exteriors of *Sunnyside*. In the hotel set for that film, Chaplin and Edna meet Crown Prince Frederick of Denmark;

Chaplin again does the walk and some business with his cane, then arranges the Prince and his entourage into impromptu film rôles, Chaplin playing an over-zealous porter with the Prince as a guest. Benny Leonard, the boxer, is seen with his manager visiting the set of *A Dog's Life*, with Syd Chaplin in attendance; the resultant comic scrap is similar to that with Jack Dempsey (see *The Funniest Man in the World*), and anticipates a time when, three years later, Leonard engaged the Marx Brothers in fisticuffs for a vaudeville sketch, 'On the Mezzanine'. Harry Lauder arrived, playing bagpipes, intending to make a film with Charlie to raise money for wounded British servicemen (details of this footage may be found under **The Bond** and **Race**). Chaplin and Lauder's William Tell routine is shown as the genesis of similar business in *The Circus*.

An early version of the golf routine from *The Idle Class* – seemingly from an uncompleted Mutual comedy and planned also for *How To Make Movies* – casts Austin as a myopic golfer whom Chaplin knocks out with a backswing. In the *Sunnyside* out-takes, noted in the main entry, Austin suffers again, this time in a barber's chair. This is shown once more as the origin of a later routine, this time from *The Great Dictator*. The flea-training idea in *Limelight* developed from an abandoned film, believed intended as the last two-reeler for First National, entitled *The Professor* (one might note that Chaplin had used similar business in *By the Sea*). The sequence, again described under **Abandoned projects**, was assembled from Chaplin's rushes by the programme makers.

The next Chaplin scenes are those deleted from the opening of *Shoulder Arms* (detailed within the main entry), showing Charlie's domestic life and army medical. Next is the extensive segment deleted from *The Circus*, again described under the main entry, in which Charlie, Merna and Rex visit a café in town. This precedes the only surviving out-take from *Modern Times*, edited by Chaplin but deleted prior to release. Charlie crosses a busy street against the lights, and is sent back by a cop who insists he should wait his turn. Charlie eventually gives up. The best deleted sequence is saved until last, that from *City Lights* in which Charlie becomes preoccupied with a piece of wood jammed in a street grating. This leisurely-paced gem, once more described in the film's main entry,

closes the show. At the very end, it is made clear that we shall never know how many other classic moments were destroyed.

In evaluating the three episodes, it is easy to regard part two as the least effective, but this is only within the context of the series as a whole. The sheer volume of rare comedy footage in the first and third episodes inevitably overshadows the second, which, in isolation, would still be considered an important Chaplin study. At the time, *Unknown Chaplin* drew enormous interest on both sides of the Atlantic. The vast bulk of its source material had never been seen in public, and even those normally averse to Chaplin often seemed compelled to praise the work represented. Its impact may have diminished slightly, owing to the subsequent availability of some of the footage from other sources, but for many this is still the prime source for Chaplin's non-mainstream film work. At the time of writing, the series has incredibly not been repeated in Britain, but has been made available in home video form.

(See also: Animals; Animation; Children; Documentaries; Epstein, Jerry; First National; Food; Marx, Groucho; Music; Mutual; Newsreels; Politics; Royalty; Sport; Suicide; Television; Trick photography; United Artists; Walk, The)

THE VAGABOND

(Chaplin film)
Released by Mutual, 10 July 1916.
Written and directed by Charles
Chaplin. Photographed by William C.
Foster and Rollie Totheroh. Two reels.
1,956 feet.

With Charlie Chaplin (himself), Edna
Purviance (the gypsy drudge), Eric
Campbell (gypsy chief), Lloyd Bacon
(the artist), Charlotte Mineau (the
artist), Leo White (Jewish bar
customer/gypsy woman), Frank J.
Coleman (fat gypsy), John Rand, Albert
Austin, James T. Kelly (in the German
band/gypsy).

Charlie, a roaming violinist, leaves a bar-
room by the front entrance. Taking up a
position by its side door, he starts to
play. Around at the front, a German
band arrives, drowning out Charlie's
efforts and impressing the customers.
Charlie finishes his tune and, in the bar,
accepts contributions intended for the
opposition. When the German band
pauses, its leader enters the bar to accept
donations; he is surprised to learn there
has already been a collection until he sees
Charlie, still collecting money. There is a
fight and a wild chase, but Charlie
defeats allcomers, allowing him time for
a free drink before finally eluding his
rivals. Meanwhile, a well-to-do but
heartbroken woman interrupts her
needlework to gaze at a photograph of
her lost child, as a companion tries to
comfort. The child, by now a young
woman, is seen scrubbing clothes in a
gypsy encampment. She pauses, and an
aged gypsy woman slaps her back to
work. Charlie the violinist wanders into
the vicinity. When the girl rebels, the

chief is summoned, a burly man who
reinforces the old woman's orders with
the threat of a whipping. Charlie,
recognizing a likely place for a busker,
entertains the girl with his music. When
Charlie's playing becomes frenetic, the
girl begins to scrub clothes at a similar
pace. Charlie's enthusiastic musicianship
lands him in the wash tub. He continues
with an unlikely piece entitled 'The
Hungarian Goulash'. Charlie takes
several 'encores', only to land in the tub
again. When it is time to offer the hat,
Charlie discovers the girl has no money,
but is persuaded to continue. The recital
is interrupted by the chief, who not only
refuses Charlie any money, but punches
him back into the tub. The girl receives a
whipping from the chief; Charlie, armed
with a hefty piece of wood, stealthily and
systematically knocks out the gypsy
band. He places the girl inside a caravan.
The chief, who is first to regain
consciousness, tries to drown Charlie in
the washtub; the girl, standing in the
caravan, brings the piece of wood down
on his head. Charlie commandeers the
caravan, and the pair escape, the gypsies
in irate pursuit. The girl knocks out the
chief, his inert form tripping over the
other gypsies. A title card takes them to
'The next morning, safe and sound'.
Charlie, who has slept in the open,
awakens to discover a cactus beneath
him. Using a rake, Charlie 'makes' his
bed of straw. A gentle knock on the
caravan door brings forth his new
companion, scratching violently. Charlie
volunteers the rake before examining her
hair for passengers. Placing his hand
inside a sock, he sets the girl down at a
bucket of water for a good wash. Suitably
tidied, she is sent off with the pail to
obtain fresh water, as Charlie cooks eggs
– breaking them with a hammer – before
setting places. Nearby is an artist,
despairing over a lack of inspiration. The
girl, curious, approaches the artist, who
finds inspiration in both her beauty and
the shamrock birthmark on her arm.
Though frightened at first, the girl soon
takes to her status as model; the portrait
completed, she takes him to the caravan.
Charlie soon realizes that her interest
now lies elsewhere. The 'Living
Shamrock' is exhibited at a prestigious
gallery. As the girl pines for her new love,
Charlie tries in vain to compete by
drawing her picture on the wall of the
caravan. Among the gallery's patrons is
the girl's mother, who faints on
recognizing the birthmark. Charlie is at a
nearby farm, collecting eggs, when a

limousine pulls up beside the caravan.
The girl is reunited with her mother and
the artist. When Charlie returns, he is so
shocked that he drops the eggs on the
artist's foot. Charlie declines to accept
money from the grateful parent, moving
her arm aside in favour of a last hug with
the departing girl. Shaking the artist's
hand, Charlie puts on a brave face, but
sinks into despair once the car has gone.
It has travelled only a short distance
when the girl realizes it is Charlie she
really wants. The car duly returns, and
Charlie, somewhat startled, has time
only to fetch his violin, hat and cane
before being dragged into the car and a
new life.

It has long been rumoured that
Chaplin inserted a happy ending solely
to accommodate popular taste, filming
for private use an alternate conclusion in
which Charlie, desolate, jumps into a
river only to be rescued by a woman. On
discovering her to be fantastically ugly,
he leaps back into the water. There was
no sign of this variant when preparing
Unknown Chaplin (qv), suggesting it may
have gone the way of a largely
decomposed fragment showing Charlie
preparing food by the caravan. There
was, however, a splendid practical joke in
which Edna Purviance (qv) unexpectedly
and prematurely burst in on her long-
lost mother during the art gallery scene.
Third in the series for Mutual (qv),
The Vagabond was Chaplin's best film up
to that point, a well-constructed tale
permitting a thoroughly unmawkish
pathos alongside adroit slapstick and an
often much subtler mime. The dramatic
device of a lost child identified by her
unique birthmark was hackneyed even in

The Vagabond: *violinist Charlie treats
Edna to the 'Hungarian Goulash'*

1916 (having been over-employed long before 'opera' meant 'soap'), but Chaplin, able to play such things with simple sincerity, could get away with it.

The Vagabond remains a charming classic, albeit a minor one in comparison with later works. Its appeal survives despite the indignities it has suffered in reissue, where it has been subjected to idiotic amendment. In the original version, the opening bar-room scene cuts to a title introducing the girl's mother, who is seen lamenting the lost child; next there is a title identifying the 'gypsy drudge', followed by an opening-iris shot of Edna at the washboard and her chastisement by the old woman (played by Leo White!). There is a straight cut to Charlie walking along a country path. The reissue fades out on the bar-room, fades up on Charlie walking into the scene and omits the initial footage of the girl. The scene of the disconsolate mother is, absurdly, moved to a position during Charlie's attack on the gypsies. This is the version to which music and effects were added in the early 1930s; one tends to imagine such butchery to date from these fledgling talkie days, when silent films were considered fair game for mutilation, yet the author has seen this arrangement in a full-frame silent reissue, with, by the way, insensitively-rewritten titles.

An earlier, American-made 'restoration' belies the term by presenting the film as edited for reissue. The recent laserdisc edition – issued in America – is a good copy with the correct sequence of events restored. The BBC *Chaplin SuperClown* copy is also as per the original, albeit slightly marred by 'cropping' the image to sound aperture. This reduces frame height and obliterates action to the left of picture; although not serious, it kills the point of one gag in the bar-room scene, where we cannot see that Charlie is helpfully switching the 'beef' and 'ham' signs when a Jewish customer (Leo White again!) helps himself to the wrong dish.

(See also: Alcohol; Cars; Kelly, James T.; Left-handedness; Music; Race; Rand, John; Reissues; Suicide; Television; Vagrancy; Video releases; White, Leo)

VAGRANCY

(Chaplin films *qv*)
In his memoirs, Charles Chaplin Jr claims that his father always referred to

his screen character as 'the Little Tramp', a phrase much recycled over the years; in the reissue of *The Gold Rush*, Chaplin uses instead the term 'the little fellow' and, at least latterly, favoured the French diminutive 'Charlot' in describing his movie persona, a reflection, perhaps, of the 'pierrot' image he favoured over that of a literal tramp. Chaplin's selection of a tramp for his consistent screen image has as much to do with the deprivations of his own childhood as with any instinct to elevate the underdog. It may be significant that he considered adopting a comic tramp persona even when touring with the 'Eight Lancashire Lads' (see **Early stage appearances**).

At the time of *The Tramp*'s release, Chaplin claimed to have drawn inspiration from an interview with a genuine vagabond. (During the 1920s, one of Chaplin's regular advisers was Jim Tully, who had chronicled his own wanderings under the title *Beggars of Life*. Tully's work was later filmed with Wallace Beery and Louise Brooks.) It was probably *The Tramp*, and its implied sequel *The Vagabond*, that consolidated in the public mind Charlie's position as wanderer. It was not necessarily always the case: *A Night in the Show*, *The Cure* and *One A.M.* are instances where Charlie is in no way tramp-like, and there are several films – *The Pawnshop*, *Sunnyside* and *The Kid* among them – in which Charlie, though evidently surviving on the economic level of a tramp, has either an at least ramshackle home, some form of occupation or, in rare instances, a family. In many instances, he is not a

tramp but simply a rather scruffy tradesman (*His Musical Career*) or some form of artisan (*Work*). There are occasions, too, when he clearly descends into vagrancy through misfortune, as in the decline of the artist in *The Face On the Bar Room Floor*, or his displaced factory worker of *Modern Times*. There is a suggestion that Charlie's reduced circumstances in *A Dog's Life* are involuntary, given his initial attempts to find employment – albeit with an admittedly enticing brewery! – and eventual acquisition of a farm.

Invariably, though, Charlie is a transient figure by choice, preserving a freedom that would otherwise be threatened by any lasting home or occupation. It does, of course, require him to sleep rough (*His Prehistoric Past*) or in even less hospitable surrounds (*Police*/*Triple Trouble*), but this same independence allows him to wander into the boxing profession in *The Champion* or become an accidental star of *The Circus*, from which he can withdraw gracefully when to remain would be untenable. Charlie is not workshy: he is willing to labour during a given stay. His 'reward' in *The Tramp*, for example, is to be given a job as farmhand, to which he applies himself with enthusiasm even though unacquainted with traditional methods. *City Lights*, which for many represents Chaplin's tramp in purest form, gives, in the person of the blind girl, incentive for Charlie to slave mightily, this time as roadsweeper and prizefighter. A number of Charlie's varied occupations are described, strange to say, under **Occupations**.

(See also: Childhood; Children; Parks; Policemen; Women)

VAUDEVILLE

See: Karno Company, The, and *Property Man, The*

VIDEO RELEASES ♠

(Chaplin films *qv*)

The market for 8mm home movie editions has been mostly overtaken by video releases. Chaplin's early, public-domain subjects proliferated on cine film, and have done so again on video, albeit to a lesser extent. A large number of minor tape releases have come and gone over the years; from the bigger leagues, Blackhawk Films offered the Mutuals on VHS before closing down in the 1980s. Among the more recent issues are editions of various Essanays and Mutuals, deriving from Canada, which have been released on both sides of the Atlantic. Magnetic Video Corporation had Chaplin's own package in the USA from the late 1970s; an equivalent British/European series appeared in the early 1980s from Spectrum, as did a few Videodiscs from RCA. Again in Britain, Channel 5 video had Chaplin's own collection – and a few earlier subjects – in the second half of the 1980s. Several collections of early Chaplin shorts were issued by Palace. PolyGram has since issued versions of many pre-1918 films. Since the beginning of the 1990s, UK and US tape releases of Chaplin's authorized collection have been from Fox, deriving from upgraded masters. *The Chaplin Revue* was first released on tape in the USA during 1982 – minus its intro – but later appeared complete; it has yet to be issued in the UK at the time of writing. Also unissued on UK video is *A Countess From Hong Kong*, to which Chaplin did not retain the rights. An American tape release was via MCA.

Today's US laserdiscs of Chaplin's package have restorations, deleted footage and other rarities, plus supplementary information. The First National films have been transferred at the correct speed, and incorporate out-takes where extant. Attention should also be drawn to David Shepard's restorations, released on laserdisc by Image Entertainment, Inc.; the present version of *Tillie's Punctured Romance* is easily the best made available to collectors. The Mutuals, with the aid of

good masters and computer technology, have been brought up to a standard comparable to the First National films. The set comprises a 'Chaplin Mutual Scrapbook', reprinting his contract and other rarities.

News film of Chaplin was used in the Parkfield Pathé series, 'A Year to Remember', offering individual tapes chronicling the years 1930–69; that for 1931 includes Chaplin's British visit for the première of *City Lights*. The series was later reissued under the British Pathé News banner, expanded beyond 1969 by the use of BBC material. Chaplin appears again in these additional tapes, as in that for 1972.

Chaplin documentaries on tape have included *The Gentleman Tramp* (Spectrum), *Unknown Chaplin* (*qv*) (VCI and, later, Connoisseur) and *Charlie Chaplin – a Celebration*. *The Funniest Man in the World* (*qv*) was available to rent in the UK in the early 1980s.

(See also: *Chaplin*; *Circus, The*; Documentaries, compilations; *Nice and Friendly*; Risqué humour; Trick photography)

VILLAINS ♠

(Chaplin films *qv*)

When playing at theatres with a childhood friend, Charlie gave himself the villainous parts, being instinctively aware of their more colourful status. Therefore, it is perhaps no coincidence that Chaplin's first films often cast him as a villain, either specifically (as in *Mabel at the Wheel*, *Tillie's Punctured Romance*) or in his overall conduct (e.g. *Gentlemen of Nerve*). In a contemporary ad for Keystone's 'Comedy Quartette' – meaning Mack Sennett, Mabel Normand, Roscoe 'Fatty' Arbuckle (all *qv*) and Chaplin – the line drawing of Chaplin shows him glaring at the reader with his best villainous scowl.

In the Keystone troupe, Mack Swain (*qv*) was more a large buffoon than a villain, something which remained true when he rejoined Chaplin at First National (*qv*). In the later *Gold Rush*, he is actually a friend, albeit sometimes a dangerously unhinged one, with the villainy handled instead by Tom Murray (*qv*) and, to a lesser degree, Malcolm Waite (*qv*).

The Essanay films sometimes pit Charlie against Bud Jamison, Fred Goodwins and Charles Insley (all *qv*), but they, along with Leo White and Billy Armstrong (both *qv*) fit more the

description of rivals than outright baddies. Chaplin seemed to veer away from stereotyped heavies in this series, but returned to them in the Mutuals in the imposing shape of Eric Campbell (*qv*), who proved not merely the best of them all, but ultimately impossible to replace.

The later features, aside from Allan Garcia's cruel proprietor of *The Circus*, often dispense with an outside villain altogether. It is interesting to note the absence of a specific villain in either *City Lights* or *Modern Times* – except, by implication, the world at large. Chaplin, of course, portrays the hero and the villain in *The Great Dictator*; in *Monsieur Verdoux* he is again both, but wrapped up into one person. *Limelight* has no villain except time, which is not on Calvero's side; *A King in New York* includes a crooked adviser who makes off with the King's fortune, but otherwise all blame is ascribed to political extremes. Nor does the plot of *A Countess From Hong Kong* have any real villain, except circumstance.

(See also: Desmonde, Jerry; Essanay; Garcia, Allan; Keystone; Mutual; Politics; Sickness)

VON STERNBERG, JOSEF

See: Baker, Nellie Bly, and Purviance, Edna

WAITE, MALCOLM
(1892 or 1894–1949)

Michigan-born actor who plays 'Jack', Charlie's rival for the heroine in *The Gold Rush* (*qv*). Other films include *Kid Boots* (1926) with Clara Bow and Eddie Cantor, *Noah's Ark* (1928), also a pre-teaming Laurel & Hardy short, *Why Girls Love Sailors* (1927).

(See also: Laurel, Stan)

WALK, THE

During Chaplin's peak years, several explanations circulated regarding the origin of his screen character's distinctive walk, a jaunty shuffle with feet turned out. John McCabe cites Chaplin's own childhood recollection, from *McClure's* magazine of July 1916, of a character known as 'Rummy' Binks owing to his weakness for rum. Binks used to walk in this somewhat pained fashion as he tended the horses left outside the Queen's Head pub by visiting coachmen. The young Chaplin was able to replicate Rummy's walk with facility, but did not use it professionally until introducing his 'tramp' character (see **Costume**). In 1915, British cartoonist Steve Drummond labelled the comedian's distinctive silhouette as the 'anchor'. Charlie's singular method of cornering at high speed, a staccato skid on one foot, was at least as famous, and may perhaps date from his stint with *Casey's Court*. Comedy producer Hal Roach, who worked alongside Chaplin at Essanay (*qv*) in 1915, cited this essentially child-like action to support his belief that the best comedians are those who imitate children.

(See also: *Between Showers*; 'Chaplin Craze', The; Childhood; Children; Early stage appearances; Risqué humour; *Unknown Chaplin*)

WALLIS, SHANI
(b. 1933)

London-born singer and dancer, with early experience in repertory, television and radio before training at RADA for two years. She later appeared in cabaret and West End musicals. She was spotted by Chaplin when appearing in pantomime at the Golders Green Hippodrome, and given the rôle as cabaret singer in *A King in New York* (*qv*).

WARD, CARRIE CLARK (CARRIE WARD OR CARRIE CLARKE-WARD)
(1862–1926)

Supporting actress, born in Nevada, who plays minor characters in two Chaplin Essanays, *The Bank* and *A Night in the Show* (both *qv*). Her later films include Valentino's *The Eagle* (1925).

(See also: Essanay)

WARTIME

(Chaplin films *qv*)
The 20th century's two World Wars are reflected in Chaplin's output by, respectively, *Shoulder Arms* and *The Great Dictator*. *Limelight* also takes the First World War as its background, but it is little emphasized. The comedian's non-participation in the first such conflict was a matter of controversy at the time, and has remained so ever since, but it is worth pausing to consider public attitudes at its outset. In the latter part of 1914, many Britons volunteered their services in the genuine belief that it would 'all be over by Christmas'. This was all the more so among expatriates, as Chaplin later recalled, who saw no need to uproot themselves for a fight destined to conclude even before their bags were packed. The war was not taken seriously until Christmas had passed, Germany had not been vanquished, and casualties had become heavy. By this time, Britons overseas were expected to return home and enlist, though many did not; *Variety*'s 'Show Biz from Vaude to Video' details a type of embargo on such Britons in

American theatre, but its impact seems to have been limited. When the British government enacted conscription in 1916 (for the first time in the country's history), it was not extended to Britons resident in the USA; they were, however, subject to America's draft on her entry into the war a year later.

Wartime: Franklin D. Roosevelt, Douglas Fairbanks, Mary Pickford, Marie Dressler and Charlie Chaplin support the Liberty Loan campaign in 1918

Chaplin and his several British colleagues were criticized for remaining in America instead of returning to enlist. In response, all effort was made publicly to support war charities, as when Chaplin and Eric Campbell (*qv*) staged a comic boxing match, or the parallel occasion where they took part in a 'tragedians v. comedians' baseball game. Chaplin had in any case been told, quite early on, that he would not be required by the military. Nevertheless, Mutual (*qv*) cautiously included a contractual requirement not to leave the USA, as reported by *Pictures and Picturegoer* at the time: 'The Chaplin contract contains more than twenty thousand words and provides conditions and clauses to cover numberless contingencies. An element of "war risk" enters into it. The comedian is a British subject, but it is stipulated that he shall not leave the United States within the life of the contract without the permission of the Corporation. There are those, of course, who whine about "Charlie's duty to his country"; but they should not lose sight of the fact that as a laughter-making genius he is almost indispensable in this darkest hour of history.' This seems to have been the dominant attitude, both from public and officialdom, but it is known that Chaplin, finally wearied of all the accusations, eventually took an army medical and was refused, or, to quote a contemporary report, 'placed in the fifth classification of the American Army draft', meaning that his services would not be required for a considerable period, if at all.

On 21 July 1917, the *Motion Picture News* quoted Chaplin's new employers, First National (*qv*), on the numerous 'unpleasant rumors' circulating about his non-involvement in the fighting. 'If the gentlemen who are publishing these scurrilous reports were aware of the extent to which Mr. Chaplin is giving his aid there would be less comments. Mr. Chaplin has been called, by the Queen of England, "F.M.O.E." When she was pressed to explain what that meant, she replied, "The Funniest Man on Earth". Mr. Chaplin's pictures are giving the soldiers in the trenches the greatest relaxation they could find. In addition to that he is buying war stocks heavily. Mr. Chaplin has a perfect right to resent being termed, in any sense, a "slacker". He is doing a thousand times more good for the world by doing what he is than if he were in the trenches. People fail to realize that at this depressing time the man who can make them smile and forget the terrible, world-wide gloom is doing a real good for humanity.'

While it is difficult to imagine the august-looking Queen Mary enthusing over a knockabout comedian, the British and American authorities shared the opinion that Chaplin was doing more good by making his films and raising funds (in the spring of 1917, the *Star* reported Chaplin as having subscribed £30,000 to the War Loan). In 1918, Chaplin toured extensively in the Third Liberty Loan, promoting the sale of War Bonds, in the company of Mary Pickford and Douglas Fairbanks (both *qv*). Film exists of them campaigning outside the Sub-Treasury building on Wall Street in 8 April 1918. Chaplin later recalled having slipped off the platform, landing

on Franklin D. Roosevelt. Theodore Huff mentions a subsequent reception at the White House, where Chaplin danced with Marie Dressler (*qv*). The news films of these occasions are mentioned elsewhere, also Chaplin's promotional film *The Bond* (made for the fourth Loan Drive) and an item in which Chaplin and Fairbanks entertain an appreciative audience of US marines.

After the conclusion of the Liberty Loan campaign, Chaplin was welcomed at a lunch by a British line officer, Captain Bealley, whose speech informed those present of the several occasions when he and his colleagues had watched Chaplin comedies as a means of relieving war stress. 'He made us laugh when it often seemed nothing else could,' said the Captain, 'and in my opinion and in the opinion of thousands of others at the Front it would be little short of a calamity to cut short the output of Mr. Chaplin's inimitable comedies.' Something of these attitudes may be gleaned from *The Wipers Times*, one of several titles given to a humorous paper published and read by Britain's front-line troops. Amid the ironic pieces are several punning references to Chaplin, usually something like 'Marley Taplin' playing at a bombed-out cinema. Generally, accusations of 'slacking' came from those who were not directly involved, as with a perhaps complacent joke in *Punch* calling him 'Chaplain to the Slackers'. A widely-told story of Chaplin's 1921 British visit concerns an ex-soldier who offered his medals to the comedian, in gratitude for the encouragement his films had provided during the war.

It was not necessarily Chaplin himself who was criticized for not fighting; *Pictures and Picturegoer* for 11 September 1915 describes a Chaplin lookalike contest at Gatti's Picture Palace in London, comprising entrants hailing mostly from Chaplin's own south London haunts. One such participant was greeted with the cry, 'Why don't you join the army?'

As history records, the First World War led to the Second in little more than two decades. *The Great Dictator* makes this connection somewhat, while Chaplin's real-life remarks on a Second Front for Russia were later seized upon as evidence of his supposed Communist sympathies. Ultimately less controversial was a transatlantic telephone call, heard over BBC Radio on 5 March 1943. It was intended to encourage the people of Lambeth, Chaplin's former home, after

the area had sustained considerable bomb damage, with the recollection that its people were constructed of 'pretty good metal'. A recording survives, and may be heard in the documentary *Our Charlie*.

As an odd postscript, one might mention a *Daily Mail* item of 3 May 1958, headed 'Chaplin signs a peace pact'. The comedian had spent more than a year battling the local council in Vevey, Switzerland, over the noise – much of it early in the morning – from a rifle range only 300 yards from his home. The case was on the point of going to court when a 'compromise' was reached over the number of people allowed to use the range at any given time.

(See also: 'Chaplin Craze', The; *The Chaplin Revue*; Childhood; Documentaries, compilations; Impersonators; *Monsieur Verdoux*; Newsreels; Politics; Public appearances; Sport; *Triple Trouble*; United Artists)

WELLS, MAE (MAI OR MAY)

See: *Pilgrim, The*

WEST, BILLY

See: Impersonators

WHITE, LEO
(1880–1948)

(Chaplin films *qv*)
British actor of Punchinello-like features, born in Manchester; he specialized as light comedian on the music-hall stage from 1898 until 1910, when he travelled to the USA under the auspices of producer Daniel Frohman. White joined Chaplin from his first Essanay release, having appeared previously in the studio's 'Sweedie' comedies, from 1914, starring Wallace Beery. White remained in Chaplin's stock company into the Mutual period, specializing in excitable Frenchmen (even when they weren't supposed to be!) sporting top hat, frock coat and Van Dyke whiskers. In his debut with Chaplin, *His New Job*, he appears, out of make-up, on the studio reception desk before donning his usual moustache and beard as one of the actors. In the next film, *A Night Out*, White is an outraged restaurant patron;

Leo White as the 'French Count'

in *The Champion*, he attempts to influence the outcome of Charlie's fight with 'Young Hippo'; *In the Park* places him in the sad plight of a distressed lover, who requests Charlie's help in drowning himself; *A Jitney Elopement* is quintessential White, presenting him as a count whose place Charlie usurps; *The Tramp*, by contrast, sees him among the thieves outwitted by Charlie; White is the paramour of a well-to-do lady in *Work*, one of the parkgoers in *A Woman*, an official in *The Bank* and an initially rebellious recruit in *Shanghaied*. He has another dual rôle in *A Night in the Show*, as both a wealthy patron and (in blackface) one of the gallery rowdies. *Carmen* casts him among the uniformed guard, while he contributes in at least three rôles in *Police*, variously as greengrocer, flophouse owner and cop. Chaplin's first Mutual film, *The Floorwalker*, sees White amid the store's customers; in the next, *The Fireman*, he is the panicky householder reporting an unattended blaze; in *The Vagabond*, White doubles as a Jewish character in the opening scene and as an old gypsy woman later on; and *The Count* echoes *A Jitney Elopement* with White as Count Broko, whose place is taken by Charlie. From here, White vanishes from the Chaplin company, the result of his having returned to Essanay. *Pictures and the Picturegoer* for the week ending 23 December 1916, while describing him as the man 'who made the French Count famous', notes also his signing with Essanay to appear alongside Max Linder (*qv*). As detailed elsewhere, Linder's Essanay films were not a great success, and White subsequently joined Chaplin's foremost imitator, Billy West (*qv*). In

1918, White assisted Essanay in the compilation of *Triple Trouble*, a 'new' Chaplin film assembled from an abandoned feature, sections of previously released subjects plus new linking segments. Leo White reappeared only once in Chaplin's career, as one of Hynkel's barbers in *The Great Dictator*; among other appearances in the intervening years are *Vanity Fair* (1923), *Ben-Hur* (1925), the Marx Brothers' *Monkey Business* (1931), plus a 1935 sound short, *Keystone Hotel*, intended as a revival of slapstick comedy's heyday. From the same year, and again with the Marx Brothers, White is one of a trio of bearded aviators in their *A Night at the Opera*. His final film appearance was as Joe Weber, of vaudeville's Weber & Fields, in Warners' turn-of-the-century piece, *My Wild Irish Rose* (1947). Leo White's birthdate has been given variously as 1880, 1883 and 1887 (the *Pictures and Picturegoer* item referred to above describes him as then being aged 33); the most plausible date is that suggested in his *Performer* obituary, which quotes his age at death as being 68.

(See also: Camera-looks; Dual rôles; Essanay; Florey, Robert; Impersonators; Marx, Groucho; Mutual; Race)

WILLIAMS, FRANK D.
(1893–?)

Reportedly Chaplin's cameraman for most of his films at Keystone (*qv*), Frank D. Williams is on-screen as the newsreel cameraman of *Kid Auto Races at Venice* (*qv*). Other credits include *Poor Rich Man* (1918), Mabel Normand's *Mickey* (1918), *Queen of the Sea* (1918), *The Tong Man* (1919), *Dragon Painter* (1919), *The Brand of Lopez* (1920), *First Born* (1921) and travelling matte work for *Ben-Hur* (1925).

(See also: Normand, Mabel; Sennett, Mack; Struss, Karl)

WILSON, JACK 🎩

(Chaplin films *qv*)
Photographer who was Chaplin's second cameraman from *A Dog's Life* in 1918 to *City Lights* in 1931, Jack Wilson also contributes on-screen to *How To Make Movies* (*qv*), plus a brief bit in *The Pilgrim* (allegedly to save the cost of

hiring an extra!), as the clergyman whose clothes are stolen by Charlie. Jack Wilson's wife, Edith, has been spotted in *The Kid* as the woman pushing a pram (reportedly containing the Wilsons' baby!) and in a deleted sequence noted under the main entry of *City Lights*. (In *My Life in Pictures*, Chaplin misidentifies 'the woman with the pram' as Phyllis Allen [*qv*].) Jack Wilson's biographical details are uncertain, but he should not be confused with the vaudeville comedian of that name who committed suicide in 1931. It is also doubtful that he is the Jack Wilson whose acting credits range from British films of the 1930s to American TV bit parts in the 1960s. Rollie Totheroh's grandson, David, has mentioned socializing between his family and the Wilsons into the 1940s. His grandfather received a visit from Jack Wilson in 1966; after Totheroh's death a year later, Wilson sent a letter of condolence to his late colleague's son. It is understood that Jack Wilson has surviving nieces in Scotland.

(See also: Totheroh, Roland 'Rollie')

WILSON, TOM 🎩
(1880–1965)

(Chaplin films *qv*)
Burly (6 feet 2 inches), Montana-born actor, earlier in a military career before becoming involved with boxing. 'Legitimate' stage work included a stint with Minnie Maddern Fiske, an early supporter of Chaplin. Wilson also appeared in vaudeville prior to entering films. His early screen rôles include two with Douglas Fairbanks (*qv*), *The Americano* and *Wild and Woolly* (both 1917). Wilson may be seen in *How To Make Movies* (*qv*) and five of Chaplin's First National films: he is a cop in *A Dog's Life* and *The Kid*; a German woodcutter in *Shoulder Arms*; Charlie's employer in *Sunnyside*; and Babe London's boyfriend in *A Day's Pleasure*. He is reported also in *Monsieur Verdoux*. Other films include *Dinty* (1920) with Colleen Moore, Lloyd Hamilton's *His Darker Self* (1924), Keaton's *Battling Butler* (1926), *His Lady* (1928), *The Big House* (1930), Cagney's *The Picture Snatcher* (1933), *Devil's Island* (1940) and *The Tall Men* (1955).

(See also: First National; Keaton, Buster; London, Jean 'Babe'; Policemen)

A WOMAN

(Chaplin film)
Released by General Film Company, 12
July 1915. Produced by Essanay. Written
and directed by Charles Chaplin.
Photographed by Harry Ensign. British
title: *Charlie, the Perfect Lady*. Two reels.
1,785 feet.

With Charlie Chaplin (himself), Edna
Purviance (girl), Charles Insley (her
father), Marta Golden (her mother),
Margie Reiger (flirtatious girl), Billy
Armstrong (gentleman with soda), Leo
White (his companion).

A 'happy family' sits in the park. The
father scowls, the mother snores, and the
daughter covers her ears. Father takes an
interest in a flirtatious girl. His daughter
has given up reading and is slumbering
beside her mother. Father pursues the flirt.
Charlie saunters into view, walking
through a lawn sprinkler. Father leaves his
new acquaintance to buy her a soda.
Charlie passes the flirt, hooking her leg on
his cane. After he takes a seat, his cane
hooks the girl's leg once more, pulling her
to the ground. He is replacing her
dislodged shoe when Father returns; he
breaks a soda bottle over Charlie's head
and escorts the girl away. Charlie regains
full consciousness, and is joined on the
bench by two gentlemen, who are also
drinking soda. The girl persuades Father
to play Blind Man's Buff. Charlie has
stolen a sip from one man's soda bottle.
Battle commences, but concludes with
Charlie breaking the bottle over its
owner's head. The other man flees. Father
is deserted by his new companion,
unaware that she has taken his wallet.
Charlie meets the blindfolded man,
allowing him to think he is the girl.
Charlie leads him to the lake and, after
selecting a suitable spot, boots him in. A
policeman arrives, but Charlie, hooking

A Woman: *Charlie is invited home by
Edna and her mother...*

him with the cane placed over his
shoulder, throws him in with Father.
Charlie passes the other gentleman, still
out cold, pausing to knock off his hat.
Next he chances upon the mother and
daughter, still asleep, as Father and the
cop clamber ashore. Father, angry, pushes
the officer back in. The ladies, awakened,
invite Charlie to sit with them. Father
greets the other gentleman, evidently an
acquaintance. The ladies have brought
Charlie home. He enjoys their hospitality,
though suffers discomfort when sitting on
a feathered hat, complete with gigantic
pin. At the park, Father and friend order
more sodas, only for Father to discover he
has been robbed. In the kitchen, the ladies
ply Charlie with doughnuts, which he
dispenses by letting them slide the length
of a carving knife. Father and the
gentleman are outside. Once Father has
been persuaded away from yet another
pretty girl, they enter the lounge. Charlie
and the girl are kissing; the arrival of
Father prompts an introduction, and
Charlie is soon being throttled. Charlie
fights off the two men, but his trousers
are torn off. He flees to the lounge, then
into the street, but returns to the house,
taking refuge in an upstairs room. Charlie
finds a female costume and puts it on.
Downstairs, Father and his chum have
recovered from the scrap and are charging
around; Father, less than pleased to see his
wife comforted by the other man, starts
another fight. Ordered from the lounge,
the girl ventures upstairs. She finds
Charlie in women's clothes but still with
moustache and boots. She finds him a
pair of shoes while Charlie goes to shave.
The girl brings Charlie downstairs,
introducing 'her' to Father. The bogus
woman scores an immediate hit with
Father, and has soon entranced both men.
The girl explains the ruse to her mother,
as they look on. Charlie turns the men's
rivalry to his advantage by persuading
them to close their eyes before planting a
kiss. On the count of three, Charlie
moves away, allowing the men to kiss each
other. The joke backfires when Father
takes a swing at the other man, hitting
Charlie by mistake. Father ejects his rival
into the street, and returns to Charlie.
Father, protesting devotion, pulls Charlie's
skirt to the floor and the ruse is over. As
Charlie declares his love for the girl,
Father slowly relents; the young couple
embrace, but a chance remark from
Charlie is enough to renew Father's anger.
Charlie joins the other man out on the
street.

... and cornered by her irate father

Available copies of *A Woman*,
divested of their original sub-titles,
render this finale unclear. At least two
restorations, with titles replicating the
Essanay design, completely omit the final
dialogue cards, in which Charlie wrests a
change of heart from the girl's father
before making a second, less discreet
remark. There is certainly no reason to
trust those in a British reissue, the
gagged-up nature of which is typified by
Edna Purviance (*qv*) introducing the
disguised Charlie as 'Nora Nettlerash'. In
this version, Charlie, at the conclusion,
says nothing worse to Father than 'And
may the Lord have mercy on you.'

In any form, *A Woman* is by no
means an outstanding film (at least by
Chaplin standards), and is something of
a regression after the Essanay two-reelers
immediately preceding it (*The Tramp* and
Work, both *qv*). The opening segment –
approximately half the film – is yet
another reworking of the 'park' theme,
while the female impersonation, though
strikingly convincing, had been done at
least as well in *The Masquerader* (*qv*).
Sime Silverman of *Variety* was by no
means an unqualified admirer of
Chaplin's work, and complained over the
seeming lack of a scenario. He also found
much to criticize in the film's alleged
vulgarity; while the film seemed to pass
quickly, Sime attributed this to possible
cutting by the censors rather than
entertainment value (it should be noted
that *A Woman* has no less a running time
than several other Essanays).

The uneven nature of Chaplin's
Essanay films made no difference to their
initial success, but in retrospect it may be
seen that perhaps two in every three
showed a marked advance in his
technique. *A Woman* saw Chaplin between
innovations, but his next, *The Bank* (*qv*),
proved to be one of the series' best.

(See also: Auctions; Essanay; Female
impersonation; *Funniest Man in the World,
The*; Parks; Policemen; Reissues; Titling)

A WOMAN OF PARIS 🎩

(Chaplin film)
Released by United Artists, 1 October 1923. Produced, written and directed by Charles Chaplin. Assistant director: Eddie (A. Edward) Sutherland. Editorial direction, Monta Bell. Business manager: Alf Reeves. Photographed by Rollie Totheroh and Jack Wilson. Research by Harry [Henri] d'Abbadie d'Arrast and Jean di Limur. Copyrighted 17 October 1923 (LP19504). Eight reels, 7,577 feet. Working titles: *Public Opinion* and *Destiny*. Reissued in 1978 by Kino International Corp., with an orchestral score composed by Charles Chaplin.

With Edna Purviance (Marie St. Clair), Clarence Geldert (Marie's stepfather), Carl Miller (Jean Millet), Lydia Knott (Jean's mother), Charles French (Jean's father), Adolphe Menjou (Pierre Revel), Betty Morrissey (Fifi), Malvina Polo (Paulette), Karl Gutman (orchestra leader), Henry Bergman (maître d'hotel), Harry Northrup (valet), Nelly Bly Baker (masseuse), Charles Chaplin (unbilled bit part as porter).

It is evening in a small village 'somewhere in France', where Marie St. Clair makes ready to leave her unhappy home. She plans to depart with Jean Millet, her lover, in the morning, but is locked in her room by her stepfather. Marie's lover helps her escape by the window. After discussing plans for their future, Marie is returned home, but discovers she has been locked out. The stepfather refuses to admit her, suggesting she spend the night at Jean's home. Marie arrives *chez* Millet, but Jean's father orders her from the house. Marie and Jean go to the railway station, intending to catch a Paris-bound train at 12:15. Marie is left to buy the tickets while Jean returns home to pack his bag. At the house, Jean's father rejects his son, but is prevailed upon by his mother to accept the young couple's impending marriage. Grudgingly, Jean's father passes her some money to give him. Ready to leave, Jean embraces his mother and is persuaded to bid his father good-bye. Entering the living-room, Jean discovers his father unconscious in the armchair. He telephones for the doctor, but it is too late. Marie, pacing at the station, calls Jean, only to be told that 'something terrible has happened' and that their trip must be postponed. Before he can continue, Jean has to let the

doctor in. Instead of waiting, Marie hangs up and boards the train for Paris. Twelve months later, an elegant Marie is seen at a plush Paris restaurant, accompanying Pierre Revel, 'a gentleman of leisure, whose whims have made and ruined many a woman's career'. Pierre is the type of gent who inspects the kitchens, carries scented handkerchiefs and orders truffles, which, according to a title card, are 'rooted up from the soil by hogs – A delicacy for pigs and gentlemen'. Marie and Pierre enjoy a sumptuous, champagne-lubricated dinner. The following morning, at Marie's luxurious apartment, there is a visit from Fifi, Marie's vivacious friend. Marie, still in bed, is playfully scattered with flowers by Fifi. She opens the curtains, encouraging Marie to get up. When asked what she is doing up so early, Fifi explains that she hasn't been to bed as yet. At Pierre's office – his bedroom – the *roué* studies the stock market by means of a tickertape machine, then peruses a magazine announcing his engagement to a wealthy society woman. When an aide asks Pierre if the 'other lady' will complicate things, Pierre has him place a call to her. The other lady – Marie – agrees to meet Pierre for dinner that evening. Pierre is thus satisfied that Marie has yet to hear of the engagement. Marie learns the truth from another visitor, Paulette. Marie makes light of it, but breaks down in tears once her friends have gone. Later, Pierre arrives at Marie's apartment, only to be told she is too depressed to go out that evening. Pierre understands why when he finds the magazine open at the relevant page. Pierre insists they can continue their relationship despite his marriage, but Marie will not accept the idea. Pierre leaves her, saying he will return the next day, when Marie is in 'a better mood'. Marie receives a telephone call from Paulette, at a wild party in the 'Latin quarter'. She invites Marie to join her at the 'quiet' gathering, taking place in an artist's studio. Among its decadent delights is a woman gradually divested of her one garment, a lengthy bandage. Thanks to Paulette's erratic directions, Marie knocks at the wrong studio, and is astonished to find Jean, working as an artist and living with his mother. Marie is entertained, but the passage of time lends formality to the proceedings. Across the hallway, a tipsy Paulette and her comparably-soused gentleman friend are ejected from the party. Jean is evidently not making a good living.

Marie sets off alone to become **A Woman of Paris**

Marie engages him to paint her portrait. He agrees to visit her apartment the following morning, and escorts Marie to her limousine. Jean keeps the appointment, and is shown in by the maid. Paulette is visiting again, and observes Jean as she makes her way out. Marie, explaining which gown she would prefer to pose in, eventually notices the black armband on the young man's shoulder. He is in mourning for his father. 'When did he die?' asks Marie. 'The night you left,' explains Jean. Pierre arrives, and Marie goes to greet him. He is aware of Jean's presence, but Marie refuses to explain. Pierre, unconcerned, claims to 'understand perfectly', recommending only caution. When Pierre has gone, Marie dispassionately tells Jean of her decision to wear the 'silver dress'. Jean makes a comparably formal exit. Marie spends several days posing at Jean's studio. When Marie sees the finished painting, she is shocked to see herself depicted as she was at the time of their betrothal. Jean justifies the work by claiming, 'I knew you better then.' Marie tries to leave, but is stopped by Jean, who says he still loves her. Jean's mother returns via the kitchen, where she overhears Jean's intention to wed Marie and start a new life. Marie, torn between marriage and a wealthy lifestyle, departs in confusion. Back with Pierre, Marie expresses dissatisfaction. She wants 'a real home, babies, and a man's respect'. Pierre contemptuously indicates a ragged woman on the street, overrun by unruly offspring. When Marie insists she gets nothing out of life, Pierre indicates her pearl necklace. Furious, Marie tears it from her neck and hurls it into the street. A passing tramp picks up the necklace, and Marie eventually rushes out to reclaim it, offering cash in

A Woman of Paris: *Marie finds a wealthy provider in Pierre*

exchange. On her return, Marie's humiliation is compounded by a broken heel. She tells Pierre that they must part. Pierre guesses who the other man might be, and is told they are to marry. He is sceptical of their love and of Marie's insistence that she will never see him again. Jean's mother has persuaded him not to go through with the wedding. Marie arrives as Jean pacifies his tearful mother by claiming to have proposed in a moment of weakness. Marie agrees it was perhaps just that, and returns to her limousine, with Jean in hopeless pursuit. That night, Pierre 'consoles' himself in the company of Paulette, but sends her home in a taxi. Marie is alone in bed, drinking tea and reading a book. The maid reports that Jean is still waiting outside. Marie and Pierre's servants pretend that each has phoned the other. Back on speaking terms, they arrange to meet the following night. Jean, finally abandoning his vigil, returns to his studio. Next morning, Marie is getting a massage while Fifi delivers the gossip, essentially that Paulette, a supposed friend, had been seen on the town with Pierre. As Paulette prattles on, the masseuse performs her duties with a look of icy contempt, the more so when Paulette arrives and is greeted cordially by Fifi. In the lounge, Paulette pours drinks while asking Fifi not to mention the previous night to Marie. She adds that Pierre has invited her to dine again that night, which Fifi immediately relays to Marie. Once dressed, Marie ostentatiously calls Pierre to verify their date that night. This established, Paulette takes her leave. Jean sinks further into depression. He loads a revolver, concealing it as his mother enters the studio. Jean goes out. He follows Marie

and Pierre to a nightclub, where he sends Marie a note asking to see her one last time. Marie shows Pierre the note, and Jean is invited to their table. Jean, seeing Pierre has the letter, reclaims it and attacks his rival. The manager escorts Jean to the foyer. Jean produces the revolver, and a shot is heard. The guests rush to the foyer, where Jean lies dead. His mother is seen briefly, cooking supper at his studio. On being told Jean is dead, Marie passes out. Jean's body is returned to his flat, where police break the news to his mother. Pierre takes Marie home. Jean's mother contemplates the note found on her son's body and the portrait he painted of Marie. Taking the revolver, she sets off for Marie's

A Woman of Paris: *a decadent party in the artists' quarter*

apartment. On arrival, she is told that Marie has gone to the studio. Once there, she finds Marie weeping over Jean's body. The gun is laid down. 'Time heals,' says a title, 'and experience teaches that the secret of happiness is in service to others.' Marie and Mme Millet share a country cottage with several young children. 'Mother, here comes Father,' announces one, heralding the entrance of the local *curé*. The priest, noting the addition of another youngster, asks Marie when she will marry and have children of her own, but the question is laughed off. Marie sets off with one of the children to fetch some milk from the village. Nearby, a limousine, en route to Paris, pauses by a signpost. In the rear seats are Pierre and a friend. Marie and the child hitch a lift in a hay wagon. In the car, the friend asks Pierre what became of Marie St. Clair. Pierre does not know. Neither is aware of the other's presence as car and hay wagon cross, travelling in opposite directions.

Although a co-founder of United Artists (*qv*) in 1919, Chaplin was initially unable to participate in the company owing to his existing contract with First National (also *qv*). On its expiry in 1923, Chaplin decided his first UA project should be a dramatic vehicle for Edna Purviance (*qv*), who by then had outgrown the *ingénue* rôles she had been playing. Some critics suggest that Marie is really the mother of *The Kid* (*qv*), her adventures here being an extension of the earlier film. While Chaplin may have considered Edna Purviance best served by a similar type of rôle, it should be noted that society girl Marie does not resemble the financially independent, benevolent actress of *The Kid* until the very end. According to historian Herman G. Weinberg, the version of *A Woman of Paris* prepared for the Continental European market did not permit Marie even this final rehabilitation, depicting instead Marie's return to Pierre following Jean's suicide. There are also reports that Chaplin's advisers, Jean de Limur and Harry d'Abbadie d'Arrast (both *qv*), dissuaded him from having Marie end her days in a leper colony.

With *A Woman of Paris*, Chaplin resolved to disprove a claim that the screen was incapable of conveying 'psychology'; his autobiography cites as example a scene where Marie feigns indifference when informed of her lover's imminent marriage, even though her shock is apparent to the audience. He describes also the frequent use of subtle suggestion, as when Marie's activities are implied by the sight of a man's collar among her effects.

Chaplin had been contemplating such a film for perhaps two years, after much-married socialite Peggy Hopkins Joyce had told him of her involvement with a wealthy French publisher. As early as 17 December 1921, *Picture Show* claimed that 'Charlie Chaplin may surprise the world by making his next picture a serious drama. This, as you may know, has always been his ambition, and it is said that he has written a really dramatic story for himself.' On 10 March 1923, the magazine reported that

Chaplin was working on a film with Edna Purviance, at that time entitled 'Destiny', and rumoured to be 'a deep, dark tragedy, with no glimmer of the famous Chaplin comedy'. Although Chaplin considered a number of serious portrayals (see **Abandoned projects**), he did not appear in *A Woman of Paris* – sub-titled 'a drama of fate' – which, in the end, was to be his only dramatic production. (Technically, he did play a part, disguising himself as a porter in the railway station. This cameo, like those made by Alfred Hitchcock in later years, has since become one of cinema's least-kept secrets.) Cautiously, he inserted into the main titles an explanatory caption:

TO THE PUBLIC:

In order to avoid any misunderstanding, I wish to announce that I do not appear in this picture. It is the first serious drama written and directed by myself.

CHARLES CHAPLIN.

He was at least as guarded in the programme notes for the film's opening, at New York's Lyric Theater on 1 October 1923. 'I've been thinking that the public wants a little more realism in pictures,' mused Chaplin, 'whereby a story is pursued to the logical ending. I would like to get your ideas on the subject, for I am sure that those of us who are producing pictures do not know — we only guess.' He described the film as containing every element which, to him, made life 'interesting', though allowing that 'it is not for me to say that I am right'. 'After all,' he added, you are the judge, and your taste must be served ... by your reception will I guide myself in the future.' The text continued in like vein even into a postscript, promising that 'a letter to Mr. Chaplin, care Lyric Theater, will be given his personal attention'. Chaplin was covering himself to the utmost, but need not have worried. *Variety* appreciated what Chaplin was trying to do, noting a 'subtlety of idea-expression ... new to film dramatization'. The New York *Times* declared that Chaplin, as a director, had revealed himself as a 'bold, resourceful, imaginative, ingenious, careful, studious and daring artist', his intentions vindicated once more in a 'marvelous depth of charm' plus the elimination of

cinematic cliché, chiefly 'flashbacks' and 'what might be termed "standardized motion-picture acting"'. 'Chaplin has studied his sets and the human possibilities,' said the reviewer. 'This film lives, and the more directors emulate Mr. Chaplin the better will it be for the producing of pictures.' Mention was also made of the careful photography of scenes that would otherwise have caused censorship problems. There was no reference to an evident lesbian in the party sequence, though the review describes the girl she is ogling, wrapped in silk but gradually undraped. Despite its exclusively adult theme, *A Woman of Paris* encountered no censorship problems except, curiously, on an intended provincial booking in England, several months after its British debut (see **Censorship**). Theodore Huff noted the film's success in large cities and among the *intelligentsia*, who welcomed it back for several reissues during the 1920s. The mass audience proved less responsive and, above all, it was felt that Adolphe Menjou (*qv*) had made far greater impact than the nominal star. It is possible that Chaplin believed he had failed Edna Purviance in some way; this may explain why, following the introduction of sound, he kept the film under wraps until finally preparing a new orchestral score in 1976. Chaplin died before this, his final work, opened at the Cinema Studio, New York, in April 1978 (a London run, at the newly-launched Gate Three Cinema, followed in 1980). Judith Crist of the *New York Post* suggested that the general public of 1923 might not have been able to evaluate either the film or its star with total objectivity. 'Though Chaplin's contemporary audience may have missed him as comedian and been cool to Purviance in a dramatic role,' she wrote, 'today the leavening of the moralistic drama and the true wit of its unfolding is as evident as Purviance's beauty and subtlety of performance.' Both this review and that in the *New Yorker* touched upon the film's influence upon director Ernst Lubitsch; the *New Yorker* piece greeted this seemingly rediscovered production as 'a king's ransom dredged up from the ocean bed of sunken movies'. *A Woman of Paris* was said to contain 'all of Chaplin's wit and none of his whimsy', which was, incidentally, a frequent grumble during the comedian's heyday. 'Strange, lively, reviving,' it continued, 'to see evidence of the innovative mind of the figure so familiar to us in the guise of the little

By courtesy of Robert G. Dickson

A Woman of Paris: *Marie and Pierre live it up ...*

...but Marie is soon united in grief with Jean's mother

man' – a remark that may have been prompted by one of the 'tramp' character's periodic falls from popular favour. Vincent Canby of the New York *Times*, who also drew comparisons with Lubitsch, revisited his paper's 1923 review, and in so doing drew a brace of misconceptions. One is that the film had been abridged, citing a running time of 83 minutes compared to an original duration of nearly two hours. The discrepancy was due less to editing than the result of an increased projection speed, as projectors in 1923 would have operated at perhaps 60 or 70 feet per minute rather than the 90 feet imposed by an added soundtrack. Among the supposed deletions was a 'picturesque prologue', which would not have been part of the film itself but instead an introductory stage presentation, of the type customarily arranged for important silent feature films at prestigious venues. (The actual cuts in Chaplin's reissue – restored in America's laserdisc copies – consist of a scant few shots plus a melodramatic introductory title, which reads: 'All of us are seeking good – We sin only in blindness. The ignorant condemn our mistakes – But the wise pity them.') Canby was precisely on target in citing the film as an opportunity to see Chaplin at the height of his directorial powers – which some believe he was not by the time of *A Countess From Hong Kong* (*qv*) – while not 'closely bound to the performer's personality'. Canby applauded the fact that Marie is 'no victim', taking quite knowingly to her shallow lifestyle. He expressed further approval of such moments as Marie's retrieval of the discarded necklace and that in which a *masseuse* expresses mute contempt through her stern countenance. 'One does not truly know the work of Chaplin,' decided Canby, 'until one has had the good fortune to see this rediscovered masterpiece.'

(See also: Baker, Nellie Bly; Knott, Lydia; Music; Northrup, Harry; Pathos; Polo, Malvina; Reissues; Suicide; Sutherland, A. Edward; Television; Trick photography; Video releases; Women)

A WOMAN OF THE SEA

See: Abandoned projects and Purviance, Edna

WOMEN

(Chaplin films *qv*)
The depiction of women posed an interesting difficulty for Chaplin; as he wrote in his memoirs, 'logically it was difficult to get a beautiful girl interested in a tramp. This has always been a problem in my films.' The Chaplinesque heroine, epitomized by Edna Purviance (*qv*), is often dismissed as outmoded in present times, as is Chaplin's gallantry, though

one could cite Vincent Canby's comments (detailed under **Pathos**) regarding the implications of this brand of idolatry.

Not all women are idealized in Chaplin's films. Wives, particularly when played by Mabel Normand (*qv*) in the Keystone films, are accustomed to disharmony and, on occasion, a marital scrap; although Charlie has fewer roles as husband in his later films, *Pay Day* offers a less than ideal picture of married bliss. Charlie dreams of a happy home with the *gamine* in *Modern Times*, but his gallic successor, *Monsieur Verdoux*, actually murders in order to care for his wife and family.

The women Charlie meets – often in the many 'park' comedies – tend to be maids or similar types, such as Edna in *Work* and *In the Park*, or the two-timing cook in *The Count*. There are occasional hints that some of them might be prostitutes (see **Risqué humour**). Charlie has little chance of success with women from the upper bracket, as illustrated by a contemporary review, quoted in the main entry for **The Idle Class**. He is sometimes entangled with the girlfriends of others (*His New Profession*) or even, inadvertently, their wives (*Caught in the Rain, A Night Out*). Though seemingly innocent, one might also query his relationship with the landlady in *The Star Boarder*.

It is well known that Chaplin's real-life experiences with women were many and varied. When aged 16, he fell for Marie Doro, leading lady of *Sherlock Holmes*, but Chaplin's age and status enforced his silence on the matter; they met again in Hollywood a decade later (see The '**Chaplin Craze**'). His first genuine romance was with a girl named Hetty Kelly, whom he had met while playing with the Karno Company (*qv*) at the Streatham Empire. Hetty was part of 'Bert Coutts' Yankee Doodle Girls', a song-and-dance troupe; she was only fifteen at the time, four years younger than Chaplin. The relationship lasted only a matter of days, but, as Chaplin admitted, would have a prolonged effect. They met only once more before Chaplin left for America. Hetty married in 1915, but died three years later in the flu epidemic. There had been sparse correspondence, but Chaplin remained unaware of her death until revisiting England in 1921. Latterly, Chaplin could not even revisit the scene of their first meeting; after being converted to cinema use, the Streatham Empire was destroyed by a flying bomb in 1944.

Women: *Chaplin and Pola Negri. She compensated for a lack of English with a great deal of enthusiasm*

Chaplin's first, brief American romance was with Keystone actress Peggy Pearce (*qv*); he established a serious relationship with Edna Purviance from 1915, but by 1918 was seeing Mildred Harris (*qv*), whom he married that year. It is easy to detect an autobiographical element when, in *Limelight*, Calvero admits to having had a few failed marriages. As noted elsewhere, Chaplin's first marriage failed quickly. A syndicated column from Louella Parsons (which reached the UK via *Picture Show* of 21 May 1921) described the journalist as 'agog' over Chaplin's intention to marry May Collins after the final decree from Mildred. The marriage never took place. Instead, Chaplin embarked on a somewhat tempestuous affair with Polish-born screen actress Pola Negri, who on 13 February 1923 was described in London's *Daily Mail* as 'Charlie Chaplin's Bride' after the recent announcement of their engagement. The same description was used by *Picture Show* on 10 March, when commencing a biography of the actress. They had first met during Chaplin's 1921 visit to Berlin, and were reunited when Paramount brought the actress to America a year later. Chaplin's autobiography suggests the announcement of their 'marriage' to have given to the press by Pola, who was made 'ill' by his reluctance to issue a corroborative statement. He describes also a visit from representatives of her studio, suggesting he should oblige. Chaplin refused to 'marry someone just to safeguard Paramount's investment', thus ending the affair. In her own book, *Memoirs of a Star*, Pola Negri refuted most of Chaplin's claims, describing instead his avid pursuit and eagerness to raise a family with her. In her version, it was she who ended the romance; among the contemporary accounts cited is a headline from the Los Angeles *Examiner* of 2 March 1923, that reads 'POLA NEGRI JILTS CHAPLIN'. It must be said that available photographs of the couple do not exactly show Chaplin fighting her off; by the same token, a later hysterical display for the press – when Pola attended the funeral of Rudolph Valentino in 1926 – does little to dispel hints of strategically-expressed emotion.

An odd postscript: in the 1930s Pola Negri took legal action after a French magazine falsely claimed she was involved with Hitler, as 'the power behind the throne'. They had not even met, and the story seems to have developed from her having been cited as Hitler's favourite film star. Thus, at different times, Pola seems to have commanded the interest of both Chaplin and the model for his 'Adenoid Hynkel'.

Chaplin's next marriage was to Lita Grey (*qv*), a youngster with none of Pola's public histrionics – at least initially. Their marriage is chronicled elsewhere, but it necessary to mention here that it overlapped with his relationships with leading ladies Georgia Hale and Merna Kennedy (both *qv*). Several commentators have remarked on the fact that most of Chaplin's leading ladies became his lovers, both off-screen and on, suggesting this to have had some bearing on his disharmonious – and strictly on-screen – relationship with Virginia Cherrill (*qv*).

Lita's account of their parting mentions Chaplin's claim to have been unfaithful to her with Merna, Edna and Marion Davies. Chaplin's friendship with Marion Davies – at that time secretly the mistress of William Randolph Hearst – was a close and long-term business, causing much gossip at the time, but never any evidence of private consummation. She and Chaplin never failed to attend each other's parties, and it was Chaplin who, reportedly, supplied a docile old lion from his own studio when Marion was required to play opposite a more dangerous specimen. In her dictated memoirs, *The Times We Had*, Marion claims that Chaplin doubled for her in this scene. Fred Lawrence Guiles' Davies biography reprints both this tale and another refuting it. Neither the Davies memoir nor Chaplin's own autobiography suggest any intimacy between them, but speculation continues. Another of Chaplin's brief flings of the mid-1920s was with Louise Brooks; still another involvement – sexual or otherwise – with

socialite Peggy Hopkins Joyce was the inspiration for *A Woman of Paris*. Carol Matthau's *Among the Porcupines* makes mention of Chaplin speaking about his various conquests, among them writer Rebecca West, a one-time mistress of H.G. Wells. It is easy to suspect that, despite public evidence of enthusiastic pursuit, Chaplin had become disillusioned with women at this time. In 1926, when Chaplin's affairs were (to say the least) complicated, *Vanity Fair* approached various famous men to detail their requirements for 'the Ideal Woman'. They were perhaps unaware that this was probably the worst possible time to broach this subject with Chaplin, whose contribution, they felt, 'strikes a rather acid note at times, for one so versed in the poignancy of simple sorrow'. One can hardly wonder at it, but his response was as follows:

1. When in my company, she never admires other men.
2. If I am obliged to leave her in order to keep another engagement, her disappointment is always keen enough to be flattering to me, but never quite keen enough to keep me from going where I am going.
3. Her diamond bracelets never need cleaning.
4. Her shoulders are never shiny.
5. She never takes advantage of a voluptuous situation to narrow her eyes.
6. She always reads all of the Sunday papers (the funny sheet first) but, having read them, she refolds them neatly and leaves them as they were.
7. She knows the words of no popular dance music, or, if she does, never sings them in my ear when dancing.
8. She uses only a faint *eau de toilette* during the day, but sprays herself plentifully with *L'Heure Bleue* upon retiring.
9. I am not exactly in love with her, but
10. She is entirely in love with me.

Chaplin's divorce from Lita the following year was as acrimonious as divorces are likely to be. His next wife, Paulette Goddard (*qv*), seemed to provide stability in the period between their first meeting in 1932 and seemingly amicable divorce a decade later. It was towards the end of 1942 that he met Oona O'Neill (*qv*), whom he married the following year. He had intended Oona to star in a film called *Shadow and Substance* (see

Abandoned projects), as replacement for another actress, Joan Barry (or Berry, among other names). Joan had been signed for the part but became unstable, breaking into the Chaplin home wielding a gun, then claiming to be carrying his unborn child, conceived during a trip to New York. In addition to the paternity case, Chaplin was prosecuted for trying to deprive Joan Barry of her civil rights and for an alleged violation of the Mann Act, a law making it illegal to transport a woman across a state line for 'immoral purposes'. This law had originally been passed to combat the trade in prostitutes, but had long been misused in the blackmail of politicians. Chaplin, represented by top lawyer Jerry Giesler, was cleared of every accusation, despite such courtroom descriptions of him as a 'Cockney cad'. A blood test proved he could not be the father of Joan Barry's baby, yet, incredibly, he was ordered to pay maintenance until the child reached adulthood.

Oona, pregnant with her first child, fainted when news of the acquittal was broadcast by radio. Despite this turbulent start, their marriage endured until Chaplin's death. Claire Bloom (*qv*) was aware of being hired partially on the strength of her resemblance to Oona, noting also how, in costuming her, Chaplin would select a type of dress worn by his mother, or a type of shawl worn by his first girlfriend; in short, he wanted her to embody a 'composite young woman, lost to him in the past'. Carol Matthau has remarked on the way Chaplin fell for Oona as if he were a boy in love for the first time, who 'really did marry the girl of his dreams'.

A frequently-held belief is that Chaplin's preference for teenage brides – Mildred, Lita and Oona were all in that category – owed its origins to a desire to recapture Hetty Kelly. Miss Bloom realized also that her character in the film was another of the 'damaged heroines' inspired by Chaplin's mother, believing further that Oona's strength had at long last eradicated 'the image of broken womanhood' left in Chaplin's mind by his tortured mother.

Just as widely accepted is that Chaplin's ousting from the US had as much to do with his love life as his alleged politics. Chaplin himself occasionally admitted that, when meeting a woman, his first thought concerned the likelihood of sex between them. It was a reflective Chaplin who, at

82, addressed the British press on the topics of money and world problems. On 11 January 1972, David Lewin of the *Daily Mail* quoted his response to the question, 'What is your weakness?' 'My weakness?' replied Chaplin, 'Women. I love them all.'

(See also: Children; Early stage appearances; *Great Dictator, The*; Keystone; Politics; Prisons; Vagrancy)

WOOD, TOM

See: *Day's Pleasure, A, How to Make Movies* and *Sunnyside*

WOOD, 'WEE' GEORGIE
(1895–1979)

Pint-sized British comedian who first made acquaintance with Chaplin while touring America during the 1920s. Wood had been asked to visit Alf Reeves (*qv*) on behalf of one of the latter's in-laws and, on arrival at the Chaplin Studio, was assured that Mr Reeves 'would see anybody and anything from London'. Reeves duly appeared, whispering, 'Would you like to see Charlie? He is in a very good mood today.' Wood declined, explaining a reluctance either to 'genuflect' or to risk his admiration of Chaplin by not necessarily liking him as a man. 'Thank God for somebody who does not want to meet me,' said Chaplin, stepping out from behind a screen. Chaplin recognized him instantly, the result of a long-forgotten encounter in Oldham, Lancashire. Wood had been touring in Levy and Cardwell's 1907 production of the pantomime *Sleeping Beauty* – with, incidentally, Stan Laurel (*qv*) also in the cast – and had been 'sprayed' by Chaplin when standing next to him in a public convenience. 'You could not have been more than 3 feet high,' recalled Chaplin, 'but you looked up with all the dignity in the world and said, "Young man, haven't you learned to pee straight yet?"' Wood claimed that Chaplin was then appearing at the local Empire, but it is difficult to reconcile *Sleeping Beauty*'s dates with Chaplin's itinerary, unless it took place early in the year and overlapped with one of the untraced weeks of the 'Casey Circus'. Having met again in somewhat drier circumstances, the two comedians formed a lasting friendship – it was Wood who seconded Chaplin's membership of the Water Rats – despite such alleged incidents as Wood stomping around the music-hall

set of *Limelight* (*qv*) claiming, 'It was not like that!'

John McCabe has quoted a further shaky start to the Chaplin–Wood relationship. When their respective shows were playing at Oldham, Lancashire, Chaplin invited several from Wood's company to an after-show tea. Their manager forbade the late-night trip, without bothering to inform Chaplin, who was left wondering what had become of his guests. The incident remained with Chaplin, who incorporated a parallel sequence into *The Gold Rush* (*qv*).

(See also: Early stage appearances; Grand Order of Water Rats, The; Menjou, Adolphe)

WOOLLCOTT, ALEXANDER
(1887–1943)

Waspish, rotund journalist, critic, broadcaster and sometime actor, Alexander Woollcott was the prototype figure of Moss Hart and George S. Kaufman's play *The Man Who Came to Dinner*. Woollcott's influence could destroy or make a theatrical production, and his more general enthusiasms (ranging from guide dogs for the blind to American involvement in the Second World War) benefited from his endorsements. The Marx Brothers' success on Broadway owed something to Woollcott's approval; he was also a considerable supporter of Chaplin (in Woollcott's effusive terminology, 'the greatest living actor'), with whom the critic formed a long-term friendship. Woollcott's comments on *The Gold Rush* (*qv*) led to the film's reissue being dedicated to him, 'In appreciation of his praise of this picture'. Woollcott was due to undergo surgery, but delayed the operation until he had seen the revived film and its singular dedication.

(See also: Introduction; Marx, Groucho; *Monsieur Verdoux*; Radio)

WORK 🎩

(Chaplin film)
Released by General Film Company, 21 June 1915. Produced by Essanay. Written and directed by Charles Chaplin. Photographed by Harry Ensign. British title: *Charlie at Work*. Reissued as *The Paperhanger*. Two reels. 2,017 feet.

'Wee' Georgie Wood visits the Chaplin studio in the 1920s
By courtesy of Roy Hudd and the Grand Order of Water Rats

With Charlie Chaplin (decorator's assistant), Charles Insley (decorator), Billy Armstrong (the householder), Marta Golden (his wife), Edna Purviance (maid), Leo White (wife's lover) Paddy McGuire (workman).

Early morning in a well-to-do household. The owner's wife potters around while the maid occupies the telephone. Reminding them the decorators are due, the husband demands breakfast. In a busy street, Charlie, a decorator's dogsbody, tows the wagon containing his employer and the tools of their trade. After knocking over a policeman, they take a 'short cut', narrowly avoiding a streetcar. This alternate route is along the steepest of hills, which Charlie cannot negotiate despite frequent whippings. They slide back, narrowly missing another streetcar. A second attempt is made, through the path of *another* streetcar. Atmosphere at the house is fraught; outside, the cart stops and Charlie's boss greets another tradesman. He is given a lift, adding to Charlie's burden. They have nearly arrived when Charlie vanishes down a manhole. The front of the cart is lowered for Charlie to grab; he is retrieved, but continues to bob up and down as the wagon teeters. On reaching the house, Charlie is left to bring in the materials. The lady of the house lists her requirements as the decorator calmly smokes a cigarette. Outside, Charlie also attempts to smoke, but is heavily burdened with ladders, buckets, barrels, trestle tables and tools. Beneath it all, Charlie makes his way to the hallway, where he collapses. The housewife, detailing where she wants work to be done, absently knocks Charlie's hat askew; he turns it sideways. Work begins in a ground floor room. The wife, in a sudden panic, puts her silverware in the safe. In response to this affront, Charlie gathers their own watches and cash, placing them in a trouser pocket secured by a safety pin. Exit the lady, huffily. Charlie, his attention taken by a small statuette, is ordered to fetch paste and brush. In the hallway, the maid is back on the telephone. Unwittingly, her feather duster tickles Charlie's rear as he bends to pick up the paste. They are both amused, but the maid is less pleased when Charlie uses the paste brush to 'dust' her face. Back to work, Charlie takes his employer's coat and cap. He brushes the coat with the paste brush, making it dirtier than ever; the cap has to be retrieved from the paste bucket. Charlie's next job is to fetch their ladder and a plank of wood. He meets the frantic householder, who is inadvertently thumped by a door and the plank. Back in the room, Charlie creates space by pushing the safe into a corner. Next he has to bring in wallpaper and whitewash. This done, the plank is set across the ladder, Charlie supporting the opposite end as his boss perches above. In the kitchen, the householder, running late, continues to demand breakfast. While supporting the plank, Charlie picks up the statuette once more, adding a lampshade 'skirt' and making it perform a bump-and-grind dance. In the kitchen, wife and maid prepare breakfast, but the stove explodes. The husband's attempt to re-light it induces a second explosion. The maid is sent to obtain help; she brings Charlie, who allows his employer to crash to the floor, his head in the whitewash bucket. Charlie re-lights the oven, and all seems well until it explodes again. His next task is to help the boss to clean up. The floor is slippery, and the boss difficult to prop up. The boss is soon even messier. There is another explosion in the kitchen. Charlie is upstairs, papering the maid's bedroom. He has applied several clumsy-looking rolls when the maid arrives. Sitting beside her on the bed, Charlie ingratiates himself with a tale of woe, casually

cleaning and buffing his nails with trowel and file. He takes the maid's hand, covering it in dirt. She departs angrily. Work continues, and the stove explodes again. Not expecting the husband to be home, the wife's secret lover arrives. The wife palms him off as one of the decorators; he obligingly totes a barrel upstairs. The maid has returned upstairs to Charlie, who, distractedly, pushes a whitewash brush into the secret lover's face. Below, householder and wife argue as Charlie and the new arrival do battle. The husband charges upstairs to confront the interloper. The decorator also heads upstairs, arriving just as the householder has drawn a gun. The lover is chased downstairs, cornered in the kitchen with the wife. Above, the decorator seeks revenge on Charlie, who hurls a bucket in retaliation. The boss is sent flying into the bathroom, landing in a full tub. Gunshots are flying around the kitchen. Charlie rushes downstairs in time to meet a final, massive explosion. The decorator is seen gurgling in the bath. Husband, wife and lover are struggling beneath the rubble; this includes the oven, the door of which opens as Charlie's head appears. He grins, is struck by hurled debris, and retreats back inside.

One of the best Essanays, *Work* is a descendant of a Karno sketch called *Repairs*. It resembles the Keystone films in its mix of basic slapstick and marital farce, but is altogether better organized. Another difference is Charlie's initial appearance as extreme underdog, something the early, defiant Charlie would not have countenanced.

Significantly, the elementary knockabout routines are punctuated by nuance, particularly Charlie's sly camera wink when telling his tale of woe, or the moment where Charlie mirrors the housewife's mistrust by securing their own valuables. *Work* was reissued under the more descriptive (but less dramatic) title of *The Paperhanger*; a large Chaplin cut-out advertising this release is used amid the period detail of a 1963 film, *All the Way Home*, based on James Agee's novel *A Death in the Family*, though the film actually shown on screen is *Gentlemen of Nerve* (*qv*). James Agee (1909–55) was one of Chaplin's prime supporters at a time when *Monsieur Verdoux* (*qv*) was pilloried alongside its creator; his 1949 *Life* magazine essay, *Comedy's Greatest Era*, would in turn do much to revive interest in silent-film comedians as a group.

A footnote: the fantastically ugly house used in the film is none other than the Bradbury mansion, then in use by Essanay's West Coast unit.

(See also: Camera-looks; Cars; *Dough and Dynamite*; Essanay; Karno Company, The; Keystone; *King in New York, A*; McGuire, Paddy; *Pay Day*; *Police*; Reissues; Risqué humour; Streetcars; Vagrancy)

THE WOW-WOWS

See: Karno Company, The

Work: *Charlie ingratiates himself with the maid*

X-CERTIFICATES

(See Censorship)

YOUNG CHARLIE CHAPLIN

The celebration of Chaplin's centenary during 1989 took various forms, one of them a high-profile Thames TV dramatization of his early life entitled *Young Charlie Chaplin*, with child actor Joe Geary in the title rôle. This series of six twenty-five minute episodes earned a place as a cover story for the ITV listings magazine, *TV Times*, despite having been placed in an early slot generally aimed at older children. Transmissions were on Britain's ITV network from 25 January 1989.

There is much impressive period detail, but the depiction of events tends rather towards the obvious, even allowing for the timeslot. There are contrived chases with various policemen and a towering landlord, which are clearly intended to foreshadow Chaplin's film work; another sequence echoes *A Dog's Life* (*qv*) where Charlie filches food from a lunch wagon with the aid of brother Syd (played by Lee Whitlock). There is also a pawnbroker's window whose frontage matches that in *The Pawnshop* (*qv*). Aside from a disputedly strong northern accent, Stan Laurel (*qv*) is presented more as a caricature of his 1930s screen persona than the youthful novice he would have been, even to the point of using the name 'Laurel' (which, in reality, was not acquired until around 1918). Charles Chaplin Sr. (*qv*), played by Ian McShane, does the bread-roll dance from *The Gold Rush* (*qv*) and, in this account, does not leave Hannah (played by Twiggy) until Charlie is about ten.

Although most of the key events are covered, it should be said that considerable dramatic licence has been allowed to influence the chronology; for example, young Charlie is seen touring in *Sherlock Holmes* prior to the death of his father in 1901, a discrepancy of more than four years. The distortion in time may possibly have been designed in part to allow co-star Ian McShane a lengthier contribution to the series; less explicable is the decision to have the same child actor portray Charlie through the entire story, with the result that an impossibly young Chaplin is selected for the Karno Company's American tour.

Some things in *Young Charlie Chaplin* are done well, notably a fictionalised meeting with Dan Leno (*qv*), and the pastiche of Karno's *Football Match* sketch (albeit with an underage Chaplin). Perhaps in homage to the period subject (or perhaps not), there are moments when the series uses shots of train wheels to represent Charlie's travels, a device for which Chaplin himself was sometimes called 'old-fashioned' when employing it in *Monsieur Verdoux* (*qv*).

Young Charlie Chaplin was produced by Colin Shindler. Episodes one and two were written by Shindler with Andrew Nickolds and Stan Hey; episodes three and four were by Shindler alone; while the concluding episodes were written by Jeremy Burnham. Executive producer was Alan Horrox; director was Baz Taylor.

(See also: Birth; *Chaplin* [1992]; Chaplin, Hannah; Chaplin, Syd; Childhood; Documentaries, compilations; Early stage appearances; Karno Company, the)

YOUNGSON, ROBERT

See: Documentaries, compilations; *Gentlemen of Nerve*; *Masquerader, the*; Politics

ZUKOR, ADOLPH

See: Pickford, Mary, and United Artists

APPENDIX 1

CHAPLIN'S FILMS, 1914–67

The following list comprises Chaplin's films either as star or director; each film is documented as a separate entry within the main text. Titles are given in order of release. Feature-length films are marked *. Readers are also directed to the entries headed Abandoned projects; Documentaries, compilations; Guest appearances, and Newsreels.

1914 (KEYSTONE):
Making a Living
Kid Auto Races at Venice, CA.
Mabel's Strange Predicament
Between Showers
A Film Johnnie
Tango Tangles
His Favorite Pastime
Cruel, Cruel Love
The Star Boarder
Mabel at the Wheel
Twenty Minutes of Love
Caught in a Cabaret
Caught in the Rain
A Busy Day
The Fatal Mallet
Her Friend the Bandit
The Knockout
Mabel's Busy Day
Mabel's Married Life
Laughing Gas
The Property Man
The Face on the Bar Room Floor
Recreation
The Masquerader
His New Profession
The Rounders
The New Janitor
Those Love Pangs
Dough and Dynamite
Gentlemen of Nerve
His Musical Career
His Trysting Place
* *Tillie's Punctured Romance*
Getting Acquainted
His Prehistoric Past

1915–16 (ESSANAY):
His New Job
A Night Out
The Champion
In the Park
A Jitney Elopement

The Tramp
By the Sea
His Regeneration
Work
A Woman
The Bank
Shanghaied
A Night in the Show
Carmen
Police
Triple Trouble (assembled in 1918)

1916–17 (MUTUAL):
The Floorwalker
The Fireman
The Vagabond
One A.M.
The Count
The Pawnshop
Behind the Screen
The Rink
Easy Street
The Cure
The Immigrant
The Adventurer

1918–23 (FIRST NATIONAL):
How To Make Movies (unreleased)
A Dog's Life
The Bond (made for the Liberty Loan drive)
Shoulder Arms
Sunnyside
A Day's Pleasure
* *The Kid*
The Idle Class
Pay Day
The Pilgrim

1923–52 (UNITED ARTISTS):
* *A Woman of Paris*
* *The Gold Rush*
* *The Circus*
* *City Lights*
* *Modern Times*
* *The Great Dictator*
* *Monsieur Verdoux*
* *Limelight*

1957 (ARCHWAY):
* *A King in New York*

1967 (UNIVERSAL):
* *A Countess From Hong Kong*

APPENDIX 2

SELECT BIBLIOGRAPHY
The following list confines itself to books consulted during preparation of this book. A full Chaplin bibliography would be difficult – if not impossible – to compile, and would probably fill a reasonably-sized volume by itself. I owe particular gratitude to David Robinson's *Chaplin: His Life and Art*, Theodore Huff's pioneering *Charlie Chaplin*, John McCabe's *Charlie Chaplin*, McDonald, Conway and Ricci's *The Films of Charlie Chaplin*, and Chaplin's own memoirs, *My Autobiography* and *My Life in Pictures*. Harry M. Geduld's study of the Keystone films also proved useful in solving a number of mysteries. From the world of periodicals, particular mention should be made of *Picture Show, Pictures and the Picturegoer, Bioscope* and *Film Weekly*, the Chaplin society magazine *Limelight*, and also the numerous Chaplin-related articles published over the years by *Classic Images* (formerly *Classic Film Collector*). Apologies to any source inadvertently neglected.

Adams, Samuel Hopkins (1946) *Alexander Woollcott*, Hamish Hamilton
Adeler, Edwin and West, Con (1939) *Remember Fred Karno?*, John Long
American Film Institute, *American Film Institute Catalog: Feature Films 1911–20; Feature Films, 1921–30; Feature Films, 1931–40*
Asplund, Uno (1973) *Chaplin's Films* (English translation by Paul Britten Austin), David & Charles
Bergen, Candice (1984) *Knock Wood*, Hamish Hamilton
Berle, Milton with Frankel, Haskel (1975) *Milton Berle*, Dell
Bessy, Maurice (1972) *Charles Chaplin*, Collections Étoiles
Bloom, Claire (1982) *Limelight and After: The Education of an Actress*, Harper & Row, New York (1996) *Leaving a Doll's House*, Virago Press
Blum, Daniel (1953) *A Pictorial History of the Silent Screen*, Spring Books
Bryan, George B. (ed.) (1991) *Stage Deaths*, Greenwood
Buchanan-Taylor, W. (1942) *Shake the Bottle*, Heath Cranton
Carey, Gary (1977) *Doug and Mary*, Dutton, New York
Chaplin, Charles (1922) *My Wonderful Visit*, Hurst & Blackett
(1964) *My Autobiography*, Bodley Head
(1974) *My Life in Pictures* Bodley Head
Chaplin, Charles Jr with Rau, N. and Rau, M.
(1961) *My Father, Charlie Chaplin*, Panther
Chaplin, Lita Grey with Cooper, Morton (1966) *My Life with Chaplin*, Bernard Geis Associates
Chaplin, Patrice (1995) *Hidden Star: Oona O'Neill Chaplin*, Richard Cohen Books
Cooke, Alistair (1976) *Six Men*, Bodley Head (reprinted by Book Club Associates, 1977)
Cotes, Peter and Niklaus, Thelma (1951) *The Little Fellow: The Life and Work of Charles Spencer Chaplin*, Paul Elek
Davies, Marion, edited by Pfau, Pamela and Marx, Kenneth S. (1976) *The Times We Had*, Angus & Robertson
Dressler, Marie with Harrington, Mildred (1935) *My Own Story*, Hurst & Blackett, London
Epstein, Jerry (1988) *Remembering Charlie*, Bloomsbury
Eyman, Scott (1990) *Mary Pickford: America's Sweetheart*, Donald I. Fine, New York
Fowler, Gene (1934) *Father Goose* (reprinted by Avon Books, New York, 1974)
Gambaccini, Paul with Rice, Tim and Rice, Jo (1987) *British Hit Singles* (6th edn), Guinness Books
Geduld, Harry M. (1987) *Chapliniana Vol. 1: The Keystone Films*, University of Indiana Press, Bloomington and Indianapolis
Gehring, Wes D. (1983) *Charlie Chaplin: A Bio-Bibliography*, Greenwood Press
(1984) *W.C. Fields: A Bio-Bibliography*, Greenwood Press
Green, Abel and Laurie, Joe Jr (1951) *Show Biz from Vaude to Video*, Henry Holt & Co
Griffith, Richard and Mayer, Arthur (1957) *The Movies*, Bonanza Books/Simon & Schuster
Guiles, Fred Lawrence (1973) *Marion Davies*, Bantam
Halliwell, Leslie (1979) *The Filmgoer's Companion* (6th edn), Granada/Paladin (1982) *Halliwell's Hundred*, Granada
Hamblett, Charles (1962) *Brando*, May Fair
Hancock, Ralph and Fairbanks, Letitia (1953) *Douglas Fairbanks: The Fourth Musketeer*, Peter Davies
Hoyt, Edwin P. (1977) *Sir Charlie*, Robert Hale
Huff, Theodore (1951) *Charlie Chaplin*, Henry Schuman (revised and updated edn published by Pyramid, 1964)
Kaufman, Beatrice and Hennessey, Joseph (eds) (1946) *The Letters of Alexander Woollcott*, Cassell
Lahue, Kalton C. (1966) *World of Laughter: The Motion Picture Comedy Short 1910–1930*, University of Oklahoma Press (2nd impression, 1972).
and Gill, Samuel (1970) *Clown Princes and Court Jesters*, A.S. Barnes
Lamparski, Richard (1967) *Whatever Became Of ...?*, Ace Books
Lee, Raymond (1970) *The Films of Mary Pickford*, Castle Books
Lister, Eric (1985) *Don't Mention the Marx Brothers: Reminiscences of S.J. Perelman*, The

Book Guild

Maltin, Leonard (1980) *Of Mice and Magic*, Plume
(1982) *The Great Movie Comedians* (revised edn), Harmony Books, New York with Bann, Richard W. (1992) *The Little Rascals: The Life and Times of Our Gang* (revised edn of *Our Gang: the Life and Times of the Little Rascals*), Crown Trade Paperbacks

Marx, Groucho (1959) *Groucho and Me*, Victor Gollancz
with Anobile, Richard J. (1973) *The Marx Brothers Scrapbook*, Grosset & Dunlap

Marx, Harpo (1961) *Harpo Speaks!*, Victor Gollancz

Marx, Maxine (1986) *Growing Up With Chico*, Limelight Editions

Le Maschere (1957) *Enciclopedia Dello Spettacolo*, Casa Editrice Le Maschere, Rome (for some details of Alice Davenport and Frank J. Coleman)

Matthau, Carol (1992) *Among the Porcupines*, Orion

McCabe, John (1961) *Mr. Laurel and Mr. Hardy*, Doubleday (republished by Signet, 1966; Robson Books, 1976)
(1975) *The Comedy World of Stan Laurel*, Robson Books
(1978) *Charlie Chaplin*, Robson Books

McCaffrey, Donald W. (1971) *Focus on Chaplin*, Spectrum/Prentice-Hall

McDonald, Gerald D. (1965) *The Picture History of Charlie Chaplin* (magazine format), Nostalgia Press
with Conway, Michael and Ricci, Mark (1965) *The Films of Charlie Chaplin*, Citadel/Bonanza

Mitchell, Glenn (1995) *The Laurel & Hardy Encyclopedia*, B.T. Batsford
(1996) *The Marx Brothers Encyclopedia*, B.T. Batsford

Moore, Colleen (1968) *Silent Star*, Doubleday

Nathan, David (1971) *The Laughtermakers*, Peter Owen

Negri, Pola (1970) *Memoirs of a Star*, Doubleday

Parker, John (ed.) *Who's Who in the Theatre* (Sir Isaac Pitman & Sons, various edns, 1912–47)

Parrish, Robert (1976) *Growing Up in Hollywood*, Bodley Head (reprinted by Panther, 1980)

Quigley, Isabel (1968) *Charlie Chaplin: Early Comedies*, Studio Vista

Ramsaye, Terry (1926) *A Million and One Nights*, Simon & Schuster (reprinted by Touchstone/Simon & Schuster, 1986)

Robinson, David (1983) *Chaplin: The Mirror of Opinion*, Secker & Warburg
(1985) *Chaplin: His Life and Art*, McGraw-Hill
(1989) *Charlie Chaplin: 100 Years* (booklet), Channel 4/Museum of the Moving Image
(1996) *Charlie Chaplin: the Art of Comedy*, Thames & Hudson

Roeburt, John (1962) *'Get Me Giesler'*, Belmont Books

Rust, Brian (1979) *British Music Hall On Record*, Gramophone

Rutherford, Margaret with Robyns, Gwen (1972) *Margaret Rutherford: An Autobiography*, W.H. Allen

Seldes, Gilbert (1937) *Movies for the Millions*, B.T. Batsford

Sennett, Mack with Shipp, Cameron (1955) *King of Comedy*, Peter Davies

Silver, Charles (1989) *Charles Chaplin: An Appreciation*, Museum of Modern Art, New York

Slide, Anthony (1970) *Early American Cinema*, Zwemmer/Barnes

Sobel, Raoul and Francis, David (1977) *Chaplin: Genesis of a Clown*, Quartet

Spears, Jack (1971) *Hollywood: The Golden Era*, Castle Books, New York/A.S. Barnes

Stewart, William T., McClure, Arthur F. and Jones, Ken D. (1981) *International Film Necrology*, Garland Publishing

Swanson, Gloria (1981) *Swanson On Swanson*, Michael Joseph

Thompson, David and LoBianco, Lorraine (eds) (1994) *Jean Renoir: Letters*, Faber & Faber

Truitt, Evelyn Mack (1984) *Who Was Who On Screen*, R.R. Bowker

Variety (1983) *Variety's Film Reviews*, R.R. Bowker

Vazzana, Eugene Michael (1995) *Silent Film Necrology*, McFarland

Walker, Alexander (1989) *It's Only a Movie, Ingrid*, Headline

Wearing, J.P. (1981) *The London Stage 1900–1909*, Scarecrow Press

Welles, Orson and Bogdanovich, Peter (ed. Jonathan Rosenbaum) (1993) *This is Orson Welles*, HarperCollins

Winchester, Clarence (ed.) (1933) *The World Film Encyclopaedia*, Amalgamated Press

Winnington, Richard (1975) *Film; Criticism and Caricatures*, Paul Elek, London

Wood, ('Wee') Georgie (undated) *Royalty, Religion and Rats!*

Woollcott, Alexander (1934) *While Rome Burns*, Arthur Barker

Yallop, David A. (1976) *The Day the Laughter Stopped*, Hodder & Stoughton

PERIODICALS

Most of these, where traceable, are identified within the text. The following articles are those which proved of particular value.

Classic Images (formerly *Classic Film Collector* and, earlier, *8mm Collector*): 'The Lost Liberty Loan Films' by Eldon K. Everett (no. 39, Summer 1973); 'Collecting Chaplin' by Dr. F.C. MacKnight (series published from Fall 1974 to Fall 1978, with additional entry in September 1983); account of 'A Great Imitation of Charlie Chaplin's Burlesque on Carmen' by Eldon K. Everett (no. 45, Winter 1974–75); 'Jay Rubin interviews Jackie Coogan' (no. 52, Fall 1976); 'Still Another Unknown Chaplin Keystone!' by Bo Berglund (no. 86, August, 1982); 'Fighting For Reappraisal: The Films of the Little Fellow' by Rick de Croix (nos 97–105, July 1983–March 1984); 'Everyone's Favourite Comedian: Charlie Murray' by George Katchmer (in two parts, nos 170 and 171, August and September 1989); 'Lost Players' (for details of Virginia Kirtley) by Billy Doyle (November 1989).

Evening News (London): *The Chaplin Legend*, a series of articles by Jympson Harman (September 1952)

Film Weekly: 'Will Charlie Talk?' (9 September 1929) (Nathan Burkan interviewed over possible dialogue in the forthcoming *City Lights*); 'Two Out of Fourteen' (23 September 1929) (Stan Laurel's extensive recollections of his friendship with Chaplin in the Fred Karno company)

Limelight, newsletter of the Charlie Chaplin Film Co., 1994 to date

Music-Hall magazine: a review of David Robinson's *Chaplin: His Life and Art*; and Leo Dryden, both by Barry Anthony (no. 33, April 1986)

Pictures and the Picturegoer: 'The Idol of the Picture World: Charlie Chaplin as He Really Was and Is' (18 September 1915) (a résumé of Chaplin's life and work up to that time plus reports of his then-current Essanay productions); 'Concerning "CC" and "IPG"' (8 April 1916) (Chaplin's remarks to the press concerning his Mutual contract); 'Charlie at his Best' by Elsie Codd (21–28 April 1917) (an appreciation of *One A.M.* and of Chaplin's screen character); 'Chase Me Charlie' (1–8 September 1917) (a detailed account of the Essanay anthology of that name); 'A Chaplin Comedy in the Making' by Elsie Codd (17–24 November 1917) (an account of Chaplin's working methods at the Lone Star Studio)

Sight and Sound: 'The Day the Tramp Was Born' by Bo Berglund (Spring 1989)

The Silent Picture: 'Babe London' (July 1972)

The Times (London) 'Entrance of a Movie Legend' by David Robinson (9 January 1989)

APPENDIX 3

Chaplin admirers may wish to know of the society dedicated to his life and work, the Charlie Chaplin Film Co., and its quarterly newsletter, *Limelight*. Contact:

Bonnie McCourt
300 South Topanga Canyon Boulevard
Topanga
CA 90290
USA